Good
Guide 1994

THE
Good Skiing
Guide 1994

— THE — Good Skiing Guide 1994

THE 400 BEST WINTER SPORTS RESORTS
IN EUROPE AND AMERICA

EDITED BY PETER HARDY
AND FELICE EYSTON

IN ASSOCIATION WITH THE
SKI CLUB OF GREAT BRITAIN

WHICH?
BOOKS

Published by Consumers' Association

Which? Books are commissioned and
researched by The Association for
Consumer Research and published by
Consumers' Association,
2 Marylebone Road, London NW1 4DF

Copyright © 1993 Consumers' Association Ltd
Maps copyright © Consumers' Association Ltd

First edition of
The Good Skiing Guide 1985

This edition August 1993

The Guide has been prepared with the help of the Ski Club of
Great Britain, which is gratefully acknowledged. But the views expressed
herein are those of the Editors, and not necessarily those of the Club.

Editors	Felice Eyston and Peter Hardy
Chief sub-editor	Caroline Ellerby
Researchers	Jo Hiles, Alex Berrill
Contributors	John Pakington, Minty Clinch, Arnie Wilson, David Goldsmith, Nigel Lloyd
Design	Editorial Design Partnership
Cover design	Paul Saunders
Cover photo	Ian Jones for Skishoot
Maps	David Perrott Cartographics

British Library Cataloguing-in-Publication Data:
A catalogue record for this book is available from the British Library

ISBN 0-340-59105-6

Typeset by	Editorial Design Partnership, Albion Courtyard, Greenhill Rents, London EC1
Printed & bound in Great Britain by	Richard Clay Ltd, Bungay, Suffolk

Contents

Foreword

Taking over the editorship of what we, together with everybody else professionally involved in skiing, have always considered to be the 'bible' of the business has been a daunting task. This is the eighth edition of *The Good Skiing Guide* and we have carried out a complete overhaul of content and introduced a number of important changes which, as newcomers, we were no doubt expected to do. However, our objective remains the same: to provide a detailed critical analysis of what each resort has to offer, as opposed to what the tourist office of each resort says it has to offer.

We were surprised to discover that *The Good Skiing Guide* has no rival in any other country. Of course there are detailed and not-so-detailed ski guides in France, Germany and the United States, but none of them to our knowledge purports to review resorts and their facilities critically. For this reason some tourist offices are deeply upset when they discover we do not agree with their piste-grading, or find their weekend queues wholly unacceptable; sometimes we entirely contradict their publicity statements. This British brand of 'warts and all' journalism comes as a shock to them, but we are encouraged to learn of subsequent changes in, for example, resort lift maps which have come about as a direct result of past editions.

Together with those of our own researchers we have based our reports on personal visits to resorts, but our views are not nearly as important, nor can they be either as impartial or as objective, as those of individual readers; it is their opinions which make up the backbone of this guide. We are also acutely aware that within the strictures of a short working trip it is not always possible to highlight all the good or bad points of any village or region.

A ski resort is a kind of living organism; some facet of it is constantly changing, be it a new hotel, a new lift, or the addition of a whole new ski area. Without regular inspection reports from readers it would be impossible to keep abreast of all these developments. A section at the end of the guide shows how you can help contribute as well as listing the key points to look for and record while you are on holiday to enable us accurately to compile the next edition. As a carrot, we offer free copies of the guide to the writers of the 200 most comprehensive reports, although such is the enthusiasm of our reporters that clearly most of you would happily contribute anyway.

It is of great assistance to us if your holiday report is on a resort outside the top 10: the Trois Vallées, Verbier, Val d'Isère/Tignes, Alpe d'Huez, Avoriaz/Morzine, Zermatt, Kitzbühel, St Anton, Obergurgl, Breckenridge and Vail. That does not, however, mean that we do not want to hear from you if you have visited these resorts; their size and popularity means that substantial changes in lifts, hotels and restaurants are even more likely in these places.

Our biggest single task has been the selection of resorts: consider that France alone has 286 villages with ski resort status. What we have done is to focus primarily on those which appear in British tour operators' brochures, plus a few sensible extras. Just because it is an established holiday destination does not mean that it is a worthwhile resort, but it does mean that it is worthy of examination. The confines of space mean that we have to curtail some entries in order to allow for radical additions which we hope will provide readers with some insight into resorts they might not otherwise have either heard of or considered. We believe there is no such beast as a bad ski resort – everywhere has its good points. Admittedly, these may sometimes be outweighed by the negative factors, but so much is dependent on snow conditions and crowds.

Always we are asked the inevitable question: 'And what is your favourite ski resort?' The answer must be almost anywhere when given a blue sky, fresh snow underfoot, 1000 vertical metres below you, and like-minded companions. For all of us who love mountains, any resort is fabulous on the right day. Our reports may sometimes appear negative to you, not entirely in agreement with what you encountered over New Year, at Easter, or in the lowest season week of January. What we have strived to do is to produce a balanced critique of each resort in which conditions (not just the snow, but the standards of hotels and the friendliness of the locals) may vary dramatically during the course of an 18-week season.

Family skiing is pinpointed by many tour operators as the biggest single area of growth within the ski market. We also confess to a personal interest here and have therefore made childcare facilities an important part of the text and of the 'at-a-glance' table in each major entry.

To make room for extra resorts we have transformed part of the reference section into *Skiing by numbers*, an essential address book and telephone directory for skiers, from which it should be possible to obtain all the necessary information for booking ski holidays. The guide to tour operators is greatly expanded to provide as much detail as possible about every bonded travel firm.

The *Good Skiing Guide* maps, not always seen at first glance to be as easily comprehensible as the piste plans you receive in resorts, have been updated to show new or upgraded lifts wherever possible. We believe them to be an indispensable method of orientating yourself within a ski area. There is no great mystery to them; like any ordinary road map, they give a bird's-eye view of the terrain and the contours. They show clearly which runs face north, south, east or west. All but a couple are drawn to a single scale and it is therefore possible to compare the sizes of different ski areas.

Introduction

Few businesses have had to tighten their belts as painfully as the ski industry at the height of the recession. Winter holidays were among the first items to be crossed off the budget of many a household. Natural culling, coupled with the new EC regulation requiring every tour operator to be bonded, has led to a small but significant drop in the number of firms and the realignment of some of the big boys. The managing director of Ski Thomson, the long-time British market leader, was reported in early 1993 to have said that the sport could be going out of fashion. Highly publicised accidents, a weaker pound and sharp rises in prices were largely responsible for an apparent seven per cent drop in numbers of skiers in the British market. The wider point that he was making was that the winter travel market will have to change in line with skiers' needs. The steady decline in the mass summer holiday market in Spain a few years ago led to a fundamental reappraisal of what holidaymakers wanted. Spain is now back as a premier destination. The same wind of change is beginning to blow through European skiing.

This prognosis was greeted with some scepticism by Crystal Holidays, which claimed its market share was up 20 per cent to around 17 per cent of the total. At the same time Airtours, Britain's third-biggest summer operator, announced its first winter programme and intention to seize an immediate 7 per cent from other operators.

When the elephants play, the grass becomes trampled even in Britain's small corner of the ski jungle. But the real surprise is that the British ski market should be so resilient as to lose only seven per cent. Rather than the sport going out of fashion, a large number of people, for whom a skiing holiday is the second annual break, have recently had to be content with only a summer holiday. Come the end of the recession they should, theoretically, be back in force. However, whether they will be is quite another matter. Problems of far greater significance than mere cost alone are blighting the slopes.

The ski industry worldwide is in a state of fundamental disarray and unless immediate steps are taken by the big-name European resorts in particular, it is hard to see how they can remain commercially viable – or even how some can survive into the twenty-first century.

Overcrowded slopes

The much-publicised deaths on piste are in fact few and far between, but overcrowding has led to a serious increase in the number of collision accidents. Faced, on a high-season weekend, with a piste so choked with skiers that it resembles the M25 on a bank holiday, even veteran exponents of the sport are now asking themselves: 'Is this really worth it? Am I actually enjoying myself?' Increasingly, the sad answer to both questions is a resounding 'no'. The skiing public is a discerning one and, quite simply, it is fed up with overcrowding, artificially high resort prices and the reticence of lift companies in some European resorts to put back into the mountain some of the millions they have reaped from it. Unless they set their houses in order, even their most devoted followers are going to realise there is other comparable and better-value skiing to be found elsewhere.

In mitigation, the primary line of defence of these resorts is either that their government's rural conservation policy forbids them to upgrade their lift systems, or indeed that their own spirit of environmental consciousness is such that they themselves want to protect their surroundings. Both arguments are laudable, but these resorts fail to nail their green colours to the mast by limiting the number of ski passes issued in proportion to the capacity of their lift system. If hot air were needed to manufacture artificial snow, none of these resorts would have need of Mother Nature at all.

Verbier stands in the dock, accused of outrageous lift queues, an antiquated lift system and high resort prices. Its main means of mountain access is a 1986 six-seater gondola, hopelessly superannuated even before it was built, to deal with the volume of skiers for which it has to cater. It deposits skiers at the second of a series of mountain bottlenecks which, on high-season Sundays, make skiing a blood pressure-raising ordeal to be avoided at all costs.

Kitzbühel, despite its formidable international reputation, has a lamentable snow record, yet it has never until now invested in snowmaking equipment. It has finally agreed to install snow-cannon along the Streif, the Hahnenkamm downhill racecourse. This will no doubt spare the blushes of the resort management at a further cancellation of the toughest downhill on the World Cup calendar, but will do precious little to benefit holidaymakers. The backbone of its lift system remains the Hahnenkamm cable car, built in 1928, for which two-hour queues are not uncommon.

Mayrhofen, the Austrian village where generations of British have learned to ski, holds the record for the longest lift queue we have encountered and verified – four hours to travel down the mountain after two hours to travel up it in the first place. Queues here are completely unacceptable. A new gondola is due to be installed for the 1994-5 season.

Alpe d'Huez has one of the most modern lift systems in the world and proudly claims to have eliminated the lift queue. This may well be true, but in its place it has introduced a less frustrating, but more dangerous hazard. The main runs immediately above the resort are so overcrowded at peak times that progress on skis becomes impossible. The resort must severely limit the number of day passes issued, at least at weekends.

These resorts are by no means the only guilty ones, but they need to undertake a fundamental reappraisal of what they are trying to achieve and how they should go about it. They should first look to America, which of course has its imperfections, although the attitude of resorts towards their customers is a more sympathetic one.

If you invest correctly in a lift system, queues disappear except at peak times. When these inevitably develop, it takes only basic public relations skills to inform paying customers of what is happening, to marshal queues in a pleasant manner and thereby to avoid the push and shove which is the daily lot of the European skier.

Ski tuition

In general we have received what at best can only be described as disturbingly mixed reports of individual ski schools, although instructors in North America appear to be uniformly helpful and cheerful. The continued emergence of alternative schools to the ESF as well as the main Swiss and Austrian ski schools must be constructive in that any competition is a healthy guard against complacency. But too many schools appear to have an attitude problem. Time and again we receive reports of teachers using the 'follow me' technique of instruction while offering only minimal advice on how to improve.

France is the worst offender. Much has been done to update what was until recently the rather tired and old-fashioned image of the ESF. However, we feel it remains a sufficiently introspective French organisation to deter many foreign visitors. They cannot be blamed for turning to the more cosmopolitan-minded teachers of alternative schools with a less Gallic and more international focus.

One reporter wrote that he felt his instructor was filling in time between two other more interesting engagements. Others have continually remarked upon the inadequacy of ski schools in general, the organisation of lessons, the time wasted by instructors' poor time-keeping, their insufficient grasp of English and lack of enthusiasm.

To be fair, there are many notable exceptions, including the ski schools in Andorra, which are lavishly praised for their high standard of tuition and for the attitude of their instructors, most of whom are native English speakers and have BASI or similar qualifications.

Small needs

Childcare is now recognised by tour operator and resort alike as a crucial factor in sales, yet compared to those in America the facilities offered in Europe are woefully inadequate. If the children are happy, the parents are happy and everyone can enjoy their holiday. The converse is all-round misery. The problem divides into two: the care of pre-ski children and of young beginners and quasi-beginners.

Most resorts offer some kind of a crèche or non-ski kindergarten which cares for babies (sometimes even from a few weeks old) up to the age of four, when children may want to ski for at least part of the day. The hours and prices vary dramatically. An increasing number of tour operators have their own qualified nanny service; alternatively it is often possible to hire a babyminder through the local tourist office. There is a strong argument for leaving small children at home with relatives when skiing, but for some families this is neither possible nor desirable.

The problems really begin for parents when children reach skiing age. The surprisingly difficult solution is to find a ski kindergarten which offers a gentle introduction to skiing combined with play. The Swiss, followed by the Austrians, manage this better than anyone outside America. But the French place an overbearing emphasis on ski lessons and for this reason we remain extremely wary of the ESF ski kindergartens. The Italians, despite (or perhaps because of!) their love of small children, clearly see little need for kindergartens in many of their resorts. Certainly the whole of Europe has much to learn from the United States, where the positive attitude towards both instruction and childcare is without parallel.

Recent snowfall

The 1992-3 European ski season began in early December with the annual Critérium International de la Première Neige in Val d'Isère coinciding with some of the heaviest snowfalls for 20 years and a white Christmas everywhere. But a steady ridge of high pressure lodged over the Alps for much of January and February provided week upon week of unbroken blue skies and sunshine and little fresh snow. Low night-time temperatures meant that cover held surprisingly well and those resorts which have invested in extensive snow-making equipment were able to use it to good effect to maintain the home runs and nursery slopes. However, the relentless sunshine gradually wore the snow cover away, leaving lowland Austrian resorts facing closure in February.

The new snow came in the nick of time, but the damage was already done. The irreparable thawing of the base and encroaching spring meant that the pistes could never be restored to their former glory. The season ended once more with heavy snowfalls in Europe, allowing the higher resorts to fulfil their hopes of staying open well into May. Across the Atlantic, California had its best season in years. The Rockies were above average and Canada below. Overall no one could seriously complain.

Trends

British skiers in the 1992-3 season found their holidays savaged by the Government's removal of the pound from the ERM. The large operators maintained their prices as they were forced to do under ABTA regulations, but skiers still found their spending money worth up to 14 per cent less than the previous year. For 1993-4 many tour operators have no choice but to pass on costs in full with overall price rises of at least 10 per cent. Italy, which has had its own currency problems and has consequently held prices against sterling, suddenly became one of the most sought-after destinations. For the same reason Eastern Europe will continue to remain popular, although reports from Bulgaria suggest that ski resort entrepreneurs are quickly learning the vices of capitalism.

Grouses

● A surprising number of resorts in Austria still do not accept credit cards either for lift passes or for payment of hotel bills. Travellers are advised to take Eurocheques.

● Self-caterers in Austria are warned that with few exceptions food shops and supermarkets close at lunchtime on Saturdays until Monday morning. This leaves new arrivals, who are unaware of this lack of concession to tourism, with no option but to eat out for the first two nights of their holiday.

● Self-caterers in general and in France in particular worry about bed-clothes. The hassle involved on arrival, especially after a delayed transfer, in obtaining sheets and towels adds unnecessary pressure to the holiday. Certainly we advise skiers to take their own towels (shortages seem frequent). Check with your tour operator whether you have to pay a deposit for linen on arrival. Several reporters said that this unexpected expense seriously ate into their spending money.

● Ski theft has reached epidemic proportions in France and Italy. Austria and even Switzerland are no longer the safe havens they used to be. The risk is only marginally less in the United States. Most of the thieving is professional and highly organised, but just where these thousands of pairs are resold is highly intriguing. Standing glumly in a two-hour queue in the High Tatras of Slovakia, we were amazed at the number of ski shop stickers from major European resorts. Superannuated hire stock, which has been sold on, would be the charitable but not always correct explanation.

Always separate your skis and twin them with a companion's of contrasting colour, make and size when leaving them even for a few minutes. We are concerned that some insurance policies specifically do not cover skis left unattended, which is when you most want insurance. Read your policy carefully.

News

Much of the basic information in the Guide has to be obtained, sometimes with great difficulty, from individual resorts and on occasion we have reason to doubt its accuracy. For example, time and again we have come across linked ski areas where the sum of the total kilometres of each resort's pistes does not match the much publicised overall total of the area. We would be pleased to hear from readers who spot any such discrepancies. Megève deserves a special award for providing the most detailed of all information on its infrastructure.

Gstaad, dropped from the last edition altogether, is back with minor resort status. While its own skiing and popularity does not alone merit inclusion, its 14 linked or nearby resorts make it worthy of mention. Adelboden, the Montafon, and Valfréjus have been dropped this year because of lack of international interest. Resorts we have expanded include Risoul, Valloire, Aspen and Whistler.

On the equipment front Fat Boys (see *Equipment news*) were the phenomenon of the season and were hailed as the greatest innovation in skiing since the safety binding 40 years ago. Atomic Powder Plus, already imitated by other manufacturers, are twice as wide as normal skis and enable any intermediate to ski off-piste, even in breakable crust. Atomic is currently experimenting with a design which should be usable on-piste as well as in deep snow. Fat Boys have in fact been around for three years but we predict a major increase in popularity in this revolutionary type of ski.

Accidents

Last winter was peppered with tales of gruesome ski accidents and deaths, attributed mainly to dangerous pistes, caused by overcrowding or lack of snow. Skiing is no more and no less dangerous than any other comparable action sport combining the hazards created by speed and the elements. Anyone going on a skiing holiday should be aware of the risks and read the 'highway code' of the slopes drawn up by the International Ski Federation (see *Ski safety*).

Statistics prepared by the FIS and insurance companies show a worrying increase in the number of collisions on piste. A high proportion of injuries are to the upper body and the head and the time has surely come for the introduction of the compulsory wearing of lightweight crash-helmets.

In no other sport would amateurs be allowed to attain speeds in excess of 30mph over often hazardous terrain without any protection. Riders, after considerable agonising, finally accepted the need for hard-hats. It is now the turn of skiers to do the same.

As an immediate measure, helmets should be made compulsory for all children qualifying for a free (usually under 4 or 5) or reduced price (usually under 14) lift pass.

Snowboarding

The increase in the popularity of snowboarding has done nothing to make the slopes any safer, but the 'shredders' with their Bad Boy image also receive an unfair press. Skiers consider snowboards to be unwieldy and dangerous and snowboarders have the same opinion of skis. In Copper Mountain, Colorado, we have seen the emergence of 'pack-boarding', a sinister game of 'chicken' in which snowboarders see how close they can ride to other snowboarders or skiers. Snowboarders would argue that every sport has its 'yobbo' element and this is nothing in comparison to the danger presented by a group of skiers weaving down the piste all the worse for a gallon of *Glühwein*. Skiers do not own the mountains just because they were there first. The two groups have to learn to live together. Although segregated slopes (at least for novices) make sense, commercial considerations are likely to prevent any such general measures in Europe.

Assistance

We are extremely grateful for the assistance of the Ski Club of Great Britain, whose reps have provided information on many of the major resorts in the book. We would also like to express our gratitude to David Hearns, head of the SCGB information department, for his valuable help. Again we would like to emphasise the importance of the facts, figures and comments provided by you, the readers of the guide. For details on how you can contribute to the next edition please refer to the *Foreword* and to the chapter entitled *Reporting on resorts*.

Choosing your resort

When to go skiing is almost as important a factor to consider as where to go, but so are companions, accommodation and travel arrangements, snow and sunshine – and without a decent amount of both, your holiday could still be a disappointment. The level of occupancy of the resort is also a major consideration: too many skiers means overcrowded lifts and pistes, too few and the resort takes on a half-closed atmosphere. Reading this Guide and the tour operator brochures should enable you to make a decision you won't regret.

When to go

Pre-Christmas

Most European ski resorts open during the second week of December, but will not necessarily run their entire lift system until the weekend before Christmas. American ski resorts traditionally open for Thanksgiving, which falls on the third Thursday of November. If you book well in advance it is possible to obtain some good early-season bargains at this time of year. Various incentives are offered, including reduced – even free – lift passes and all-inclusive, low-cost packages. Tour operators will have already paid for their beds and can only fill them by offering rock-bottom prices. On top of this, the slopes are wonderfully uncrowded. However, the all-important question is: 'Will there be snow when I go?'

It is essential to choose a resort with a high top lift station and preferably a glacier, where at least some skiing is guaranteed. Val d'Isère traditionally hosts the first World Cup downhill of the season in early December and is a sound choice. Val Thorens, Les Deux Alpes, Saas Fee, Zermatt, Sölden and Obergurgl are all good bets.

Christmas and New Year

These are the early high-season dates when resorts are at their busiest. The first is the less crowded of the two weeks. Again it is important to go for altitude to be sure of snow cover, but you have to weigh this against the attractions of a pretty Christmas-card resort. Alpbach, Kitzbühel, Megève, Mürren and Grindelwald are always popular, despite their sometimes limited snow. New Year queues in most major resorts make it a week to be avoided by serious skiers. The Trois Vallées, with its efficient lift system, copes better than most.

January

The low season begins in early January, again a good time for holiday bargains. Although it used to be a safe snow time, new snow in January has been lacking in three out of the last six seasons (1987-93). It is often the best time to visit the big-name resorts like Verbier, Chamonix, Zermatt and Kitzbühel, while most Europeans stay at home in January. Similarly, off-season prices make North America appealing in January, although it can be extremely cold (particularly in New England and in Canada).

February

European slopes should be at their best in February, although such was the lack of fresh snow in 1993 that the low Austrian resorts had to consider closure. Snow finally fell at the end of the month. Unfortunately, the normal peak conditions are invariably coupled with peak crowds, which coincide with school holidays.

In 1994 the first two weeks in Europe are expected to be relatively uncrowded. However, the week beginning Saturday 12 February is not only British half-term, but also the start of the two-week Paris school holidays. Belgium, Holland, Spain, Sweden and Denmark have also chosen this week.

March

There is still plenty of skiing to be found in March, even in some of the lower resorts, but spring is on the way and it is sensible to bear in mind that the best snow will be above 1800m. The weather is generally warmer with a lot of sunshine and longer days. Off-piste skiing can be exceptionally good, providing the temperature remains cold enough to reduce avalanche danger. German school holidays begin on 19 March. The British, Spanish, Swedish and Danish holidays commence one week later.

April

The one consistency in the weather pattern over nearly the whole of the last decade has been the heavy snowfall in April. The Davos Institute for Snow and Avalanche Research has confirmed that, although the amount of precipitation remains much the same during the winter in the Alps, more of it now falls in April. This month therefore offers some of the best skiing of all, with the magic of off-piste spring snow, together with plenty of powder pockets. High-altitude is essential, with only limited skiing found below 2000m during the latter half of the month. In 1994 Easter falls on 3 April and the high altitude resorts will be extremely crowded. The Paris school holidays end on 23 April, but most of the higher French resorts will try to stay open until all the regional holidays end on 7 May.

Where to go

After deciding when to go you then have to decide where you want to take your holiday. This depends on your individual preferences and requirements. Consequently a host of variables come into play. The choice may be influenced by the budget available, your skiing ability and experience and that of others in your holiday party.

● Complete beginners face the hardest task of all, not helped by the inundation of advice from well-meaning friends. A course of lessons on a dry ski slope will save some of the time wasted getting to grips with the basics during the first days of the holiday. Do not be put off by how difficult it all seems and remember that a real slope is much easier than an artificial one.

The resort you choose should have a gentle nursery slope served by an easily manageable slow lift. These slopes may either be in the resort or up the mountain and reached by gondola or cable car. The higher slopes usually have the advantage of more reliable snow and sunshine

Modern equipment and teaching methods mean the novice outgrows the nursery slopes within a couple of days. You therefore need to choose a resort with plenty of easy runs for the next stage of progress. Large resorts with extensive ski areas and consequently expensive lift passes are generally not suitable for novices.

A percentage of beginners are not hooked for life as soon as they put on skis. Indeed, a few of them give up even before the end of their first week. It is therefore important to choose a resort with some atmosphere and off-slope fun. It is also advisable to take a budget holiday instead of spending a fortune to discover you do not like skiing. Particularly recommended are the lowland Austrian resorts, including Söll and Westendorf. Andorra has an extremely high standard of tuition; Romania and Bulgaria are good value and well-suited to beginners.

● Intermediates make up the vast majority of skiers. They range in ability from quasi-beginners to those who have reached a plateau of competence. Intermediates will find plenty of runs suitable to their ability in most resorts. As they progress, most will seek out the motorways of the giant linked ski circuses like the Portes du Soleil, the Trois Vallées and the Milky Way. But not every intermediate is a piste-basher who is obsessed with clocking up a high number of kilometres per day. Plenty of skiers like a gentle meander down the slopes before a long, relaxing lunch, followed by a little sedate exercise before the lifts close for the day.

Choice of resort should be dependent on the type of holiday you want and the importance of the ski area *versus* the village and off-slope activities. We feel that most intermediates (and therefore most skiers) choose the country first and the resort second.

● Experts should by definition know what they want and where to find it. In this guide we have indicated the resorts, the ski areas and the runs of interest. It should be pointed out that given good snow conditions most European black (or, in America, single black diamond) runs can be managed by a good intermediate who wants a challenge.

Access

Unlike most summer package-holiday destinations, few ski resorts are near airports and the final leg of the journey is usually a long one. La Clusaz is 90 minutes from Geneva and Barèges only 30 minutes from Lourdes, but these are exceptions. The transfer time from your destination airport is more likely to be over two hours, culminating in a tortuous climb up roads which can be affected by heavy traffic and winter weather conditions.

The legacy of the Albertville Winter Olympics is a vastly improved access route to the major group of resorts in the Tarentaise, which has dramatically reduced journey times to the Trois Vallées and Val d'Isère from both Lyon and Geneva. Similarly the Austrian motorway network is so efficient that resorts like Obertauern are no longer isolated. But you must expect an appreciably longer than average journey time to Italian resorts east of Milan as well as to some Swiss resorts (notably St Moritz).

Driving from Britain is simple enough nowadays. For the main French and Austrian resorts you travel by motorway to within minutes of your destination. It is worth remembering that in mid-winter road conditions may deteriorate over the final kilometres. Chains are not an optional accessory but a necessity. Under the laws of the main alpine countries it is a serious traffic offence not to be so equipped. Practise putting them on before you leave home and pack a pair of gardening gloves and a torch. Reading the instructions for the first time in a blizzard at midnight is not advisable. The Euromatic, obtainable from Rudd Chains of Whitstable, is the new concept in chains and takes only a couple of minutes to fit.

Rail travel becomes easier every year and in the table at the end of each major chapter we state the nearest station to the resort. The majority of Swiss resorts are directly accessible by rail. The charter snow train (see *Skiing by numbers*) leaves Calais on Friday evening for French and Austrian resorts.

Setting and convenience

No one actually likes plodding along icy roads wearing awkward boots and carrying heavy skis. The ideal resort has ski-in ski-out convenience from your hotel or apartment. Unfortunately, only a handful of resorts (Valmorel, Risoul and Belle Plagne) manage to combine this with any level of village charm. The purpose-built resort bears little resemblance to a real village, has no proper summertime population and therefore no community feel to it. Traditional resorts are usually more attractive.

Time and again reporters comment that they were drawn to a particular resort 'because it has a life away from skiing'. You have to decide whether the skiing or the village is your priority, although you must bear in mind that given plenty of resort-level snow, even the monsters like Tignes visibly soften. Fortunately the French have learned from their architectural mistakes of the 1960s and new resorts (La Tania in the Trois Vallées is a good example) have been constructed in a much more sympathetic manner.

A picturesque setting is all important. The prettiest resorts are neither too exposed (Val Thorens) nor too enclosed (Champéry), but are at the same time surrounded by trees. Those situated up the mountain (Mürren) have better views and more sunshine than those on the valley floor (Chamonix). Traffic fumes do not mix with skiing and an absence of cars, or at least a pedestrianised resort centre, is a distinct advantage.

Those in search of an all-round winter sports holiday should look to the long-established resorts like St Moritz and Arosa, where horse-drawn sleighs, skating and tobogganing are of equal status to skiing. Non-skiers, apart from the keenest of walkers, will find it difficult to occupy their daylight hours for a full week in all but a few resorts. Especially good are those close to a city of interest (Sierra Nevada for Granada, Igls for Innsbruck).

Accommodation

Where you stay within a chosen resort is largely dictated by your budget. In Austria, Italy and Switzerland most accommodation is in hotels, which range from the simplest of bed and breakfasts and pensions to luxury four- and five-star establishments. Half-pension board is unquestionably the most economical. France leads the field in self-catering apartments, although they are also available in other countries. The American condominium is an altogether more luxurious affair.

Shopping facilities are an important factor; ski resort supermarkets are expensive and prone to serious early-evening queues. If driving to a self-catering apartment, it is advisable to buy your main supplies in a valley hypermarket.

The chalet is a uniquely British and increasingly popular concept with its origins in Switzerland, but now found in most alpine resorts. You can take over the entire chalet as a group, or join a chalet party as an individual or a couple. Gone are the days of no hot water and bowls of half-cooked spaghetti. The standard is now generally high, with more and more operators offering 'luxury' or 'gourmet' weeks.

Nannies

The all-inclusive staffed chalet formula is ideal for families, particularly those with young children. A growing number of operators employ their own qualified nannies, usually based in one of the chalets. The nannies look after pre-skiing children and babies, and will often collect older children from the ski school while their parents are still skiing. The standard of hotel or chalet nanny service can vary, so it is wise to check whether the crèche is run from a well-equipped playroom in the building. If in doubt, ask the tour operator for the names of former clients who have used their service and ask their opinion.

Après-ski

The length of the skiing day varies by month, resort and country. It may finish as early as 3pm (in the United States) or as late as 5.30pm, and there are plenty of off-slope hours to be filled. An increasing number of resorts have swimming-pools and sports centres where the pre-dinner hours can be happily whiled away by those with energy left after the day's exertions. Night-time entertainment traditionally centres around bars of varying degrees of rowdiness and sophistication. As a rule of thumb, Austria has the liveliest nightlife and the warmest atmosphere. Holidaymakers who have started skiing here before moving on to the greater challenges of France are invariably disappointed at the comparative lack of evening entertainment in all but a handful of villages (Courchevel, Megève, Les Deux Alpes). Italy and Switzerland are more lively. Late-night revellers should seek out major resorts (St Anton, Kitzbühel, Verbier, Zermatt), where groups of like-minded people will also be eager to socialise.

Cost

Whichever way you look at it, skiing is an expensive activity – and it is becoming more so. For the majority the cost can be broken down into three parts: the holiday package, overheads and incidentals. The 'package' comprises transport, accommodation and dinner (if half-board). 'Overheads' include clothing, skis and boots, lift pass, tuition, kindergarten and food shopping (for self-caterers). 'Incidentals' are mountain lunches, refreshments and entertainment.

Choosing the right package to suit your budget is extremely difficult. Remember that the 'bargain' offer of the £99 apartment for four has its drawbacks. Firstly you have to get there and driving is not necessarily cheaper than flying. In general, chalets or pension-type hotels are the most economical and convenient.

Eastern Europe and Andorra are by far the cheapest destinations. Of the main alpine countries, Italy provides the best value for 1993-4 for British holiday-makers owing to a favourable exchange rate. However, no country today can truly be singled out as cheaper than another. North America continues to prove extremely good value, with incidentals cheaper than in Europe.

Major resort verdicts

The tables on the next ten pages show our verdicts on the advantages and disadvantages of the European and North American resorts we have covered in detail in the Guide. They are intended to help you choose your resort, although you should not rely exclusively on them for resort selection, as much depends on personal tastes and views. Also remember that there are plenty of good smaller resorts in the Guide which, for reasons of space, are not included in the chart. Having drawn up a short list from the tables, you should read the relevant chapters thoroughly.

For most aspects of a resort we use a simple measure of good or bad (a tick or a cross). Where it is average we have left a blank. But for some aspects, where the cross or 'bad' qualification has little meaning, we use only the tick or 'good' rating, e.g. *off-piste skiing*, *summer skiing* and *tree-level skiing*.

Most headings are self-explanatory, but a few need further clarification. *Snow probability* is based on the likelihood of skiing in or around the resort, especially at the beginning of the season. Some resorts receive a tick despite their relatively low altitude, because of their own micro-climates. *Tree-level skiing* denotes those resorts which offer sheltered skiing on bad weather days, with the subsequent improvement in visibility.

Ugly mountain scenery does not exist, so we have only used the affirmative tick for particularly *beautiful scenery*. *Resort charm* applies to villages which have beautiful architecture, like Kitzbühel, or are rich in atmosphere like Alpbach or Jackson Hole. Aesthetically unpleasing resorts and busy towns with heavy traffic receive a cross.

By a *large ski area*, we mean a linked lift network making it possible to cover plenty of terrain without removing your skis, as in the Trois Vallées resorts. Gstaad and Mayrhofen may have numerous lifts covered by their lift passes, but the areas are not linked, so they receive a blank. *Big vertical drop* applies to resorts which have a difference of at least 1500m from the top to the bottom of the ski area. In assessing how good or bad a resort is for *tough runs*, we have concentrated on whether a resort as a whole is likely to appeal to skiers who relish a challenge. Mürren, for example, has the tough Schilthorn run but is overall better suited to intermediates, so it receives a blank.

Après-ski receives a tick not only for a lively nightlife, but also for a large choice of restaurants, as in Aspen. *Family skiing* refers to a family of mixed ages. *Children's facilities* refers to the availability of ski and non-ski kindergartens, babysitting facilities and good nursery slopes. A resort receives a tick only if it offers all four of these. Resorts rated good for *easy road access* are ones which offer no local difficulties for drivers. Arosa, for example, has 244 hairpin bends on the way up from Chur, so it receives a cross.

	Large ski area	Tough runs	Intermediate skiing	Easy runs	Nursery slopes	Off-piste	Summer skiing	Cross-country	Children's facilities	Lift queues
Alpbach	✗	✗		✔						✔
Alpe d'Huez	✔	✔	✔		✔	✔	✔		✔	✔
Andermatt		✔		✗	✗	✔			✗	✗
Andorra	✗	✗		✔	✔				✔	✗
Aspen	✔	✔	✔	✔	✔			✔	✔	
Les Arcs	✔		✔			✔			✔	
Arosa	✗	✗		✔						
Aviemore	✗		✔					✔		✗
Avoriaz	✔	✔	✔	✔	✔				✔	✗
Badgastein		✔	✔						✗	
Banff		✔	✔	✔					✔	
Barèges		✗	✔	✔						✗
Beaver Creek			✔	✔	✔				✔	
Bormio			✔					✔	✗	
Borovets	✗	✗		✔	✔	✗				✗
Breckenridge		✔		✔	✔				✔	
Cervinia	✔	✗	✔	✔	✔		✔			✗

Long runs	Tree-level skiing	Big vertical drop	Skiing convenience	Snow probability	Non-skiing	Mountain restaurants	Beautiful scenery	Resort charm	Compact village	Traffic	Road access	Rail access	Late holidays	Low prices	Après-ski	Family skiing
			✗	✔				✔			✔		✗			✔
✔		✔	✔			✔	✗						✔		✗	✔
	✗		✗	✔	✗	✗	✔	✔				✔			✗	✗
						✗		✗					✗	✔	✔	✔
	✔				✔	✔		✔		✗	✗					✔
		✔	✔	✔	✗	✗		✗		✔			✔	✔	✗	
			✔		✔	✔			✗		✗	✔				✔
			✗	✔		✗		✗								
			✔		✗			✗		✔	✔					✔
	✔		✗							✗		✔		✔	✔	
			✗	✔												
				✗	✗						✔		✗	✔		
	✔		✔			✔			✔							
✔	✔	✔		✔	✔	✔		✔		✗	✗		✔			
				✔	✗			✗					✗	✔		✔
	✔		✗	✔				✔	✗	✗	✔	✗			✔	✔
✔	✗	✔		✔	✗				✗	✗			✔			✔

23

	Large ski area	Tough runs	Intermediate skiing	Easy runs	Nursery slopes	Off-piste	Summer skiing	Cross-country	Children's facilities	Lift queues
Champéry	✔		✔	✔						
Chamonix	✔	✔		✗		✔			✗	✗
Châtel	✔		✔	✔						
La Clusaz		✗	✔	✔	✔			✔	✔	
Cortina d'Ampezzo	✔	✔	✔	✔	✔	✔		✔	✔	
Courchevel	✔	✔	✔	✔	✔	✔		✔	✔	
Courmayeur			✔	✔		✔	✔		✔	
Crans-Montana			✔	✔	✔	✔	✔	✔	✔	
Davos	✔	✔	✔		✗	✔		✔		
Les Deux Alpes			✔			✔	✔		✔	
Flaine	✔		✔	✔	✔	✔			✔	
Flims		✗	✔	✔				✔		
Grindelwald	✔	✗	✔	✔		✔				
Gstaad		✗		✔				✔		
Innsbruck/Stubai			✔	✔			✔			✗
Ischgl/Galtur	✔	✗	✔	✔		✔				✗
Isola 2000		✗		✔	✔				✔	

Long runs	Tree-level skiing	Big vertical drop	Skiing convenience	Snow probability	Non-skiing	Mountain restaurants	Beautiful scenery	Resort charm	Compact village	Traffic	Road access	Rail access	Late holidays	Low prices	Après-ski	Family skiing
				✗	✗			✔			✔	✔	✗		✗	
✔		✔	✗	✔	✔	✗	✔			✗	✔	✔	✔		✔	
				✗					✗	✗	✔		✗		✗	
				✗		✔				✗	✔		✗			✔
	✔	✔	✗			✔	✔			✗	✗		✗		✔	
✔	✔		✔	✔	✗	✔							✔		✔	✔
	✔		✗		✔	✔	✔	✔	✗		✔	✔			✔	
	✔	✔			✔			✗	✗	✗	✔	✔				
✔	✔	✔		✗	✔	✔		✗	✗	✗		✔	✗		✗	
	✗	✔		✔	✗	✗	✔	✗	✗	✗			✔		✔	✔
			✔	✔	✗			✗			✔	✔		✔	✗	✔
	✔		✗	✔		✔			✗	✗			✗		✗	
			✗			✔							✔	✗		
			✗		✔			✔		✗	✔					
			✗	✔	✔			✔			✔	✔			✔	
							✔	✔							✔	
			✔	✔	✗			✗			✔	✗		✔		✗	✔

	Large ski area	Tough runs	Intermediate skiing	Easy runs	Nursery slopes	Off-piste	Summer skiing	Cross-country	Children's facilities	Lift queues
Jackson Hole		✔	✔	✘	✔	✔			✔	
Killington			✔	✔	✔	✘		✘	✔	
Kitzbühel	✔	✘	✔	✔				✔		✘
Klosters	✔	✔	✔		✘	✔		✔		✘
Lech/Zürs			✔	✔		✔				✘
Lenzerheide		✘		✔				✔		
Livigno				✔	✔				✘	
Mammoth Mountain	✔		✔		✔				✔	✘
Mayrhofen		✘	✔	✔	✔		✔			✘
Megève	✔	✘	✔	✔	✔			✔	✔	
Les Menuires	✔	✔	✔	✔		✔			✔	
Méribel	✔	✔	✔	✔	✔	✔		✔	✔	
Montgenèvre	✔	✘	✔	✔		✔				
Morzine	✔		✔	✔				✔		
Mürren			✔	✘	✘	✔				✔
Niederau	✘	✘		✔	✔					
Norway	✘	✘		✔				✔		

Long runs	Tree-level skiing	Big vertical drop	Skiing convenience	Snow probability	Non-skiing	Mountain restaurants	Beautiful scenery	Resort charm	Compact village	Traffic	Road access	Rail access	Late holidays	Low prices	Après-ski	Family skiing
	✔				✔	✗	✔	✔				✗	✗			
	✔		✗	✔	✗			✗	✗				✔			✔
			✗	✗	✔			✔		✗	✔	✔	✗		✔	
✔	✔	✔	✗	✗		✔		✔		✗		✔	✗			
					✗			✔			✗	✗				✔
	✔		✗		✔										✗	
				✔	✗					✗	✗		✔	✔		✗
					✔	✗		✗	✗			✗	✔		✗	
	✗		✗								✔				✔	✔
✔	✔			✗	✔	✔		✔	✗	✗	✔		✗		✔	✔
	✗		✔		✗		✔	✗		✗				✔	✗	✔
✔					✔					✗						✔
	✔		✔		✗	✗		✔		✗			✗		✗	
					✔			✔		✔			✗			✔
		✔	✔		✔		✔	✔	✔	✔		✔				
✗	✔											✔	✗	✔	✔	✔
✗	✔			✔			✔									✔

27

	Large ski area	Tough runs	Intermediate skiing	Easy runs	Nursery slopes	Off-piste	Summer skiing	Cross-country	Children's facilities	Lift queues
Obergurgl	✗	✗		✔	✔	✔	✔		✔	
Obertauern			✔	✔	✔	✔			✔	✔
Park City		✗	✔	✔	✔			✔	✔	
La Plagne	✔	✗	✔	✔	✔	✔	✔		✔	
Risoul/Vars		✗	✔	✔					✔	
La Rosière			✔	✔	✔	✔				✔
Saalbach/Hinterglemm			✔	✔	✔				✔	✗
Saas-Fee			✔		✔		✔		✔	
Sauze d'Oulx	✔	✗	✔			✔			✔	✗
St Anton	✔	✔		✗		✔			✔	✗
St Johann in Tirol	✗	✗		✔	✔			✔		
St Johann im Pongau	✔	✗	✔	✔				✔	✔	✔
St Moritz	✔	✔	✔	✔	✗	✔	✔	✔		✗
Schladming		✗	✔	✔	✔	·			✔	
Seefeld	✗	✗	✗	✔	✔	✔		✔		
Selva	✔		✔	✔		✔		✔		
Serre Chevalier	✔		✔	✔		✔			✔	✔	✔
Sestriere	✔	✔	✔			✔				

Long runs	Tree-level skiing	Big vertical drop	Skiing convenience	Snow probability	Non-skiing	Mountain restaurants	Beautiful scenery	Resort charm	Compact village	Traffic	Road access	Rail access	Late holidays	Low prices	Après-ski	Family skiing
			✓	✓	✗		✓	✓					✓			✓
			✓	✓	✗				✗				✓		✗	✓
	✓		✗		✓							✗			✓	
		✓	✓	✓	✗					✓			✓		✗	✓
	✓		✓	✓	✗						✗			✓	✗	✓
	✗		✗												✗	✓
						✓			✗	✓	✓					✓
	✗		✗	✓	✓		✓	✓		✓	✗		✓			
	✓		✗	✗	✗	✓		✗			✓	✓	✗	✓	✓	✗
✓			✓						✗		✓			✓		
	✓		✗	✗		✓		✗	✗		✓	✓	✗		✓	✓
	✓		✗		✗	✓		✗	✗		✓	✓			✓	
✓		✓	✗	✓	✓	✓	✓		✗	✗	✗	✓	✓		✓	
	✓		✗	✗		✓		✓			✓	✓	✗		✓	
			✗		✓		✓	✓			✓	✓	✗		✓	✓
✓		✓	✗	✓	✓	✓				✗	✗					
	✓			✗					✗	✗	✗		✗			
✓								✗								

	Large ski area	Tough runs	Intermediate skiing	Easy runs	Nursery slopes	Off-piste	Summer skiing	Cross-country	Children's facilities	Lift queues
Snowbird		✔	✔	✔		✔			✔	✔
Sölden			✔	✔		✔	✔			
Söll	✔		✔	✔				✔		✔
Stowe		✔	✔			✔	✗		✔	✗
Telluride		✔	✔					✔	✔	✔
La Thuile			✔	✔	✔	✔			✗	
Tignes	✔	✔	✔			✔	✔			
Vail	✔		✔	✔	✔	✔			✔	
Val d'Isère	✔	✔	✔	✗	✗	✔	✔			
Valloire			✔			✔			✔	
Valmorel		✗	✔	✔	✔	✔			✔	✔
Val Thorens	✔					✔	✔		✔	
Verbier	✔	✔	✔			✔	✔		✔	✗
Villars		✗	✔	✔				✔	✔	
Wengen	✔	✗	✔	✔	✔					
Whistler/Blackcomb	✔	✔	✔	✔	✔	✔	✔		✔	✗
Zell am See/Kaprun		✗		✔			✔	✔		✗
Zermatt	✔	✔	✔	✗	✗	✔	✔		✗	

Long runs	Tree-level skiing	Big vertical drop	Skiing convenience	Snow probability	Non-skiing	Mountain restaurants	Beautiful scenery	Resort charm	Compact village	Traffic	Road access	Rail access	Late holidays	Low prices	Après-ski	Family skiing
			✔	✔	✗			✗					✔		✗	
			✔						✗	✗			✔		✔	
	✔			✗	✗		✔	✗			✔				✗	✗
	✔	✗	✔					✔								
	✔			✔	✗		✔	✔			✗				✔	
	✔		✔		✗			✗	✔			✔		✔	✗	
✔	✗	✔	✔	✔	✗			✗					✔		✗	
	✔							✔			✔				✗	✔
✔		✔	✗	✔	✗				✗				✔		✔	
					✔	✗		✔				✗			✔	✔
			✔		✗			✔		✔	✔					✔
	✗		✔	✔	✗										✗	
✔		✔	✗		✔			✔		✗	✔	✔	✔		✔	
								✔			✔	✔			✗	✔
	✔			✗	✔	✔	✔	✔		✔		✔				✔
	✔	✔	✔					✔			✔		✔			✔
			✗	✔	✔		✔	✔		✗	✔	✔	✔		✔	
✔	✔	✔	✗	✔	✔	✔	✔	✔					✔	✗	✔	

31

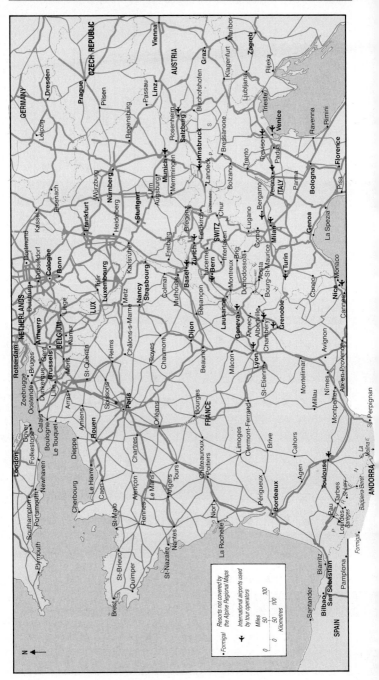

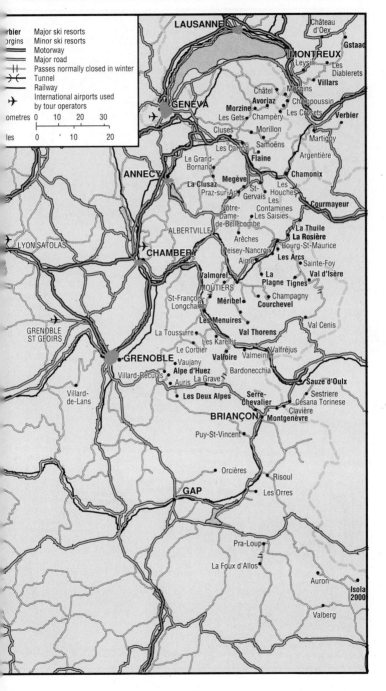

Major ski resorts
Minor ski resorts
Motorway
Major road
Passes normally closed in winter
Tunnel
Railway
International airports used by tour operators

rbier — Major ski resorts
orgins — Minor ski resorts

ometres   0   10   20   30
les   0   ·   10   20

LAUSANNE
Château d'Oex
Gstaad
MONTREUX
Leysin
Les Diablerets
Villars
Châtel
Morgins
Avoriaz
Champoussin
GENEVA
Morzine
Champéry
Les Crosets
Verbier
Les Gets
Champéry
Cluses
Morillon
Martigny
Les Carroz
Samoëns
Argentière
Le Grand-Bornand
Flaine
ANNECY
Megève
Chamonix
La Clusaz
St-Gervais
Les Houches
Praz-sur-Arly
Courmayeur
Nôtre-Dame-de-Bellecombe
Les Contamines
Les Saisies
ALBERTVILLE
Arêches
La Thuile
La Rosière
LYON SATOLAS
Peisey-Nancroix
Bourg-St-Maurice
CHAMBERY
Aime
Les Arcs
Valmorel
Sainte-Foy
La Plagne
Val d'Isère
MOÛTIERS
Tignes
St-François Longchamp
Méribel
Champagny
Courchevel
Les Menuires
La Toussuire
Les Karellis
Val Thorens
Val Cenis
GRENOBLE ST GEOIRS
La Corbier
Valfréjus
Le Corbier
Valloire
Valmeinier
Vaujany
GRENOBLE
Alpe d'Huez
Bardonecchia
Villard-Reculas
Auris
La Grave
Sauze d'Oulx
Villard-de-Lans
Les Deux Alpes
Serre-Chevalier
Sestriere
Cesana Torinese
BRIANÇON
Clavière
Montgenèvre
Puy-St-Vincent
Orcières
Risoul
GAP
Les Orres
Pra-Loup
La Foux d'Allos
Auron
Isola 2000
Valberg

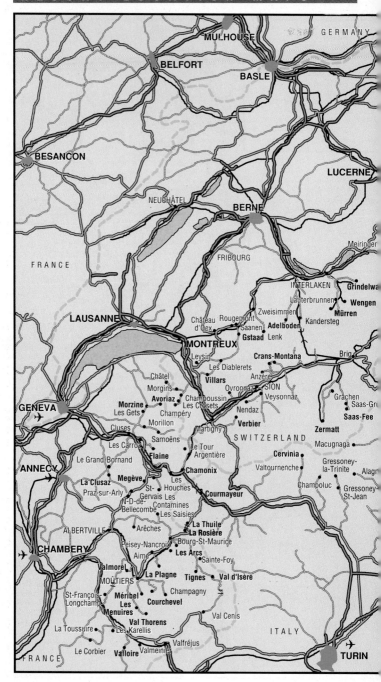

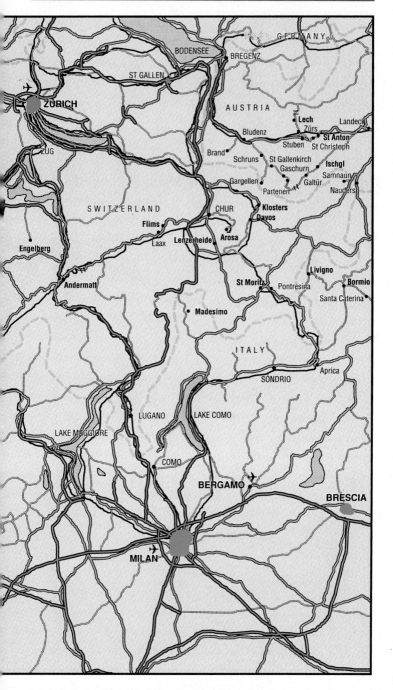

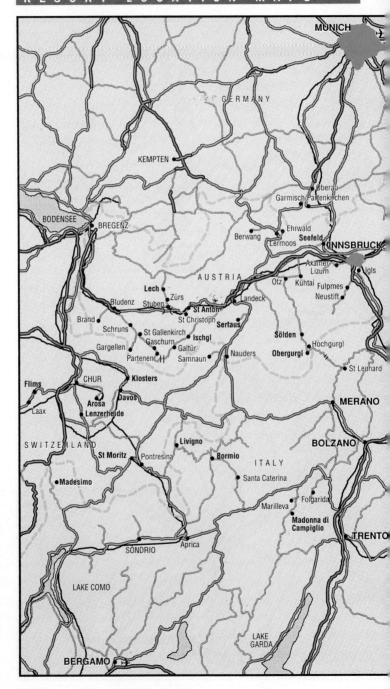

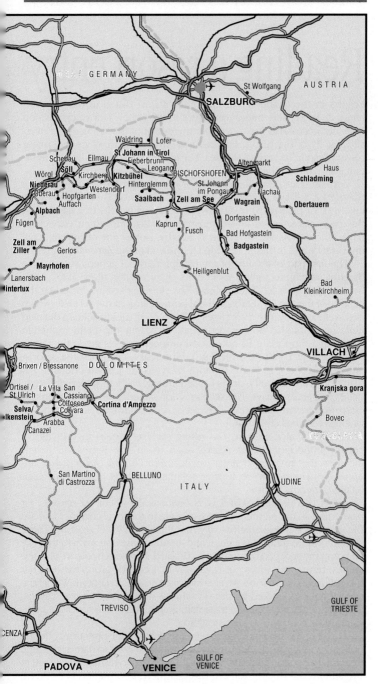

Reading a resort entry

Resorts in the Guide are divided into 'major' (listed in our table on pages 22 to 31) and 'minor' ones (not in the table). This categorisation does not necessarily indicate either the extent of the skiing or the over-all capacity of the resort. For example, Obergurgl qualifies as a major resort, despite its limited ski area, because it continues to be an important international skiing destination, for British skiers in particular.

Zermatt is also classified as a major resort. After its name and canton (district) is a list of its good points and bad points. This is followed by linked (l) or nearby (n) resorts which might be worthy of a day trip. In this case, Cervinia is a linked resort and is also important enough to have its own chapter. Grächen is nearby, but is not of international importance and is therefore added to the end of the Zermatt chapter.

The first part of the text of each chapter gives a general summary of the area, aiming to convey some of its character and more of its attractions and drawbacks. Then follows *The skiing*, a section including the heights of the top lift station and the bottom limit of the ski area (which may well be below the resort itself). This section incorporates a detailed description of the ski area or areas, including the main mountain access. It is important to note that European resorts grade their runs black (difficult), red (intermediate), blue (easy) and, in some resorts, green (beginner). In North America the runs are graded double black diamond (very difficult), single black diamond (difficult), blue (intermediate) and green (easy). The skiing section includes smaller sections on *Mountain restaurants* and *Beginners and children* (ski tuition and facilities for small children).

Another major section, *The resort* (or *The resorts* in the case of equally important linked resorts such as in the Portes du Soleil) includes the smaller sections on *Accommodation*, *Eating out* and *Après-ski*. There may be further separate sections describing minor linked or nearby resorts.

A fact box entitled *Skiing facts* contains details of ski schools, lift passes and so on. All the prices we give are in the local currency and are the most recent available (usually based on the 1992-3 season). These should only be treated as a guideline. For lift passes we say whether the lift company accepts payment by credit card. For ski schools we give the names, times and prices per hour, day or week for group lessons. For the children's ski schools we also indicate the ages accepted. We list the special courses offered by the ski schools, the cost of private lessons, and state whether there is a mountain guiding company for those interested in ski-touring and off-piste skiing.

At the end of the fact box we list the British tour operators offering holidays in the resort. Our list of tour operators is up to date at the time of going to press in June 1993, but liable to change during the course of the summer and early winter. There is more information about each operator in the tour operators section towards the back of the book, including addresses and numbers for further information.

We also summarise major changes in the resort *(What's new)* and quote typical prices for food and refreshments. Again, it must be emphasised that this is just a guideline to the prices you can expect to find.

Regular readers will notice a major departure from previous editions in that resorts are now listed not in geographical groups, but in alphabetical order country by country. Major linked ski areas are sometimes called by their area name rather than by a long string of the resort names, as in the case of the Jungfrau region and the Portes du Soleil. Where an area crosses a border we have been obliged to choose one country as its 'base'. In the case of La Thuile-La Rosière and for the Milky Way it is Italy; and in the case of the Portes du Soleil it is France. All resorts in the book are also listed in the index.

The 'minor' resorts, for example Maria Alm and Copper Mountain, are often not minor in importance at all within the context of their country. These are resorts which we feel at present do not generate sufficient international interest for promotion to the premier league. The text for these 'minor' resorts is broken down into fewer sections – *The skiing* (with mountain restaurants, beginners and children), *The resort* (including accommodation) and *Après-ski* (with village restaurants, suitability for non-skiers and other sports).

In the *Best of the rest* section each of the chapters includes a number of resorts and begin with an introduction to the country or area. In some cases the major resort has a table.

The ski area of many of the 'major' resorts (and linked 'minor' resorts) is shown on a map. All but a couple of these maps are drawn to a consistent scale and use colour tints to show height above sea level – see the scale and key below. The arrows on the runs indicate the resorts' own gradings, not our assessment of difficulty. The maps are intended to help you compare resorts, not to find your way around the mountains. Both the text and the maps are based mainly on the 1992-3 ski season.

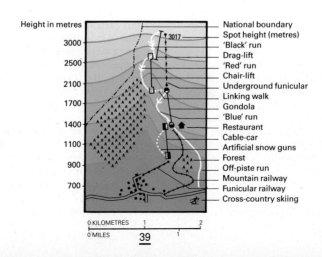

Height in metres		National boundary
	3017	Spot height (metres)
3000		'Black' run
		Drag-lift
2500		'Red' run
		Chair-lift
2100		Underground funicular
		Linking walk
1700		Gondola
		'Blue' run
1400		Restaurant
		Cable-car
1100		Artificial snow guns
		Forest
900		Off-piste run
		Mountain railway
700		Funicular railway
		Cross-country skiing

0 KILOMETRES 1 2
0 MILES 1

Alpbach, Tyrol

ALTITUDE 1000m (3,280ft)

••

Good points attractive village, ideal for family skiing, lack of queues, ideal for non-skiers, long vertical drop
Bad points lack of challenging pistes, limited late-season skiing, access to slopes, limited number of pistes
Linked or nearby resorts Reith (n)

Alpbach is a tiny, typically Tyrolean hamlet of traditional wooden chalets and farmhouses. In its time it has been voted Austria's prettiest village. Tourism came to Alpbach in the 1930s, and the village has managed to win over generations of visitors who come to ski here year after year. In fact, it is not unusual to see three generations skiing together.

The ski area is limited both in size and in its variety of runs, and is best suited to beginners and less adventurous intermediates. On top of this there is the slight inconvenience of having to take a bus from the village to the main slopes and back again each day. Having a car helps, not least because it means you can make day-trips to other resorts such as Mayrhofen, Söll or Kitzbühel for a bit of variety. Parking can, however, be a problem in the village.

Alpbach is not the place for intermediates who are trying to clock up the kilometres, nor is it for advanced skiers searching for new challenges. It is essentially a small family resort, ideal for a Christmas or early-season holiday, but snow in the village cannot be guaranteed.

The skiing
Top 2000m (6,560ft) bottom 830m (2,723ft)

Apart from the nursery slopes next to the village, and the Böglerlift with its south-facing red (intermediate) run, which is rarely open, all of Alpbach's skiing is on the slopes of the Wiedersberger Horn, a five-minute bus ride from the village. One reporter comments: 'It's a great resort if you don't mind doing the same run over and over again.' Mountain access from Alpbach is on the two-stage, six-seater Achenwirt gondola across the wooded north-facing slopes to Hornboden at 1850m. Queuing is not a problem here, although the number of skiers increases at weekends.

Alpbach has a large vertical drop compared to other Austrian resorts of a similar village altitude and there are a number of long runs. From Hornboden, a couple of wide pistes run back down to the Kriegalm half-way station, including a black (difficult) FIS racecourse which is one of the two black runs on the mountain; the other is Brandegg. From here a red run carries on down to the bottom, creating a good, fast course of over 1000m vertical, which is used by British racing clubs for

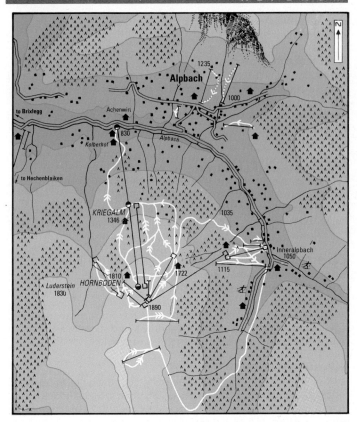

their competitions. The views around Hornboden are superb and the terrain open and gentle, with several short drag-lifts suitable for near-beginners.

It is interesting to note that although Alpbach has always had the reputation of being a beginners' resort, all but a couple of the runs on the mountain are marked red, and only one, the Familienabfahrt, is blue (easy). This is a long path from Gmahkopf to Kriegeralm, which reporters claim is often icy.

Mountain access is also possible by chair-lift from Inneralpbach along the valley. Here the lifts join up with the skiing above Hornboden, and there is a long, easy red run from Gmahkopf back down to Inneralpbach. The top lift here, Hornlift 2000, opens up some higher altitude and more challenging intermediate skiing. There is more skiing at Reith, 7km down the valley from Alpbach, which includes mainly red runs and some beginners' skiing served by several more lifts to the nursery slopes.

The long, red itinerary route from Gmahkopf down to Inneralpbach is not pisted, though it is usually well skied and conditions are not generally difficult. There is some interesting off-piste skiing to be found around the Wiedersbergerhorn, and the ski school runs special tours for this on Saturdays.

Mountain restaurants

Hornboden is a self-service and à la carte restaurant at the top station of the gondola and is also easily reached by non-skiers. Rossmoos is above the village and offers typical Tyrolean food. The Gmahstuben is recommended by one reporter for 'very good food' but, as can be expected up the mountain, it is 'not cheap'. The restaurants in the valley at Inneralpbach and Achenwirt are also popular.

Beginners and children

We have favourable reports of the ski school here. It is said to be 'well organised' and 'The instructors spoke good English.'

The nursery slopes close to the village centre are good, varied, and sunny. Beginners are taken up to Hornboden when the snow cover lower down is poor.

The resort

Alpbach is a small, sunny village set on a steep hillside. The compact resort has a pretty green-and-white church at its centre, which is surrounded by old wooden chalets. A few new buildings have recently been added, though all new additions have to be built in the traditional style. Many of Alpbach's regulars are British and there is a British ski club, the Alpbach Visitors, for children's race training.

Accommodation

Most of Alpbach's accommodation is in hotels, ranging from basic bed and breakfast to the very comfortable. The three most luxurious hotels, all with pools, are the Böglerhof, the Alphof and the Alpbacherhof. The latter is centrally placed and several reporters found the food and service to be excellent here. The Alphof is for heartier skiers as it is reached by a 15-minute uphill walk from the village. Its restaurant is warmly recommended. Less expensive hotels include the Post, Haus Angelika, Haus Elisabeth, Haus Erna and Haus Max. The keenest skiers may find the Galtenberg and the Gasthof Achenwirt well positioned for the gondola. Inneralpbach, 4km along the valley, is another convenient and quiet place to stay. There are two Spar supermarkets in Alpbach and one in Inneralpbach which, according to reporters, 'sell everything you could possibly need'.

Eating out

The restaurants do not offer much variety, although the recommended ones include the Gasthof Jakober, Alpbacher Taverne and the Gasthof Wiedersbergerhorn. The most luxurious is the restaurant in the four-star Hotel Böglerhof.

Après-ski

The nightlife in Alpbach is not too expensive, according to our reporters. Typical Tyrolean evenings, sleigh rides, skating, curling and bowling are the main post-skiing occupations. The public swimming-pool and sauna are about five minutes' walk from the village centre and there is a long toboggan run at Reith, 7km away.

There are some lively tea-time places in hotels such as the Messnerwirt and the Jakober. The pubs, namely the Hornbeisl next to the lifts in Inneralpbach, the Waschkuchl and the Birdies Pub in Alpbach village centre are all recommended. The Schneeloch disco is recommended, as is the Weinstadl disco which is 400m from the village centre. One reporter recommends the horse-drawn sleigh rides up to the 300-year-old inn at the head of the valley. The seventeenth-century farmhouse, Unterberg, at Inneralpbach is a museum of the history of the area. Shopping in Alpbach is limited.

Skiing facts: Alpbach

TOURIST OFFICE
A-6236 Alpbach 604, Tyrol
Tel 43 5336 5211
Fax 43 5336 5012

THE RESORT
By road Calais 1127km
By rail Brixlegg 10km, 7 daily post-buses to Alpbach
By air Innsbruck 1 hr, Munich 2 hrs
Visitor beds 2,400 (50% guesthouses, 25% hotels, 25% apartments)
Transport free bus between village and gondola runs every 15 mins

THE SKIING
Longest run Kafner, 3km (red)
Number of lifts 22
Number of trails/pistes 16 (6% easy, 81% intermediate, 13% advanced)
Total of trails/pistes 45km
Nursery slopes 10 lifts (3 in resort, others at Reith and Inneralpbach)
Summer skiing none
Snowmaking 10 hectares covered

LIFT PASSES
Area pass (covers Alpbach and Reith) ÖS1,170-1,210 for 6 days
Day pass ÖS260
Half-day pass ÖS195 after midday
Beginners free baby-lift for ski kindergarten, points tickets
Children 40% reduction up to 15 yrs
Pensioners 31% reduction over 65 yrs
Credit cards accepted no

SKI SCHOOLS
Adults Alpbach Ski School and Innertal Ski School, ÖS1,150 for 6 days

Children as adults
Private lessons ÖS1780 per day
Special courses snowboarding, mono-skiing, off-piste skiing, ski-touring
Guiding companies through Alpbach Ski School

CROSS-COUNTRY
Ski schools Alpbach Ski School
Loipe location and size 17km at Inneralpbach

CHILDCARE
Non-ski kindergarten organised by tourist office for 3 yrs and over, 9.15am-4.15pm, ÖS150 per day plus ÖS50 for lunch
Ski kindergarten through ski school for 4 yrs and over, 9.30am-4.15pm, ÖS1800 for 6 days including lunch
Babysitting list from tourist office

OTHER SPORTS
Skating, sleigh rides, paragliding, swimming, fitness centres, tobogganing, indoor tennis in Kramsach (12km away)

WHAT'S NEW
● Drag-lift on the Wiedersbergerhorn, the Hornlift 2000, goes up to 2000m

FOOD AND DRINK PRICES
Coffee ÖS24, bottle of house wine ÖS170, beer ÖS25, dish of the day ÖS150

TOUR OPERATORS
Enterprise, GFT Tours, Inghams, Made to Measure, Neilson, Ski Thomson

Badgastein, Salzburgerland

ALTITUDE 1100m (3,608ft)

••

Good points large intermediate ski area, tough runs, tree-level skiing, thermal baths, variety of après-ski, easy rail access, low prices
Bad points lack of skiing convenience, awkward for families with small children, heavy traffic
Linked or nearby resorts Bad Hofgastein (l), Dorfgastein (n), Sportgastein (n), Grossarl (n)

Legend has it that the thermal springs which abound in the Gasteiner region of Austria were discovered in the seventh century when two hunters pursuing a wounded stag found it nursing its injuries in a steaming pool. Gold and silver were mined here for Rome a century before Christ, and the rich ore of the Tauern mountains continued to be the major source of revenue for the area until the sixteenth century. Apart from its recent fame as a conference centre and ski destination, its reputation as a resort is founded on its curative thermal baths. Schubert composed his D Major Piano Sonata (Deutsch no.850) here while taking the cure in the summer of 1825. By coincidence, Mozart's widow and mother were here at the same time. The Gasteinertal has four ski areas: Badgastein, Bad Hofgastein, Dorfgastein and their modern neighbour, Sportgastein. Between them they offer 250km of bus- and mountain-linked skiing in a magnificent winter sports setting.

Badgastein, dramatically stacked on a steep hillside, is the best-known village of the quartet. It is no alpine charmer, but a town of that slightly faded grandeur associated with spas, boasting impressive-looking and rather formal hotels looming above the River Ache. With a smart casino and many first-class hotels, it still attracts a well-heeled clientele, but that does not mean it is purely a resort for wealthy gamblers. Unfortunately it has in recent years, like Saalbach, suffered from a blight of noisy Swedish holidaymakers and an increasingly large number of British, particularly families, prefer the more peaceful and traditional Austrian village ambience of Badhofgastein, a spacious and comfortable spa without any grandiose pretensions.

Similarly Dorfgastein, situated just inside the narrow gateway to the valley, is an unspoilt rustic village with direct access to plenty of easy and intermediate skiing. Sportgastein at the head of this narrow boxed valley remains largely undeveloped beyond a couple of restaurants and is strictly a ski area, which because of its altitude can be cold and bleak.

It does, however, come into its own when snow elsewhere in the valley is poor.

In Badgastein, which has an annoyingly complicated one-way system, traffic is heavy and parking can be difficult; the bus service between the resorts is efficient but 'hideously overcrowded' during high season. Because of the steepness of Badgastein itself, transport within the resort is preferable to walking. Taxis are plentiful and rates negotiable. Reporters say a car is handy for visits to the Graukogel ski area on the other side of the valley as well as to Bad Hofgastein and Dorfgastein. A growing number of reporters enthuse about the region and as one reporter put it: 'There is nothing you can find that is bad about Badgastein.'

The skiing
Top 2686m (8,810ft) bottom 850m (2,788ft)

In addition to the main ski area on the west side of the valley between Badgastein and Bad Hofgastein, there are three other separate areas, all with differing attractions. The Graukogel runs above Badgastein on the far side of the valley are few in number, but long and satisfying descents for good skiers. Sportgastein has high-altitude skiing over vast open expanses of mountainside. The friendly skiing shared by Dorfgastein and Grossarl is a confidence-building, but at times challenging little area for beginners and intermediates.

The main **mountain access** is via a two-stage gondola, which climbs from above the station to the Stubnerkogel at 2246m, a tangled junction of lift arrivals at the top of a long ridge. The east-facing runs to Badgastein provide good, tough skiing, with a mixture of open ground above half-way, and woods below mostly graded red (intermediate), but difficult when conditions are poor. The blue (easy) run winds down the mountain and is usually crowded and often icy. The wide top-half of the slope gives plenty of opportunity for off-piste variations. The Ahorn drag-lift back up is particularly steep like many others in the valley and reporters comment on how difficult they can be to ride.

The west-facing backside of the ridge is broken ground with some impressive rocky drops and gullies on the way down to Jungeralm. The piste here again carries considerable skier traffic. The north-facing runs down into the Angertal provide some of the best skiing in the region. From Jungeralm a long, undulating black (difficult) run drops directly through the woods. The alternatives are to take the easy serpentine Skiweg path from Jungeralm, or to take the much more satisfying red run from Stubnerkogel. Both the Angertalbahn and the Jungeralmbahn, which take you back up, are modern high-speed chairs. From the Angertal, a chair and a drag-lift go up over south-facing slopes to the Schlossalm ski area, also accessible by the Kitzstein funicular railway, which starts a bus-ride from the centre of Badhofgastein.

Schlossalm is a spacious basin above the tree-line, which offers a lot of rather similar intermediate runs, none of them of any great length and generally easier than those on the Stubnerkogel. The new Sendleitenbahn quad chair has reduced congestion here. Good skiers will mainly be interested in the long run around the back of the moun-

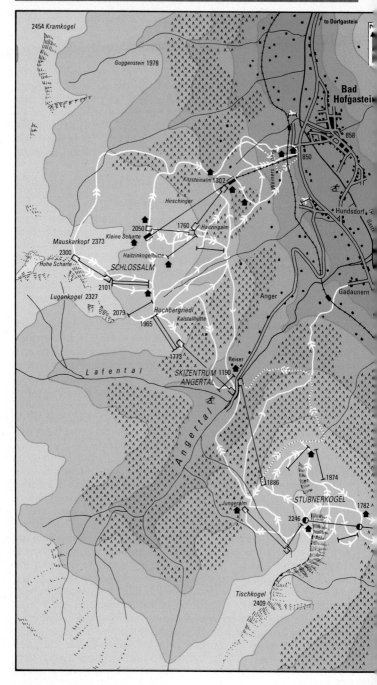

tain, which is reached either from Höhe Scharte at 2300m or from Kleine Scharte at 2050m. In good snow conditions it is possible to ski 1450m vertical over eight kilometres all the way to the bottom of the railway.

The thickly wooded, north-west facing slopes of Graukogel are served by a slow two-stage chairlift. This is the local racing hill and, apart from one easy run around the top of the mountain, all the trails are challenging variants of the direct descent under the chairs of 900m vertical. Some of the best snow in the region is to be found here and at least a couple of the runs are left purposefully ungroomed. Grading and piste maintenance is excellent throughout the region. Skiing is possible with only a minimum of snow cover, as most of it is on pastureland, with few rocks and stones. One veteran reporter describes them as 'the best-kept pistes I've ever skied on'. There are small artificial snow installations at the bottom of the Stubnerkogel and on the long Angertal run, as well as at Dorfgastein.

Sportgastein, at the head of the valley, is an icy place to find yourself when the weather closes in. However, on a fine day the piste skiing is varied enough to be interesting and the off-piste can be quite exceptional. If snow conditions are poor elsewhere in the valley, Sportgastein can become very crowded. A chair, followed by a drag, takes you up from 1600m to Kreuzkogel at 2686m, most of it above the trees and very exposed. The main attraction for good skiers is the north-facing

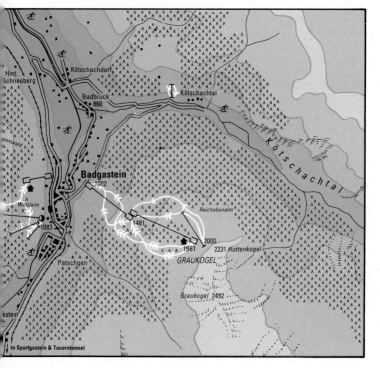

off-piste descent off the back, down to the tollgate above Böckstein, from where it is necessary to take a bus back to the lifts. The slopes beneath the chair-lift are quite steep, with some good off-piste skiing among the thinly scattered trees as well as a testing red piste.

Dorfgastein and Grossarl share a wooded family ski area. A double chair from Dorfgastein takes you up to Wengeralm, where a gondola brings you to Fulseck, which at 2033m is the highest point. Although most of the runs are classified as red and some are of over 1000m vertical, few of them can be described as steep except the black back down to Dorfgastein from Wengeralm. The Grossarl side is mostly gentle with long wide runs and some easy off-piste between the trees. It is served by a gondola from the village, which takes you up to Kreuzhöhe at 1827m.

Mountain restaurants

The area is plentifully served with pleasant huts on the slopes as well as self-service cafeteria at the lift stations. Prices appear to be no higher than in the valley, and there they are low by Austrian standards, which is surprising in a resort of this standing. Reporters particularly recommend the Wengeralm above Dorfgastein for its 'very good traditional fried potato pancakes'. The Jungerstube on the far side of the Stubnerkogel is praised for its 'wicked hot chocolate'. The Aeroplanstadl is a continuing favourite. The Schlossalm has a warm cosy atmosphere and is famed for its thick *Gulaschsuppe*. The Hamburger Skiheim above Badhofgastein has a barbecue and ice-bar. The Panorama at Kreuzkogel has a children's slide between floors. Toni's Almgasthaus at the top of Graukogel serves garlic soup in bowls hollowed out of loaves of bread.

Beginners and children

We have generally good reports of both the Skischule Pflaum and the Skischule Luigi, although one correspondent did complain that his instructor turned up drunk on the last day in Bad Hofgastein: 'The school was most apologetic and refunded ÖS50; apart from this lapse the chap was very good.' Size of classes seems to vary between 4 and 12 with the standard of English high, ('the instructor even understood our jokes').

Like all resorts with a disparate ski area of this nature Badgastein is difficult to recommend for children. All the villages have ski kindergarten taking children from three years old, but finding someone to care for younger ones is more difficult. Hotel Grüner Baum in Badgastein does run a crèche, although we have no reports of it. The nursery slopes are 10 minutes from the centre.

The resort

Badgastein is built in a cramped, claustrophobic position on the steep, wooded slopes which abruptly close the southern end of the Gastein valley. The main road and railway bypass the resort centre, which is more simply negotiated by the steep footpaths and stairways than by car. The focus of the resort is a smart complex including hotel, shopping precinct, casino and conference hall projecting from the hillside beside the waterfall. Expensive boutiques pander to the tastes of the wealthy clientele who come here not only to ski. The resort's upper level, a steep but short climb away, is a rather ordinary collection of unfashionable spa hotels which attract skiers in winter because of their convenient location, and newer accommodation which has sprung up here for the same reason.

Accommodation

Most of the accommodation is in hotels, of which there are quite literally hundreds in the valley, some of them with hot and cold thermal water. Among the hotels at the top of the resort within easy walking distance of the Stubnerkogel lifts, the Bärenhof is the most comfortable and expensive. The Krone and Goethehof are ideally placed but rather uninspiring middle-range hotels. Much more charming and in a quieter position is the simple Fischerwirt. The Hotel Mirabell is praised, but the position is not so convenient as there is 'a long tiring walk to the lift'. Hotel Mozart is recommended as comfortable and spacious and 'well-positioned for the skiing and the nightlife'. The Tannenburg is said to be in an excellent location, comfortable but 'in need of a good coat of paint'. The recently renovated Salzburgerhof is a luxurious five-star which is recommended for its 'exceptional attention to detail'. At the foot of the Graukogel lift is the Schillerhof, recommended for its 'splendid views, clean and comfortable rooms'. The Grüner Baum, built in 1831 by Archduke Johann as a hunting lodge, is a resort within a resort in the beautiful setting of the Köschachtal. It has its own thermal indoor swimming-pool.

Eating out

The choice of restaurants is limited mainly to the hotels, but the Bahnhof restaurant is particularly recommended as good value-for-money. The Mozart on Mozartplatz is praised for its fondue. The Pizzeria am Wasserfall is 'inexpensive and cheerful'. The China-restaurant on Kaiser-Franz-Joseph 'makes a pleasant change from *Wienerschnitzel*'.

Après-ski

Nowhere in Austria do reporters' views on the quality and quantity of the après-ski vary so much as they do in Badgastein. Opinions run the full range from 'quiet' to 'fantastic, better than Mayrhofen'. Certainly there has been an invasion of young Swedes in recent years who do not believe in quiet evenings with a good book after a day on the slopes. However, their sometimes rowdy behaviour is not to everyone's taste in a resort which does on the other hand attract an older and more sedate kind of visitor. The Gatz Music Club is recommended at tea-time and again much later in the evening. Most other bars seem similarly to be run and frequented by Swedes. Eden's Pub is said to be usually crowded, 'not least because a giant moose head takes up most of the room'. For night owls the Blockhäusl Club near Mozartplatz begins to liven up after 1am. The Salzburgerhof Hotel bar has live music ('everything from UB40 to Glenn Miller'). The thermal baths are said to be 'the best cure ever for aching limbs and a bruised body and ego', but they are not cheap with prices starting at ÖS174 for a dip.

Badhofgastein 870m (2,854ft)

Badhofgastein has neither the inconveniently steep and dark setting, nor the faded grandeur of its neighbour. It is smaller, but still a sizeable resort with 18 hotels spread along the broadest part of the valley. The Kitzstein funicular is a long walk or a bus ride away. It is a good base for the valley's walks and cross-country trails, and busy skating and curling rinks complete the winter scene. There is an outdoor, naturally heated

· ·

Skiing facts: Badgastein

TOURIST OFFICE
A-5640 Badgastein,
Salzburgerland
Tel 43 6434 25310
Fax 43 6434 253137

THE RESORT
By road Calais 1220km
By rail station in resort
By air Salzburg 1½ hrs
Visitor beds 7,519 (68% hotels, 32% pensions and apartments)
Transport buses run between Badgastein and Dorfgastein

THE SKIING
Longest run Hohe Scharte Nord (Bad Hofgastein), 7.8km (red)
Number of lifts 52
Number of trails/pistes 60 (30% easy, 40% intermediate, 30% difficult)
Total of trails/pistes 250km
Nursery slopes 4 lifts
Summer skiing none
Snowmaking 38km covered

LIFT PASSES
Area pass Gastein Super Ski (covers Schossalm-Angertal-Stubnerkogel-Graukogel-Grossarl and all Gastein resorts), ÖS1,430-1,680
Day pass ÖS300-340
Half-day pass ÖS270 after 11.45am
Beginners points tickets
Children 40% reduction for 6-13 yrs, free for 6 yrs and under
Pensioners 10% reduction for women 60 yrs and over and men 65 yrs and over
Credit cards accepted yes

SKI SCHOOLS
Adults Werner Pflaum and Luigi, 10am-3.15pm, ÖS1,450 for 6 days
Children as adults
Private lessons ÖS400 per hr
Special courses snowboarding, off-piste skiing
Guiding companies Hans Zlöbl

CROSS-COUNTRY
Ski schools Werner Pflaum
Loipe location and size 37km in Badgastein and Sportgastein

CHILDCARE
Non-ski kindergarten none
Ski kindergarten Werner Pflaum, 3 yrs and over, 9am-4pm, ÖS2,000 for 6 days including lunch
Babysitting list available from tourist office

OTHER SPORTS
Skating, curling, indoor tennis and golf, squash, swimming, fitness centre, sleigh rides, tobogganing

WHAT'S NEW
● Sendleiten quad chair-lift at Schlossalm ● extension of snowmaking

FOOD AND DRINK PRICES
Coffee ÖS22, bottle of house wine ÖS200, beer ÖS27, dish of the day ÖS150

TOUR OPERATORS
Crystal, Enterprise, Inghams, Made to Measure, Neilson, Ski Miquel

· ·

swimming-pool as well as a modern sports centre with tennis and squash. Reporters complain that the funicular holds 100 while the cable car above it has a capacity of only 40; this leads to annoying 30-minute queues at peak times. Wise skiers take the chair from the top of the train. The resort has a strong conservation policy and anyone who deliberately skis through sapling plantations is liable to forfeit his lift pass. Buses circle the northern part of the resort every 10 minutes and the southern section every 20 minutes. The kindergarten takes children from three years old. Thermal baths here are said to be a must, as are the evening sleigh rides.

Accommodation is mainly in hotels. The Gasthof zum Boten is described as an 'excellent old posthouse with big, clean comfortable rooms'. The Kaiser Franz and the more expensive Hotel Norica both receive good reports, as do the Hotel Moser and the Salzburgerhof. The most convenient hotels are mostly new ones lining the road from the centre to the river. Francky's Kneipe is said to be the place for après-ski along with Sonia's Pub. The one disco is not usually busy. The bowling alley is recommended as 'great fun for a rowdy night out – the best excursion I've ever been on'.

TOURIST OFFICE
PO Box 136, A-5630 Bad Hofgastein,
Salzburgerland
Tel 43 6432 7110 0
Fax 43 6432 7110 31

TOUR OPERATORS
Austrian Holidays, Crystal, Enterprise,
Neilson, Ski Thomson

Dorfgastein 835m (2,739ft)

Dorfgastein is the first of the settlements you come to on entering the Gasteinertal. Too many visitors to the area drive through without stopping. What they miss is a delightful little village with a charming main street lined with arcades. It remains untouched by the slightly depressingly health-conscious image of its bigger brothers. Horses and carts clatter along the narrow street past the old church, more often taking local folk about their business than taking tourists for joy rides. There are several well-kept, friendly and comfortable hotels in the centre. The Steindlwirt and Kirchenwirt are two of the larger ones. The skiing begins at least a five-minute walk from the village. The Gasthof Schihäusl stands at the foot of the slopes. Evenings are said to be livelier than you might expect in a village of this size.

TOURIST OFFICE
A-5632 Dorfgastein, Salzburgerland
Tel 43 64 33 277

TOUR OPERATORS

Innsbruck, Tyrol

ALTITUDE 575m (1,886ft)

••

Good points attractive town, short airport transfer, variety of skiing in area, summer skiing, activities for non-skiers
Bad points small separate ski areas, weekend lift queues, lack of skiing convenience
Linked or nearby resorts Axamer Lizum (n), Fulpmes (n), Igls (n), Mieders (n), Mutters (n), Neustift (n), Telfes (n), Tulfes (n)

The capital of the Tyrol is not only one of the most beautiful and historic cities in Austria, but is also a ski resort in its own right. It has twice hosted the Winter Olympic Games, has the advantage of its own international airport and a variety of good skiing is to be found within easy commuting distance.

Innsbruck stands at the crossroads of western Austria and is well served by a network of motorways fanning out towards the Arlberg, through the Inn valley towards the German border, and up towards the Brenner Pass and Italy. Nearby outlying villages can easily be reached by post-bus, but you do really need a car to take full advantage of all the surrounding skiing.

The Ötztal and the snow-sure skiing of Obergurgl and Sölden can be reached in under 90 minutes. The journey to Kitzbühel and the Ski-World takes an hour. Compared to what one might call a conventional ski resort, the costs of staying in the city are considerably lower. The choice of restaurants is wide and nightlife is both lively and varied. One reporter comments that not many places can include *Die Fledermaus* at the opera as après-ski on New Year's Eve.

Anyone staying over three days is entitled to a Club Innsbruck discount card giving a reduction on the area ski pass, which covers Igls, Mutters, Tulfes, Axamer Lizum and Hungerburg. Free ski-buses depart from the Landestheater and the Hauptbahnhof each morning and bring skiers back at the end of the day. Reporters are impressed with the service. The most challenging local skiing is to be found across the Inn above the city at Hungerburg on the south-facing slopes of the 2334m Hafelekar. The black (difficult) Karrine and the red (intermediate) Langes Tal runs are particularly challenging.

Igls 893m (2,929ft)

Igls, five kilometres up towards the Europabrücke and the Italian border, has the best skiing in the immediate area and is a fine example of a traditional Tyrolean village. The skiing goes up to 2247m and is served by a cable car, a chair-lift and four T-bars. The ski area consists of four runs cut through the trees. The red Olympic downhill presents a challenge on the front face of the mountain. It was here that Franz Klammer threw caution to the wind and hurled himself down the mountain to win the greatest Winter Olympics Gold of all time. The blue (easy) Familienabfahrt follows a less direct route. There are off-piste opportunities from the top of the Gipfel lift.

Igls has four mountain restaurants, most of them criticised by our reporters for their high prices, although the restaurant at the top of the cable car receives considerable praise.

The resort manages to support two ski schools, Igls 2000 and Schischule Schigls; instructors at both speak good English. The two nursery slopes are covered by snow-cannon and are a five-minute walk from the village centre. A non-ski kindergarten operates from 9am to 5pm. Ski-age children are catered for all day, between 10am and 4pm, with lunch in the Skikindergarten.

The village is small and uncommercialised. It has sedate hotels and coffee houses, excellent walks for non-skiers, and the Olympic bob-run, which is open to the public and, according to one reporter, 'totally brilliant.' The Astoria is a sound family hotel, the Sporthotel and the Schlosshotel are upmarket and expensive, while the Gasthof Stern is more middle-of-the-road. Hotel Alt Igls is recommended and described as 'very comfortable', the Pension Gstrein is a 'simple, but good' guesthouse. Two main supermarkets look after the needs of self-caterers.

Après-ski is not the strongest point of Igls, but the bars at the Bon Alpina and the Astoria, as well as the cellar bar of the Alt Igls, are the liveliest spots. Happy Night in the Gasthof Stern and the Sporthotel disco are for the later crowd.

TOURIST OFFICE
Hilberstrasse 15, A-6080 Igls
Tel 43 5123 77101
Fax 43 5123 78965

TOUR OPERATORS
Austrian Holidays, Equity Total Ski,
Inghams, Neilson, Ski Airtours

Axamer Lizum 1600m (5,248ft)

This is a somewhat characterless ski station of 12 hotels and a huge car park set in the heart of the most interesting and the largest all-round ski area beneath the peaks of the Hoadl (2343m) and Pleisen (2236m). Two discos, the Alte Mühle and the Axamer Klause, are the centre of the nightlife. Weekend lift queues, as in all the Innsbruck ski areas, can be a problem, but the 10 lifts provide piste possibilities, which are both extensive and varied. The 6.5km Axamer, graded black but red by most resorts' standards, takes you all the way down to the quiet village of Axams (874m).

Across the narrow valley, a long chair serves either the black Riesenslalom Herren run back to Axamer Lizum, or it gives access to the sunny and easy pistes above Mutters. Expectations of an improved link to form a ski circus here have not yet been met, and now seem likely to have evaporated in the light of the growing environmentalist lobby in the Tyrol. One reporter points out that this resort gets extremely cold in mid-winter when the sun disappears after midday, and that the quiet slopes are very civilised with none of the speed merchants playing on the Olympic slopes at Igls and Axamer.

Tulfes makes up the fifth Innsbruck ski area and consists of two blues and two reds on the slopes beneath the 2677m Glungezer and the 2305m Schartenkogel, 20 minutes from Innsbruck city centre along the Inn valley in the direction of Munich.

TOURIST OFFICE
Sylvester-Jordan Strasse 12,
A-6094 Axams, Tyrol
Tel 43 5234 8178
Fax 43 5234 7158

TOUR OPERATORS
Seasun School Tours, SkiBound,
Ski Partners

Fulpmes 937m (3,073ft)

Slightly further away, but still within easy post-bus travel, the Stubaital offers some of the best skiing in the area. Mieders, Telfes, Fulpmes, and Neustift all share a lift pass. Above Fulpmes, but not directly accessible from it, there is good skiing in a sheltered bowl now branded as Schlick 2000 Skizentrum. Lifts include a four-seater chair going up to 2200m. Some of the runs are tough and unpisted, but the majority are easy and confidence-building, and good for lower intermediates. The small, sunny nursery area receives favourable reports and Innsbruck can be reached by a scenic train/tram ride.

The Hotel Stubaierhof and the Hotel Alte Post are both recommended. Restaurants include the Leonardo Da Vinci ('very popular and good value'), and the Gasthaus Hofer, which serves 'simple, plain Austrian farmhouse fare.' The Café Corso, the Ossi-Keller, Platzwirt and Dorfalm discos make it a lively place by night.

TOURIST OFFICE
Gemeindezentrum, A-6166 Fulpmes, Tyrol
Tel 43 5225 2235/2892
Fax 43 5225 3843

TOUR OPERATORS
AlpineTours, Crystal

Neustift 1000m (3,280ft)

The main community and the centre of the broad and lush Stubaital, Neustift is a large, spread-out village, which has seen great expansion in recent years. Nevertheless, it remains very much at heart the traditional Tyrolean village, centred on one of the more magnificent and ornately decorated churches in this corner of Austria.

Recommended hotels include the Tirolerhof, which offers 'excellent food and a warm welcome', and the budget-priced and quaint Hotel Angelika in the centre of town. Nightlife is noisy in the Romanastübl with 'strange music, but a great, fun atmosphere'. Neustift has its own gentle ski area on wooded north-facing slopes, but it is also the hotel base for the more important skiing on the Stubai Glacier, 20 minutes away at the end of the valley. A free ski-bus operates regularly.

The skiing here is 365 days a year at a top altitude of 3200m and is one of the most extensive summer ski areas in Europe. The old four-seater gondola from the base station at Mutterbergalm (1750m) has been supplemented by a six-person gondola running in parallel to the first stage at Fernau. From here you can either continue by gondola or chair to a network of drags, which take you up to the top of the ski area. When snow is short elsewhere, the slopes can become unbelievably crowded and, out of season, German bank holidays are to be avoided. The glacial ski area is also extremely well-equipped and efficiently run. The ski shop at the top station is highly recommended for repairs, as most of its customers outside the winter months are international racing teams.

Keen skiers will probably stay in the Alpensporthotel Mutterberg, which is a comfortable establishment right at the base of the lifts. It has its own swimming pool, disco and bowling alley, which is just as well as it is particularly isolated.

Separate ski schools operate in both Neustift and on the glacier. There are kindergarten in both.

TOURIST OFFICE
Dorf A-6167, Neustift, Tyrol
Tel 43 5226 2228
Fax 43 5226 2529

TOUR OPERATORS
Alpine Tours, Crystal, Inghams,
Made to Measure, Neilson, Ski Hillwood,
Ski Thomson, Ski Trax

Ischgl, Tyrol

ALTITUDE 1400m (4,592ft)

••

Good points variety of easy runs, big ski area, beautiful scenery, alpine charm, ski-touring possibilities, sunny slopes, ski excursions into Switzerland, lively après-ski
Bad points long lift queues, lack of challenging runs
Linked or nearby resorts Samnaun (I), Galtür (n), Kappl (n)

For an increasing number of skiers, Ischgl and neighbouring Galtür in the remote and beautiful Paznaun valley, provide the near perfect mix of skiing and snow reliability together with alpine charm, an extensive ski area, and some of the wildest nightlife in Austria. As if that were not enough, the duty-free Swiss resort of Samnaun is linked across the border. Apart from bargain shopping, the Swiss side also has excellent mountain restaurants and some of the best skiing in the region. All of this was known to Ernest Hemingway, who dropped in here one afternoon in 1925 and became so entranced with the place that he stayed and found the inspiration to write the short story *An Alpine Idyll*.

Some of Hemingway's resting places on his literary lurch through life owe their subsequent spot on the map in part to his pen. Others merely shrugged off the transitory mantle of fame, named a bar after him, and got on with life. So it was with Ischgl, which has relied little on international publicity over the years to extol its virtues as a ski resort. Most of its clients are German, with an increasing number of Scandinavian and British visitors. We have been receiving detailed reports of the region, practically all from satisfied customers.

Ischgl's skiing contains few really difficult runs although many of the red runs are long enough to test most intermediate skiers. The off-piste and more exacting touring possibilities in the region are extensive and, because Ischgl does not have the fashionable cachet of St Anton, it does not immediately become 'skied out' after a proper snowfall.

The lift system comes in for some just and unjust criticism. It is better than in many comparable Austrian resorts, but too much emphasis is still placed on old-time T-bars that should have long since been recycled in this environmentally conscious corner of Austria.

Galtür is a peaceful and very friendly village at the head of the valley. It has long been known as an excellent ski-touring base and more recently it has added greatly to the size of its own small but varied ski area. Queuing is not a problem in Galtür, but sadly the same cannot be said for Ischgl and Samnaun, which suffer terribly from overcrowding at peak times. As one reporter, who inadvertently picked the worst fortnight of the season, put it: 'The pistes were like the alpine answer to Brighton beach on a hot August Bank Holiday.'

The skiing

Top 2864m (9,396ft) bottom 1377m (4,517ft)

The skiing principally consists of open slopes above Ischgl; long descents through woods to the village and a series of high, rocky bowls above with plenty of open, easy pistes. A long mountain crest which forms the Austro-Swiss border is reached by lift and easily breached on skis in a number of places, opening up a less extensive, but delightful area on the Swiss side, above the duty-free resort of Samnaun. The slopes on the Ischgl side face north-west and west, while on the Samnaun face they are mainly south and east.

Mountain access from Ischgl is from both ends of the village. One gondola takes you up to Idalp, a broad, sunny, open plateau with a ski school, restaurants, hotel and nursery slopes. A second gondola rises to Pardatschgrat, 300m higher, with runs back down to Ischgl or an easy connection with the rest of the lift system via Idalp.

The runs down to Ischgl from Pardatschgrat are among the best for good skiers, some of them giving an uninterrupted and demanding 1200m vertical across open slopes and on down through swathes cut through the trees. These runs are graded red (intermediate) or black (difficult), and it seems a pity there is no blue (easy) run. Black 4 down to the middle station seems more worthy of red classification. In the late afternoon these runs are crowded with skiers who cannot always handle the terrain, making it hazardous for themselves and for those skiers who can. Elsewhere in the resort piste-grading seems mixed.

At Idalp an assortment of lifts takes you up to different points around a fairly shallow, unevenly shelving, rocky bowl. The lower part provides good altitude nursery slopes. For better skiers this is not an area in which to linger, but it serves as a staging post to other parts of the region. Velillscharte offers one of the most beautiful and least skied of all the descents to Ischgl, down a valley of its own. However, it is not always open. From Idjoch, there are easy runs down into the sunny Swiss Alp Trida, and a long, panoramic traverse to the narrow Hölltal beside Idalp. The lifts up the Hölltal serve a variety of short runs, and also give access to some of the better skiing. Behind Palinkopf (2864m), which is the high point of the system, are some excellent reds and blacks, which in average snow conditions should present few problems to anyone. A long, enclosed chair-lift, which provides necessary protection against the weather in mid-winter, has been built from Gampen Alp, down in the Fimbatal, back up to Palinkopf. It is relatively little-used, and its runs (900m vertical both on- and off-piste) are a useful playground for accomplished skiers.

The run down a Swiss valley to the scattering of woods around Samnaun can be reached from any of the three lifts near Palinkopf. It is long and extremely beautiful, but not very interesting skiing, being mostly wide and gentle unless you start from the Schwarzwand drag.

After a visit to the duty-free emporia of Samnaun, which helpfully sell small backpacks, an awkward route beside the road or a short bus ride from the tourist office brings you to the cable car at Raveisch. This takes you up to the southern upper rim of the Alp Trida basin with its wide easy and intermediate skiing. The run down from the Alp

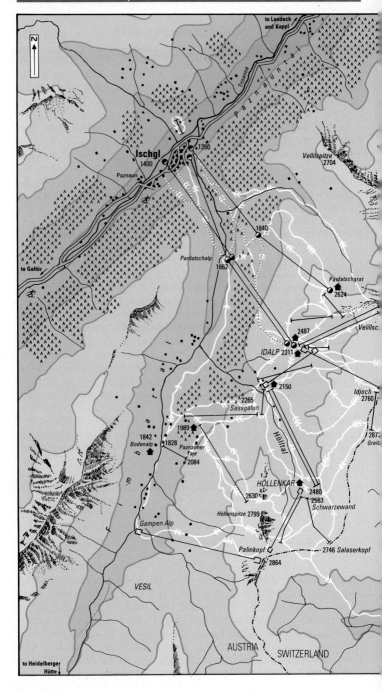

Trida restaurant ends up at Compatsch. From Alp Trida a double T-bar links up with Idalp and the return to Ischgl via Austria's highest customs post.

Ischgl has one enormous disadvantage: except during the lowest weeks of the season, huge queues are prone to develop and the home runs suffer from serious congestion: 'Your "bad" rating for lift queues was an euphemism', wrote one reporter; 'We felt ill at ease because of the hazard of skiing among excessively fast downhillers intermingled with slow and uncertain learners – in a seething mass'. Even in mid-January another encountered queues of up to 15 minutes and said the only way to avoid them was to ski the black runs in the morning and skip lunch. One reporter queued for nearly two hours to get back across the Swiss border from Samnaun. He stoically commented: 'The answer is to grin and bear it as the visit on a sunny day is a must.' However, it must be noted that another correspondent said he found no queues during an entire February week. Most of the lower pistes back to Ischgl are covered by artificial snow over the last few hundred metres.

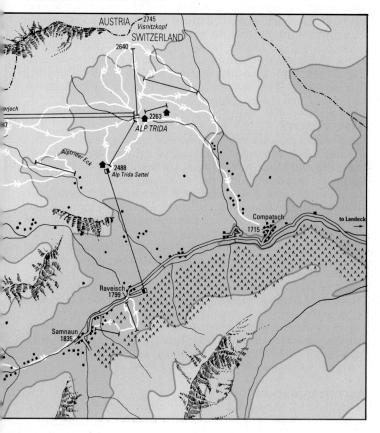

Mountain restaurants

The Paznauer Taja is recommended, if only for its 'truly wonderful panoramic views', and it sometimes has a live band on the terrace. Nearby Bodenalp is an attractive alternative, as is the pleasant hut at the bottom of the Höllenkar. The restaurant at the foot of the baby slope in Alp Trida is reportedly good, provided you avoid peak hours. All reporters found a noticeably higher standard of cuisine on the Swiss side ('try the *Rösti*'). The absence of tax is not noticeable in restaurant prices, which are in Swiss francs, although Austrian schillings are accepted everywhere.

Beginners and children

The Ischgl Ski School has had a solid reputation over many years. However, according to some reports, the lack of competition can lead to complaisance. One reporter encountered an English-speaking instructor who insisted on conducting the class only in German. Another spoke of 'chaos and time loss' as the classes were organised at the beginning of the week. In fact, most instructors speak good English. The average size of classes is as high as 10 to 12 pupils. Off-piste tours can be arranged through the ski school in what is exceptional touring terrain, particularly late on in the season.

Ischgl has good childcare facilities. The ski school takes children of four years and over for the whole day. The main nursery slopes are a 20-minute cable car ride up the mountain, but there is also a baby-drag near the village. Three hotels have crèches as well as the kindergarten, which takes potty-trained children.

The resort

Ischgl is an old village which has developed in a smart and harmonious way with a high standard of new buildings and accommodation and a high price level to match. More recent building is said to be less, rather than more, environmentally conscious in conception and some hotels are in danger of losing their traditional character with the addition of charmless modern extensions. The centre, bypassed by the main road, positively bustles with activity and excitement in the early evening. The remainder of the village sprawls along the valley in the shadow of the steep, wooded mountainside, which makes up the ski slopes. Parts of the village are hilly, with several staircases and steep paths, which can become dangerously icy.

A free ski-bus service links Ischgl, Kappl, and Galtür infrequently during the day and not in the evening. A post-bus service also operates between them as well as to the railhead at Landeck 30km away. Non-skiers can enjoy good walks, both in the valley and up the mountain to the restaurants at Bodenalp. The Silvretta Sports Centre houses a swimming-pool and a bowling alley. The farming museum at Mathon on the bus route to Galtür is also reportedly worth a visit.

Accommodation

Much of the accommodation is centred on the two lift departure points at either end of the village. Although Ischgl has grown in recent years, it takes only a few minutes to walk from one end to the other and therefore location is not a priority in choosing where to stay. The Goldener Adler, near the Silvretta gondola, receives good reports as 'a fine example of a proper Austrian hostelry in the old style'. The Post is centrally positioned. The Antony, on a hillside opposite the village, is 'very pleasant, with spacious rooms and excellent food'. Hotel Solaria, praised in the past for its comfortable rooms and facilities including a swimming-pool and sauna, receives a couple of adverse reports. One correspondent speaks of the atmosphere being 'gloomy and fraught', and there were claims last season that the management attitude did not appear to be entirely pro-British due to the alleged bad behaviour of some former guests. The Pension Paznaunhof is said to be 'very clean with a good breakfast in a pleasant atmosphere'. Some of the outlying gasthofs operate a courtesy mini-bus service.

Eating out

Most of the restaurants are in the hotels and one reporter comments on the 'sameness' of both menus and prices. The best eating places are tucked away off the main street. The Trofana-Alm bar-restaurant has a warm atmosphere and 'delicious pizza cooked on a wood-burning stove, and a good salad table'. The Goldener Adler is recommended for delicious fresh trout and other gourmet food in its wonderful traditional setting. The Nikis Stadl in the Piz Buin Hotel and the restaurant at the Hotel Tyrol are also worthy of note. The Sports Centre is suggested for value-for-money food and 'the lack of atmosphere was compensated for by the lack of cigarette smoke'. Popular fondue expeditions to the Heidelberger Hütte by snowcat or horse-drawn sleigh are organised most evenings.

Après-ski

Ischgl has a lively, but not necessarily rowdy, air to it when the lifts are closed for the night. Action starts at the outside bar of the Hotel Elisabeth. Later on the Tenne is popular. Tea-dancing, that ancient Austrian courtship ritual from which, no doubt, the Manhattan singles bar was derived, is alive and flourishing in Ischgl. There is also plenty of traditional entertainment of the yodel-and-*Schühplatte* variety complete with log-chopping. For a quieter coffee and cake, reporters recommend the Konditorei Salner and the Dorfcafé. Thommy's Bar is suggested for those who want to enjoy a quiet drink. The disco beneath the Hotel Madlein is the hot-spot later on.

Galtür 1585m (5,200ft)

This pleasing Austrian village is only a few minutes' drive from Ischgl but offers an altogether more relaxing, crowd-free environment coupled with limited, but interesting, skiing. It is small, but with a total capacity of 3,500 visitor beds, it is certainly not tiny. It enjoys a sunnier position than Ischgl at the widening head of the valley. The lifts are a bus ride away at Wirl (1635m). Buses are reliable and frequent, but only during peak hours. Given the energy, you can pole your way home at the end of the day. Avalanche slopes on both sides of the village mean that it can be completely isolated for short periods after a major storm. Galtür is recommended for relaxed family holidays.

The main access to the slopes is by a covered chair and the skiing goes up to 2464m at Saggrat with a series of interesting red and black runs down a wide, undulating bowl to the shore of the Kopssee. The skiing immediately above Wirl is of a more intermediate nature with a couple of long blues giving nearly 600m vertical, and an assortment of easy reds. Lift queues are non-existent and one reporter describes the skiing as 'the perfect example of how skiing should be everywhere: no queues, well organised, pretty, and reasonably varied for a small resort'. The nursery slope in Wirl is covered by snow-cannon.

The two mountain restaurants are said to be adequate, with the one near the main chair-lift offering the best food and prices. The ski school is recommended for 'friendly and competent teaching'. The kindergarten takes children of three years old and over, and the ski school gives lessons from three-and-a-half years upwards. Again we have glowing reports of the standard of child instruction.

The nightlife is much quieter here, but there are a number of cheerful bars, some with live music and tea-dancing, including the popular La Tschuetta. The Hotel Rössle is recommended for its comfortable rooms and 'the best restaurant in the village'. The Hotel Post and the Fluchthorn are both centrally located. The Ballunspitze is slightly further out, but an equally sound choice. The family-run Alpenrose is 'quiet, very welcoming, and offers excellent food'. We have good reports of the Alp Aren apartments ('very luxurious with colour television, coffee machine, and dishwasher'). The hotels at Wirl are isolated, but have their own excellent facilities and are popular at lunchtime. The Almhof in particular is said to serve good, cheap lunches and has a swimming-pool open to non-residents. The Wirlerhof is also recommended as a place to stay with children.

There are skating and curling rinks, a floodlit toboggan run and a smart sports centre with swimming-pool, squash, tennis and bowling. The centre is open until midnight and the pool is free to holders of a Silvretta lift pass bought in Galtür.

TOURIST OFFICE
A-6563 Galtür
Tel 43 5443 521
Fax 43 5443 52176

TOUR OPERATORS
Crystal, Enterprise, Made to Measure,
Ski Thomson, Ski Unique

Samnaun 1840m (6,036ft)

Samnaun is one of those anomalous communities in high, dead-end corners of Europe which has stayed alive thanks to their duty-free status coupled with ski resort facilities. This Swiss village is not exactly booming; it is little more than a large cluster of shops, hotels and supermarkets. Unless the price of spirits and electrical goods is your primary consideration it is not outstanding as a winter holiday centre. Petrol is also cheap, but ski equipment and perfume are not such good bargains.

Samnaun's attraction is that you can ski the Ischgl circuit and avoid much of the queuing and overcrowding you would experience on the Austrian side. It has a 10km cross-country track, a ski school, which specialises in organising ski tours, and a kindergarten at Alp Trida. Access by car is from the Inn valley south of Landeck.

TOURIST OFFICE
CH-7563 Samnaun
Tel 41 84 95154
Fax 41 8495652

TOUR OPERATORS
Ski Unique

Skiing facts: Ischgl

TOURIST OFFICE
Postfach 24, A-6561 Ischgl, Tyrol
Tel 43 5444 5266
Fax 43 5444 5636

THE RESORT
By road Calais 1017km
By rail Landeck 30km, frequent buses from station
By air Innsbruck 1½ hrs
Visitor beds 7,396 (63% hotels, 26% apartments, 11% guesthouses)
Transport bus service links Ischgl, Kappl and Galtür

THE SKIING
Longest run Palinkopf, 12km (red)
Number of lifts 37
Number of trails/pistes 50 (20% easy, 60% intermediate, 20% difficult)
Total of trails/pistes 200km
Nursery slopes 2 lifts at Idalp
Summer skiing none
Snowmaking 12km covered

LIFT PASSES
Area pass Silvretta (covers Ischgl/Samnaun, Galtür, Kappl and See), ÖS2,080 for 6 days. Ischgl/Samnaun lifts only, ÖS1,665 for 6 days
Day pass Ischgl/Samnaun, ÖS410
Half-day pass ÖS310 after 11.30am
Beginners book of tickets available
Children Silvretta, 6-14 yrs, ÖS1,170 for 6 days. Ischgl/Samnaun, ÖS1,020 for 6 days
Pensioners 60 yrs and over, as children
Credit cards accepted no

SKI SCHOOLS
Adults Ischgl, 10.30am-12.30pm and 1.30-3.30pm, ÖS1,230 for 6 days
Children 4 yrs and over, times and prices as adults
Private lessons ÖS1,000 for 2 hrs
Special courses snowboarding
Guiding companies through ski school

CROSS-COUNTRY
Ski schools Ischgl Ski School
Loipe location and size 25km in Ischgl/Galtür

CHILDCARE
Non-ski kindergarten
Gästekindergarten Ischgl, all ages, 10am-4pm, ÖS220 per day including lunch
Ski kindergarten Ischgl Ski School, 4 yrs and over, ÖS520 per day including lunch
Babysitting list available from tourist office

OTHER SPORTS
Parapente, skating, indoor tennis, bowling, fitness centre, climbing wall, swimming, tobogganing at Kappl

FOOD AND DRINK PRICES
Coffee ÖS27, bottle of house wine ÖS175, beer ÖS40, dish of the day ÖS150

TOUR OPERATORS
Bladon Lines, Crystal, Enterprise, Inghams, Made to Measure, Ski Thomson

Kitzbühel, Tyrol

ALTITUDE 760m (2,493ft)

••

Good points big ski area, beautiful architecture, alpine charm, lively après-ski, facilities for non-skiers, short airport transfer, extensive cross-country skiing
Bad points antiquated lift system, lack of tough runs, lift queues, poor snow record, heavy traffic outside pedestrian centre
Linked or nearby resorts Kirchberg (l), Jochberg (l), Pass Thurn (l), St Johann in Tyrol (n)

Kitzbühel remains the most beautiful ski town in Europe. Its walled medieval streets are lined with heavy buttressed buildings and delicate frescoes. Tourists come here from all over the world, not just to ski, but also to bask in its copious alpine charm. It takes its name from the Chizzo family who, in the twelfth century, ruled the trade route subsequently known as Chizbuhel. The story goes that Franz Reisch, the mayor of Kitzbühel from 1903 to 1913, first introduced skis into this part of Austria when he obtained a pair by mail order from Norway. He tried them out in January 1893 and later wrote: 'The new, totally strange fascination of this sport stimulated me to such an eagerness, which one can almost call enthusiasm, and in a short time I learnt to conquer both up and downhill slopes'.

The main mountain on which he practised was the Hahnenkamm, home each January since 1931 (war years excepted) to the international downhill race of the same name. Contrary to popular belief, the actual racecourse is not called the Hahnenkamm at all, but the Streif. World Cup racers treat it with the greatest respect of all. Former British champion Konrad Bartelski once described the top couple of turns as 'the six most difficult seconds of skiing in the world'. The town has prospered over the years to cater for its international clientèle, which continues to be drawn here at least in part by the glamour and excitement of the race which is televised in a hundred countries around the world.

Unfortunately the same cannot be said of its lift system, which is disgracefully antiquated and utterly out of keeping with Kitzbühel's cosmopolitan image. The Hahnenkamm cable car was built in 1928. It was the first cable car in Austria – and by Zeus it looks it. Two-hour queues are not uncommon during high-season mornings for the dubious privilege of being one of the 48 skiers transported like a sardine for all of a measly 870 vertical metres. Given the revenue generated by it, it is completely unforgivable that this antique has not been moved to some pre-war transport museum and replaced with a modern 160-person cable car or jumbo gondola. However, there is alternative mountain access (explained overleaf).

Sadly, too, Kitzbühel, along with much of the Tyrol, has not basked in the best of snow records in recent years. If this once great resort is to be great again and is to retain its winter guests (23 per cent of them British) into the twenty-first century, then it must stop living off past glories. The town fathers can do nothing about the snowfall, but they would do well to look, not just around Austria, but to other countries beyond its borders to see just how far they have allowed Kitzbühel's lift system to fall behind in world rankings.

The skiing

Top 2000m (6,561ft) bottom 760m (2,493ft)

Kitzbühel's skiing is divided into three quite separate areas, the intermediate Kitzbüheler Horn, the small Aurach sector, and the much larger and more challenging Hahnenkamm. The Kitzbüheler Horn is a big and beautiful mountain, which towers against the sky like a distorted pyramid. It rises 1200m from the valley floor and the views from the top of the rocky Wilder Kaiser peaks are spectacular. The skiing is pleasant and gentle, but experienced skiers will quickly find the Horn a disappointment with pistes much easier than they are graded.

Mountain access is via an expensive new cable car which undoubtedly would have been better placed reducing lift queues on the other side of the valley on the Hahnenkamm. The skiing is reached by a 20-minute walk from the town centre or ski-bus (free if you have a lift pass). Most flanks of the Horn are steep and rocky, which in part explains the lack of a lift link with nearby St Johann, although a strong reluctance from Kitzbühel to join forces with its mass market neighbour is nearer the mark.

Aurach, a 10-minute ski-bus ride away from Kitzbühel is served by a single chair and a couple of drag-lifts, which provide access to three gentle blue (easy) runs and a marginally steeper reddish alternative. It is an area that is hardly skied and, if there has been a fresh fall or you just cannot face the queue for the Hahnenkamm, it is worthy of a morning's skiing.

The real business is the Hahnenkamm area itself. Wise skiers make an early start unless they do not mind the queues. In peak season, any arrival at the cable car later than 8.50am involves a wait of 10 to 20 minutes. Arriving later than 9.15am or before 11am can involve queuing for an hour or more. There are two alternative means of **mountain access**, which often prove quicker and are certainly less frustrating. A 15-minute plod across the nursery slopes takes you to the Streifalm double chair which, in two stages, carries you to a higher point than the cable car, from which you can access all lifts. The second alternative is to take the ski-bus to Klausen, three kilometres away on the road to Kirchberg. From here, the modern Fleckalm gondola takes you swiftly up into the system.

From this point you can explore a wide variety of pisted terrain spread over the Ehrenbachhöhe, Steinbergkogel and Pengelstein sectors. Again, too many of the lifts here (chairs and drags) need upgrading and the linking is poor, with too many paths and too much poling required. But, unlike many resorts, such is the layout of the terrain that

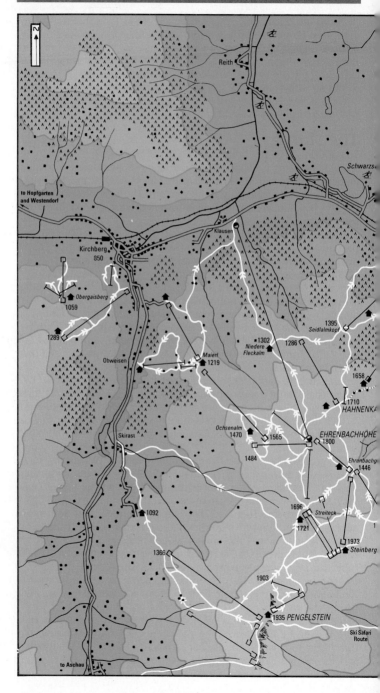

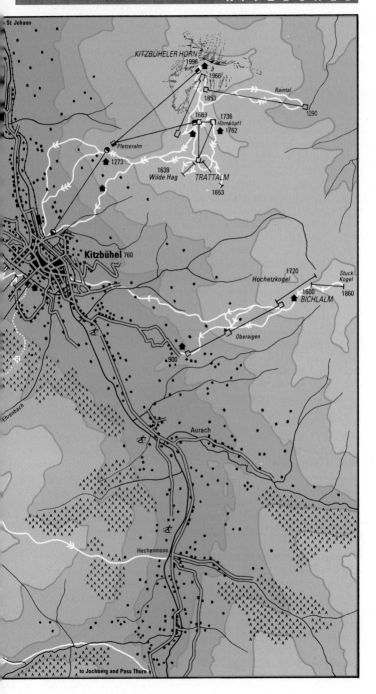

St. Johann

KITZBÜHELER HORN
1996
1966
1853
Raintal
1290

1669
1736
Hornköpfl
1762
1639
Wilde Hag
TRATTALM
1653

Pletzeralm
1273

Kitzbühel 760

1720
Hochetzkogel
Stuck
Kogel
1600
1860
BICHLALM
Oberaigen

900

Aurach

Hechenmoos

Ehrenbach

to Jochberg and Pass Thurn

you really feel you are going somewhere even if you remain within the confines of this part of the ski circus.

The Hochsaukaser red (intermediate) run is a wide, fast piste with wonderful lips and rolls. The one side which is usually left unpisted becomes a steep mogul field between new snowfalls. Other good, long runs are the Kälberwald and the Pengelstein, both blues, together with the Schwarzkogel, Hieslegg and the Brunn red runs. Maierl by Three is a long, enjoyable run down to Kirchberg. The Streif, which is now to be armed with artificial snow-cannon along its entire length, is specially prepared as a racecourse with horrendous jumps each January.

Kitzbühel is famous for its Ski Safari. A short walk links the Hahnenkamm ski area, Jochberg and Pass Thurn. The latter, with skiing up to 2000m, is the high point in the area above the valley town of Mittersill, home of the Blizzard ski factory. On the plus side, the Safari, indicated by elephant symbols on the piste map, makes an interesting day out, which can be accomplished by anyone with two weeks' skiing experience. On the down side, it can only be skied in one direction and you have to take a bus back from Pass Thurn. It is possible to ski back as far as Jochberg, but you may not get a place on the bus because most skiers will have already boarded at Pass Thurn. Too many people ski the Safari without pausing to explore the different runs on the way. Above Jochberg, in particular, it is important not to miss the descents back down from Wurzhöhe to the bottom of the Wagstätt double chair, or the runs down from Bärenbadkogel, which are hardly ever skied.

The Safari starts at the Kasereck triple chair. When the links are closed (quite often) due to lack of snow, this chair is a particular bottleneck on the mountain. If you take Pengelstein-Sud, a gentle but long red all the way down to Trampelpfad, a short run will bring you to the Hausleiten drag. It is impossible to get lost here.

Pass Thurn can be cold and bleak in bad weather, but this is where you will find the best snow for much of the season. At weekends it tends to become very crowded indeed waiting for the double chair, which is the sole means of mountain access from the road. The higher runs, a broad band of blues interspersed with the odd red pitch are all much the same, but provide some high-mileage skiing. The Zweitausender double chair gives access to an interesting red run, of the same name. The Rettenstein, a short sharp black (difficult) run which brings you back to the bottom of the Zweitausander from the top of the Trattenbach triple chair, certainly gets the adrenalin going.

Mountain restaurants

These are numerous and the standard is generally high, with plenty of praise from reporters for the Alpenrose on the Horn for its 'very cheerful staff cleaning up your plate almost before you have finished', and for the 'sumptuous *Apfelstrudel*' at the Ochsalm. The Pengelstein restaurant has been expensively extended, but still tends to be crowded. One reporter recommends the Ehrenbach at the bottom of the Steinbergkogel summit chair for its good food and because 'it is always empty, but don't tell anybody'. The Trattenbergalm, between Jochberg and Pass Thurn, has a strong following. The Brandseit, 'cheap and uncrowded', is situated near the bottom of the Fleckalm gondola. The new Panorama-Alm at Pass Thurn has a glass-walled bar outside to keep out the wind, a cosy wooden interior with a roaring log fire and 'modern self-service with an unlikely amount of charm'.

Beginners and children

Kitzbühel has four separate ski schools including the famous Red Devils. All have a generally good reputation, and the resulting competition between them is healthy indeed. However, we have mixed reports of the Red Devils, which, it seems, must look to the opposition. One reporter in a class of 13 notes that 'the instructor was a gloomy soul, older than usual, and his English was pretty basic.' There are a number of complaints regarding oversized classes, and instruction that amounted to little more than guiding, with no individual tuition.

Five lifts make up what is an extensive nursery slope on the golf course at the foot of the Hahnenkamm. There is a ski kindergarten, but no crêche facilities and anyone wanting to bring non-skiing children to Kitzbühel must hire a local babysitter.

The resort

Kitzbühel now has a traffic-free centre fringed by a complicated one-way system. It is a great improvement, but traffic remains a problem as cars circle the town in search of a parking space. A shuttle bus service, supposedly running every 10 minutes, operates around town and to the ski areas, but all too often buses are bogged down in the heavy traffic, on the ring-road. Getting to the ski areas can still involve a long walk or a slow bus ride, depending on where you are staying. The buses to surrounding villages are seriously over-subscribed at peak times. A day out on the Safari, which begins with a wait for the Hahnenkamm cable car, usually ends with a matching one for the bus at Pass Thurn. Taxis are plentiful and, shared with other skiers, a sensible option.

But none of Kitzbühel's shortcomings should be allowed to detract from the overall charm of this medieval town, which attracts tourists throughout the year. Serious shoppers will, however, be disappointed.

Accommodation

The Weisses Rössl, the Kitzbüheler Hof and the Tiefenbrunner are all praised as sound, four-star hotels with service to match their ratings. Hotels near the Hahnenkamm include the Haselberger and the Montana, both recommended as good value. Two regular visitors recommend the family-run Mühlberghof, on the edge of town.

Eating out

There is no shortage of good restaurants in Kitzbühel, although few serve other than the ubiquitous Austrian fare. One of the best restaurants of all is the Goldener Greif, an atmospheric fourteenth-century hotel in the centre of town. Frescoes of knights in armour adorn the walls and the chef is famed for his *Salzburgerknockerl*, a kind of meringue soufflé. The Hotel Zur Tenne restaurant, on the high street, is recommended by two reporters for 'delicious fresh trout'.

Chinarestaurant Peking in the Kirchplatz makes a pleasant change of cuisine from the endless *Wienerschnitzel*. The existence of a McDonald's seems a shame in such beautiful surroundings, but its presence is muted and even a Big Mac rings the changes from *Zwiebelrostbraten*.

Après-ski

Kitzbühel never sleeps, nor indeed do the returning dawn revellers allow occupants of the village centre hotels to do so. The raucous behaviour of drunken Scandinavians is still a problem here as in many Austrian resorts, although the noisiest are no longer the young, but the 30-somethings still determined to drink the barrel dry and still wearing ski boots at 3am. The Londoner, appropriately opposite McDonald's, is the gathering point for young Brits and is reported to be 'noisy, smoky, but with great music and loads of atmosphere'. Big Ben is another pub run on similar lines, while Seppi's Pub is where Austria meets the Old Kent Road. Praxmair, Kitzbühel's oldest coffee house, is more of a 'caff' these days. It serves good, cheap food, the locals gather here, and it is one the best after-skiing spots. The Goldener Gams is for the older clientèle, a discreetly lit bar and restaurant with live music and dancing. S'lichtl is a noisy bar with disco lights and incredibly uncomfortable seating. The Zur Tenne has a live band and dancing and is described as having 'pricey drinks, although the lead singer had a great voice'. Discos include Royal Dancing ('fun but young') and the Drop In, both in the Old Town. The Aquarena swimming-pool is free to those with a ski pass.

Kirchberg 850m (2,788ft)

This large satellite village, six kilometres from Kitzbühel, is at the entry to the Brixental and gives direct and usually easier access to the Hahnenkamm. It has grown over the years from a charming, traditional Austrian backwater into a busy sprawl dissected by river and railway line. It shares some of its more interesting neighbour's problems as well as its skiing; it has serious traffic congestion and the lifts are a bus ride from the centre. The notion that you could stay in Kirchberg and do Kitzbühel on the cheap is no longer true – prices are much the same in both resorts. Kirchberg is, however, a lively place with plenty of nightlife, traditional Tyrolean or otherwise.

Kirchberg has good cross-country skiing along the valley floor towards Westendorf, as well as a short, difficult track at high altitude. Other facilities include skating, curling, 40km of prepared paths for walkers, as well as tennis, squash, sleigh rides and swimming. Most of the hotels and guesthouses are in the centre, but if you are staying on bed and breakfast terms be prepared for queues and early closing in the village restaurants. Kirchberg has its own nursery slopes and kinder-garten and there is a choice of two ski schools. The village has its own small ski area, independent of the Hahnenkamm, with nursery lifts and a baby tow. Recommended hotels include the medium-priced Gasthof Unterm Rain, the much smarter Alpenhotel Tiroler Adler, and Hotel Landhaus Brauns.

TOURIST OFFICE
A-6365 Kirchberg, Tyrol
Tel 43 5357 2309
Fax 43 5357 3732

TOUR OPERATORS
Crystal, Enterprise, Falcon, Neilson,
Ski Thomson, Top Deck, Ski Choice

Skiing facts: Kitzbühel

TOURIST OFFICE
A-6370, Kitzbühel, Tyrol
Tel 43 5356 2155
Fax 43 5356 2307

THE RESORT
By road Calais 1130km
By rail mainline station in resort
By air Salzburg 90 mins, Munich 2½ hrs
Visitor beds 7,500 (63% hotels, 37% chalets and apartments)
Transport free ski-bus, in theory every 10 mins

THE SKIING
Longest run Pengelstein Sud, 6.8km (red)
Number of lifts 67
Number of trails/pistes 61 (39% easy, 46% intermediate, 15% difficult)
Total of trails/pistes 158km
Nursery slopes 8 lifts
Summer skiing none
Snowmaking only on the Streif

LIFT PASSES
Area pass (covers Kitzbühel, Kirchberg, Jochberg, Pass Thurn) from ÖS1,490-1,650 for 6 days
Day pass ÖS280-340, depending on month and starting time
Half-day pass ÖS200-220 from 1pm. Other starting times available
Beginners points cards
Children 5-16 yrs, ÖS825 for 6 days
Pensioners 10% reduction for women over 60 yrs and men over 65 yrs
Credit cards accepted no

SKI SCHOOLS
Adults Red Devils and Total Ski School both ÖS1,200 for 6 days
Children Red Devils and Total as adults, Kitzbüheler Horn ÖS1,590, Hahnenkamm ÖS1800 for 6 days
Private lessons Total Ski School,

ÖS500 per day, Kitzbüheler Horn, ÖS1,750 per day, Hahnenkamm, ÖS1,750 per day, Red Devils, prices on application
Special courses telemarking, snowboarding
Guiding companies through ski school

CROSS COUNTRY
Ski schools Red Devils Langlaufschule
Loipe location and size 30km around Kitzbühel, 200km in whole valley

CHILDCARE
Non-ski kindergarten Hechenberger babysitting service, 4 yrs and under, 8am-4pm, prices on application
Ski kindergarten Total Ski School, 3 yrs and over, ÖS1,100. Kitzbüheler Horn, groups only, ÖS1,590. Red Devils, ÖS1,200. Hahnenkamm, groups only, ÖS1,800. All prices for 6 days plus ÖS80 per day for lunch
Babysitting list available from tourist office

OTHER SPORTS
Curling, skating, bowling, squash, swimming, and hot-air ballooning

WHAT'S NEW
● Artificial snow cannon on the Streif for 1993/94

FOOD AND DRINK PRICES
Coffee ÖS20-25, bottle of house wine ÖS120-140, beer ÖS25-30, dish of the day from ÖS120

TOUR OPERATORS
Austrian Holidays, Bladon Lines, The Club, Crystal, Enterprise, GFT Tours, Inghams, Kings Ski Club, Made to Measure, Neilson, Ski Airtours, SkiBound, Ski Choice, Ski Europe, Ski Thomson

Lech, Arlberg

ALTITUDE 1450m (4,756ft)

••

Good points alpine charm, sunny slopes, plenty of easy skiing, varied
off-piste skiing, good artificial snow cover, high standard of hotels,
facilities for family holidays
Bad points difficult road and rail access, lack of mountain
restaurants, long lift queues, high prices
Nearby or linked resorts Zürs (l), St Anton (n), Stuben (n),
St Christoph (n)

Every skiing nation has at least one ultra-smart resort, which lures the
Beautiful People to its manicured slopes and the pampered luxury of its
hotels. Austria has Lech, with Princess Diana as its star annual visitor,
and the higher neighbouring village of Zürs, much patronised by
Princess Caroline of Monaco. Back in the 1920s, the tiny hamlet of Zürs,
no more than a cluster of huts and an inn at the top of the Flexenpass
around the shoulder of the Valluga from St Anton, was one of the cradles of modern alpine skiing. The great Hannes Schneider was born
around the corner in Stuben and Victor Sohm gave the first ski lesson in
Zürs as long ago as 1906. Visitors were an eclectic blend of stolid Swiss
Burger and upper-class British, drawn by the open slopes of the
Trittkopf and Hexenboden, as well as the towering Madloch on the far
side of the frozen Zürsersee.

Today Zürs is still little more than a cluster of buildings astride the
pass, albeit the huts have been replaced by four and five-star hotels and
an assortment of marginally less exotic establishments. Lech, which nestles beside the river of the same name in what in winter is a boxed valley
beyond, has grown into the larger and more cosmopolitan resort of the
two. It is the text-book example of the charming Austrian village, a farming community centred on its onion-domed church which, despite
major expansion into a complete dependency on tourism over 35 years,
has still managed to retain its rural character. It continues to be no
stranger to the international stage. In the 1960s Egon Zimmerman, then
a hotel chef, became ski world champion. In 1992 the church bells rang
out to celebrate the surprise Olympic downhill gold medal of Patrick
Ortlieb, born and raised in Oberlech.

This satellite, once the summer home of herdsmen and shepherds,
is on the open pastureland above, and is reached by cable car from the
village. The collection of chalets and hotels here are ideally placed for
the skiing and provide an attractive car-free centre for families with
small children. It has more accommodation, but similar rural charm to
Zug, three kilometres away through the woods from Lech up a pretty,
closed valley. Oberlech was once accessible only in winter by horse-

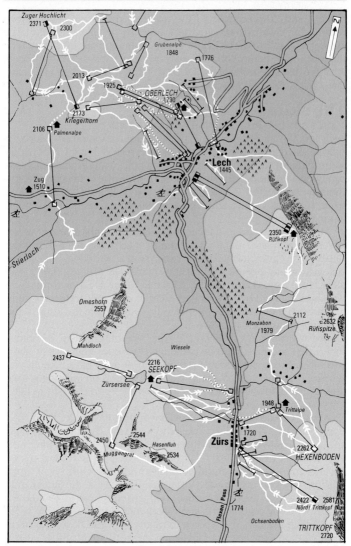

drawn sleigh from Lech – still a delightful evening excursion to the old village inn, now a major hotel, but it is now well-linked into the lift system which joins Zürs with Lech.

The resorts share a long-established ski area, which is varied, extensive, and open but has not been upgraded to the standard you might expect of a community which generates so much wealth from its fur-clad clientèle. Consequently it lends itself to beginners and lower intermediates rather than to cruising intermediates. Advanced skiers will be more interested in the off-piste in the area. St Anton, with its larger choice of expert piste terrain, is a short drive away.

73

Lech and Zürs lie close to the major road and rail link between Austria and Switzerland, but the journey is an awkward one. The Flexenpass can be blocked for hours or, on rare occasions, days, after a major storm. Parking in both villages is restricted and ruthlessly policed. A car is of assistance if you want to visit St Anton. The bus service is regular, but extremely slow, while taxis are expensive.

The skiing
Top 2450m (8,036ft) bottom 1445m (3,439ft)

Lech and Zürs share a ski circus spread over three mountains which can only be skied in a clockwise direction. This results in crowds of people all heading for the same lifts at the same time, with resultant high-season queues. Although the valleys are not wide, the connections across them are not perfect. Zürs is high, with all its skiing above the tree-line, while Lech has a more attractive arrangement of gentle lower slopes among the trees.

Mountain access to the circus is via the Rüfikopf cable car, which scales an impressive wall from the centre of Lech, too steep to be skied directly (except in springtime by experts), but with long, difficult and spectacular unprepared runs off the shoulder which are often closed after a heavy snowfall. These lead down in either direction through the woods to the road by Zürs, or back to Lech via a long and scenic itinerary through the Wöstertäli. Alternatively, you can take the long, beautiful pistes towards Zürs.

Lech's main skiing area, on the other side of the valley, is contrastingly open and mostly gentle, although the slopes immediately above the village are uncomfortably steep for those who have recently progressed from the nursery slopes. Mountain access on this side is by an assortment of four lifts, including a detachable quad chair, from different points in or near the village.

Above Oberlech, lifts and pistes are spread in a wide, fragmented basin below the peaks of the Kriegerhorn and the Zuger Hochlicht. The two are linked by a cable car with spectacular views. Easy and intermediate motorway pistes branch off in all directions, but there are also some tougher runs, especially from the Kriegerhorn. These include a couple of short, steep off-piste routes down towards Lech and the Steinmahder chairs, as well as a long, attractive south-facing run down to Zug; it is steep, but easily negotiated in good snow conditions.

Off-piste skiers have a choice of routes from the Zuger Hochlicht, including long traverses before skiing down to Oberlech or even to Stubenbach and Warth further along the Lech valley floor. It should be pointed out that most of these itineraries involve a fair amount of hiking. In the other direction, the open slopes beside the Steinmähder chair-lift are much favoured after a fresh snowfall. From the bottom a long schuss, on a route which is often closed because of avalanche danger, takes you around to Zug.

The skiing above Zürs is also split into two areas by the village and the road, and the west-facing slopes are themselves divided except at the bottom. The Hexenboden chair-lifts serve fairly ordinary intermediate pistes, with plenty of off-piste opportunities in the right conditions. The Trittkopf cable car climbs higher and gives access to much more demanding runs, with some difficult and exciting off-piste descents reached by long traverses. The most testing of these approaches involves skiing over the concrete gallery protecting the road for the run down to Stuben. Beside Hexenboden there is a link lift by quad chair for skiers coming up from Lech, or for those who have skied the north-facing off-piste slopes from Hexenboden down into the Pazieltal.

The east-facing Seekopf slopes are served by a long drag-lift from above the centre of the village near the Zürserhof, and a roadside chair-lift starting below the village. At the north end of the sector one long, fairly easy run takes you down to the village. A variety of off-piste descents which end up on the road between Lech and Zürs are accessed by a short climb. On the other side of the lift there are a couple of more difficult pistes, graded red and, as elsewhere, off-piste variants. From Zürsersee, just below the Seekopf, a chair-lift climbs a secluded north-facing bowl behind the 2540m Hasenfluh; its easy piste usually holds the snow. An alternative route is to drop over the back into a steep bowl and on down the Zürsertäli back to Zürs. The other chair-lift from Zürsersee gives access to good long runs, on- and off-piste, behind the Omeshorn to Lech and Zug.

The standard of piste-grooming is impressive. Lech has artificial snow on all the main lower slopes and Zürs has snow-cannon on the lower pitches of the heavily skied runs from the Seekopf chair. The lift system is still in severe need of improvement despite some cosmetic upgrading in recent years, and as a result queues can be a serious problem throughout most of the season in these two extremely popular resorts. The lifts from below Zürs to Seekopf and from Zug up to Palmenalpe have been replaced and are no longer the bottlenecks that they were, but the sheer volume of skiers still leads to queues. The Seekopf lifts have priority lanes for local residents as well as the ski school. Other notable bottlenecks are the chairs from Zürsersee up Madloch-Joch and up to the Zuger Hochlicht. The Trittkopf cable car gets crowded in the morning rush and throughout the afternoon. Heli-skiing is available for those who want to get away from the crowds and can afford to do so.

However, Lech and Zürs deserve praise for being the first major resorts to limit the number of skiers allowed on the mountain (to 14,000). Hotel residents and day visitors arriving by public transport have priority. Skiers arriving by car at peak times will in future be warned via motorway information boards if the resorts are full.

Mountain restaurants

The choice of mountain eating places is extremely limited, surprisingly so in an area which attracts so many potentially discerning lunchers. The Palmenalpe self-service above Zug is one of the better ones, provided you avoid peak hours. The Burg hotel has waiter- and self-service restaurants. The Sonnenburg is another quite reasonable self-service. The best choice is among the hotels of Oberlech. The other alternative is to take off your skis and walk into Lech, Zürs or Zug.

Beginners and children

The Austrian ski school in Lech, Oberlech and in Zürs has a particularly fine reputation and we have received no adverse reports. Most instructors speak good English, a necessity because of the very international clientele here. The resort, particularly Oberlech, lends itself well to family skiing. The main nursery slopes are here. A number of hotels run their own crèches and we have good reports of the ski kindergarten, which has a mainly English-speaking staff and a sympathetic attitude.

The resort

Lech is a delightful Austrian village centred on its church on the banks of the river of the same name. Originally it was called Tannberg im Lech after the fir trees *(Tanne)* which grow in the valley. It was first settled by Swiss immigrants in the fourteenth century and this corner still looks more towards Switzerland, its nearest neighbour, than to the main part of Austria. The modern expansion of the resort has been unobtrusive and Lech still has a real village feel to it, despite the presence of luxury hotels and designer boutiques. Regular, but not frequent, post-buses connect Lech, Zürs, Stuben, and St Anton, as well as the railhead at Langen.

Accommodation

Accommodation is mostly in comfortable and expensive hotels, plus some apartments and the odd tour operator-run chalet. The village is fairly compact and location is not particularly important (although we recommend Oberlech for families with small children). The smartest hotel, indeed one of the most celebrated five-stars in Austria, is the ornately frescoed Hotel Post. It has only 40 rooms and you need to book a year in advance. The Arlberg and the Almhof Schneider are both warmly recommended by regulars. The Tannbergerhof is popular with the British and is the centre of Lech's social life. There are numerous less formal hotels and plenty of *Fremdenzimmer* (bed and breakfast) but nowhere is cheap. In high season rooms can be extremely hard to find at any level on the scale.

Oberlech has several comfortable hotels near the cable car station and chalets spread widely around the hillside. The main attraction of staying here is to avoid ski school crowds on the Schlegelkopf lifts out of Lech itself, and to holiday in a car-free environment. The Sporthotel Petersboden is known for its piste-side Red Umbrella bar. In Zug the original inn, the Rote Wand, is now a luxury four-star hotel. Hotel Elisabeth is also recommended.

Eating out

Good restaurants abound, as you might expect in a resort of this character, but none is cheap. The Brunnenhof is strongly recommended as is the Bistro Caserole. The Käsknöpfle's food is described as 'a bit too Austrian, but the restaurant is good fun and friendly'. Pizzeria Charly is consistently popular with reporters for 'sound Italian fare served with a smile, not as schilling-snatching as others'. In Oberlech the Ilga Kellerstübli and the Goldener Berg are famous for fondue.

Après-ski

In Lech, après-skiers prefer to put their hair up, rather than let it down. The Tannbergerhof is where it all begins, at the bar (ice-bar, weather permitting) on the pavement outside. Guests filter inside to join in the tea-dancing, which begins as the lifts close. There is live music later in the evening here and at a number of other hotels. The Rüfikopf cable car transforms into a moving cocktail bar at dusk. Sleigh rides to Zug for dinner are popular. You can take the cable car up to Oberlech and toboggan down after dinner (the cable car closes at 1am).

Skiing facts: Lech

TOURIST OFFICE
A-6764 Lech, Arlberg
Tel 43 5583 2161
Fax 43 5583 3155

THE RESORT
By road Calais 970km
By rail Langen 15km, frequent buses daily
By air Innsbruck 2 hrs, Zurich 3½ hrs
Visitor beds 6,771 (89% hotels, 2% apartments, 9% guesthouses and chalets)
Transport buses to Zürs, Stuben and St Anton not included in lift pass price

THE SKIING
Longest run Madloch-Lech, 5.2km (red)
Number of lifts 34 in Lech and Zürs
Number of trails/pistes 62 in Lech and Zürs (30% easy, 40% intermediate, 30% difficult)
Total of trails/pistes 110km in Lech, 300km in Arlberg area
Nursery slopes 4 lifts in Lech
Summer skiing none
Snowmaking 50 hectares covered

LIFT PASSES
Area pass Arlberg pass (covers Lech, Zürs, Stuben, St Anton), from ÖS1,660
Day pass from ÖS370
Half-day pass from ÖS585, from midday
Beginners points tickets
Children 7-14 yrs, Arlberg pass from ÖS990, free for 6 yrs and under
Pensioners no reduction
Credit cards accepted no

SKI SCHOOLS
Adults Lech and Oberlech, 9am-midday or 1.30-5pm, from ÖS1,280 for 6 days
Children Lech and Oberlech, 9am-noon or 1.30-5pm, from ÖS1,200 for 6 days
Private lessons ÖS1,950 per day
Special courses snowboarding, telemark
Guiding companies through ski school

CROSS-COUNTRY
Ski schools Lech and Oberlech
Loipe location and size 19km, practice track to Stubenbach (3km), to Zug and beyond

CHILDCARE
Non-ski kindergarten some hotels offer facilities
Ski kindergarten Ski School Lech and Oberlech, 2½ yrs and over, 9am-4pm, from 3½-12 yrs, 10am-midday and 2-4pm, from ÖS1,200 for 6 days not including lunch
Babysitting list available from tourist office

OTHER SPORTS
Parapente, skating, swimming, indoor tennis, squash, bowling, toboganning, sleigh rides

FOOD AND DRINK PRICES
Coffee ÖS25, bottle of house wine ÖS250, beer ÖS40, dish of the day ÖS150

TOUR OPERATORS
Austrian Holidays, Bladon Lines, Inghams, Made to Measure, Ski Choice, Ski Tal, Ski Unique

Zürs 1720m (5,642ft)

The village stands in an isolated position above the tree-line astride the Flexenpass and lacks much of the charm of Lech, although resort-level snow is guaranteed for most of the season. It is little more than a collection of extremely smart hotels. While it may completely lack the showy gaudiness of St Moritz or Gstaad, the degree of opulence of its clientele is often even greater – it just wears it more discreetly. The Zürserhof is strongly recommended, both for its facilities and its restaurant. The Alpenrose Post and the Arlberhaus, marginally less expensive, both receive glowing reports. Zürs has its own ski school. The kindergarten takes children from three years old and teaches skiing from four.

TOURIST OFFICE
A-6763, Zürs am Arlberg
Tel 43 55 83 22 45
Fax 43 55 83 29 82

TOUR OPERATORS
Austrian Holidays, Bladon Lines,
Made to Measure, Ski Unique

Mayrhofen, Tyrol

ALTITUDE 630m (2,066ft)

••

Good points reputable ski school, lively après-ski, short airport
transfer, sunny slopes, varied skiing in area, extensive family
facilities, snow-safe glacier at Hintertux
Bad points horrendous lift queues, little challenging skiing, lack of
skiing convenience, lack of tree-level skiing
Linked or nearby resorts Finkenberg (l), Fügen (n), Gerlos (n),
Hintertux (n), Kramsach (n), Lanersbach (n), Ramsau (n), Schwendau
(n), Kaltenbach (n), Vorderlanersbach (.∴.), Zell am Ziller (n)

Mayrhofen remains one the most popular resorts in Austria with the
British although, with the wide choice of destinations open to all standards of skier, it is not always easy to understand why this should continue to be. Its setting in the heart of the Zillertal is certainly a beautiful
one: a long and steeply wooded offshoot of the Inn Valley and the
Munich-Innsbruck *Autobahn*. Its hotels are numerous, clean and comfortable. Away from the slopes there is much to do, and the nightlife in
Dutch- and British-dominated bars and discos is both raucous and energetic. The ski school has the finest of reputations for coping with beginners who do not speak German and this whole valley, of which
Mayrhofen is the unchallenged ski capital, is geared towards families,
with a particular emphasis on childcare. The skiing is neither convenient for novices nor challenging enough for experts, but there is a substantial amount for all standards in nearly a dozen other ski areas all
within a bus ride.

Mayrhofen has one major failing: completely unacceptable queues
during the main weeks of the year which in the words of one reporter
'turn skiing into such a misery. I would frankly rather be at home in
Stoke'. We have one exceptional and verified report of a skier who, on a
bank holiday weekend, waited for four hours to catch the Penkenbahn
cable car down the mountain. Waits of 90 minutes or more in the morning for this antiquated sardine tin are the norm: 'Beginners get the
impression that all ski resorts are like this, mercifully they are not.'
However, the good news is that the lift company has finally bowed
under pressure and agreed to supplement it with a high-capacity gondola system which, now that plans have been approved by the regional
government, will be in operation for winter 1994-5.

The Ski-Zell-Superski pass covers the entire valley and opens up the
possibility of an enormous range of skiing; tuition hours are staggered
to relieve the pressure on the main lifts. Mayrhofen does not generally
suffer the snow problems common to many other low Tyrolean resorts,
if only because it does not have lower slopes; you have to take a cable

car both to and from the skiing, which takes place at nearly 2100m on sunny, open slopes above the tree-line.

South of Mayrhofen the Zillertal splits into three smaller valleys, one of which leads on into the Tuxertal, along a narrow steeply wooded passage between the mountains, at the end of which is the Tuxer Glacier, Austria's steepest all-year-round skiing. Just above Mayrhofen, the compact little village of Finkenberg, home of former Olympic downhill champion Leonard Stock, shares Mayrhofen's main Penken ski area. Further on, Vorderlanersbach and Lanersbach have their own ski areas which are tentatively planned to link into the system. For keen skiers who are happily prepared to put up with little or no après-ski, these resorts have the advantage of easy access to the snow-sure skiing on the glacier. A regular bus service operates from Mayrhofen to Hintertux but, like the lifts, it is grossly oversubscribed during too many winter weeks.

To the north of Mayrhofen, back towards the river Inn and along the banks of the Ziller which flows into it, lies an assortment of small resorts with their own ski areas. Zell am Ziller (not to be confused with Zell am See in Salzburgerland) is the most important of these, followed by Kaltenbach and Fügenberg. All of them can easily be reached by bus.

The skiing
Top 2250m (7,381ft) bottom 630m (2,066ft)

The skiing takes place on both sides of the mountain. **Mountain access** is by ancient cable cars from separate stations on either side of town, both of which rise steeply over heavily wooded slopes. The main skiing is on the Penken, which can also be reached by gondola from the village of Schwendau, a bus ride away to the north, or from Finkenberg, an inconvenient journey of equal length further up the Zillertal. The secondary area is the Ahorn, on the other side of Mayrhofen, a long walk from most of the accommodation. For all these lifts, with the exception of the Finkenberg gondola, there is a free bus service which is often disastrously overcrowded. In particular, it cannot cope with the influx of visitors who want to return in the afternoon from the Horbergstal gondola at Schwendau.

The gentle slopes of the Ahorn at 2000m serve as an excellent beginner and lower intermediate area surrounded by outstanding views down the Zillertal. Wide confidence-building pistes are served by five short drag-lifts and a chair. An intermediate trail goes down through the woods to the Wiesenhof restaurant, which is served by occasional buses. It is possible to ski on down from here to the bottom of the Ahornbahn on the bank of the Ziller.

The 2095m Penkenjoch provides Mayrhofen's main skiing. The cable car (now to be replaced) climbs over an unskiable, wooded mountainside to a sunny Penken balcony just above the tree-line. Two awkwardly linked chair-lifts take you on up to the top of this rounded mountain, which naturally lends itself to varied bowl skiing. From the bottom of the chairs it is possible to ski all the way down to the Horbergbahn gondola station via an interesting and ungraded route through the trees, which is steep and awkward in places. In good snow this is one of the best runs in the resort for accomplished skiers.

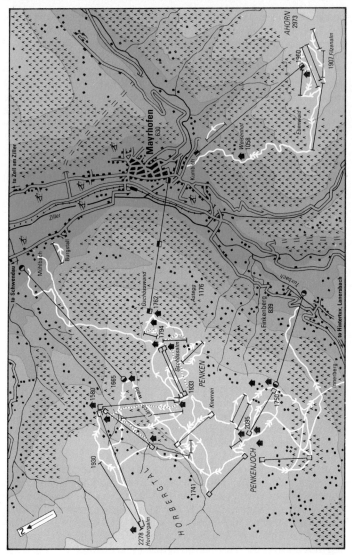

The main skiing area consists of a relatively narrow band of open and lightly wooded skiing on the north and south sides of the Penkenjoch. The runs are short, generally more red than blue, with the easiest ones back along the ridge towards Penken. An easy run links the top of the Penken chairs and the Horberg gondola, allowing inexperienced skiers to take the lift down at the end of the day. From just below the gondola top station, a double chair climbs up to 2250m on the sunny Gerent side of the Horberg valley. The unpisted run down beneath the lift is long and steep with pitches of around 27° which can become heavily mogulled. Half-way down it branches right to the top of the Tappenalm double chair, from where it is possible to make your way back up to Penkenjoch. The other branch merges with an easy blue which returns to the top of the Horbergbahn.

On the Finkenberg side of the mountain, the Almbahn gondola and a double chair give often easier access to Penkenjoch with its cluster of restaurants and lively ice-bars. The Katzenmoos double chair at the southern extremity of the ski area serves a variety of easy red runs, one of which winds down to Finkenberg. There is a considerable amount of artificial snow on Penken's nursery slopes and intermediate runs.

Mountain restaurants

Vroni's Skialm at Penkenjoch receives the most favourable reports out of a cluster of eating places offering much the same standard of Austrian fare. The Almstüberl by the middle station of the Finkenberg gondola is recommended for its *Gulaschsuppe* and home-made bread. Hilde's Schitenne, a third of the way down the Tappenalm chair on Piste 8, is praised for its cosy atmosphere. Crowds are again a problem and one reporter suggests that you 'eat early or not at all if you want to ski in the afternoon and beat the lift queues down before supper time'. The Ahorn now has three restaurants as well as the Weisenhof on the way down.

Beginners and children

Mayrhofen has earned a strong reputation over many years as one of the foremost learning centres in the Alps. Generations of British have mastered the basics here on the gentle nursery slopes of the Ahorn and Finken before moving on to other resorts which offer more of a challenge. Mayrhofen itself boasts no less than three schools, which are healthily competitive; Finkenberg has a further two schools. The standard of all is said to be high, but encouragingly we still have particularly warm reports of the original Uli Spiess school in Mayrhofen, which seems to thrive under the challenge. Large classes in all remain a high-season drawback.

Because of the severe queuing problems here the crèche operates for longer than normal hours: Wuppy's Kinderland opens at 8am and parents do not have to return until 6pm. All three ski schools run their own all-day ski kindergartens. However, despite its good facilities, it is hard to recommend Mayrhofen as a family resort because the fallibilities of the lift system make it difficult for parents to see their children during the course of the day while being able to ski themselves.

The resort

Mayrhofen is a large, traditional village with chalet-style buildings and ornately frescoed walls. Despite the village's huge expansion into a major tourist centre, it still manages to retain its charm. It is a lively place, full of young people, and this 'fun resort' atmosphere is the enduring reason for its popularity. The valley road bypasses the main part and, although traffic can be heavy around the outskirts and parking is a problem, congestion in the streets is not a major drawback. Action centres on the long, wide main street, between the market place near the station and the Penken cable car, which is busy and bustling by day and night. There is no public transport in the evening.

Mayrhofen has a newly built health centre with pools, sauna, solarium and a restaurant within the complex. Non-skiers can enjoy good walks on clearly marked trails along the valley floor and up into the mountains. There are plenty of attractive excursions to Innsbruck and Salzburg.

Accommodation

Most accommodation is in traditional hotels, gasthofs, and small pensions with the usual high standards of service and cleanliness, if not necessarily of haute cuisine. We have favourable reports of the Hotel Neuhaus and the Landhaus annexe opposite it ('everything you expect of a fine Austrian hotel'). Hotel Strass by the Penken cable car has lively après-ski. The interconnecting and more expensive Sporthotel has its own squash courts. One reporter praised the Strass Chalets, family-run guesthouses at various locations throughout the village, as 'the best value I have every found in Austria'. Hotel Pramstraller is also strongly recommended 'although rather inconveniently situated a long walk from either cable car'. Gasthof Scheulinghof is said to be 'cosy, cheap and clean'.

Eating out

The 400-year-old Wirtshaus zum Griena, an old beamed farmhouse, is recommended for its traditional Austrian food and 'marvellous atmosphere'. The Neuhaus and the Alpenhotel Kramerwirt restaurants are recommended for good four-course dinners, and Die Gute Stube is a gourmet restaurant. Pizzerias are Mamma Mia, Pizzeria Manni, Pizza and Strudl and the pizzeria at the Hotel Rose. Other eating places include the Edelweiss, Mount Everest and the Sporthotel. The restaurant in Hotel Strolz caters for special diets.

Après-ski

Evening entertainment is lively by any standard, with the full range on offer from tobogganing and sleigh rides to Tyrolean evenings of thigh-slapping and yodelling, through to late-night discos. The Sporthotel bar is most popular with the British ('not exactly dripping in atmosphere, but a nice crowd'). Scotland Yard is more of a pub and usually heavily packed throughout the evening. The Aven and Schlüssel discos are less British-orientated and are popular late in the evening. The Hotel Kramerwirt's Andreas Keller has a live band for more sedate dancing. The Elizabeth has an expensive, but stylish nightclub where you can drink and hear yourself talk.

The Tuxer Glacier 1500m (4,920ft)

This provides Austria's steepest year-round skiing and for that reason is much favoured by national team downhill trainers. There is no village of Tux as such; the community is made up of Lanersbach, Juns, Madseit and Hintertux. Lanersbach has 20km of interesting open skiing on the

2300m Eggalm slopes of the Beilspitz, as well as a further 13km of generally easier skiing on the sunny Lämmerbichl plateau. A free shuttle
bus runs every 30 minutes to and from Vorderlanersbach to the bottom
of the Tuxer.

The glacier is a cold and forbidding place on a harsh winter's day,
but snow cover is guaranteed here when much of the rest of the Tyrol is
green. A rather tired gondola and parallel double chair start a kilometre
beyond the small village of Hintertux. They climb over steep wooded
slopes to the summer pastureland of Sommerbergalm, a sunny platform with restaurants beneath the Tuxerjoch and an easy, east-facing
ski area served by two drag-lifts and a new quad chair for 1993-4. The
main glacier area is separated from here by a narrow gorge.

The second stage of the gondola and cold parallel chair take you up
to the Tuxerfernerhaus restaurant at 2660m, the bottom of the summer ski area. Two more slow and bitterly cold chairs take you on up to
3250m just below the top of the aptly named Gefrorene Wand (frozen
wall). The broad, open slopes here are served by a number of T-bars
and a central chair-lift, and a triple chair off the back has opened up
350m vertical of sunny skiing at the top of the Schlegeisgletscher.

While the runs on both sides are generally easy, the glaciers are considerably steeper than most. On the western side, in particular on the
long runs down both above and below glacier level, there are more
demanding stretches than you might expect. A short T-bar returns you
to Sommerbergalm from which point you can either take a tricky
ungraded route which is steep and narrow in places, or a red down the
western flank of the mountain through the trees. A more attractive
alternative for experienced skiers is to take the Tuxerjoch chair-lift and
then traverse an unnervingly steep slope to reach what is a delightful
run down the bowl of the Schwarze Pfanne. It is all off-piste, but an
extremely popular and by no means difficult run.

TOURIST OFFICE
Tux, A-6293 Lanersbach, Tyrol
Tel 43 5287 606
Fax 43 5287 60629

TOUR OPERATORS
Alpine Tours, Crystal, Made to Measure

Zell am Ziller 600m (1,968ft)

Zell is a large and not particularly remarkable village downstream from
Mayrhofen and has long been a popular summer resort. It has gained
considerable popularity in winter, more owing to the desire of tour
operators to maintain favourable two-season contracts with hoteliers
than to any particular merit as a ski centre. Neither the main Kreuzjoch
ski area, which opened in 1978, nor the minor Gerlosstein/Sonnalm is
conveniently situated and both have to be reached by ski-bus. The
Kreuzjoch gondola, which starts from a large car-park on the Zillertal
highway takes you up the Wiesenalm. It is not possible to ski back down
to the bottom. A chair-lift takes you on up to Rosenalm at 1744m. From
here a choice of lifts fan out across a sunny bowl up to Kreuzjoch which,

at 2559m, is the top of the ski area. The runs down are a mixture of blue (easy) and flattering reds. The Sportbahn Karspitz double chair from Wiesenalm serves a more challenging black (difficult) run which takes you back to Wiesenalm.

The Gerlosstein area, five kilometres away from the centre, is accessed via a cable car which takes you up to 1650m and a choice of routes on up to the Arbiskogel at 1830m. Runs down are a mixture of

Skiing facts: Mayrhofen

TOURIST OFFICE
A-6290 Mayrhofen, Zillertal
Tel 43 5285 2305
Fax 43 5285 2305 33

THE RESORT
By road Calais 1200km
By rail station in resort
By air Innsbruck 1 hr, Munich 2 hrs
Visitor beds 7,930 (61% guesthouses, 19% chalets, 14% hotels, 6% apartments)
Transport free bus service

THE SKIING
Longest run Skiroute Schwendau, 6km (red)
Number of lifts 30
Number of trails/pistes 45 (32% easy, 49% intermediate, 19% difficult)
Total of trails/pistes 90km
Nursery slopes 5 lifts
Summer skiing extensive skiing on the Hintertux Glacier
Snowmaking 16km covered

LIFT PASSES
Area pass Zillertal (covers whole Zillertal valley, including Hintertux glacier) ÖS1,900 for 6 days.Mayrhofen/Finkenberg ÖS1,450 for 6 days
Day pass Mayrhofen/Finkenberg ÖS300
Half-day pass ÖS215 from midday
Beginners no free lifts
Children 40% reduction for 6-14 yrs, free for 6 yrs and under
Pensioners no reduction
Credit cards accepted no

SKI SCHOOLS
Adults Ski School Mayrhofen Uli Spiess, Manfred Gager and Max Rahm, 10am-midday and 1.30-3.30pm, ÖS1,300 for 6 days
Children 4-14 yrs, Spiess, Gager and

Rahm, 10am-midday and 1.30-3.30pm, ÖS1,300 for 6 days not including lunch
Private lessons ÖS430 per hr, ÖS2,000 per day
Special courses snowboarding, ski-touring, Yeti Club-High-Life
Guiding companies Peter Habeler

CROSS-COUNTRY
Ski schools Spiess, Gager and Rahm
Loipe location and size 20km in and around Mayrhofen

CHILDCARE
Non-ski kindergarten Wuppy's Kinderland, 3 mths-7 yrs, 8am-6pm, ÖS1,600 for 6 days including lunch
Ski kindergarten Riki's (Spiess) 4-12 yrs at the Ahorn, Dwarfland (Gager) 4-14 yrs at the Penken and Rahm nursery at the Ahorn and Penken, 9am-4pm, ÖS1,900 for 6 days including lunch
Babysitting list available from tourist office

OTHER SPORTS
Hang-gliding, skating, curling, sleigh rides, squash, indoor tennis, swimming, fitness centres, bowling, tobogganing

WHAT'S NEW
● Adventure pool ● gondola at Penken for 1994/95

FOOD AND DRINK PRICES
Coffee ÖS22, bottle of house wine ÖS200, beer ÖS27, dish of the day ÖS150

TOUR OPERATORS
Crystal,Enterprise, Equity,Total Ski, Falcon, Inghams, Made to Measure, Neilson, Sally Holidays, Seasun School Tours,Ski Airtours, Ski Choice, Ski Thomson, Snowcoach

mainly undemanding reds and easy blues. One mostly north-facing red offers a pleasant cruise of 1000m vertical all the way to the bottom station. This area can also be reached from the village of Ramsau via a chair which takes you up to Sonnalm half-way down this road. A double chair from Sonnalm takes you on up to Arbiskogel.

TOURIST OFFICE
Dorfplatz 3A, A-6280, Zell am Ziller
Tel 43 5282 2281
Fax 43 5282 228180

TOUR OPERATORS
Neilson, Ski Europe,
Snowcoach Club Cantabrica

Niederau, Tyrol

ALTITUDE 830m (2,722ft)

• •
Good points easy runs, gentle and extensive nursery slopes, excellent for beginners, tree-level skiing
Bad points limited skiing, lack of challenging skiing, short runs, not suitable for late holidays
Linked or nearby resorts Oberau (n), Auffach (n), Mühltal (n), Roggenboden (n), Thierbach (n)

Niederau is the capital of a small, quite separate group of Tyrolean resorts south of the Inn Valley between Alpbach and Söll, which are collectively known and marketed as the Wildschönau. Despite this savage-sounding name the skiing here is extremely gentle. The few runs are best suited to beginners and early intermediates, but Niederau itself has a long historical association with the UK market and generations of British skiers have taken their first tentative steps here before moving on to more comprehensive ski areas which offer a greater challenge. There is, however, a kind of Niederau fan club which is made up of skiers who return year after year to Niederau because they know every inch of every run and are on first-name terms with every village barman.

Niederau has easy nursery slopes where, as one reporter put it, 'you are not constantly bombarded by experienced skiers swishing past to the lifts at the end of a long run, and skiers of different standards can easily meet for lunch'. Prices are five per cent lower than in other resorts in the region and you will find a considerable proportion of skiers are British. Oberau and Auffach are a bus ride away.

The skiing
Top 1900m (6,232ft) bottom 830m (2,722ft)
The skiing immediately above Niederau is in two small areas, with **mountain access** for both by an ancient double chair-lift from the valley. You can ski from the higher Lanerköpfl to the lower Markbachjoch. The chair-lift for Lanerköpfl leaves from the western extremity of Niederau. The two runs from it are graded red (intermediate), and the more westerly one, which connects with the Lanerköpfl drag, is given the status of a 'ski-route', meaning that while it is not groomed it should be still periodically checked by the ski patrol. Both runs are sound intermediate trails cut between the trees and offer no surprises, but plenty of confidence-building terrain for timid intermediates.

The short run above them from Lanerköpfl (1600m) is graded black (difficult), although it is not noticeably steeper. Alternatively, from the top an intermediate run with some poling links with Markbachjoch (1500m) where, beyond the hotels and restaurants and linking nursery lifts, two drags serve a sunny slope correctly graded blue (easy). From the lower of these two lifts at the eastern extremity of the ski area a piste, starting with a choice of red or blue, but briefly merging into a tricky red section, descends through the trees to the top of the Tennladenlift. An easy blue from here takes you either to the bottom of the lift or on down to the bottom of the Markbachjochbahn. Steeper runs from the top of Markbachjoch include a direct, but not too diffi-cult, black descent directly under the chair-lift.

Oberau and neighbouring Roggenboden are a few kilometres along the valley floor and are served by eight short drag-lifts, which offer noth-ing more than nursery slopes, except for the one red run down from the Riedlberg lift, which one reporter argues is not as difficult to cope with as the rutted track of the actual T- bar itself.

Auffach is again a bus ride away. It has a gondola going up from a busy car park area to the south of the village, which offers more, although not necessarily more interesting skiing, including one long red run from Schatzberg (1903m) providing over 1000m vertical. The top section of the gondola is backed up by a long drag-lift, and a series of four parallel drags serve easy, but red-graded, quite short runs, as well as giving access to some long off-piste variations down to the valley which are not marked on the piste map. The northern flanks of the mountain are interspersed from both the middle and top stages of the gondola with short drags-lifts serving blue runs, but there are no easy ways down to the valley. Lift queues throughout the area can be as long as 25 minutes at the ski school's 10am starting time. There is no artifi-cial snow.

Mountain restaurants
Overcrowding is a problem in the small number of mountain eating places available. Most reporters choose to eat in the easily accessible restaurants at the bottom of the lifts in Niederau. We have, however, good reports of the 'elderly establishment' above the Hotelhanglift. The top of the drag-lift restaurant at the Auffach gondola middle station is said to be 'reasonably priced, clean, and not crowded'.

Beginners and children
Good instruction is what has given Niederau its reputation and we con-tinue to receive enthusiastic reports. As one correspondent says: 'The care taken in bringing on the starters was excellent, but really ambitious up-and-coming intermediates would not choose Niederau as it lacks the ability to stretch this level of skier.' English is well and widely spoken; indeed, a number of the instructors are native English speakers.

The children's ski school here is equally well known and takes chil-dren from four years for the entire day. Younger non-skiers, from two years old, are cared for in the *Gästekindergarten*. The nursery slopes are gentle and convenient. More extensive slopes can be found at Oberau.

The resort
The village, which sprawls away from the foot of the two main ski areas, has modern hotels and gasthofs built in traditional style as well as a vil-

lage square, but somehow seems to lack the real heart of so many similar villages in this part of Austria. While it is not particularly charming, the skiing is certainly convenient to the point of being door-to-door from some hotels. Non-skiers who are not content to potter along gentle paths between the villages will find activities in the Wildschönau extremely limited. Cross-country trails run for 38km along the valley floor. Shopping is limited beyond the usual sports outfitters to a few local craft shops.

Accommodation

The most convenient hotels are the Austria and the Alpenland, situated at the base of the nursery slopes and close to the main mountain access double chair. The Hotel Staffler is nearby and is 'basic but efficiently run'. However, a couple of reporters complain that 'the dining-room doubles as the main sitting area, so if you dislike eating in a smoky atmosphere, avoid it'. Pension Lindner is said to have larger bedrooms, separate dining- and living-rooms, and to be better value. The Hotel Vicky remains popular with the British and is one of the focal points of the nightlife. The four-star Sonnschein, a few minutes' walk from the centre, is said to shine above others ('excellent, quiet, elegant service, and the food is good'). It has an indoor swimming-pool, a children's playroom, and its kitchen also caters for vegetarians. The friendly Pension Diane is run by an Englishwoman and her Austrian husband.

Eating out

As is usual in most of Austria, the restaurants are mainly in the hotels, and these can vary from those serving typical Austrian dishes to pizzas and pasta. Hotel Austria has an à la carte restaurant, hotels Wastlhof and the Harfenwirt are among the best value, and the pizzas in the Café Lois are said to be substantial.

Après-ski

Small it may be, but Niederau has a lively choice of entertainment after the lifts close for the night. Swimming is available at some of the hotels, including the Austria and the Sonnschein, and the Hotel Sportklause has a bowling alley. The Vicky is popular with British visitors and has live music two nights a week, ('go early if you want a seat'). The Dorfstübn Café and the Cave Bar beneath the Staffler are for late-night drinkers. The latter also has a disco, as does Gasthof Schneeberger. The Alm Pub is a more traditional nightspot. Sleigh rides are popular, and Oberau has floodlit skiing.

Oberau   935m (3,067ft)

Oberau is an attractive and friendly little village with its own extensive nursery slopes, but no access to the main skiing. A free ski-bus runs every 15 to 20 minutes to and from Niederau. It is a resort strictly for beginners, with good nursery slopes and its own ski school. Hotel Tirolerhof, in the centre by the beginner's lift and the ski school, is said to be extremely comfortable with live entertainment most evenings. The hotel's Sno'Blau Bar is the centre of what limited nightlife there is.

The attractive Gasthof Kellerwirt, which was once a monastery, has a popular restaurant, a Kellerbar, and organises harp music evenings.

TOURIST OFFICE
A-6311 Oberau, Tyrol
Tel 43 5339 82 55/22
Fax 43 5339 24 33

TOUR OPERATORS
Enterprise, Inghams, Ski Europe,
Ski Sutherland, Ski Thomson

Skiing facts: Niederau

TOURIST OFFICE
A-6311 Niederau, Wildschönau
Tel 43 5339 8255
Fax 43 5339 2433

THE RESORT
By road Calais 1114km
By rail Wörgl 7km
By air Salzburg 2 hrs
Visitor beds 8,931 in Wildschönau area (72% hotels, 17% guesthouses and chalets, 11% apartments)
Transport bus service to Oberau and Auffach (included in lift pass)

THE SKIING
Longest run Schatzberg, 7km (red)
Number of lifts 36
Number of trails/pistes 37 (5% beginner, 60% easy, 30% intermediate, 5% difficult)
Total of trails/pistes 42km
Nursery slopes 3 lifts in Niederau
Summer skiing none
Snowmaking none

LIFT PASSES
Area pass Wildschönau (covers Niederau, Oberau, Auffach) ÖS1,280 for 6 days
Day pass ÖS265
Half-day pass ÖS150 from 1pm, ÖS180 from midday, ÖS200 from 11.30am or before 1pm, ÖS220 after 11am
Beginners coupons available
Children 5-14 yrs, ÖS770 for 6 days, free for 5 yrs and under
Pensioners 60 yrs and over, as children
Credit cards accepted yes

SKI SCHOOLS
Adults Ski School Wildschönau, 10am-midday and 2-4pm, ÖS1,150 for 6 days
Children Ski School Wildschönau, 10am-midday and 2-4pm, ÖS1,100 for 6 days
Private lessons ÖS380 per hr
Special courses snowboarding
Guiding companies through Ski School

CROSS-COUNTRY
Ski schools Wildschönau
Loipe location and size 38km total, links Niederau, Oberau, Möhltal and Auffach

CHILDCARE
Non-ski kindergarten
Gästekindergarten, 2 yrs and over, 9.30am-4.30pm, ÖS800 for 6 days not including lunch
Ski kindergarten Ski School Wildschönau, 4 yrs and over, ÖS1,100 for 6 days, extra ÖS110 per day for lunch
Babysitting list from tourist office

OTHER SPORTS
Parapente, skating, curling, bowling, swimming, tobogganing, sleigh rides

FOOD AND DRINK PRICES
Coffee ÖS20, bottle of house wine ÖS144, beer ÖS28, dish of the day ÖS90

TOUR OPERATORS
Enterprise, Equity Total Ski, Inghams, Made to Measure, Neilson, Seasun Ski Tours, Ski Airtours, Ski Austria, Ski Europe, Ski Thomson

Auffach 870m (2,854ft)

Auffach has developed relatively little as a resort, despite laying claim to the major lift, indeed the only gondola, in the area. It consists mostly of a gathering of chalets around the church as well as a line of hotels and gasthofs along the road beyond the gondola station. Hotel Bernauerhof and Gasthof Platzl are both recommended. The Schönangeralm restaurant is also praised for its 'great local venison and cheerful staff'. The Avalanche Pub is the main après-ski gathering point.

TOURIST OFFICE
A-6316 Auffach, Tyrol
Tel 43 5339 82 55/20
Fax 43 5339 24 33

TOUR OPERATORS
Ski Europe

Obergurgl, Tyrol

ALTITUDE 1930m (6,330ft)

••

Good points excellent for beginners and children, ski-touring, ideal for families, reliable snow record, late-season skiing, resort atmosphere
Bad points lack of tough runs, limited for non-skiers, small ski area
Linked or nearby resorts Hochgurgl (n), Sölden (n), Untergurgl (n), Vent (n)

Obergurgl made its mark on the European map of skiing on 27 May 1931 when Swiss aviation pioneer Professor Auguste Piccard force-landed his hot-air balloon on the Gurgler-Ferner Glacier. What he had just achieved was the world altitude record of nearly 16000m, what he was to bring about was world recognition for one of Austria's most exclusive ski resorts. Local mountain guide Hans Falkner spotted the balloon land in the last light of the day. The following morning he carried out a triumphant rescue of the explorers, leading them between the crevasses to Obergurgl and glory for the village and all concerned. Set at the head of the isolated Ötztal, with its 21 glaciers, it was and is one of the best ski-touring centres in Austria. The lift system later installed was state-of-the-art and Obergurgl became the ideal ski resort.

Today it has 13 four-star hotels, but little else has really changed from the ski boom years of the 1960s, apart from the modern gondola and quad chair. While elsewhere in Austria villages have sought to expand and combine their ski areas, isolated Obergurgl has remained upmarket, but not aloof, still successfully maintaining its small village identity. Development has remained largely in the hands of three families who have neither sought nor needed outside investment and, sensibly, they have largely limited the number of beds in proportion to the capacity of the lift system.

Obergurgl's geographical position, an hour's drive up the Ötztal Valley, positively discourages day-trippers and keeps its beautifully unspoilt terrain exclusively for its paying guests. It is almost as if there is a sign on the final approach road saying: 'Keep out (unless you can afford it) – exclusive famly ski area.' It is interesting to note that the resort is devoid of coach parking facilities.

Hochgurgl, just a few kilometres away by regular free ski-bus, is in reality an entirely separate resort, with a different character and a different clientèle. While Obergurgl draws families like a moth to a searchlight, Hochgurgl has a more serious ski image. Both have in common an exceptional snow record. Obergurgl claims, along with Val Thorens, to be the highest ski village with a church in Europe. Hochgurgl, according to our statistics, is in fact the winner. Good snow cover is usually assured from early December to late April.

What is remarkable is that 21 per cent of skiers who find their way to Obergurgl are British. Generations of the same families have spent their winter holidays here since Piccard dropped in so unexpectedly. It seems that Austrian village charm and quaint skiing, boosted with lashings of luxurious accommodation, remain a winning formula.

Only limited Vent and mass-market Sölden are within easy reach for a day out. Lift passes are not compatible and most Obergurgl visitors are more than content to remain secure in their elegant eyrie at the head of the valley.

The skiing
Top 3064m (10,050ft) bottom 1793m (5,881ft)

For a resort with this kind of international reputation it comes as a surprise to discover that the ski area is both small and lacking in any serious challenge. The slopes of both Obergurgl and Hochgurgl occupy a north-west facing area at the southern end of the Ötztal on the Italian border. Most of the skiing is above the tree-line and runs are intermediate. Not all of the handful of black runs justify their gradings and expert skiers, unless they are interested in ski-touring, will soon tire of the limited pistes. However, there is plenty to keep less adventurous skiers and families occupied in these truly magnificent surroundings.

The skiing takes place over three small areas naturally divided by the contours of the terrain. Hochgurgl offers the greatest vertical drop off the glacier and adds the variety of a wide, wooded hillside down to Untergurgl, little more than a roadside lift station and car park. Obergurgl's two sectors have greater off-piste potential, more interesting slopes, and steeper runs at the top.

From near the village centre **mountain access** is via a two-seater chair which rises lazily over gentle slopes to the Gaisberg area. Attractive, short red (intermediate) runs here take you down through a scattering of trees to the Steinmann mountain restaurant and a couple of short, steeper gullies under the Nederlift. A long, antique single chair takes you up to the Hohe Mut at 2670m. The only official run down is black, but the 1.8km descent is not difficult when snow cover is good, and you cannot but suspect that the grading and lack of alternative piste is designed to reduce traffic and avoid bottlenecks at the outdated lift.

An alternative off-piste run off the back takes you down through what in good powder conditions is a glorious descent, which ends up near the Schönwiesehütte. Off-piste opportunities at this end of the sector are numerous, but most involve the use of skins.

Access to the Festkogl area is via a modern gondola from the beginning of the village. Skiers coming from Gaisberg take a long blue (easy) traverse behind the ice-rink; a short baby drag-lift to provide the necessary height to schuss to the station. Alternatively the two access points are linked by ski-bus. The gondola rises steeply to a sunny plateau with a restaurant and a couple of drag-lifts. The area of mainly red (but not difficult) intermediate skiing has been vastly improved by the building of a modern quad chair which takes you up to the highest point of the skiing at 3035m. Less confident skiers will enjoy the blue run down from the gondola station down to the bottom of the Rosskar double

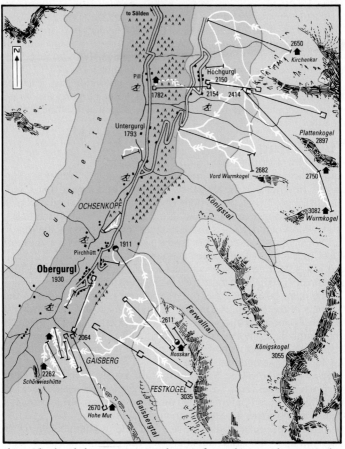

chair. The local ski map is somewhat confusing here, with run number 2 marked 3 on the mountain, 3 marked 3a, and 8 on the map appearing to be 7 in reality; the errors are irritating rather than dangerous.

Experts will enjoy the black itinerary down the Ferwalltal from the top of the gondola. The two Obergurgl ski areas are linked on the mountain from this direction; from the top of the gondola a blue run which later becomes red takes you under the quad chair across the bottom of the Gaisberggletscher to the foot of the Hohe Mut lift.

Hochgurgl's skiing is mostly very gentle, on broad, open slopes above the resort reached by road or by chair from Untergurgl. A double chair gives access to a choice of easy pistes served by long drag-lifts at either end of the ski area. The top of this long glacier is served by two chairs, one a high-speed covered quad which affords protection against the elements, often severe at this altitude. Even on a sunny day in February extremely low temperatures can be the price you pay for high-quality snow. The last section is a steep drag which takes you up to just below the 3082m summit of the Wurmkogel and to a short black run.

The less powerful Schermerspitz chair gives access to a wide, easy red piste, the start of nearly 1500m vertical to Untergurgl.

The drag-lift on the southern side of the ski area, with a short, steep second section to it, serves an interesting long and varied red run, with moguls on the bottom half. One reporter describes the bottom half as 'much more difficult than any other red runs in the resort'. There is a black variation from half-way down which dips into the scenic Königstal and ends up in the same place.

Mountain restaurants

The Hohe Mut Hütte at the top of the single chair at Gaisberg provides magnificent views of the Ötztal and the Dolomites. The ability to ski the black run from here is necessary, which means that the old wooden chalet is the least crowded restaurant in the area. On fine days there is an ice-bar and barbecue on the terrace. The Schönwieshütte is a 10- to 15-minute walk from the Sattellift piste and is a touring refuge which serves simple meals ('best *Gulaschsuppe* and *Kaiserschmarren* ever'). David's Schihütte is recommended for its *Tirolergröstl*.

In Hochgurgl the three altitude restaurants are reasonable, but usually overcrowded. Reporters warn that restaurants in Hochgurgl itself are nearly all attached to the smart hotels and are considerably more expensive.

Beginners and children

We have generally favourable reports of the Austrian ski school which operates in Obergurgl and Hochgurgl. Some reporters have complained that classes, in theory restricted to 12 pupils, can have as many as 15 during high season and division into language groups is not always well organised.

As might be expected from a ski resort which has founded its reputation on family holidays, Obergurgl is well served with child facilities. Eight hotels operate their own crèches, usually free of charge, and the minimum age accepted varies from hotel to hotel. These include the Alpina, Austria, Bellevue, Bergwelt, Crystal, Hochfirst, Hochgurgl and Mühle. Obergurgl's kindergarten takes children all day long from two years old. Surprisingly there is no ski kindergarten as such; ski lessons begin in the ski school from five years old.

The resort

Building in Obergurgl has reached capacity within the avalanche-safe area and despite the large number of luxury hotels it is still a small village set on the lower level around the church and a handful of shops, and on the upper area around an open-air ice rink. At the heart of it all is the Edelweiss und Gurgl Hotel, once the local inn and now the focal four-star around which much of village life rotates.

A regular free bus service operates from the centre to Untergurgl and to Hochgurgl. Post- buses run to Sölden and beyond. Cars are banned from the village between 11pm and 6am, and parking is not easy. The handful of shops is strictly limited to sports and souvenirs. Two small supermarkets look after the needs of self-caterers.

Eating out

Dining is largely confined to the main hotels, most of which have separate à la carte restaurants. Pizzeria Romantika in the Hotel Madeleine provides some respite from the ubiquitous rounds of *Wienerschnitzel*. The Edelweiss has a comfortable candlelit *Stübli* and the Bergwelt is recommended for its nouvelle cuisine. One reporter speaks warmly of fondue evenings organised at the Nederhütte.

Skiing facts: Obergurgl

TOURIST OFFICE
A-6456 Obergurgl, Ötztal
Tel 43 5256 258
Fax 43 5256 35377

THE RESORT
By road Calais 1083km
By rail Ötz 48km, regular buses from station
By air Innsbruck 1½ hrs
Visitor beds 3,680 (66% hotels, 34% apartments and guesthouses)
Transport free bus to Untergurgl and Hochgurgl

THE SKIING
Longest run Wurmkogl-Untergurgl, 8km (blue/red)
Number of lifts 23
Number of trails/pistes 22 (35% easy, 47% intermediate, 18% difficult)
Total of trails/pistes 110km in area
Nursery slopes 6 in area
Summer skiing none
Snowmaking 1km covered

LIFT PASSES
Area pass (covers Obergurgl, Untergurgl, Hochgurgl) from ÖS1,790 for 6 days
Day pass from ÖS370
Half-day pass from ÖS330 after 11am, from ÖS280 after midday, from ÖS200 after 2pm
Beginners coupons available
Children 6-14 yrs, from ÖS1,240 for 6 days, free for 6 yrs and under
Pensioners 60 yrs and over, as children
Credit cards accepted no

SKI SCHOOLS
Adults Obergurgl, 10am-midday and 2-4pm, ÖS1,300 for 6 days, Hochgurgl, 10am-midday and 2-4pm, ÖS1,320 for 5 days

Children Obergurgl, 10am-midday and 2-4pm, ÖS1,200 for 6 days, Hochgurgl, 10am-midday and 2-4pm, ÖS1,320 for 5 days
Private lessons Obergurgl ÖS2,050 per day, Hochgurgl ÖS2,390 per day
Special courses snowboarding, monoskiing, telemark, Big Foot, ski-touring
Guiding companies Hochgebirgsschule Obergurgl

CROSS-COUNTRY
Ski schools Ski School Obergurgl
Loipe location and size 13km-4km Obergurgl, 7km Untergurgl, 2km Hochgurgl

CHILDCARE
Non-ski kindergarten 2 yrs and over, 9.30am-4.30pm, ÖS180 per day including lunch and supervision, ÖS1,200 for 6 days not including lunch
Ski kindergarten Ski School Obergurgl, 5 yrs and over, 10am- midday and 2-4pm, ÖS1,200 for 6 days. Ski School Hochgurgl, 5 yrs and over, 10am-midday and 2-4pm, ÖS1,320 for 5 days
Babysitting list available from tourist office

OTHER SPORTS
Skating, curling, squash, swimming, shooting range, bowling

FOOD AND DRINK PRICES
Coffee ÖS22, bottle of house wine ÖS140, beer ÖS25, dish of the day ÖS100

TOUR OPERATORS
Austrian Holidays, Bladon Lines, Crystal, Enterprise, Inghams, Made to Measure, Neilson, Ski Airtours, Ski Thomson

Accommodation

Most of the accommodation is in smart hotels and, to a lesser extent, in gasthofs and pensions. It is also possible to rent attractive and spacious apartments by contacting the resort direct. Obergurgl is not by any stretch of the imagination large, and location is of relative unimportance. Those who want to enjoy the nightlife are ill-advised to stay at the Festkogl end, a 15-minute walk from the main bars and discos. Hotel Crystal is a monster of a building, completely out of keeping with the resort character, but extremely comfortable inside. The Deutschmann has nothing to do with the predominant nationality of its guests, but is the name of the old Obergurgl family which owns it. The second group of hotels is clustered around the ice-rink, on high ground above the centre. The Bergwelt ('art deco furniture and a great pool') and the Austria are both warmly recommended. Down in the centre the Edelweiss and Gurgl is highly thought of although rooms are not as large or as well-equipped as in the new four-stars. The Jenewein is also praised for its friendly service and 'quite exceptional demi-pension food'.

Après-ski

Obergurgl is surprisingly active in the evenings. The Nederhütte at the top of the Gaisberg lift becomes crowded as the lifts close for the day. Tea-dancing and copious measures of *Glühwein* prepare you for the gentle run down to the village. The outdoor bar of the Edelweiss at the foot of the Gaisberg lift continues to attract customers until darkness falls. The Joslkeller has a cosy atmosphere and good music, which gets louder with dancing as the evening progresses. You find the odd person in ski suit and boots still here in the early hours. The Krump'n'Stadl is noisy with yodelling on alternate nights. The Edelweiss has live music in the lobby bar. Late in the evening its cellar disco is said by most reporters to be the best in town ('good music, reasonable prices, and you can actually talk between dances').

Hochgurgl 2150m (7,052ft)

Hochgurgl is little more than a collection of modern hotels perched by the side of the road leading up to the Timmelsjoch Pass, which is closed in winter. It has a loyal following among reporters who admit they return here 'to ski, and only to ski'. We have good reports of the Hotel Riml and the less expensive Hotel Ideal ('it is, as the name implies'). The three-star Alpenhotel Laurin is recommended for its excellent food ('superb Farmers' Buffet'). Shopping is limited to little more than skis and postcards. What nightlife there is centres on hotel bars.

TOURIST OFFICE
as Obergurgl

TOUR OPERATORS
Crystal, Inghams, Neilson,
Ski Thomson

Obertauern, Salzburgerland

ALTITUDE 1740m (5,707ft)

Good points excellent snow record, reliable resort-level snow, sunny slopes, skiing convenience, extensive nursery slopes, lack of lift queues, interesting off-piste skiing, variety of easy runs
Bad points limited activities for non-skiers, quiet après-ski, spread-out village
Linked or nearby resorts Schladming (n)

Obertauern is what the Austrians call a *Schneewinkel*, a snow pocket in the Niedere Tauern mountains which separates Villach and Klagenfurt in southerly Carinthia from northerly Salzburg. While other resorts in Austria and elsewhere struggle to cope with a lack of cover during lean winters, Obertauern is usually rolling in metres of the stuff. It was for this reason that 60 years ago a group of local enthusiasts built a stone refuge at the highest point of the pass. From here they could climb the surrounding peaks and ski down, certain of good snow even when the resorts of the Tyrol were green. In the 1930s a handful of huts, devoid of running water or electricity, sprang up on the roadside of this arterial throroughfare.

Today Obertauern is a thriving, effectively purpose-built ski resort, in the Austrian top three for tourism, but still more popular with the German and Dutch market than with the British. Thanks to a motorway tunnel, the Tauern Pass, once an important Roman trade route at the only point in the range where altitude falls below 2000m, is now a quiet backwater. The impressive peaks of the Niedere Tauern ring the road, allowing the construction of lifts from a central point to fan out into a natural ski circus. It is possible to ski the arena in either direction, and unlike most Austrian ski resorts, it is also possible to ski to and from the doorsteps of most hotels.

Although the village is far higher than most Austrian resorts, the skiing only rises a further 573m, and pistes extend 100m below village altitude. The area is not particularly extensive, but there is more to it than most resorts of its size and an interesting variety of gradient and terrain, mainly suited to intermediates but with enough to keep most advanced skiers happy for a week. Pistes can become heavily mogulled around the rim of the bowl and a couple of runs are positively steep. In powder conditions the off-piste is spectacular with long runs both above and below the tree-line.

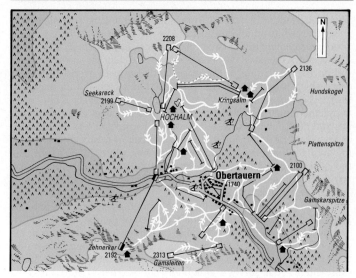

The resort itself is no classic beauty. If you are expecting a chocolate-box Austrian village with onion-domed church, frescoes and ornately fretworked balconies, you will be disappointed. Under its usual blanket of snow the long straggle of roadside hotels and bars looks more like a Wild-West town. But it has its own particular charm. The range of non-skiing activities is limited to the point of absence.

A car is not necessary for getting about the village, but it is an advantage for making use of some of the other skiing in the area. Schladming and a host of other resorts are included in the Top-Tauern Skischeck lift pass. Obertauern's favourable micro-climate has one disadvantage: when other resorts are suffering from lack of snow its easy accessibility means a large daily influx of coaches and cars, particularly at weekends. However, such is the high standard of the lift system that serious queues are a rarity.

The skiing
Top 2313m (7,587ft) bottom 1640m (5,379ft)

The skiing circuit is concentrated on the north side of the resort, spread around a broad undulating, mainly treeless bowl ringed by rocky peaks. Four main lifts group around the bowl to points near the rim. Two of them ascend to approximately 2000m from almost the same point at Hochalm (1940m); the Seekareckbahn quad chair-lift takes you up over a steep east-facing slope, and the Panorama triple chair over a more varied south-facing one. As the altitude suggests, neither run is long, but both are challenging and entertaining, often with moguls. The triple chair also gives access to a couple of longer, varied runs down to Kringsalm.

The Hundskogel chair serves a slightly longer slope offering a choice of routes down, with a moderately steep piste away from the lift on the north side and off-piste routes more directly down on the south side. The Plattenkar drag-lift, now supplemented by a parallel quad chair, goes up from a point just below the village to 2100m, giving a good intermediate run of over 400m vertical. Beyond these lifts, a little further down the pass, the Schaidberg double chair serves the steepest run on the north side of the resort and also gives access to a short drag, which is gentle enough to be used as a high-altitude beginner slope. There is an easy run back to the village from here. Supplementing these lifts going up to the outer edges of the skiing are lifts and pistes linking one with another. These offer less experienced skiers plenty of scope and a clockwise circuit of this northern part of the area need not involve any of the higher, more difficult runs. But the pistes of most interest to timid skiers are the easy, open runs across the middle of the bowl, served by drag-lifts including the long Zentral lift from just below the village.

On the south side of the resort the mountains rise more immediately, keeping the village in shade for much of the day in mid-winter. The major lift is the Zehnerkar cable car, climbing over 500m from the western extremity of the village and giving access to a long, moderately testing run branching to various points along the pass. The lower Gamsleiten 1 chair serves a straightforward blue (easy) piste across the mountain to the bottom of the cable car, which is part of the clockwise circuit. More challenging red (intermediate) runs lead back to the base of the lower Gamsleiten. The upper Gamsleiten 2 chair serves a seriously steep, unprepared run from the high point of the system. When snow is in short supply, this rocky slope may lack adequate cover despite its north-east orientation.

With multiple **mountain access** points scattered throughout the village, queueing is not a problem in Obertauern. Even at peak times when snow is poor elsewhere and tour operator 'bus-ing' is in operation, waiting time is unlikely to exceed 10 minutes. The bottlenecks used to be the Zehnerkar cable car on the anticlockwise circuit and the nearby Grünwaldkopfbahn double chair. But this has now been replaced by a detachable quad chair, which has greatly alleviated the problem. You can now ski back down over a road-bridge at the bottom directly to the cable car. However, even at off-peak times the short Seekar drag-lift just below Kringsalm restricts the clockwise flow.

In recent years much has been done to improve the piste-marking and some have been more sensibly re-graded. One reporter said he felt a number of the blues appeared more taxing than the reds, but much depends on the prevalent snow conditions. The new local lift map is an improvement, but it still fails to show piste names or numbers. Signposting of the clockwise and anticlockwise circuits is generally good. Thanks to the fact that no less than seven different lift companies share the ski area, the quality of grooming brought about by competition between them is unsurpassed anywhere in Austria. There is substantial artificial snowmaking both on one long piste from Seekarspitze down to Kringsalm, and on the short Schaidberg black (expert) run at the eastern end of the village. Snow-cannon also operate on the blue run down from the Edelweisshütte served by the Kurven lift.

Mountain restaurants

Because of the ski-in ski-out layout of Obertauern it is quite easy to ski back into the village to eat at lunchtime, but nevertheless the supply of mountain restaurants is more than adequate. The Seekarhaus at Kringsalm is a cosy spot with good food, but it can get crowded with consequent slow service. Similarly, the Sonnhof is overcrowded at peak times, with its 'busy and chaotic self-service system that entails a scrum and a long wait'. The Schaidberg Liftstube has an extensive menu. The small Achenrainhütte at Gamsleiten is 'very pleasant, but small'. The open-air grill at the top of the Grünwaldkopbahn serves four kinds of sausage with tarragon mustard and 'a wonderful garlicky dish in a fry-ing-pan that you could smell halfway down the red run at the back of the restaurant'. Gamsmilch bar at the top of the cable car and Edelweisshütte at the top of Lift 12 is the scene of lively tea-dancing; both have only easy blue runs left to negotiate on the way home.

Beginners and children

Obertauern now has three ski schools: the Krallinger Obertauern-Süd, which has a higher than average number of female instructors and is much favoured by tour operators, Schischule Koch in Obertauern-Nord, and CSA (also known as Ski On Grillitsch) in Obertauern-Nord.

We have mixed reports of the Krallinger; classes of up to 15 are reported, but the general standard of tuition is good. One reporter who had specifically asked to join a beginners' class with other English-speakers, found himself alone with 10 Germans: 'Everyone helped with the translation, but I feel much was lost in the process.'

The nursery slopes are excellent. There is a short, gentle drag-lift in the heart of the village, just north of the road, and another longer one on the lower slopes at the east end. There is an even longer one parallel to and just south of the road, although it is out of the sun for much of the day in mid-winter. The high Gamskarlift, at the top of the steep Schaidberg chair, also provides gentle skiing suitable for children. The terrain lends itself, in general, to family skiing.

The resort

The main part of the resort is spread along the road gently dropping down to the south-east from the summit of the pass. Three large car-and coach-parks at either end absorb most of the weekend traffic. It takes about 20 minutes to walk from one end to the other of this long, strung-out resort. The main buildings, which constitute the centre, are around the village nursery slope and the tourist office. A lot of the build-ings are in a modern chalet style and as one of Austria's only stabs at a purpose-built resort the overall look, if not impressive, is certainly not offensive. Shopping is strictly limited to a couple of supermarkets and the usual sports shops. Obertauern is not a place for non-skiers.

Accommodation

Nearly all the accommodation is in hotels and guesthouses, few of them cheap by Austrian standards. Location is not particularly critical unless you have small children (choose a hotel within easy walking distance of one of the kindergartens). Hotel Krallinger, across the road from the Gamsleiten chair and close to the Kurven lift, is recommended as a good ski-in ski-out base with satellite television in the rooms. The Hotel Kärntnerland is said to be 'clean, comfortable, and friendly with exceptional food'. The four-star Hotel Rigele is praised for its four-course dinners. The recently built Alpenrose apartments in the village centre are said to be 'cosy and well-appointed'. The lavish Marietta remains a favourite with reporters. Hotel Enzian is also mentioned for its excellent location for skiing.

Skiing facts: Obertauern

TOURIST OFFICE
A-5562 Obertauern, Salzburgerland
Tel 43 6456 252
Fax 43 6456 515

THE RESORT
By road Calais 1222km
By rail Radstadt 20km, connecting buses
By air Salzburg 1½hrs
Visitor beds 4,500 (71% hotels, 18% apartments, 11% guesthouses)
Transport no bus system

THE SKIING
Longest run Zehnerkarseilbahn, 3km (blue)
Number of lifts 25
Number of trails/pistes 47 (49% easy, 36% intermediate, 15% difficult)
Total of trails/pistes 120km
Nursery slopes 5 lifts
Summer skiing none
Snowmaking movable, no figures available

LIFT PASSES
Area pass Top-Tauern Skischeck (covers Obertauern, Schladming, Wagrain, Pongau, Dachstein), ÖS1,700 for 6 days (Obertauern only, ÖS1,480 for 6 days)
Day pass ÖS320
Half-day pass ÖS245, 9am-1pm or mid-day-5pm
Beginners points tickets
Children Top-Tauern Skischeck, 6-13 yrs, ÖS960, Obertauern, ÖS935
Pensioners no reduction
Credit cards accepted no

SKI SCHOOLS
Adults CSA (Nord), Krallinger (Sud), Koch (Nord), all ÖS1,350 for 6 days

Children CSA, 3 yrs and over, Krallinger, 4 yrs and over, Koch, 3 yrs and over, both 10am-midday and 2-4pm, ÖS570 per day, lunch on request
Private lessons ÖS450 per hr
Special courses snowboarding
Guiding companies none

CROSS-COUNTRY
Ski schools through CSA, Krallinger and Koch ski schools
Loipe location and size 15km, from top of village into downhill ski area

CHILDCARE
Non-ski kindergarten Hotel Alpina (public crèche), 2 yrs and over, 9am-4pm, ÖS300 per day, including lunch
Ski kindergarten CSA, Koch, 3 yrs and over, Krallinger, 4 yrs and over, 10am-3.30pm, ÖS1,350 for 6 days, lunch on request
Babysitting list available from tourist office

OTHER SPORTS
Swimming, indoor tennis, squash, bowling

WHAT'S NEW
● Plattenkar, Seekarspitzlifte and Seekarecklift are now quad chairs
● ski-bridge ● sports centre

FOOD AND DRINK PRICES
Coffee ÖS25, bottle of house wine ÖS350, beer ÖS30, dish of the day ÖS130

TOUR OPERATORS
Crystal, Inghams, Made to Measure, Neilson, Ski Austria, SkiBound, Ski Thomson

Eating out

Most of the restaurants are in hotels. The Stüberl restaurant in the Hotel Regina is reported to be extremely good value ('quiet, candlelit, and serves enormous portions'). The Lurzeralm requires reservations and serves 'well-presented, good food, although the service is slightly on the sniffy side'. The Latsch'n'Stüberl has friendly service and well-prepared food.

Après-ski

This is centred on the main hotel bars, of which more than 15 claim to offer music and dancing. The Edelweisshütte is the place to go at the end of skiing, along with the Gamsmilch Bar. The Gasthof Taverne reportedly has the most lively disco later in the evening. The Enzian has a lively bar.

Saalbach-Hinterglemm, Salzburgerland

ALTITUDE 1000m (3,280ft)

Good points extensive intermediate ski area, short airport transfer, extensive nursery slopes, traffic-free village centres, large choice of accommodation
Bad points lift queues, sprawling village, high prices, late-season skiing, noisy at night, too many old T-bars
Linked or nearby resorts Hinterglemm (l), Leogang (l), Kaprun (n), Zell am See (n)

The two villages of Saalbach and Hinterglemm have grown so much over the years that they now stretch along the valley almost meeting. Indeed they refer to themselves by the collective name of Saalbach-Hinterglemm. However, those looking for two cheap and cosy little Austrian villages are in for a disappointment. Saalbach-Hinterglemm is expensive, bustling, and its size means it no longer has much in the way of alpine charm. Saalbach is the larger and more attractive village of the two, offering more activities for the non-skier and better après-ski. A third village, Leogang, is a quiet, attractive little spot in the next valley, which offers a back-door into the ski area. What the Saalbach-Hinterglemm complex does offer, however, is a network of more than 200km of easily accessible intermediate skiing known as the Ski Circus.

The skiing
Top 2100m (6,888ft) bottom 1000m (3,280ft)
The skiing is spread along two sides of the valley, with interlinking lifts enabling you to ski from one village to the other and from one side of the valley to the other. The Ski Circus can be skied in both directions, although the anti-clockwise route is longer. On one side of the valley the slopes are north-facing and offer most of the steeper skiing, while on the other the south-facing slopes are wide and gentle, though they can deteriorate quickly in the sunshine in spite of snowmaking efforts.

Schattberg Ost, Schattberg West and Zwölferkogel are the north-facing slopes, which group together to make up the area's most challenging skiing, although there is some good off-piste skiing here too.

Mountain access is via a large, 100-person cable car rising 1000m from Saalbach centre to the summit of Schattberg Ost. It is here that you will find some of the worst queues when the snow is scarce on the sunny slopes across the valley.

Up the mountain, there is easy skiing behind the peak, served by two drags and a beginners' lift. Beneath the cable car is the Nord trail, a good 4km black run to the village, which is not too steep but can be icy and crowded. For the fainter-hearted there is an alternative 7km blue run through the woods to Jausernalm, where a gondola across the road links with the Wildenkarkogel slopes on the other, sunnier side of the valley. This ends with an easy run back to Saalbach and makes a good long trip for near-beginners. Better skiers can carry on from the Wildenkarkogel Hütte to Leogang via a number of drag-lifts.

Another possible route from Schattberg Ost is to head towards the connecting lift for Schattberg West at 2096m. The link is an easy black run. A good wide red takes you 5km down to the nursery slopes of Hinterglemm from where you can return to Saalbach by taking the chair.

From Hinterglemm's nursery slopes there is a short walk to the two parallel Zwölferkogel chair-lift stations, which rise to 1984m at the Zwölferkogel peak, venue for the men's downhill in the 1991 Alpine World Championships. The main run back to Hinterglemm is a wide intermediate trail, the last part of which is the men's slalom course for the World Championships. A varied black run also takes you down to the valley, and you can come back up in the usually uncrowded gondola.

Mountain access at Hochalmspitze, Bernkogel and Kolmaiskopf is near the bottom of the Zwölfer gondola station where the Hochalm chair takes skiers to the south-facing side of the valley. This serves some good, wide red runs and you can take a series of drag-lifts towards Reiterkogel above Hinterglemm. A chair and a red piste connect the top of Reiterkogel with the top of the triple Bernkogel chair. At the latter, several reporters noted extremely undisciplined jams to get onto the lift. From the top of the Bernkogel a number of unpisted routes lead down to the valley. From the bottom of the Bernkogel another triple-chair and a parallel cable car lead up to the Kolmaiskopf, site of most of the women's races for the World Championships in 1991. Bottlenecks are reported at the Sonnhof and Sportalm chair-lifts.

Leogang is a small village with beginner slopes as well as some good intermediate skiing, but the queues can sometimes be heavy on the return to Saalbach at the end of the day. From Schönleiten, at the top of the Poltenlift between Leogang and Saalbach, a very long blue run goes all the way down to the village of Viehhofen. Unfortunately there is no lift back from here, so it is necessary to take a taxi when returning to Saalbach-Hinterglemm.

Piste-marking and maintenance in the whole area are varied. Reporters mentioned that grooming is not much in evidence and complained of 'grossly overcrowded' pistes and 'non-existent piste-marking in some places'.

Mountain restaurants

These are spread all over the slopes and range from cosy huts to larger

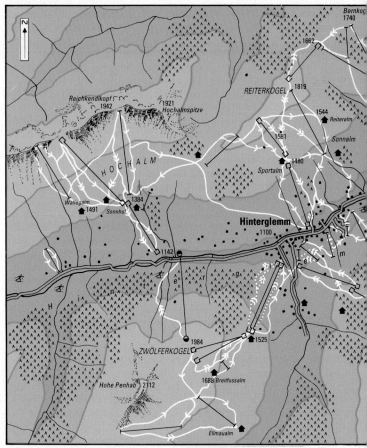

self-service establishments. Most of them are built in traditional style and offer hearty Austrian food. Rosswaldhütte, beside the Rosswald lift in the Hochalmspitze area, is recommended for its good-value food. The friendly staff wear their local costumes. The rather twee Wildenkarkogel Hütte, at the top of the Vorderglemm gondola, is also accessible for non-skiers. It offers good pasta, as well as a special children's menu. Barnalm is a small, attractive restaurant at the top of the triple chair at Bernkogel and serves very good-value lunches. Dishes include the Austrian speciality of *Kaiserschmarren* (pancakes accompanied by stewed plums and sugar).

Beginners and children

A total of eight ski schools operate in Saalbach-Hinterglemm. We have reports on three of them. At Zink in Saalbach one reporter experienced between six and ten to a class, the instructor had a very good command of English and lessons were well explained. He described it as one of the best classes he had attended. Fuerstauer in Saalbach is less well spo-

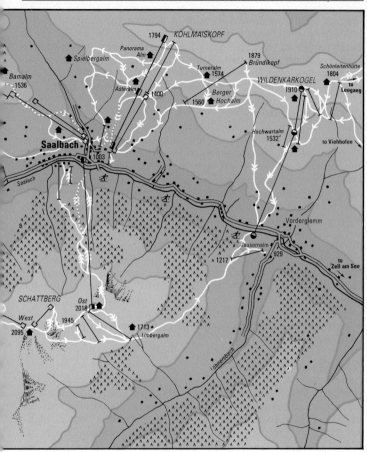

ken of with about 15 to a class: 'The instructor spoke reasonably good English, but he often disappeared out of sight and lost members of the group on T-bar falls on several occasions.' Wolf in Hinterglemm met with the comment: 'You had to have an English teacher otherwise you could be disappointed.'

Nine nursery slope lifts in the valley offer easy skiing for beginners and small children, and from Saalbach lifts up to the easy south-facing slopes at Bernkogel prove useful when snow is scarce lower down. Beginners' skiing is better in Hinterglemm, while Saalbach sports few easy runs. Children are well catered for with a choice of five kindergarten locations in Hinterglemm: the Aparthotel Adler, Hotel Lengauerhof, Kinderhotel Egger, Hotel Theresia, and Miniclub der Partnerhotels. No kindergartens operate in Saalbach.

The resort

Saalbach is a post-war, purpose-built village in the traditional Austrian style. The centre is traffic-free between 9am and 6pm, with glitzy gift and clothing shops, hotels and restaurants all lining the main street. The atmosphere is lively and friendly, often bordering on the over-lively with large amounts of boisterous Scandinavians. Several reporters have mentioned rowdiness in the early hours of the morning when the revellers return to their hotels shortly followed by the noise of 6am deliveries being made to hotels and restaurants before the traffic curfew starts at 9am.

Accommodation

The Hotel Ingonda and the Alpenhotel in Saalbach, as well as the Theresia in Hinterglemm, are the most luxurious hotels. The fact that there are over 30 four-star hotels and nearly as many three-stars shows the wealth of the average clientele here. Shops and restaurants reflect this in their high prices. Of the four-stars, one reporter mentions the Hotel Dorfschmiede in Hinterglemm as having an 'unimpressive' restaurant, and another recommends the Reiterhof in Saalbach as centrally positioned for the shops, ski schools, and village amenities with 'excellent food, small but adequate rooms, and helpful staff'.

The resort does also have a wide selection of pensions, private rooms, and 50 youth hostels at budget prices. The Berger Sporthotel in Saalbach has a *Stübli* for après-ski and a reporter notes that 'the dining room is on two floors, doubled up as disco, so non-smokers should avoid the ground floor, which is smoke-filled following après-ski drinks'. One reporter stayed in Chalet Bergland which was 'attractive on the outside, but very basic inside; the lounge was a box room with no décor to speak of.'

Eating out

Most reporters stayed half-board and our feedback on restaurants is somewhat limited. Recommended for those not counting the Schillings is the Gourmetstube in the Ingonda hotel. Pizzeria Wallner, and Haider's Pizzeria in the Hotel Haider in Saalbach, were both acclaimed for their good value. Others include the Berger Sporthotel where 'the food is good, but nouvelle cuisine is not to everyone's liking'.

Après-ski

We have received a lot of comments on the après-ski in Saalbach-Hinterglemm, most of it not very flattering: 'Resort would suit young, well-heeled people looking for loads of noisy après-ski', 'not a place to attract older people', 'seems to be attracting the younger Scandinavian and German skiers who have been driven out of other Austrian resorts' as well as 'a number of wealthy fur-coated Germans in their Mercedes who go to be seen and don't ski'. Drink prices vary between being 'very high' and 'generally a rip-off'.

Cafés abound in Saalbach-Hinterglemm for après-ski hot chocolate, and later on in the evening 16 discos start pounding away into the early hours, the Londoner in Hinterglemm being one of the most popular ('reasonable atmosphere, but a rip-off'). The resort has 28 bars, although few are traditional Austrian stube. The Bar Old Fashion in Saalbach is warmly recommended, and Lumpi's Bla Bla in Hinterglemm has a good atmosphere.

A wealth of non-skiing activities is to be had in Saalbach-Hinterglemm. Miles of marked walks make the resort ideal for those who do not want to ski every day.

Skiing facts: Saalbach-Hinterglemm

TOURIST OFFICE
A-5753 Saalbach, Salzburgerland
Tel 43 6541 7272
Fax 43 6541 7900

THE RESORT
By road Calais 1193km
By rail Zell-am-See nearest station.
Buses 11 times a day from station to
Saalbach-Hinterglemm
By air Salzburg 1½ hrs, Munich 2 hrs
Visitor beds 18,231 (44% hotels, 26%
guesthouses, 20% apartments, 10%
youth hostels)
Transport free ski-bus

THE SKIING
Longest run Jausernabfahrt, 7km (blue)
Number of lifts 24
Number of trails/pistes 62 (43% easy,
47% intermediate, 10% difficult)
Total of trails/pistes 200km
Nursery slopes 9 lifts
Summer skiing nearest is at Kaprun
Snowmaking in 5 areas, longest run
covered 4km

LIFT PASSES
Area pass (covers
Saalbach-Hinterglemm, Leogang)
ÔS1,700 for 6 days
Day pass ÖS335
Half-day pass ÖS230 from midday
Beginners no free lifts. Hourly day
passes, ticket books and some single
tickets available
Children 6-10 yrs, ÖS750 for 6 days,
11-15 yrs, ÖS1,010 for 6 days. Free for
under 6 yrs
Pensioners reductions for women over
60yrs, men over 65yrs
Credit cards accepted yes

SKI SCHOOLS
Adults in Saalbach-Hinterglemm, from
ÖS400 per day, ÖS1,290 for 4-6 days
Children 4 yrs and over through local
ski schools, 10am-4pm, ÖS400 per
day, ÖS290 for 4-6 days
Private lessons ÖS500 per hr

Special courses telemarking,
snowboarding, ski-touring, ski safaris,
race technique
Guiding companies none

CROSS-COUNTRY
Ski school bookings through local
ski schools
Loipe location and size from
multi-storey car park to Vorderglemm
and back (8km), by tennis hall in
Hinterglemm to the end of the valley
(10km)

CHILDCARE
Non-ski kindergarten (all in
Hinterglemm) Aparthotel Adler by
appointment. Hotel Theresia, 2-7 yrs,
for guests. Hotel Lengauerhof, Mon-Fri,
9.30am-4pm. Miniclub der
Partnershotels, Mon-Fri, 9am-5pm,
for guests. Prices on application
Ski kindergarten 4 yrs and over
through local ski schools,10am-4pm
ÖS400 per day, ÖS1,290 for 4-6
days. extra ÖS100 for lunch-time
care and meal
Babysitting list available from tourist
office

OTHER SPORTS
Indoor tennis, swimming, sleigh rides,
curling, indoor shooting gallery,
tobogganing, bowling, fitness centres,
skating, ice hockey, squash,
telemark

FOOD AND DRINK PRICES
Coffee ÖS20-24, bottle of house wine
ÖS150-170, beer ÖS34, dish of
the day ÖS120-150

TOUR OPERATORS
Austrian Holidays, Crystal, Enterprise,
Inghams, King's Ski Club,
Made to Measure, Masterski, Neilson,
Ski Austria, SkiBound, Seasun School
Tours, Ski Choice, Ski Europe,
Ski Sutherland, Ski Tal, Ski Thomson,
The Club

Schladming, Styria

ALTITUDE 745m (2,444ft)

• •

Good points big ski area, lively après-ski, extensive nursery slopes, alpine charm, tree-level skiing, excellent cross-country facilities, short airport transfer, easy road and rail access, variety of mountain restaurants
Bad points short skiing season, unreliable resort-level snow, lack of tough runs, lack of skiing convenience
Linked or nearby resorts Haus (n), Obertauern (n), Rohrmoos (n), Ramsau/Dachstein (n), St Johann im Pongau (n)

Schladming claimed international fame as a ski resort when it hosted the World Championships in 1982. Its FIS downhill course is a regular feature on the World Cup circuit, and this attractive town and surrounding mountains are therefore familiar to thousands of armchair skiers, as well as an increasing number of British holidaymakers. The town lies in the middle of a broad valley on a main east-west road and rail route. To the north are the spectacular rocky peaks of the Dachstein, with summer skiing (both alpine and cross-country) on its extremely gentle glacial slopes.

Schladming's own skiing forms the heart of this area of 140km of pisted runs marketed under one lift pass as the Skiparadies. It takes place in the wooded foothills of the Tauern mountain range and offers a series of long, broad runs through the woods from a top altitude of 2000m down to the valley floor at 745m. The area is a large one by any standard, a complex of blue (easy) and red (intermediate) runs stretched across six mountains and the Dachstein glacier. There is, unfortunately, a pronounced lack of variety in this intermediate skiing, which some reporters found disappointing. Apart from a lift link between two, the mountains are all separate and you have to transfer tediously from one to the other, by what is admittedly an efficient free ski-bus system. Much talk has gone on over too many years of on-mountain links being provided between the four main ones, but nothing has, as yet, materialised.

Further substantial ski areas including Obertauern and the St Johann im Pongau ski circus are all within easy reach by car. Several reporters comment that a car is advisable, even for the local skiing.

The skiing
Top 2015m (6,609ft) bottom 750m (2,460)
The four mountains lined up on the south side of the valley form four entirely separate ski areas, which together provide a collection of useful red (intermediate) and blue (easy) cruising runs but which individually

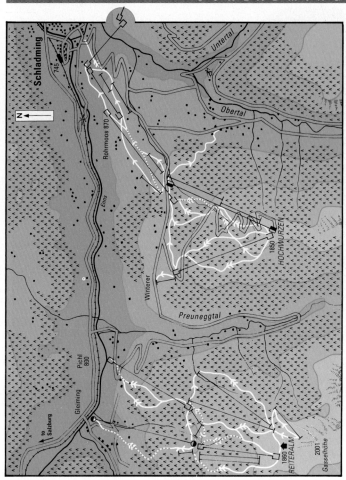

leave you with a sense of dissatisfaction. Planai (1894m) and Hochwurzen (1850m), the two central mountains and those closest to Schladming, are linked by two-stage chair, but not by piste. The lie of the land is such that improvements in this link will be difficult to achieve.

In contrast there is obvious scope for linking Planai to Hauser Kaibling (2017m) and Hochwurzen to Reiteralm. The growth of the environmentalist lobby in this unspoilt corner of Austria means that these links may now never be built. Most of the slopes are north-facing and gentle. Such is the lack of variety in the terrain that it is often diffi-cult to tell one from another. At higher altitudes there is some skiing to be found above the tree-line on the west- and east-facing flanks of Planai and Hauser Kaibling and there is a network of artificial snow-can-non on all of the main mountains.

For Schladming-based visitors the closest skiing is on Planai. **Mountain access** is via a two-stage gondola from the edge of town, an

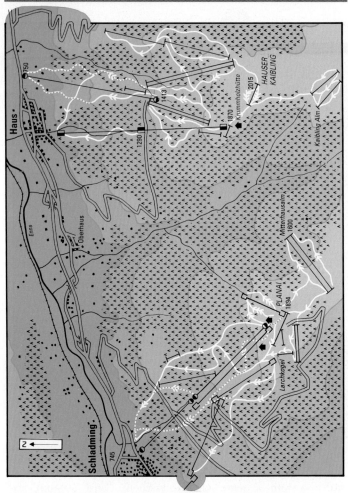

easy walk from the centre. The Kessleralm middle station of the gondola can also be reached by car, and a chair-lift running parallel with the second stage helps to ease weekend congestion. From the top a quad-chair and a couple of drag-lifts give access to some open, easy slopes. A long blue run takes you down into an area of wooded pistes served by four drag-lifts that take you back up above the gondola station.

Hauser Kaibling (2115m) towers over the pretty village of Haus in Ennstal. The main mountain access is a gondola from a huge car-park reached after a long walk to the east from the village. This takes you up to the mid-station, which is also accessible by bus. Motorists can also drive up to Knappl (1100m) on the eastern side of the mountain and avoid queues by working their way into the system via two drag-lifts. Beyond the gondola a quad-chair now takes you directly up to the Krummholzhütte (1870m), a great improvement on the alternative net of three drag-lifts, which reach the same place via the western face of the mountain.

Krummholzhütte can also be reached directly from the western end of Haus via a small and inefficient cable car. A gentle path leads from here along the side of the mountain to the Gipfellift, serving an easy black (advanced) slope, and on to a remote area of gentle skiing at Kaiblingalm, with two short drags, no crowds, usually good snow, and a friendly restaurant. The Gipfellift also gives access to a short, well-marked and popular off-piste route down to the lifts at the eastern extremity of the system. It is slightly awkward at the top and quite steep, although not terrifying.

Hochwurzen offers several long red runs (and a toboggan run) up to 1850m, served by two steep drags, a jumbo gondola, and a double chair. Below the main lift station, a choice of chairs and drags serve a reasonable network of easy and beginner slopes around the village of Rohrmoos and on down to the western edge of Schladming. At the western end of the local ski area the slopes of the Reiteralm (1860m) offer a variety of red and blue tree-line runs down to the villages of Pichl and Gleiming on the banks of the River Enns. Access is either by gondola from the edge of Gleiming or by double chair from an isolated riverside lift station across the valley from Pichl. This in turn links with a quad chair for the journey on up to Reiteralm. Plans to build a quad chair up to the Gasselhöhe (2001m) are still stuck on the drawing board. At the eastern end of the valley the Gaistbergalm (1976m) offers a few further, mainly gentle slopes reached by cable car from above the village of Pruggern (680m). This in turn gives access to a couple of T-bars for some open skiing above the tree-line.

On the other side of the valley from Schladming the commune of Ramsau Ort at 1200m has no less than 19 lifts scattered around the hills on either side of the village. All are short beginner and easy slopes with 100 to 580m in vertical. Turlwand, outside Ramsau, is the starting point for the cable car up to the Dachstein Glacier, which has limited all-year skiing that is too gentle to be of much more than scenic interest for alpine skiers. It is served by a chair and three drag-lifts.

Mountain restaurants

'Never,' said one reporter, 'have I been to a resort with so many mountain restaurants.' Indeed, they are so numerous that they are not all featured on the piste map. The Krümmelholze at Haus received particular recommendation. On Planai the Mitterhausalm and Schladmingerhütte are praised, along with Ski-Willy's Hütte for live music and a sunny terrace. The Eiskarhütte on Reiteralm, the Seiterhütte and the Hochwurzenhütte on Hochwurzen are all recommended.

Beginners and children

Reporters are consistent in their praise of the Keinprecht Kahr, Franz Tritscher and the new Hoppl ski schools. 'Our instructor spoke excellent English because he was Australian,' said one reporter. Another commented that the attitude of the entire school (Hoppl) was 'refreshingly one of enthusiasm – all the staff are really happy people'.

The number of nursery and beginner slopes in the region makes Schladming an excellent area in which children can learn and gain confidence.

The resort

Schladming is an ordinary Austrian town with a life of its own outside tourism. As well as wooden chalets with painted shutters there are sober, old stone buildings, including the remains of the town walls, which date back to 1629. It is a fairly compact town, with most of its shops and a good many of its hotels, restaurants and bars concentrated around the broad and attractive main square, the Hauptplatz. Anyone looking for the *Lederhosen*-and-oompah *Gemütlichkeit* will discover that it still thrives here.

Accommodation

Most guests stay in hotels and guesthouses in the Enns valley. Without a car, location is of crucial importance and many of our reporters found themselves staying too far from either the town centre or the lifts, or both. The Sporthotel Royer receives rave reviews, as do both the Neue Post and the Alte Post, both in the main square. Haus Stangl is recommended as a simple bed-and-breakfast place, Gasthof Kirchenwirt, according to reports, has variable service in its dining-room and the reception is seldom manned.

Eating out

The restaurants are mainly in the hotels. We have good reports of the Rôtisserie Royer Grill in the Sporthotel Royer and of the Restaurant Bachler ('friendly staff and good food at not ridiculous prices'). The Neue Post has two recommended à la carte restaurants, the Jägerstüberl and the Poststüberl.

Après-ski

The Siglu in the Hauptplatz attracts the biggest crowd after skiing and is said to be 'very lively, but reasonably priced compared to similar establishments in other resorts'. The Planaistub'n, also known as Charly's Treff, draws large crowds. One reporter favoured Ferry's Pub in the Steirergasse, another the Hanglbar. The bowling alley behind the latter is said to offer a good night out. The toboggan run from top to bottom of Hochwurzen down the hairpin road is open only at night (when the road is closed) and offers great entertainment. Most of the après-ski centres on the numerous bars, but there are also a couple of discos including one under the Hotel Rössl.

Rohrmoos 870m (2,854ft)

This diffuse satellite suburb has easy skiing to and from many of its hotel doorsteps. Among the choice of good-value hotels and guesthouses is the Austria, well-placed at the point where the lower, gentle slopes of Rohrmoos meet the steeper slopes of Hochwurzen. The smarter Schwaigerhof has a good position on the edge of the pistes, and is one of the few places with a swimming-pool. The après-ski is informal and based on hotel bars. The café at the Tannerhof is a tea-time favourite. Barbara's and the Alm Bar are busy later on.

TOURIST OFFICE
A-8970 Rohrmoos, Styria
Tel 43 3687 61147
Fax 43 3687 6114713

TOUR OPERATORS
none

Skiing facts: Schladming

TOURIST OFFICE
A-8970 Schladming, Styria
Tel 43 3687 22268
Fax 43 3687 24138

THE RESORT
By road Calais 1235km
By rail station in resort
By air Salzburg 1 hr, Munich 2½ hrs
Visitor beds 3,375 (66% hotels,16% guesthouses, 6% apartments, 12% other)
Transport free bus with ski pass

THE SKIING
Longest run Hochwurzen FIS-Abfahrt/Primsabfahrt, 7.7km (red/blue)
Number of lifts 78
Number of trails/pistes 68 in area (31% easy, 59% intermediate, 10% difficult)
Total of trails/pistes 140km
Nursery slopes 15 lifts in area
Summer skiing nearest on Dachstein Glacier at 3000m
Snowmaking 46km covered

LIFT PASSES
Area pass Skiparadies (covers Dachstein-Tauern region) ÖS1,470-1,630 for 6 days, Top-Tauern Skischeck (covers Obertauern, Schladming, Wagrain, Pongau, Dachstein) ÖS1,700 6 days for adults and ÖS960 for 6 days for children
Day pass ÖS305-335
Half-day pass ÖS335 from 11am
Beginners 'Try-out' ticket valid for 2½ hrs, ÖS345, ÖS110 refunded if returned within the 2½ hrs
Children 50% reduction for 15 yrs and under
Pensioners reductions available
Credit cards accepted no

SKI SCHOOLS
Adults Keinprecht Kahr, ÖS1,150, Franz Tritscher and Hoppl, ÖS1,600 both for 5 days
Children as adults
Private lessons ÖS800 for 2 hrs
Special courses Franz Tritscher snowboarding clinics
Guiding companies through ski school

CROSS-COUNTRY
Ski schools Keinprecht Kahr, Franz Tritscher and Hoppl
Loipe location and size trails down the valley to Pruggern and beyond, at Rohrmoos and Ramsau, 180km

CHILDCARE
Non-ski kindergarten Huberta's, 1-10 yrs, times and prices on application
Ski kindergarten through the 3 ski schools, 4 yrs and over, 9am- 5pm, ÖS1,600 for 5 days including lunch
Babysitting through Huberta's

OTHER SPORTS
Curling, skating, hot-air ballooning, sleigh rides, parapente, bowling, indoor tennis, swimming, squash, tobogganing

FOOD AND DRINK PRICES
Coffee ÖS23, bottle of house wine ÖS150, beer ÖS28, dish of the day ÖS145

WHAT'S NEW
● Hauser Kaibling chair-lift at Planai
● quad chair-lift Quattralpina ● Vital luxury apartments

TOUR OPERATORS
Austrian Holidays, Crystal, Enterprise, Kings Ski Club, Neilson, Seasun School Tours, Ski Bound, Ski Partners, Ski Airtours, Ski Thomson

Haus in Ennstal 750m (2,460ft)

Haus is a quiet village with its farming origins still in evidence, although it has a considerable amount of holiday accommodation in guesthouses and apartments. There are a couple of shops and cafés, one of which has jazz nights. The upmarket Hauser Kaibling has a swimming-pool and is recommended for its good food. Gasthof Kirchenwirt is a traditional hotel in the village centre, the Gasthof Reiter is a fine old chalet, much cheaper than most, and the Gürtl is a quiet family-run hotel well situated for the cable car. There is a gentle, open nursery slope between the village and the gondola station.

TOURIST OFFICE
A-8967 Haus in Ennstal, Styria
Tel 43 3686 2234
Fax 43 3686 2430

TOUR OPERATORS
Ski Thomson

Seefeld, Tyrol

ALTITUDE 1200m (3,936ft)

Good points village atmosphere, variety of après-ski, activities
for non-skiers, short airport transfer, superb cross-country facilities,
beautiful scenery
Bad points very limited piste skiing, long distance from village to
slopes
Linked or nearby resorts Garmisch (n), Lermoos (n), Mittenwald (n)

Seefeld is a tiny version of Salzburg, Innsbruck, Kitzbühel and the other
beautiful towns of Austria, with its frescoed houses and medieval architecture. Everything about the village shouts style and sophistication:
the six luxury hotels, a casino, an extensive health centre with a
Hollywood-style grotto and waterfalls, horse-drawn sleighs and a pedestrianised village centre complete with exclusive jewellery shops, sports
shops and boutiques. In winter, Seefeld's main activity is cross-country
skiing, though there are also three small pisted ski areas for those who
want to try their hand at alpine skiing in beautiful surroundings, and
with a variety of other activities.

The skiing
Top 2200m (7,217ft) bottom 1200m (3,936ft)
In the past it has been said that Seefeld is not the place to go for downhill skiing. This is not strictly so. The three ski areas are limited in size,
but there is enough for the unadventurous lower intermediate who
wants an all-round winter sports holiday. There is also some off-piste
skiing to occupy experts. Of the three ski areas, Geigenbühel is the
nursery slope area, Gschwandtkopf a low peak used mainly by the ski
school, and Rosshütte the more extensive with the slightly steeper
runs. All three areas are reached from the village centre by the free bus
service. **Mountain access** to Gschwandtkopf is by chair-lift at the
south of the village. Three drag-lifts and the chair serve one slope with a
number of blue (easy) runs on it and there is also a chair-lift from Reith
on the eastern side of the mountain with a good red (intermediate)
run. A reporter describes the main slopes here as 'well groomed, but
the popular red run down the back of the Gschwandtkopf is quite
bumpy'.

Access to Rosshütte is via a mountain railway starting in a car-park
one kilometre out of town. The top of the railway is the middle station
and the busiest part of the slopes. From here there is a choice of a drag-
lift or an ancient cable car taking you slightly higher up the mountain to
Seefelder Joch at 2074m. The advantages of the cable car over the drag
are the view from the top and the extra height, which enables skiers to

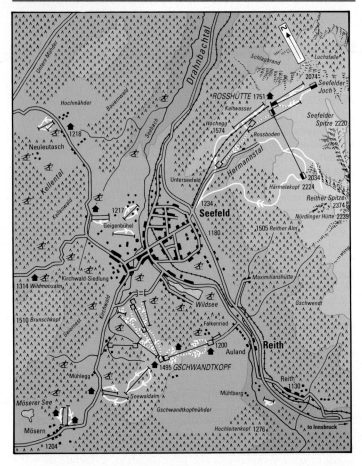

cross the ridge to some good off-piste opportunities. The runs down from both are all easy red and there are several variations. From below the middle station two drags and a chair take you back up again. The queues, even in high season, are usually short. Reporters comment that the only reason queues form at all here is because skiers have to insert their computerised tickets into a machine at every lift, rather than just once at the bottom. If one person can't produce his ticket instantly, a small bottleneck is the immediate result. A choice of a long blue or red run brings you back down to the base of the railway.

A more exciting option from the middle station is the Härmelekopf cable car, which goes every 15 minutes. This takes you up to 2000m, where a long red run begins, winding down through the trees back to the railway base. Experts can choose to ski one of two off-piste options around the shoulder of the mountain. These runs start either with a traverse with a very steep drop to one side and a jump off a cornice, or a climb of 200m vertical. Skiers should be extremely careful and sure-footed here, as a fall at this point could be extremely nasty. The runs join up in a steepish gunbarrel, so well skied that it often has small moguls on it. This is followed by a choice of narrow and interesting gullies through rocks and trees, finally ending back on the piste close to the railway base.

Mountain restaurants

Rosshütte is the main eating place in the area of the same name. It has both waiter-service and self-service on a large sun-terrace filled with a throng of skiers and non-skiers at lunchtime. Prices are average for the resort with soft drinks costing ÖS20. Lower down the slopes there is a small self-service hut where drinks and snacks are taken at outdoor tables and benches. On the Gschwandtkopf mountain the restaurant of the same name is recommended, as is the Café Christina, which is waiter-service only.

Beginners and children

Reporters talk of Seefeld as 'a good place to learn to ski, particularly for families'. The ski school, run by Erwin Seelos and meeting daily in the village centre, receives mostly good reports, although some reporters found the grading tests were not very successful. We also have some reports of middle-aged skiers being pushed too hard. There is one nursery slope lift at the base of the Gschwandtkopf area, which is described by a reporter as 'the most crowded lift of the area, although even then it was only a few minutes' wait'. The advantage of this nursery slope is that it is part of a bigger area, so friends or families of mixed standard can easily arrange to meet up at lunchtime. The other, bigger but separate, nursery slope area is at the ski school meeting place at Geigenbühel at the north-east end of the village.

The kindergarten, operating on weekdays and based in the Olympia Sport and Congress Centre, is praised by reporters, who mention that English is widely spoken. The attitude of staff is friendly with flexible teachers ('no one seemed to mind us being late because we had to get across town from the other mountain').

Cross-country skiing

Seefeld describes itself as 'Eldorado for cross-country skiers'. It has twice hosted the Winter Olympics cross-country events, in 1964 and 1976, and in 1985 the Nordic World Championships were held here for the first time. Seefeld also has some excellent facilities for the recreational cross-country skier, with the Nordic ski school based at the Olympia centre including a team of specialist cross-country instructors. The 200km of loipe is mechanically prepared and a special cross-country trail map is available from the tourist office.

The resort

Seefeld was originally a busy thoroughfare for merchants and pilgrims between the fifteenth and eighteenth centuries. Later on, in the 1920s, the village saw a swing towards tourism as it grew into a health resort and winter sports centre. Tourism, in both summer and in winter, has been flourishing ever since. A combination of beautiful scenery, excellent health and leisure facilities, and a good position between Innsbruck and Munich, have all helped to make Seefeld a popular tourist spot.

Accommodation

Seefeld boasts some unusual and exotic hotels, utterly unexpected in an alpine resort. The five-star Hotel Klosterbräu in the heart of the

Skiing facts: Seefeld

TOURIST OFFICE
Klosterstrasse 10, A-6100 Seefeld, Tyrol
Tel 43 5212 2313
Fax 43 5212 3355

THE RESORT
By road Calais 989km
By rail station in resort, Innsbruck 35 mins
By air Innsbruck 25 mins, Munich 2 hrs
Visitor beds 8,600 (75% hotels, 13% apartments, 12% guesthouses)
Transport free bus service between village and ski areas

THE SKIING
Longest run Rosshütte to Talstation, 4km (blue)
Number of lifts 18
Number of trails/pistes 19 (74% easy, 26% intermediate)
Total of trails/pistes 25km
Nursery slopes 6 lifts
Summer skiing none
Snowmaking 50 hectares covered

LIFT PASSES
Area pass Happy Ski Card (covers 11 villages including Lermoos, Garmisch and Mittenwald, and 50 lifts), ÖS1,580 per wk,
Day pass ÖS260
Half-day pass ÖS210 (after midday or before 1pm)
Beginners points cards
Children 17 yrs and under, ÖS1,140 per wk, ÖS385 for 2 days
Pensioners no reduction
Credit cards accepted no

SKI SCHOOLS
Adults Seefeld Ski School, ÖS1,190 for 5 days, from 10am-midday and 2-4pm
Children Seefeld Ski School, 4-16 yrs,

ÖS1,080 for 5 days, hrs as adults
Private lessons ÖS400 per hr plus ÖS100 for each additional person
Special courses snowboarding
Guiding companies none

CROSS-COUNTRY
Ski schools Langlaufschule Seefeld, based at the Olympic Centre
Loipe location and size 200km circuit, Seefeld to Reith, Mösern, Leutasch, Scharnitz and back

CHILDCARE
Non-ski kindergarten crèches in hotels Kaltschmidt, Klosterbräu, Schönruh, Veronika, and Waldhotel. Prices on application
Ski kindergarten through Seefeld Ski School, ÖS1,520 for 5 days, 4 hrs per day including supervision and lunch, or ÖS570 per day
Babysitting list available from tourist office and hotels

OTHER SPORTS
Hang-gliding, swimming-pools, indoor tennis, tube sliding, squash, fitness centres, indoor golf, sleigh rides, snow rafting, 60km of prepared walks, curling, skating, tobogganing, ski jumping

WHAT'S NEW
● Snow-cannon from Seefelder Joch down to Seefeld ● 4-star hotel St Peter

FOOD AND DRINK PRICES
Coffee ÖS22-25, bottle of house wine ÖS108, beer ÖS28-32, dish of the day ÖS100-150

TOUR OPERATORS
Austrian Holidays, Crystal, Enterprise, GTF Tours, Inghams, Made to Measure, Ski Thomson, Snowcoach

pedestrian district is a former sixteenth-century monastery. It has indoor and outdoor pools and a Roman sauna with steam grotto. Another five-star, the Creativhotel Viktoria, is not as well placed on the busy main road going out of town, but its rooms are certainly out of the ordinary, reflecting different periods and places as far flung as Tibet and New York. The Gartenhotel Tümmlerhof is set in its own huge park. It has a crèche, the Kid's Club, with all-day childcare and a playground. The two spa hotels are just as unusual: the Hotel Schneeweiss has thermal baths, nutrition programmes and physiotherapy among its many health options, and the Vital Hotel Royal bases its healthcare on holistic medicine (acupuncture, ozone therapy, and meditation), together with health food.

On a more reasonable price scale the family-run Hotel Bergland and Hotel Haymon are in a quiet location on the edge of the pedestrian zone. The Kaltschmidt has 'palatial apartments' and is 'very handy for the nursery slope with a nice pool on the fourth floor'. The two-star Krinserhof is reported as being 'small and friendly with good food, but a long walk from the village'. Village apartments are well-equipped and self-caterers can shop for provisions at Kaufhaus Albrecht and Julius Meindl. The newest apartment building is St Martin.

Eating out

The Alte Stube is a gourmet restaurant in the Hotel Karwendelhof's casino. Beim Jörg has grilled specialities, the Diana Stüberl serves local dishes and the Seefelderstuben has a good, varied menu of pizzas, pasta and typical Austrian dishes. A handful of pizzerias are available for those who do not appreciate Austrian food, including Da Pino's, Pizzeria Angelo and Pizzeria Don Camillo.

Après-ski

The popular Café Corso on Bahnhofstrasse was teeming with elderly cross-country skiers on our visit and the service was rushed and unfriendly. Café Nanni is a popular after-skiing place for a drink or snack, as is the Café Moccamühle just outside the pedestrian area on Olympiastrasse. English-style pubs seem to be popular here, though a little out of place in the upmarket village. The Big Ben bar is as English as you would expect, complete with an old red telephone box on display. The Brittania Inn is another popular English pub.

Monroe's disco-bar attracts the late-night crowd along with the Miramare and the Postbar in the Hotel Post. The Kanne in the Hotel Klosterbräu, the centre of the village's social life, has live music at night as well as tea-dancing. Reporters also recommend the Lamm and the Siglu. The bar Fledermaus has live jazz in the evenings. The casino is worth a visit if only to watch the punters.

Shopping opportunities in Seefeld are extensive with a dozen boutiques, nine sports shops, a number of jewellers, shops selling leather goods, traditional costumes, ceramics and children's fashion. One of the best all-round shops is the Kaufhaus Albrecht, which is on two floors and is more of a department store, selling everything from discount ski wear and clothing to toys and books.

Sölden, Tyrol

ALTITUDE 1380m (4,5264ft)

••

Good points late-season holidays, summer skiing, modern lift
system, lively après-ski
Bad points lack of skiing variety, crowded pistes, long and strung-out
village
Linked or nearby resorts Hochsölden (n), Untergurgl (n),
Hochgurgl (n), Obergurgl (n), Vent (n), Zwieselstein (n)

Sölden, near the end of the isolated Ötztal, 90 minutes by road from
Innsbruck, has a well-established reputation as a major Austrian ski
resort. Much has been done to improve the lift system, two nearby but
by no means interlinked glaciers ensure a level of snow security, the
vertical drop is substantial by Austrian standards, and at least in high
season, the après-ski entertainment is lively to the point of being raucous. It is surprising therefore that we come away from Sölden with a
lingering feeling that, for a resort of its calibre, it falls short of justifying
its reputation. There are, it has to be said, many who would disagree
with this opinion and who return year after year to this long, strung-out
village, which has no real heart to it.

The off-piste and touring opportunities are extensive, but the piste
skiing itself is simply not good enough to earn Sölden a top-10 placing
in Austria. The runs off the top stage of the gondola are limited for most
of the people, most of the time. Publicity about the resort somehow
fails to mention that the two glaciers are a good bus-ride away, neither
one of them is connected to the main ski area, and both often remain
closed until the early spring. The rest of the skiing is lacking in variety
and prone to nasty overcrowding during the main holiday weeks.
Hochsölden is a collection of hotels 700m up the mountainside set on a
shelf with dramatic views of the Ötztal. From here there is easy access
to the slopes at the more mundane and busy end of the mountain.

The skiing

Top 3058m (10,030ft) bottom 1377m (4,517ft)

Sölden's ski area is in two sections linked by chairs up both walls of the
narrow Rettenbachtal, which provides the toll road up to the two glaciers. Both sectors are reached by gondolas at either end of the village
which are in turn linked by a regular, but often oversubscribed, ski-bus.
The skiing is extensive, with a drop of nearly 1700m vertical, half above
and half below the tree-line, but less varied in difficulty than the piste
map suggests. Most of the slopes are east-facing.

The main **mountain access** is via the Gaislachkogel gondola at the
far end of the resort. Open slopes around the middle station provide

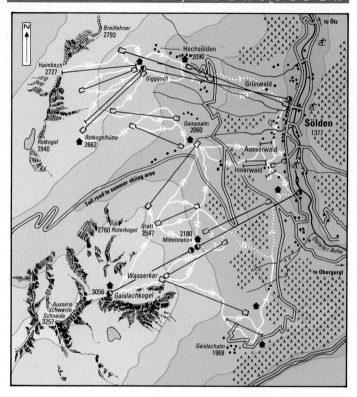

easy intermediate skiing served by a couple of chair-lifts, one of which gives access to a long red (intermediate) run down to Gaislachalm at 1982m where the sunny terraces of the restaurants prove popular lunching places. A long path takes you back on to the lower pistes of Sölden at Innerwald. The main run down through the trees from the middle station can be icy and overcrowded, especially at the end of the day, and care should be taken. Once you get to know the lower slopes it is possible to find all kinds of off-piste variations to end up on the road in the most convenient part of the resort for you. The second chair from near the middle station gives access to a variety of undemanding red runs which, in good snow conditions, could pass for blue (easy).

The top stage of the gondola rises steeply over 850m to the craggy peak of the Gaislachkogl at 3058m. The normal run from the top gives beautiful views, but only the top pitch justifies its red grading. However, the front face directly beneath and to the south of the gondola cable is an exciting off-piste descent on which enormous care should be taken. The top is deceptively easy, but after a couple of hundred metres the bowl divides into two. The southern couloir (to the right as you descend) is the wider and therefore easier of the two. It is not dauntingly steep, 33° at its worst, but the length is such that any fall would be serious.

Hochsölden ski area can be reached either via a flat traverse from the gondola middle station, or via a continuation of the red run from Gaislachkogel from the top of the Stabele double chair, which starts at the bottom of the Rettenbachtal. There are considerable off-piste opportunities from the top of this chair and, given good snow conditions, on the sunny slopes accessed by the Langegg I chair and the Silberbrünnl chair on the other side of the valley. Return in both cases is along paths at the edge of the road to the chair-lifts.

Alternative mountain access to Hochsölden is via a 20-minute chair-lift from the other end of Sölden or a gondola up to Giggijoch above it. Above this gondola is a wide, open expanse of gentle mountainside served by a variety of drag-lifts and chairs. This part of the mountain is prone to the worst congestion, although the quad chair to the top of the Hainbachjoch has relieved some of the pressure, at least for good skiers who will enjoy the small mogul field at the top and the over-graded black (difficult) run down. The runs on down to Hochsölden are graded blue and black, although both should be red. The only really serious queues on the mountain tend to develop at Giggijoch and skiers do best to avoid this area altogether at weekends. There is artificial snow on the lower parts of the runs to the valley from both ends of the resort.

The Rettenbach and Tiefenbach glaciers are reached by toll road and separated by a dramatic tunnel through the mountain. A total of 10 lifts serve the usual selection of mainly blue runs, which are more enjoyable for their panoramic views than the actual challenge of the skiing.

Mountain restaurants

The choice of mountain restaurants is more than reasonable, although like the slopes, they do tend to get overcrowded. The Giggijoch is a large modern complex with a new sun terrace ('lots of choice, but to be avoided during peak hours'). The Rotkoglhütte has 'sound Austrian fare if you can stomach the queue for the Silberbrünnl chair to get there'. Most reporters prefer eating away from the main lift stations. The Gamperalm has a scenic outside bar. Both the Gaislachalm and the Silbertal at Gaislachalm have sun terraces, a wide variety of food, and live accordion music.

Beginners and children

We have mixed reports of the two ski schools and more dissatisfied reporters than we would expect. The chief criticism is of the main Austrian ski school where the number of instructors who speak good English appears to be very low indeed. Visitors agree that, this apart, the actual instruction is good, but organisation is poor. 'We had to ask a passing instructor where we should be waiting', complained one correspondent. Innerwald has a nursery area without sun for much of the day and the snow is often poor here. The best beginner runs are above the gondola at Giggijoch. One reporter who used the alternative school Total Vacancia said she was 'very impressed with their attitude'.

A non-ski kindergarten operates in the Sporthotel Schöne Aussicht for babies and children up to three years old. The ski kindergarten takes children from three to eight years old all day including lunch.

The resort

Sölden stretches for more than two kilometres on either side of the road and river along the valley floor, an unmemorable collection of hotels, restaurants and bars that cannot be described as being in the traditional chocolate-box style. Nevertheless it would be uncharitable to dismiss the whole as unattractive. Most visitors come here by car and traffic is a real hazard throughout the day. Once in the resort, a car is

....

Skiing facts: Sölden

TOURIST OFFICE
Postfach 80, A-6450 Sölden, Tyrol
Tel 43 5254 22120
Fax 43 5254 3131

THE RESORT
By road Calais 1000km
By rail Ötz 30km, 12 daily buses from station
By air Innsbruck 2 hrs
Visitor beds 8,940 (49% guesthouses and pensions, 28% hotels, 23% apartments)
Transport bus runs between north and south lifts

THE SKIING
Longest run Gaislachkogl, 10km (red)
Number of lifts 23
Number of trails/pistes 23 (41% easy, 44% intermediate, 15% difficult)
Total of trails/pistes 101km
Nursery slopes 4 lifts
Summer skiing 10 lifts on Rettenbach and Tiefenbach glaciers
Snowmaking 10km covered

LIFT PASSES
Area pass Ötztal Arena (covers Sölden, Hochsölden, Zwieselstein), from ÖS1,600 for 6 days
Day pass from ÖS360
Half-day pass from ÖS290 after 11.30am
Beginners points tickets
Children 6-14 yrs, ÖS1,060 for 6 days, free for 6 yrs and under
Pensioners women 60 yrs and over, men 65 yrs and over, ÖS1,440 for 6 days
Credit cards accepted no

SKI SCHOOLS
Adults Sölden/Hochsölden, 10am-midday and 1-3pm, ÖS1,290 for 6 days. Ski School Total Vacancia, 9.30am-midday or 1-3.30pm, ÖS870 for 6 days

Children Sölden/Hochsölden, 85% of adult rate if one of the parents joins ski school. Ski School Total Vacancia, as adults
Private lessons ÖS2,000 per day
Special courses snowboarding, monoskiing, telemark
Guiding companies Ski School Sölden/Hochsölden, Ski School Total Vacancia

CROSS-COUNTRY
Ski schools Sölden/Hochsölden
Loipe location and size 16km-3km near Sölden, 5km at Zwieselstein, 8km Untergurgl

CHILDCARE
Non-ski kindergarten Sporthotel Schöne Aussicht, 9am-4pm, 3 yrs and under, ÖS100 per hr, 4 yrs and over ÖS70 per hr
Ski kindergarten Sölden, Hochsölden, Zwieselstein, 3-8 yrs, 9am-4.30pm, ÖS1,590 including lunch, tuition and baby-lift
Babysitting list available from tourist office

OTHER SPORTS
Parapente, skating, curling, indoor tennis, indoor rifle shooting, swimming, fitness centre, bowling, tobogganing

WHAT'S NEW
● Underground car-park at the Gaislachkogl cable car

FOOD AND DRINK PRICES
Coffee ÖS23, bottle of house wine ÖS180, beer ÖS30, dish of the day ÖS90

TOUR OPERATORS
Alpine Tours, Crystal, Enterprise, Inghams, Made to Measure, Neilson, Ski Thomson, Ski Airtours

....

neither necessary nor desirable except for visits to Vent, the glaciers, and the Gurgls, and parking is extremely difficult. Ski-buses run regularly around the resort and the post-bus service in the valley is efficient. Hochsölden is served by morning and afternoon buses, but there is no service after dark and taxis are expensive.

After Austria, Sölden draws its clientèle partly from Germany, but Dutch and Scandinavians make up a large proportion of visitors.

Accommodation
Location is moderately important here; better skiers should choose the southern end of town, which is within easy reach of the Gaislachkogel gondola, while more inexperienced visitors will need access to Giggijoch at the other end. The Hotel Regina, right by the Gaislachkoglbahn, is strongly recommended ('good sized rooms, friendly staff, ample good food'). Gästehaus Sonneheim in the same area is praised for being 'extremely cheap and reasonably sited – we shall come here again'. Gästehaus Paul Grüner is also described as a 'more than adequate' bed and breakfast establishment. The Stefan and the Tirolerhof both have good reputations and a loyal following. The Alpenhotel Enzian in Hochsölden is highly recommended: 'The atmosphere and food are both intimate and unpretentious.'

Eating out
Most of the restaurants are in hotels and serve traditional Austrian food. The Kupferpfanne in the Hotel Tirolerhof is famed for its venison and steaks. The Café Corso serves the best pizzas in town. The Ötztaler Stub'n in the Hotel Central is recommended, as is the restaurant Saitensprung for its 'inexpensive food in an unusual setting'. Hotel Sonne has a *Stüberl* with a cosy atmosphere.

Après-ski
Once the lifts close Sölden swings into life. Café Philip at Innerwald, reached via an often rocky run down, has a lively atmosphere and is a gathering point for young people. The single chair down from here runs until 6pm for those whose legs are wobbly from the skiing or otherwise. The party then carries on across the road at the Après Ski Bar. The Obstlerhütte below Hochsölden is equally lively; revellers must negotiate an easy piste down in dusk. The Hinterher pub and disco is usually packed to the gunnels with all nationalities. Dancers from Dominic's Bla-Bla, a large glass-fronted bar, regularly overflow into the street. The resort is lacking in coffee houses. Nightly tobogganing after dinner and *Glühwein* at the Gaislachalm restaurant is a much recommended diversion. There is little on offer here in Sölden for non-skiers.

Söll, Tyrol

ALTITUDE 700m (2,296ft)

••

Good points large linked ski area, attractive scenery, efficient lift
system, short airport transfer, tree-level skiing, cross-country
Bad points limited après-ski, lack of alpine charm, unreliable bus
service, facilities for families, nothing for non-skiers, low altitude
Linked or nearby resorts Brixen (I), Ellmau (I), Going (I), Hopfgarten
(I), Itter (I), Kelchsau (n), Kirchberg (n), Kitzbühel (n), Scheffau (I),
Westendorf (n)

Söll is the best known resort of a vast ski circus made up of a total of 9
resorts with 90 lifts, and hilly skiing best suited to the intermediate, but
with enough varied on- and off-piste skiing to keep the expert happy
too. The resorts in the area have officially changed the area name from
Grossraum to Ski-World, but most people prefer to stick to the more
recognisable former name.

The resort has suffered for years from the unflattering image of
being a harbour for British lager-louts, all-night partying ending in
police intervention, and skiers with such bad hangovers that they are
unable to tackle more than a couple of basic blue runs each day. These
rumours came to a head in January 1992 when two of our correspondents individually witnessed a British tabloid newspaper reporter and
photographer baiting a group of British youths with free pints of beer in
return for some 'action', as they described it. What occurred was a
deliberately provoked confrontation between the British and a group of
locals ending in a fight, for the benefit of a newspaper story.

Söll does attract the budget, and therefore the younger end of the
market, but anyone looking for a wild time here is in for a disappointment. Certainly we found no sign of it ourselves, and the resort seems
mournfully quiet in comparison with the fleshpots of Kitzbühel a few
kilometres down the road. You have to wonder whether, in the minds
of the public, Söll becomes confused with Sölden or even with Soldeu.
Both the latter, in Austria and in Andorra, are considerably more prone
to the "'ere-we-go, 'ere-we-go' school of skier.

Söll aims itself, with not inconsiderable success, at a clientele mainly
in their twenties to early thirties, although it is not ideal for families or,
according to reporters, for those in search of 'a quiet drink after a long
day's skiing'. The one frequented disco may thump away through the
night, and the main three bars are full until the early hours, but their
main clients are Dutch rather than British. For non-skiers the resort
offers good alternative sporting activities, but nothing at all for non-
sports enthusiasts, with disappointing shops and the village deserted
during skiing hours.

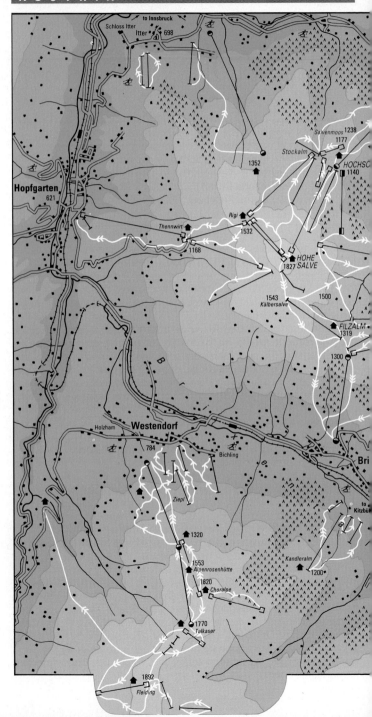

to Innsbruck
Schloss Itter
Itter 698

Salvenmoos 1238
1177
Stockalm
HOCHSÖ
1140
1352

Hopfgarten
621

Rigi
Thennwirt 1532
1168

HOHE
1827 SALVE

1543
Kälbersalve   1500

FILZALM
1319

1300

Holzham   Westendorf
784
Bichling   Bri

to
Kitzbü

Ziepl

1320

1553
Alpenrosenhütte

1820
Choralpe

Kandleralm
1200

1770
Talkaser

1892
Fleiding

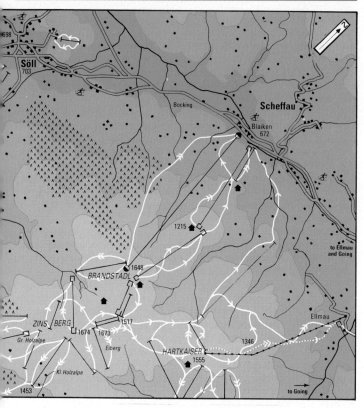

The skiing is some of the most underrated in the whole of the Alps. Kilometre upon kilometre of varied piste will take an average intermediate from one typically Tyrolean village to the other, with the chance to stop en route at a number of pleasant little mountain restaurants, many of them with panoramic views over the pretty valley scenery.

The skiing

Top 1829m (5,999ft) bottom 622m (2,040ft)

The whole Ski-World area ranges from 622m at Hopfgarten to 1829m at the top of the Westendorf section. Söll's skiing is on north-facing slopes, a brisk walk from the village or reached by a free bus service, which one reporter complains is 'crowded and unreliable, though the drivers are more pleasant than in the past'. A car is useful, with the added bonus of allowing you to visit other nearby resorts.

The smart modern gondola from the valley up to the ski area has significantly reduced queuing. Bottlenecks do, however, still exist higher up the mountain and to avoid these you can take a mini-bus taxi to neighbouring Scheffau, which appears to suffer least, especially when the skiing connections are closed due to lack of snow. Prices are said to be reasonable, provided there are enough of you to fill the mini-bus.

Mountain access is on the fast and efficient Hochsöll gondola. A curious optional addition to the lift is a shiny, black detachable cabin with tinted glass windows, owned by Formula One racing driver Gerhardt Berger, who comes from nearby Wörgl. Berger hires the gondola out at ÖS1,000 per hour for private business meetings or a romantic rendez-vous. It has a black interior, a table, a radio, and included in the price is a bottle of Champagne.

At the top of the gondola is Salvenmoos, the hub of Söll's ski area where a cluster of lifts start, including a single chair and a covered bubble-chair. The single chair takes you up to Hohe Salve which, at 1829m, is the highest point of the Söll sector of the ski circus. From here there is a good black (difficult) mogul slope, Grundried, back down to the Salvenmoos area. Apart from this higher piste and a red (intermediate) run close to it, the longest and most interesting descents are the red run and the blue Family Run through the trees from Hochsöll to Söll. Both can be icy at times.

Good off-piste skiing is to be found under the single chair from Hohe Salve. The little bowl here usually holds its snow in good condition for longer than any of the neighbouring pistes. The unpisted run down through the trees at Kasbichl, between Rigi and Salvernmoos at Hopfgarten, can also be challenging. Innere Keat above Söll has a number of off-piste opportunities, including an itinerary route to Brixen. Advanced skiers should try the challenging black at Scheffau, which is marked with a skull-and-crossbones sign at the starting point, while Westendorf has a black mogul field from the top of the Alpenrose chair and a run to Santenbach and Kandler. Ellmau's off-piste is on the Lederbauernalm. Many of the red runs in the area are steep enough to qualify as blacks elsewhere, including the Abfahrt in Ellmau, and the runs down from the four-seater chair in Söll.

Access to Westendorf from Söll is via the covered bubble-chair from the middle station, which bypasses Hohe Salve, then skiing the excellent runs from here down to Brixen via Hoch Brixen, after which you take the bus to Westendorf gondola station. Apart from the short bus connection to Westendorf, or another to the much smaller area of Kelchsau, the rest of the huge circus is all fully connected on skis. One of the few remaining bottlenecks is the Kälberalm drag-lift in the Brixen area.

The lift system is, on the whole, fairly modern by Austrian standards. The Ski-World lift companies insist that their policy is only to build new and larger lifts when they are quite sure about the safety of allowing extra skiers in that part of the ski area. More probably it is the local goverment's 'green' policy which forbids further expansion. The lack of piste hazard warning signs is a persistent complaint, especially when snow cover is insufficient, with reporters continually coming across bare pistes: 'I lost count of the number of runs I came down only to find that half-way down I had to negotiate mud for about 200 metres.'

Mountain restaurants

In the Söll mountain restaurants queues of up to half-an-hour to be served are not uncommon during busy weeks, but most restaurants are reported to be comfortable, reasonably priced and to serve a wide variety of food. The Rigi mountain restaurant at the top of the Kasbichl chair above Hopfgarten has a wonderful view of the valley and some of the neighbouring resorts. Similarly, from the Gipfel self-service restaurant above Hopfgarten you can soak up the sunshine and the awesome panorama of the Wilder Kaiser. Owner Georg Arger, a former professional ski champion, uses the restaurant walls as a showcase for his cups and medals. All grades of skier can meet up here as it is easily reached by the gondola and chair from Söll. Kraftalm, at the top of the Itter gondola, is one of the area's original restaurants, which remains the most popular stop-off point after skiing. Fitzalm, in Brixen, is an attractive old hut, run by an elderly farmer with home-made bread and home-cooked food his specialities. Jochstube at the top of Zinzberg in Scheffau is another old hut, with a large, open fireplace and several tiny rooms.

Beginners and children

The nursery slopes are in the open fields between the village and the bottom of the mountain. The low altitude (622m) means snow here is uncertain and in the event of poor cover, beginners are taken to Salvenmoos. Reports are of friendly instructors, but 'too many classes in the first few days of the week were crowded on to a limited nursery area'.

The bus transfer to the slopes, coupled with a general lack of childcare facilities, means this is not a resort for families with young children. It is, however, an excellent place for young teenagers.

The resort

Söll has a small centre based around a church and a pedestrian precinct which, although it has won prizes as the safest and most attractive pedestrian area in Austria, looks as though it might have seen better days; a further face-lift is taking place. Chalets and guesthouses sprawl out from the middle of town. The resort and ski area base are set low in a valley, divided by a trunk road. This makes Söll ideal for easy transfers to Innsbruck and Munich, but otherwise cuts an unpleasant swathe across the pastures. Although there is a lack of typical Tyrolean atmosphere found in nearby resorts such as Kitzbühel, the locals have a sensible, cosmopolitan attitude towards tourism.

Accommodation

The main hotel in the pedestrian zone is the Postwirt. A comfortable modern annexe has now been added to the old traditionally furnished hotel. We have good reports of both the Greil and the Austria, also in the town centre. The Hotel Tyrol is recommended, with 'rooms not exactly large, but comfortable and clean', and 'meals were excellent and well worth the cost'. Hotel Maria at the northern end is 'fairly basic, but has a very friendly and helpful personal service and superb food'.

Restaurants

The majority of Söll skiers tend to eat at their hotels on half-board terms. The choice of restaurants is limited, but the cost of eating out is by no means as prohibitive as in some resorts. The Schindlhaus and the Greil are renowned for their Austrian nouvelle cuisine and the Postwirt restaurant is also recommended. At the cheaper end of the scale, the Venezia Pizzeria and the Christophorus offer value for money. The Hotel Tenne is reported as 'basic, but good value', while the Dorfstube offers traditional Austrian cooking. The hotels Postwirt and Gänsleit serve vegetarian meals on request.

Après-ski
The après-ski starts at 4pm with the focus on the village's three main bars. Pub 15 is, in the view of one reporter, 'loud and horrible – it is best to walk past it. The crowds were packed in like sardines.' However, lots of visitors clearly do like it. Whisky Mühle, housed inside a giant beer barrel in the pedestrian zone, has established itself as a Söll landmark over the years, but has also started to weather as one. It badly needs a facelift and a fresh coat of paint. Pub Austria and the Elbow Room are said to be 'more civilised'. The Gasthof Christophorus has live music.

Ellmau 820m (2,690ft)
Ellmau's once compact centre has over recent years been expanding and now straggles the whole 400m up to the ski area. It has more shops, bars and general après-ski facilities than the other Ski-World resorts, and is a livelier place to stay at than Söll. In terms of location, where you stay is no longer of any real importance as the maximum walk to the centre or the lifts is 10 minutes. There is a nursery slope T-bar in the village centre and five other nursery slope lifts in the main ski area. The resort supports three different ski schools.

Mountain eating places include the self-service Bergrestaurant Hartkaiser ('over-busy at peak times, but great *Gulaschsuppe*'). The Alte Post is one of the more comfortable hotels. Après-ski venues include Café Widauer, the Helden bar, Café Breit, Café Kaiserman, Café Monica and the Memory Pub. Recommended restaurants include Pizzeria Sojer, Renates Bistro and Café Restaurant Hermann. Discos are the Rendezvous, Ellmauer Tenne and the Helden.

TOURIST OFFICE
A-6352 Ellmau, Tyrol
Tel 43 5358 2301
Fax 43 5358 3443

TOUR OPERATORS
Crystal, Inghams, Kings Ski Club,
Neilson, Sally Holidays, SkiBound,
Ski Airtours, Ski Thomson

Going 800m (2,624ft)
A quainter place than most of the others in the Ski-World, it is a village of attractive, old wooden chalets at the far end of the valley towards St Johann in Tyrol. The north-facing slopes, although they start at a low 800m, hold their snow longer than some of the neighbouring resorts.

TOURIST OFFICE
A-6353 Going, Tyrol
Tel 43 5358 2438

TOUR OPERATORS
Enterprise

Hopfgarten 622m (2,040ft)

Hopfgarten recently had its application for snow-cannon turned down by the Austrian government. The reason was that the resort's ski runs are all south-facing and, given the low altitude, it is rarely cold enough here to produce snow at the times of year when it is most needed. The village, between Westendorf and Itter, has an ancient feel to it with its steep, cobbled streets and compact centre. For no known reason beyond the sheep principle, it attracts a disproportionate number of South Africans, Australians and New Zealanders. This gives the village an unexpectedly international air. Café Mayer and the Old English Pub are popular, and the restaurant Brixental is recommended.

TOURIST OFFICE
A-6361 Hopfgarten, Tyrol
Tel 43 5335 2322
Fax 43 5335 2630

TOUR OPERATORS
Contiki, SkiBound, Ski Europe,
Ski Hillwood

Scheffau 750m (2,460ft)

Scheffau is not as well placed for skiing as some of its neighbours. The actual village is a short bus ride away from the slopes on the far side of the main road. However, the rustic solitude of the village with hotels dotted around the pastures and a pretty green and white church, more than makes up for this inconvenience. Reporters speak warmly of it: 'Small, quiet and friendly, ideal access point for the Ski-World.' The free bus to and from the slopes runs regularly. The slopes area reached by gondola or chair-lift and the runs back down to the base station are open and wide.

The chair-lifts at Eiberg are fast and usually uncrowded. The only queues are for the gondola in the morning and the Brandstadl chair at lunchtime and in the evening. Scheffau is known for holding its snow better than any of the other Ski-World villages, and access to Ellmau and Söll's skiing, on either side of Scheffau, is straightforward. The Alpin Hotel has a swimming-pool and the Gasthof Weberbauer in the village centre is recommended for its 'excellent bedrooms and bathrooms, and very good evening meal'. The main nightspot, Pub Royal, is a friendly place with live music The Kaiseralm disco is expensive and Conny's Corner attracts mainly locals.

TOURIST OFFICE
Postfach 10, A-6351 Scheffau, Tyrol
Tel 43 5358 8137
Fax 43 5358 8539

TOUR OPERATORS
Crystal, Enterprise, Ski Thomson

Westendorf 800m (2,624ft)

Westendorf is next in line along the valley from Brixen and is linked with the whole ski area by a free bus link. An efficient six-person gondola starts in the village, and beside it is an immense beginner's ski area, well covered by snow-cannon, at the foot of the principal slopes. The main

• •

Skiing facts: Söll

TOURIST OFFICE
Postfach 21, A-6306, Söll, Tyrol
Tel 43 5333 5216
Fax 43 5333 6180

THE RESORT
By road Calais 1114km
By rail Wörgl, 2 hrs from Munich or Salzburg
By air Munich 1½ hrs, Salzburg 1½ hrs
Visitor beds 4,200 (36% guesthouses, 30% chalets, 24% hotels, 10% apartments)
Transport free bus between village and ski area

THE SKIING
Longest run Hohe Salve-Kraftalm-base area, 8km (red)
Number of lifts 12 in Söll, 90 in whole Ski-World area
Number of trails/pistes 12 in Söll (33% easy, 42% intermediate, 25% difficult), 96 in Ski-World area (38% easy, 53% intermediate, 9% difficult)
Total of trails/pistes 250km
Nursery slopes 3 lifts
Summer skiing none
Snowmaking 17km covered

LIFT PASSES
Area pass Ski-World (covers all lifts in area, and bus connection with Westendorf), OS1,395
Day pass Söll ÖS270, Ski-World ÖS300
Half-day pass Söll ÖS170-240, Ski-World ÖS230-270, prices depend on starting time
Beginners points tickets, single ascent tickets
Children Söll, free for 5 yrs and under, 6-15 yrs ÖS640 for 6 days. Ski-World, ÖS790 for 6 days
Pensioners no reduction
Credit cards accepted yes

SKI SCHOOLS
Adults Söll Schischule, Hohe Salve Ski School, both ÖS1,150 for 6 days

(4 hrs per day)
Children Söll Schischule, Hohe Salve Ski School, both 5-14 yrs, ÖS450 per day (4 hrs), ÖS1,100 for 6 days, ÖS100 extra per day for lunch
Private lessons ÖS400 per hr
Special courses snowboarding, race training, guided Ski-World tour, telemarking, mogul skiing
Guiding companies through Ellmau tourist office

CROSS-COUNTRY
Ski schools Söll Schischule
Loipe location and size 30km in Söll, 100km with Bocking and Schloss Itter, also all over Ski-World area

CHILDCARE
Non-ski kindergarten none
Ski kindergarten Söll Schischule, Hohe Salve Ski School, both for 5 yrs and over, ÖS450 per day (4 hrs), ÖS1,100 for 6 days, extra ÖS100 per day for lunch
Babysitting difficult

OTHER SPORTS
Skating, curling, sleigh rides, tobogganing, swimming, bowling, rifle range, squash, hang-gliding, parapente, 120km cleared walks, fitness centre

WHAT'S NEW
● Enlarged pedestrian area

FOOD AND DRINK PRICES
Coffee ÖS20, bottle of house wine ÖS100, beer ÖS22-40, dish of the day ÖS65-75

TOUR OPERATORS
The Club, Crystal, Enterprise, GFT Tours, Inghams, Neilson, Sally Holidays, Ski Airtours, Ski Austria, Skibound, Ski Thomson, Ski Falcon, Snowcoach

• •

runs are generally more demanding than those elsewhere in the region. One reporter comments that they were 'steeper, icier and more difficult than we expected'. Much, of course, depends on snow conditions. The only lift queues of more than a few minutes seem to be for the nursery slope drag, an indication of the immense popularity of this resort for beginners. The tourist office claims that more British have learned their skiing here than anywhere else in the Alps. Recommended mountain eating places include Alpenrose and Breckhornhaus. The Talkaiser at the top of the gondola is said to lack charm.

Westendorf is one of the most compact and attractive of all the Ski-World villages and has a genuine Tyrolean atmosphere coupled with a liveliness lacking in resorts such as Scheffau and Going. The general standard of accommodation appears to be high, with the most expensive hotels the most conveniently placed. Hotel Jakobwirt is recommended for its 'friendly staff, good food, good facilities and central location'. The Schermerhof apartments are described by reporters as suitable for families.

The après-ski has plenty of variety and is very lively. The Cow Shed at the bottom of the gondola is recommended and Café Angerer is a popular meeting place. Skiers dine early here with restaurants filling up by 7pm; reservations are recommended. Chez Yves is good for pizza and steaks, the Schermer for fresh farm produce and local venison, and Pizzeria Toscana is also recommended. The Bichlingerhof and the Jacobwirt restaurant, are more expensive. Gerry's Inn attracts the young disco crowd.

Westendorf has all the makings of a good family resort. It is traffic-free, the slopes are a five-minute walk from the centre of the village (free bus available) and both ski schools (Ski School Westendorf and Ski School Top) have non-ski and ski kindergartens catering for children from two years and over. We have mixed reports of the larger of the two, Ski School Westendorf. One reporter complains that: 'The sole playing point consisted of a mountain of ice made from previously piled-up snow. No sledges, toys or other such useful items were available.' Reporters said that the smaller Ski School Top appears to offer a more personal service for adults and children alike.

TOURIST OFFICE
Pfarrgasse 1, A-6363 Westendorf, Tyrol
Tel 43 5334 6230
Fax 43 5334 2390

TOUR OPERATORS
Crystal, Enterprise, Inghams, Neilson,
SkiBound, Ski Thomson

The remaining Ski-World resorts are Brixen im Thale at 800m (the bus connection point for Westendorf), Itter at 730m, between Söll and Hopfgarten, and Kelchsau, a small, unconnected farming village between Hopfgarten and the Wildschönau area.

St Anton, Arlberg

ALTITUDE 1300m (4,265ft)

••

Good points challenging slopes on extensive sunny terrain, wide
choice of off-piste opportunities, excellent après-ski, easy resort
access, cosmopolitan atmosphere
Bad points long lift queues, limited for easy runs, inconvenient
layout, unsuitable for beginners
Linked or nearby resorts St Christoph (l), Lech (n), Pettneu (n),
Stuben (l), Zürs (n)

In a country where alpine charm is the major attraction, St Anton stands
alone as a tough skier's town. There is nothing seductive about the setting, a meandering valley along the main railway line between Zurich
and Vienna. There is not much that is distinguished about the architecture, a blend of old and new that owes little to planning and a lot to
those who had an eye to the main chance before the current strict zon-
ing regulations came into force. There is certainly not much to enjoy
about the raucous behaviour in the streets when the bars and discos
close around 3am.

Yet, for those who love skiing and the traditions that go with it, St
Anton is incomparably the best resort in Austria. When it comes to variety and degrees of difficulty, its slopes are world-class, on a par with
those in Val d'Isère, Verbier and Chamonix.

Skiing came to the Arlberg before the turn of the century. The
Pastor of Lech visited his parishioners on skis as early as 1895 and the
first races were held in St Christoph in 1903 under the aegis of the
newly formed Arlberg Ski Club, but St Anton's star only began to rise in
1921 when Hannes Schneider opened the Arlberg Ski School. It proved
to be the father of all ski schools, a role model that underpinned subsequent advances worldwide. Generations of Britons grew up with the
distinctive Arlberg technique – skis clamped together, shoulders facing
down the hill – a contrived yet elegant style that dominated the sport
until the French declared technical war in the 1950s and 1960s.

St Anton took its place in racing history when Hannes Schneider
and Arnold Lunn established the Arlberg Kandahar in 1928. The downhill course on the Kapall, currently used in alternate years, is still considered one of the most gruelling on the World Cup circuit. In 1937, the
opening of the Galzig cable car provided a new challenge for local hot-
shots as they attempted to race this revolutionary form of transport
back to base. Piste preparation, courtesy of two men and a roller, was
pioneered in the resort in 1949. Today 38 snow-cannon, 22 drivers and
16 snow-cats work for up to 9 hours a night to ensure good coverage
right down to the town.

The skiing

Top 2650m (8,695ft) bottom 1300m (4,265ft)

As far as skiing is concerned, geography is firmly on St Anton's side. For a relatively low and, for the most part, south-facing resort, it has remarkably good snow records. However, the resort's downside is the high avalanche risk, evident in 1988 when a slide swept into the town in the early morning killing several people as they lay in bed. There are dramatic slopes on both sides of the steep-sided valley, with a rich variety of terrain, which includes bowls, woods, chutes and ridges.

The heart of St Anton's ski area is the Valluga, with **mountain access** by a two-stage cable car that is less than state-of-the-art. The first stage stops at Galzig, the centre of a network of lifts and runs suited to all grades of skier. One of the most popular is the attractively varied blue (easy) descent to the exclusive hamlet of St Christoph. Less negotiable, even by experts, is the notorious Osthang, a fierce bump-run with a hostile camber, on the way back to St Anton.

The second stage of the cable car swings out dramatically across the Steissbachtal to the Vallugagrat, the shoulder just below the dome of the Valluga. This can be reached by a third 15-person cable car, which provides access to panoramic views of Austria's most impressive peaks. Only those accompanied by guides are permitted to take their skis to the top for the testing descent over the back of the Valluga to Zürs ('huge powder bowls and some fairly steep stuff'). From the Vallugagrat, three of St Anton's finest long runs lead back to the broad flat valley of the Steissbachtal, a corridor between the Valluga runs and those on the adjoining Kapall.

The toughest of the three is the Schindlerkar, a wide, 30° mogul marathon that seems to go on forever. Nowadays it can be repeated all day, by those who are strong enough, by riding the Schindlergratbahn high-speed quad, but its south-facing aspect makes it vulnerable to early-morning ice and late-afternoon slush. The Mattun is a series of mogulled bowls linked by traverses, less steep in pitch but more intriguing because of the variety of its challenges. The third much easier option, the long dog-leg via the Ulmerhütte, opens the Valluga up to confident intermediates. It is also the starting point for the descent to the high, cold outpost of Stuben.

Stuben's skiing on the steep slopes of the Albona, on the other side of the road over the Arlberg Pass, is accessed by a two-stage chair-lift that offers much-needed blankets to its clients. In a north-facing area, the snow is often exceptional, but only the run back to Rauz is suitable for intermediates. Experts will enjoy the off-piste descent to St Christoph and, to an even greater extent, the excursions from the Maroikopf to Langen and down the heavily wooded Maroital to the restaurant at Verwalltal, a long walk from St Anton. Reporters particularly praise the former descent: 'If you are prepared to climb for an hour, the runs are superb.'

Officially, St Anton's less demanding skiing lies on the Kapall side of the Steissbachtal but, in a resort of this calibre, difficulty is very

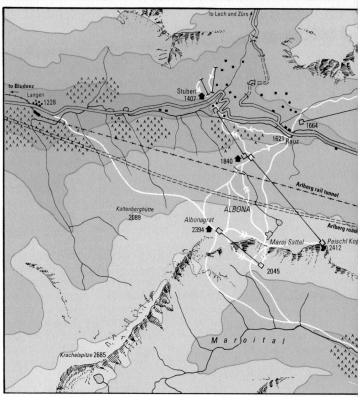

much a question of degree. Unlike most of its Austrian rivals, St Anton is looking to increase its quota of blue runs, which means that there can be some nasty surprises on slopes that are graded easy. This is particularly true of the runs under the two Kapall chairs above the Gampen mid-station. Keen but inexperienced powder-hounds will be drawn to the east-facing slopes near the top station and to the spectacular descents in the Schöngraben valley to Nasserein.

St Anton's newest area lies on the other side of the valley at Rendl, a long walk or a short, crowded shuttle-bus ride from the town cen-tre. It is served by a long gondola that takes skiers up to a restaurant with a terrace that catches the full impact of the afternoon sun. From here there is a fan of drag-lifts serving intermediate slopes, plus two chairs to the top of the area. The main run is graded red (intermedi-ate), but the snow is often sparse on its west-facing slopes and it is usually crowded when skiers head back to the resort at the end of the day.

Rendl's greatest pleasure is the easy access to its off-piste runs, especially on the ridge below Gampenberg and the secluded bowl behind it. An easy two-hour hike on skins from the top of the chair-lift is the start of an all-day adventure circuit that ends up in the small

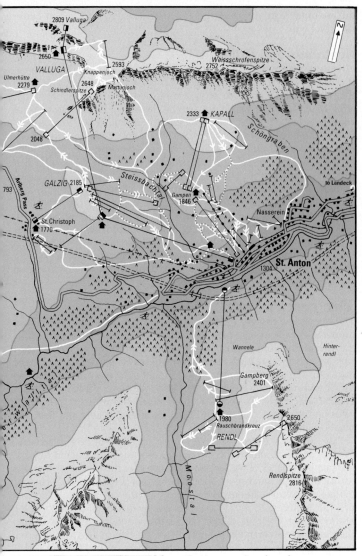

resort of Pettneu on the road from St Anton to Innsbruck.

Mountain restaurants

Out of a wide selection, the least desirable is the large, bleak self-service cafeteria at the Galzig mid-station. Recommendations include the Ulmerhütte, one of the oldest mountain restaurants in the Alps, the Rodelalm above Nasserein (the starting point for hair-raising, night-time toboggan rides down to the resort) and the Kapallstube which concentrates on simple Austrian fare. On the whole reporters found the mountain eating places 'good but expensive', and 'much better than average'.

Beginners and children

After some years in the doldrums when classes rose to 15 and more, the Arlberg Ski School is getting its act back together. Pressure from the Tiroler Ski School, recently established by Franz Klimmer, has already reduced the maximum size of classes to 10. Arlberg director Harald Rofner employs 200 instructors to Klimmer's 30, but competition is fierce, which can only help maintain standards on both fronts. Recent reports found the Arlberg Ski School to be very good. One reporter was surprised to see instructors still skiing 'with both feet locked together'.

Although St Anton is not recommended for beginners of any age, children are well catered for on the nursery slopes near Nasserein. The ski kindergarten includes basic instruction for children aged two-and-a-half years and over, and the Arlberg Ski School runs regular classes for those of five years and over. Conscious of its limitations when it comes to safe, easy skiing, the resort opened two new children's practice lifts for the 1992-3 season, one in St Christoph and one by the Marchen piste on Gampen mountain.

The resort

The opening of St Anton to the outside world began when the railway tunnel under the Arlberg pass was completed in 1884. In the first half of the twentieth century, what had been little more than a hamlet grew steadily into a village, with its narrow main street running parallel to the tracks. In the days before the road tunnel under the Arlberg pass and the St Anton bypass were opened in 1977, the street was a traffic nightmare. Today it is a relatively peaceful pedestrian zone lined with shops, cafés and St Anton's most handsome traditional hotels, the Post, the Alte Post and the Schwarzer Adler.

The rest of the town straggles along the road in both directions, towards Mooserkreuz at the top of the resort to the west and towards the satellite villages of Nasserein and St Jakob to the east. British clients without their own transport should beware of package holidays in low-budget Nasserein, frequently featured in the St Anton section in brochures. Access to the ski area was greatly improved by the opening of the Mulden chair-lift in 1992 but, as the shuttle-bus does not run in the evening, the nightlife is limited to local bars unless you are prepared for a long walk. Reporters found 'a lack of the "here to serve" ideal. They switched the Nasserein Slalom lift off with people on it one afternoon at 4.45pm.'

St Anton is aggressively youth-oriented, with a rich, cosmopolitan mix of skiers out to get the most for the least. It cultivates a macho image, so much so that the ratio of men to women works out around four to one. This, combined with its popularity with the British, Australians and Scandinavians, leads to disturbing levels of late-night rowdiness but, as yet, the authorities have failed to come up with an acceptable means of curbing such unacceptable behaviour.

Accommodation

The area has two five-star hotels, the historic and expensive Hospiz at St Christoph and the modern St Antoner Hof near the bypass. The four-star options are headed by the Post ('accommodation excellent, but staff snotty'), the Alte Post and the Schwarzer Adler, all much richer in tradition and much closer to the lifts. The Bergheim, right at the point where the road crosses the railway, is even more convenient. The Valluga hotel is criticised for its employees' attitude: 'The clients were obviously just a nuisance to the staff.' Hotel Fahrner is praised ('looks as if the decorators moved out the previous week – full marks'), and the Hotel Grieshof has a good swimming-pool. For the independent traveller, there are numerous family-run pensions offering simple bed and breakfast accommodation, often at surprisingly reasonable rates, but it is wise to check the exact location because walks can be long. Haus Pangratz and Ludwig Strolz are warmly recommended. Those who find themselves uncomfortably far away from the slopes can leave skis and boots overnight in the storage at the bottom of the Galzig lift.

Eating out

With the exception of the Hospiz at St Christoph, which is renowned for its gourmet dining and its well-selected wine list, eating out in St Anton is substantial rather than sophisticated. The emphasis is on such local specialities as boiled meats and dumplings, followed by sickly creamy puddings. The restaurants in the Post and the Alte Post do these things rather better than more contemporary rivals. Café Sailer is a reasonably priced establishment. Fondue is also popular, especially at the family-run Montjola. So too are the candle-lit dinners at the Ferwall, never more so than when they are reached by a brisk 45-minute sleigh ride along one of the most beautiful valleys in the Alps.

Après-ski

St Anton's undeniably vibrant nightlife begins at the end of skiing, in the Krazy Kangaruh, a large bustling Australian-inspired bar just above the final descent to the resort. Those who survive both the crowds and the last run through the snow-cannon in darkness often head for the cavernous Piccadilly Bar, which habitually buzzes until closing time just before dawn.

A new addition to the scene is the Chic Bar in the Hotel Schwarzer Adler. It offers cocktails, fresh pizza until 3am and what it claims is the first karaoke in Austria. Another popular meeting place is the Underground Bar, which has an extended Happy Hour from 4pm to 7pm, followed by live guitar music and 'all you can eat' piste bashers' specials. Hotel Post Keller is reported to be good for 30-year-olds and under. The Drop Inn and the Hazienda are recommended.

Pettneu   1275m (4,182ft)

The free ski-bus will take skiers from here to St Anton and back, making this traditional village an economical alternative place to stay. Pettneu has its own, limited skiing.

TOURIST OFFICE
A-6574 Pettneu am Arlberg
Tel 34 5448 221

TOUR OPERATORS
Crystal

● ●

Skiing facts: St Anton

TOURIST OFFICE
A-6580, St Anton am Arlberg
Tel 43 5446 22690
Fax 43 5440 253215

THE RESORT
By car Calais 970km
By rail Innsbruck 75 mins, Zurich 3-4 hrs. Orient Express stops here en-route to Venice
By air Innsbruck 104km, Munich and Zurich 208km each

THE SKIING
Longest run 8km, from the top of the Vallugagrat via the Ulmerhütte and Steissbachtal to the resort (black/blue)
Number of lifts 42 (88 on the Arlberg Ski Pass, including Lech and Zürs)
Number of trails/pistes 40, plus 41 ski routes, (20% easy, 34% intermediate, 46% difficult)
Total of trails/pistes 208km of groomed piste, plus 179km of off-piste runs
Nursery slopes 2 lifts
Summer skiing none
Snowmaking 18km covered

LIFT PASSES
Area pass Arlberg Special (covers St Anton, St Christoph, Stuben, Lech, Klösterle) ÖS1,660-1,840 for 6 days
Day pass ÖS370-410
Half-day pass ÖS310, from midday
Beginners no free lifts
Children Arlberg Special, 5-14 yrs, ÖS220-245 per day, ÖS1,100-1990 for 6 days
Pensioners men 63 yrs and over, women 58 yrs and over, ÖS345-385 per day, ÖS1,490-1,660 for 6 days
Credit cards accepted no

SKI SCHOOLS
Adults Arlberg Ski School St Anton, St Christoph and Nasserein, ÖS1,300 for 6 days. St Anton Ski School, ÖS1,200 for 6 days
Children Arlberg Ski School,5-14 yrs,

ÖS590 per day, ÖS2,030 for 6 days, including lunch
Private lessons ÖS1,800-1,850 per day
Special courses snowboarding, telemark
Guiding companies Arlberg Ski school

CROSS-COUNTRY
Ski schools Arlberg Ski School at Nasserein
Loipe location and size 40km on 4 tracks

CHILDCARE
Ski kindergarten Jugendcenter, 5-14 yrs, 9am-4.30pm, öS590 per day, ÖS2,030 for 6 days including lessons and lunch (closed on Saturdays)
Non-ski kindergarten Jugendcenter, 2½yrs and over, 9am-4.30pm, ÖS980 for 6 days including lunch (closed on Saturdays)
Babysitting list available from tourist office

OTHER SPORTS
Curling, swimming, indoor tennis at the Raiffeisen Tennis Centre, squash, sleigh rides, tobogganing, bowling, skating

WHAT'S NEW
● 2 children's lifts, one in St Christoph and one on Gampen

FOOD AND DRINK
Coffee ÖS25, bottle of house wine ÖS250, beer ÖS40, dish of the day ÖS200

TOUR OPERATORS
Activity Travel, Austrian Holidays, Bladon Lines, Crystal, Enterprise, Inghams, Made to Measure, Mark Warner, Neilson, Sally Holidays, Ski Beach Villas, Ski Choice, Ski John Wyatt, Ski Partners, Ski Total, Ski Thomson, Ski Unique, Ski West

● ●

Stuben 1410m (4,625ft)

Stuben is a small village on the western side of the Arlberg Pass. It is known for its often harsh weather conditions, but is one of the most convenient places to stay for enjoying not only St Anton, but also Lech and Zürs without the queues for mountain access. Stuben has its own skiing and nightlife, the former quiet and traditional. Reporters praise the skiing as being 'not too busy, with north-facing, good off-piste'.

TOURIST OFFICE
A-6762 Stuben, Arlberg
Tel 43 5582 761

TOUR OPERATORS
SkiBound

St Christoph 1780m (5,838ft)

St Christoph is no more than a few hotels and bars, with the famous old Hospiz hotel and gourmet restaurant in its midst. The ski school is well thought of and much in demand. The myth that St Bernard dogs were used for avalanche rescue with restorative baby barrels of brandy around their necks is reputed to have started here. A grand old canine used to sit thus attired in the snow outside the Hospiz, but is not known ever to have strayed on to the slopes.

TOURIST OFFICE
as St Anton

TOUR OPERATORS
Inghams

St Johann im Pongau, Salzburgerland

ALTITUDE 650m (2,132ft)

••

Good points large ski area, plenty of easy and intermediate skiing, tree-level skiing, minimal queuing, extensive cross-country skiing, easy road access, mountain restaurants, child facilities
Bad points unattractive town (but see alternatives), lack of advanced skiing, poor facilities for non-skiers
Linked or nearby resorts Alpendorf (l), Altenmarkt (n), Eben (n), Filzmoos (n), Flachau (n), Flachauwinkl (n), Kleinarl (n), Mayrdörfen (l), Moardörfl (l), Neuberg (n), Radstadt (n), Wagrain (l), Zauchensee (n)

St Johann im Pongau, not to be confused with the popular Tyrolean resort of the same name, is one of the few ski resorts with a cathedral. This small city, 45 minutes from Salzburg by road or rail, is the capital of Austria's greatest unsung ski area. Die Drei Täler (the Three Valleys) of St Johann, Wagrain and Flachau predates its better-known namesake in the French Tarentaise and, while not as challenging, offers some impressive statistics: a dozen resorts with 350km of on- and off-mountain linked skiing, served by 120 lifts all accessible on one ski pass.

The circuit is hugely popular with almost every nationality, bar the British who have still scarcely heard of it. The reason is simple: few tour operators come here because they cannot contract beds for the season in sufficient numbers to make its inclusion in the brochures a commercial viability. Do not be deterred; the skiing is excellent and the villages are delightful. You always get that pleasant feeling of actually going somewhere while skiing. A car is useful, but not essential.

Alpendorf, 4km away by ski-bus and 150m higher, is the gateway to the ski circus. The pretty village of Wagrain is the Méribel of the Drei Täler, the central resort in the heart of the system, from which it is easy to access both ends. In our opinion this is the best of the centres for those without a car. Flachau is an equally attractive alternative option. Bus connections to the outlying areas are efficient, but time-consuming. Overall, the area, which calls itself the Sportwelt Amadé, offers one of the better-value lift passes in Austria.

The skiing
Top 2188m (7,177ft) bottom 650m (2,132ft)
St Johann does have its own Hahnbaum ski area by the town and the **mountain access** by double chair takes you up to 1200m. Together

with a couple of drag-lifts this serves a by no means unenjoyable collection of fairly short red (intermediate) runs over undulating terrain. There are nursery slopes both at the bottom and higher up. Alpendorf, a hamlet with a few hotels, is where most skiers head each morning. The main mountain access is by six-person gondola up to Obergass-Alm at 1550m, and a quad chair on up to Hirschkogel at 1750m. Alternatively, you can take the old two-stage chair-lift, which rises over the woods to reach almost the same point. The runs back down again are red and more than a little testing for the timid intermediate, but ahead lies a series of marvellous blue (easy) cruising runs, spiced with the odd steeper pitch, as you work your way across the mountain above the tree-line to Sonntagskogl at 1850m, and to Grafenberg at 1702m.

There is little here to challenge the good skier, but a couple of pistes are certainly testing: the short black (difficult) run from the top of Sonntagskogel II down to the double drags at Strassalm, and the red run back down from the top of these lifts. From Grafenberg a long blue run takes you down into Wagrain. Return is direct via an efficient six-person gondola back up to Grafenberg. The top three-quarters of this wide, open, sunny family piste is also served by a chair and twin drags.

A bus link takes you from here either to Kirchboden for the runs down to Flachau from the top of the lifts to Griessenkareck (1991m) or to Kleinarl for the Mooskopf (1980m) and over the top to Flachauwinkl, which in turn links into the Zauchensee ski area. One reporter correctly points out that the local lift-map suggests that the Kirchboden-Flachau circuit is connected to the Kleinarl-Flachauwinkl circuit behind it – they are not. Kirchboden is a spacious suburb of Wagrain a few hundred metres east of the centre. The first stage is by chair, although plans for an additional gondola are at an advanced stage.

Above here, a 12-person gondola serves the skiing on the Flachau side. From the top you can also ski a worthwhile little bowl beneath the Saukarkopf (2014m) served by two drags; the one which takes you up to the summit gives access to a short, moderately challenging slope which is rightly graded black.

All the runs from Griessenkareck are broad swathes through the woods, which are of intermediate difficulty. The reds are not particularly testing, while the occasional blue is more challenging than it should be. One veteran reporter to the area sums it up: 'We have always felt the colour-grading of the pistes to be unhelpful, probably even misleading. It is sometimes hard to justify the distinction between blues and reds. There are true blues and true reds, but most runs fall somewhere in between.' Most of the five blacks in the region could well be classified as steepish reds. There are no alternatives to the red runs through the trees down to Flachau itself or to its suburb of Moardörfl, but it is possible to ride down by lift.

From Flachau there is an efficient free bus-service to Flachauwinkl, where the Tauern motorway divides the south-easterly three-valley lift chain into two: Zauchensee to the east, and Kleinarl to the west. The two halves are in turn linked by a toy train shuttle via a subway. A gondola and a chair take you up to the Rosskopf at 1929m and still further to Zauchensee, or you can head homewards via Mooskopf to Kleinarl and bus to Wagrain. The bus runs only once an hour but is now included in the lift pass. A new 4-person covered chair above Kleinarl has greatly eased west-east congestion on the Mooskopf. Zauchensee in its own right has some excellent, mainly intermediate and easy skiing with long runs down from the Gamskogel 2188m. Off-piste opportunities in the area abound. The smaller areas of Eben, Altenmarkt/Radstadt and Filzmoos/Neuberg are all at this end of the Three Valleys circuit and can be reached by an efficient bus service.

There is a considerable amount of artificial snow cover, in particular on the middle and lower runs down to Alpendorf from Gernkogel, and on the main Wagrain piste on the Grafenberg side. Floodlit night skiing at Flachau is a must. Most reporters agreed there was simply not enough time in even a fortnight to explore every corner. Schladming and Obertauern are also within easy reach by car.

Mountain restaurants

The area is well supplied with eating places, from small huts to larger self-service establishments. The Strass-Alm is to be avoided at peak times. The Alpenhof Edelweiss at the top of the Wagrainer Höhe double chair is 'more off the beaten track and less crowded'. One reporter suggests the pizzeria in the Wagrain gondola station ('waiter service and we

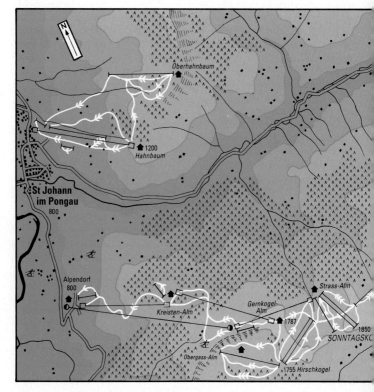

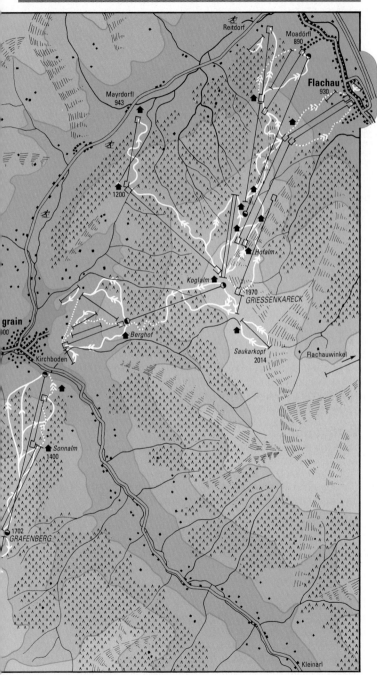

could be sure of a table'). The Stegbach Alm is an afternoon sun-trap.
The Latschenhof is praised for the quality of its *Gulaschsuppe*.

Beginners and children

We have good reports of nearly all the ski schools in St Johann,
Wagrain, and in Flachau. The only complaint comes from Wagrain
where beginners, we are told, are now normally taken up the
Grafenberg gondola, rather than to Kirchboden on the other side of the
valley. This necessitates a lift pass of which they cannot make full use.
The ski schools in Alpendorf are commended for their number of
English-speaking instructors and sympathetic approach to clients.

St Johann is not at first glance geared towards the young family
because of the inconvenient bus journey to Alpendorf. However, the
Alpenland Sporthotel has a crèche, and all the ski schools take children
from three years and mix ski lessons with games.

The resort

St Johann itself is a busy county town, which has little of the usual air of
a ski resort apart from a good choice of hotels, restaurants, and a couple of enjoyable evening bars. You get the feeling that it has an existence quite independent of the tourism industry, which of course it
does. It was largely rebuilt after a disastrous fire in 1852, so it lacks the
medieval charm of Austria's other county towns.

Accommodation

We have good reports of the Gasthof Taxenbacher ('small, comfortable,
serving home-made food'). The more expensive Sporthotel Alpenland
has a swimming-pool, and satellite television in all bedrooms. Hotel
Wielander is praised for its 'spacious rooms and happy staff'. The
Tennerhof is typically Austrian and 'nothing was too much trouble'.

Eating out

St Johann has a reasonable choice of good restaurants, mainly attached
to hotels. The Alpenland has a gourmet restaurant as well as a pizzeria
and a *Stübli*. The Stöcklwirt is recommended for its *cordon bleu*
(breaded chicken stuffed with ham and cheese) and the Hirschenwirt
for *duck à l'orange*. The Bächerstube has fine pizzas.

Après-ski

St Johann's après-ski is lively and good-value, although it is limited to a
handful of cheerful bars. The Baradox Pub and Amadeus Pub attract the
younger teenage set. Studio 31 is a smarter disco for late-night revellers.
Indoor tennis, as well as squash and skating are all popular.

Wagrain 900m (2,952ft)

The village is a tight, compact, busy little place with a fair amount of traffic on the minor road from St Johann to Flachau and Radstadt.
Fortunately the village has been able to develop away from the road
along the closed valley up to Kleinarl, as well as into Kirchboden at the
foot of the Griessenkarech lifts. Parking and traffic do, however, remain

a niggling problem. The village has a ski kindergarten.

Location within the resort is not critical. A free bus service links the two ski areas and the town, but because both buses tend to arrive simultaneously it is important to check you are on the right one. Most of the accommodation is in hotels and pensions. Hotel Grafenwirt is recommended for its 'quiet and upmarket atmosphere', although some of the rooms are small. One reporter claims the Enzian is the best hotel in town. The Wagrainerhof has a sound reputation and excellent facilities. Après-ski is varied with the Café Bosek for after-skiing coffee and cakes, ('definitely a café and not a bar'). The California bar is said to be overpriced, the Hubertus has traditional decoration and a friendly bustle of activity. The Wagrainerhof usually has live music. The Tenne and the California also have dancing.

TOURIST OFFICE
Box 14, 5602 Wagrain, Salzburgerland
Tel 43 6413 8265/8448
Fax 43 6413 8449

TOUR OPERATORS
Ski Thomson

Flachau 930m (3,050ft)

Flachau is an attractive, old farming village, a spacious, relaxed place spreading along the valley and up the slopes away from its somewhat nebulous centre. There are a number of comfortable and large chalet-style hotels and gasthofs, as well as apartment blocks. The village seems to attract wealthy German and Dutch tourists in particular. No British tour operator is currently using the resort because of the difficulty in obtaining favourable seasonal contracts with hoteliers.

The nursery slopes here are good, consisting of a gentle piste in the village separated from the proper mountain, and a more extensive and slightly steeper area at the foot of the main ski area. There is a non-ski kindergarten and the Griessenkar ski school takes children from three years old. Cross-country skiers have 160km of all standards of loipe throughout the valley. The centrally-located Reslwirt is recommended, along with the Gasthof Salzburgerhof in the medium-price range. The resort is undergoing considerable expansion with two new four-star hotels last season, the Hotel Vierjahreszeiten beside the cable car, and the new Tauernhof, as well as two new apartment blocks with upmarket accommodation for two to five persons. Recommended restaurants include the Flachauerhof, Unterbergalm, and the Pizzeria Jagdhof and Kaiserstube for more budget-conscious evenings. There is dancing at the Yeti, Jagdhof, Kitzbar, and in the Weinstadl.

TOURIST OFFICE
A-5542 Flachau, Salzburgerland
Tel 43 6457 2214
Fax 43 6457 2536

TOUR OPERATORS

Altenmarkt 856m (2,808ft)

This a pretty little market town, straddling the border between Salzburgerland and Styria, with its own small ski area linked to neighbouring and slightly larger and livelier Radstadt. The main skiing is a bus ride away at Zauchensee (or Flachau). It has, with Zauchensee, three ski schools, all of which are recommended for the standard of English spoken by instructors and the small size of classes. A correspondent who took an off-piste course with Fun Ski gave a 9 out of 10 rating and was impressed by the emphasis on safety. Altenmarkt's kindergarten takes

....

Skiing facts: St Johann im Pongau

TOURIST OFFICE
A-5600 St Johann im Pongau,
Salzburgerland
Tel 43 6412 6036
Fax 43 6412 6036

THE RESORT
By road Calais 1210km
By rail station in resort
By air Salzburg 1 hr
Visitor beds 2,513 (hotels,
apartments and chalets – no
breakdown available)
Transport bus covers all resorts in the
Amadé region

THE SKIING
Longest run Gernkogelabfahrt, 6.5km
(red)
Number of lifts 17 in St
Johann/Alpendorf, 120 in area
Number of trails/pistes 11 in St
Johann/Alpendorf (36% easy, 46%
intermediate, 18% difficult), 130 in
area
Total of trails/pistes 25km in St
Johann/Alpendorf 320km in area
Nursery slopes 5 in area
Summer skiing none
Snowmaking 20 hectares covered

LIFT PASSES
Area pass Salzburger Sportwelt Amadé
(covers 8 resorts including Wagrain,
Flachau, Altenmarkt), from ÖS1,380 for
6 days
Day pass from ÖS290
Half-day pass from ÖS205 after midday
Beginners free baby-lifts or points
tickets
Children 6-14 yrs, from ÖS760 for 6
days, free for 6 yrs and under
Pensioners 10% reduction for men 60
and over and women 65 and over

Credit cards accepted no

SKI SCHOOLS
Adults Ski School St Johann/Alpendorf,
ÖS1,250 for 6 days. Toni's Ski School,
ÖS1,100 for 6 days
Children ÖS540 per day, ÖS1,560
for 6 days, including lunch
Private lessons ÖS1,650 per day
Special courses snowboarding,
telemark
Guiding companies through all ski
schools and Gernot Werner

CROSS-COUNTRY
Ski schools Ski School St
Johann/Alpendorf
Loipe location and size 21km in and
around St Johann/Alpendorf

CHILDCARE
Non-ski kindergarten Alpendorf Mini-
Club, 4 yrs and under, 5 hrs per day
ÖS2,020 for 6 days including lunch
Ski kindergarten through ski school,
3 yrs and over, 10am-4pm
Babysitting Alpendorf Mini-Club or
Alpenland Sporthotel

OTHER SPORTS
Hang-gliding, skating, curling, indoor
tennis, squash, fitness centre, bowling,
sleigh rides

WHAT'S NEW
● Alpendorf Mini-Club

FOOD AND DRINK PRICES
Coffee ÖS23, bottle of house wine
ÖS180, beer ÖS28, dish of the day
ÖS80

TOUR OPERATORS
Enterprise, Masterski, Ski Partners

....

children from three years old. All the ski schools will take children all day and provide lunch. Cross-country opportunities are extensive.

Several reporters have commented on how pleasant it is to stay in a resort which does not exist just for tourism, but has an independent village life of its own ('full of atmosphere and very Austrian'). The local industry is the Atomic ski factory. We have good reports on the Hotel Schartner, one of the main village rendezvous points and the best restaurant. The Lebselter and the Platz are also praised. After-skiing action begins at 5pm with tea-dancing in the Hotel Alpenhof in Zauchensee. Back in Altenmarkt the spotlight switches to the Areche Noah, Almbar, Tauernstuben and the Gamsbar.

TOURIST OFFICE
Sportplatzstrasse, A-5541 Altenmarkt,
Salzburgerland
Tel 43 6452 5511
Fax 43 6452 6066

TOUR OPERATORS
Alpine Tours, Made to Measure

Filzmoos 1057m (3,467ft)

Filzmoos is a small village with lots of *Gemütlichkeit* and a permanent population of only 1,150. It has its own interesting ski area on both sides of a little valley, linked to the neighbouring hamlet of Neuberg, with a top altitude of 1645m and 17 lifts. Year-round skiing on the Dachstein Glacier is only 18km away, and access to the Drei Täler skiing at Flachau is by bus. We have no reports of the two ski schools here, Schischule Filzmoos and Schischule Bögei. The kindergarten takes children from three years old and has English-speaking staff. The history of Filzmoos as a tourist resort dates back to Edwardian times, when it was a popular holiday area for wealthy Viennese.

The choice of accommodation is surprisingly large for the size of the village. It has over 3,000 guest beds in 25 hotels and a number of apartments. The extremely comfortable Alpenkrone, run by the brother of actress Susan Hampshire, is the most popular with British guests. Recommended restaurants include the Oberhofalm, Reithof and Gseng ('great value, real Austrian dumplings'). Pinocchio is praised for its pizzas and spaghetti. One reporter recommends the Hotel Hubertus restaurant 'very smart, very good food and service, and a very big bill'. Après-ski centres on the Happy Filzmoos and other bars. The Mühlradl is for late-night revellers. The area is particularly popular with hot-air balloon enthusiasts and, as Château d'Oex is to Switzerland, Filzmoos has the title of hot-air ballooning capital of Austria.

TOURIST OFFICE
5532 Filzmoos, Salzburgerland
Tel 43 6453 235
Fax 43 6453 685

TOUR OPERATORS
Inghams

St Johann in Tirol

ALTITUDE 650m (2,132ft)

••

Good points easy runs, ample mountain restaurants, lively après-ski, short airport transfer, easy resort access, extensive cross-country tracks, facilities for family holidays, variety of tree-line runs, extensive snow-making
Bad points poor resort-level snow, lack of skiing convenience, limited tough runs, heavy traffic
Linked or nearby resorts Fieberbrunn (n), Kitzbühel (n),Oberndorf (l), St Jakob (n), St Ulrich (n), Waidring (n)

St Johann in Tirol, easily confused with the other ski resort St Johann im Pongau, has grown in recent years from a compact Tyrolean village into a sprawling industrial town and has thereby sacrificed much of its undoubted charm. It lies off a busy road-junction only 10 minutes by car or train over the hill from Kitzbühel, but there the similarity ends. The hill in question is the Kitzbüheler Horn, Kitzbühel's second ski area and St Johann's only one. An on-mountain link between the two is technically feasible and not particularly costly, but fashionable Kitzbühel has no desire for any closer contact with its more mundane neighbour, which attracts a different clientele. Like its skiing, which best suits beginners and early intermediates, St Johann's appeal is much more straightforward. Away from the industrial estate suburbs it offers a pleasant, chalet-style setting for a lively and quite varied winter holiday at a reasonable price.

The skiing
Top 1700m (5,576ft) bottom 680m (2,230ft)
Mountain access is by a two-stage gondola, which goes up from a point on the fringes of the resort all the way to Harschbichl at 1700m. From this point, runs fan out down three gentle rounded ridges, separated by wooded glades, some of which split and link further down the mountain. Practically all the skiing on the top half of the mountain is graded red (intermediate), and properly so. These are good intermediate slopes and the terrain is both varied and occasionally challenging. Most runs go all the way down to the valley, snow permitting, but plentiful drag-lifts and chairs allow you to stay high. The lower half of the mountain is generally easier and more suited to less confident intermediates.

The Penzing quad chair gives access to a long and attractive black (difficult) run, the Saureggabfahrt. This has an FIS downhill course rating, but you should not be deterred. Like all downhill courses it only becomes truly testing when prepared for a race. In normal conditions,

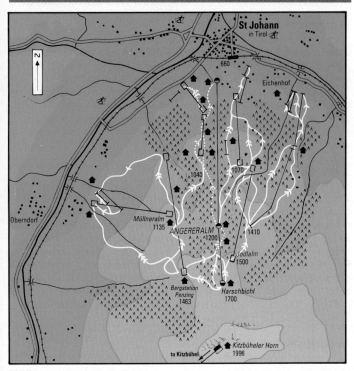

with the exception of one steep pitch half-way down, which can provide a few problems in poor snow, the run can be managed by any intermediate skier. There are also some interesting off-piste variations. Back at the top, the main run down to the village is of similar length, but over terrain which is ideal for building the confidence of near-beginners.

Queues are generally not a problem either at village level or up the mountain. But the balance can be upset by weekend visitors from Innsbruck and Munich when conditions are good, in a resort which has a reputation for being a snow-trap, although not as good as its neighbour, Fieberbrunn. The main gondola has a 'singles' lane to ensure cars leave full, and waits of more than 10 minutes are uncommon. There is artificial snow on the main piste down from above Angereralm to the town, and on the piste of the short Hochfeld chair nearby. This, combined with the northward orientation of the slopes and good grooming, generally keeps slopes in fine condition.

Mountain restaurants

The choice of 18 mountain restaurants is way above average for a resort of this size. Practically every piste has a welcoming hut at the top or bottom, part-way down, or all three. On the main run down it is possible to stop off at no less than 8 bars or restaurants, if you have the stamina. One reporter waxed lyrically about Hochfeld, half-way down the gondola mid-station: 'Popular with instructors, less quaint but good food.'

Beginners and children

Both the St Johann ski school and a second school based at Eichenhof at the foot of the eastern extremity of the ski area have sound reputations. Eichenhof's policy of including native English-speaking instructors among its staff has to be of advantage to all learners.

St Johann is a suitable resort for families apart from the major drawback of the distance across town to the lifts. There is a non-ski kindergarten as well as an efficient babysitting service organised by the tourist office. Older children can have lunch as well as lessons with their ski school class.

The resort

St Johann stands at a junction of valleys, rivers and roads, and has a railway line running through it. The attractive centre is a triangle neatly defined by the railway on the south side and by the confluence of two rivers to the north. The ski slopes are on the far side of the railway line and the sprawl of suburbs in the remaining two directions is grim. Light industry and tourism are not necessarily the best of bed companions. Eichenhof, the eastern satellite, is conveniently situated for the lifts but is 'an unattractive 15- to 20-minute walk from the town centre along a busy, dusty road'. Mercifully, the main trunk road to Kitzbühel is bypassed. The medieval centre still remains attractive, but the changing face of St Johann is not a welcome one.

Accommodation

Most guests stay in hotels, no-frills pensions and private rooms. The Hotel Post, which dates from 1225, is the beautifully frescoed central feature of St Johann. It is warmly recommended for its breakfast buffet and three-course dinners. The Hotel Park, situated near the gondola, is a more modern addition in the luxury class. We have good reports of the Hotel Moser ('pleasant family owners who know how to cook'), and the Hotel Fischer ('staff couldn't do enough to help'). The Goldener Löwe is strongly recommended for families with children: 'The staff seemed genuinely fond of them, and were unfazed by headbutts at groin level.' The Pension Kaiserblick is quietly located off the main street.

Eating out

The Speckbacherstub'n and the Rettenbachstüberl are both praised for their value for money. The Pizzeria Masianco and Pizzeria Rialto prove popular with what is a generally a young skier here. One reporter speaks warmly of the Löwengrill on Speckbacherstrasse.

Après-ski

It is noisy and there is a lot of it, but the après-ski is mainly aimed at the younger crowd. After skiing the action starts at the Café Rainer, Max's Pub near the station and in Bunny's Pub nearby. Later on the scene moves to Holzschuh, Schickeria and the Tatoo and Caprice discos. Thigh-slapping evenings can be enjoyed at the Huberbrau Stalle.

Fieberbrunn 800m (2,624ft)

Ten kilometres up the road from St Johann, along the Pillerseetal, lies the sprawling village of Fieberbrunn. The centre is set back from the road and has typically Tyrolean hotels and guesthouses, a pretty church, and a lively après-ski atmosphere. Dutch visitors are very much in evidence. The resort overall is inconveniently strung-out for nearly two kilometres along the road and not close to the skiing.

The small but attractive ski area is north-facing, and prides itself on being the eastern Tyrol's *Schneewinkel* (snow pocket). Indeed, the resort is lucky enough to receive big snowfalls, which are generally heavier than those received by its neighbours St Johann and Kitzbühel. The main skiing is in the tree-line and goes up to Lärchfilzkogel at 1655m. There are several long and easy runs, some varied off-piste skiing including treks over to Kitzbühel (the ski school specialises in pow-

Skiing facts: St Johann in Tirol

TOURIST OFFICE
Postfach 114, A-6380, St Johann
in Tirol
Tel 43 5352 2218
Fax 43 5352 5200

THE RESORT
By road Calais 1133km
By rail station in resort
By air Salzburg 1½ hrs
Visitor beds 5,586 (50% hotels, 27% apartments, 23% guesthouses)
Transport free bus service

THE SKIING
Longest run Penzing, 7km (black)
Number of lifts 18
Number of trails/pistes 20 (41% easy, 47% intermediate, 12% difficult)
Total of trails/pistes 60km
Nursery slopes 4 lifts
Summer skiing none
Snowmaking 7km covered

LIFT PASSES
Area pass Schneewinkl (covers St Johann in Tirol, Oberndorf, Fieberbrunn, St Ulrich, Waidring), ÖS1,540 for 6 days St Johann only ÖS1,380
Day pass St Johann in Tirol, ÖS295
Half-day pass ÖS230 until 12.30pm or starting after 12.30pm
Beginners points tickets
Children Schneewinkl, 6-14 yrs, ÖS920. St Johann in Tirol, ÖS730. Free for 6 yrs and under
Pensioners no reduction
Credit cards accepted no

SKI SCHOOLS
Adults Schischule St Johann and Eichenhof, ÖS1,200 for 6 days
Children as adults
Private lessons ÖS1,950 per day for 1-2 people
Guiding companies through tourist office

CROSS-COUNTRY
Ski schools Schischule St Johann and Eichenhof
Loipe location and size 74km on east and west sides of the town

CHILDCARE
Non-ski kindergarten none
Ski kindergarten 2 yrs and over, 9.30am-4.30pm, ÖS450 per day
Babysitting list available from tourist office

OTHER SPORTS
Parapente, hot-air ballooning, skating, curling, tobogganing, indoor tennis, bowling, swimming, fitness centre, sleigh rides

FOOD AND DRINK PRICES
Coffee ÖS22, bottle of house wine ÖS140, beer ÖS27, dish of the day ÖS120

TOUR OPERATORS
Crystal, Enterprise, Seasun School Tours, SkiBound, Ski Europe, Ski Partners, Ski Thomson

der skiing), and there are steeper slopes down to a broad and empty valley. The only black (difficult) run is Reckmoos, which is steep and narrow with moguls.

TOURIST OFFICE
A-6391, Fieberbrunn, Tyrol
Tel 34 5354 6305

TOUR OPERATORS
Enterprise, SkiBound

Waidring 780m (2,558ft)

This unspoilt village is less than 20km from St Johann in Tirol. Situated in the same snow pocket as Fieberbrunn, Waidring is known for its family skiing, with the Hausberg nursery slopes right in the village. The rest of the skiing is at Steinplatte, 4km from the village, which rises to 1860m offering mainly beginner to intermediate skiing. There are 5 mountain restaurants on the slopes. The best hotel is the Waidringerhof, with a swimming-pool, a cosy dining room, and live music on some evenings. Hotel Tiroler Adler is also in the village centre. The nightlife is relaxed and informal, with the Schniedermann bar and the Alte Schmiede both popular.

TOURIST OFFICE
A-6384 Waidring, Tyrol
Tel 43 5353 5242
Fax 43 5353 527072

TOUR OPERATORS
Ski Thomson

Zell am See, Salzburgerland

ALTITUDE 750m (2,460ft)

••

Good points variety of easy runs, easy road and rail access, facilities
for non-skiers, short airport transfer, extensive cross-country skiing,
pleasant town, lively nightlife, resort charm
Bad points heavy traffic, poor skiing convenience, horrendous
peak-season lift queues, lack of challenging skiing
Nearby or linked resorts Schüttdorf (l), Thumersbach (n), Kaprun (n)

Zell am See sits on a natural promontory at the edge one of the prettiest
lakes in Austria, at the foot of the 2000m Schmittenhöhe. As a geographical setting it is hard to beat and, together with the neighbouring
glacier resort of Kaprun, Zell am See markets itself, under the horribly
unoriginal name of Europa Sport Region, as one of Austria's major year-
round ski resorts. In the summer, skiing is confined to the upper slopes
of the Kitzsteinhorn above Kaprun, while in winter the mainly gentle
slopes of the Schmittenhöhe add to what is a thoroughly pleasant intermediate playground with snow guaranteed on the glacier. Cross-country skiing is extensive, the panorama exceptional, non-skiers are kept
busy, and nightlife is loud and lively. It therefore comes as somewhat of
a surprise that the reality of this little lakeside town, easily reached by
road or mainline railway and famed for its golf course, should fall a full
eight- iron short of being the perfect winter sports centre.

The town is savagely separated by the busy main road from both
mountain access points. But Zell's biggest fault is its lift queues which,
in high season, destroy much of the enjoyment of what is otherwise a
pleasant intermediate area. The Kitzsteinhorn Glacier at Kaprun, 20
minutes away by ski-bus, is open for skiing all year. In times of poor
snow cover it becomes a daily point of pilgrimage for thousands from
other resorts in Salzburgerland, and the overcrowding here can be
unacceptable. However, off-season and in summer this is, with the
exeption of Tignes, the best-developed and organised glacier for skiing
in Europe.

If Zell am See is to maintain its reputation as a major resort then it
must look to a rapid upgrading of its inadequate lift system. The official
reply to this criticism is that Zell is a conservation area and the lift company prides itself on its green policy. During the summer months a
team of eight *pisteurs* is employed full time to tend to the slopes. To
avoid soil erosion and to protect saplings, skiing outside the marked

pistes is forbidden except in designated areas.

All this is highly laudable. If no more lifts are to be constructed then Zell am See should truthfully pursue this policy by ruthlessly restricting the number of lift passes issued by linking them to the number of hotel beds. Unfortunately it is likely that commercial considerations will continue to dictate otherwise.

The skiing
Top 1965m (6,445ft) bottom 750m (2,460ft)

The Schmittenhöhe looks like a *Germknödl*, the rounded sweet dumpling to be found in its mountain restaurants. The gentle slopes provide long, red (intermediate) runs both back down to the village itself and along the southern flank to the satellite of Schüttdorf. Steeper slopes drop down from a bowl scooped out on the lakeside of the mountain to provide the most challenging skiing, and off-piste if it were allowed.

The main **mountain access** is on the 'wrong' side of the road where a gondola rises to the middle station at 1320m. This is also reached by a six-seater gondola and a quad chair from Schüttdorf. A third lift station is 2km from the centre of Zell at Sonnenalm-Pfiff in the pit of the bowl, from where, snow permitting, you can ski back to the resort. One of the two cable cars from here takes you directly into the Schmittenhöhe Berghotel on the summit, from where an elevator deposits you on the sunny plateau. A small area of blue (easy) and red runs behind the summit is served by a chair and a couple of drag-lifts. Turning right at the top takes you along a gently sloping ridge to a collection of runs of varying difficulty on the sunny side of the bowl. This Sonnalm area, served by two more chairs and a drag-lift, can also be accessed via the second cable car from Sonnenalm-Pfiff. Two more lifts open up the skiing around the shoulder at the top of the north face of the mountain. None of the skiing could be classified as difficult in good snow conditions, although a steepish pitch in the black (difficult) run below Sonnalm can present problems when it is worn and icy. Lifts and pistes link back to the top of Schmittenhöhe.

South of Schmittenhöhe a succession of gentle, broad and sunny pistes descend along the ridge and on down to Schüttdorf. A right fork takes you to Areitalm, arrival point for the Schüttdorf gondola; the cruising piste down to the bottom does not keep its snow in warm weather. The left fork brings you down to the Zell am See middle station. Higher up, two black runs branch off over the lip of the bowl. These soon steepen into testing, but not intimidating, long runs with the occasional pitch of almost 30°. The other two runs to the bottom stations are less severe, but get more sun. The Ebernberglift, above the road between Zell and Schüttdorf, is mainly used for slalom practice. The run down is short and fairly steep, offering panoramic views of the town. Colour-grading on the piste map is confusing. There is artificial snow on the black runs down into the pit of the bowl (which without snow can be become dangerously icy) and on the nursery slopes.

Queues during peak weeks are horrendous. Over New Year we have reports of 40- to 50-minute waits for the Schmittenhöhe and Sonnalm

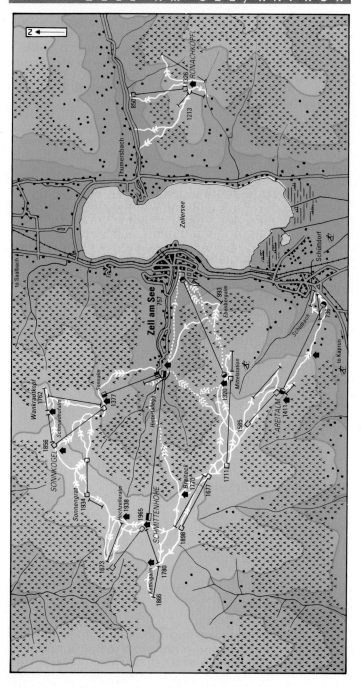

cable cars. Runs down under Areitbahn and Zeller Bergbahn become seriously congested ('late-afternoon crowds, including head-banging snowboarders, turn a relatively acceptable red run into a nightmare'). The worst bottleneck is at the top of the Bergbahn where the sole means of upward progress is an antique double chair-lift.

Beating the base queues by taking the bus to Schüttdorf for alternative access via the six-person Areitbahn gondola relieves the symptoms, but fails to cure the disease. Queues here are generally much shorter and the bubble is followed by a fast quad chair. From here the only means of gaining altitude is to take the antique double chair. Another reporter said that even in the last week of January queues were awful: 'One morning it took from 9.20am until 12.10pm to get up to Schmittenhöhe.' However, visitors in March said that apart from rush-hour queues at the base, there was little waiting on the mountain.

Thumersbach, on the other side of the lake, has a chair-lift and three short drags which provide a couple of gentle, uncrowded runs back down the wooded slopes with wonderful views of Zell am See.

The pretty village of Kaprun, a 5-minute journey on the ski-bus, also has its own larger ski area above the village with mainly blue (easy) runs. But the best of its skiing is on the Kitzsteinhorn Glacier, 20 minutes from Zell. A choice of gondola followed by quad chair, or the original underground funicular, takes you up to the Alpincenter at 2450m from where lifts takes you on up to the top of the ski area at 3029m.

The Alpincenter includes a modest hotel, restaurants and a first-class ski shop. The glacier offers good, but exposed, blue and red runs, most of which are open nearly all year (August skiing is usually limited to a couple of T-bars). A cable car takes you to the Aussichtsrestaurant at the top and gives access to the only difficult run: a short, steep mogul field. There is also an all-year-round cross-country circuit below the ridge at the top of the bowl. In winter, a long and interesting red takes you down to the middle station of the funicular and ends in a push along the plastic floor of a long tunnel. The building of the gondola up to the glacier has reduced queuing, but when snow cover is poor here the extensive car-parks fill up with coaches at first light.

Mountain restaurants

Zell am See has a good choice of eating places on the mountain, although again these are crowded during busy weeks. Prices are reasonable. The black run down from Sonnalm has a pleasant hut for those who can get to it. The Sonnenalm-Pfiff is praised for its 'delicious hot chocolate'. Schmiedhofalm has amazing views from its sunny terrace. The middle station restaurant serves 'huge and excellent *Kaiserschmarren*'. Glocknerhaus, on the way down to Schüttdorf, is also popular. The Berghotel terrace bar has loud music and attracts a young crowd.

Beginners and children

Ski schools in the valley seem to vary in quality and we have mixed reports of the eight schools in the region. None of them have priority in the lift lines, so it not worth taking lessons just to jump the queues. The Wallner Prenner in Zell am See is most recommended with 'excellent instructors, all of whom speak good English'. The Zell am See/Schmittenhöhe has a number of Australian teachers and also receives considerable praise. The Kitzsteinhorn ski school operates all-year-round and has a high standard of instruction, particularly for advanced skiers. Nursery slopes are situated at the bottom of the cable car and at Schüttdorf, as well as on top of the Schmittenhöhe. Kaprun operates its own ski school.

The children's facilities are generally good with a kindergarten taking 1-year-olds and upwards from 9am to 4pm. Ski lessons are given from the age of three. One parent reporter described it as better than the adult ski school he attended: 'We have no complaints about the standard of tuition or care of the children.' The Mövenpick Grand Hotel and the Feriendorf Hagleitner both run crèches.

The resort

Zell am See, at the gateway to Austria's highest mountain, the Gross Glockner, is an established town first settled by a monastic order in the eighth century. In recent years it has done much to smarten up its image. The whole of the centre has been pedestrianised, the investment in hotels has been mighty, and it has an altogether more upmarket feel to it as it strives with its nucleus of medieval buildings to be a kind of mini-Kitzbühel in Salzburgerland, rather than the chocolate-box Austrian village. The range of shops is wide, as you would expect in a market town of this size, which has an even larger summer trade centred on watersports. Buses run every 15 minutes to the lifts and regularly to Kaprun and the Kitzsteinhorn. Reporters complain that they tend to become very crowded, and if snow conditions confine skiing to the Kitzsteinhorn then a car is a necessity. There is a regular bus service to Thumersbach, but you can also walk across the lake in mid-winter. Cross-country skiing is extensive and non-skiers will find plenty of attractions in and around the town.

Accommodation

The luxurious Mövenpick Grand Hotel, jutting out over the lake, receives much acclaim, although even by five-star standards prices are said to be very high. The duplex rooms with private sauna and hot tub are described as 'the last word in hedonism'. The Tirolerhof is highly recommended ('friendly staff with good English, and the four-course meals were excellent with individual attention to a vegetarian in our party'). One reporter stayed in Thumersbach: 'Apartment comfortable, but taxis necessary to enjoy the nightlife.' Pension Daxer at the top end of the village, close to the cable car stations, is said to be convenient for the skiing, though not for the après-ski, but otherwise 'small and friendly, and highly recommended'. Also well positioned for the lifts are the Schwebebahn and the Waldhof St Georg. The three-star Traube in the pedestrian zone is small and comfortable. The Neue Post, Hotel zum Hirschen, and the expensive Salzburgerhof are also praised. For those hotels with television sets in bedrooms, fixed weather cameras on both the Kitzsteinhorn and the Schmittehöhe allow you to check the weather on top before you get out of bed in the morning.

Eating out

The Neue Post is praised for its 'amazing fresh trout'. The Alpenkönig and the Chataprunium are considered the best value for money along with the Kupferkessel and the Saustall. Waldhof St Georg, Hotel Erlhof, and the Salzburgerhof are all recommended for their high standards of

Skiing facts: Zell am See

TOURIST OFFICE
A-5700 Zell am See, Salzburgerland
Tel 43 6542 2600
Fax 43 6542 2032

THE RESORT
By road Calais 1184km
By rail station in resort
By air Salzburg 1½ hrs
Visitor beds 14,380 (73% hotels, 27% apartments) – in Zell am See and Kaprun
Transport bus service between Zell am See and Kaprun

THE SKIING
Longest run Nordabfahrt, 6.1km (blue)
Number of lifts 25 in Zell am See, 54 in area
Number of trails/pistes 31 in Zell am See, 54 in area (38% easy, 50% inter-mediate, 12% difficult)
Total of trails/pistes 80km in Zell am See, 130km in area
Nursery slopes 3 lifts
Summer skiing extensive area on Kitzsteinhorn, above Kaprun
Snowmaking 20km covered

LIFT PASSES
Area pass Europa Sport Region (covers Zell am See and Kaprun), from ÖS1,520 for 6 days
Day pass from ÖS330
Half-day pass Zell am See only, from ÖS270 after midday
Beginners points tickets
Children 6-15yrs, from ÖS990 for 6 days, free for 6 yrs and under
Pensioners women 60 yrs and over, men 65 yrs and over 10% reduction
Credit cards accepted yes

SKI SCHOOLS
Adults Schmittenhöhe and Wallner Prenner, from 9.30am for full day, Areitbahn, from 10am for full day, all ÖS1,260 for 6 days. Thumersbach, ÖS700 for 6 half-days

Children as adults
Private lessons Schmittenhöhe, Wallner Prenner, Areitbahn, ÖS1,800 per day. Thumersbach ÖS1,200 per day
Special courses snowboarding, monoskiing, telemark
Guiding companies through ski school

CROSS-COUNTRY
Ski school Langlaufschule at the Langlauf Centrum at Tennishalle Schuttdorf, Langlaufschule Eckbert Stöphasius at Thumserbach
Loipe location and size 200km along the valley floor

CHILDCARE
Non-ski kindergarten guest kindergarten, 3 yrs and over, 8am-4pm, ÖS200 per day. Snow Kindergarten, 3 yrs and over, 9am- 4pm, ÖS1,200 for 6 days. Kindergarten Ursula Zink, 1 yr and over, 9am-4pm, ÖS1,200 for 6 days including lunch
Ski kindergarten Schittenhöhe, Wallner Prenner, Areitbahn, 4 yrs and over, ÖS1,260 for 6 days. Thumersbach, any age, 6 half-days, ÖS700
Babysitting list from tourist office

OTHER SPORTS
Parapente, hang-gliding, luge-ing, ice-driving, hot-air ballooning, sleigh rides, skating, indoor tennis, swim-ming, fitness centre, bowling, shooting range, climbing wall, tobogganing

FOOD AND DRINK PRICES
Coffee ÖS25, bottle of house wine ÖS150, beer ÖS30, dish of the day ÖS50

TOUR OPERATORS
Austrian Holidays, Crystal, Enterprise, Inghams, Made to Measure, Masterski, Neilson, Seasun School Tours, Ski Austria, SkiBound, Ski Choice, Ski Europe, Ski Falcon, Ski Thomson, Ski Trax

cuisine. The Pizza House is said to be great value, and the ubiquitous McDonald's in the town centre has prices much the same as home.

Après-ski

Zell am See is lively by any standards. Once the lifts have closed for the day the zither music starts, *Schuhplatte* commences and the beer flows. Tea-dancing still exists, and a number of reporters have enjoyed watching major league ice hockey matches. Action begins at 4pm in the Kellerbar of the Hotel Schwebebahn near the lifts. The Feinschmeck and the Mösshammer in the main square both have good coffee and cakes, but away from the traditional Austrian entertainment there are bars and discos to suit all pockets. Crazy Daisy's is a focal point for Anglo-Saxon visitors, but said by one reporter to be 'very expensive and unpleasantly crowded'. Another commented that the local Austrian bar game which involves driving nails into logs enlivened many an evening.

The Pinzgauer Diele is popular with the British. The Kellerbar of the Hotel zum Hirschen is lively and the main bar of the Tirolerhof is a good place to relax and at the same time hear yourself think. The Wunderbar, a glass conservatory on the roof of the Mövenpick Grand Hotel, has views of the lake and mountains. Sugar Shake and the Schnelle Bier are popular. Late-night action switches to Visage, Disco 'Nr 1' Taverne, and half-a-dozen other discos.

Kaprun 770m (2,526ft)

Kaprun is a delightful, typical Austrian holiday village a few kilometres back into the mountains from the lakeside, which has seen considerable expansion in recent years as it has developed into an all-year-round ski resort. But despite new hotel and apartment developments it has managed to retain its essential village atmosphere based on the church and stream. It has a handful of sports and gift shops, the odd tea-room, and makes a good attempt at providing a nightlife for its visitors, who range from lakes-and-mountains walkers to winter holiday skiers and on to the professionals who use the glacier as their workbench during the summer months. The Baum Bar on the edge of town is worthy of special mention as the liveliest nightclub in the valley.

The four-star Orgler has the best accommodation and one of the best restaurants. The Barbarahof and the Sportkristall are both recommended. The Sonnblick and the Kaprunserhof cater specially for families. The Pension Salzburgerhof has 'pleasant, spacious bedrooms', and Hotel Toni has some of the best food and friendly staff.

TOURIST OFFICE
A-5710 Kaprun
Tel 43 6547 8643
Fax 43 6547 8192

TOUR OPERATORS
Austrian Holidays, Crystal, Enterprise,
Made to Measure, Neilson,
Ski Partners, Ski Thomson

Alpe d'Huez, Dauphiné

ALTITUDE 1860m (6,100ft)

....

Good points big ski area, sunny position, beautiful high alpine scenery, extensive artificial snow, ideal for family skiing, varied off-piste skiing, child facilities
Bad points lack of alpine charm, limited tree-skiing, traffic, crowded pistes at weekends
Linked or nearby resorts Auris (l), Oz-en-Oisans (l), Vaujany (l), Villard-Reculas (l), Les Deux Alpes (n), La Grave (n)

Despite being one of France's top five high alpine ski areas, Alpe d'Huez is better known abroad for what takes place here on one of the hottest days of summer. Each July, riders in the Tour de France climb through 1130m and 22 agonising hairpin bends from the valley town of Bourg d'Oisans to this hotch-potch of a resort perched on a sunny balcony in the Oisans mountain range 90 minutes from Grenoble. The Big Burn, generally considered to be one of the toughest endurance tests in any sport, makes or breaks the top riders who push themselves through the pain barrier and battle against fatigue and heat exhaustion to complete what is the Blue Riband stage of the Tour. In winter Alpe d'Huez has an altogether less malevolent image as a ski resort, with 220km of linked piste served by 86 lifts making up an area marketed as Les Grandes-Rousses.

Back in 1934 a young engineer called Pomagalski invented the drag-lift here just a few days ahead of a rival in Davos, and its lift system remains one of the most up-to-date in France. Alpe d'Huez itself, a venue for the 1968 Olympics (they managed to construct the only south-facing bob-run in the world here) has grown without design, an architectural mélange that is painful to behold but which functions flawlessly. It is one of the few resorts which can be reached directly by aircraft into its own altiport. Les Deux Alpes is a few minutes away by helicopter, or 45 minutes by road. In recent years, the Alpe d'Huez satellites of Auris, Oz, Vaujany, and Villard-Reculas have emerged as resorts in their own right and, to some extent, are in danger of eclipsing their grizzled old master.

Through mass marketing, Alpe d'Huez has lost much of the rather exclusive cachet it held in the 1960s and 1970s, when it saw itself as a potential Megève or a Courchevel. Its clientèle is predominantly French and its proximity to Grenoble means that it suffers heavily from over-crowded pistes on high-season weekends, but it is proving increasingly popular with British families. It is that rare commodity: a genuine all-round resort with excellent nursery slopes, good intermediate runs, long black runs (difficult) and extremely demanding off-piste opportunities.

The skiing
Top 3330m (10,922ft) bottom 1100m (3,608ft)

Mountain access is multiple. Two main modern gondolas feed traffic out of the village into the Pic Blanc sector, but there are plenty of alternatives at peak times. Such is the efficiency of the lift system, capable of shifting 90,000 people an hour, that Alpe d'Huez claims to have dispensed with lift queues. Indeed, even on peak days you will not have to wait for more than a few minutes for access to the main jumbo gondola. However, the pistes immediately above the resort can become so overcrowded you find yourself nostalgically remembering the M25 during the rush hour. Skiing becomes near impossible.

First glances can be deceptive and none more so than here. Having finally negotiated the 22 hairpin bends up from the valley floor, the skiing facing one at Les Bergers lift station looks disarmingly mild; an open mountainside served by an array of gondolas and chairs. But skiers who have cut their teeth on the gentle pastures of the Tyrol will be shocked by the severity of the skiing here. Much of the real mountain, Pic Blanc, is hidden from sight by the lie of the land. A cable car takes you up to its 3330m summit and from here it is possible to ski over 2000m vertical down to well below Alpe d'Huez itself. The off-piste opportunities from the top are superb, but should be attempted only in the company of a qualified guide.

The area divides naturally into four main sectors: Pic Blanc, Signal de l'Homme/Auris, Signal/Villard-Reculas, and Oz/Vaujany. The central part of the skiing takes place immediately north-east of the resort on the sunny lower and middle slopes of Pic Blanc, served by the impressively efficient two stages of the 25-person DMC jumbo gondola. The first section climbs only 240m over the enormous area of green (beginner) runs and pedestrian trails close to the resort. It links in here with the two-stage Poutran jumbo gondola coming up from Oz-en-Oisans. Above it, the rocky massif markedly steepens and the second stage serves red (intermediate) and blue (easy) runs of 600m vertical, interestingly varied but often too busy for comfort. The second stage gives access to the cable car to the summit of Pic Blanc itself.

From the top, two black runs, the Sarenne and the Château Noir, take you all the way down into the Sarenne Gorge and are, at 16km, the longest black runs in the Alps. However, it should be pointed out that they accrue most of their length from the long run-out along the bottom of the gorge before you take the Alpauris chair to return to the resort. Only pitches of the Sarenne are really black (34°). Both runs are narrow in places and can produce awkward bottlenecks, but the views are quite spectacular. Off-piste variations include the Grand Sablat further round the shoulder of the mountain, the Combe du Loup and a long and tricky descent via the Couloir de Fiole.

The glacier also provides a small summer ski area. The front face of the mountain is accessed via a tunnel 200m below the summit and an awkward path at the end of it. The mogul field which follows can be extremely daunting when snow has not fallen for some weeks. It is prone to ice and is often closed until the moguls have softened in the afternoon sunlight. A 20-minute climb from the cable car station takes

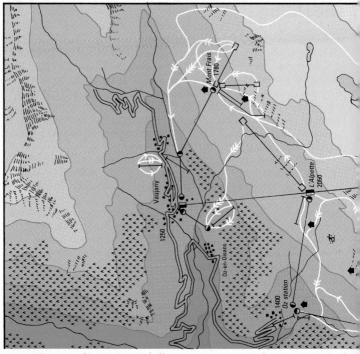

you to the top of La Pyramide, off-piste starting point for over 2000m of vertical bringing you down through a range of gulleys and open snow-fields all the way to Vaujany or Oz. The top can be extremely icy and ropes may be needed to negotiate the steeper couloirs in packed snow conditions.

From the mid-station of the main gondola (2100m), the Lièvre Blanc chair gives access to a lot of good, challenging skiing. It serves its own red piste, but also leads to another more notable red, the satisfyingly secluded Balme, which takes you all the way down to Alpe d'Huez. Above it another chair goes on up to Clocher de Mâcle, starting point for a choice of interesting black runs. These include a beautiful long run (the Combe Charbonière) past Europe's highest disused coal mine and from there either down into the Sarenne gorge or round to the resort. The short run down from Clocher de Mâcle to Lac Blanc is steep (33°), but the snow is usually good and there are some interesting off-piste variations.

The mid-station of the main gondola (2100m) is also accessible from the eastern end of Alpe d'Huez, via the Flèche Sarenne gondola, which takes you up to the Plat des Marmottes at 2300m. The second stage is planned to provide alternative access to the glacier. It serves a series of worthwhile blues and reds of its own, including the red Canyon run back down into Alpe d'Huez.

The Signal de l'Homme/Auris sector is on the eastern side of the steep Gorge de Sarenne. Auris, the first and the poorest of the Alpe

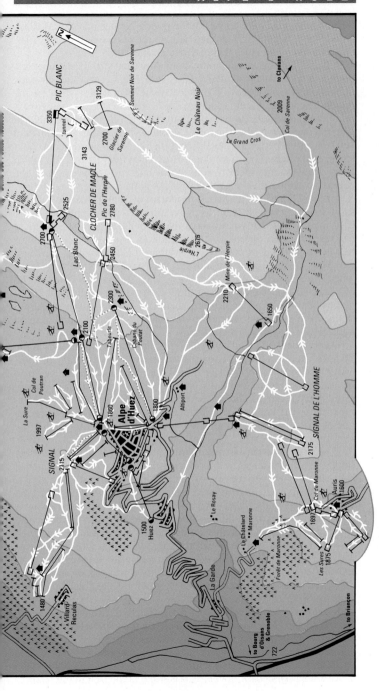

d'Huez offspring, used to be rather poorly connected. Alpe d'Huez-based skiers faced a difficult and slow journey home at the end of the day. However, the Auris Express detachable chair, which opened in 1991-2, has cut the journey time from 30 minutes to 15 minutes and done much to make this under-skied sector more attractive. Its wide open north-facing slopes often keep some of the best snow in the region. The whole mountainside is of intermediate steepness and much of it becomes covered in moguls, both on- and off-piste. A magnificent long red goes down from the top of Signal de l'Homme to the hamlet of Le Chételard. The return drag-lift and the black run beside it are both steepish in places. Return to Alpe d'Huez is via the Chalvet chair which gives access to intermediate runs down into the Bergers end of the resort, or via the path along the floor of the gorge and the Alpauris chair.

Signal (2115m) is the second mountain of Alpe d'Huez, a rounded snow-covered peak adjacent to the resort itself which provides open, easy, intermediate runs easily accessible from the heart of the village. It has recently been covered by snow-cannon. The front face becomes heavily mogulled. A motorway around the shoulder provides a fast and easy blue, much loved by second- and third-week skiers. Behind Signal, longer runs drop down the open west-facing slopes above the satellite of Villard-Reculas. Gentle runs at the top are served by the Petit Prince drag, but there is no easy route all the way down for faint-hearted skiers. Even the green run alongside the lowest drag (Cloudit) can be transformed into a small mogul field.

Oz-en-Oisans and Vaujany have some of the most modern lifts in the ski area. Vaujany's home slopes are on a mainly gentle mountain shelf, with much steeper and rockier terrain above and below, reached by a six-seater gondola to Montfrais, the nursery slopes and main congregation area. It can also be reached by the first stage of the 160-person cable car to the higher point of l'Alpette. In 1992-3, 85 new snow-cannon at a cost of £2 million greatly improved the snow coverage in the sector.

Four short lifts fan out from Montfrais serving wide, easy nursery slopes, together with a few intermediate variants, and an abundance of light off-piste between the trees, which is fun to ski after a snowfall. The Vallonet chair at the northern extremity of the area gives access to red and black runs to the valley. The black Roche Melon is a local favourite in good winter snow conditions. These runs merge with the blue from Montfrais to terminate at the gondola mid-station near La Villette. A chair-lift connects Montfrais with the cable car mid-station at l'Alpette, with an easy blue taking you back down. Vaujaniate, the run down into La Villette, has been completely rebuilt as a wide blue piste and is served by a battery of snow-cannon. A gondola links the hamlet with Vaujany itself.

A red run, open at the top, but narrowing to a path with some usually rocky off-piste options from it, takes you down from l'Alpette to Oz Station. A 12-person gondola brings you back up again. Alternatively, you can ski across the resort to the Poutran gondola, which takes you up in two stages to the mid-station of the DMC gondola above Alpe d'Huez. The skiing back down to Oz is some of the best in the resort, a wonderful variety of easy blue or a really testing red down a long gulley. The off-piste alternative from the ridge separating Oz from Alpe d'Huez, known as Le Magicien, is a gloriously steep powder field, which filters into the tree-studded gorge at the bottom. It is prone to avalanche and should only be attempted in the morning and with a guide. The bottom half of the runs to Oz have suffered greatly in the past from poor snow conditions throughout a substantial part of the winter, although the installation of snow-cannon has now alleviated this.

Skiers based in Vaujany or Oz can also join the Pic Blanc sector via the second stage of the Vaujany cable car to the Dôme des Petites Rousses (2808m), slightly above the starting point for the Pic Blanc cable car and linked by an easy red piste. There are numerous off-piste opportunities from here down towards Vaujany.

Mountain restaurants

The ski area is dotted with reasonable mountain restaurants. The Poutran and the Piano Bar in Oz are particularly praised for the quality of their food with 'prices half those of anywhere else'. Auberge de l'Alpette, a stone hut below the top of the Alpette gondola on the Oz piste, offers simple farmhouse fare and home-made cheeses. Les Airelles at the top of the Les Airelles nursery drag is good value for money in a rustic atmosphere. La Bergerie at Villard-Reculas is a farm-house museum, which doubles as a restaurant in a particularly attractive setting. Le Tetras in Auris is said to produce 'the finest pizzas in the Alps'. We have also had glowing reports of the Forêt de Maronne below Auris, as well as the Chalet du Lac Besson on the cross-country trail between the DMC and Alpette. Combe Haute in the Sarenne Gorge has a welcoming feel to it and is renowned for its salads.

Beginners and children

The ESF has 300 instructors with offices in Alpe d'Huez, Auris, Oz and Vaujany. The International Ski School teaches in English and there is a snowboard school, Planète Surf. Reports of the ESF are mixed. Lack of English-speaking instructors is a repeated criticism however: 'There were 14 pupils at the start of the week, and none at the end', said one disgruntled reporter. Another commented that it was a 'waste of money: my girlfriend learned more from me'. One group of complete beginners was unlucky with its instructor and did not get a particularly good introduction. However, intermediates from the same party who took a private instructor had a totally different story and were full of praise. The International Ski School offers classes restricted to eight.

The ESF Club des Oursons takes children from four years at Grandes Rousses and at Bergers. Both have playgrounds and their own drag-lifts. The International Ski School runs the Club des Mickeys et Papotines which starts at three-and-a-half years old and the Club des Marmottes for 5- to 12-year-olds. The Club des Eterlous, next to the Club Med building, takes children from 2 to 14 years. There is a particularly well-equipped ski kindergarten in Vaujany starting at three months up to three years, and a garderie in Oz.

The resort

Alpe d'Huez first opened as a resort in 1931 with a handful of beds. At the time of the 1968 Olympics it was little more than a one-street alpine village dominated by a futuristic modern church. The massive, apparently uncontrolled, building surge that followed saw the resort spread out in all directions in a profusion of styles.

Traffic remains a problem, although it must be pointed out that as there is no through-road from the resort to anywhere else, it is more a question of overcrowded parking than busy main roads. A shuttle bus service takes skiers up to the slopes from the lower reaches of what is a steep resort for pedestrians. A bucket lift and a cross-resort chair also act as people-movers.

Shops are limited to a few designer boutiques, standard ski shops and some remarkably tacky T-shirt and souvenir establishments.

Accommodation

Accommodation in Alpe d'Huez is split between a wide range of self-catering apartments, a few tour operator chalets and a number of medium-priced hotels. Basically, the higher up the hill you are, the easier it is to get to and from the skiing. The hard core of one four-star and eight three-star hotels is supported by numerous family establishments. The Christina is friendly and charming and one of the few attractive chalet-style buildings at the top of the resort. The Chamois d'Or is a bright and comfortable hotel with a highly regarded restaurant. Supermarkets are considered adequate by reporters, but serious self-caterers drive down to the Ralleye supermarket in Bourg d'Oisans.

Eating out

Dining is an altogether important business in Alpe d'Huez, perhaps a legacy from its more exclusive days. Au P'tit Creux, Le Chamois d'Or, La Pomme de Pin, and the Lyonnais all vie with each other as the best centres for haute cuisine in town. Less exotic restaurants include Chez La Mère Michel and Le Coin Chaud ('great crêpes') and the Pinocchio for pizzas.

Après-ski

The Lincoln Pub, the Underground, and Apples and Pears are all popular, together with La Belle Etoile and Le Grizzly. The Eclipse, Sporting Patinoire and Le Chalet have a rather smarter image. Alpe d'Huez sports four discos, two of which are the Igloo and Crystal. All were considered 'overpriced with boring music; there are better ways of getting rid of what was a lot of money'. A week's lift pass covers entry to the swimming pool, ice rink and sports hall. Other sports on offer include ice-driving, parapente, hang-gliding, snow-mobiling and indoor climbing.

Oz Station 1350m (4,429ft)

This small village is purpose-built above the old village of Oz-en-Oisans. It is reached by a fast all-weather road from the valley in only 20 minutes, thereby providing an excellent back-door into the lift system. At present the resort consists of two large apartment blocks built of stone and wood in pleasing harmony with the environment, and two gondola stations branching upwards in different directions. Shops are limited to a surprisingly reasonably priced supermarket, two sports shops, and a newsagent. It has its own ski school and nursery slopes as well as a crèche. Nightlife is limited to a couple of bars.

TOURIST OFFICE
As Alpe d'Huez

TOUR OPERATORS
none

Auris-en-Oisans 1600m (5,249ft)

Auris is again a collection of apartments and the Beau Site hotel which mainly attracts French guests. The resort has 4,000 guest beds and is marginally more exciting by night than the other satellites. It is somewhat isolated from the bulk of the skiing in Les Grandes-Rousses, but well positioned for outings to Les Deux Alpes, Serre Chevalier, La Grave and Briançon. Down the hillside in the old village are the more traditional Auberge de la Forêt and Les Emeranches hotels, as well as chalets and gîtes to rent. Over the hill behind the resort and served by pistes and a lift is the Forêt de Maronne hotel.

TOURIST OFFICE
As Alpe d'Huez

TOUR OPERATORS
none

Villard-Reculas 1500m (4,921ft)

The rustic old village is linked by chair and drag into the ski area. Much has been done in recent years to renovate the village, and plans are afoot to build a gondola down here. It has one hotel and a number of quite new apartments to add to the converted cowsheds and barns. Sustenance is provided by one small supermarket and a couple of small bars and restaurants. The one-track road between here and Oz/Vaujany should not be attempted in any but the driest of conditions.

TOURIST OFFICE
As Alpe d'Huez

TOUR OPERATORS
none

Vaujany 1250m (4,101ft)

Vaujany is a sleepy farming community which, but for a quirk of fate, would have faded into oblivion. Compensation for a valley hydro-electric scheme made the village rich beyond its residents' wildest dreams. Oz benefited to a lesser extent from the scheme and the two villages plunged their millions into the winter sports industry. This explains why, in the case of Vaujany, an apparently impoverished mountain village manages to own a state-of-the-art 160-person cable car which ranks among the top three in the world. No one has yet seen a queue here,

Skiing facts: Alpe d'Huez

TOURIST OFFICE
38750 Alpe d'Huez, Dauphiné
Tel 33 76 80 35 41
Fax 33 76 80 69 54

THE RESORT
By road Calais 916km
By rail Grenoble 65km
By air Lyon 2 hrs, Grenoble 90 mins
Visitor beds 26,000 (84% apartments, 11% hotels, 4% guesthouses, 1% chalets)
Transport free ski-bus

THE SKIING
Longest run the Sarenne, 16km (black)
Number of lifts 86
Number of trails/pistes 107 (36% beginner, 28% easy, 26% intermediate, 10% difficult)
Total of trails/pistes 220km
Nursery slopes 8 including extensive nursery runs immediately above Alpe d'Huez. All satellites have nursery slopes
Summer skiing limited, open for 1 mth in July
Snowmaking 100 hectares covered

LIFT PASSES
Area pass (covers whole Grandes-Rousses area) 696-870FF for 6 days, includes entry to swimming-pool and option of day's skiing in either Les Deux Alpes, Serre Chevalier/Briançon, or the Milky Way. Reduction at La Grave
Day pass 180FF weekdays, 168FF weekends
Half-day pass 125FF weekdays, 117FF weekends
Beginners 2 free lifts at Alpe d'Huez
Children under 13 yrs, 557-696FF for 6 days. Free for 5 yrs and under
Pensioners 60 yrs and over, as children. Free for 70 yrs and over
Credit cards accepted yes

SKI SCHOOLS
Adults ESF, 5½ hrs per day, 800FF for 6 days. International (SEI), 4 hrs per day, from 1,010FF. Planète Surf, 990FF for 6 days
Children ESF, 5½ hrs per day, 650FF for 6 days. International 4½ hrs per day, from 845FF for 6 days

Private lessons ESF, 150FF per hr for 1-2 people. International from 165FF per hr. Planète Surf, 160FF
Special courses snowboarding, monoskiing, moguls, freestyle, slalom, off-piste skiing, competition
Guiding companies Bureau des Guides

CROSS-COUNTRY
Ski school ESF
Loipe location and size 50km divided into 2 difficult and 2 easy circuits

CHILDCARE
Non-ski kindergarten Les Eterlous, 2 yrs and over, 205FF including lunch. Crèche Vaujany, 3 mths-3 yrs, 500FF for 6 days, extra 20FF per day for lunch
Ski kindergarten ESF Club des Oursons at Bergers and at Grandes-Rousses, 3 yrs and over, 650FF per wk, 60FF per hr, 9.45am-12.45pm and 2.30pm-5pm, 3pm-5.30pm after mid-Feb.
International Ski School Club des Mickeys et des Papotines, 3½ yrs and over. Club des Marmottes, 5-12 yrs. Les Eterlous, 2-14 yrs, 205FF per day, 8.30am-6pm
Babysitting list available from tourist office

OTHER SPORTS
Ice-driving, snow-mobiling, snow-shoeing, parapente, hang-gliding, swimming, helicopter rides, skating, curling, indoor tennis, indoor climbing, fitness centre

WHAT'S NEW
● 85 snow-cannon covering Vaujany/Oz sector ● skating rink at Vaujany

FOOD AND DRINK PRICES
Coffee 7FF, bottle of house wine 70FF, beer 12FF, dish of the day 50FF

TOUR OPERATORS
Activity Travel, Bladon Lines, Brittany Ferries, Club Med, Crystal, Enterprise, Equity Total Ski, Hoverspeed, Inghams, Kings Ski Club, Made to Measure, Neilson, Ski Airtours, SkiBound, Ski Miquel, Ski Thomson, Skiworld, STS, Touralp

but who is complaining? Considerable, but considered, development is taking place and a number of new chalets and apartments are being built, but the community retains its rural atmosphere.

There are four simple hotels in the village centre. The Etendard, closest to the lift station, is the après-ski hub. The Rissiou is under British winter management and produces a much higher standard of food and accommodation than you might expect in a village of this size. The Hotel Cîmes, across the road, is a friendly little hostelry. The Grandes-Rousses Hotel is less central. The Voltige disco is crowded with mainly Belgian teens and twenties and positively swings. The Sabot is the more sophisticated alternative. Shopping is limited to a single grocery store and a ski shop.

TOURIST OFFICE
As Alpe d'Huez

TOUR OPERATORS
Ski Peak

Les Arcs, Savoie

ALTITUDE 1600-2000m (5,248-6,560ft)

● ●

Good points big ski area, *ski évolutif*, skiing convenience, child facilities, extensive off-piste skiing, late-season holidays (Arc 2000), reliable resort-level snow, easy access, car-free resort
Bad points little for non-skiers, lack of alpine charm, inadequate mountain restaurants, limited après-ski
Linked or nearby resorts Bourg-St-Maurice (l), Peisey-Nancroix (l), La Plagne (n), Le Pré (l), Vallandry (l)

Les Arcs was founded in the 1960s by Robert Blanc, one of the fathers of modern French skiing and the European sponsor of *ski évolutif*, the graduated-length teaching method which is still used in the resort today. At a time when there were more skiers than beds in the French Alps, Blanc together with ex-Olympic racer Emile Allais conceived the idea of a purpose-built resort divided into separate accommodation units at different altitudes on the slopes above his home town of Bourg-St-Maurice.

Robert Blanc died tragically in 1980 in an avalanche while searching for two German skiers believed to be missing above Les Arcs (the skiers turned up alive and well at home in Germany). Had he lived, he would have seen Les Arcs celebrate its 25th anniversary in 1993 as one of the most popular resorts in France. What would have pleased him still more was that the style of architecture he chose, which was modern and yet in counterpoint to the Savoyard environment, has worn its years well and in the environmentally conscious world of today is still not displeasing.

Les Arcs is not one, but three quite separate, predominantly self-catering resorts linked by 150km of skiing served by 77 lifts, a good intermediate snow-sure playground with some steep skiing to be found on the slopes of the 3226m Aiguille Rouge. Arc 1600, the lowest village, first opened in 1968. Arc 1800 is the heart of the resort with most of the accommodation and shops and almost all the après-ski life. It also provides the best access to the ski area. Arc 2000, which opened in 1979, is one of the very few resorts in Europe at this altitude and is of limited appeal to all but the most dedicated of skiers. If you want to ski in early May, then this is the place to be. One reporter succinctly describes it as 'a totally characterless garage in the sky'.

The skiing is extensive, interesting and suitable for all grades of skier, with plenty of easy runs above 1800 and 2000 and more than enough challenge on the slopes of the Aiguille Rouge for most skiers. The lift system is well thought out and the accommodation is nearly all conveniently placed for skiing. Les Arcs has two great selling points: *ski*

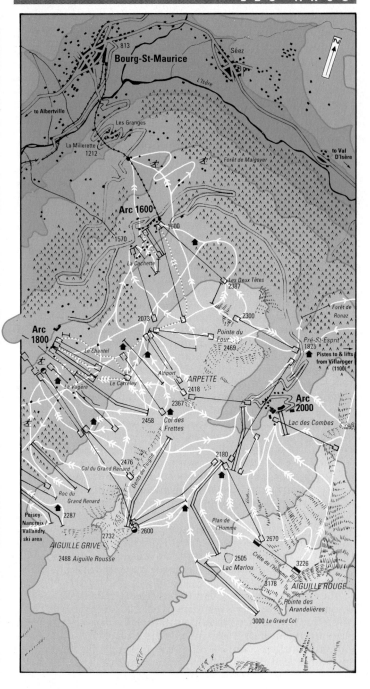

évolutif and what the French call *les nouvelles glisses*.

Ski évolutif is the European mutation of an American learning method where you begin on one-metre skis and progress in length as you improve in technique. *Les nouvelles glisses*, for which there is no real translation, are all the other on-snow activities which first became popular in Les Arcs. These started with monoskiing (now largely defunct) and progressed to snowboarding and speed-skiing by way of a host of intermediaries. For reasons that are not always clear, Les Arcs has managed to act as a sounding board for all that is new in the sport.

All three resorts are served by a road up from Bourg-St-Maurice. The construction of the funicular to Arc 1600 has, however, transformed communications. It departs from behind the railway station and takes seven minutes, with one mid-way stop at the village of Les Granges. Bourg is a real town with a good Saturday market, real locals and reasonable prices, not least in its restaurants and hotels. Les Arcs also has piste links with the neighbouring wooded ski area of Peisey-Nancroix-Vallandry, which provides the best bad-weather skiing in the region. There is extensive (and expensive) parking at all three resort centres, but a car is of little use in the resort itself.

The skiing
Top 3226m (10,581ft) bottom 850m (2,788ft)

The broad north-west-facing mountain flank above Arc 1600 and Arc 1800 is well served by chairs and drag-lifts to a ridge of rocky peaks, with skiing up to about 2400m. **Mountain access** is via a choice of chairs or the Transarc gondola from Villards up to the Col de la Chal. On the other side of this ridge is a wide bowl with Arc 2000 in the pit; from here lifts rise to the 3226m summit of the Aiguille Rouge, which offers long and serious runs down to the hamlet of Le Pré outside Villaroger as well as back to Arc 2000.

The runs above Arc 1800 are open and generally provide gentle, cruising skiing, a satisfying mixture of blue (easy) and red (intermediate) runs, which make you feel that you are getting mileage out of your holiday. However, these slopes, which are extremely popular with Arc 1800-based skiers, catch the afternoon sun and particularly late in the season tend to be icy in the morning and slushy in the afternoon. The ski area naturally connects with lifts up from Vallandry, Plan Peisey and Nancroix, between Les Arcs and La Plagne. This is an excellent area for skiing in bad weather, with plenty of good runs on- and off-piste through the trees. Off-piste links to Montchavin give access to the whole of La Plagne. Plans to link the two continue to meet a level of opposition from both resorts, which argue correctly that big is not necessarily beautiful.

The skiing directly above Arc 1600 is steeper and equally wooded, although the snow cover is not nearly as reliable. Given the right conditions, there is some excellent off-piste through the trees as well as some broad, interesting trails. These are served by a fan of chair-lifts from Arc 1600; from the top of these it is possible to ski right the way down to Bourg or at least to the funicular station at Les Granges. The Gollet chair gives access to an easy blue run to Arc 1800.

The bowl above Arc 2000 has easy runs down into it from several points along the ridge reached from Arc 1600 and Arc 1800. There are some more difficult pistes including l'Ours (from Arpette), which deserves its black grading. The run to Pré-St-Esprit through the Comborcières valley has some exciting off-piste variants reached by chair-lifts from both sides of the ridge. The red run down from Col des Frettes has challenging options near the top, and goes through a scenic, often crowded, narrow valley lower down.

The terrain around Arc 2000 provides wide, open intermediate skiing with good snow against the spectacular backdrop of the Aiguille rouge, served by a fast chair and a cable car. Unfortunately the summit is closed when conditions are not good, which is often. From the exposed open peak there are magnificent views across to the glaciers of Mont Pourri (3779m). The off-piste is steep and rocky and the pistes are long and challenging. The red run from the top is not in itself difficult, but skirts some very steep slopes marked with dramatic warning signs, unnerving if visibility is poor. An exceptional black run of over 2100m vertical descends from the top the whole way down to Le Pré. It covers an enormous variety of terrain, from steep moguls and narrow gulleys to open pastureland. The lower half can be reached from Arc 2000 via the Lanchettes chair-lift.

The face of the Aiguille Rouge above Arc 2000 is the setting for the Olympic speed-skiing run. High altitude, combined with a 45° slope and a long run-out towards the resort, has produced a world record speed of 229.299kph. The women's record stands at 219.245kph. The racers in their plastic-skin suits and streamlined helmets use 240cm skis for their death-defying descents, which can be viewed from the Dou de l'Homme chair-lift in the spring. Anyone can have a go for 50FF, which includes the loan of helmet and downhill skis; novices start from much lower down.

The Dou de l'Homme chair gives access to several black pistes offering long slopes of sustained steepness and usually formidable bumps. The drags to the Grand Col on the south shoulder of the mountain serve good, high red and black pistes; and the red from there back to the middle of the bowl has the option of a big mogul field, which keeps its snow very well. Exciting off-piste runs start from the Grand Col and go behind the Aiguille Rouge to Villaroger. Equally, you can ski with a guide in the opposite direction from below the 2732m peak of the Aiguille Grive to Nancroix and Plan Peisey.

Despite the comprehensive network of lifts, queues can be annoying at peak holiday times, particularly out of Arc 1600 in the mornings and in the Arc 2000 bowl at lunchtime. The Aiguille Rouge cable car attracts mighty crowds in fine weather and snow conditions. Snow-cannon operate on two runs directly above 1800, on the long piste to 1600 served by the Cachette chair and on one nursery slope in 1600. Each part of the resort has a floodlit piste.

Mountain restaurants

Eating places on the mountain are the weak spot in a resort which otherwise caters well for almost everyone's needs provided they are skiers.

Restaurants are few and far between and most skiers tend to return to Les Arcs for lunch or ski down to one of the low-lying villages. The runs below 2000 and down to Le Pré are the best equipped in the whole area with the Belliou la Fumée at Pré-St-Esprit, the cosy little Solliet on the Villaroger run, and the Aiguille Rouge and La Ferme in Le Pré. The latter is a charming little satellite of Villaroger, which links into the ski area via a chair-lift.

Prices are markedly lower in the Peisey-Nancroix-Vallandry sector and reporters here recommend the Poudreuse above Vallandry, Chez Felix ('the best in this area'), Le Blanchot and Le Poudreuse ('spartan, with a good chef and large portions'). La Tanière, on the piste above 1600, has 'loads of atmosphere and good food'.

Beginners and children

The thinking behind *ski évolutif* is that starting with one-metre skis and gradually moving up to longer ones as your skiing progresses, speeds up the whole learning process. Its critics argue that if you never learn the snowplough you have no technique to fall back on when conditions become difficult. Whatever the answer, it is certainly a much faster tuition method for adults who want to be able to move around the mountain and enjoy themselves on skis as soon as possible. Indeed, one reporter writes of her 'absolute amazement' at her husband's ability to attempt a steep black run 'albeit with more confidence than style' after only one week.

The three ski schools all teach *évolutif* and there seems little to choose between them. Reporters complain that classes can be too large in high season, but the standard of tuition seems to be extremely high. It is perhaps just as well that *ski évolutif* does not involve long days spent on nursery slopes, as Les Arcs is not ideally provided with these. Areas are roped off near the resort for the first stages of *ski évolutif* and for children's ski playgrounds. Arc 1800, in particular, caters well for near-beginners, with a long, wide and varied slope above the resort.

We have glowing reports of off-piste guiding by the ski schools. There are skiing and non-skiing kindergartens in 1600 and in 1800, but not, to the chagrin of one reporter, in 2000. The ski schools offer lessons for 3-year-olds and upwards at 2000 and in the other villages, 'but you cannot expect a 5-year-old to want to ski all day, every day, for a whole week'. Hotel La Cachette at 1600 has a crèche for babies from four months old and upwards, with a fine reputation over many years. It also runs its own ski kindergarten.

The resort

Arc 1600 is situated in a stand of pine trees. It is the first of the accommodation centres you reach as you climb the serpentine road from Bourg-St-Maurice. It is also served by the high-speed funicular railway. It is a friendly little resort with its own devotees, mainly French families, who return here year after year. Its major drawback is the height, or rather lack of it, which means poor or no resort-level snow for a large part of the season. At the heart of it is a horseshoe of buildings around the Hotel La Cachette, with sunny terraces in front of the shops and restaurants; it has a more personal feel to it than its neighbours. Arc 2000 is a cluster of undistinguished apartment buildings and a couple of hotels, dominated by Club Med.

To the south-west in the heart of the ski area lies Arc 1800, the undisputed capital of Les Arcs. This cosmopolitan resort is divided into the three sub-villages of Charvet, Charmettoger and Villards. Nearly all the apartment blocks are ski-in ski-out. Charmettoger is the most recent development, a series of modern chalet-style buildings clad in wood, on the edge of the forest. Villards is the ski school meeting place right on the slopes. Charvet is the commercial core of the resort containing most of the shops and restaurants, a hotel and the original apartments.

Both Arc 1600 and Arc 1800 command magnificent views north-west across to Mont Blanc and west along the valley into the setting sun. They are both compact clusters, with curving forms hugging the mountain, designed to ensure that many of the apartments and hotels have sunny terraces and balconies. Wood has been widely used, but the original buildings are now showing their age. Each centre has an adequate range of shops, but we have reports of post-skiing supermarket queues in all three villages of 1800.

There are several supermarkets in Bourg and a hypermarket on the outskirts of the town. Frequent day-time buses run between Arc 1600 and Arc 1800 until 8pm and occasionally to Arc 2000 until 6pm. If driving, it is wise to leave your car in the huge, free car-park at the Bourg-St-Maurice funicular station and buy your pass at the office there. The funicular runs every 20 minutes from approximately 7.30am to 7.00pm. A free shuttle operates from 1600, although arrangements for getting luggage across each resort are far from perfect.

Accommodation

Most of the accommodation is in apartments and most of those are in Arc 1800. The older *résidences*, particularly in Charvet and 1600, are distinctly tacky and their compact 1960s design was clearly borrowed from the standard Portuguese sardine tin. The newer ones in the other two sub-villages are altogether more superior. La Nova and Tournavelles in Villard are said to be of a high standard, together with the whole Charmettoger village. Studios in Grand d'Arbois in Villards are described by one of our reporters as 'warm, with lots of hot water and four minutes' walk across the shopping mall from the ski school meeting place'.

However, the resort has now sold off nearly all of its accommodation to outside property companies. Pierre et Vacances has acquired the lion's share, followed by Maeva; we are therefore likely to see a very welcome upgrading of most of the apartments over the next couple of years. The Golf Hotel in 1800 has now been completely renovated and the reception and bar area has finally emerged from its 1960s time-warp. Hotel Les Latitudes in Charmettoger is also strongly recommended by reporters. At 1600, Hotel La Cachette has a formidable reputation (see *Beginners and children*) for good service and excellent food. Hotel Trois Arcs at 1600 has been improved, but is still 'only an adequate two-star'.

At Arc 2000, the Hotel Aiguille Rouge is forever popular with reporters ('excellent value hotel with good food – very much the hub of the resort'). The Hotel Eldorador, also in 2000, is described as 'comfortable, but the food is not a patch on that of its sister hotel in La Plagne'. Club Med and Club Aquarius, now both under the same ownership, are also popular. The self-catering apartments here are generally in poor repair and their new ownership should bring the much needed redecoration.

Eating out

Les Arcs has a reasonable choice of restaurants, nearly all of them expensive. In Charvet, the Green restaurant in the Hotel du Golf is a formidable gourmet experience. L'Equipe specialises in fondue and other Savoyard dishes. The Laurus is also recommended. Pizzeria Le Flambadou is popular. In Villard, the Gargantus ('gigantic portions of pizza and pasta') and the Triangle Noir are both highly rated by reporters. In Arc 1600, La Cachette is recommended along with Restaurant l'Arcelle. La Tanière on the piste above the village is also open in the evening. In 2000, the Red Rock ('casual bar/formal dining room, live music') and St Jacques ('small, cosy, instructors' hangout') are both recommended. The Marloup is good for fondue and live jazz.

Après-ski

Arc 1800 and Arc 2000 both have skating rinks. The resort is not recommended either for cross-country skiers, except at Nancroix, or non-skiers. Several reporters have regretted the lack of a swimming-pool. There is a bowling alley in 1800 as well as a luge run which starts at the top of the Chantel lift; floodlit skiing takes place here two evenings a week. The three squash courts need to be booked. All three resorts have cinemas and horse-riding can be arranged close to the village of Arcs1600.

Later evening entertainment is livelier, although not exactly riotous, in 1800 than in the other two villages. Hotel du Golf has live jazz in the bar and is one of the main meeting places. Young British congregate at the Pub Russel and at the Arc en Ciel bar. The Carré Blanc in Villard together with Le Fair Way in Charvet are noisy and expensive discos. The nightlife in 2000 is described by one reporter as 'limited to non-existent'. The centre of action in 1600 is the Abreuvoir piano bar.

Bourg-St-Maurice 840m (2,755ft)

Visitors who enjoy France as opposed to French resorts and want to ski on a budget can consider staying in Bourg-St-Maurice. The construction of the funicular, which takes seven minutes to reach Arc 1600, conferred semi-resort status on the town. It has 10 small hotels including the comfortable l'Autantic, Au Bon Repos, Concorde, the Relais de La Vanoise, Le Petit St Bernard and La Petite Auberge. It is also possible to rent apartments by contacting the tourist board. The nightlife centres on a few bars including the inevitable Café de la Paix.

TOURIST OFFICE
73700 Bourg-St-Maurice, Savoie
Tel 33 79 07 04 92
Fax 33 79 07 24 90

TOUR OPERATORS
none

Skiing facts: Les Arcs

TOURIST OFFICE
BP 45, F-73706 Les Arcs, Savoie
Tel 33 79 41 55 45
Fax 33 79 07 45 96

THE RESORT
By road Calais 937km
By rail Bourg-St-Maurice 15km,
frequent buses and direct funicular to
Arc 1600
By air Geneva 3 hrs, Lyon 3 hrs,
Chambery 2½ hrs
Visitor beds 31,807 (89% apartments,
11% hotels)
Transport free shuttle bus between Arc
1600, 1800 and 2000

THE SKIING
Longest run L'Aiguille Rouge, 7km
(black)
Number of lifts 77
Number of trails/pistes 112 (22%
beginner, 31% easy, 31% intermediate,
16% difficult)
Total of trails/pistes 150km
Nursery slopes 11 lifts
Summer skiing none
Snowmaking 20 hectares covered

LIFT PASSES
Area pass (covers Les Arcs, Villaroger,
Peisey and Vallandry) 875FF for 6 days
Day pass 190FF
Half-day pass 135FF after 1pm
Beginners 3 free lifts – Combettes
(Arc 1600), Charvet (Arc 1800),
Lac des Combes (Arc 2000)
Children 7-12 yrs, 745FF for 6 days
Free for 7 yrs and under
Pensioners no reduction
Credit cards accepted yes

SKI SCHOOLS
Adults ESF (Arc 1600, 1800 and
2000), ESI/Arc Adventures (Arc 1800),
Virages (Arc 1800), all 108-120FF for a
half-day, 720-790FF for 6 days

Children ESF, ESI/Arc Adventures,
Virages, all 110-120FF for a half-day,
680-790FF for 6 days
Private lessons 170-185FF per hr
for 1-4 people
Special courses *ski évolutif*,
snowboarding, monoskiing
Guiding companies Vincent Terrisse

CROSS-COUNTRY
Ski schools ESF, ESI/Arc Adventure,
and Virages
Loipe location and size 15km total at
the 3 villages

CHILDCARE
Non-ski kindergarten Les Pommes de
Pin (Arc 1800), 1-6 yrs, 8.30am-6pm,
730FF for 6 days including lunch. Hotel
La Cachette (Arc 1600), 4 mths-12 yrs,
8.30am-6pm, 219FF per day
including lunch
Ski kindergarten Les Pommes de Pin
(Mini Club), 3-9 yrs, 9am-5pm,
1,255FF for 6 days including lunch.
Hotel La Cachette, 4-9 yrs, 219FF per
day, 75FF per day extra for lunch
Babysitting list available from tourist
office

OTHER SPORTS
Parapente, luge-ing, skating, squash,
freestyle snowboarding, bowling,
fitness centres, climbing wall

FOOD AND DRINK PRICES
Coffee 8FF, bottle of house wine 45FF,
beer 15FF, dish of the day 65FF

TOUR OPERATORS
Club Med, Crystal, Direct Ski,
Enterprise, Equity Total Ski,
Hoverspeed, Made to Measure,
Neilson, Optimum Ski Courses,
SkiBound, Ski Choice, Ski Europe,
Ski Tal, Ski Thomson, Skiworld,
Touralp, UCPA

Peisey-Nancroix-Vallandry 1350-1600m (4,428-5,248ft)

This cluster of villages at the extreme south-western end of the ski area has been a small winter holiday centre since 1945, unknown to all but a few French families who wanted some peace and quiet coupled with undemanding skiing. Its linkage into the Les Arcs system changed it little, but it does offer a rural and much cheaper accommodation base for the region. Peisey is the more traditional farming community and Nancroix is the starting point for 40km of cross-country trails. Plan Peisey and Vallandry are the ski resorts connected by gondola to Peisey at 1350m in the valley below. It has its own ski school, as well as non-ski and ski kindergartens.

The hotels are simple; we have a good report of Le Bon Acceuil and a poor one of the Emeraude ('a slightly glorified youth hostel, strictly functional with no carpets. The food was reminiscent of school, but less edible'). Nightlife is confined to drinking with the locals in a few bars. There is, however, quite a wide choice of restaurants. A car is an advantage.

TOURIST OFFICE
Syndicat d'Initiative,
73210 Savoie
Tel 33 79 07 94 28
Fax 33 79 07 95 34

TOUR OPERATORS
Ski Tal, Touralp

Chamonix, Haute Savoie

ALTITUDE 1040m (3,411ft)

••

Good points spectacular scenery, large ski area, tough runs, extensive off-piste and ski-touring, variety of après-ski, late-season holidays, short airport transfer, suitable for weekend skiing, facilities for non-skiers
Bad points lack of skiing convenience, lift queues, limited easy runs, antiquated lift system, limited mountain restaurants, heavy traffic
Linked or nearby resorts Argentière (n), Courmayeur (l), Les Houches (n), Megève (n), St-Gervais (n)

Chamonix claims with some justification to be the climbing and skiing capital of the world. Certainly it offers some of the toughest challenges of both disciplines and it is not a place for beginners at either. The headstones in the little churchyard, from Victorian *alpiniste* Edward Whymper to modern-day guides Patrick Vallençant and Jean-Marc Boivin, serve as benchmarks to the eternal struggle of man against mountain.

In 1741 two English explorers, William Windham and Richard Pococke, took three days to reach the Chamonix Valley from Geneva, rather than the 90 minutes it now takes along the Autoroute Blanche. Their party of 13 expected to encounter 'savages' along the way and was consequently armed to the teeth; Pococke, further to confuse the harmless peasants they actually encountered, was fresh from a trip to the Levant and was for reasons best known to himself, dressed as an Arab.

What they discovered was the Mer de Glace, the awesome tumble of seracs from the glacier above the hamlet which has acted as a magnet over the centuries for tourists from all over the world. Towering over the whole region is the majestic peak of Mont Blanc. It was eventually conquered, according to the history books, by a young Chamonix crystal hunter called Jacques Balmat in 1786, although the honour quite probably belonged to his companion, Dr. Paccard.

Victorians and Edwardians viewed Chamonix as an essential port of call on the Grand Tour. A collection of large and elaborate holiday mansions sprang up on the hillside above the town and its railway station. In 1924 it was chosen to host the very first Winter Olympics, a fact which the tourist board still trumpets today. Not a lot of people know that the Games failed to include a single alpine ski event, nor was skiing actually accorded Olympic status until two years after the competitors had

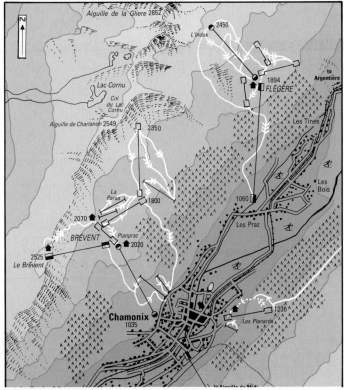

packed up and gone home. Today Chamonix thrives on its dual season for sightseers, skiers and summer climbers.

In fact, Chamonix like Zermatt derives more of its income from non-skiers than skiers. Its greatest draw is the Aiguille du Midi cable car, the top of which at 3842m is still 1000m below the summit of Mont Blanc. Its passengers are not skiers (except those undertaking the Vallée Blanche and other more radical off-piste), but camera-toting tourists.

Chamonix's popularity as a destination for British skiers continues to increase and accounts for over 20 per cent of winter visitors, most of whom come here, secure in the knowledge of what awaits them, to seek the serious off-piste offered in particular on the Grand Montets above the neighbouring village of Argentière. Others are frankly disappointed at the six main and three minor separate ski areas, most of which have to be reached on usually crowded buses.

Chamonix is the definition of skiing inconvenience. A number of reporters complain that the piste-grooming is poor, 'runs are simply not up to the standard of Austria and we found all sorts of hazards'. Chamonix aficionados grin with delight at these words. It is precisely this untamed mountain environment which is so attractive to its devout communicants, although the accompanying level of machismo is often hard to stomach. The town makes no secret of the fact that it has the

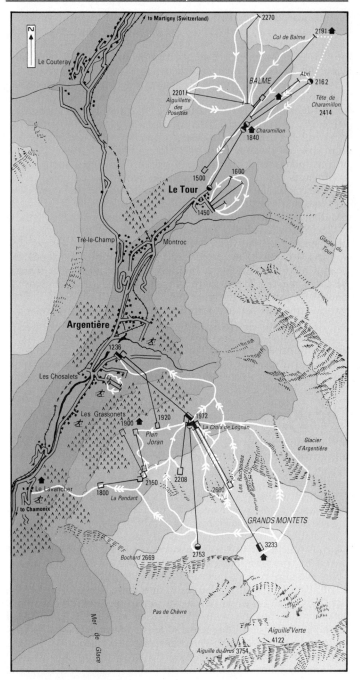

highest accident mortality rate among tourists of any comparable resort, albeit mostly among climbers. The skiing is superlative, but the drawback is that to realise 50 per cent of the potential available you need to be, if not an expert, at least a solidly competent off-piste skier. Quite simply, there is more convenient piste-skiing elsewhere.

Chamonix stands permanently in awe of the might of its mountain. It also stands, quite literally, in its shadow for a considerable part of the winter. It can be a cold and forbidding place with its own, not always agreeable, microclimate dictated by Mont Blanc. Before the onset of bad weather a distinctive hat-shaped cloud hovers around its peak and from up to 200km away skiers will be forecasting fresh snow. Chamonix attracts more than its fair share of storms. It can be a sunny day in Courmayeur 35km away through the Mont Blanc tunnel, while Chamonix stoically bears the brunt of a blizzard. But the converse is also true, and when the sun shines on the glaciers there are few more beautiful alpine panoramas, and the snow is exceptional.

The main alternative to staying in Chamonix itself is the small village of Argentière up the valley towards the pass into Switzerland (and Verbier). Its much sunnier position, convenient nursery slopes and nearby intermediate skiing at Le Tour make it a much more sensible base for families. A main road running through the village centre is the principal drawback. At the other end of the valley, Les Houches has its own intermediate ski area with good nursery slopes. St-Gervais and Megève are nearby. All these resorts are linked by an efficient, if at peak times somewhat oversubscribed, ski-bus network and are included in the main Chamonix lift pass, which covers 600km of skiing. Distances are large; it is possible, but not advisable, to switch areas during the course of a day. A car is of major assistance, some would say a necessity, in exploring the region.

The skiing
Top 3790m (12,431ft) bottom 1035m (3,395ft)

The Chamonix Valley has six real ski areas as well as four more small nursery and lower intermediate slope developments scattered along its length. The most serious skiing and the most awesome glacial terrain is on the south side of the valley on the lesser peaks of Mont Blanc. **Mountain access** is by a cable car and a quad chair from Argentière to the Grands Montets and by cable car from Chamonix itself to the Aiguille du Midi, completely renovated in 1990.

Chamonix's original reputation as a ski resort was based on Brévent, which is reached by a six-seater gondola reached by a steep walk from the edge of the town (or it can be accessed with less effort from the top of the two nursery slope button-lifts). Planpraz, the top of the gondola, is the start of a couple of blue (easy) runs down to the bottom of the Col Cornu chair, which in turn serves various pleasant red (intermediate) runs including the Combe de la Charlanon, which is patrolled but not necessarily pisted. The second stage is a dramatic cable car journey up to Le Brévent itself at 2525m, which offers spectacular views of the summit of Mont Blanc.

From here there is a choice of a moderate red or a more direct and consequently more challenging black (difficult) run, the Charles Bozon. The top-half of the black, which leads down towards Planpraz, is an impressive descent with an exposed and usually mogulled wall; the red follows a slightly more leisurely and longer line. From Planpraz you can ski down the blue trails on either side of the Parsa chair before picking up the new Nants black run, which falls away steeply through the trees before cutting sharply right and across the top of the nursery slopes to the bottom of the gondola. The alternative is to follow the old black (no longer a piste) from Planpraz down a long, narrow and demanding gulley followed by a seemingly endless, wide bumpy section. Whichever route you choose gives an impressive 1500m vertical.

La Flégère ski area, the next ridge along from Col Cornu, is in many ways similar terrain and the combination of the two would add up to a reasonable-sized ski area, although the much-vaunted and technically easy link between the two seems never to materialise. The area is reached by cable car from Les Praz, a suburb of Chamonix and a bus ride up the valley from the centre. The top section, served by enclosed chair, is less daunting, but has a greater variety of runs, mostly tough blues and some reds, which would be graded black elsewhere. There is only one run down to the valley, which starts off black with a near parallel red alternative and which later becomes all black and difficult. The off-piste in both areas is good, given the right snow conditions.

Argentière is the point of pilgrimage for all ski-bums and for others who want to experience some of the best off-piste skiing in the world. To do this you also have to cope with one of the worst and most overcrowded two-stage cable cars in the Alps. To be fair, valley queues to the 2000m Croix de Lognan have been greatly reduced at peak times and all but eliminated at others by the building of a quad chair, which takes you up to Plan Joran. From here you take a further chair and cut across back to Croix de Lognan; it can often be the quicker of the two routes and is the less stressful. Lognan is the bottom of the ski area, and the only pisted route to the valley is a single red, which becomes icy and rocky as much through over-use as from weather conditions.

From Lognan, the Bochard covered chair goes up to 2800m and serves a usually unprepared red with a welter of off-piste variants back down again. Particular care should be taken here as the off-piste is deceptively crevassed. Most of the main face between 2800m and 2000m is a wide open area of ridges and bowls interspersed with gullies and the occasional pitch so heavily tracked that it becomes a mogul field. The distinction between piste and off-piste is often in the eye of the beholder. It is easy to get lost in poor visibility, particularly off the Herse chair. For safety and also to realise the potential of this extraordinary area, a guide is a worthwhile investment. Do not be surprised to be waved through the queue for this chair by ski-bums in front of you – they know that every fifth chair has a hood, which affords useful protection against the elements. None of the runs is easy and few are pisted.

An alternative itinerary from Bochard is to take the 4.5km black Chamois across the Combe de la Pendant, which leads to steep wooded slopes above the hamlet of Le Lavancher, although the bowl is now served by a chair and a partially prepared piste; the opportunities for off-piste here are enormous and the terrain is extremely steep in places. The off-piste run down through the woods has several testing sections and the snow conditions at this altitude are often difficult. There is a free bus back from the bottom to Argentière.

But it is the Grands Montets cable car, the second stage from Lognan, which is the focus of attention. It carries only 700 passengers per hour. Not only can queues be horrific, but you have to pay a supplement for the privilege of riding it. When the two black pistes down are closed, only skiers with a guide are allowed to travel. This is serious alpine territory and the risks to anyone who strays out of the marked area are great indeed. Arrival is followed by an exposed 200-step metal staircase down to the departure point or by a shorter staircase up to a viewing platform, also the start of a vertiginous off-piste alternative.

The views from here are extraordinary and the runs, both the piste and the multitude of off-piste variations, are long (over 4km) and consistently challenging. The joint start of the pistes is steep, narrow and awkwardly mogulled, but soon flattens out to a more acceptable, but still seriously black, gradient. The Pylones run, as the name indicates, follows the line of the cable car. The Point de Vue skirts the edge of the glacier, giving an incredible view of this awesome panorama. Experts with a guide will tackle the steep, open powder fields on the top of the glacier itself before threading their way with extreme care through the tangled skein of seracs and crevasses.

Other off-piste descents include the Pas de Chèvre, an even more demanding west-facing slope. It is studded with a choice of severe couloirs leading down to the Mer de Glace and the Vallée Blanche run to Chamonix. No one should attempt any of these off-piste runs without a local qualified guide; the couloirs have gradients of 35° to 45°. There are other less radical off-piste descents.

Le Tour, beyond Argentière at the head of the Chamonix valley, is a sunny intermediate area which is prone to overcrowding at peak times. The three Vormaine drag-lifts are the best nursery slopes in the valley, but annoyingly the day passes for these are not valid on the main lift and *vice versa*. Main access to the ski area is via the Tour-Charamillon gondola to 1850m. From here a new detachable quad chair provides direct access to the Col de Balme. The runs, served by a series of drag-lifts, are all pleasant intermediate terrain. In good snow conditions the front-face run down to the gondola station offers some interesting off-piste opportunities. It is possible to ski with a guide over the back of the Col de Balme down into Switzerland.

Les Houches is a delightful and often under-rated ski area, which tends to lose its identity in the overall might of the Chamonix Valley but could qualify as a resort in its own right. The skiing is reached either by the newly renovated cable car with a 40 per cent capacity increase, or a gondola from either end of the village over steep, tree-lined slopes to either side of the 1653m Col de Voza. It is also accessible two or three times a day by a scenic mountain railway from Le Fayet and St-Gervais.

From the two main arrival points of Bellevue (1820m) and Prarion (1860m), long, wide trails lead down through the trees back to Les Houches. The Noire des Houches is an exacting international downhill course, which starts near Prarion. The alternative and much longer Bleue des Houches meanders gently down to the bottom of the gondola. A small network of drag-lifts between Col de Voza and Prarion serves a wide slope of about 300m vertical; these are suitable for beginners and often have cover when Le Tour does not. Off the back of Prarion the Plancerts drag-lift serves two interesting red runs through the trees down to the 1350m. It is possible to ski down to St-Gervais, which is included in the lift pass, but the only way back is by bus or the infrequent mountain railway.

The Vallée Blanche, reached via the Aiguille du Midi cable car, is the most famous of Chamonix off-piste runs and one that every skier aspires to conquer. The only real enemy is the weather. Given a sunny day and fresh snow conditions anyone who can ski parallel and has enough nerve to overcome the first sticky moments of access from the cable car can achieve a relatively flat descent across three glaciers against the most magnificent of alpine backdrops. Many good skiers are actually disappointed to discover that the technical challenge is minimal. But when the weather closes in, all visibility is lost and so too are a number of skiers every year down crevasses. On blue sky days so many set off on what is a 24km descent of 2770m vertical that queues can form at the tricky bits. Dangerously, the run becomes pounded into a piste, which it is not. It is important to remember never to ski it without a guide and never to stray off the beaten track. So many fall down crevasses that the helicopter rescue service claims to have found lost skiers by chance while searching for someone else.

The journey up in the two-stage Aiguille du Midi cable car (the highest in Europe) is one of the area's most spectacular. At the top a tunnel cut into the ice leads to a long, steep and narrow ridge with terminal drops on either side. The Steps, spoken of in awe by all who have climbed not up them, but down them, have to be negotiated before skis can be attached. A fixed rope provides little comfort to non-mountaineers. In icy conditions a guide may insist on roping up his party and fitting crampons to ski boots. To descend gingerly in this manner and to be passed by an accomplished mountaineer with skis on shoulder may be humiliating, but better over-kill than kill.

Courmayeur-based skiers *(see separate chapter)* do not have to submit to this ordeal. From the bottom of the steps the Vallée Blanche is nothing more than a long cruise through a wilderness of snow and rock, with long stretches of controlled schuss to avoid arduous poling. It is important to follow the tracks of your guide; a drift of even five metres out of line could lead you over a concealed crevasse. The most awkward section is the junction of glaciers known as the Salle à Manger, where crevasses yawn uninvitingly on either side of the path and queues build up on sunny weekends. But even here the skiing is not technically difficult, requiring more from nerves than from knees. The glacier section of the run ends with an uphill walk off the Mer de Glace on to terra firma. The long ski on down to Chamonix is mostly on a path on the steep hillside, which is icy, stony and short of snow when it is skiable at all. However, the Montenvers funicular railway, originally built in 1908 to take summer sightseers to the Mer de Glace, was opened in winter 1992 and has greatly added to the appeal of the Vallée Blanche by avoiding what is normally a 45-minute trudge in ski boots.

Other alternative routes from the Aiguille du Midi require a greater level of expertise and must again only be undertaken in the company of a guide. It is possible to climb on skins up to the Col de Toula, ski down on the Italian side of the massif, return by lift and then ski the Vallée Blanche back to Chamonix. It is a long but rewarding day's skiing for those who have the stamina.

Queuing in Chamonix remains a serious problem. The wait for the Grands Montets cable car can be horrific and other lifts in Argentière can involve a long delay. When the valley runs from Brévent and Flégère are closed, the queues to download can be exasperating. The single-sheet local piste map covering the whole valley gives you only a rough idea of the lifts. There is a much better alternative published yearly in booklet form, entitled *Cham' Ski*. This incorporates descriptions of pistes as well as individual maps of each area.

Mountain restaurants

Mountain restaurants are the weak point in the Chamonix armour. 'Uninteresting and overpriced, dreadful, almost without exception' is the consensus of opinion among reporters, with a few notable exceptions. Plan Joran is recommended for both waiter- and self-service, but is 'nevertheless very pricey'. The Charamillon gondola station at Le Tour is a special target for criticism: 'Outrageous prices for mediocre fodder to be eaten with plastic cutlery' and 'the *potage du jour* was instant soup in a plastic cup'. Flégère is said to have the best-value mountain restaurant in Chamonix. At Les Houches, La Chalette at Bellevue has waiter-service and is reportedly 'less of a rip-off than most'.

Beginners and children

Chamonix is the headquarters of the ESF and tries to keep up with modern trends by offering snowboarding, monoskiing, ski-ballet, tele-marking and off-piste courses, as well as basic technical training. We have few reports of these: most British skiers who visit Chamonix do not take lessons. Our own recent experience of the ESF during high season in Argentière was extremely negative. A 14-year-old novice, despite assurances that she would be put in a class of teenagers, found herself up on the mountain with six middle-aged Frenchwomen and an instructor who spoke no English. Remonstrations were met with the all too familiar Gallic shrug of indifference.

Chamonix, as this experience reinforced, is not a place for beginners or indeed for timid intermediates. There are nursery slopes in Chamonix itself and at various points throughout the valley including Le Tour and Les Houches, but there are other more convenient and pleasurable resorts in Europe in which to get to grips with the basics.

Similarly, Chamonix prides itself on its childcare facilities, with ski and non-ski kindergartens in both Chamonix and Argentière. We have had a number of negative reports on both with particular concern over the Panda Club ski kindergarten in Argentière beside the Lognan lift: 'Complete indifference by overworked staff, our child cried every day.'

Our own experience confirmed this view: the childcare as such was adequate, but the attitude of the staff was of the couldn't-care-less variety with a distinct bias towards French-speaking children. Again, constructive complaints were met with complete indifference.

The Compagnie des Guides de Chamonix is the oldest and most respected body of its kind in the world and offers every conceivable course from basic off-piste to heli-skiing and ski mountaineering. Independent guides include Roland Stieger and Fred Harper.

The resort

Chamonix is a bustling town with a permanent population of 10,000 and is the centre of day-to-day life in the valley. A large proportion of its inhabitants make their living out of the mighty mountains that watch over them, either by guiding or by supplying the clothing and equipment for those who pay to venture on them. Nevertheless, it has little of the atmosphere expected of a ski resort: 'What we liked was the relatively normal atmosphere in the town – more than just skiers on holiday.' Part of the centre is a pedestrian zone, but traffic remains a serious problem. Drivers are advised to use the pay car-parks on the edge of the town or risk being towed away. There is substantial free parking at the Argentière-Lognan cable car and at other valley lifts.

The old town with its one main shopping street and a village square has expanded hugely over the years. The resultant suburbs, including the whole new town of Chamonix Sud, are not attractive. On the hillside, villas built by wealthy Geneva businessmen at the turn of the century remain in private hands, although a handful are rented out as tour operator chalets. Visitors have to rely upon the valley ski-bus system, which basically works efficiently although is prone to overcrowding. Large queues form at the end of the day at the bottom of the cable car in Argentière for Chamonix-bound buses, which are already half-full from Le Tour. By the time they reach the passengers waiting at La Flégère there is no room left. At peak times some extra buses do run, but the wait can be a long one. One reporter points out that an annoying feature is the number of locals who buy tickets on the bus, 'an old-fashioned process, which takes a great deal of time'. Buses run regularly to Les Houches and St-Gervais.

Accommodation

Chamonix has a wide choice of hotels, from the simplest of youth hostels and dormitories up to four-star hotels like the Albert 1er ('wonderfully comfortable, furnished with antiques and the food is exquisite'), the Auberge du Bois Prin and Hotel Mont-Blanc. Hotel International is a 'rather overpriced three-star with all rooms on the roadside and consequently very noisy, but conveniently situated'. Hotel Alpina is a 'good three-star, with excellent food, but an expensive bar'. The Sapinière-Montana is 'charming if slightly scruffy in the old part of the hotel. Serves excellent four-course set dinner'. Hotel Eva is 'very basic and English-run'. The Richemond is 'old-fashioned, but loveable', the Aiglons has good views and the Hermitage Paccard is centrally situated.

A considerable amount of tour operator accommodation is also in chalets and self-catering apartments. Villa Terrier, run by British tour operator The Ski Company, is a classic Edwardian town-house with views of the Glacier des Bossons. Chalet la Grande Savoyarde, run by Enterprise, has 'much atmosphere, panelling and oil-paintings'. The Chamonix Sud apartments are said to be 'very cramped'.

Eating out
The Albert 1er, once described as 'one of the great undiscovered secrets of France', has since been discovered and is priced accordingly. However, the food is 'beyond dreams'. Restaurant Atmosphère and the National are strongly recommended. The Matafan in the Hotel Mont-Blanc is famous for its wine cellar and Savoyard specialities. The Eden at Les Praz is praised and Le Chaudran is also singled out. Besides the usual pizzerias and crêperies, Chamonix boasts Spanish, Mexican, Italian, Alsatian, Chinese and Japanese eating places.

Après-ski
Non-skiers will find plenty to do here. There is an excellent sports centre with a competition-size pool; reporters have complained, however, that it does not open until 3pm even on days when the lifts are closed because of adverse weather conditions. There are also indoor and outdoor skating rinks as well as covered tennis courts, interesting mountain walks and substantial cross-country skiing between Les Praz and Argentière. Those in search of wilder entertainment will not be disappointed. The bars stay open into the small hours, with Le Choucas the most popular. The Blue Night is the best of the four nightclubs.

Argentière 1240m (4,067ft)
Argentière is a small, attractive, but strung-out village up the valley, set beneath the glacier of the same name and the towering peak of the Grands Montets. The main street is the Chamonix-to-Martigny road and traffic is a major problem and a continual hazard to ski-carrying pedestrians. Away from the main road the village still has pretensions to the farming community it once was and has a considerable and far greater charm than urban Chamonix. Shopping is limited to a few sports retailers, the odd delicatessen and a reasonable supermarket.

In the evening you can eat and drink in congenial surroundings. The Hotel Montana is just across the car park on the other side of the river from the cable car ('pleasant modern rooms with bath, and the food is good: we had an excellent rabbit casserole'). The Grands Montets is also recommended by reporters. Chez Luigi is a good Italian restaurant with huge wooden menus; the Dahu and the Stone are also both praised.

TOURIST OFFICE
as Chamonix

TOUR OPERATORS
Activity Travel, Bladon Lines, Collineige,
Crystal, Sally Holidays, Ski Esprit,
Ski Trax, Ski Weekend,
Susie Ward Travel, White Roc

Skiing facts: Chamonix

TOURIST OFFICE
BP 25, F-74400 Chamonix, Haute
Savoie
Tel 33 50 53 00 24
Fax 33 50 53 58 90

THE RESORT
By road Calais 900km
By rail station in resort
By air Geneva 1½ hrs
Visitor beds 16,547 (67% apartments
and chalets, 33% hotels)
Transport free bus from Le Tour to
Les Houches

THE SKIING
Longest run Vallée Blanche, 20km
(itinerary)
Number of lifts 45
Number of trails/pistes 64 (23%
beginner, 31% easy, 31%
intermediate, 15% difficult)
Total of trails/pistes 136km in
Chamonix, 600km in Mont Blanc area
Nursery slopes 2 lifts in Chamonix,
1 in Argentière
Summer skiing limited
Snowmaking 45 mobile snow-cannon

LIFT PASSES
Area pass (covers 13 resorts in
Mont Blanc region), 775-860FF for
6 days.
Lift pass for 2 days or more valid for a
day in Courmayeur
Day pass 160FF
Half-day pass 42-82FF, depending on
area
Beginners coupons available
Children 4-11 yrs, 580-645FF for 6
days. Free for 4 yrs and under
Pensioners 60 yrs and over, as children
Credit cards accepted yes

SKI SCHOOLS
Adults ESF Argentière and Chamonix,
Ski Ecole International, 75FF for a 2 hr
lesson, 600FF for 6 days
Children ESF Argentière and Chamonix,
Ski Ecole International, 65FF for a 2 hr
lesson, 480 for 6 days
Private lessons 170FF per hr
Special courses snowboarding,
monoskiing, ski-ballet, telemark, off-
piste
Guiding companies Compagnie des

Guides, Association Independante

CROSS-COUNTRY
Ski schools ESF and ESI
Loipe location and size 41km total in
Chamonix and Argentière

CHILDCARE
Non-ski kindergarten Panda Club
Argentière and Chamonix,
3 mths-3 yrs, 8.30am-5.30pm,
250FF per day including lunch. ESF
Bébé, 3 mths-3 yrs, 275FF per day,
1,350FF for 6 days
Ski kindergarten ESF Argentière,
3-12 yrs, 9am-5.30pm, 200-245FF
per day, 1,275FF for 6 days, including
lunch. ESF Chamonix, 3-12 yrs,
210FF per day, 1,050FF for 6 days.
Panda Club Argentière and
Chamonix, 4-12 yrs, 8.30am-5.30pm,
3,650FF for 7 days, including
lunch
Babysitting list available from tourist
office

OTHER SPORTS
Parapente, snow-mobiling, ice-driving,
skating, curling, indoor tennis, squash,
swimming, climbing wall

WHAT'S NEW
● Montenvers railway open in winter
● detachable quad chair-lift des
Autannes (Charamillon to Balme) in
Le Tour area ● three-star hotel Le
Morgane ● fitness centre in the
swimming-pool complex

FOOD AND DRINK PRICES
Coffee 13FF, bottle of house wine
60FF, beer 15FF, dish of the day 50FF

TOUR OPERATORS
AA Motoring Holidays, Activity Travel,
Bladon Lines, Brittany Ferries,
Club Med, Collineige, Contiki, Crystal,
Enterprise, French Impressions,
Fresh Tracks, Hoverspeed, Inghams,
Made to Measure, Neilson,
Sally Holidays, Ski Airtours, Ski Esprit,
Ski Jean Stanford, Ski Savoie,
Ski Thomson, Ski Trax,
Ski Weekend, Susie Ward Travel,
The Ski Company, Touralp, Ultimate
Holidays, White Roc

La Clusaz, Haute Savoie

ALTITUDE 1100m (3,608ft)

••

Good points extensive cross-country skiing, variety of skiing for beginners, easy road access, short airport transfer, beautiful scenery, variety of mountain restaurants
Bad points unreliable snow cover, heavy traffic, lack of skiing convenience, not suitable for late holidays
Linked or nearby resorts Chamonix (n), Le Grand-Bornand (n), Megève (n)

La Clusaz is a large and established resort 32km from Annecy and an hour by car from Geneva. It has the shortest airport transfer of any resort in the Alps and this factor on its own makes it extremely attractive to weekend skiers from Britain, some of whom have invested in property in the area. The layout of the resort is messy and inconvenient, the atmosphere is unspoiled French and it has a considerable amount of beginner and intermediate skiing. Its major disadvantage is that all this takes place beneath 2600m and most of it at below 2000m; snow cover is therefore unreliable throughout the winter. However, in the right conditions the skiing, including some good off-piste runs, is enough to keep any category of skier satisfied here for a full week's holiday.

La Clusaz has none of the cachet of its stylish neighbour Megève and its skiing is less extensive, but the village has an honest rural and un-affected French charm and its slopes are more varied and challenging.

At weekends and during the holidays the proximity to Geneva and Annecy means that the resort is prone to overcrowding. On off-season weekdays it can be delightfully deserted. The 40 lifts of nearby Le Grand-Bornand are included in the regional lift pass. A car is useful for access to the different sectors of the inconveniently arranged ski area, or for excursions further afield into the Chamonix Valley.

The skiing
Top 2600m (8,528ft) bottom 1100m (3,608ft)
La Clusaz has five ski areas spread around the sides of several valleys and facing north, east and west. **Mountain access** to Beauregard and l'Aiguille is by lifts from the resort centre. The other three are accessed from various points along the valleys via a not particularly efficient ski-bus network. Despite roads and rivers, all five are linked by lift or piste, although some of these connections are long green (beginner) pistes, which involve a plod; another is a trans-valley cable car shuttle.

Beauregard, served by a single cable car from the bottom of the resort, is a 1690m flat-topped, wooded mountain with attractive and easy skiing in pastoral surroundings at the top. It is ideal for beginners.

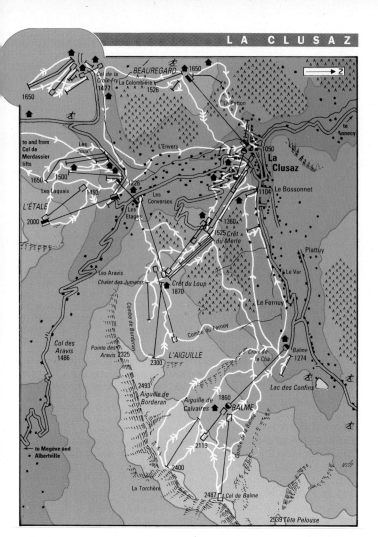

It also has a cross-country loipe and pleasant paths for walkers. Two long blue (easy) and green runs take a line around both shoulders back to the resort. La Noire, one of the resort's three black (difficult) runs, follows the fall-line down the front face. The run starts gently, but becomes steeper with a couple of awkward pitches. A chair-lift beside the road down from Beauregard to the foot of l'Etale has created a link with the enjoyable area of short, gentle runs through the trees spread over a knoll between the cols of La Croix-Fry and Merdassier. The most westerly runs at La Croix-Fry face almost north; they are shaded by trees and therefore hold their snow well. These include a red (intermediate) run, which is not at all steep, but is fairly narrow. There are steeper and more open runs on the other side of Merdassier (not included in our map) as well as a gentle run across to l'Etale providing the return link. The area is well supplied with restaurants beside the two cols.

L'Etale, like Beauregard, is mainly served by a single cable car, which takes you up to the top at 1960m. Skiing is limited to the north-west-facing flank of the mountain, which is open and fairly steep on the upper half, with a network of drag-lifts serving the gentler and more spacious slopes at the bottom and giving access to an easy run across to Merdassier. From the bottom station the Trans-Val cable car shuttles skiers to and from the Aiguille area.

L'Aiguille is the largest of the different sectors and is directly accessible from the village by efficient chair- and drag-lifts. The Crêt du Merle mid-station has a small nursery slope, ski school assembly area and restaurants. None of the runs down from here offers any real difficulty. From the next stage the Crêt du Loup, the long west-facing run to the valley, offers more than 600m vertical. In deep snow the area beneath the chairs offers good off-piste skiing. The bowl above Crêt du Loup is mostly gentle, but the lifts give access to some interesting off-piste itineraries, including the Combe de Borderan and the Combe du Fernuy, both long, steep gullies in the wall of the Chaîne des Aravis.

The north-west-facing Balme slopes provide La Clusaz's highest and most challenging pistes with long runs down the Combe de la Balme and the Combe de la Torchère providing over 1200m vertical with plenty of scope for off-piste variations. Part of the main black run, Le Vraille is steep enough to be used as one of France's top speed-skiing courses. Moderate red runs descend from both top stations and a long blue winds its way down from the top of the Bergerie chair. Two long, flat green runs lead back to the resort, with the lower one requiring a lot of poling.

Mountain restaurants

La Clusaz is well served with mountain eating places, although a lot of the better ones are on the lower pistes and are not always accessible because of scant snow cover. In the main they are attractively old-fashioned and inexpensive in comparison to other French ski areas, especially at La Croix-Fry/Merdassier. Le Vieux Ferme at Merdassier is lavishly praised by all reporters who have stopped there ('outstanding cuisine in a wonderful setting'). The Beauregard, beside the cross-country track, has 'good food, a wonderful sun-terrace and spectacular views'. Both restaurants in the Crêt du Merle sector are reportedly good. Balme does not offer such a high standard, with both restaurants at the top and the bottom of the gondola 'disappointing and expensive'.

Beginners and children

There are small but good nursery slopes close to the village centre and at the bottom of each sector. However, the best are at Crêt du Merle and on the top of Beauregard. Reports on the ski school, which in the past has had a sound reputation, are not good. Correspondents tell of large classes of up to 18 in number with instructors 'apparently taking the view that their pupils were capable of skiing, but didn't want to'. The Club des Mouflets crèche takes children from eight months to four-and-a-half years, the Club des Champions ski kindergarten gives lessons for 3½- to 6-year-olds. We have no recent reports of either.

The resort

La Clusaz is a reasonably attractive but rather enclosed village beside a river at the meeting point of several steep-sided wooded valleys. As one reporter enthuses: 'The scenery is as impressive from the town as it is from the slopes. Resorts which have an independent life away from skiing are much more interesting places.' But La Clusaz has expanded in every direction over the years and no longer fits comfortably into its natural setting. The resultant sprawl of buildings along the valley and up its sides is complicated by a series of road junctions and roundabouts. It is a confusing place to find your way around and traffic can be a serious problem in the late afternoon and at weekends. Parking is difficult and well policed, but there is an underground car-park.

The heart of the village is pleasantly traditional, built around a large bulbous-towered church, with a stylish modern shopping precinct beside it and a fast-flowing stream below. The shops are attractively varied and you can still find the ordinary French café of the lowland villages, unusually in a ski resort. The disparate nature of the skiing makes La Clusaz dependent on an efficient bus service, which it by and large has, although reporters complain of long waits on some routes. The hourly service to Col de Merdassier seems hopelessly inadequate. The heavy traffic does not contribute to its smooth operation.

Accommodation

Most of the accommodation is in tour-operator chalets scattered around the resort. It is important to relate where you are staying to the lifts and to discover whether there is a bus stop nearby. The skiing convenience factor here is one of the lowest in this guide and any visit here involves considerable clomping about in ski boots. In the centre of the resort there are lots of simple, reasonably priced hotels. The Alpenroc (formerly the Vita) is strongly recommended ('really good rooms with satellite television, splendid food which is varied, but with a local accent'). The Hotel Nouvel is also praised. The Beauregard is a new three-star in the hamlet of Le Bossonet, above the village on the edge of the slopes. We have favourable reports of the Résidence du Centre apartments, which are close to the church and conveniently situated 100m from the Praz chair-lift to l'Aiguille.

Eating out

La Clusaz has a wide choice of restaurants, larger than you would expect in a resort of this size. Recommendations include Le Vieux Chalet, which also has rooms. Le Foly is a particularly attractive and expensive log-cabin in the Confins valley. The Symphonie in the Hotel Beauregard is praised by one reporter. Other popular choices are the Calèche, l'Ourson and l'Outa.

Après-ski

Its identity as a real village, rather than just a *station de ski,* makes La Clusaz a reasonable choice for non-skiers. There is swimming, skating and curling along with snow-shoe excursions and scenic walks. The scenic cross-country tracks around Lac des Confins reportedly hold the snow well and are served by a regular bus service. The area on top of Beauregard is well laid out and signposted, but it is much busier and there is more chance of conflict with downhill skiers.

The shops of Annecy are 32km away by regular bus service. Après-ski is quiet during the week, some would say too quiet, but becomes extremely lively at weekends. Most of the action centres on a few bars. Le Pressoir and Le Montmartre are the busiest, but even these close early mid-week out of season. L'Ecluse is said to be the best of the three discos, with a glass dance floor over the river.

Skiing facts: La Clusaz

TOURIST OFFICE
F-74220 La Clusaz, Haute-Savoie
Tel 33 50 02 60 92
Fax 33 50 02 59 82

THE RESORT
By road Calais 820km
By rail Annecy 30km, frequent bus service to the resort
By air Geneva 2 hrs
Visitor beds 8,900 (78% apartments, 22% hotels)
Transport free bus service with a ski pass of 4 days or more

THE SKIING
Longest run La Motte, 4km (green)
Number of lifts 56
Number of trails/pistes 75 (33% beginner, 37% easy, 26% intermediate, 4% difficult)
Total of trails/pistes 130km
Nursery slopes 10 lifts
Summer skiing none
Snowmaking none

LIFT PASSES
Area pass Aravis (covers La Clusaz and Le Grand-Bornand), 690FF for 6 days. La Clusaz (covers Croix Fry/Merdassier), 650FF for 6 days
Day pass La Clusaz, 128FF
Half-day pass 39FF after 12.30pm
Beginners points tickets
Children La Clusaz, 4-12 yrs, 520FF for 6 days
Pensioners 60 yrs and over, as children
Credit cards accepted yes

SKI SCHOOLS
Adults ESF, 9-11am and 3-5pm, 690FF

for 6 days
Children ESF Jardin des Neiges, 5-11 yrs, 9-11am and 3-5pm, 310FF for 6 half-days, 550FF for 6 full days
Private lessons 160FF per hr
Special courses snowboarding
Guiding companies through ski school

CROSS-COUNTRY
Ski schools ESF
Loipe location and size 70km of trails around Beauregard and in Les Confins valley

CHILDCARE
Non-ski kindergarten Le Club des Mouflets, 8 mths-4½ yrs, 8.30am-6pm, 899FF for 6 days including lunch
Ski kindergarten Le Club des Champions, 3½-6 yrs, 8.30am-6pm, 974FF for 6 days including lunch and 2 hrs instruction
Babysitting list available from tourist office

OTHER SPORTS
Parapente, snow-shoeing, skating, curling, swimming, fitness centres

WHAT'S NEW
● Three-star hotel Le Beauregard

FOOD AND DRINK PRICES
Coffee 6FF, bottle of house wine 70FF, beer 14FF, dish of the day 50FF

TOUR OPERATORS
Activity Travel, Brittany Ferries, Crystal, Enterprise, French Impressions, Made to Measure, Neilson, Sally Holidays, Silver Ski, SkiBound

Les Deux Alpes, Dauphiné

ALTITUDE 1650m (5,412ft)

••

Good points choice of intermediate runs, off-piste skiing, beautiful
scenery, sunny slopes, extensive après-ski, summer skiing, efficient
lift system
Bad points heavy traffic, lack of alpine charm, lack of tree-line skiing,
difficult pistes to village, crowded pistes
Linked or nearby resorts La Grave (l), Alpe d'Huez (n),
Serre Chevalier/Briançon (n), St-Christophe-en-Oisans (l), Venosc (l)

Les Deux Alpes has a strong British following, and yet it is hard to work
out why this large resort off the Grenoble-Briançon road should be so
popular. Certainly it is not for the long, straggly village itself, which has
no architectural merit and is plagued by traffic. But the piste skiing is
pleasantly varied, the off-piste is extraordinary, and its top altitude of
3568m means that, even in a bad season, there is always snow on the
glacier. However, in these circumstances, of which there have sadly
been too many in recent years, those who come here from other
greener resorts make the skiing unbearably crowded. As developed
glaciers go – summer skiing is popular here – Les Deux Alpes has a particularly flat one. The scenery of the Ecrins National Park to the south is
truly spectacular.

The lift system is highly efficient and comprehensive, but anyone
coming here expecting to find a small Trois Vallées or an area as varied
as nearby Alpe d'Huez is in for a major disappointment. The skiing does
go very high, up to 3568m, but many find that their enjoyment of these
high-altitude, easy runs is spoilt by difficult conditions on the lower
slopes at the end of the day. Because of their steepness and vulnerabil-
ity to sunshine, down-loading is often the only (crowded) option.
Indeed, crowded pistes are too often the norm here, not from any
major fault in the lift system, but from the sheer volume of skiers.

However, the safety valve is La Grave, the linked mountaineering
resort to the north-east of the glacier, which offers some of the most
spectacular and radical off-piste skiing to be found outside the Mont
Blanc massif. Many were the complaints from La Grave aficionados when
the two resorts were tenuously linked a few years ago. La Grave's ski
area, served by one large cable car, is unpisted and offers an infinite variety of stunningly beautiful itineraries. But pressure to homogenise the
slopes of La Meije, the last major peak in Europe to be climbed, and to

turn them into a series of manicured pistes for the benefit of escapees from the overcrowded runs of Les Deux Alpes, has so far been success-fully averted. La Grave remains an unspoilt haven for expert skiers.

The skiing

Top 3568m (11,703ft) bottom 1270m (4,166ft)

The western side of the skiing climbs only a few hundred metres above the resort to the shoulder of Pied Moutet (2100m) and is not heavily used, despite the attraction of a long, north-facing, unprepared run down to the small village of Bons (1300m). The blue (easy) run down to the Venosc end of Les Deux Alpes is steep. The main skiing is on the eastern side of the resort with the principal **mountain access** via the two-stage Jandri Express jumbo gondola. Alternatives include a chair and another gondola from the Venosc end of the village.

The lower slopes are wide, running the whole length of this long resort, and above nursery-slope level are quite steep; the remote upper ones on the glacier are broad and gentler. The middle area, from 2200m to 3200m, offers some good north-facing slopes, although these are prone to congestion in the afternoons. There are some interesting off-piste couloirs close to the marked trails.

The first section of skiing immediately above the resort is a broad, steep, west-facing mountainside, terraced for safety with a spacious open ridge at the top where very easy runs and a number of lifts link the two gondola stations. There is little variety in the runs down to the vil-lage itself. All are steep except for a narrow track, wrongly graded green (beginner), which zigzags down at the northern end of the ridge and from which it is possible to cross to most areas of this large resort at the end of the day. When crowded, this run is no fun at all (especially for a 'green' skier) and even comparative novices will find themselves ven-turing out on to an unpisted traverse.

Behind the ridge above the village is the Combe de Thuit, a deep, steep bowl with the peaks of Rachas, Tête Moute and Diable at its head. The four-seater Diable gondola from the south end of the village, and the chair above it, lead directly to Tête Moute, from where the black (expert) Diable run offers an equally direct 1200m descent to the vil-lage. The top pitch of this run is seriously steep (about 35°) and it exceeds 30° for much of its length down to the bottom of the Diable gondola. Below that the gradient eases off, but the run is often covered in big moguls, which are inclined to be icy at both ends of the day.

The Thuit chair, from the bottom of the bowl up to the top of the Diable gondola, introduces some quite steep off-piste as well as serving a long blue run, which is gentle after a mogulled start. From Tête Moute there are some good, steep north-facing runs off-piste between the rocks, as well as a more roundabout blue piste, down to Lac du Plan. From here, chairs go back up to the shoulder of Tête Moute and to the major mid-mountain lift station at 2580m for access to the gondolas up to the Col de Jandri and the glacier beyond. The alternative is to carry on down to the Thuit chair, or to take the broad run around to the eastern side of the ridge. Beyond this gondola station at 2580m a diverging pair of chairs serve open, north-facing runs on La Toura. These are steeper than their

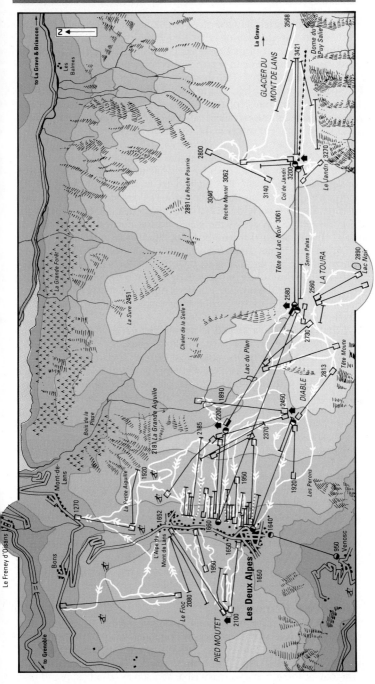

blue gradings suggest and the off-piste variants are challenging. The tops of these lifts provide amazing views across the Vénéon Valley.

The top section of the gondolas up to Col de Jandri span a larger open area of intermediate skiing centred on a good and long (but too often crowded) arterial. The short, awkward section at the end can be avoided by branching left. To the north of the Col are gentle, north-facing runs on the fringe of the glacier which are served by chair-lifts. Above it, to the south, a chair serves a short but challenging mogul field. This is high alpine territory and these chairs can be very cold indeed to ride in mid-winter.

The Glacier du Mont-de-Lans, to the east of the Col, is the summer ski area which is served both by drag-lifts and by the Dôme Express underground funicular. The high-speed train whisks you up to the Dôme de la Lauze, only 200m above the Col de Jandri, but almost 2km distant. The runs back to the Col constitute a vast nursery slope. There is a less gentle run across the glacier to the Roche-Mantel chair, and good off-piste skiing down to the lower Signal chair.

From the higher train station, a short drag-lift takes you on up towards the top of the Glacier de la Girose and the top of La Grave's skiing. The two areas are separated by a gentle 15-minute hike, long enough to deter the average Les Deux Alpes piste basher from venturing into what the purists consider this sacred, untamed terrain in the shadow of the mighty 4000m La Meije.

The Glacier de la Girose is heavily crevassed and prone to slab avalanche so the greatest care should be taken. La Grave has built a drag-lift from the top of its cable car at Col des Ruillans (3200m) to the Dôme de la Lauze. No one should attempt to ski outside this unbashed piste which, with neighbouring runs on the Deux Alpes Glacier, provides some of the best summer skiing in Europe. The many ways down to La Grave are neither obvious nor easy, but offer some of the best off-piste skiing anywhere. In the right conditions you can notch up 2300m vertical here. The easy route, all of it manageable by an intermediate, in favourable conditions, is down on the Deux Alpes side to Mont-de-Lans. Expert skiers will relish the challenges offered by the routes down to La Grave against a backdrop of dramatic ice-falls.

A wonderful alternative is the Vallon de la Selle, a steep descent off the far side of the Dôme de la Lauze, which takes you down to the hamlet of St-Christophe-en-Oisans. A taxi from here takes you back to Venosc from where an elderly two-seater gondola brings you back up to the southern end of Les Deux Alpes. La Grave's gondola does not normally open until the end of January and its hours of operation are erratic. When it is closed it is still possible to ski La Grave from Les Deux Alpes, although the return taxi costs 200FF.

Mountain restaurants

This is not the place for serious lunchtime eating. 'Uninviting' and 'overpriced' were two of the politer comments from our reporters. La Pastorale at the bottom of the Diable run received kinder commendation for its good atmosphere and more reasonable price structure. The one at the top is also reasonable and serves 'good soup and tasty omelettes'. The restaurant at the top of Jandri 1 receives heavy criticism for its high prices. Le Panoramic at 2600m is 'friendly, but a bit crowded at peak hours'. The higher mountain restaurants charge 10FF for the use of the loo.

Beginners and children

The general standard of instruction is high. However, not all instructors have a sound knowledge of English. One reporter said he was not in a position to judge this as his ESF instructor never spoke more than one sentence each lesson in any language. The establishment of the International Ski School of St-Christophe means there is healthy rivalry between the two, which is of obvious benefit to the skier.

The ESF operates a good kindergarten slope with a lift right in the centre of the village by the Jandri Express and is convenient for parents. The International Ski School also has its own kindergarten.

The resort

Les Deux Alpes is a long, straggly resort of modern hotels and apartment blocks not entirely pleasing to the eye, but not entirely unpleasing either. Traffic is a serious problem and it can surely be only a question of time before it is completely pedestrianised; the Venosc end is already partially car-free. The setting is a remarkably symmetrical one, with steep drops to the north and south of the flat col on which it rests, and steep walls climbing evenly to the east and west.

Originally two communities, the summer pastures of Mont-de-Lans to the north and Venosc to the south, Les Deux Alpes has now merged into one long village, with concentrations of development around the central gondola station. Alpe-de-Venosc is the smarter and much livelier end of town, dramatically perched on a ledge above which is the Vénéon valley.

At the northern end in Clos-des-Fonds the satellite of Le Village is fast developing on the eastern hillside. It is linked to the resort centre by a free bus service which works well during the peak hours but is unreliable outside them: 'A 45- to 60-minute wait was common in the afternoons.' Shopping is still limited and reporters spoke of the inconvenience of the 20-minute walk ('never attempt it in ski boots') into the resort centre.

Accommodation

The Hotel Edelweiss is praised for its plentiful breakfasts and four-course dinners, but rooms are said to be in need of refurbishment. Les Marmottes is out of the way although it runs a courtesy bus, can be reached on skis, and offers 'excellent food, facilities, accommodation and service'. Both the Berangère and the Farondole receive equal praise, but are also equally expensive. The Brunerie is singled out along with the Amethystes for their friendly staff. Much of the accommodation is in tour operator chalets, some of it in apartments masquerading as chalets. The Chalet Tetras beneath Le Village is described as 'very comfortable, with good twin rooms with en suite shower and wc'. Self-caterers have a choice of six food shops.

Eating out

The range of restaurants is surprisingly varied. We have good reports of La Spaghetteria, L'Ours Blanc, and L'Abri pizzeria. The Chalet Mounier has good food at good prices. Other places include Les Capricornes, La Petite Marmite, Chez le Gaulois, La Bel'Auberge, and Le Break.

Skiing facts: Les Deux Alpes

TOURIST OFFICE
BP 7, 38 860 Les Deux Alpes,
Dauphiné
Tel 33 76 79 22 00
Fax 33 76 79 01 38

THE RESORT
By road Calais 910km
By rail Grenoble 75km, 4 buses per day
By air Lyon 2 hrs, Grenoble 1½ hrs
Visitor beds 24,765 (85% chalets and apartments, 15% hotels)
Transport free bus service

THE SKIING
Longest run Mont de Lans to village, 10km
Number of lifts 64
Number of trails/pistes 76 (29% beginner, 33% easy, 28% intermediate, 10% difficult)
Total of trails/pistes 196km
Nursery slopes Coolidge Nord and Coolidge Sud, both free for beginners
Summer skiing mid-June to early September
Snowmaking 7 beginner slopes covered (no figures available)

LIFT PASSES
Area pass 742-825FF for 6 days, including 1 free day in either Alpe d'Huez, Serre Chevalier/Briançon, Puy-Saint-Vincent, the Milky Way
Day pass 75-165FF (depending on number of lifts covered)
Half-day pass 125FF
Beginners 2 free lifts, 75FF per day for 20 lifts
Children 4-13 yrs, 550-610FF for 6 days
Pensioners 60 yrs and over as child
Credit cards accepted yes

SKI SCHOOLS
Adults ESF, 635FF for 6 mornings, 500FF for 5 afternoons. St-Christophe

International Ski School, 575FF for 6 half-days
Child ESF, 500FF for 6 mornings, 400FF for 5 afternoons
Private lessons ESF, 160FF per hr for 1-3 people. ESI, 180FF per hr for 1-4 people
Special courses race training, mono skiing, snowboarding, telemark, ski-touring
Guiding companies Bureau des Guides in Les Deux Alpes and in La Grave

CROSS-COUNTRY
Ski schools ESF and ESI
Loipe location and size 4 loipe totalling 20km, including the 15km Vénéon valley track

CHILDCARE
Non-ski kindergarten crèche for 6-23 mths, 170FF per day including lunch. 2-5 yrs, 190FF per day including lunch, 900FF for 6 days
Ski kindergarten ESF, 4-6 yrs for 6 days at 2 locations, 820FF for 6 days, lunch by arrangement. ESI, 840FF, lunch extra
Babysitting list available from tourist office

OTHER SPORTS
Skating, curling, parapente, snow-shoeing, helicopter flights

FOOD AND DRINK PRICES
Coffee 6FF, bottle of house wine 70FF, beer 14-17FF, dish of the day 40-70FF

TOUR OPERATORS
Bladon Lines, Brittany Ferries, The Club, Crystal, Enterprise, Hoverspeed, Inghams, Made to Measure, Neilson, Sally Holidays, Ski Airtours, Seasun School Tours, SkiBound, Ski Thomson, Ski Tracer, Skiworld, Touralp, UCPA

Après-ski

Les Deux Alpes has some of the better nightlife to be found in compara-ble French resorts, although that is not to say it is exactly wild. Mike's Bar near the Jandri lift is a 'very British, ESF prize-giving venue' and 'noisy, but loads of fun and not too expensive'. Smokey Joe's has a strong following immediately after skiing as well as later in the evening. The Rodeo at the Venosc end of town is 'loud, cheap and a bit dirty. The mechanical bull is quite a crowd puller'. Le Windsor is the ubiqui-tous London pub now found in many resorts. Le Pressoir and Le Tonic were both named as 'useful watering holes'. The resort has four discos (entry fee is usually 100FF) of which l'Avalanche seems to be the more popular.

La Grave 1450m (4,756ft)

This ancient village straddling the road up to the Col de Lauteret is more famous as a mountaineering centre than a ski resort. It lies in the shadow of the soaring peak of La Meije and the spectacular ice-falls of the glaciers which tumble down below it. As we have said, the only real lift does not usually open before late January and the best time to visit is in March or even April.

La Grave has only 1,500 beds, 33 per cent in hotels and the remain-der in apartments and chalets. Its hotels are all simple and small. Prices here are far below those of a 'real resort' and more in keeping with those of a lowland French village. The dish of the day at most of the handful of restaurants is under 50FF and a coffee costs 6FF. Babysitting, arranged through the tourist office, costs only 10FF an hour or 70 to 80FF a day. There is extensive (29km) cross-country skiing in the area.

TOURIST OFFICE
05320 La Grave
Tel 33 76 79 90 05
Fax 33 76 79 91 65

TOUR OPERATORS
Fresh Tracks, Ski Weekend

Flaine, Haute Savoie

ALTITUDE 1600m (5,248ft)

••

Good points big ski area, excellent family facilities, skiing
convenience, short airport transfer, freedom from cars, variety of
easy and intermediate runs, reliable resort-level snow, suitable
for skiing on a budget, variety of off-piste skiing
Bad points ugly architecture, lack of alpine charm, limited après-ski,
nothing for non-skiers
Linked or nearby resorts Les Carroz (l), Morillon (l), Samoëns (l),
Sixt (n)

Flaine is the core of the large, linked ski area called Le Grand Massif.
The purpose-built resort was laid out in the 1960s in an unimaginative
architectural style of depressing, unfinished grey concrete to rival
London's South Bank. It was, like Les Menuires, Isola 2000, Chamrousse
and countless other French resorts of its generation, designed to be
completely functional. Its aim was to provide doorstep skiing at affordable prices, but with no regard for appearance and little for the other
qualities which give the older (and, more recently, the newer) resorts
their broader appeal.

However, Flaine's good points outnumber the bad, making the
whole a not entirely unattractive proposition. It benefits from a lack of
cars, good-value accommodation, excellent nursery slopes and, in general, a lack of queues. Add to these ingredients a short transfer from
Geneva Airport, and the resulting popularity with British families and
budget-conscious skiers is easy to understand. Unfortunately the compact no-walking convenience of the original Bauhaus school design no
longer exists for much of the village, due to expansion. Nevertheless,
the centre at least is traffic-free and user-friendly for children, as well as
convenient for parents.

Flaine's bowl skiing connects with the three lower and more traditional villages of Samoëns, Morillon and Les Carroz. These areas
greatly add to Flaine's skiing and replace some of its vital missing ingredients: sheltered tree-line skiing, long runs and atmospheric mountain
eating places. Unfortunately, the lift links can sometimes close in bad
weather or poor snow cover, although on our many personal visits we
have never found this to be the case.

For skiers who would prefer to stay in a village of character, Les
Carroz provides the best all-round alternative base to Flaine. It is rather
inconveniently set on the road up to Flaine, albeit in attractive surroundings. Samoëns and Morillon are valley communities. Morillon has
a few hotels and, in 1986 an additional satellite village of wooden buildings, Morillon-Grand-Massif, was added.

The skiing

Top 2561m (8,400ft) bottom 690m (2,263ft)

The Grand Massif skiing is distributed into several segments, each linked to the next. Most of Flaine's immediate skiing is ranged around the north-facing part of the bowl, with several lifts soaring to nearly 2500m around the rim. Most of the skiing is open and unsheltered above the tree-line. The main **mountain access** point from the village centre is a huge gondola up to Grandes Platières, a high and wide plateau with panoramic views. A large number of runs go from here down to the resort, most of them graded red (intermediate) and blue (easy), with exotic names such as Lucifer, Faust and Belzebuth. For quasi-beginners there are some wide, snaking blues to the bowl's west-facing slopes. These are served by a sequence of drag- and chair-lifts. The most difficult drops are on the fragmented terrain in the centre of the bowl and, if the off-piste skiing looks tempting here, it should be tackled only with a local guide: powder hunts in this area can all too easily end on a cliff edge.

The more advanced skiing sections are in the middle, graded black (difficult) under the gondola and red to each side. The black Diamont Noir is a fun run for mogul skiers. The Combe de Gers is one of the most interesting off-piste areas, although it is frequently closed due to avalanche danger. When open it is certainly worthwhile for anyone in search of a challenge. One benefit of an area served by a long drag-lift is, in the eyes of a reporter, that it keeps out the surfers.

A good off-piste descent starts at the foot of the lift and goes round via the back of the Tête de Pelouse. The shorter Véret lift serves another steep and sometimes dangerous bowl, reached from the Grand Vans chair. The terrain on the popular blue Serpentine run from the top of Grand Vans to Le Forêt has recently been greatly improved to hold the snow more successfully.

A gondola from the resort or a run down from Grandes Platières gives access to the Aujon skiing on the east-facing part of the bowl. Reporters complain that the blue runs in the Aujon area are narrow, and often icy, making them more difficult than some of the wider reds elsewhere in the resort. There is an area of intermediate runs above and below the tree-line, with a bumps course and several other competition pistes going down to the valley. A chair takes you up to the highest point, Tête des Lindars at 2561m, from where a red run round the shoulder or a more direct black down the face provide some testing skiing. Close to the gondola base, the Téléski du Bois, which leads up to an easy blue area, is particularly steep, and if you do fall off you have to negotiate a severe obstacle course through the trees to get down again.

The remaining and most varied part of the skiing is reached via the valley of the Lac de Vernant, often with a bottleneck caused by skiers travelling between the villages. The Tête du Pré des Saix on the far side is the central point of the whole Grand Massif system. From here north-facing runs drop down steep mogul slopes towards Samoëns. Half-way down the descent is broken by the lifts, which go up a short distance to Samoëns 1600. Then there is a further 800m drop down to Vercland on the outskirts of Samoëns itself; the steeper black option goes through

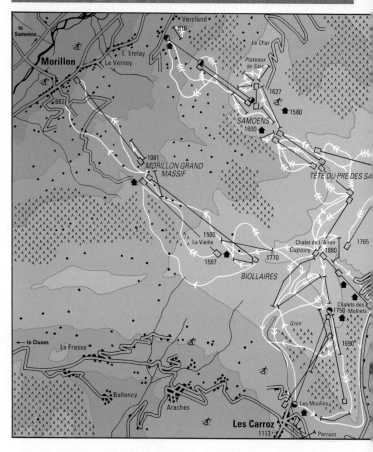

the trees, but unfortunately it does not hold its snow well and quickly becomes patchy. On the other side of the valley the easier pistes towards Morillon run in parallel, comprising long and gentle trails in the tree-line, with a couple of restaurants along them. There is an efficient gondola from Morillon village to Morillon Grand Massif.

The runs to Les Carroz are short, but give a wide variety of tree-level trails, including some more difficult sections at the top of the reds and some good off-piste. The blue run to the village is often crowded and bare. We have received complaints that l'Airon chair, which provides the best link to Flaine, is often closed. Without it a long traverse or a 180m uphill walk are needed to link up with Flaine. Access to the slopes is on Le Kédeuse gondola, which is reported to have a queue in the morning. Sixt, along the road from Samoëns, has its own small ski area and a cross-country track linking it with Samoëns and Morillon.

The Grands Vans and Lac de Vernant drags can be bottlenecks at peak times. We have received complaints of inconsistent lift informa- tion, with some noticeboards stating that certain pistes were closed,

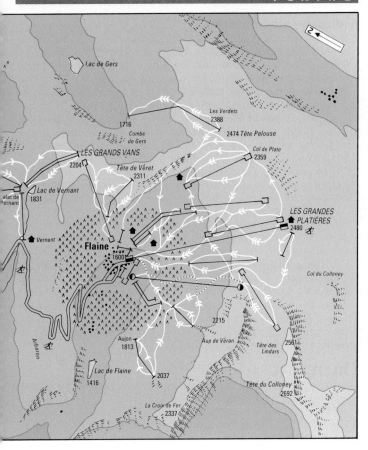

while others said they were open. Other complaints were of runs lacking variety, too much poling, and overcrowded pistes. The slopes are swarming with snowboarders, including on the lower nursery slopes while classes are in progress.

Mountain restaurants

Those in the immediate Flaine vicinity are limited, especially in the Aujon area. The Blanchot and Chalet Bissac are recommended, as is La Combe in the Morillon area. The Oréade at the top of La Kédeuse gondola is recommended for its good food and large, sunny terrace. The restaurant on the Chariande piste at Samoëns has reasonable prices and an excellent view from the terrace.

Le Pativerdans at Verclands, near the foot of the gondola, is reported to be good value, with English hosts who have absorbed themselves into the local community. The Chalet Les Molliets is said to be cheaper than most and the bar at the Pré de la Tête de la Saix sells 'the biggest and hottest hot chocolate in the resort'.

Beginners and children

ESF classes are criticised: 'The instructor taught in French all the time even though there were 6 British pupils in our class of 15 beginners.' A reporter praises the International Ski School for its English-speaking instructors and 'plenty of positive and negative feedback'.

Flaine is among the top alpine resorts which specialise in catering for families with small children. It is car-free and safe, with a large central playground, good nursery slopes, a short airport transfer and sympathetic hotels. The Green Mouse Club (Souris Verte) at the International Ski School is recommended by several reporters, with staff speaking reasonable English and 'happy to accommodate children's wishes to ski or not'. The staff were also praised for 'playing with the children rather than sticking them in front of the video'. Both the ESF Rabbit Club and the Green Mouse will pick up and drop off children from their accommodation each day.

The kindergarten in the Hotel Les Lindars, one of the best-known nurseries in the Alps, unfortunately appears to be resting on its laurels. Some dissatisfaction is creeping into recent reports, with children undeniably well looked after, but staff failing either to play with them or to organise any activities, preferring to leave the children to their own devices. One reporter said that 'the children were sitting outside in a very small area doing nothing, with one bored-looking young girl watching over them'. The Green Mouse Club has easier access to the slopes than Les Lindars' nursery. From the latter, children have to 'struggle with steps and an awkward lift'.

The resort

The first view down into Flaine is a surprising one; it nestles in an isolated bowl where you would not expect to find any centre of habitation at all. The grey concrete matches the grey rock formation in what some would call an ugly, at best inoffensive, purpose-built village. Reporters' opinions of Flaine vary from 'no soul' and 'a ski ghetto, which does not give one the feeling of being in France', to 'a pleasant atmosphere because it is so compact'. In counterpoint to this grey image, Flaine has recently developed a reputation as a centre for fine art. Works by Picasso, Dubuffet and Vasarely are dotted around the village street and also housed in the resort's arts centre.

Two people-mover enclosed lifts operate day and night between the higher and lower villages. The newest Hameau area is served by a free bus, which runs from the chalets to the nursery slopes every 15 minutes during the day, but is apparently not reliable at night.

Accommodation

Flaine Forum is the heart of the resort where the main gondola begins. The Hotel Totem, with Picasso's statue of the same name standing outside, incorporates its one-time neighbour, the smart Hotel Gradins Gris. Reporters' views range alarmingly from 'expensive with clinical, modern décor' and 'still living on its old reputation' to 'a truly grand establishment'. Les Lindars is a family-orientated hotel. The Aujon is conveniently located, cheerful, but the rooms are very basic. Flaine

Forêt, on a shelf above Flaine Forum, has mainly self-catering accommodation and its own shops and bars.

The Hameau de Flaine on the mountain at 1800m is the latest development of attractive Scandinavian-style chalets inconveniently situated for the ski area. There are several well-stocked supermarkets open until late each day and a good bakery in the shopping complex at Flaine Forêt.

Eating out

Chez La Jeanne is 'small and friendly with excellent pizzas and good house wine'. La Perdrix Noire has a good early-evening family menu. The rustic Chalet du Michet is one of the few original buildings in the valley, converted from a cowshed to an excellent restaurant specialising in fondue and raclette. La Pizzeria is ever popular and La Trattoria has a 'pleasant, almost Italian atmosphere and good wine'.

Après-ski

People do not come to Flaine for the nightlife and many tend to opt for quiet evenings in, especially those with small children. The Diamont Noir bar attracts the locals, the Eve Pub has pool tables and a giant video screen. The White Grouse Pub, that little piece of Scotland that is forever France, is sadly reported to be expensive and 'of a very poor standard'. The Shelby is the main disco.

Les Carroz 1140m (3,739ft)

Les Carroz is big and, in the view of most correspondents, more pleasing to the eye than Flaine. It spreads across a broad, sunny slope on the road to Flaine and attracts many families and weekend visitors who use it as an access point for this substantial ski area. The gondola and chairlift are a steep walk from the centre of the village, but within easy reach of some attractive, simple old hotels including the Airelles and the Croix de Savoie. The well-located Hotel des Belles Pistes, run by an English couple, is said to have been 'decorated Cotswolds-style, so there is little French character. However the chef is French and very good.' The Front de Neige is said to cope well with the needs of small children. Most of the self-catering accommodation is much less conveniently placed. Cross-country skiing is very good. The bus is not included in the lift pass and there are only three services per day to Flaine. Late-night taxis between the two are hard to find.

TOURIST OFFICE
F-74300 Les Carroz-d'Araches, Haute Savoie
Tel 33 50 90 00 04
Fax 33 50 90 07 00

TOUR OPERATORS
SkiBound, Ski Tal

Samoëns 720m (2,362ft)

The beautiful old town of Samoëns in the Giffre Valley has been a ski resort since 1912 and is the only one in France to be listed as a historical monument. It was once a thriving stone-cutting centre and twice a

Skiing facts: Flaine

TOURIST OFFICE
F-74300 Flaine, Haute Savoie
Tel 33 50 90 80 01
Fax 33 50 90 86 26

LONDON AGENT
Erna Low Consultants, 9 Reece Mews,
London SW7 7HE
Tel 071-584 2841
Fax 071-589 9531

THE RESORT
By road Calais 877km
By rail Cluses 25km, frequent bus
service
By air Geneva 1½ hrs (70km)
Visitor beds 5,200 (67% apartments,
23% hotels, 10% chalets)
Transport traffic-free, all cars left in car
park

THE SKIING
Longest run Serpentine, 7.5km (blue)
Number of lifts 31 in Flaine, 81 in area
Number of trails/pistes 46 in Flaine
(6% beginner, 28% easy, 55%
intermediate, 12% difficult), 120 in
area
Total of trails/pistes Flaine 150km,
Grand Massif area 260km
Nursery slopes 4 lifts, 500m
Summer skiing none
Snowmaking 4km covered

LIFT PASSES
Area pass Grand Massif (covers Flaine,
Les Carroz, Morillon, Samoëns and
Sixt), 720FF for 6 days. Flaine only,
136FF per day
Day pass Grand Massif, 156FF
Half-day pass Flaine 110FF, Grand
Massif 130FF, after 12.30pm
Beginners 4 free lifts
Children 4-12 yrs, Flaine 105FF per
day, Grand Massif 120FF per day,
520FF for 6 days, free for 4 yrs and
under
Pensioners 60 yrs and over, as children
Credit cards accepted yes

SKI SCHOOLS
Adults ESF, 170FF for 4 hrs, 660FF for
6 days, Ski Ecole International, 120FF
for 2 hrs, 595FF for 6 days, Flaine
Super Ski (advanced skiers only)

Children ESF, 150FF for hrs, 560FF for
6 days, Ski Ecole International, 100FF
for 2 hrs, 475FF for 6 days
Private lessons 160FF per hr, 1,200FF
per day
Special courses snowboarding
Guiding companies through ski schools

CROSS-COUNTRY
Ski schools ESF, Ski Ecole International
Loipe location and size 2 tracks of
4km, situated at L'Arbaron, ending at
Vernant, and a 700m beginners' circuit

CHILDCARE
Non-ski kindergarten Hotel Les Lindars
(priority to residents): nursery,
2 yrs and under, 230FF per day,
kindergarten, 2-7 yrs, 170FF per day,
both 9am to 5pm
Ski kindergarten ESF Rabbit Club,
7-12 yrs, 9am to 5pm, 240FF per day,
1,120FF for 6 days, both including
lunch. ESF Flaine Junior (based at Les
Lindars), 3-7 yrs, 170FF per day, extra
60FF per day for lunch. SEI (based at
Les Lindars), 2-7 yrs, 210FF per day,
990FF for 6 days, both including lunch.
SEI Club de la Souris Verte (based
at Résidence de la Forêt and Hotel
Aujon), 3-12 yrs, 9am to 5pm, 210FF
per day, 1,040FF for 6 days, both
including lunch
Babysitting Hotel Les Lindars, or
through the tourist office

OTHER SPORTS
Parapente, hang-gliding, snow-mobiling,
ice-driving, climbing wall, swimming

WHAT'S NEW
● Résidence de la Fôret and Hotel
Aujon renovated ● additional shops at
Flaine Fôret

FOOD AND DRINK PRICES
Coffee 7FF, bottle of house wine 40FF,
beer 15FF, dish of the day 60FF

TOUR OPERATORS
Bladon Lines, Crystal, Direct Ski,
Enterprise, Fresh Tracks, Inghams,
Made to Measure, Neilson, Sally
Holidays, Ski Airtours, Ski Thomson,
Ski West, Snowpiper, Touralp

week the tourist office organises guided tours around the town's architectural sites.

In the centre of town is a botanical alpine garden with over 4,000 species of mountain plants from all around the world. Traditional-style bars and restaurants abound in what is a resort largely undiscovered by other nationalities, the British in particular. The hotels Neige et Roc and Les Sept Monts are recommended, together with Les Drugères. One reporter spoke highly of the restaurant Le Pierrot Gourmet. Samoëns has its own ski school, crèche for children from 6 months old, and ski kindergarten for children aged 3 to 6. It also has a cross-country school.

TOURIST OFFICE
F-74340 Samoëns, Haute Savoie
Tel 33 50 34 40 28
Fax 33 50 34 95 82

TOUR OPERATORS
Alpine Expressions, Brittany Ferries

Isola 2000, Alpes-Maritimes

ALTITUDE 2000m (6,560ft)

••

Good points extensive nursery slopes, skiing convenience, resort-level snow, well-linked lifts, late season holidays, sunny slopes, tree-level skiing, ideal for family holidays, traffic-free resort
Bad points lack of alpine charm, limited for non-skiers, lack of tough runs, limited après-ski, difficult road access
Linked or nearby resorts Auron (n)

Isola is the most southern alpine resort, a snowy island in the sunny South of France. On a good day it is 90 minutes from Nice up the dramatic road beside the Tinée ravines. The resort is not accessible from the north, which is in part the reason why so few British tour operators offer it in their brochures. British skiers do, however, make up a big slice of the winter business, many of them having bought their own apartments here in its early years.

The resort was built by a British property company in the 1960s. It was created with families in mind, as a convenient complex of shops, bars, economically designed apartments and hotels next to the lift station and a large, sunny nursery area. The original building, Front de Neige, is as convenient as it ever was, but also just as unattractive. In an attempt to dress up the soulless centre, the more attractive, wood-clad additions of Le Bristol, Le Hameau and Les Ardets have been built behind Front de Neige. These are less convenient, but contain bigger and better apartments and a luxurious hillside hotel. This has greatly helped the overall look of Isola, dissipating some of its claustrophobic atmosphere.

The ski area is limited in size, but varied enough for beginners, intermediate skiers and families with small children. Unlike other southern resorts, Isola is high enough not to warrant snow-cannon. Instead it offers a reimbursed lift pass to apartment occupiers if they are unable to ski back to the nearest apartments. Most of the lifts are packed into the heavily mechanised central segment of the ski area above Front de Neige, so it is possible for two out of the three segments to be closed without bringing the guarantee into action. On our visit, there was actually too much snow. Isola also offers a unique sun guarantee only to self-caterers: a free week's accommodation another time, if the resort's heliograph registers no sun for more than three consecutive days in a week.

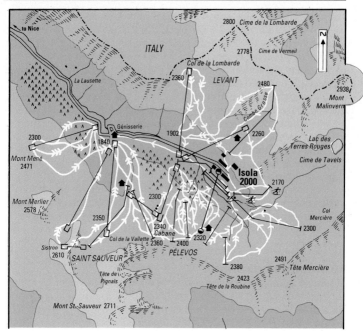

Despite its name, Isola is not an island, although it can feel like it when the approach road is blocked by snow. Auron makes a feasible day-trip for skiers with a car.

The skiing
Top 2610m (8,560ft) bottom 1800m (5,904ft)

The local piste map divides the skiing into three areas, although all of these are linked: the Domaine du Pelevos (immediately above the resort), the Domaine du Levant and the Domaine du Saint Sauveur.

The Pelevos area is densely furnished with lifts and pistes, the major lift being a gondola, which provides the main **mountain access** from the resort; secondary access is via a chair-lift. We have reports of bottle-necks on both these lifts. From the top (2320m) there are easy and intermediate runs back down through the trees, with links in both directions to drags which go slightly higher. Travelling eastwards, you reach a long green (beginner) run, away from the lifts, which is perfect for near-novices, in the right conditions, but hard work if there is new snow. Westwards, a drag-lift gives access to further varied runs to the resort and links into the Saint Sauveur area. Skiing down to the big car park at 1900m (the main way into the skiing for day visitors) brings you to a chair, which forms a second link with the Saint Sauveur area, as well as serving its own red (intermediate) and black (difficult) runs.

Saint Sauveur is the more serious sector, with satisfying skiing for intermediates and experts and the most interesting off-piste possibilities. A drag and short chair-lift take you to the highest point of Isola's skiing, the Cîme de Sistron (2610m), on the flank of Mont Saint Saveur.

There are red and blue (easy) variations of the run back down. Off the back of the mountain is a short black run leading to a long red down and a return drag-lift. Further across the mountainside is the chair-lift towards Mont Ménć, where black and red runs descend to the bottom of the chair. The return from here to the slopes above the resort is via the recently enlarged Genisserie chair.

Once up the Genisserie chair, a choice of lifts takes you back over La Cabane to the Pelevos slopes, with runs either to the resort or down to 1900m, where the main chairs go up to the Levant area where the Col de la Lombarde and Combe Grosse lifts serve south- and south-west-facing slopes. These are mainly on the open mountain above the trees. Easy traverses from this area link with drag-lifts serving long, flat green runs which are the extension of the nursery slopes.

The lift system works well enough, although we have complaints of misleading piste grading: 'Parts of green runs were difficult for beginners, whereas the blue runs were not always as difficult as expected.' On two evenings a week the Belvedere slope immediately above the resort is floodlit.

Mountain restaurants
Mountain restaurants are few and far between, but adequate for a small ski area with a good lift system, enabling skiers to return to the resort for lunch. The Genisserie at the bottom of Saint Sauveur is rustic. The Schuss self-service restaurant is recommended.

Beginners and children
The nursery slopes are superb, running the length of the resort, and the progression to real pistes is gradual. Beginners' instruction appears to be good, using both the *ski évolutif* (short ski) and traditional teaching methods. A couple of middle-aged beginners report: 'Tuition with the ESF was friendly, patient and we all had good fun.' We do, however, have some complaints about the ESF intermediate classes ('12 per class, poor "follow me down the hill" instruction, with very little stopping'). Ski instruction is also provided by some tour operators, often with a mixture of British and local instructors.

The children's village has indoor and outdoor activities, and for younger children there is a nursery. Reports are favourable.

The resort
The resort consists mainly of a zig-zag series of modern blocks linked by a twisting corridor, which takes you wherever you want to go within the main complex, including no fewer than 30 shops. These are flashy enough to betray Isola's second rôle as a venue for weekend sprees from the Côte d'Azur. Residents of Le Hameau are poorly served by shops, with only a supermarket, a ski shop and one restaurant. To get to and from the apartments they are now provided with a free funicular.

Accommodation
Accommodation is mainly in apartments. The three original hotels are spaced along the Front de Neige building arranged in price order from

up-piste, starting with Le Druos, leading on via the Pas du Loup to the more upmarket Le Chastillon. A short traverse away is the fairly new and expensive Diva hotel, with pleasant bedrooms, good service and excellent food. Apartments are at Les Adrets ('quite spacious and clean'), Le Hameau and Le Bristol. There are also a number of individual chalets.

Eating out

Of the restaurants in and around Front de Neige, the Cow Club in the middle of the nursery slope is highly praised by reporters for its good atmosphere, although it is not cheap. Le Starving at Le Hameau serves pizzas and Les Aviateurs is also recommended. La Buissonerie is reported to be good value and the Yeti is recommended. La Bergerie is cosy but expensive ('they even charged 5FF for a carafe of ordinary water').

Skiing facts: Isola 2000

TOURIST OFFICE
Le Pelevos, F-06420 Isola 2000,
Alpes-Maritimes
Tel 33 93 23 15 15
Fax 33 93 23 14 25

THE RESORT
By road Calais 1325km
By rail Nice 90km
By air Nice 1½ hrs
Visitor beds 10,000 (88% apartments, 12% hotels)
Transport traffic-free village centre

THE SKIING
Longest run Sistron to Genisserie, 6km (black/red)
Number of lifts 24
Number of trails/pistes 46 (15% beginner, 39% easy, 35% intermediate, 11% difficult)
Total of trails/pistes 120km
Nursery slopes 4 lifts
Summer skiing none
Snowmaking none

LIFT PASSES
Area pass Isola 2000, 513-619FF for 6 days
Day pass 134FF
Half-day pass 94FF after 12.30pm
Beginners points tickets
Children 12 yrs and under, 487FF for 6 days. 12-24 yrs 557FF for 6 days
Pensioners 60 yrs and over, as children
Credit cards accepted yes

SKI SCHOOLS
Adults ESF, 2 hrs am and/or pm,

460FF for 6 days
Children ESF, 2 hrs am and/or pm, 460FF for 6 days
Private lessons 162FF per hr
Special courses snowboarding
Guiding companies Bureau des Guides

CROSS-COUNTRY
Ski schools none
Loipe location and size 4km above the village

CHILDCARE
Non-ski kindergarten Les Pitchouns, 6 yrs and under, 8am-8pm, 800FF for 6 days, extra 43FF per day for lunch
Ski kindergarten Le Caribou, 3-8 yrs, 9am-5.15pm, 920FF for 6 days, extra 43FF per day for lunch
Babysitting Les Pitchouns or through tourist office

OTHER SPORTS
Heli-skiing, parapente, ice-driving, snow-mobiling, swimming, skating, curling, fitness centre, floodlit skiing

WHAT'S NEW
● Grands Vallons quad chair-lift

FOOD AND DRINK PRICES
Coffee 6FF, bottle of house wine 50FF, beer 15FF, dish of the day 60FF

TOUR OPERATORS
Made to Measure, Neilson, Seasun School Tours, Ski Thomson

Après-ski

Apart from the piano bar of the Diva, après-ski is confined to Front de Neige. The bars are busy in the early evening with the Rendezvous ('very friendly'), Le Crocodile ('crowded, but with a good atmosphere') and La Marmotte ('quite a relaxed atmosphere and live bands') recommended by reporters. There are two discos, which liven up at weekends and in high season. At other times, Isola's nightlife barely exists, apart from the odd torchlight descent and weekly fireworks display.

Isola is not recommended for cross-country skiers or non-skiers. There is a swimming-pool in the original Isola village, a bus ride away, and the skating rink is unattractively positioned in the shade of the main resort building. The shops are on the whole disappointing.

Megève, Haute Savoie

ALTITUDE 1100m (3,608ft)

....

Good points long and easy runs, activities for non-skiers, large choice of restaurants, ideal for beginners, lively and varied après-ski, short airport transfer, tree-level skiing, attractive village centre, ideal for families and children
Bad points lack of tough runs, low altitude, unreliable resort-level snow, heavy traffic outside pedestrian centre
Linked or nearby resorts Chamonix (n) – *see separate chapter*, Combloux (l), Flumet (n), Le Bettex (l), Les Contamines-Montjoie (n), Les Saisies (n), Notre-Dame-de-Bellecombe (n), Praz-sur-Arly (n), St- Gervais Mont-Blanc (l), St-Nicholas-de-Véroce (l)

Pretty Megève has seen major growth in recent years, but has still managed to retain the polish and natural charm, which made it one of France's most fashionable resorts in the early days of skiing. Once it gloried in the fact that, at the height of the season, it was the holiday home of more crowned heads of state than any other ski resort in Europe. Today, however, royalty extends no further than the princes of Arabia, with the Saudi royal family having a sumptuous chalet above the town at Rochebrune.

The Beautiful People who holiday in their private villas at St Tropez in the summer still come here for Christmas, New Year and high-season February. Along with Courchevel 1850, Megève is the place to see and be seen in the French Alps. The continued patronage of the Rothschild and Citroën families has much to do with it, but its success in instituting exclusivity is largely the consequence of keeping prices high in the restaurants and nightclubs, thereby keeping the mass market out of the resort.

The backbone of Megève's visitors are families, albeit of the well-heeled variety. The rest of its clientèle is made up of non-skiers who wear designer ski suits never likely to touch the snow, or furs to walk around the town and travel up the lifts for lunch.

The old village centres on a fine medieval church and carefully restored old buildings. The streets are rich in designer boutiques straight from the Faubourg St Honoré, and the sound of sleigh bells is everywhere. The downside is that Megève is not small, but an expanding mass of suburbs suffocating in the heavy traffic and it is a resort where much care should be given to selecting the location of your accommodation. Après-ski is taken almost more seriously here than the skiing, and the choice of venues is enormous, ranging from the simplest of bars through incredibly noisy discos to the most exotic of nightclubs.

219

The skiing

Top 2350m (7,708ft) bottom 850m (2,788ft)

The skiing takes place in three very separate areas on smooth, well-groomed and generally delightfully easy pistes. **Mountain access** is by joint gondola, for both the Mont d'Arbois and Rochbrune areas, which takes you out of the town to the base of Rochbrune. From here, a cable car followed by a gondola takes you up to Mont d'Arbois, the best-known and most extensive of these areas, on the eastern side of a crescent of peaks in the lee of Mont Blanc. Mont d'Arbois is also accessed by separate gondolas from La Princesse outside Combloux as well as from Le Bettex above St-Gervais. On the crest where all the lifts meet there is a series of small link drags and runs, plus a scattering of hotels and restaurants and panoramic walking paths.

The skiing around Mont d'Arbois is predominantly on the gentle side although there are some more challenging runs higher up on Mont Joux, the next peak along from Mont d'Arbois, on the ridge which climbs towards Mont Joly, with increasingly steep slopes around the bowl. The scope here has been greatly increased by the chair-lift going up over an impressive open slope of about 33° in places to the high point of the area at 2350m. A choice of long and fairly gentle red (intermediate) runs and some excellent off-piste takes you down into the attractive little village of St-Nicolas-de-Véroce.

From Mont Joux long, easy runs descend to Les Communailles near Le Bettex, with drag-lifts back up to the ridge. The runs into Megève itself are mostly wide and easy, including a long green (beginner) piste. The slopes on the north-facing La Princesse side of the mountain are wooded and more challenging than the runs to Megève, but the black (difficult) grading is not altogether justified. The off-piste through the trees often provides some of the best skiing; the Bureau des Guides de Megève is warmly recommended.

The Rochebrune area is served by Megève's oldest cable car, which starts outside the town centre, as well as the gondola from the centre. Future plans include replacing the cable car with a 12-person gondola to Alpette. The area offers arguably the most attractive runs in delightful tree-lined settings. Reporters recommend this as being less crowded than Mont d'Arbois. From the top stations of the cable car and gondola, parallel drag- and chair-lifts take you on up to Alpette, the start of Megève's downhill course. The highest point, Côte 2000, also provides the toughest skiing, including the women's downhill course and some good off-piste. Two fairly new high-speed quad chairs have added to the appeal and accessibility of the area. A detachable quad replaces the two-stage drag-lift between the altiport and the top of Côte 2000 for the 1993-4 season, and snowmaking is being introduced at the altiport.

Megève's third skiing area is Le Jaillet, completely self-contained and reached by gondola only after a lengthy walk, or ski-bus, from the centre of town. The runs are both gentle and pleasant, mainly suited to beginners and early intermediates. Nearly all reporters are full of praise for the quality of the piste-grooming. Piste-marking is said to be insufficient, with descending numbers given, but no indication of which run you are actually on. A lack of information noticeboards was also a complaint. Piste-grading is not always consistent; some black runs are said to be easier than the reds due to good grooming, and some blues have difficult sections. The local piste map is not one of Megève's strongest points. Lift queues of up to 20 minutes long are commonplace in high season. In common with other European resorts, reporters complain of chairs going up empty or half-full; the lift company could reduce much of the waiting time simply by operating more efficiently.

Mountain restaurants

With a total of 30 restaurants in the ski area, Megève certainly has no shortage of interesting lunch venues. Reporters do, however, note that mountain eating is expensive, with prices sometimes even higher than in Swiss resorts. L'Alpette, on the crest of the same name, offers a unique view of the surrounding area. The self-service La Caboche is good value by local standards. The Chalet Ideal Sports, a popular place for the fur-coated, has excellent food and 'not prohibitive' prices. L'Auberge du Grenard offers typically French cooking and local specialities. The Jaillet Supérieur has a cosy atmosphere and serves traditional alpine meals. The Côte 2000 restaurant has 'fresh, well-cooked food'.

Beginners and children

The nursery slopes at Mont d'Arbois are good and easily accessible by cable car or bus. The resort also abounds in green and gentle blue runs for the next stage of learning. There is a new beginners' drag-lift in the trees at the top station of Jaillet. Megève has four ski kindergartens (each one next to a main lift station), and one non-ski kindergarten.

The resort

Megève has grown to become one of France's largest ski resorts, with suburbs stretching out in all directions. The attractive medieval centre is traffic-free and, according to one reporter, is 'the perfect place to parade, pose and show off your dog'. There are no noticeable eyesores created by large modern buildings and all the new ones have been built in a sympathetic chalet style.

Traffic is a major problem, particularly from 4 to 7pm; a main road runs through the town although the actual centre is bypassed. Ski-buses link the centre with the lifts, and coaches run to other nearby resorts covered by the Mont Blanc lift pass. There are several covered car-parks.

Reporters praise the 'wonderful shops'. The pedestrian mall in the heart of the old village contains most of them: jewellers, perfumeries, delicatessens, chocolate-makers, luxury boutiques and sports equipment retailers are numbered among the resort's 200 retail outlets.

Accommodation

Megève has a wide range of more than 50 hotels, as well as sumptuous and more utilitarian private chalets. The standard of its six four-stars and some of its fifteen three-stars is outstandingly high. The Parc des Loges has art deco rooms each with its own fireplace. The Chalet du Mont d'Arbois is owned by Baron Edmond de Rothschild and located some distance from the town near the Mont d'Arbois cable car. Les Loges du Mont Blanc is the town's showpiece, set in the centre. At the bottom of La Princesse ski area is the Hotel Princesse de Megève, which has only 11 rooms. At the top of Mont d'Arbois and reached by gondola is L'Igloo, again with only 11 rooms. Les Fermes de Marie is a modern hotel built in traditional style with a fitness centre and swimming-pool. In the three-star category hotels recommended by reporters include Le Fer à Cheval, one of the resort's biggest hotels, and Au Coin de Feu.

Eating out

A reporter comments on the 'extensive quantity and variety of available eating places to suit all budgets'. This is certainly true; Megève has more than 70 restaurants and is, along with Courchevel 1850, one of the gourmet dining resorts of the French Alps. But it also offers a good choice of less exotic places. The Chamois is a lively bistro with good local white wines and fondue. At the Piano à Bretelles you can eat and dance the night away. Good-value restaurants include Les Griottes, which has à la carte specialities, and the Michel Gaudin, which combines Mediterranean and alpine cooking. The Sapinière is an unpretentious bistro with some of the best food in town and comes highly recommended. La Maisonette is also popular.

At the top of the range, the Hotel Mont Blanc's Les Enfants Terribles, with interior design by Jean Cocteau, has delicious but expensive food. La Rotonde serves Lyonnais cuisine in 1930s surroundings. The Chalet du Mont d'Arbois used to be the Rothschild family home and is now a high-quality restaurant with one of the most interesting wine cellars in Europe. The Fermes de Marie offers good Savoyard cooking and Le Fer à Cheval serves a fine dinner, but is also recommended for its English breakfast. Two unusual eating places are Le Phnom Penh, which offers unusual Cambodian food, and the Viking, which has atmospheric surroundings of dark wood beams and roughly hewn tables.

Après-ski

After skiing Le Prieuré and the Milady are recommended for tea and cakes at 5pm. The Milady has 'delectable apple tart'. Le Chamois is a traditional place with a warm atmosphere. The Village Rock Café is popular with teenagers.

Later on the nightlife is pricey, but none the less generally worth the expense, revolving around Megève's nine nightclubs and piano bars. Les Cinq Rues is a jazz club set in a cosy chalet, complete with open fire. Les Caves de Megève has a young atmosphere. Les Enfants Terribles is a popular bar in the centre of the village. The most popular nightclubs include L'Esquinade, which is also a casino. Sacha Distel and Charles Aznavour are among its regulars. Le Rols Club is the place for those who like their evening entertainment on the decadent side. The Glamour is half-piano bar and half-disco. The Pallas and the Cocoon keep going until dawn. The large sports centre contains a good swimming-pool.

Les Contamines-Montjoie 1164m (3,818ft)

This unspoilt Savoyard village is near the head of the narrow Montjoie valley just over the hill from Megève. It has a keen following, despite the fact that the whole set-up is badly planned: the long village is on one side of the river and the ski area on the other, and the base station Le Lay is a long uphill walk from the centre. Prices here are, on the whole, below average for this area of France and the accommodation is modest.

Two efficient gondolas take skiers up to a plateau at 1500m where a sole gondola can become a bottleneck to Le Signal and the start of the main skiing. There is a small nursery lift at Le Signal at 1900m, which can often be busy when snow is poor lower down. There is little challenging skiing, although we have experienced some excellent off-piste all over the area after a fresh snowfall. A large number of runs are spread around a vast, mainly north-east facing bowl behind Le Signal. The Col du Joly (2000m) separates the main bowl from a smaller, but also open, area of intermediate runs. The ski-bus is not covered by the lift pass.

The rather basic mountain restaurant at Signal has stunning views of Mont Blanc and the addition of an indoor picnic area. The restaurant at the bottom of the Roselette is rustic and cosy; one reporter experienced the proprietor taking everyone's beers away during a visit by the *gendarmerie*.

The village runs along a single street with an old church, old fashioned hotels and a few shops and cafés. The best location is on the east side of the river near the gondola. Both the Chemenaz and the Christiania hotels have swimming-pools. The Gai Soleil, Le Miage and the centrally placed Chamois are all recommended. Two well-stocked supermarkets cater for those staying in apartments. Nightlife is almost non-existent, according to reporters, with the village 'virtually dead after 7pm'.

TOURIST OFFICE
74170 Haute Savoie
Tel 33 50 47 01 58
Fax 33 50 47 09 54

TOUR OPERATORS
Ski Falcon, Ski Total, Ski Trax

Notre-Dame-de-Bellecombe 1130m (3,707ft)

This small village at the base of Mont Reguet has always attracted school parties and those looking to ski on a strict budget. The skiing is in two parts, the west-facing slopes of Mont Reguet and a more extensive area on Mont Rond. The latter is best reached from Le Planay, which in turn is reached by car or free bus from Notre-Dame. From Le Planay the main lift up Mont Rond is a long chair going to 2010m, serving blue, red and black runs back down again. The top section connects with a drag-lift on the west-facing slopes above the village of Les Frasses. On the other side of Mont Rond more challenging pistes are served by drag-lift and descend to Plan Dessert. The longest runs in this area are from the top of the Vorès drag back to Plan Dessert. There are no mountain restaurants, but the surrounding villages have a choice of eating places.

The village is fairly busy, with the main Flumet/Les Saisies road running around it. A car is essential for those staying at neighbouring Le

Planay at the base of Mont Rond's skiing. Accommodation at Notre-Dame is mainly in apartments including the spacious Equipe. The half-dozen simple hotels include Le Tétras, out of town on the road to Les Saisies, Les Armailles and the Bellevue. There are several bars and a few restaurants including Le Chamois and La Mollinière.

TOURIST OFFICE
73590 Savoie
Tel 33 79 31 61 40
Fax 33 79 31 67 09

TOUR OPERATORS
none

Praz-sur-Arly 1036m (3,398ft)

Two chair-lifts take you to the main ski area below the Crêt du Midi at 1900m where several drags serve mainly blue runs above the tree-line. A chair-lift goes to 2000m where there is more taxing skiing, including a black run. A chair and drag take you from the nursery slopes to the Roc des Evettes and Mont Reguet skiing, with mainly easy runs in the tree-line except for a black run beside the drag-lift. A chair-lift links Mont Reguet with Mont Rond, where several lifts serve a variety of pistes.

Accommodation is mainly in hotels and chalets, with l'Edelweiss and Mont Charvin the main hotels; neither has a restaurant. Others include Les Quatres As, Le Darbello and Les Deux Savoies. The Cannibal's, Auberge d'Amou and Les Dryades restaurants are recommended. Nightlife centred on a handful of bars. The kindergarten takes children from 18 months old. Praz also has a couple of cross-country trails and 15km of cleared walks.

TOURIST OFFICE
74120 Haute Savoie
Tel 33 50 21 90 57
Fax 33 50 21 98 08

TOUR OPERATORS
none

St-Gervais Mont-Blanc 850m (2,788ft)

As a spa, St-Gervais has attracted tourists since 1806. The town is an informal if busy one ('full of traffic, even during the night') on two sides of a river gorge. It is popular with families wanting a cheaper alternative to Megève. A reporter recommends it as an ideal base for visiting other resorts in France, Italy and Switzerland. Nearby Le Bettex is a quieter village with a few comfortable hotels and some cross-country skiing. The main ski area of St-Gervais is on the slopes of Mont d'Arbois and linked with that of Megève. It is accessed by a fast, 20-person gondola from the edge of the resort to Le Bettex. The second stage goes up to what is known on this side of the mountain as St-Gervais 1850. This is a popular and often crowded entrance into Megève's ski area. Skiing on the Mont Blanc side of St-Gervais is served by the Tramway, a funicular which climbs slowly to the Col de Voza at 1653m, where it links to the skiing

Skiing facts: Megève

TOURIST OFFICE
BP 24, F-74120 Megève, Haute Savoie
Tel 33 50 21 27 28
Fax 33 50 93 03 09

THE RESORT
By road Calais 890km
By rail Sallanches 12km, regular bus service to resort
By air Geneva 1½ hrs
Visitor beds 14,105 (74% apartments and chalets, 26% hotels)
Transport bus links centre with access lifts, coach shuttles run between the 13 ski resorts in the Mont Blanc region

THE SKIING
Longest run Milloz, 3.6km (red)
Number of lifts 82
Number of trails/pistes 121 (30% easy, 45% intermediate, 25% difficult)
Total of trails/pistes 300km (Evasion Mont Blanc)
Nursery slopes 3 lifts
Summer skiing none
Snowmaking 3 hectares covered

LIFT PASSES
Area pass Evasion Mont Blanc (covers Megève, St-Gervais, St- Nicholas, Combloux), 653-764FF for 6 days. Skipass Mont Blanc (covers 13 resorts including Chamonix and Argentière, and a free day at Courmayeur), 775-860FF for 6 days
Day pass Evasion Mont Blanc 148FF
Half-day pass 115FF after midday
Beginners no free lifts
Children Evasion Mont Blanc, 12 yrs and over, 540-634FF for 6 days. Skipass Mont Blanc, 12 yrs and over, 580-645FF for 6 days. Free for 4 yrs and under with pass required only on cable cars
Pensioners 60 yrs and over, as children
Credit cards accepted yes

SKI SCHOOLS
Adults ESF, 9.30-11.30am and 3-5pm, 710FF for 6 days. SEI, 10am-midday or 3-5pm, 475FF for 6 days
Children ESF, 5-12 yrs, 9.30-11.30am and 3-5pm, 650FF for 6 days. SEI, 5-12 yrs, and SE1 Souris Club, 4-6 yrs, 10am-

midday or 3-5pm, 500FF for 6 days
Private lessons ESF 165FF, SEI 175FF, both per hr
Special courses snowboarding, telemark, monoskiing, race training, artistic/acrobatic skiing
Guiding companies Bureau des Guides de Megève, and through SEI

CROSS-COUNTRY
Ski schools ESF (Mont d'Arbois)
Loipe location and size 70km in and around Megève

CHILDCARE
Non-ski kindergarten Meg'Loisirs (on route du Palais des Sports), 12 mths-6 yrs, 8am-6pm, 190FF per day, 800FF for 5 days. Both prices include lunch
Ski kindergarten Alpage (next to Mont d'Arbois cable car) 3-6 yrs, 9.15am-5.30pm, 345FF per day. Princesse (next to Princesse cable car), 3-6 yrs, 9am-5pm, 220FF per day. Caboche (next to Caboche cable car), 3-10 yrs, 9am-5.30pm, 265FF per day. Montjoie (next to Jaillet cable car), 3-12 yrs, 8.45am-5.30pm, 180FF per day. All prices include lunch
Babysitting list available from tourist office

OTHER SPORTS
Parapente, skating, curling, indoor tennis, climbing wall, fitness centres, swimming

WHAT'S NEW
● Cross-country trail (10km) at Maz-Côte 2000 ● snowmaking on Côte 2000 ● chair replaces two drags at Côte 2000

FOOD AND DRINK PRICES
Coffee 8FF, bottle of house wine 29.50FF, beer 15FF, dish of the day 59FF

TOUR OPERATORS
Bladon Lines, Brittany Ferries, Jean Stanford Ski Holidays, Made to Measure, Sally Holidays, Ski Campus, Ski Esprit, Ski Savoie, Touralp, White Roc Ski

above Les Houches. The only run back to St-Gervais is off-piste and sometimes unskiable. Hotel-Restaurant Igloo and the Terminus in Le Fayet both have good reputations.

St-Gervais has three nursery slope lifts and its own kindergarten, which takes children between six months and six years old. The two ski schools (ESF at St-Gervais and ESI at Le Bettex) teach snowboarding, monoskiing, telemarking, slalom skiing and off-piste, as well as the usual group classes. There is also a local guiding organisation: St-Gervais Val Montjoie Mountain Guides. Other sports in the resort include skating, curling, sleigh rides, parapente, hang-gliding, and a climbing wall.

Hotels here include the Carlina with a swimming-pool, the Val d'Este, L'Adret (without a restaurant) and the Edelweiss. A reporter recommends the Regina with its simple rooms, reasonable prices and friendly staff. At Le Bettex, the quiet Arbois-Bettex has a swimming-pool and the Flèche d'Or is also recommended. St-Gervais has a moderate range of restaurants with three of particularly good value: L'Eventail and L'Eterle pizzerias and the Dômes de Miage. Le Four, La Grangni and Le Robinson are all popular eating places serving a variety of local specialities. Val d'Este and Carlina are the more upmarket establishments in the town, La Tanière and La Chalette are traditional. The family-run Chalet Remy in Le Bettex is recommended.

Après-ski is said to be 'extremely limited'. The only disco is La Nuit des Temps, although the Chardon Bleu restaurant in Le Fayet has a dance floor.

TOURIST OFFICE
BP 5, 74170 St-Gervais Mont-Blanc
Tel 33 50 78 22 43
Fax 33 50 47 76 08

TOUR OPERATORS
Brittany Ferries, Ski La Vie, Ski Savoie,
Ski Trax, Snowcoach

La Plagne, Savoie

ALTITUDE 1250m (4,100ft) – 2050m (6,724ft)

Good points large intermediate ski area, skiing convenience, resort-level snow in the higher villages, variety of easy runs, extensive off-piste skiing, ideal for family skiing, extensive nursery slopes, freedom from cars, facilities for beginners
Bad points limited après-ski, lack of challenging skiing, peak season lift bottlenecks, limited for non-skiers
Linked or nearby resorts Les Arcs (n), Champagny-en-Vanoise (l), Les Coches (l), Courchevel (n), Montalbert (l), Montchavin (l)

La Plagne is not one, but eleven separate villages which collectively form France's premier ski resort for her domestic market. The satellites, varying from ugly purpose-built through pleasant modern to traditional farming hamlet, are all perched at different altitudes on the Tarentaise mountainside above the small and undistinguished valley town of Aime. Curiously La Plagne came into existence as the result of a youth employment scheme dreamed up by Pierre Borrione, a former mayor of Aime in the early 1960s. Borrione was so concerned by the decline in local light industry and agriculture and the consequent migration of youth to the cities that he commissioned a feasibility study on winter tourism. A new road was carved into the mountain up to what is now Plagne Centre and the resort opened for business with 3,000 beds. Today that figure has swelled to 41,000 and the network of 112 interlinking lifts covers 210km of piste.

La Plagne is a large and very fragmented place, an ugly duckling which has given birth to some surprisingly appealing offspring as well as one unpresentable mistake in Aime la Plagne. The area is initially confusing to the newcomer, but straightforward in its appeal. The skiing is enormous in extent and vertical range; few of the pistes are challenging, but the off-piste skiing is excellent. The area is topped by a 3250m glacier with summer skiing and snow conditions are reliable except at the lower extremes of the network. Nursery slopes are abundant and immediately accessible and childcare facilities are good in most of the villages. Nearly all accommodation is in modern apartments, conveniently placed for getting to and from skiing. Apart from some lift bottlenecks, which manifest themselves in the peak season, La Plagne is a perfect recipe for the sort of winter holiday that suits many skiers.

Here, more than in any other resort in Europe, choice of holiday location is of crucial importance and before booking it is essential to discover just how your travel agent or tour operator interprets 'La Plagne'. The main resort centres are set on gentle slopes above and below the tree-line. In descending order of altitude from 2100m to

1800m they are: Aime La Plagne, Belle Plagne, Plagne Villages, Plagne Soleil, Plagne Centre, Plagne Bellecôte and Plagne 1800. In the most modern of these centres the designers have tried, with some success, to reproduce a village atmosphere. Most of our reporters have visited Bellecôte and 1800 and are in general impressed with this manufactured ambience.

There are also smaller resort components much lower down, some of them modified old villages, others new developments. These lower resorts – Montchavin, Les Coches, Champagny, Montalbert – are not directly below the main parts of La Plagne, but are reached by first taking lifts up to the rim of the wide bowl around the resort centre. In bad weather these lifts are liable to close, making the low, sheltered skiing inaccessible to centrally based skiers. The lift pass is wide-ranging and a car is helpful in making full use of it on excursions to Les Arcs, Tignes and Val d'Isère as well as other nearby resorts.

The skiing
Top 3250m (10,660ft) bottom 1250m (4,100ft)
The core of La Plagne's skiing is an area above Plagne Centre and its similar altitude neighbours Plagne Villages, Bellecôte and Belle Plagne, all of them set between 1930m and 2050m. The western side of this basin is dominated by the giant all-purpose building of Aime la Plagne at 2100m, from which it is easy to ski down to Centre. Below it is Plagne 1800, a more modern and sympathetic resort unit. There are three other aspects to the skiing: runs through woods behind Aime la Plagne as far as Montalbert; south-facing slopes above Champagny; and a high altitude area of glacier skiing leading down to runs in the tree-line above Montchavin and Les Coches. The top of the glacier down to Montchavin is an enormous descent of 15km and 2000m vertical, but there are no prepared pistes down and an indirect chain of six lifts up.

The main **mountain access** points are too numerous to mention in this, the definitive ski-in ski-out resort. The central basin above the main residential units provides timid skiers with an extensive range of not very long and not at all steep runs with a vertical range of about 500m. Above Plagne Bellecôte and Belle Plagne is a big area of almost entirely gentle runs, some of them satisfyingly long. More challenging terrain can be explored on the slopes below the 2700m Roche de Mio.

The pistes converging on Plagne Villages and Plagne Centre are steeper and include some genuine red (intermediate) runs down from the rim of the bowl and lower points. Immediately above Centre is an unusual area of mini-canyons, with on- and off-piste routes winding through them. On the open slopes between Centre and Aime la Plagne are some of the most consistently challenging red runs, with roundabout blue (easy) alternatives.

The long Emile Allais black (difficult) piste from Aime la Plagne is one of the best and least-skied runs on the mountain. It takes you down through woods past Plagne 1800 all the way to 1400m; the return is via two drag-lifts. Behind the Biolley lifts above Aime la Plagne there are stiff runs with pitches of over 30°, initially west-facing and liable to be icy and very difficult in the mornings. After this steep open slope, a gentle trail through woods links with the Emile Allais run or with the Les Adrets lift to the rounded peak of Le Fornelet (1970m) for a gentle run through the woods to Montalbert. A chair-lift from Montalbert takes you back up to Le Fornelet. The link with Aime and Centre has also been improved by the new Coqs chair out of the intervening valley to a point high above Aime.

The south-facing slopes above Champagny can be reached from several points above the central resort units without any great difficulty. From Grande Rochette, Col de Forcle and particularly from Roche de Mio there are long confidence-building intermediate runs away from the lifts. For good skiers, the toughest skiing and usually the best snow is in the area beside the long, steep Verdons lifts; from here an interesting red run goes all the way down to Champagny and an efficient gondola takes you back up as far as the tree-line from where you take the Borselier drags. The remainder of the Champagny skiing is easy, sunny and not very extensive.

The Bellecôte Glacier is the key to La Plagne's success as a good intermediate ski area. Unlike many glacial ski areas it opens up plenty of challenging skiing, with long and wide black runs of nearly 1000m vertical down to 2300m from where the isolated Chalet de Bellecôte drag-lift takes you back up into the system. Off-piste you can ski even further, all the way to Les Bauches at 1800m, where there are lifts back toward Plagne Bellecôte and an easy piste down to Montchavin. In the company of a guide the off-piste opportunities are excellent, including long runs down towards Peisey and the Champagny valley. There is also a moderately easy red run from the glacier to the Col de la Chiaupe. The glacier lifts are unfortunately often closed, particularly early in the season.

The Montchavin/Les Coches runs are most directly reached from the main bowl by a chair-lift from Plagne Bellecôte to Arpette. This sector can also be accessed by a good, long, open red from Roche de Mio; the top half can be repeated by taking a chair back up. They provide plenty of variety of tree-line skiing, with a drop of over 1000m vertical from the Arpette chair-lift to Montchavin. Returning to Arpette from Montchavin or Les Coches is slow, involving four lifts. The pistes below Pierres Blanches above these two villages provide some of the best tree-level skiing when visibility is poor. They are graded red and blue, but none of the blues is easy; at their steepest they tend to be narrow, to the discomfort of timid intermediate skiers. Given the right snow conditions the off-piste between the trees here can be truly exceptional.

The two drags above Pierres Blanches serve broad open slopes, gentle except for tricky bits above the restaurant. The runs down from the flanks of Dos Rond into the bowl above Les Bauches are steeper than their blue grading suggests; further round the bowl the run served by the Crozats chair is easier and usually has better snow. The Crozats chair also provides a link with Belle Plagne when it is open, which is not always as the steep start of the run is vulnerable to sunshine.

In general the lift system runs smoothly, even if you do spend a disproportionate length of time on lifts getting around this widely spread ski area. Queuing can be a problem during the main French school holidays. Around 80 per cent of the resort's beds are in the central area,

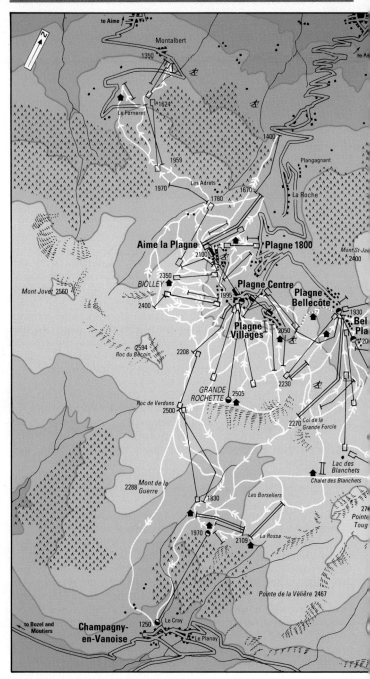

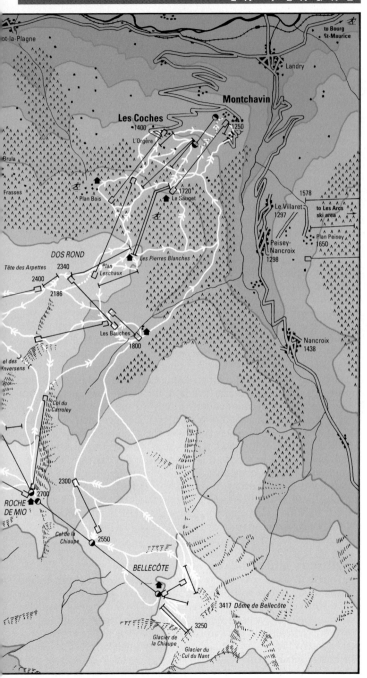

to Bourg
St-Maurice

Landry

Montchavin

Les Coches
1400
L'Orgère
1250

Brula

Frasses

Plan Bois
1720
Le Sauget

1578

Le Villaret
1297

to Les Arcs
ski area

Plan Peisey
1650

Peisey-
Nancroix
1298

DOS ROND

Tête des Arpettes
2340
2400
2186

Plan
Leschaux
Les Pierres Blanches

Les Bauches
1800

Nancroix
1438

el des
nversens

Col du
Carroley

ROCHE
DE MIO
2700

2300

2550

Col de la
Chiaupe

BELLECÔTE

3417 Dôme de Bellecôte

3250

Glacier de
la Chiaupe

Glacier du
Cul du Nant

which means a lot of skiers set off at much the same time in the mornings and return en masse at the end of the skiing day. Plagne Bellecôte is a bottleneck; the improved chair-lift to Arpette seems to have eliminated serious queues to reach the Montchavin sector and by offering an alternative roundabout route to Roche de Mio it has even reduced, but by no means removed, the queues for the gondola. Queues for the Grande Rochette gondola out of Plagne Centre (after lunch as well as in the mornings) have been relieved only partly by the recently built chair-lift to Verdons, giving an alternative route to Champagny.

When snow cover is poor on the lower slopes here, or in nearby resorts, the glacier can become dismally crowded. Snow-cannon are used to good effect on a short length of piste at Belle Plagne and the final approach to Montchavin from a point level with Les Coches.

Mountain restaurants

Eating places on the mountain are by no means the strong point of La Plagne, which is surprising for a resort of this magnitude. One reporter goes so far as to dismiss them as 'uniformly dreadful' and the only place he said he could tolerate was the English bar in Plagne Soleil where the draught Guinness made up for everything else. This extreme view apart, the restaurants are adequate, but the real gastronomic experiences in the region are to be found in small traditional restaurants in the lower outlying villages.

Plan Bois above Les Coches is recommended for its 'excellent *vin chaud*' and 'tasty French cooking'. Most reporters found the restaurant just below Roche de Mio to be the best at altitude, with 'plenty of seating and reasonable prices'. The crêperie in Plagne Bellecôte is lavishly praised, 'but only worth visiting on sunny days because there is no seating inside'. The restaurant at the bottom of the Rossa drags above Champagny is also recommended, 'if only for the view from the sundeck'. The Bar Soleil at Centre is right on the slopes and offers 'nourishing pasta meals'. The restaurant inside the Grande Rochette gondola station is praised for its 'good, filling pizzas'. The nearby Bistroquet de St Trop has 'excellent food and is reasonable value'. Le Bec Fin and Le Chaudron in Plagne Centre are said to be good value.

Les Bauches, on the long run down from Bellecôte to Montchavin, is 'excellent, with a sunny terrace'. L'Alpette, last stop before Bellecôte on the way back from Montchavin, is 'nothing special, but perfectly reasonable in both quality and price'. The chalet at 1830m on the way down to Champagny is reportedly 'authentic'.

Beginners and children

The nursery slopes are generally very good. Plagne Centre, Plagne Villages, Belle Plagne and Bellecôte are the most suitable of all, with gentle surrounding slopes which are reliable for snow cover. We have continuing positive reports on the ESF at Belle Plagne. Reporters do, however, comment on the surprisingly poor standard of English spoken by instructors, given the high number of English-speaking visitors. The reason relates to the volume of French skiers who come here compared to the small percentage of English. One correspondent rightly notes that 'you only get as much out of group lessons as you are prepared to put in' and skiers should not necessarily be deterred by the overtly French attitude of the ESF. However, one reporter remarked that 'the attitude of the instructors we encountered was thoroughly pleasant – no arrogant boy-racers here.' Another spoke warmly of his week in an advanced class.

In startling contrast the ESF at Plagne 1800 brought a postbag of complaints. One disgruntled reader comments: 'Only a mutiny plus pressure by reps got us less than 20 in a group.' Another said of his class: 'We had the impression of being ski fodder, filling time between more interesting and rewarding engagements.' Facilities for children are generally excellent, with nurseries and ski kindergartens in all the resort units.

The resorts

All the altitude villages are linked by bus or lift from 8am until 1am. Each resort unit has its own character (or lack of it) and is entirely self-contained. Plagne Centre, the original 1960s development is still the main centre for shopping, entertainment and après-ski. The buildings are big, square blocks, many of them linked by covered walkways. The hub is a dark and dank underground commercial precinct with lots of shops, bars and restaurants in little cubicles.

Aime la Plagne at 2100m is the highest satellite and the ugliest, a giant single building which looks like the beached hulk of some mighty ocean liner. The odd reporter who found himself on board was decidedly unimpressed. Happily, it is not popular with British tour operators. Plagne Bellecôte is also a single development, well placed for the skiing and recommended by several reporters. But it is irritatingly inconvenient, with the lifts starting uphill of the building. Plagne Villages is more pleasingly constructed in neo-Savoyarde style with mainly privately owned chalets and apartments.

Plagne 1800 has the attraction of individual chalet-style buildings and the standard of apartment is said to be high, although it is situated slightly out of the mainstream. Plagne Soleil is the latest development: a couple of blocks of apartments and shops situated a 10-minute walk up the mountain from Centre. Reporters speak enthusiastically of both its comfort and its convenience ('Although expansion is inevitable, it will remain much smaller than the other Plagnes and it is really quite impressive. Our apartment was spacious compared with other French apartments we have stayed in. We could not fault it, or the building in which it was housed').

By far the majority of our reporters and British holidaymakers stay in Belle Plagne, which has a more colourful and sympathetically conceived design than the others; it is convenient for skiing, especially for Roche de Mio, and has adequate, comfortable and quiet apartments. There is, however, little for those looking for a high-profile nightlife. One reporter points out that in all the altitude resorts you tend to feel isolated despite the regular mountain bus service: 'The connection between Belle Plagne and the rest of the world is tenuous – the coach journey down to Aime has to be pre-booked and so it is difficult to decide spontaneously to have a day off.'

Accommodation

More than 90 per cent of all accommodation is in apartments, which vary little in size and facilities. Nowhere more than La Plagne does the rule of thumb for French apartments apply: 'sleeps four comfortably' really means 'just adequate for a couple'. To be fair, most tour operators do not try to fill them to recommended capacity. Some of the newer apartments, in Plagne Soleil and in 1800, are more spacious.

In Belle Plagne those recommended by reporters include the residences Agate, Centaur, Maeva, Croix du Sud and Nereides. The Maeva are said to be 'excellent by French standards, really spacious and comfortable'. The Nereides is well positioned right at the top of the resort ('the secret is to have a seventh-floor apartment, which gives direct access to the snow at the back of the building, otherwise the scrum for the lifts at the end of the day can be annoying'). The Agate is described as 'standard French'. The only real complaint is that the baths are too small. The new Winform health centre in Belle Plagne offers special half-board health packages: you stay in the La Carène apartments and eat in the health club restaurants. The Eldorador Hotel receives lavish praise: 'I cannot praise it enough, it is the only place to stay,'and 'the restaurant was very cosy and the food excellent.' The one supermarket is small, but adequate, although 'not as good as the one in Bellecôte'.

Résidence Le Cervin in Plagne Soleil is generally considered comfortable although one reporter complained of inadequate hot water and troublesome electrics. The Lauze apartments in Plagne 1800 are said to be very small. Several reporters complained of having to pay a 1,000FF deposit on arrival to ensure their apartments were left clean and tidy. The three-star Hotel Graciosa, on the edge of Plagne Centre, is small and friendly and its restaurant, the Etoile d'Or, is highly regarded.

Eating out

Le Matafan in Belle Plagne has live music and is a firm favourite over many years, although we have a couple of reports suggesting food and service are not always as good as they used to be. Le Mouflon and Au Vieux Tyrol are warmly praised. La Cloche is 'informal, reasonably priced and has excellent pizzas and *pierrade*'. Le Bec Fin, Le Bistroquet, Le Chaudron and La Cheminée in Centre are also recommended. La Bartavelle in La Plagne 1800 is 'exceptional value, but not cheap'. Froggies is 'cheap, cheerful and fun'. La Savoia is a popular new restaurant with cabaret in Bellecôte.

Après-ski

La Plagne is not the place for those who view a riotous nightlife as an integral part of their holiday. There are bars and restaurants in all the residential units, piano bars in Centre and Bellecôte and a few overpriced discos, mainly in Centre. It does, however, lack places with any character or animated atmosphere. The Hotel Eldorador has a jazz band and its staff put on a nightly cabaret, which includes karaoke and a magician. Belle Plagne has the new Winform health centre with a ten-pin bowling alley and an electric golf clinic, sauna, steam room and gym. Matt's Pub is the new gathering place for young British in Belle Plagne. Bellecôte has an outdoor skating rink. The Grande Rochette gondola is sometimes open in the evening, with fondue and *brasserades* served at the mountain restaurant at the top. Tom's bar in 1800 is a favourite with the young British. It has its own disco after 10pm.

There is little for non-skiers, apart from extensive cross-country skiing and the Olympic bob run. The bob costs 600FF to travel down as 'ballast' sandwiched between an experienced driver and brakeman, or 500FF for a slightly slower descent on 'a kind of inflatable raft – for 90 seconds of pleasure the price seems to be about as steep as the run, but worth every penny'. One reporter warns against offers of cut-price runs as 'these do not include either return transport or insurance, both of which are essential'.

Montchavin 1250m (4,100ft)

Montchavin is a small old village which had most of its rustic wrinkles ironed out when it was transformed into a miniature ski resort in the early 1970s, but it is still undeniably attractive, with the pistes down from Arpette ending in an orchard in front of pleasant restaurant terraces. It manages to retain a level of village atmosphere in its bars and restaurants in the evening. La Boule de Neige and Le Moulin à Poivre are both recommended dining places. Le Friolin offers 'wicked crêpes'.

Nearly all accommodation is in apartments and chalets; much of it is up the steep slope to the east of the home pistes. The Bellecôte is a small, simple hotel near the centre ('pleasant rooms, friendly staff, good food'). There are adequate shops and a kindergarten.

This all sounds appealing for families and perhaps for novice skiers who would be happier in a backwater than in the mainstream of La Plagne, but there are snags, not only with the skiing, but also with the lifts: access to the gentle upper slopes is normally via an unnerving dog-leg drag, difficult for children. When snow is short at village level, beginners go up to Plan Bois, above Les Coches. Young children are looked after at the Chat Bleu nursery.

TOURIST OFFICE
as La Plagne

TOUR OPERATORS
Made to Measure, Simply Ski, Ski Esprit

Les Coches 1450m (4,750ft)

Les Coches was purpose-built in the early 1980s in a sympathetic and attractive style not unlike Belle Plagne. Small though it is, the village is broken into three hamlets; the main one is Hameau du Carreau, at the foot of the main lift, with a sunny restaurant terrace facing up the wooded slopes. All the accommodation is in apartments and chalets. The Club Pirouette non-ski kindergarten has a good reputation. A regular ski-bus links Les Coches to Montchavin. We have good reports of the Pierre et Vacances apartments in Hameau de la Forêt, which are 'compact, but space is efficiently used'.

A car is a great asset in all the lower resorts and one reporter suggests a saving on self-catering costs of 30 to 50 per cent by driving down to the hypermarket at Bourg-St-Maurice. La Taverne du Monchu is repeatedly recommended for excellent food at modest prices and friendly service. Les Bognettes is good for crêpes and the Origan for pizzas. When snow is short on the village nursery slopes, classes move up to a large area of gentle skiing at Plan Bois, at the top of the chair-lift out of the village. There is nothing here for non-skiers apart from plenty of walks. It is not a resort either for après-ski or for quick access into the main La Plagne ski area.

TOURIST OFFICE
as La Plagne

TOUR OPERATORS
AA Motoring Holidays, Brittany Ferries,
Hoverspeed, Ski Olympic, Simply Ski, Ski Esprit

Champagny-en-Vanoise 1250m (4,100ft)

This is a peaceful collection of hamlets, some of them old, in a secluded valley. The main community (Champagny-le-Bas) is linked to the La Plagne ski area by a modern and efficient gondola. Hotel Les Glières is said to be 'simple, but convenient'. The Club Alpina apartment hotel has a choice of self-catering or half-board and is recommended by reporters ('good apartments, good food, good chalet atmosphere').

Beyond the village the mountains form a narrow gateway into a beautiful, lonely upper valley (Champagny-le-Haut), an excellent place for cross-country skiing. Champagny has a disco and 10 ski instructors, some of them English-speaking. Le Cabris nursery looks after pre-ski children and registered childminders can be contacted through the tourist office.

TOURIST OFFICE
as La Plagne

TOUR OPERATORS
Sally Holidays

Montalbert 1350m (4,428ft)

Montalbert is a small purpose-built satellite below Aime la Plagne, on the western extremity of the ski area. Its position is a key factor; the skiing immediately above the resort is limited and exposed to afternoon sun and connections with the more extensive areas beyond Plagne Centre are time-consuming. All the accommodation is in apartments. A long cross-country trail climbs through woods along the mountainside past Les Coches to Peisey-Nancroix. Les Bambins non-ski kindergarten looks after young children.

TOURIST OFFICE
as La Plagne

TOUR OPERATORS
Ski Tal

Skiing facts: La Plagne

TOURIST OFFICE
BP 62, F-73211 Aime, Savoie
Tel 33 79 09 79 79
Fax 33 79 09 70 10

LONDON AGENT
Erna Low Consultants
9 Reece Mews
London
SW7 7HE
Tel 071-584 2841
Fax 071-589 9531

THE RESORT
By road Calais 930km
By rail Aime 20km
By air Geneva 3 hrs
Visitor beds 41,000 (93% apartments, 7% hotels)
Transport bus service or cable car link between each station

THE SKIING
Longest run Roche de Mio to Montchavin, 10km (red)
Number of lifts 112
Number of trails/pistes 119 (10% beginner, 55% easy, 29% intermediate, 6% difficult)
Total of trails/pistes 210km
Nursery slopes 1 free lift
Summer skiing Bellecôte Glacier served by 5-9 lifts
Snowmaking 3km covered in Montchavin, also at Belle Plagne

LIFT PASSES
Area pass La Plagne (covers 10 stations), 875FF for 6 days. Six-day pass offers 1 free day in Les Arcs, L'Espace Killy or Trois Vallées
Day pass 190FF
Half-day pass 135FF after 1.30pm
Beginners 1 free lift
Children 6-13 yrs, 660FF for 6 days, free for 6 yrs and under
Pensioners 60 yrs and over, as children
Credit cards accepted yes

SKI SCHOOLS
Adults ESF in all stations, 680FF for 6 days (5 hrs per day)
Children ESF in all stations, 3 yrs and over, 570FF for 6 days (5 hrs per day)
Private lessons 150-170FF per hr
Special courses snowboarding
Guiding companies through ESF

CROSS-COUNTRY
Ski schools ESF
Loipe location and size 96km in Plagne Villages, Plagne Bellecôte, Champagny-en-Vanoise, Montalbert and Montchavin

CHILDCARE
Non-ski kindergarten Garderie Marie-Christine (Plagne Centre), 2-6 yrs, 9am-5pm, 1,050FF for 7 days including lunch. Garderie (Belle Plagne), 18 mths-6 yrs, 995FF for 6 days including lunch
Ski kindergarten in all stations, tuition available with ESF, 9am-5pm: Plagne 1800, 3 yrs and over, 420FF for 6 days; Plagne Centre, 570FF for 6 days; Plagne Villages/Plagne Soleil, 2-6 yrs, 570FF for 6 days; Aime, 2-7 yrs, 630FF for 6 days; Bellecôte, 2-6 yrs, 1,055FF for 6 days including lunch; Belle Plagne, 1,015FF for 6 days including lunch
Babysitting difficult

OTHER SPORTS
Parapente, bob-sleigh, skating, snow-mobiling, bowling, swimming, fitness centre

FOOD AND DRINK PRICES
Coffee 10FF, bottle of house wine 60FF, beer 15FF, dish of the day 55-70FF

TOUR OPERATORS
AA Motoring Holidays, Brittany Ferries, Club Med, Crystal, Direct Ski, Enterprise, Equity Total Ski, Ski Falcon, Hoverspeed, Inghams, Made to Measure, Neilson, Sally Holidays, Ski Airtours, Silver Ski, SkiBound, Ski John Wyatt, Ski Tal, Ski Thomson, Ski Tracer, Skiworld, Touralp, UCPA

The Pyrenees

Resorts included Barèges, Cauterets, Font-Romeu, La Mongie, Superbagnères, St-Lary

The large and varied Pyrenees ski area covers 166km² of piste, 38 separate resorts and 1000km of cross-country trails. However, there is one big disadvantage. Snowfall in the Pyrenees is a subject which always produces much disagreement. There is no proof that the mountains receive any less snow than the Alps; if anything, they receive more in winter. But the Pyrenean winter is milder than in the Alpine one as the mountains are further west and closer to the warm Atlantic.

The resorts on the northern side of the chain (those in France and Baqueira-Beret in Spain) are much more reliable for snow than those on the southern side. On the eastern side are the Pyrénées-Orientales, also known as the Mediterranean Pyrenees because of their proximity to the coast. This area is much drier than the Atlantic side and includes the resorts of Font-Romeu and Les Angles.

The main French resorts are concentrated in a relatively small area in the middle of the range, the Hautes-Pyrénées. These include Barèges, Cauterets, La Mongie and St-Lary. The Spanish resorts are more spread out and there may be greater difference between their snowfall. On the Spanish side the ski area closest to the Mediterranean is La Molina, an infamously hazardous place for snow.

One of the major attractions of the Pyrenees is the people, who seem genuinely pleased to see visitors and keen for them to enjoy themselves – a rare occurrence in some of the French alpine resorts. This, plus a relaxed atmosphere, helps to compensate for the lack of the facilities of, for example, Austria. The locals have retained their traditional way of life and do not view holidaymakers just as people with money to spend. The Pyreneans are also pleased to see the British because we represent the only foreign business they can hope to attract.

Following the example of Andorra, where the British-run ski schools have made a great success of ensuring that people enjoy learning to ski, several of the French Pyrenean resorts are making a lot of effort to improve their ski school classes for English-speakers. The instructors are learning English and there are separate classes for British skiers.

The Pyrenees may come as a bit of a shock if you are expecting the chalet-style prettiness of Switzerland and Austria. Stone is used in all local building, so the villages look drab. In France you face an unappealing choice between grey spas (Barèges and Cauterets) and purpose-built resorts (La Mongie, Piau-Engaly and Pla d'Adet), no more attractive than their alpine counterparts. Only St-Lary has charm as a village. In Spain the purpose-built villages (Formigal and Baqueira-Beret) are more stylish and the old village resorts such as Cerler are more rustic.

Barèges, Hautes-Pyrénées

ALTITUDE 1250m (4,092ft)

••

Good points large intermediate ski area, short airport transfer, sunny slopes, low prices, variety of easy skiing, small and unspoilt village
Bad points lift queues, limited tough runs, lack of resort-level snow, not suitable for late-season holidays, few activities for non-skiers, limited choice of restaurants, not suitable for self-caterers, town noisy at night, insufficient bus service
Linked or nearby resorts La Mongie (l)

Skiers disenchanted by the anonymity of so many of the French alpine resorts find themselves in search of that illusive combination of an unspoilt French country village and the varied runs of a large ski area. Barèges, which is one of the friendliest Pyrenean resorts and is part of the largest ski area in the Pyrenees, manages to fill these requirements. At first sight it is a dour grey spa in a narrow valley, but it is not at all institutional and has a friendly atmosphere, largely due to its small size. Prices are low by French standards, but there is little to do except soak in the thermal spa.

Barèges was one of the original ski resorts of the Pyrenees. The village also receives attention in the summer months when it becomes part of the Tour de France route. It has a long lift system following the course of the road, which in summer leads over the Col du Tourmalet to the modern resort of La Mongie. Although hardly the Portes du Soleil, the area offers plenty of variety of terrain.

La Mongie is larger, higher, but considerably less charming than its neighbour. It offers no more facilities than Barèges and it is set in the less interesting half of the ski area. It is, however, the better place for beginners, with easy slopes around the resort that keep their snow relatively well. The lifts linking the two resorts sometimes close in bad weather.

The skiing
Top 2350m (7,708ft) bottom 1250m (4,100ft)
Barèges and La Mongie share 100km of wide, cruising pistes served by more than 50 lifts. The upper slopes are mainly open and sunny, while the lower ones just above Barèges offer the only tree-level skiing. The slopes are reached by either of two **mountain access** lifts from the resort. The two-stage Ayré funicular climbs steeply through the woods and serves red (intermediate) and black (difficult) runs down to the Lienz

clearing, which is some of the best skiing in the area when conditions are favourable. Although these broad runs are not too steep, there is no easy way down from Ayré. Inexperienced skiers can make their way across from the mid-station to Lienz. Of the two runs from there down to Barèges, the green (beginner) is a rarely used road starting with an uphill section and the red is more convenient, although the snow is not always reliable near the bottom.

La Laquette gondola is the most popular access lift and is the direct route towards La Mongie as well as the way up to the ski school meeting place. A variety of short intermediate pistes covers the sides of the hill, west-facing down to Lienz and east-facing down to Tournaboup where the Col du Tourmalet road ends in winter. There is a small nursery area beside a large car park and a long chair-lift over a wide, fairly steep west-facing mountainside, which is left unpisted although it is much skied in good conditions. From the top of the lift an easy link run leads on to Superbarèges, which is little more than a restaurant.

There are some fairly sheer west-facing slopes below the Col du Tourmalet, including short but steep mogul fields and some blue (easy) and green runs. A new development to the north of Superbarèges, below the Lac d'Oncet, adds to the size of the area. Below Superbarèges is a long path straddling both road and river. It is often crowded and it can be hard work returning to Tournaboup and Barèges late in the season in sticky end-of-the-day snow.

Although the mountains are not renowned for their beauty, there are some pleasant views east and west from the ridge beside the Col du Tourmalet. The eastern slopes are gentler and the runs to La Mongie are wide and easy. The rocky slopes bordering the resort and road are steeper and although there are lifts, the terrain does not give much scope for pistes. A gondola is the main lift on the north-facing side, serving a long and sunless blue gully. The 4 Termes chair-lift has added to the run and gives access to a long off-piste itinerary down the Aygues Cluses valley, ending up at Tournaboup. The most challenging piste skiing in this area is beneath the Prade Berde chair-lift, on steep runs, which are often closed.

On the south-facing side of La Mongie, the Pic du Midi cable car is only designated for skiers up to its half-way point at 2340m. There are vague plans to allow skiers up to and down from the observatory on top (2877m), which would add an exciting new dimension if it ever happens. The slopes beneath the nearby Sud chair-lift are not gentle and the blue run contains a narrow section. On this sunny side of the mountain, the most interesting runs are reached from the top of the Coume Louque drag and chair. One trail follows a valley down to La Mongie, the other leads down to Superbarèges; the beginning of the run is rather exposed before becoming steep enough to be graded black. It can also be icy in the morning. Another variation is the off-piste itinerary round to the Lac d'Oncet, a good place for spring snow even in mid-winter. The proposed development up this valley has begun with the construction of the Toue drag-lift.

The mountain restaurants are inexpensive by alpine standards, but not particularly appealing. Chez Louisette at Lienz and the restaurant at the Col du Tourmalet are the exceptions and Le Yeti in La Mongie is rec-ommended. Queues can be a serious weekend problem, especially on Sundays; as Barèges cannot cope with many cars the lifts from the top of the village and from Tournaboup are crowded and the Col du Tourmalet can be a bottleneck in both directions.

The Ecoloski offers, among other classes, tuition in off-piste skiing and moguls. The ESF also operates in Barèges. There are nursery slopes in all the main areas, except on the edge of the village itself; the main one is at the top of La Laquette gondola. There are plenty of long green runs for quasi-beginners. The ESF and Ecoloski both have ski kinder-gartens and Les Marmottes non-ski kindergarten takes children from three to six years old.

The resort

Barèges is little more than a single street climbing steeply beside a river, enclosed by the tree-lined mountainsides. There is no place for a village and none would have appeared had it not been for the sulphur springs, which became famous in the seventeenth century. But it was only quite recently that avalanche barriers allowed the construction of permanent buildings, which stand today grey and unmemorable except for the spa itself, a mixture of renovated and grand old build-ings at the top of the village.

The nearest airport is Lourdes, 25km from Barèges. This narrow village has restricted parking space and the ski-bus, covered by the lift pass, cannot cope when runs to the village are closed and many skiers end up at Tournaboup.

Most of the simple, inexpensive hotels have a two-star rating. The fam-ily-run Europe and Richelieu are recommended, both of which are just below the funicular station and about five minutes' uphill walk from the main lift station. The Igloo is run by a former ski champion and is close to La Laquette gondola. The Central is pleasant but old-fashioned, the Poste rather run-down. The English-run Les Sorbiers is a popular small hotel.

Après-ski

After-skiing entertainment consists of a few bars, a handful of restau-rants and two discos. The liveliest places are L'Oncet, L'Isba and the Café Richelieu. The restaurants include Le Ranch for five-course meals, La Rozelle for fondue and crêpes and the Downstairs Pizzeria. The main event of the week is an evening at Chez Louisette organised by the ski school, culminating in a torchlight descent. The discos open at 11pm and do not fill up until 1am; L'Hibou and Le Club Jonathan are popular. Hotels facing on to the main street are frequently disturbed by the return of late-night party-goers.

There is cross-country skiing in the woods around Lienz and there are some interesting walks, but on the whole Barèges is not recom-mended for non-skiers unless they are here for the spa treatment.

TOURIST OFFICE
65120 Barèges, Hautes-Pyrénées
Tel 33 62 92 68 19
Fax 33 62 92 66 60

TOUR OPERATORS
Ski Thomson

La Mongie 1800m (5,904ft)

La Mongie is a modern roadside resort in a bleak setting. The two parts of the resort are linked by a day-time bucket lift and an expanse of almost flat nursery slopes, which suffer from being a popular thoroughfare. The lower village is the main one, its focus a south-facing half-moon of restaurants, shops and hotel buildings with a car park in the middle, lift stations nearby and a large number of dogs.

La Mongie is an untidy and charmless place, but it has a greater variety of bars, shops and restaurants than most small purpose-built resorts. There are few activities for non-skiers. The upper resort, La Mongie Tourmalet, is a long jagged complex with a three-star hotel, a restaurant and apartments. There are ski school and lift pass offices at both centres, as well as a kindergarten at the lower one. The road up from Bagnères-de-Bigorre is extremely busy on Sundays and can be closed when the resort is full.

TOURIST OFFICE
65200 Bagnères-de-Bigorre,
Hautes-Pyrénées
Tel 33 62 91 94 15
Fax33 62 95 33 13

TOUR OPERATORS
none

Cauterets 1000m (3,280ft)

This pleasant thermal resort became a ski station in 1962 and today it has 22,000 visitor beds in a large selection of hotels. The nearest airport at Lourdes is 40km away. The skiing is in the Cirque du Lys bowl, accessed by a two-stage cable car, which also brings skiers back to the resort at the end of the day. The terrain is best suited to beginners and intermediates. There are 25 runs and 29km of piste serviced by 18 lifts going up to the highest point of 2400m at Col d'Ilheou. Five mountain eating places are scattered around the pistes.

The ski school offers instruction in freestyle skiing, snow-shoeing, snowboarding, parapente, monoskiing and off-piste skiing in addition to ordinary group and private lessons. Les Marmottes non-ski kindergarten takes children from 3 months to 6 years old; lunch is not provided. Children from 4 to 10 years old are taught in the ski school. There are 36km of cross-country tracks.

The extensive choice of accommodation ranges from gîtes, chalets and simple one-star hotels to three-star establishments. The Bordeaux is recommended as a comfortable hotel with a good restaurant. The Aladin and Astérides are the other three-stars. The Royalty pub is a popular place, as is the St Trop video bar. Other resort facilities include two discos, a swimming-pool, skating, tennis, squash, luge-ing and a range of health treatments in the spa.

TOURIST OFFICE
65110 Cauterets, Hautes-Pyrénées
Tel 33 62 92 50 27
Fax 33 62 92 55 58

TOUR OPERATORS
Ski Thomson

Font-Romeu 1800m (5,906ft)

The resort, 19km from Perpignan and 200km from Toulouse, is set on a sunny plateau known for its mild climate, making it unreliable for snow at the beginning and end of the season. The skiing is 4km from the village, linked by a bus service. The slopes, which rise to a top height of 2204m at Roc de la Calme, suit beginners to intermediates as well as families. Weekend queues are a problem, as the resort is popular with both French and Spanish skiers and is situated on the junction of three French national routes and two Spanish. The ski school also offers special children's classes.

There are two dozen hotels and pensions, over a dozen youth hostels and self-catering apartments. Après-ski activities include a casino, cinemas, discos and bars. Other sports catered for in the resort are tobogganing, cross-country, skating and ski-jumping.

TOURIST OFFICE
Ave Emmanuel Brousse, BP 55, 66120
Font-Romeu, Pyrénées-Orientales
Tel 33 68 30 02 74
Fax 33 68 30 29 70

TOUR OPERATORS
Inntravel

St-Lary 830m (2,722ft)

St-Lary is a typically Pyrenean village of stone-built houses and one main, rather narrow street. The skiing is suitable for beginners to intermediates and it begins a four-minute walk from the village centre at the cable car to St-Lary Pla d'Adret (1680m), itself a small but dull modern ski station with some accommodation. From here a bus runs to two other small centres, St-Lary La Cabane and St-Lary Espiaube. The ski area is serviced by a chain of lifts, but is mainly tree-less and lacks variety. There are six nursery slopes and a ski school. Ski-touring is popular here and a list of overnight huts is available from the tourist office.

Hotel Mir is recommended, as well as the Altea Cristal Parc and Motel de la Neste. Andredena is in a quiet position and has a swimming-pool. At Espiaube there is La Sapinière.

TOURIST OFFICE
65170 St-Lary-Soulan, Hautes-Pyrénées
Tel 33 62 39 50 81
Fax 33 62 39 50 06

TOUR OPERATORS

Superbagnères 1800m (5,904ft)

Luchon is a thermal spa town with shops and three nightclubs, Superbagnères is the quieter ski station 17km away by road and, from 1994, 7 minutes by cable car. Spain is just half-an-hour from Luchon, and Toulouse (France) is the nearest airport.

Superbagnères is one of the highest resorts in the Pyrenees, with a top point of 2260m. Ten drag-lifts, six chair-lifts and one cable car make up the ski area with its 24 pistes. There are two mountain restaurants, Céciré and La Hount, and two nursery slopes. There is an ESF ski school, which also runs a comprehensive ski kindergarten with its own slope and ski lift. Non-skiing children from two years old are also cared for here.

Superbagnères has 1,360 visitor beds, of which 88 per cent are in apartments and the remainder in the two hotels, the Isard and the Aneto. Club Med has a hotel in the resort. The two restaurants are Plete and Isard and there are two cafeterias and a supermarket. Activities outside skiing are a disco, swimming, two indoor tennis courts, parapente and a thermal centre. Luchon has more than 30 hotels including a three-star, the Corneille, and over a dozen restaurants ranging from pizzerias to those serving local cuisine.

TOURIST OFFICE
18 Allées d'Etigny, 31110 Luchon,
Haute-Garonne
Tel 33 61 79 21 21
Fax 33 61 79 11 23

TOUR OPERATORS
Club Med

Portes du Soleil

Avoriaz, Haute Savoie
ALTITUDE 1800m (5,904ft)

Good points large ski area, skiing to suit all standards, facilities for beginners and children, car-free resort, short transfer
Bad points lift queues, crowded pistes, lack of alpine charm, limited for non-skiers
Linked or nearby resorts Abondance (n), Champéry-Planachaux (l), Champoussin (l), La Chapelle d'Abondance (l), Châtel (l), Les Crosets (l), Les Gets (l), Montriond (l), Morgins (l), Morzine (l), Saint Jean d'Aulps-La Grande Terche (n), Torgon (l)

Champéry, Valais
ALTITUDE 1055m (3,460ft)

Good points small and traditional farming village, large intermediate ski area, well-positioned for best skiing on the circuit
Bad points low altitude, limited après-ski, limited activities for non-skiers

Châtel, Haute Savoie
ALTITUDE 1200m (3,936m)

Good points large intermediate ski area, short airport transfer, attractive scenery
Bad points poor snow record, strung-out resort, heavy traffic, limited après-ski

Morzine, Haute Savoie
ALTITUDE 1000m (3,280ft)

Good points attractive small town, large intermediate ski area, tree-level skiing, short airport transfer, varied choice of hotels and restaurants, suitable for non-skiers, family holidays
Bad points lack of skiing convenience, low altitude, heavy traffic

---

Les Portes du Soleil is a 2000m col which separates the French Haute Savoie from the Swiss Valais above the small Swiss resort of Les Crosets. Its name comes from the way in which the first rays of morning sunlight touch the peak before illuminating the pretty Illiez valley below and the granite incisors of Les Dents du Midi beyond. For the past 20 years it has lent its name to the joint marketing operation of a dozen ski resorts on both sides of the border. Much credit is due to Jean Vuarnet, founder of its most important resort Avoriaz, who is remembered by the French for his Olympic Gold Medal at Squaw Valley in 1960 and immortalised elsewhere for his sunglasses. He was one of the two founders of what was, and is, a truly remarkable and successful *entente cordiale* between two 'tribal' groups of mountain folk.

This massive ski area is little more than an hour's drive from Geneva airport and includes every type of resort from isolated hamlet to busy market town and purpose-built *station de ski*. If it has one serious fault it is its lack of altitude. With a top height of only 2500m and the main villages mostly below 1200m, snow cover is by no means guaranteed at any stage of the season. The region as a whole has suffered badly in recent years with the links more often broken than not for large parts of the winter.

But when the snow is good there are few better playgrounds in Europe for intermediate skiers who enjoy fast cruising and want to feel that they are going somewhere each day. The circuit, which takes all

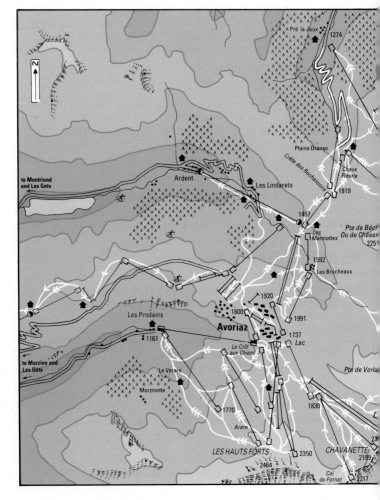

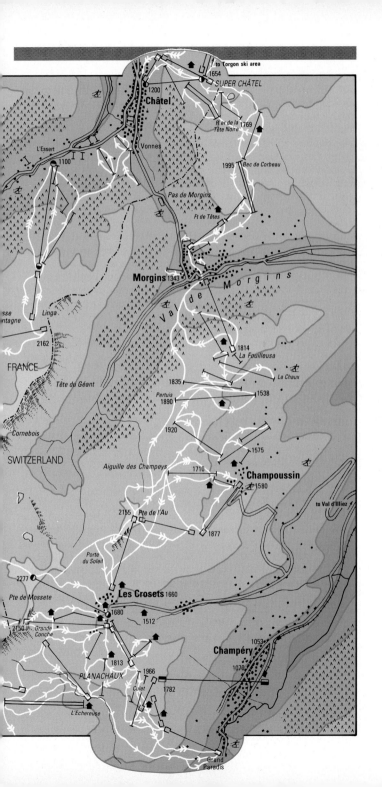

day with much of your time spent on lifts, can be completed by any early intermediate with a sense of adventure. There is also a linear link between Avoriaz and the Morzine/Les Gets area. Keen skiers will want to base themselves at this, the higher and more demanding end of the circuit. For this reason the region does suffer from serious congestion at peak times and in particular when cover in the lower resorts is poor or non-existent. Sign-posting has been vastly improved, as has the overall Portes du Soleil piste map, which indicates the links from area to area, as well as a rather over-optimistic figure for the suggested time it takes. But skiers who want to explore more than the main circuit still, infuriatingly, have to obtain separate piste maps on arrival in each resort.

Seven hundred slope markers should tell you where you are, the difficulty of the run and where it is taking you. Champéry, an attractive old farming village over the Swiss side of the border, attracts a number of visitors from Britain, but the second (although fading) centre of interest is the French resort of Châtel at the other end of the circuit. Unless you are staying in Avoriaz itself, a car is extremely useful in the Portes du Soleil for visiting other parts of what vies with the Trois Vallées for the title of largest linked ski area in the world.

There are no border controls, but skiers are advised to carry their passports with them as well as two sets of currency; both countries accept both types of franc, but not always at an advantageous rate. Customs controls do exist, with border patrols on the snow and in countryside where smuggling is a centuries-old profession, we have heard tales of rucksacked skiers being chased by excise men.

The Portes du Soleil lift pass covers 224 lifts comprising 134 drag-lifts, 75 chair-lifts, 11 gondolas and 4 cable cars. They serve 750km of piste and 230 runs, but we must confine ourselves here to the main circuit. The **mountain access** points are too many to mention.

The skiing
Top 2275m (7,462ft) bottom 1100m (3,608ft)

The skiing around Avoriaz itself can be divided into four main areas. Above the village is an upward extension of the main nursery slopes, Le Plateau, with a variety of drag-lifts serving a series of confidence-building green (beginner) runs, which link with the series of lifts coming up from Morzine. The pistes from the top lifts in this chain are again suitable for novices. In the opposite direction are pistes down to Les Marmottes from where lifts branch off towards Châtel; these runs are by no means as easy and are often crowded. From Les Marmottes a satisfyingly easy red run goes on down to Ardent, from where you can take a jumbo gondola back up. This also provides a useful access point into the best skiing for those staying in Châtel, Torgon, and the other lower resorts at this end of the system.

At the bottom of Avoriaz you are faced with essentially three choices. Directly to the south is the main Arare sector, which from Avoriaz looks steeper than it really is. There are some trees towards the bottom, but the skiing is mainly above the tree-line. Such is the volume of traffic that the separate marked runs amalgamate to form a whole pisted face to

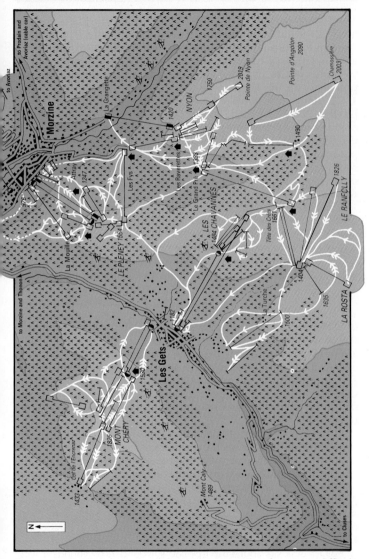

the mountain. The runs are all basically easy with a few more difficult pitches towards the bottom. This sector is much frequented by the ski school, parts are often closed for slalom practice and it does become seriously congested. A long chair starting from the same area at the bottom of the village takes you up to Hauts Forts, the most challenging skiing in Avoriaz and the most interesting for good skiers.

Several routes take you down all or part of the way towards Les Prodains, 650m below Avoriaz and a full 1300m vertical from Les Hauts Forts. The often heavily mogulled pistes here narrow considerably as you descend into the trees, and are prone to ice. The blacks are genuinely black (difficult), and the main red (intermediate) run from the Arare sector has an extremely difficult pitch, which causes major problems for otherwise confident intermediates. The lower runs are usually congested in late afternoon and extremely popular when visibility is poor above the tree-line.

The third direction is by chair and drag to the north-west facing bowl between Pas de Chavanette and the Col du Fornet. This is another area of wide, open intermediate skiing above the tree-line. In powder conditions you can virtually ski wherever you want off the edge of the marked piste and it is an ideal introduction to off-piste. There is an easy trail back to the bottom of the village. More adventurous skiers can return from Chavanette through the next valley; after an initial mogul field a pleasant gentle but satisfying run takes you down to Les Marmottes.

Champéry/Les Crosets/Champoussin Chavanette is where the skiing of Avoriaz meets the big, open and sunny alpine pastures of these three Swiss resorts. It starts with the Swiss Wall, alternatively known as the Wall of Death, the most notorious black run in Europe, where the hype is considerably greater than the degree of difficulty. A sign at the top warns that it is only to be attempted by experts and certainly the initial angle of descent is such that you cannot see what lies ahead. But the wall is wide and after the first 50m it flattens out considerably, though it still maintains an average gradient of 34°. Like all black runs the degree of difficulty depends on snow conditions; it is normally heavily mogulled within hours of a major dump of snow. Great care should be taken, not least because of the volume of less competent skiers who attempt it; any fall is liable to be a long one and you need at all times to be conscious of what skiers around you are doing. The faint-hearted or the plain sensible can take the chair down during the frequent icy conditions. An alternative black run to the left and off-piste variations are usually more rewarding.

Below the wall, acres of open snowfield are served by the lifts on either side of the Chavanette chair, connecting with the slopes of Planachaux above Champéry and with the adjacent bowl of Les Crosets. Planachaux is now reached from Champéry by cable car or by chair-lift from Grand Paradis. The run down at the valley end is a delightful one, winding its way gently down through sleepy hamlets and across the river against the dramatic backdrop of the Dents du Midi; snow disappears early in the season here. Mini-buses connect Grand Paradis with Champéry.

Les Crosets sits above the tree-line surrounded by abundant wide pistes, some of them north-facing, but most of them sunny. There are lifts up to the French border. The connection with Champoussin and Morgins is via the Pointe de l'Au and a series of linked drags and easy to intermediate pistes. The mountainside above Champoussin is broad and sunny, but with little variety of terrain; the addition of a quad chair from above Champoussin to the ridge has greatly improved the skiing. The pistes here are ideal for intermediates in need of some confidence-building. Good skiers will be interested in exploring the extensive off-piste opportunities here.

Morgins has little skiing on the approach side from Champoussin, but it includes an excellent north-facing intermediate run cut through the woods above the village. Skiers wanting to continue the circuit walk across the village or take a short bus ride to the nursery slopes and the lifts for Super-Châtel and France. In strong contrast to the sometimes bleak ski-fields of Avoriaz and Planachaux, the pistes here wind through the trees and are connected by a series of short drag-lifts.

The Morclan chair from Super-Châtel up to 1970m serves the most challenging slope, a moderately difficult mogul field. The black piste down the village presents no real problems provided snow cover is reasonable. The top of this chair is the departure point for Torgon, one of the further extremities of the Portes du Soleil back across the border again in Switzerland. The remainder of the skiing around Super-Châtel is mostly blue (easy) and red, on wide areas both above and below the lift station and main mountain restaurant. The valley runs catch the afternoon sun and can be tricky in poor snow conditions when those who care about their skis will download by gondola.

The Portes du Soleil circuit breaks down at Châtel and whichever way you are travelling the link cannot be made on skis. If going in a clockwise direction, a green (beginner) traverse from the Linga lift delivers you to Châtel's nursery slopes, leaving you with a walk across the village to the jumbo gondola for Super-Châtel. If travelling anti-clockwise, a bus ride is needed from Châtel to the 10-person gondola up to Linga. This is the first of a long chain of lifts and pistes towards Avoriaz and to the chair from Pré-La-Joux. The skiing in this sector offers more variety than other major legs of the circuit and includes a long, challenging, but not severe black beside the Linga gondola for clockwise skiers or those with time to play en route.

The fairly steep slope above the gondola, served by chair-lift, has a blue traverse cut into it as well as the red and black routes shown on the local piste map. The run down the Combes chair-lift towards Avoriaz is a satisfying and pleasant red; the Cornebois chair, which goes up from the same point, has good intermediate pistes of its own. It also connects with the top of the Chaux des Rosées chair-lift from Plaine Dranse. The runs down this chair are seriously challenging: the black offers a choice of routes down a difficult mogul field with a gradient of 35° on one pitch and the red takes a more scenic roundabout route. One more lift and one easy run bring you down to Les Marmottes for the return to Avoriaz.

Morzine is the market town above which the original concept of Avoriaz was evolved by Jean Vuarnet in the 1960s. A cable car from the satellite of Les Prodains connects the two as well as a series of lifts and pistes between Morzine itself and Avoriaz, which now link this end of the circuit into the main Portes du Soleil.

On the other side of Morzine, a gondola and a cable car climb steeply to Le Pleney (1500m), more of a sunny ridge than a peak, with a cross-country trail on it. From the lifts you look down on the less enticing sections of the direct black run down from Le Pleney, fairly steep and often scraped to an icy glaze by too many skiers. Easy skiing is to be found on the north-west side of the mountain, including a long blue down to the resort; the bottom section is covered by snow-cannon. An attractive area on the eastern side provides a series of mainly red runs complicated only by a number of piste crossroads.

From Les Fys at the eastern end of this area, a quad chair gives access to Plateau de Nyon. The Fys chair climbs back to the top of the ridge (Belvedere) from which easy link runs go down both wooded flanks of the ridge: south-westwards takes you to the village of Les Gets, south-eastwards to the junction of Le Grand Pré, where a chair and a drag-lift link with Nyon and the long Charniaz chair climbing gently to the Tête des Crêts. This lift is the usual access route to the Les Gets ski area and the runs beneath it; a red, which is mostly a schuss, followed by a green along the road, are the only ways back to Morzine.

The Plateau de Nyon can be reached by cable car from outside Morzine. Its main appeal is for good skiers: the Pointe and Chamossière chairs reach the high points of the system and serve its most challenging summits, shadowy north-facing ridges beneath the sharp peaks, which tower over Morzine's ski area and keep the early sun off much of it. Of the two black runs Aigle, which descends from the Pointe, is the narrower and the steeper. The wide bowl below the Chamossière lift offers plenty of off-piste opportunities; experts sometimes tackle the steep slopes between the two lifts (Nant Golon). Behind Chamossière there is a pleasant, sunny red run, which offers interesting off-piste alternatives before following a summer road through the woods to Le Grand Pré. From the Plateau de Nyon you can either ski down to the bottom of the cable car or the whole 11.5km directly back to Morzine via a flimsy-looking, but well-protected, bridge over a gaping river gorge.

The Tête des Crêts is near the top of the north-facing half of the Les Gets ski area. This is gentle and pleasantly pastoral, with long, easy runs over lightly wooded slopes to the resort. These pistes pass through Les Chavannes, a cluster of restaurants and hotel buildings with an area of nursery slopes, paths and cross-country loipes, which link up with Le Pleney. It is accessible by road as well as by lift from Les Gets. Only one of the Les Chavannes drags climbs to Tête des Crêts, for access not only to Morzine but also to a broad, upper bowl where a fan of six lifts offers a variety of short intermediate runs as well as one moderate black. The direct blue run to Les Gets from here is not obvious; the piste down the La Turche drag to the edge of the village is an equally gentle alternative.

The south-facing skiing of Les Gets is on Mont Chéry, reached by a six-seater gondola; its bottom station is a short walk across the road from the Chavannes lifts and runs. Good snow on the lower red and black runs is a rarity for much of the winter. The black starts gently, but has some steep moguls immediately below the mid-station, which can prove tricky when icy. The top-half of the mountain has easier, open skiing with magnificent views to the south of the Mont Blanc massif. The fairly steep, open slope behind Mont Chéry has good black and red runs of about 400m vertical down to the Col de L'Encrenaz. These runs are usually uncrowded and worth the journey from Morzine. Alone on the bleak north side of the mountain, Bouquetin is a short, sharp run, which tempts even fewer skiers. The bowl at the top is genuinely steep.

Most queuing problems in the Portes du Soleil are in the Avoriaz area, largely because of the greater volume of skiers here rather than any major deficiencies of the lift system in this quarter. Reporters suggest heading out towards Châtel and Les Lindarets on Sundays to avoid the crush. The Swiss resorts tend to be less busy at all times.

Mountain restaurants

The Portes du Soleil has a mixed bag of restaurants ranging from overcrowded self-services to wonderful old huts off the beaten track. Prices are generally high on both sides of the border and on one point all our reporters are agreed: there are simply not enough restaurants. Coquoz at Planachaux has a circular open fire and offers wonderful local Swiss specialities. Les Lindarets, the hamlet just north of Avoriaz, has the best concentration of eating places with La Cremaillère considered to be outstanding ('delicious *chanterelle* omelettes and wild *myrtilles* tart'). Les Marmottes here is also praised.

Les Prodains at the bottom of the Vuarnet run from Avoriaz is much praised, not least for its reasonable prices. The restaurants at Plaine Dranse are singled out as 'inexpensive and good'. Two at the top of Le Pleney are said to be always busy, 'but the wait is worth it'. The one at the top of the Super Morzine gondola is highly recommended for its 'good food, good prices and a spectacular view'. Les Raverettes at Les Gets is a handy stop before skiing back to Morzine. There is a good eating place half-way down the blue piste returning from Le Pleney to Morzine. Pas de Chavanette on the Swiss border charged one irate reporter 35FF for a plate of chips. The Perdrix Blanche at Pré-la-Joux is recommended for its warm atmosphere and good-value food.

Beginners and children

Views on The ESF in Avoriaz range from 'miserable' to 'superb'. Regardless of the not always positive attitude of instructors, the standard of teaching, particularly for beginners, seems high in both resorts. Les P'tits Loups crèche in Avoriaz has a good reputation, but it is essential to book well in advance. The Children's Village, right in the centre of Avoriaz and well isolated from the skiing, is considered one of the best in the Alps. Lack of cars here is a distinct safety factor, although skiers and sleighs crossing the resort remain a hazard.

Children in Champéry are well catered for with the Snoopy non-ski kindergarten, which takes babies from 6 months old. Older children who want to combine skiing with play go to the Mini Club. In Châtel, the Village des Marmottons takes babies from 14 months and skiers from 3 to 10 years old.

The Morzine ESF comes in for a fair amount of criticism. One reporter said his 4-year-old child had 4 different teachers in 6 days and lessons always started 15 minutes late. Another said his child was unhappy at the 'unsympathetic attitude of the instructor. We found a class of 17 here in the last week of March'. L'Outa kindergarten is particularly praised as being 'well run by friendly staff who speak some English'. It is also recommended for its wide variety of indoor and outdoor facilities.

The resorts

Avoriaz is a collection of mainly apartment blocks perched on the edge of a cliff far above Morzine and built in what for the 1960s was a truly amazing futuristic style. Unfortunately, many of the older blocks are showing their age and no amount of face-lifts can improve the lack of space in the interiors of the units. The resort is reached from the valley either by a narrow, winding road or by cable car from Les Prodains. You are strongly advised to leave your car 'downstairs', or indeed to leave it at home. One reporter comments: 'There are too many cars already in Morzine, so don't spoil the environment even further by bringing one'. Certainly it has no useful application in a car-free resort and the charges in either the open or covered *parkings* in Avoriaz are iniquitous. It is apparently legal to leave your car on the roadside on the outskirts of the resort, but you run the risk of it being buried or damaged by a snowplough and it is not recommended.

Transport to your apartment block or hotel is on foot or via expensive horse-drawn sleigh or piste machine. It is worth discovering exactly where you are staying before embarking on a ride, which may last for 100m. Between snowfalls the amount of horse manure combined with dog-dirt deposited on the resort 'roads' does little to improve the ambience. When not on skis moving around is made easier by public lifts within the apartment blocks to different levels of this steep resort. The busiest part is the middle section, around the foot of the nursery slopes; there are lots of bars and restaurants linking the slopes and shops for ski gear, clothes and food. The best supermarket is, by consensus, the Codec near the tourist office. All three supermarkets rent out fondue sets for easy in-apartment dining.

Châtel is still a farming village, but caring for livestock and tilling the fields takes a poor second place behind the more lucrative business of tourism. Unfortunately, precious little planning has gone into the development of the village. The result is a huge, ungainly straggle of buildings up towards the Morgins Pass and Switzerland, as well as down the hillside and along the valley towards the Linga lift, which is its connection with the skiing of Avoriaz. Its poor snow record in recent years has caused many operators to pull out of the resort.

The valley lift departures are linked by free *navettes*, which are crowded in the afternoon and have to fight their way through a village centre which at busy times and at weekends in particular is choked with traffic. Despite this, the disparate nature of the resort makes having a car an advantage for reaching the out-of-town lift stations and for travel to the other unlinked resorts on the circuit. The resort has an interesting little market on Tuesdays, selling jewellery and leather goods.

Champéry is an attractive, but quiet traditional Swiss village set in dramatic surroundings at the foot of the Dents du Midi. The one-way main street lined with wooden chalets runs the length of the village, with most of the hotels, shops and restaurants along its length. But the focus of development has moved down the hill to the valley road, which skirts the village. The sports centre is here with excellent facilities for skating, curling, swimming and bowling. The 125-person cable car up to Planachaux is also situated here. It is less convenient for many of the hotels than the old lift station at the end of the main street, but better able to cope with non-residents. The newer lift is served by a free mini-bus, which circles the village. The railway has been extended from its original terminus at the entrance to the village to a new station right next to the cable car.

Morzine is a market town and long-established resort with a very French atmosphere at the foot of the road up to Avoriaz. It has all the appeal of an old-style chalet resort set in charming, wooded surroundings. Its biggest fault is its lack of altitude (1000m), which means that resort-level snow is a scarce commodity. It is a confusing town covering a large area on both sides of a river gorge and on several levels. It has a serious traffic problem, but a high footbridge over the river makes getting around less tortuous for pedestrians than for motorists. The main congested shopping street climbs from the old village centre beside the river to more open ground at the foot of Le Pleney, where the resort has developed with hotels and shops around the tourist office.

Such is the diffuse nature of the resort that buses are an essential form of transport. The Red Line bus runs every 15 minutes in a circle around the main parts of town and to the Avoriaz cable car at Les Prodains. The Yellow Line is said to run less regularly in a circle and out to La Grangette for the Nyon cable car. A Green Line also links hotels and chalets on the opposite side of the town to Le Pleney. All buses in the resort are free. Horse-drawn taxis are an alternative means of transport, although one reporter said he felt guilty when the horse ran out of steam on the steep hills.

As Morzine is a proper town, the range of shops is far above the standard of most ski resorts. Morzine also has a large sports centre with an indoor ice rink.

Accommodation

The **Avoriaz** accommodation is nearly all in apartment blocks, which vary in quality according to their age. Alpage 1 apartments are said to be 'clean, but fairly cramped'. La Falaise units are similarly well-scrubbed but 'seriously short of clothing storage space and maybe a bit cramped'. The Thuya apartments are 'rather dilapidated'. In general it seems prudent to halve the number of advertised bed spaces. Hotel des Hauts Forts is recommended as being 'surprisingly cheap'. Location within the resort is of no importance for skiing purposes, although some of the village streets, which are also pistes, may prove difficult for novices.

Champéry's accommodation is in hotels and chalets. Pension Souvenir is well located in the resort centre ('average, with no en suite showers or baths, but very cheap'). The Hotel de la Paix is said to be 'rather expensive and rooms slightly cramped for the price, but it serves a very good breakfast'. Hotel de Champéry is centrally located and said to be 'very comfortable, with all the facilities you would expect of a four-star, plus the bonus of friendly staff'. Chalet Dents du Midi and Chalet des Amis are both highly recommended for their 'wonderful, high standard of service and cuisine'.

Châtel has a wide choice of hotels, most of them chalet-style and simple. Location is important and it is well worth checking out the distance from a main lift before booking. The Amethyste is said to be 'excellent and cheap'. The Résidence Yeti is recommended. Hotel Fleur de Neige is praised for its 'wonderful food' and 'homely atmosphere'. The Flèche d'Or apartments are said to be 'clean and comfortable, provided you halve the recommended occupancy figure'.

Morzine has a plentiful supply of hotels in each price bracket. Most of the hotels are chalet-style buildings and none is luxurious. In the central area near the tourist office the Airelles, with pool and sauna, is one of the more comfortable. The Hotel Concorde is family-run and has a relaxed atmosphere. We continue to receive rave reports of the Hotel Dahu: 'Excellent, very friendly, lovely rooms and the children loved the pool.' In the Hotel Sporting 'staff could not do enough for us, even buying our 15-month-old son a new high chair'. Hotel Viking at the top of the Morzine gondola receives poor reports for its food, which was 'sparse and the worst possible'. Hotel Les Côtes is also not recommended, either for comfort or location.

Eating out

Avoriaz has a choice of around 30 restaurants, most of which are rather overpriced as you would expect in a *station de ski* of this type. Les Intérêts is a favourite with three reporters for its raclette, fondues and *pierrades*. Le Petit Vatel serves rustic fare including fresh trout, frogs' legs and snails. Chez Hans 'does a wicked *choucroute* and *tarte flambée*'. The Bistro opposite the Children's Village is 'good, but expensive'.

The Bee-Bop in **Champéry** is described as 'good, cheap and serves free wine'. The Grand Paradis, just out of town, is still recommended, although the chef has moved to the refurbished Hotel National, where the food is said to be outstanding. Other choices include the Farinet, the Café du Centre and Le Pub, which serves 'great pizzas'.

In **Châtel**, La Bonne Menagère is popular, as is the Vieux-Four ('slow service, but food is good, basic French)'. The Fleur de Neige has some of the best cuisine. Le Kitchen, out of town, is recommended for raclette and has 'a great atmosphere created by its English owner'.

In **Morzine**, Le Dahu is again recommended for its 'mouth-watering dinners, night after night'. The Neige Roc at Les Prodains and Le Tremplin are also rated highly by reporters. L'Etale serves regional specialities in a 'wonderful, authentic mountain atmosphere'.

Après-ski

In **Avoriaz**, broomball is a popular form of after-skiing entertainment. For the uninitiated, you organise yourselves in teams of five on the ice rink in normal footwear and do battle with broom and ball. The Place has live non-French music (a band from California last season) and an 'excellent atmosphere'. Le Choucas is recommended by reporters, has live music and usually is not too crowded. Bar Tavaillon has two happy hours. Nightclubs are said to be overpriced and largely empty, except for striptease nights, when audience participation is invited. The discos Le Festival and Le Roc Club both have entrance fees, while the Midnight Express only has a cloakroom fee. The Midnight Express has a 'bucking bronco', which can be used free of charge. All three have taken to holding sponsored evenings. At Le Roc, where the seats are covered in animal skins, one reporter was bemused to find his evening was commercially endorsed by a condom company: 'Bucketsful were thrown at us. As a result there were probably two dozen packets on our small table at any one time and the dance floor was covered in them.'

Champéry is not famous for its nightlife. Le Pub bar and restaurant is often the liveliest place in town and much patronised by the locals. Reporters also recommend the Farinet bar ('quiet, friendly atmosphere, not expensive'). Its nightclub can be crowded at weekends; entry is free and drinks are said to be not too expensive. One reporter recommends Charly's Bar in Val d'Illiez as the best in the area ('very comfortable with pool and videos').

Châtel has a bowling alley and an ice rink, but otherwise the after-slopes activity is mainly limited to a handful of bars including the popular l'Isba, which has a lively atmosphere and shows ski videos. One reporter claimed they all shut too early: 'There was nothing to do, nowhere to go after 2.30am.' The Slalom bar is British-owned. The cinema shows English-language films three times a week.

Morzine abounds with civilised tea-rooms and bars. The Wallington complex houses a bowling alley, pool hall, bar and video disco. Le Pacha is another popular disco which becomes extremely lively late on.

Abondance 930m (3,050ft)

This tiny historic village lies seven kilometers from La Chapelle and is not linked into the main Portes du Soleil system. It has its own small ski area on the slopes beneath the Col de l'Ecuelle, served by a gondola and a series of drags.

TOURIST OFFICE
F-74360, Haute Savoie
Tel 33 50 73 02 90
Fax 33 50 73 04 76

TOUR OPERATORS
none

Les Crosets 1660m (5,445ft)

Les Crosets is a ski station in the heart of the open slopes on the Swiss side of the Portes du Soleil circuit. It is a tiny place with some attractive modern chalets, a couple of hotels and a handful of restaurants. It is fairly functional and with no obvious appeal to anyone but serious skiers who want an early night apart from a visit to the Sundance Saloon disco. The walk into Champéry takes around two hours. There are four daily buses to Val d'Illiez, which is one train stop from Champéry. The Hotel Télécabine, which as the name suggests is in the lift station, is simple, but serves excellent food and is British-run.

TOURIST OFFICE
CP 28, Val d'Illiez, CH-1873
Tel 41 25 772077
Fax 41 25 773773

TOUR OPERATORS

Champoussin 1580m (5,182ft)

Champoussin represents more of an attempt to create a mini-resort than Les Crosets. Its new buildings, in rustic style, are almost all apartments under the skin, but most of our reporters have stayed in the main hotel, the Alpage, which is highly impressive. It has a sauna, a pool with a superb view of the Dents du Midi and a disco. Après-ski is 'almost non-existent'. The Alpage Ambassador apartments are highly recommended, as is the small ski school. The village has a skating rink and a parapente school. The one supermarket is said to be inadequate.

TOURIST OFFICE
as Les Crosets

TOUR OPERATORS
Snowline Holidays

La Chapelle d'Abondance 1010m (3,313ft)

This little resort lies 6km down the valley from Châtel. It is an old farming community straddling both sides of the road without any defined centre. On one side, two long chairs take you up to Crêt Béni at 1650m and a series of drags, which serve a choice of mainly easy runs through the pine forest of the Mont Grange nature reserve. On the other side of the road are a recently built gondola and chair link into Torgon, Châtel and the main Portes du Soleil system. La Chapelle also has 22km of loipe, which offer some of the best cross-country skiing in the whole region. The hotels Les Cornettes du Bis and the Alti Mille both have pools and fitness centres. The Cornettes restaurant provides one of the best gastronomic experiences in the Abondance valley.

TOURIST OFFICE
F-74360, Haute Savoie
Tel 33 50 73 51 41
Fax 33 50 73 50 66

TOUR OPERATORS
Enterprise

Les Gets 1175m (3,854ft)

Les Gets straddles a low mountain pass 6km from Morzine, with lifts and pistes on both sides and good nursery slopes on the edge of the village and higher up at Les Chavannes (1490m), reached by road or gondola. This rather attractive village, an old farming community which has expanded almost out of recognition, also has a large and under-used floodlit piste. Parts of the ski area and many of the restaurants within it are accessible on foot; there are 25km of cross-country trails around the half-way stations on both sides of the resort. There is a bus service to Morzine for access to Avoriaz, but it is not frequent.

Les Gets has three ski schools and we have generally favourable reports of them all. Ski Plus specialises in 'excellent private tuition in good English' and there is a choice of kindergarten; Ski Espace ('lots of fun, they don't take the skiing too seriously') receives better comments than the ESF one. The non-ski Bébé Club takes children from three months to two years old.

Much of the accommodation is in tour operator chalets. Hotel l'Ours Blanc is said to be 'very comfortable, has good service, and we would go back there again'. The Régina is well placed on the quieter of the main streets. The Labrador and the Alissandre are both said to offer a high standard of service. Le Meridien, La Cachette and the Clé des Champs chalets are recommended along with the Soleil and La Bouillandire apartments. Recommended restaurants include Le Tyrol for its pizzas and Le Gallichou for 'excellent cider and crêpes'.

Most of the nightlife centres on hotel bars, but there are also three

Skiing facts: Avoriaz

TOURIST OFFICE
F-74110 Avoriaz, Haute-Savoie
Tel 33 50 74 02 11
Fax 33 50 74 18 25

THE RESORT
By road Calais 889km
By rail Cluses 40km, Thonon 45km
By air Geneva 2 hrs
Visitor beds 15,330 (97% apartments, 2% chalets, 1% hotels)
Transport traffic-free

THE SKIING
Longest run Jean Vuarnet Coupe du Monde, 2.7km (black)
Number of lifts 41 in Avoriaz, 224 in Portes du Soleil
Number of trails/pistes 49 in Avoriaz (6% beginner, 49% easy, 35% intermediate, 10% difficult), 230 in Portes du Soleil
Total of trails/pistes 150km in Avoriaz, 650km in Portes du Soleil
Nursery slopes 7 lifts in and around village centre
Summer skiing none
Snowmaking 4 mobile snow-cannon

LIFT PASSES
Area pass Portes du Soleil (covers 12 resorts), 805FF for 6 days
Day pass Avoriaz 140FF, Portes du Soleil 175FF
Half-day pass Avoriaz 110FF, Portes du Soleil 123FF from midday
Beginners 90FF per day
Children Portes du Soleil, 5-12 yrs, 531FF for 6 days, free for 5 yrs and under
Pensioners 60 yrs and over, 100FF per day
Credit cards accepted yes

SKI SCHOOLS
Adults ESF, 730FF for 6 days
Children ESF, 4 yrs and over, 575FF for 6 days
Private lessons 152FF per hr
Special courses snowboarding, telemark
Guiding companies through ski school

CROSS-COUNTRY
Ski schools ESF
Loipe location and size 45km at Super Morzine

CHILDCARE
Non-ski kindergarten Les P'tits Loups, 3 mths-5 yrs, 9am-6pm, 1,137FF for 6 days including lunch
Ski kindergarten Annie Famose Children's Village, 3-16 yrs, 9am-5.30pm, 1,010FF for 6 days including lunch
Babysitting list available from tourist office

OTHER SPORTS
Parapente, hang-gliding, sleigh rides, snow-mobiling, skating, swimming, squash, fitness centre, bowling

WHAT'S NEW
● Special ski pass for beginners

FOOD AND DRINK PRICES
Coffee 10FF, bottle of house wine 50FF, beer 15FF, dish of the day 50FF

TOUR OPERATORS
AA Motoring Holidays, Brittany Ferries, Club Med, Crystal, Direct Ski, Enterprise, Inghams, Made to Measure, Neilson, Nickski, Sally Holidays, Ski Thomson, Touralp, White Roc Ski

noisy discos. The English-run Pring's and the piano bar in the Hotel Régina are both popular. There is an open-air skating rink in the centre.

TOURIST OFFICE
BP27, 74260 Les Gets, Haute Savoie
Tel 33 50 75 80 80
Fax 33 50 79 76 90

TOUR OPERATORS
French Impressions, Made to Measure, Neilson, Ski Total

Skiing facts: Champéry

TOURIST OFFICE
CH-1874 Champéry, Valais
Tel 41 25 791141
Fax 41 25 791847

THE RESORT
By road Calais 900km
By rail station in resort
By air Geneva 2 hrs
Visitor beds 7,630 (92% apartments and chalets, 8% hotels)
Transport free mini-bus service

THE SKIING
Longest run Jean Vuarnet, 1km (black)
Number of lifts 17 in Champéry/Les Crosets, 224 in Portes du Soleil
Number of trails/pistes 32 in Champéry/Les Crosets (47% easy, 47% intermediate, 6% difficult), 230 in Portes du Soleil
Total of trails/pistes 80km in Champéry/Les Crosets, 650km in Portes du Soleil
Nursery slopes 2 lifts, 200m
Summer skiing none
Snowmaking 4 mobile snow-cannon

LIFT PASSES
Area pass Portes du Soleil (covers 12 resorts), SF195 for 6 days
Day pass Champéry (covers Les Crosets, Champoussin and La Foilleuse), SF33. Portes du Soleil SF42
Half-day pass Champéry SF23, Portes du Soleil SF29 after midday
Beginners no free lifts
Children Champéry, 6-16 yrs, SF22 per day. Portes du Soleil, SF129 for 6 days. Free for 6 yrs and under
Pensioners women 62 yrs and over and men 65 yrs and over, as children
Credit cards accepted yes

SKI SCHOOLS
Adults Swiss Ski School, 3 hrs per day, SF120 for 5 days
Children Swiss Ski School, 4 yrs and over, 3 hrs per day, SF110 for 5 days
Private lessons SF50 per hr
Special courses snowboarding, telemark
Guiding companies through ski school

CROSS-COUNTRY
Ski schools Swiss Ski School
Loipe location and size 7km at Grand Paradis

CHILDCARE
Non-ski kindergarten Snoopy, 6 mths-5 yrs, 9am-5pm, SF35 per day, SF156 for 6 days, both including lunch
Ski kindergarten Mini Club, 4-7 yrs, SF55 per day, SF230 for 5 days, both including lunch
Babysitting list available from tourist office

OTHER SPORTS
Heli-skiing, parapente, skating, curling, swimming, fitness centre

WHAT'S NEW
● Les Mossettes gondola replaced with a quad chair-lift from Les Crosets for 1993-4 season ● new chair-lift from Les Lindarets to Les Mossettes

FOOD AND DRINK PRICES
Coffee SF2.40, bottle of house wine SF25, beer SF2.80, dish of the day SF14

TOUR OPERATORS
Kuoni, Made to Measure, Ski La Vie, Ski Scott Dunn, Ski Unique, Ski Weekend, Snowline Holidays

Montriond 950m (3,116ft)

Montriond is little more than a suburb of Morzine, with no discernable centre and a number of simple and reasonably priced hotels. A bus links you to the resort's gondola, which provides access to the main lift system.

TOURIST OFFICE
F-74110, Haute Savoie
Tel 33 50 79 12 81
Fax 33 50 79 04 06

• •

Skiing facts: Châtel

TOURIST OFFICE
F-74390 Châtel, Haute-Savoie
Tel 33 50 73 22 44
Fax 33 50 73 22 87

THE RESORT
By road Calais 896km
By rail Thonon 45 mins, regular bus service to resort
By air Geneva 2 hrs
Visitor beds 18,000 (83% apartments, 8% hotels, 8% hostels, 1% other)
Transport free bus between village and Pré-la-Joux lift

THE SKIING
Longest run Linga, 1km (red/black)
Number of lifts 50 in Châtel, 224 in Portes du Soleil
Number of trails/pistes 47 in Châtel (27% beginner, 30% easy, 32% intermediate, 11% difficult), 230 in Portes du Soleil
Total of trails/pistes 65km in Châtel, 650km in Portes du Soleil
Nursery slopes 13 runs
Summer skiing none
Snowmaking 7 mobile snow-cannon

LIFT PASSES
Area pass Portes du Soleil (covers 12 resorts), 805FF for 6 days. Châtel only 530FF
Day pass Châtel 128FF, Portes du Soleil 175FF
Half-day pass Chatel, 90FF from midday
Beginners no free lifts
Children Châtel, 4-13 yrs, 371FF. Portes du Soleil, 4-11 yrs, 531FF for 6 days. Free for 4 yrs and under
Pensioners women 62 yrs and over, and men 65 yrs and over: Portes du Soleil, 531FF for 6 days, Châtel, 412FF for 6 days
Credit cards accepted yes

SKI SCHOOLS
Adults ESF, 400FF for 2 hrs. International Ski School (Portes du Soleil), 9am-5pm, 930FF with video. Stages Henri Gonon (3 hrs), 600FF for 5 days with video
Children ESF, 5-14 yrs, 10am-5pm, 1,380FF for 6 days. International Ski School (Portes du Soleil), 8 yrs and over, 9am-midday, 485FF for 5 days
Private lessons 165FF per hr
Special courses snowboarding, telemark, monoskiing, slalom courses
Guiding companies through ski schools

CROSS-COUNTRY
Ski schools ESF
Loipe location and size 24km, largest loipe 5km at Super-Châtel

CHILDCARE
Non-ski kindergarten Le Village des Marmottons, 14 mths-3 yrs, 8.30am-5.30pm, 600FF for 6 days including lunch
Ski kindergarten Le Village des Marmottons, 3-10 yrs, 8.30am-5.30pm, 950FF for 6 days including lunch
Babysitting list available from tourist office

OTHER SPORTS
Parapente, dog-sledding, snow-shoeing, skating, bowling, fitness centre

FOOD AND DRINK PRICES
Coffee 8FF, bottle of house wine 45-49FF, beer 13FF, dish of the day 43FF

TOUR OPERATORS
Alpine Expressions, Enterprise, Freedom Holidays, French Impressions, Hoverspeed, Interski, Masterski, SkiBound, Ski Thomson, Ski Total, Snowpiper, Susie Ward Travel

• •

TOUR OPERATORS
none

Morgins 1350m (4,428ft)

Morgins is situated a few kilometres from Châtel, just over the pass of the same name, and is the border post with Switzerland. It is a spacious, residential resort spread across its broad valley, but is not an ideal base for keen skiers because, quite simply, the best of the Portes du Soleil skiing is elsewhere. A car is definitely an asset for visiting other resorts

• •

Skiing facts: Morzine

TOURIST OFFICE
F-74110 Morzine, Haute-Savoie
Tel 33 50 79 03 45
Fax 33 50 79 03 48

THE RESORT
By road Calais 880km
By rail Cluses or Thonon 30km
By air Geneva 1½ hrs
Visitor beds 16,300 (80% apartments and chalets, 20% hotels)
Transport free bus service throughout Morzine and to Avoriaz (Les Prodains)

THE SKIING
Longest run Piste B du Pleney, 7km (blue)
Number of lifts 26 in Morzine, 224 in Portes du Soleil
Number of trails/pistes 30 in Morzine (13% beginner, 24% easy, 50% intermediate, 13% difficult), 230 in Portes du Soleil
Total of trails/pistes 43km in Morzine (Pleney/Nyon), 650km in Portes du Soleil
Nursery slopes 2 lifts
Summer skiing none
Snowmaking 7km covered

LIFT PASSES
Area pass Pleney/Nyon/Les Gets, 650FF for 6 days. Portes du Soleil (covers 12 resorts), 805FF for 6 days
Day pass 130FF, Portes du Soleil 175FF
Half-day pass 97FF, Portes du Soleil 123FF, from 12.30pm
Beginners special price for certain lifts
Children 488FF for 12 yrs and under. Portes du Soleil, 531FF for 6 days. Free for 5 yrs and under
Pensioners 65 yrs and over, as children
Credit cards accepted yes

SKI SCHOOLS
Adults ESF, 2½ hrs (6 lessons), 460FF

for 6 days. 5 hrs (11 lessons), 700FF for 5½ days
Children ESF, 2½ hrs (6 lessons), 390FF for 6 days. 5 hrs (11 lessons), 650FF for 5½ days
Private lessons 150FF per hr
Special courses race-training
Guiding companies through ski school

CROSS-COUNTRY
Ski schools ESF
Loipe location and size 80km in Vallée de la Manche, Super-Morzine, Pleney and around Lac de Montriond

CHILDCARE
Non-ski kindergarten Outa Nursery, 2 mths-4 yrs, 8.30am-6pm, 815FF for 6 days, extra 30FF per day for lunch
Ski kindergarten Leisure Centre/Outa, 4-12 yrs, 8.30am-6pm, 1,183FF for 6 days including 2½ hrs lessons (ESF) per day, extra 35FF per day for lunch
Babysitting list from tourist office

OTHER SPORTS
Hang-gliding, parapente, dog-sledding, snow-shoeing, ski jumping, ice hockey, skating, curling, climbing walls, swimming, bowling

WHAT'S NEW
● Les Lans three-star hotel

FOOD AND DRINK PRICES
Coffee 6FF, bottle of house wine 35FF, beer 12FF, dish of the day 60FF

TOUR OPERATORS
Beach Villas, Crystal, Enterprise, Made to Measure, Neilson, Sally Holidays, SkiBound, The Ski Company, Ski Esprit, Ski Falcon, Ski Jeannie, Ski Thomson, Ski Weekend, STS, Top Deck Ski, Touralp, White Roc Ski

• •

in the region. Most of the accommodation is in chalets and apartments. We have received poor reports of the once popular Hostellerie Bellevue, which is described as 'rather tatty' and 'dinners were uninspiring at best'. The resort is relaxed, perhaps relaxed to the point of being short of any real character of its own. It has a crèche of which we have extremely positive reports.

Après-ski is limited to a natural skating rink, good indoor tennis courts and a few bars. The Bellevue disco provides some measure of lively late-night entertainment in season. The small swimming-pool at the Bellevue is open to the public. Several reporters have enjoyed the thermal baths at Val d'Illiez. The three cross-country loipes amount to 15km and there is a long, marked but not prepared route to Champoussin. The village has three supermarkets as well as a butcher and a baker.

TOURIST OFFICE
VS-1875 Morgins, Valais
Tel 41 25 772361
Fax 41 25 773708

TOUR OPERATORS
Kuoni

St Jean d'Aulps/La Grande Terche   900m (2,952ft)

St Jean is the village, while La Grande Terche is the name given to a tiny development of apartments at the foot of the lifts a 15-minute drive from Morzine. The skiing is not as yet fully linked into the system, but it is surprisingly good and well worth the visit if staying elsewhere in the area. It recently combined its ski area with Bellevaux.

TOURIST OFFICE
F-74430, Haute Savoie
Tel 33 50 79 65 09
Fax 33 50 79 67 95

TOUR OPERATORS
none

Torgon   1100m (3,608ft)

Torgon is perched above the Rhône close to Lake Geneva on the outer edge of the Portes du Soleil circuit. Although in Switzerland, it is linked in one direction with La Chapelle and in the other with Châtel, both of which are in France. Access is only possible by road from the French side of Lake Geneva, which makes it somewhat isolated. The distinctive and none too pleasing A-frame architecture houses comfortable apartments. There is little else to do here but ski.

TOURIST OFFICE
CH-1899, Valais
Tel 41 25 813131
Fax 41 25 814620

TOUR OPERATORS

Risoul, Hautes Alpes

ALTITUDE 1850m (6,068ft)

Good points large ski area, beautiful scenery, reliable snow record, ideal for family holidays, uncrowded pistes, skiing convenience, intermediate skiing, low prices, children's facilities, tree-level skiing
Bad points resort accessibility, limited for non-skiers and après-ski, lack of tough runs
Linked or nearby resorts Vars (l), Sainte-Marie-de-Vars (l)

Risoul and Vars are two completely different resorts sharing the same ski area 35km from Briançon. The Domaine de la Forêt Blanche is one of the biggest ski areas in the Southern Alps. One of the drawbacks to Risoul is the long transfer from the nearest airports of more than three hours, and often nearer five due to the very narrow road into the resort, which can only take one coach at a time. Risoul 1850 is a compact resort of large wood-and-stone buildings, a purpose-built yet attractive place constructed on the lines of a real village with a main street, and the cars to go with it. It is situated above the original village of Risoul further down the valley.

Reasonable prices mean the resort is growing in popularity with British tour operators. When one of our reporters first visited 10 years ago, Risoul 1850 was a quiet resort with nothing to offer except skiing. It had no mountain restaurants and no lift queues. It has not changed much according to more recent reports. There is still nothing for non-skiers and the après-ski is limited, lift queues are rare and easily avoided, but the area does now support half-a-dozen mountain restaurants.

The skiing
Top 2750m (9,020ft) bottom 1650m (5,412ft)
The open, bowl-shaped ski area around Risoul 1850 also has some wooded areas which are good for bad-weather skiing. The runs are mainly short and present few challenges. Several of the higher slopes are steeper, as are some of the slopes around Vars, but generally the skiing is perfect for intermediates.

From the top of l'Homme de Pierre at 2361m, what starts as a wide red (intermediate) schuss gradually become a steeper run as you enter the trees.

The double Mélezet drag gives access to several easy blue runs, which sweep through the trees into Risoul. The top of Mélezet links onto a path into Risoul with access to a steeper red route down. Pinatiaux Superior, from the top of Platte de la Nonne, is a long red run combining schusses, moguls and some steeper narrow sections. It is voted one of the best runs here, as well as 'an ideal last run of the day'.

The double Valbelle drags are two of the **mountain access** points, as is the Cezier drag. Queues were reported at these points only during the morning peak hour.

Access to Vars is on a short, slow drag on the Pointe de Razis, followed by a long, easy blue run. The steeper skiing of the area is immediately above Vars on the 'wall' of the Grand Ubac and also on La Casse above Sainte-Marie. Two more lifts above Vars are planned which will extend the skiing further in the near future and add several more blue (easy) and red runs, including a very long blue down to Sainte-Marie. Mountain access from Vars to the slopes is on the Chabrières gondola as well as on three alternative drags from different points in town. Runs back to Risoul 1850 start on a narrow and windy ledge with steep drops on either side. It is important to start heading back to Risoul by 3pm. If you miss the last lift it is an expensive taxi ride around the mountain to get home again. It is also worth noting that links to and from Risoul/Vars are sometimes closed due to high winds.

The Crête de Chabrières, the highest point of the area, is where you will find the speed-skiing slope, which is well worth a look when the racers are in action.

Three separate reporters criticise the area's piste-marking as being inconsistent, with 'blues more difficult than some of the reds', 'some blue runs could have been green', and 'some of the red runs easier than the blues'. Piste-grooming is reported to take place only between 5pm and 9pm, resulting in 'ungroomed pistes after a heavy snowfall overnight'.

Mountain restaurants

There are half-a-dozen of them, more than are shown on the rather confusing local lift map. Three of the restaurants are in Risoul's ski area: Le Vallon, Le Prarond and the Refuge Valbelle. Chez Plumot in Vars is a recommended restaurant for lunch with a good atmosphere, but is not cheap by the area's standard with a 170FF set menu and a 60FF children's menu. Most people found that eating in a mountain restaurant cost under 60FF for lunch and around 13FF for a small beer or Coke. La Licorne, next to the pistes, is a good place for lunchtime pizzas, salads and crêpes.

Beginners and children

Reports on the ESF at Risoul 1850 vary wildly, with some very unfavourable comments: 'Nobody visibly in charge – we were left to hawk our ski school cards round the instructors at three different congregation points to find instructor at the right level/language.' Happily, the same reporter's eventual class size varied between three and five people (low season). Another reporter (in high season) commented that the 'class sizes exceeded 10 in all groups and more than 15 in some cases. The instructor actually left three people from the beginners' class at the top of a red run on the third day. When they eventually got down two were absolutely terrified and didn't put skis on for the rest of the week.' We have also received a worrying report of instructors leaving people behind because they couldn't keep up, follow-the-leader tuition, and of individuals reshuffled throughout the week to reflect the progress of more able skiers.

On the plus side, private lessons are highly recommended by several reporters and the instructors' standard of English seems to be high. We have no reports on the International Ski School.

Risoul 1850 has extensive kindergarten facilities, as it is a truly family-orientated resort. Les Pitchous is for non-skiing children from six months, and both the ESF and the International Ski School have mini clubs for children of three years old and upwards. The nursery slopes are right next to the resort, with two short lifts. Another longer one gives access to the secluded area of green (beginner) runs. Unfortunately the lack of other green runs in the ski area means that advancing beginners and small children have either to stay within the confines of the resort or branch out on a more difficult blue run. The drags linking with Vars are also reported as being too steep for children.

The resort

Risoul 1850 is still a relatively new resort and has the advantage of having been built in a sympathetic wood-clad and stone design. It is set in an open position in attractive surroundings. At the top of the village, next to the slopes, is a crescent of apartment buildings and cafés. Shopping for souvenirs is limited to a couple of shops, but there are more than a dozen sports retailers.

Accommodation

Le Dahu is Risoul 1850's only hotel, recently built with a sauna and gym, children's games room and 20 bedrooms. Risoul village, lower down the valley, connected by bus service to to Risoul 1850, has three more hotels, Le Rochasson I, Le Rochasson II and La Bonne Auberge. Vars has three recommended hotels: Les Escondus, Le Caribou (in the best location) and L'Ecureuil (without a restaurant). Village Leo Lagrange holiday centre in Risoul has 500 beds.

Over 90 per cent of Risoul's visitors stay in self-catering accommodation. Les Melèzes apartments are well located for the slopes but with the disadvantage of a 10-minute uphill walk back from the village centre. A reporter notes the lack of space in the four- to six-person apartments, with only enough seating for three. And complains of very loud, late-night music from the ground floor, which was heard on the sixth floor. Another reporter talks of the Melèzes as being 'not very large apartment, but well equipped', and 'corridors and stairs of the block generally not kept very clean'. The Christiana studios for two are reported as being convenient, quite spacious and well-equipped, although they poorly maintained.

The three supermarkets have a good range of supplies for self-caterers and are open until 10pm. Reporters found the wine and beer to be cheap and the food of a high quality, though they noted a shortage of meats at reasonable prices. There is also a take-away pizza establishment.

Eating out

La Licorne is a lively meeting place in the evenings and the Bergerie is recommended by several reporters for its good-value food, although its menu is limited. L'Assiette Gourmande has good quality and value-for-money food but tends to be very crowded in the evenings. L'Ecureuil is also recommended.

Après-ski

Le Pick-Up and Le Dahu are the two discos, but other après-ski revolves around bars such as La Licorne and the Rocking Bar in the Melèzes building. Other activities are limited. The cinema is the focal point of evening cultural activities.

Skiing facts: Risoul

TOURIST OFFICE
Risoul 1850, 05600 Guillestre, Hautes Alpes
Tel 33 92 46 02 60
Fax 33 92 46 01 23

THE RESORT
By road Calais 1024km
By rail Montdauphin 15km from Risoul and Vars. TGV connection
By air Marseille 3 hrs, Grenoble 3 hrs
Visitor beds 11,700 (93% apartments, 5% hostels, 1% chalets, 1% hotels)
Transport local bus service

THE SKIING
Longest run Côte Belle 2.4km (blue)
Number of lifts 54
Number of trails/pistes 104 (9% beginner, 47% easy, 40% intermediate, 4% difficult)
Total of trails/pistes 160km
Nursery slopes 2 lifts
Summer skiing none
Snowmaking 8 hectares covered

LIFT PASSES
Area pass (covers Risoul and Vars) 700FF for 6 days
Day pass 130FF
Half-day pass 95FF from 9am-1pm, 99FF after 12.30pm
Beginners 1 free lift
Children 5-11 years, 520FF for 6 days, free for under 5 yrs
Pensioners free for 70 yrs and over
Credit cards accepted yes

SKI SCHOOLS
Adults ESF Risoul, 370FF for 6 lessons (2 hrs each). Ski School International (ESI), 400-480FF for 6 lessons (2 hrs each)

Children ESF, 4 yrs and over, 70FF for 2 hrs. Ski-Resto (ESI), 6-14 yrs, 185-290FF per day, 1,050-1,680FF for 6 days (small groups of 3-8 children)
Private lessons 140-170FF per hr
Special courses snowboarding, monoskiing
Guiding companies none

CROSS-COUNTRY
Ski schools through ESF
Loipe location and size 30km

CHILDCARE
Non-ski kindergarten Les Pitchous, 6 mths-6 yrs, 9am-5pm daily, 150FF per day, 560FF for 6 days, not including lunch
Ski kindergarten Mini-club ESF, 3-5 yrs, 180-250FF per day, 1,230FF for 6 days including lunch. Chocoski (ESI), 3-5 yrs, 1,320FF for 6 days including lunch
Babysitting difficult

OTHER SPORTS
Snow-shoeing, parapente, skating, squash

WHAT'S NEW
● 200-place car park ● Bergerie ski-lift ● leisure centre housing cinema, restaurant, and tourist office

FOOD AND DRINK PRICES
Coffee 6FF, bottle of house wine 40FF, beer 12FF, dish of the day 60FF

TOUR OPERATORS
Crystal, Enterprise, Kings Ski Club, Neilson, Sally Holidays, SkiBound, Ski Airtours, Ski Thomson

Vars 1850m (6,068ft)

Vars is a mainly wood-built, though not particularly attractive, resort situated above the town of Sainte-Marie-de-Vars, where the skiing goes
down to 1650m. It attracts a largely French clientele and is connected to
Risoul by a windy ridge. Hotels include the Caribou (which has a swimming-pool), Les Escondus, and l'Ecureuil at Vars 1850, as well as Le
Vallon, Le Mayt and the Edelweiss at Sainte-Marie-de-Vars. Chez Plumot
at Sainte-Marie is a restaurant worth visiting.

TOURIST OFFICE
05560 Vars, Haute Alpes
Tel 33 92 46 51 31

TOUR OPERATORS

Serre Chevalier, Hautes-Alpes

ALTITUDE 1200-1500m (3,936-4,920ft)

••

Good points large ski area, varied off-piste skiing, tree-level skiing, minimal queuing, extensive cross-country facilities, children's facilities
Bad points heavy traffic, strung-out resort with no real centre, unreliable resort-level snow
Linked or nearby resorts Briançon (l), Montgenèvre (n), La Grave (n), Les Deux Alpes (n), Puy-St-Vincent (n)

You will not find the resort of Serre Chevalier on any map for the simple reason that it does not exist. 'Serre Che' as the French call it, is a 2491m peak in the Hautes Alpes above the ancient garrison city of Briançon not far from the Italian border. It is also the name given to the extensive ski area shared by no less than 13 villages which line the Guisane valley along the main Grenoble-Briançon highway. It has an extraordinary amount of good skiing to offer, a choice of modern and traditional villages, or even the more cultured atmosphere of Briançon itself, which these days has direct gondola access into the ski area.

On the downside, the resort of Serre Chevalier, if it can be described as such, has been allowed to develop in a thoroughly messy way with no actual centre. The growing band of reporters who are converts to its skiing agree that a car is a necessity if you are to use the on- and off-slope facilities to their fullest potential. The skiing suits every standard of skier, with good nursery slopes and extensive off-piste opportunities with a guide. But the skier who will benefit most is the high-mileage cruiser, who will find 250km of linked skiing served by a highly respectable 77 lifts.

The three main villages are marketed as Serre Chevalier 1350, 1400 and 1500, but are in reality known only by their proper names of Chantemerle, Villeneuve and Monêtier-Les-Bains. The lower two share most of the accommodation, resort facilities and the larger half of the ski area. But Monêtier is the only one of the three with any real village atmosphere. It also offers the most difficult skiing, but is unfortunately the least convenient. All the main villages suffer seriously from traffic on what is a very busy international arterial road. Briançon is pleasantly different from the run-of-the-mill ski resort, its medieval fortifications enclosing a maze of ancient and narrow streets.

There are complicated lift-pass sharing arrangements with several other major ski areas in the region, which operate under the Grande

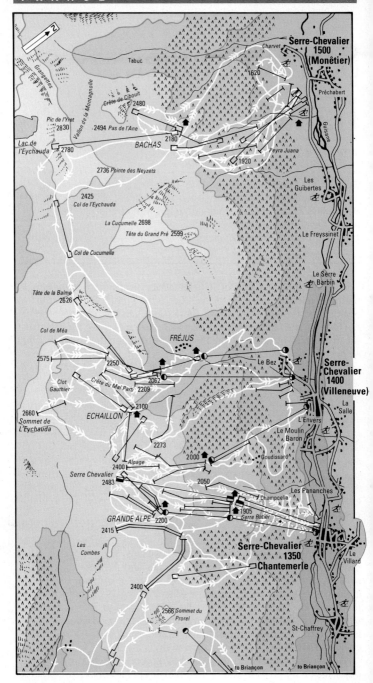

Grangettes

Tabuc

Crête de Cibouit 2480

Pic de l'Yret 2830

2494 Pas de l'Ane

Lac de l'Eychauda 2780

BACHAS

2180

2736 Pointe des Neyzets

2425 Col de l'Eychauda

La Cucumelle 2698

Tête du Grand Pré 2599

Col de Cucumelle

Tête de la Balme 2626

Col de Mêa

2575

2250

Crête du Mal Part

2209

2062

Clot Gauthier

2660 Sommet de L'Eychauda

2100

ECHAILLON

2273

2400

Alpage

Serre Chevalier 2483

2050

2000

GRANDE ALPE 2200

2415

Les Combes

1905 Serre Ratier

Champcella

2566 Sommet du Prorel

2400

FRÉJUS

Le Bez

Serre-Chevalier 1400 (Villeneuve)

La Salle

L'Envers

Le Moulin Baron

Goudissard

Les Pananches

Serre-Chevalier 1350 Chantemerle

Le Villard

St-Chaffrey

Serre-Chevalier 1500 (Monêtier)

Charvet

1620

Préchabert

Guisane

Peyra Juana

1920

Les Guibertes

Le Freyssinet

Le Serre Barbin

to Briançon

to Briançon

Galaxie umbrella. If you have a car you can ski in Montgenèvre and the Milky Way to the east, in Les Deux Alpes and Alpe d'Huez to the west, and even in Puy-St-Vincent to the south. Up the road, just over the Col de Lauteret lies La Grave and some of the best off-piste skiing in the Alps *(see Les Deux Alpes)*.

The skiing
Top 2800m (9,184ft) bottom 1350m (4,428ft)

The **main mountain** access is by a choice of cable car and gondolas from Chantemerle and neighbouring Villeneuve. Most of the lifts and pistes are concentrated above these two villages in a linked network covering a series of valleys of open, mostly intermediate skiing between 2000m and 2500m. Longer runs of varying difficulty go down through thinly wooded lower slopes dotted with chalets and farm buildings; and rough roads make easy alternatives to the more direct descents to the valley floor. The Monêtier sector at the western end of the area is in many ways the most appealing, with some good red (intermediate) runs through the woods, a couple of seriously testing blacks (difficult) and the best of the easily accessible off-piste.

Above Grand Alpe is an open basin of rather featureless intermediate runs with a good, but congested, nursery area at the top of the gondola. The double Prorel drag-lift serves intermediate pistes, and below it is an isolated quad chair serving two 'magnificent and often deserted' red pistes dropping 500m through the woods. Serre Chevalier itself is a rather unremarkable peak, but the views from the top are spectacular and a fast racecourse takes you down through the trees.

Prorel is also the top station of the Briançon lifts. A 12-person gondola, which starts from the edge of the town centre, serves an east-facing red piste of 1150m vertical back into town, natural or artificial snow permitting. There is a nursery area at 1625m at the mid-station and a black slalom course, which is served by a drag-lift finishing at the same point. On the open south-east facing flank there are long runs, red at the top, but merging into blue (easy) and green (beginner) later on.

The Fréjus/Echaillon sector directly above Villeneuve provides some of the more interesting runs for good skiers, with short, fairly steep, unprepared pistes beneath the crest of the mountain chain. There are spectacular views southwards and an exciting black run called l'Isolée, which starts along the narrow ridge from Eychauda and plunges down towards Echaillon. In good snow conditions skiers of all standards can enjoy long, interesting runs down to the valley.

Monêtier's network of lifts is linked to the Fréjus sector by a series of high chair-lifts, one of which goes to the high-point of the system on the shoulder of the Pic de l'Yret at 2830m, giving runs of 1300m vertical all the way down to the valley. The black and red pistes from here towards Fréjus are good runs when conditions are right and both get a lot of sun. The link as a whole is high and exposed, which makes it either unpleasant or impossible in poor weather. The wide and beautiful east-facing bowl above Fréjus now has a piste, the red Vallon de la Cucumelle. The Yret chair makes some favoured off-piste runs easily accessible, including the steep face under the lift which has a gradient of 35° at its harshest point. It is much skied, even when it is fenced off for safety reasons, and presents a formidable mogul field, which most reporters agree is the most difficult in the resort.

From Bachas at 2180m down to the valley there is a wide choice of intermediate pistes through the larch woods, with plenty of off-piste variants for those who want to try them. None of these runs, either on- or off-piste, is particularly easy, including the token blue. Tabuc is a rewarding, long black run through the woods away from the main ski area, with one or two awkwardly narrow and steep pitches.

Queuing does not appear to be a major problem on what is an efficient and modern lift system. Ski-buses are reportedly efficient, but not frequent enough; they stop running over the lunchtime period. Other buses operate the length of the valley. Snowmaking on the lower runs is extensive. The run from the Grand Alpe mid-station down to Chantemerle is covered, along with the lower slopes at Monêtier and more recently the top of the Casse du Boeuf down to Villeneuve.

Mountain restaurants

The choice of eating places is not large considering the size of the area, but the quality is high. The Pï Mai at the foot of the Vallon de la Cucumelle run is highly rated: '10 out of 10 for what a mountain restaurant should be.' Jacques A also receives lavish praise, as does Le Bachas.

Beginners and children

We have generally good reports of the ESF in Briançon, which is by no means geared towards British visitors, but most instructors have a good stab at speaking English and the standard of tuition is said to be 'much higher than the ESF in comparable resorts'. Similarly, in Serre Chevalier we have nothing but positive comments on the ski school. Nursery slopes are extensive, with open areas at the foot of both the Monêtier and Villeneuve slopes as well as higher up at the top of the Fréjus and Grand Alpe gondolas.

The childcare facilities are particularly good: in Chantemerle Les Poussins takes babies of eight months old and over, Les Schtroumpfs in Villeneuve six months and over, and Pré-Chabert in Monêtier 18 months old and over (or six months outside the French school holidays). The kindergarten at Briançon takes babies six months old and over.

The resort

Chantemerle (1350m) is the closest of the Serre Chevalier villages to Briançon and serves mainly as a base station for skiing commuters staying elsewhere along this long valley. The space between the main road and the river is limited and parking space is wholly inadequate. Villeneuve (1400m) is more spread out, with a narrow high street on one side of the river and more spacious resort development, including a commercial centre and large blocks of apartments beside what was the main road at the foot of the slopes on the other side (a bypass now skirts the area). If Serre Chevalier has a centre, then this is it. Near the Fréjus lifts, the ancient hamlet of Le Bez outwardly looks much as it did before tourism came to the valley, apart from its once neatly tiled roofs which have been replaced sadly by rusting corrugated iron. However, many of the buildings, linked by narrow and often icy streets, have been converted into twee holiday homes and tour-operator chalets. It has managed to retain its charm and reporters recommend it as a good place to stay.

Monêtier (1500m) is a quiet, rural spa village with some delightful huddles of old buildings between the road and the river. The lift starts a few minutes' walk away on the far side of the river.

Accommodation
Most of the accommodation is in apartments and around 40 hotels spread between the three villages, as well as a further 20 in Briançon. Location is very much a matter of personal choice rather than ease of lift access. Le Clos de Chantemerle is a popular, traditional two-star with 'very good food and a real French atmosphere'. Le Sporting in Villeneuve is said to have very friendly staff and, 'excellent food, although a slightly out-of-town location'. The Plein Sud in Chantemerle is said to be 'very comfortable, but with no ski resort atmosphere'. The two-star Alliey in Monêtier is charming and centrally located. The smarter Auberge du Choucas, also in Monêtier, is renowned for its restaurant. Self-caterers are well-served by supermarkets, which one reporter describes as 'the best in the Alps'.

Eating out
The good restaurants are spread throughout the valley and you do really need a car. Le Bidule in Le Bez is recommended for its 'excellent fresh fish'. The Serre Barbin and the Marotte in Villeneuve are both praised. The Pizzeria des Neiges and La Benoîte crêperie in Monêtier both provide good food at reasonable prices.

Après-ski
This is mainly confined to bars. Le Clos bar and disco in Chantemerle draws a large British crowd as does the Lièvre Blanc in Villeneuve ('excellent bar with open fire, very reasonable prices'). Le Frog and l'Iceberg in Villeneuve are both lively. Le Caveau disco hardly functions until after midnight.

Briançon 1200m (3,936ft)
This old garrison town had no pretensions to being a ski resort until the recent construction of the Prorel gondola, which starts from the edge of the town. Briançon was content to act as the major commercial centre of the region, a not insignificant summer tourist attraction and staging post on the road to Italy, as well as a winter dormitory for skiers wanting to explore the different villages of the Guisane valley. It therefore lacks any of the normal, sometimes stifling, ski resort atmosphere. You feel you are staying in a proper town with all the conveniences of non-tourist restaurants, the wide range of food shops that are the delight of provincial France and realistically priced hotels. Exploring the picturesque narrow streets of the old fortified town up on the hill is an unusual type of après-ski occupation. The ramparts give a spectacular

view, past the towers of the church and across the roofs of the town, of the ski area and the remainder of the Serre Chevalier ridge.

The 12-person gondola has covered and open car-parks nearby and is a short walk from the centre. The Auberge Le Mont-Prorel is a simple

Skiing facts: Serre Chevalier

TOURIST OFFICE
BP 20, F-05240 La Salle Les Alpes, Hautes-Alpes
Tel 33 92 24 71 88
Fax 33 92 24 76 18

THE RESORT
By road Calais 1000km
By rail Briançon 6km, regular bus service to resort
By air Lyon 3 hrs, Grenoble 2½ hrs
Visitor beds 21,540 (63% apartments and chalets, 17% other, 11% hostels, 9% hotels)
Transport buses run from Monêtier-Les-Bains to Briançon

THE SKIING
Longest run L'Iret, 1.3km (red)
Number of lifts 77
Number of trails/pistes 112 (19% beginner, 23% easy, 46% intermediate, 12% difficult)
Total of trails/pistes 250km
Nursery slopes 5 lifts
Summer skiing 20km away at La Grave
Snowmaking 60 hectares covered

LIFT PASSES
Area pass Serre Che (covers 1350 and 1400), 650FF for 6 days. Grand Serre Chevalier (covers all centres), 750FF for 6 days. Passes of 6 days or more include 1 day in Alpe d'Huez, Les Deux Alpes, Puy-St-Vincent, and the Milky Way
Day pass Grand Serre Chevalier, 150FF
Half-day pass 105FF after 12.30pm
Beginners no free lifts
Children Juniors, 9-16 yrs, Serre Che, 500FF for 6 days, Grand Serre Chevalier, 575FF for 6 days. Children, 4-8 yrs, Serre Che, 300FF for 6 days, Grand Serre Chevalier, 390FF for 6 days. Free for 4 yrs and under
Pensioners 60 yrs and over, as Juniors
Credit cards accepted yes

SKI SCHOOLS
Adults ESF (1350/1400/1500), International Ski School (1350/1400), both 3 hrs per day, 495FF for 6 days
Children ESF (1350/1400/1500), International Ski School (1350/1400), both 3 hrs per day, 430FF for 6 days
Private lessons 150FF per hr
Special courses snowboarding, telemark, ski-touring
Guiding companies Bureau des Guides (1350), Montagne à la Carte (1400), Compagnie des Guides de l'Oisans (1500)

CROSS-COUNTRY
Ski schools ESF and International Ski School
Loipe location and size 45km along valley floor from Briançon to beyond Village du Casset

CHILDCARE
Non-ski kindergarten Les Poussins (Chantemerle), 8 mths and over, 9am-5pm, 185FF per day including lunch. Les Schtroumpfs (Villeneuve), 6 mths and over, 9am-5pm, 155FF per day not including lunch. Halte de Pré-Chabert (Monêtier), 2-15 yrs, 9am-6pm, 135FF per day not including lunch
Ski kindergarten ESF, International Ski School, both 4 yrs and over, 3 hrs per day, 430FF for 6 days
Babysitting list from tourist office

OTHER SPORTS
Parapente, hang-gliding, ice-driving, skating, climbing wall, swimming, fitness centres

FOOD AND DRINK PRICES
Coffee 6FF, bottle of house wine 25FF, beer 12FF, dish of the day 40FF

TOUR OPERATORS
UCPA, Alpine Options, Bladon Lines, The Club, Crystal, Enterprise, Kings Ski Club, Made to Measure, Neilson, Sally Holidays, Seasun School Tours, SkiBound, Ski Europe, STS, Ski Thomson, Snowbizz Vacances, Snowcoach

Logis de France right next to the lift station. The Parc Hotel is near the central crossroads ('smart, modern but a bit soulless; you could be anywhere in the world, not necessarily in France'). The Vauban, slightly further away, is probably the most comfortable. One reporter strongly recommends Le Relais de la Guisane as the most convenient for the skiing. A group of self-caterers who rented an apartment in the town warn that the supermarket does not open until 9am. Most of the best restaurants are in the old town. L'Entrecôte is warmly recommended, along with Le Passé Simple and Le Péché Gourmand. Sports facilities are good, with a swimming-pool and a skating rink.

TOURIST OFFICE
05105 Hautes-Alpes
Tel 33 92 21 08 50
Fax 33 92 20 56 45

TOUR OPERATORS
Sally Holidays, Seasun School Tours,
Snowbizz Vacances

Trois Vallées, Savoie

Courchevel
ALTITUDE 1300-1850m (4,264-6,068ft)

Good points big vertical drop, excellent nursery slopes, caters for all standards of skier, long cruising runs, tree-level skiing, resort-level snow (1850m), gourmet restaurants, wide choice of luxury hotels, skiing convenience, big ski area,
Bad points limited activities for non-skiers, high prices in Courchevel 1850
Linked or nearby resorts La Tania (l), Méribel (l), Val Thorens (l), Les Menuires (l), St-Martin de Belleville (l)

Méribel
ALTITUDE 1450-1700m (4,756-5,576ft)

Good points superb mountain access, big ski area, chalet-style architecture, resort-level snow (1700m), large beginner area, all standards of skiing
Bad points heavy traffic, pay-bus system

Les Menuires
ALTITUDE 1850m (6,068ft)

Good points all standards of skiing, big ski area, long cruising runs, sunny slopes, off-piste skiing, well-run children's village, budget prices, extensive snowmaking
Bad points ugly buildings in centre, heavy traffic, limited après-ski, lack of tree-level runs, limited for non-skiers

Val Thorens
ALTITUDE 2300m (7,544ft)

Good points resort-level snow, big ski area, summer skiing, ski-in ski-out convenience at its best, children's facilities
Bad points lack of tree-level skiing, exposed and cold in mid-winter, limited for non-skiers, limited après-ski

---

The Trois Vallées are considered, at least by the French, to form the biggest ski area in the world, *'le plus grand domaine skiable du monde'*. This marketing statement is debatable, but some 200 lifts and 600km of well-linked pistes make a formidable argument in favour of it. Certainly it is one of the most important of the great ski circuses, if only because of the variety of skiing, and of resort, within one area. The sheer size of the Trois Vallées (somehow the name doesn't translate) is daunting to the visitor and most holidaymakers will barely come to terms with one corner of it in a week of hard piste-bashing. Truly to explore the on- and off-piste possibilities takes a season based in at least two different locations.

What we have here is the best overall lift complex in the world, an annually improving combination of cable cars, gondolas, detachable chairs and tows. Even on the busiest days of the season you rarely have to queue anywhere for more than 15 minutes. Critics point out that the runs are mainly intermediate in standard, but so are the vast majority of the skiers who come here every year. There are plenty of harsh black pistes for those who want them, including three in Courchevel which are among the hardest blacks (difficult runs) in the world. The off-piste is not as rugged as Val d'Isère or Chamonix, but much of the Trois Vallées provides an excellent and safe introduction after a new snowfall to the delights of deep powder. Those who want bigger challenges know where to find them: on Mont Vallon, off the Cîme de Carron and around La Masse.

The Trois Vallées are the three neighbouring valleys of Les Allues (Méribel), Bozel (Courchevel) and Belleville (Val Thorens, Les Menuires). They are reached via two mountain roads from Moutiers or by an under-used gondola from Brides-Les-Bains. The Trois Vallées ski area now stretches from Val Thorens into a fourth valley, the Maurienne. Mercifully, while there is a lift on the far side, there is no actual resort. Otherwise, the Trois would officially have to become the Quatres Vallées.

Each resort has its own character as well as its individual ski area aside from the hundreds of shared kilometres. Méribel has such a strong British chalet holiday tradition that there are bars where French is either the second language, or not spoken at all. Courchevel is ultra-chic and international, at least at 1850, with designer ski suits outnumbering chain-store versions on the visitors browsing in the designer boutiques. Les Menuires could not be a bigger contrast, a budget resort where the main evening entertainment for the hardcore of bourgeois French who make up its winter inhabitants is watching the rented television set in their rented apartment, or walking the dog which also came with them on holiday. Val Thorens, architecturally slightly more pleasing, is for skiers who want to be as sure of finding snow in early December as in late April.

The skiing
Top 3300m (10,850ft) bottom 1300m (4,264ft)

We have not mentioned **mountain access** here as there are simply too many access points to list throughout the Trois Vallées. The ski area is an uneasy alliance between seven different lift companies, each of which looks after itself extremely well and pays lip service to its agreement with the others. This provides an explanation, but no degree of comfort, to those skiers who are exasperated by the shortfalls of the whole lift ticket structure which, for example, does not include half-day Trois Vallées lift passes. Multiple ownership also explains why passes are checked on almost every lift.

Each resort sells its own local pass, which is adequate for skiers with only a couple of weeks' experience behind them. You do, however, have to be careful to stay within what are not always well-defined boundaries of the resort. The Trois Vallées lift pass which covers all lifts, is not hugely more expensive and is generally a better buy for the com-

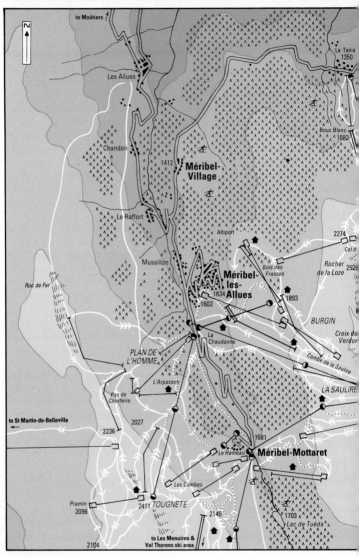

petent intermediate and upwards. However, the biggest single gripe from reporters is that they were encouraged unnecessarily by tour operator reps to buy Trois Vallées passes when a single-resort pass would suffice. Much discussion is now taking place about the introduction of a computerised ticket system with most of the lift companies favouring a pay-as-you-ski operation. It is a discussion that should, of course, have taken place years ago. Méribel claims to have improved its ticket sales operation at Chaudanne, yet on our visit only half the windows were open and the complex is serviced by one grossly inadequate

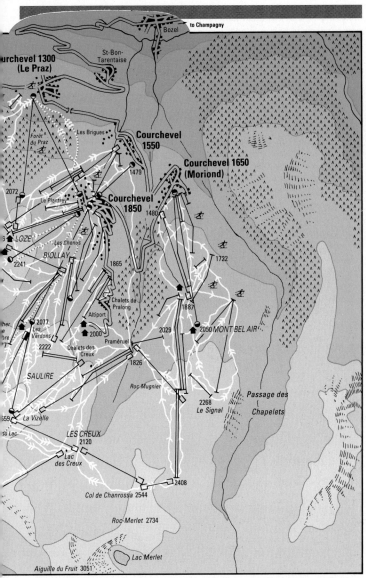

photo-machine. One-hour queues are the norm at Christmas, so forgetting to bring your photograph is a truly punishing experience.

The Méribel and Courchevel valleys are well linked by lifts and pistes up and down the craggy ridge separating the two via Saulire, as well as the Col de la Loze above the new resort of La Tania. Les Menuires and St-Martin de Belleville also have easy connections with Méribel for anyone who can ski parallel. Val Thorens, however, is connected by a harsh black and an often bumpy red.

The skiing at Courchevel is spread widely across the mountainside

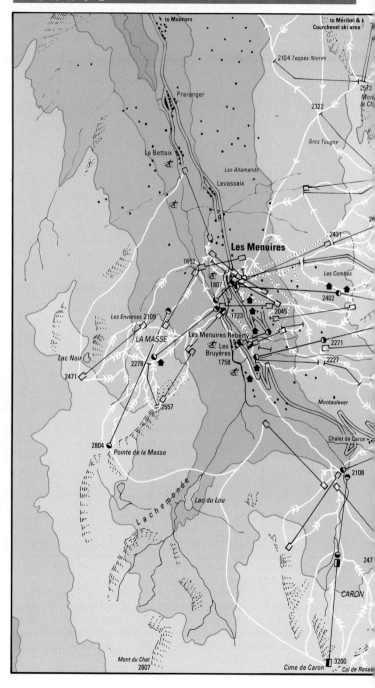

to Moûtiers

to Méribel &
Courchevel ski area

2104 *Teppes Noires*

2573
Mora
la Ch

Prarânger

2322

Gros Tougne

Le Bettaix

Les Allamands

Levassaix

Les Menuires

1652

2431

Les Combes

1807

2402

Les Enverses 2109

1723

2045

LA MASSE

Les Menuires Reberty

2271

Les
Bruyères

2227

Lac Noir

2278

1758

2471

Montaulever

2557

Chalet de Caron

2804   *Pointe de la Masse*

2108

Lac du Lou

L a c h e m o n d e

247

CARON

Mont du Chat
2807

Cime de Caron

3200
Col de Rosaë

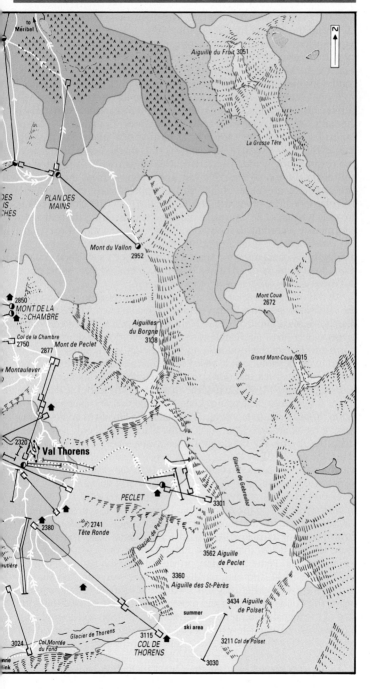

to Méribel

Aiguille du Fruit 3051

La Grosse Tête

PLAN DES MAINS

DES IS CHES

Mont du Vallon
2952

Mont Coua
2672

2850
MONT DE LA CHAMBRE

Aiguilles du Borgne
3138

Grand Mont-Coua 3015

Col de la Chambre
2750   Mont de Peclet
2877

Montaulever

2320

Val Thorens

Glacier de Gebroulaz

PECLET

3301

2380   2741
Tête Ronde

Glacier de Peclet

3562 Aiguille de Peclet

3360
Aiguille des St-Pères

3434 Aiguille de Polset

summer ski area

3024   Col Montée du Fond

Glacier de Thorens   3115
COL DE THORENS

3211 Col de Polset

nne link

3030

281

with an enormous variety of terrain. The shape of the mountains is concave, with the steeper runs at the top of the rocky ridge around Saulire flattening out and draining into a long motorway which takes you down into Courchevel 1850. This can be very crowded and wise skiers will head for the long and separate ski area above Courchevel 1600 or, snow conditions permitting, the tree-line runs down to Le Praz and La Tania.

From Courchevel 1850 a gondola takes you to Verdons where a 150-person cable car whips you up to the top of the skiing at Saulire. This is the only lift which gives access to the three Courchevel couloirs. Experts sneer that they are neither narrow nor steep, but they are among the most radical black (difficult) runs marked on a piste map in any resort in the world. They are reached by a narrow, and often icy, path from the top of the cable car. The steepest drops away directly beneath it at an angle of 38° and is appropriately called Sous la Téléphérique. The other two, the Emile Allais and the Grand Couloir, are only a 'modest' 36°. As in all couloirs, the difficulty of descent varies enormously according to snow conditions. You can always ski down the red (intermediate) piste around the shoulder and watch your friends making fools of themselves. Apart from the three established couloirs there are a number of variations if you are prepared for a short climb, but these should only be explored with a guide.

All the other runs served by the cable car can also be reached from the alternative gondola from Verdons to Vizelle from where you have the choice of continuing over to Méribel, taking one of the steepish red or genuinely black alternative ways back to Verdons, skiing the black north-east face of the mountain under the high-speed Suisses chair, or entering the beautifully wide Vallée des Creux and from there either skiing the tediously flat trail down to 1550, or taking the linking lifts back to 1850 or over to 1650. Each of the three chair-lifts from Lac des Creux serves interesting, challenging skiing. The Creux Noirs chair also opens up an off-piste run to Mottaret. The Chanrossa lift serves an impressive wide slope of around 500m vertical; the black piste is only moderately steep but the heavily skied off-piste area is steeper. A half-hour climb along the ridge of Roc Merlet gives access to a wonderful off-piste run which eventually takes you back down to 1650. On-piste, a series of easily negotiable reds also bring you down into 1650's ski area.

Courchevel 1650 is in the main gentle cruising country with wonderful nursery slopes on the Altiport, but there are some more challenging pitches, particularly down the Roc Mugnier combe. A gondola, accessible by two-way escalator from road level, climbs from the village to Mont Bel Air. Below this knoll, where lifts from the lower slopes converge, the short Petite Bosse drag provides a link with Prameruel for the trip back to 1850, and long parallel drags give access to Roc Mugnier and connect with other drag-lifts serving the confidence-building runs below the Col de Chanrossa and more interesting ones down the north face of the Signal. The right-hand gondola from 1850 and several drag-lifts serve the skiing below the Col de la Loze, the most recently developed ski area of the Trois Vallées. Long black runs take you down to Le Praz, which is also called Courchevel 1300.

La Tania is served by a jumbo gondola which gives access to two chairs and a drag-lift. As the newest it is also the least skied corner of the Trois Vallées and in flat light conditions provides some of the best tree-line skiing. After a heavy snowfall the long runs down offer superb powder conditions. But be warned, La Tania is a horribly cold spot for much of the winter and gets little sunlight. Back on the top of the Col you can return to Courchevel via an easy blue, or carry on to Méribel Altiport, from where a four-seater chair takes you back to the Col.

The main Méribel skiing used to be largely confined to the two flanks, facing roughly east and west, between Méribel and its higher satellite Mottaret, making it ideal for sunny skiing morning and afternoon. In this area there is absolutely no difficulty in getting across from one side to the other or making the links along the mountainsides above the two resorts. The slopes are open and wooded only above Méribel. Mottaret and Méribel are linked by a very easy, wide green (beginner) run, the Truite. Sensibly the resort has now built an artificial bend into it to slow down good skiers who use it as a path to return to the Chaudanne, the central lift station in Méribel. It should be noted that Méribel can now be reached from the valley town of Brides-Les-Bains by a three-stage gondola which takes you straight into Chaudanne. According to several reporters this lift is hardly ever used.

The Roc de Fer chair and the high-speed Olympic Express detachable quad are important recent additions serving what was the very difficult women's downhill course for the Olympic Games. Even without the jumps, it is still a tough black which tends to become heavily mogulled, but this sector, which includes the parallel Plan de l'Homme chair, is usually pleasantly free of crowds even at peak times.

The skiing extends above Mottaret to the head of the valley. The triple-stage Plattières gondola takes you up to Roc des Trois Marches above Les Menuires and on the other side of the valley a jumbo gondola has opened up the whole of the Mont Vallon area. It should be pointed out that, except in designated areas, off-piste skiing is forbidden here for conservation reasons. However, this area and the neighbouring Aiguille du Fruit, both of which provide exceptional powder opportunities, are skied regularly. We have, to date, not heard of any warnings or prosecutions and the general feeling is that such activities are 'discouraged' rather than 'forbidden'. From the top (2952m) there is a legitimate choice of two reds, the Combe du Vallon on the Aiguille du Fruit side, and Campagnol which skirts the Glacier du Borgne and brings you back to the lift station. From here a chair links with the top of Plattières 2.

The Côte Brune detachable chair takes you up to the top of the Mont de la Chambre. Working back through the network of lifts along the Belleville Ridge, the Mont de la Challe and Tougnette give access to a whole range of reds and easy blues of which the Mouflon, from Plattières 3 down to the top of Plattières 1, deserves special mention as a truly excellent and varied piste. The long two-stage gondola to Tougnette serves an interesting black (difficult) run back to the base station – a short, steep mogul field at the top, an easy middle section with connections to Mottaret, and a steeper run down through the woods under the bottom of the lift, often short of snow.

Moving across to Saulire on the other side of the valley there are many variants of the open runs directly down into the village, mostly taxing reds but with some winding routes, which just get away with being called blue. The slopes face south-west and snow conditions are often treacherous, despite the large numbers of snow-cannon in the area. In good conditions the Grande Rosière run is a good sustained black which becomes blue just above the tree-line. The alternative red and blue motorways suffer severely from overcrowding by skiers too unadventurous to explore other possibilities in the Trois Vallées.

The runs in the Burgin sector immediately above Méribel are mostly shorter and easier, accessed by a two-stage jumbo gondola at the top of the altiport which, like Courchevel, provides superb nursery runs. However, these are served by two drag-lifts and a chair which present major problems for beginners. The drags, one short and one long, run between trees and there are no escape trails for those who fall by the wayside. The chair takes you up into what is initially red (intermediate), rather than green, territory. From the bottom of the lift you can now follow an itinerary skirting the cross-country course down to Morel, where a newish chair serves those staying in the Chez Kiki, the French Connection quarter of town where many of the British tour operators have their chalets. Plans are afoot to develop further this side of the resort's skiing with a network of lifts up from the hamlet of Méribel Village. At the moment you can get down to the apartments, snow permitting, but you can't get back.

From the top of Tougnette at Les Menuires you have a choice of a series of sunny drags and their pistes which take you gently down into the Belleville Valley. After a major snowfall they offer an easy and fun introduction to powder, but they quickly become skied out. Similarly in spring snow conditions the whole valley is opened up. The long cruise down into St-Martin de Belleville is well worth contemplating if snow conditions are really good and a long lunch in one of the pubs in the old village is your aim. The two-stage chair back takes a boring, and often cold, half-hour to complete.

Moving along the ridge, Le Gros Tougne, a blue (easy) path takes you slowly all the way to Les Menuires. More adventurous skiers will ride the series of drags and chairs as they make their way to the Roc des Trois Marches for the series of 100m vertical choices into the resort. The Mont de la Chambre also provides a main link with Méribel, accessed by two different two-stage gondolas, one from La Croisette, the centre of Les Menuires, and the other from the satellite of Les Bruyères up the valley towards Val Thorens. The best run down from here into Les Menuires is the bumpy black (difficult), les Pylones, or via a less exacting red.

The pistes immediately above the resort were used for the men's slalom in the Olympics and have consequently been inundated with snow-cannon. These prove very necessary as the mountain is a south-facing sun trap. However, the best of the Les Menuires skiing is in its own separate area, reached by three different snow bridges over the road from La Croisette or Bruyères. La Masse, at 2807m is no hill and it can provide some of the great off-piste of the Trois Vallées as well as its own recognised runs. Two basket lifts connect the two sides of the valley and two chairs bring skiers back from the bottom of La Masse to the Mont de la Chambre side. A two-stage chair serves the shoulder and gives access to Dame Blanche, which in certain winter conditions is one of the harsher blacks in the Belleville Valley. A two-stage gondola takes you from the bottom to the peak, which is the starting point for excellent itineraries, either down the valley towards St-Martin or around the back into the vast open spaces of the Lac du Lou area in the direction of Val Thorens, bigger in dimension than the whole of Courchevel.

Val Thorens, at the head of the valley, provides the highest skiing in the Trois Vallées. It nestles, rather coldly, beneath a tight horseshoe of peaks with slopes facing south-west and north. It is, on its own, the smallest of the ski areas in this giant complex, but snow is guaranteed here from late November or early December right through until long after Easter. The Funitel de Péclet giant gondola takes you up above the resort to the summer ski area on the Aiguille de Péclet at 3561m and a whole range of chairs and drags. Runs back down to the resort, including a long red, can be tricky in poor weather conditions.

On the other side of the Aiguille a second summer area can be reached by the Moraine and Col chairs. The runs down are pleasant blues. Moving along the ridge via a series of chairs the skiing becomes much tougher with some heavily mogulled reds. But the serious focus of the Val Thorens skiing is on the 160-person Cîme de Caron cable car which climbs swiftly to the highest point of the Trois Vallées winter skiing and opens up some magnificent runs, on- and off-piste, of almost 900m vertical.

A gentle run takes you down into the Vallée du Lou between Caron and La Masse, but there are plenty of more exciting off-piste adventures to be had with a guide. The black (difficult) north-facing piste is a long, open, but steep slope reached by a slightly imposing shelf, and the main red on the shoulder of the mountain is very challenging. A chair east of the Caron access gondola goes up to La Moutière and the Boismint and Plan de l'Eau chairs give access to wide-open expanses of mainly red (intermediate) runs which add to the resort's attractions.

· The ski area has now been extended over the back into the Maurienne Valley. This was always a great off-piste itinerary involving a long climb or a very long taxi back. The red run down is still not pisted, although it is quickly packed by skiers. A run of 660m vertical takes you down to a mountain hut and restaurant called the Chalet Refuge de Plan Bouchet. A fast chair takes you back up to the Col de Rosaël. Expansion plans here include a series of chairs and a huge valley car-park designated not so much for the inhabitants of the Maurienne, but for the thousands of Italians from Turin who can reach this link to the Trois Vallées through the Fréjus Tunnel. The overcrowding does not bear contemplation.

Mountain restaurants

Prices everywhere vary from 'high' to 'astronomical'. Reporters speak of beer for 50FF a glass. Courchevel, as you would expect, is steeped in fabulously expensive mountain eating places on the edge of the piste, like the Chalet de Pierre which is strongly recommended for its puddings. The Bistrot du Praz at 1300m is worth the long ski down and thanks to Charlie, its *bon viveur* owner, it has acquired a huge international following. It is worth noting that menus begin at 280FF and go up to 665FF. A *dégustation* of four different types of *fois gras* is the house speciality. Mere mortals will look elsewhere. Pierre Plats, at the top of Saulire, has received mediocre reports and grumbles about high prices and hostile service. Budget skiers should head down into 1650 and lunch in any of the restaurants along the main road. The Casserole receives glowing reports as a 'cheap self-service'. Altitude 21 above the altiport, Le Bel-Air and La Bergerie are all recommended.

The Méribel valley is better served at the cheaper (by Trois Vallées standards) end of the scale. Les Castors, on the right at the bottom of the Truite, has great spaghetti served in individual copper saucepans and is the best-value lunch spot in the area. In contrast, the Rhododendron, situated at the top of the Rhodos 2 lift, proved one of the most expensive of the mountain restaurants and has attracted complaints about the standard of the food and size of the portions. Reports on Yorkie's, just below the top of the Rhodos 1 gondola, are greatly varied, from 'terrible' to 'excellent value'. Roc des Trois Marches is a fast and efficient self-service in a sunny spot. Les Verdons and the Mont de la Chambre are both criticised for 'hostile service'. The Côte Brune in Mottaret appears to have lost its high standard in recent years. Reporters speak of 'overcrowding leading to poor service for food that is overpriced'.

Over in the Belleville Valley serious eaters say it is worth skiing down to St-Marcel, near St-Martin de Belleville, for the delights of La Bouitte. You have to take a taxi back afterwards or walk to St-Martin to catch the lift. La Mascotte and Chalet Necou are the culinary corners of St-Martin itself. La Marmite du Géant, an attractive restaurant beside the open-air swimming-pool at Les Bruyères, is slammed by one reporter who spoke of 'two staff coping with 100 customers. It took 90 minutes to get served and by then half the dishes were off'. Le Panoramic, at the top of La Masse, is a new eating place.

In the centre of Val Thorens Le Galoubet is recommended for its dish of the day. Restaurants at the bottom of the Moutière 1 and Moutière 2 lifts are good but expensive with a large beer costing 50FF. The small self-service at the bottom of the Caron is praised for its atmosphere and food.

Beginners and children

The ESF functions in all resorts with very mixed reports. In Méribel we twice counted classes of 18, admittedly at Christmas. One reporter in Mottaret speaks of 'teachers arriving 15 minutes late or not at all', and 'the class varied between 9 and 15 in number'. On the plus side, video was used as a teaching aid. Its international section, run by Pat Graham in Méribel, is consistently classed as 'efficient and generally good'. Ski Cocktail, which also uses the name Ecole du Ski des Trois Vallées, operates from Méribel and gets the best overall rating for 'good teaching' and 'making classes fun', although for a company which concentrates on the English market the level of linguistic proficiency among teachers was heavily criticised. A breakaway from Cocktail called White Magic is to be seen on the slopes, but no reports have been received. Cocktail has ceased to operate as such in Courchevel after an unsuccessful season there in 1991-2 and has been replaced by Masterclass, run by Scottish BASI instructors. The ESF charges different prices at different altitude locations here, with 1550 being surprisingly the most expensive for groups, and 1850 for individuals.

The ESF runs children's villages in all resorts. The best reports came from Les Menuires, where staff at Les Schtroumpfs are praised for their friendliness and dedication in looking after children from three months to two-and-a-half years in the nursery and up to seven years in the kindergarten section. The village has a rope lift for beginners and a longer drag. ESF teachers also take classes out on the mountain and there are good play facilities and a video room for non-skiing children.

Its equivalents in Courchevel 1850 and in 1650 take children from two years. Both are criticised as 'too serious' in their approach. One mother, while praising her four-year-old's progress at 1850, said children sat 'in Dickensian silence on a bench' between lessons. The Club des Pingouins in Mottaret takes children from three years, and the Club Saturnin in Méribel from two years. ESF group lessons start at four years in Méribel. In Val Thorens the Marielle Goitschel Club, run by the former French racer, takes children from three to sixteen years. The ESF Mini Club here looks after babies from three months and starts ski lessons at three years. Lift tickets in the Trois Vallées are complimentary for children under five years on proof of identity.

The resorts

As in a number of French resorts you need to ascertain exactly what is meant by Courchevel before booking a holiday here. Courchevel is not one, but four quite different resorts on the road up the mountain. A bus service (not included in the lift pass) links the different villages and runs hourly until about 10pm.

Courchevel 1850 is the international resort with the jet-set image and prices to match which, together with Mégève, is the most fashionable of all French resorts – a place in which to see and be seen for much of the season. For all that, it is not a particularly charming resort in aspect. Its heart is the central lift station, a kind of village square with a bell tower on a bend in the road, and a cluster of cafés on the edge of the piste. A covered mall houses expensive boutiques and a motley collection of other shops around the village caters for ordinary skiers and the more mundane needs of self-caterers. Higher up the mountain the Jardin des Alpins sector, reached by road or by its own gondola, is Millionaires Row. Sumptuous chalets lie tucked back between the trees and the main four-star de luxe hotels are here.

The second Courchevel is 1650, 200 vertical metres lower with prices to match. Many would argue that it is much more of a ski resort with a year-round population and the feel of a village, despite lining the main road. Courchevel 1550 is little more than a cluster of apartments off the beaten track, isolated from the heart of the lift system and popular only with the French. Courchevel 1300, or Le Praz, is an old farming village at the bottom of the lift system where accommodation prices are lowest. However, for a substantial part of the season it is not possible to ski back all the way.

La Tania is the newest of the Trois Vallées resorts, a pleasing collection of wood-clad apartment blocks and moderately priced hotels. It was originally built to provide extra accommodation for the Olympic Games back in the heady days when the French believed that the world would be homing in on the French Alps in February 1992. In the event, people stayed at home and watched the Games on television, if they watched it at all.

Méribel has grown rapidly in recent years. While the architectural style is strictly wood and local stone, it is a confusing and badly planned development which is now plagued by heavy traffic and resultant fumes. The snow in the resort turns a ghastly shade of grey within hours of a major fall. Parking meters have been introduced in the centre and part of it is now closed to traffic for three hours of the peak morning and afternoon rush. When a resort reaches that level of congestion the only solution is for the village fathers to make it traffic-free and build basket lifts for transport around the village. At the moment buses are supposed to run every 20 minutes and the fact that these are not included in the basic lift pass remains one of the great scandals of the Alps.

Méribel itself at 1450m seems to have dropped the name Les Allues in favour of Méribel Centre. The remainder of the resort divides into different sectors and before booking you should check on convenience of situation. Méribel Village is a lower, separate hamlet not yet on the lift system. Morel, on the back road up towards Rond Point des Pistes now has a chair-lift. Belvédère, at 1600m, is the smartest new development of hotels and luxury chalets, reached by the Rhodos 1 gondola from Chaudanne. The altiport sector lies at the top of the road. Mottaret, reached by a continuation of the main road from Méribel Centre has in the past been referred to as a satellite of Méribel. In 1992-3 it celebrated its twentieth birthday and must soon get status in its own right as a resort. It is a development of apartments, hotels, and a shopping centre set on the piste at 1700m. A gondola takes people to and from the Le Hameau district above the resort, but it closes at 7.30pm. The bus fare (10FF) between Mottaret and Méribel, adds to holiday costs and the alternative long walk limits après-ski opportunities.

Poor **Les Menuires** gets slammed regularly as the ugliest resort in the Alps, a blot on the mountain landscape. La Croisette, the centre, is a sad indictment with its monstrous apartment blocks, of French alpine planning laws as they were in the 1960s before the environmentalist lobby came to the fore. However, a small fortune was spent in cleaning up and recladding the resort for the Olympics. The old beast is still there, but it has a kinder face. No longer do you get the feeling that you are about to be mugged while wandering La Croisette by night.

The recent satellites of Les Bruyères and Reberty with their own hotels, shops and restaurants are much more pleasing and once there the visitor has little need to venture back to La Croisette except, annoyingly, for the chemist. For those wanting to ski the Trois Vallées on a budget it is a sensible place to stay. St-Martin de Belleville is an old farming village a few kilometres down the Belleville Valley which seems out of place in the high-tech atmosphere of the Trois Vallées. The village has a population of 2,000 goats and they still make cheese here.

Val Thorens used to claim to be the highest ski resort in Europe, while Obergurgl, which has a church, purported to be the highest ski village in Europe. At the end of 1992 Val Thorens celebrated its twentieth birthday with the dedication of its own church, and now claims both titles (although Hochgurgl seems to have been forgotten). On a sunny day it is a pleasant resort. However, in bad weather you may be forgiven for thinking you have been stranded amid the mountains of the moon. The resort's height guarantees good snow, but it can be one of the colder spots in the Alps. The resort itself is a mixture of modern architectural styles laid out along the piste. It is now car-free, although you are allowed to drive to your hotel or apartment and unload.

Accommodation

In **Méribel** the majority of skiers stay in tour-operated chalets or self-catering apartments. L'Antares is probably the best luxury hotel, although the Grand Coeur is more personal and has a warmer feel to it. In Mottaret visitors spoke highly of Le Hameau apartments and the four-star Hotel Mont Vallon. Les Arolles, on the piste above Mottaret, is 'convenient, comfortable, and good-value half-board'.

Most of **Courchevel**'s accommodation is in staffed chalets and apartments. Luxury hotels abound. The Byblos des Neiges and the Airelles are members of the Leading Hotels of The World group. Alpes Hotel Pralong 2000 and the Hotel des Neiges are both Relais et Châteaux. The three-star Ducs de Savoie is reported to be 'extremely comfortable'. The two-star Courcheneige is popular with regulars.

The accommodation in **Val Thorens** is mainly split between apartments and a wide choice of hotels. Le Bel Horizon and Le Sherpa ('best hotel in town, very friendly') are reporters' favourites, along with Le Val Chavière where 'staff are actually pleased to see you'. The Hotel Fitzroy is described as 'the last word in luxury, with prices to match'. The Temples du Soleil apartments on the piste at the lower end of the resort are self-contained with their own restaurant and supermarket. Apartments here are described as 'clean, but quite small'. The complex is divided into two and connected by an unheated walkway 'often with snow on the floor'.

Les Menuires' apartments are criticised as being 'cramped in the usual French style; apartments for six were really just big enough for four.' One reporter describes the newer Reberty apartments as 'exhausted by the end of the season'. The Hotel Les Latitudes in Les Bruyères won approval as 'a great find, don't tell anyone else'.

La Tania's Hotel Le Montana is recommended as 'simple, but more than adequate', along with the Christiania apartments. The Alp-Hotel in St-Martin is on the piste and has a warm, friendly atmosphere.

Eating out

Courchevel is rich in haute cuisine. The Chabichou Hotel has two coveted Michelin stars, as does Le Bateau Ivre. The seafood restaurant at Byblos de Neige is a wonder to behold. However, few reporters found themselves in this enviable price bracket. On a more mundane level Jack's Bar (La Saulire) in the square at 1850 is a resort institution serving modestly priced French food in a warm atmosphere. Le Tremplin pizzeria is said to offer 'good value on the chalet girl's night off'.

In **Méribel** the Taverne de Morel and Chez Kiki are recommended, the Cro Magnon for 'good-value steaks', the French Connection for 'a varied international menu at affordable prices'. The Aspen Park has a sushi bar and an outstanding Moroccan restaurant, but the hotel's future seemed uncertain at the time of writing. Crêperie Chez Patrick in Mottaret is ever popular, as are Le Grenier and Le Pizzeria du Mottaret.

Les Menuires is no gastronomic delight, but the half-board food in the Latitudes Hotel is described by one reporter as 'much more exciting than we could have hoped for'. The Ours Blanc at Reberty is recommended for 'a great evening out'. La Potinière in Les Bruyères is seen as 'a great place for a family evening out, delightful staff'. The crêperie Bar du Lou on La Croisette is 'very good for children and inexpensive'. The Chalet du Necou at Reberty and the Chalet La Ruade are both on the slopes but also open in the evening and prove popular. Some of the better restaurants are to be found in St-Martin and St-Marcel *(see Mountain restaurants)*.

In **Val Thorens**, the pizzeria in the Temples du Soleil is recommended. The choice of restaurants from gourmet to snack bar is surprisingly extensive in what is a small resort. El Gringo's Café in the Péclet shopping centre receives one reporter's approval as does Le Matafan in the Place de Péclet.

Après-ski

Courchevel 1850 is home to some spectacularly expensive nightclubs. However, hideous prices at La Grange and Le Saint Nicholas fail to keep the crowds away. Le Maquis and Le Refuge are popular bars with music.

Méribel has Le Pub in the centre and the French Connection pub run by Snowtime. The latter seems to provide some of the best nightlife at reasonable prices. Yorkie's proves very popular with the under 25s. Most reporters speak of disappointment at the lack of après-ski variety: 'Poor, with no good discos or night clubs.' was one comment. 'All the bars we tried were expensive, and almost all had little atmosphere.'

Les Menuires has live music most nights in Les Latitudes. La Mousse attracts teenagers and Le Calgary, Le Pub and Le Wagon Jaune all have live music. The Piano Bar Pourquoi Pas in St-Martin is recommended.

Val Thorens has a limited number of bars, but it is a resort which tends to be early to bed. The Lincoln Inn is 'very British, but has a good atmosphere'. The underground Malaysia Bar has music, but is 'very expensive'. The Agora disco proves most popular although it is 'quite small and very expensive'. The Bar in the Temples du Soleil complex has live music.

Skiing facts: Courchevel

TOURIST OFFICE
BP37, La Croisette, 73122 Courchevel, Savoie
Tel 33 79 08 00 29
Fax 33 79 08 33 54

THE RESORT
By road Calais 925km
By rail TGV Moutiers 25km, frequent buses
By air Lyon or Geneva 2½ hrs
Visitor beds 32,500 (80% chalets and apartments, 20% hotels)
Transport free bus with lift pass

THE SKIING
Longest run Les Creux, 4.2km (red)
Number of lifts 67 in Courchevel, 190 in Trois Vallées
Number of trails/pistes 95 in Courchevel (25% beginner, 26% easy, 38% intermediate, 11% difficult), 276 in Trois Vallées
Total of trails/pistes 150km in Courchevel, 600km in Trois Vallées
Summer skiing at Val Thorens
Snowmaking 23.7km covered

LIFT PASSES
Area pass Courchevel, 786FF for 6 days, Trois Vallées, 960FF for 6 days
Day pass Courchevel 160FF, Trois Vallées 195FF
Half-day pass 112FF (Courchevel only)
Beginners 11 free lifts
Children Courchevel, 5-16 yrs, 565FF for 6 days, Trois Vallées, 720FF for 6 days. Free for 5 yrs and under
Pensioners 60 yrs and over as children
Credit cards accepted yes

SKI SCHOOLS
Adults ESF 1650 780-910FF, ESF 1850 880FF, ESF 1550 1,090FF, all for 6 days
Children ESF 1650 610-700FF, ESF 1850 690FF, ESF 1550 950FF, all for 6 days
Private lessons 1,100FF-1,400FF per day
Special courses ski-touring, snowboarding, telemarking, mono-skiing, competition courses
Guiding companies Compagnie des Guides ESF at 1850

CROSS-COUNTRY
Ski schools at 1850 and 1550
Loipe location and size at 1300, above 1650, and from 1850 to Méribel Altiport. Total of 110km tracks in Trois Vallées

CHILDCARE
Non-ski kindergarten ESF 1850 Village des Enfants, 2 yrs and over, 192FF per day, 1,050FF for 6 days, both with lunch and tea. ESF 1650 Garderie les Vacances des Petits, 2-7 yrs, 234FF per day, 1,050FF for 6 days, both with lunch and tea. ESF 1550 Jardin de Neige, 3-6 yrs, 160FF per day, 850FF for 6 days
Ski kindergarten ESF 1850 Village des Enfants, 4-12 yrs, 1,050FF for 6 days including lunch, prices as non-ski. ESF 1650, 3-5 yrs, prices as 1650 ski school. ESF 1550, 3-6 yrs, prices as non-ski
Babysitting list including registered maternity nurses available from tourist office

OTHER SPORTS
Parapente, tobogganing, flying club, skating, luge-ing, ice-climbing, squash, swimming, snow-shoeing, snow-mobiling, fitness centres, hang-gliding

WHAT'S NEW
● Beginners' drag-lift at Le Praz 1300
● Espace Olympic Savoie: Trois Vallées pass (6 days and over) entitles skiers to one day in each of the Olympic resorts

FOOD AND DRINK PRICES
Coffee 15FF, bottle of house wine 70FF, beer 30FF, dish of the day 60-80FF

TOUR OPERATORS
Activity Travel, Bladon Lines, Brittany Ferries, Crystal, Enterprise, Flexiski, French Impressions, Hoverspeed, Inghams, Le Ski, Powder Byrne, Neilson, Sally Holidays, Silver Ski, Simply Ski, Ski Airtours, Ski Equipe, Ski Choice, Ski Esprit, Ski Olympic, Ski Savoie, Ski Scott Dunn, Ski Unique, Ski Val, Ski Weekend, Ski West, Skiworld, Lotus Supertravel, Touralp

Skiing facts: Méribel

TOURIST OFFICE
BP1, 73551 Méribel, Savoie
Tel 33 79 08 60 01
Fax 33 79 00 59 61

THE RESORT
By road Calais 920km
By rail TGV Moutiers 17km, regular
bus service 53FF
By air Geneva or Lyon 2½ hrs
Visitor beds 28,000 (91% apartments
and chalets, 9% hotels)
Transport bus service not included in
standard lift pass

THE SKIING
Longest run Campagnol (Mont Vallon),
3.6km (red)
Number of lifts 47 in Méribel, 190 in
Trois Vallées
Number of trails/pistes 67 in Méribel,
(19% beginner, 33% easy, 33%
intermediate, 15% difficult), 600km in
Trois Vallées
Total of trails/pistes 120km in
Méribel, 600km in Trois Vallées
Nursery slopes at Rond Point des
Pistes and Mottaret
Summer skiing at Val Thorens
Snowmaking 110 hectares

LIFT PASSES
Area pass Méribel Valley, 800FF for 6
days, 960FF for whole of Trois Vallées
Day pass Méribel 140-164FF,
Trois Vallées 195FF
Half-day pass 98-114FF (Méribel only)
Beginners no free lifts
Children Méribel, 5-16 yrs 565FF for
6 days, Trois Vallées 720FF. Free for
under 5 yrs
Pensioners over 60 yrs as children
Credit cards accepted yes

SKI SCHOOLS
Adults ESF, 152-180FF per day, 608-
800FF for 6 days. Ski Cocktail, 895FF
for 6 days
Children ESF, 3 yrs and over, 130-
150FF per day, 525-630FF for 6 days.
Ski Cocktail, 895FF for 6 days
Private lessons 180FF per hr
Special courses snowboarding, slalom

clinics, mogul clinics with ESF
Guiding companies Bureau des Guides
de la Compagnie de la Vanoise

CROSS-COUNTRY
Ski school ESF in Méribel and in
Mottaret
Loipe location and size 8km in the
Tueda Nature Reserve, 17km in the
forest around the altiport, and 8km trail
linking Méribel to Courchevel above
La Tania

CHILDCARE
Non-ski kindergarten ESF Jardin de
Neige, 2-8 yrs
Ski kindergarten ESF Jardin de Neige,
4-12 yrs
Babysitting list available from tourist
office

OTHER SPORTS
Skating at Olympic ice rink, snow-
shoeing, parapente, hang- gliding,
tobogganing, telemarking

WHAT'S NEW
● Espace Olympic Savoie: Trois Vallées
pass (6 days and over) entitles skiers
to one day in each of the Olympic
resorts

FOOD AND DRINK PRICES
Coffee 8-15FF, bottle of house wine
60-80FF, beer 20-30FF, dish of the day
60-80FF

TOUR OPERATORS
AA Ski Driveaway, Activity Travel,
Bladon Lines, Brittany Ferries,
Crystal, Direct Ski, Enterprise,
French Impressions, Hoverspeed,
Inghams, Lotus Supertravel,
Made to Measure, Mark Warner,
Meriski, Neilson, Sally Holidays,
Silver Ski, Ski Beach Villas, SkiBound,
Ski Choice, Ski Jeannie, Ski John
Wyatt, Ski Olympic, Ski Peak,
Ski Savoie, Snowtime, Ski West,
Skiworld, The Ski Company,
Super Solitions, Ski Thomson,
Touralp, Ultimate Holidays,
White Roc

Skiing facts: Val Thorens

TOURIST OFFICE
73440 Val Thorens, Savoie
Tel 33 79 00 08 08
Fax 33 79 00 00 04

THE RESORT
By road Calais 928km
By rail Moutiers 34km from Geneva.
Regular buses 70FF
By air Geneva or Lyon 1½ hrs.
Direct buses to resort
Visitor beds 19,900 (93% apartments
and chalets, 7% hotels)
Transport free resort buses from 8am-
7.30pm

THE SKIING
Longest run Piste de Caron, 4.5km
(red)
Number of lifts 37 in Val Thorens, 190
in Trois Vallées
Number of trails/pistes 55 in Val
Thorens (18% beginner, 29% easy, 40%
intermediate, 13% difficult) 276 in
Trois Valées
Total of trails/pistes 120km in Val
Thorens, 600km in Trois Vallées
Summer skiing on Péclet Glacier
Snowmaking 15 hectares covered

LIFT PASSES
Area pass Val Thorens, 675-715FF for
6 days, Belleville Valley, 870FF for 6
days, Trois Vallées, 960FF for 6 days
Day pass Val Thorens 150-154FF,
Belleville Valley 180FF, Trois Vallées
195FF
Half-day pass 105FF after 12.30 (Val
Thorens only)
Beginners 2 free lifts
Children 5-16 yrs, 105FF per day, 470FF
for 6 days. Free for under 5 yrs
Pensioners reductions for 60 yrs and
over, 50% reduction for 75 yrs and over
Credit cards accepted yes

SKI SCHOOLS
Adults ESF, 610FF for 6 half-days,
Ecole de Ski International (ESI), 580FF
per day
Children ESF, 3-12 yrs, 460FF for 6
half-days, ESI 550FF per day
Private lessons 180FF per hr

Special courses Ski Safari Pepi Prager,
12 Valleys Tour, telemark, race
training, ski évolutif, moguls, snowboarding, monoskiing
Guiding companies The Mountain
Guides Association

CROSS-COUNTRY
Ski school ESF cross-country school
Loipe location and size Le Zenith, 3km

CHILDCARE
Non-ski kindergarten ESF Babyclub,
3 mths-3 yrs, 1,000FF for 6 days
including lunch
Ski kindergarten ESF Miniclub, 3-12
yrs, 460FF per day, 1,180FF for 6 days
including lunch. Marielle Goitschel
Village, 260FF per day, 1,450FF for 6
days, both including lunch
Babysitting list available from tourist
office

OTHER SPORTS
Microlighting, car racing on snow and
ice, sports centre with fitness rooms,
swimming, gym, indoor tennis, squash,
golf simulator, volleyball, climbing wall,
aqua gym, hockey

WHAT'S NEW
● Savoie-style church ● Espace
Olympic Savoie: Trois Vallées pass (6
days and over) entitles skiers to one
day in each of the other Olympic resorts
● four-star Hotel Résidence Montana,
Résidence Les Niverolles, chalets Les
Montagnettes

FOOD AND DRINK PRICES
Coffee 7.50FF, bottle of house wine
15-50FF, beer 10-20FF, dish of the
day 70FF

TOUR OPERATORS
AA Ski Driveaway, UCPA, Bladon Lines,
Brittany Ferries, Crystal, Direct Ski,
Equity Total Ski, Enterprise, Falcon,
Hoverspeed, Inghams, Made to
Measure, Neilson, Sally Holidays, Ski
Airtours, SkiBound, Ski Choice, Ski
Thomson, Ski Unique, Skiworld, Touralp

Skiing facts: Les Menuires

TOURIST OFFICE
BP22, 73440 Les Menuires
Tel 33 79 00 73 00
Fax 33 79 00 75 06

THE RESORT
By road Calais 960km
By rail TGV Moutiers 25km, frequent buses
By air Geneva or Lyon 2½ hrs
Visitor beds 22,000 (83% apartments, 9% holiday centres, 8% hotels). 1,000 in St-Martin de Belleville
Transport free ski-bus around resort. Basket lifts link parts of the resort during ski hrs only

THE SKIING
Longest run La Masse, 3km (red)
Number of lifts 52 in Les Menuires, 190 in Trois Vallées
Number of trails/pistes 61 in Les Menuires (9% beginner, 21% easy, 52% intermediate, 18% difficult), 276 in Trois Vallées
Total of trails/pistes 120km in Les Menuires and St-Martin, 600km in Trois Vallées
Nursery slopes in Village des Schtroumpfs, in resort centre, and at Les Bruyères. Total 500m
Summer skiing 5 runs on Péclet Glacier from end of June
Snowmaking 60 hectares covered

LIFT PASSES
Area pass Les Menuires 670FF-790FF, Belleville Valley 870FF, Trois Vallées 960FF, all for 6 days
Day pass Les Menuires 135FF-160FF, Belleville Valley FF180, Trois Vallées 195FF
Half-day pass 107FF-112FF (Les Menuires only)
Beginners no free lifts. Points card 67FF
Children Les Menuires, 5-16 yrs, 570FF, Belleville Valley 710FF, Trois Vallées 720FF, all for 6 days. Free for 5 yrs and under
Pensioners 60 yrs and over as children
Credit cards accepted yes

SKI SCHOOLS
Adults ESF, 830FF for 6 days
Children ESF, 695FF for 6 days, from 4 yrs
Private lessons 155FF per hr for 1-2 people
Special courses snowboarding, monoskiing
Guiding companies guides available through ESF

CROSS-COUNTRY
Ski schools ESF cross-country ski school
Loipe location and size 28km along bottom of valley

CHILDCARE
Non-ski kindergarten ESF Village des Schtroumpfs nursery, 3-30 mths, 720FF for 6 days, 70FF extra per day for lunch and care. Village des Schtroumpfs Stage Ourson, 2-4 yrs, 1,200FF for 6 days including lessons, lifts, lunch, tea, and shuttle bus from accommodation
Ski kindergarten ESF Village des Schtroumpfs, 3-6 yrs, 1,495-1,680FF for 6 days including lessons, lifts, lunch, tea, and shuttle bus from accommodation
Babysitting list available from tourist office

OTHER SPORTS
Parapente, skating, swimming, snow-mobiling, hang-gliding, snow-shoeing, tobogganing, fitness centres

WHAT'S NEW
● Le Panoramic mountain restaurant at the top of La Masse ● Espace Olympic Savoie: Trois Vallées pass (6 days and over) entitles skiers to one day in each of the Olympic resorts

FOOD AND DRINK PRICES
Coffee 6-10FF, bottle of house wine 60FF, beer 12-20FF, dish of the day 50-60FF

TOUR OPERATORS
AA Ski Driveaway, Club Med, Crystal, Direct Ski, Enterprise, Falcon, Hoverspeed, Inghams, Made to Measure, Neilson, Ski Bound, Ski Thomson, Ski Tal (St-Martin), Touralp

Val d'Isère-Tignes, Savoie

....

Val d'Isère
ALTITUDE 1850m (6,068ft)

Good points large ski area, variety of intermediate and expert skiing, plenty of off-piste skiing, early and late season skiing, reliable snow record, extensive lift system, lively après-ski, tough runs
Bad points strung-out village, limited skiing for beginners, restricted choice of mountain restaurants, limited for non-skiers, lack of skiing convenience
Linked or nearby resorts Tignes (l), Sainte-Foy (n)

Tignes
ALTITUDE 2100m (6,888ft)

Good points large ski area, variety of intermediate skiing, plenty of off-piste skiing, year-round skiing, reliable snow record, skiing convenience, tough runs
Bad points resort architecture, lack of ambience, limited for non-skiers, lack of tree-level runs, limited après-ski
Linked or nearby resorts Val d'Isère (l), Sainte-Foy (n)

Val d'Isère and Tignes share a joint ski area which, in terms of size and vertical drop, coupled with the variety of the terrain, makes it one of the best in the world. It is the most popular resort in France for the French and the most popular resort in Europe for British skiers. If skiing is to have a future a hundred years from now, it is probably best represented by these 20,000 acres of linked skiing with 128 prepared pistes served by 102 lifts. Pressure from ecologists has already driven the main means of uphill transport underground in both resorts and the general standard of maintenance and safety is extraordinarily high. The area, justly chosen to host the men's downhill, the Blue Riband event of the 1992 Winter Olympic Games, is marketed as l'Espace Killy after its most famous son. In actual fact, Jean-Claude, who swept the board of Olympic Gold in 1968, is a local by adoption as he comes from Alsace.

The marketing marriage of Tignes and Val d'Isère has been an uncomfortable one, but the two have learned to live and work together with great international success. The skiing in Chamonix is tougher, the après-ski in Aspen and Zermatt is better, Jackson Hole has more character, but l'Espace Killy captures the imagination of today's younger generation, albeit as many on snowboards as on skis.

If the skiing in either has a drawback it is that the authorities have a frank disregard for the needs of timid skiers. There seems little point in adopting the system of four grades of piste colouring – green (beginner), blue (easy), red (intermediate), and black (difficult) – when some of those listed as green are steep enough to become mogul fields. The reason is that the classification system in ski resorts is usually based on the average gradient of the run. If your level of proficiency suggests that you will be happiest on a green run, you don't want to encounter a single frozen bump, let alone a whole pasture of them at La Daille.

Piste-grooming, once casual, is becoming much better in these post-Olympic years. During November and December 1992 when five metres of snow fell (combined total of the previous five seasons) the army of pisteurs and machines managed to keep the clearance of it under control.

Both Val d'Isère and Tignes are skiers' resorts. You don't have to be an expert, but it certainly helps. You do, however, have to be keen. If your idea of a skiing holiday is to eat, drink and dance, with just the occasional potter down the slopes between meals, then these are not the resorts for you. According to some dubious French statistics, the average skier in Courchevel skis for one hour a day, his or her counterpart in Val d'Isère and Tignes for over five hours.

On paper there is more to find fault with in Val d'Isère than Tignes. It is very spread out, the lifts are not central and, with the exception of La Daille, the runs down to the valley are difficult. But it does have the feel of a village, greatly enhanced by the addition of Val d'Isère Village, a stone- and wood-built heart to the resort completed in time for the Olympics. It is also becoming increasingly lively in the evenings with a wide choice of bars and late-night spots.

The Olympics were a bitter commercial disappointment to the inhabitants of the Haute Tarentaise, the Avalins and the Tignards in particular. The crowds stayed away to watch it all on television, if they watched at all. However, controversial improvements to the road up the valley have left a lasting legacy to be enjoyed by skiers. The journey time from Lyon and Geneva has been cut from four hours to way under three in good traffic conditions.

Buses between the two resorts are neither frequent nor cheap and taxis can be extortionate. A reporter notes that the bus system within Tignes is efficient. If you have driven out and want a change of scenery, day-trips to Les Arcs, La Plagne, La Rosière and Sainte-Foy are possible.

The ski area is a joint one, but it is here that the similarity ends. Each resort has its individual and completely separate character. Both resorts, which share this almost inexhaustible high-altitude ski area, have the strongest of partisan following from the scores of reporters who are united in their approval of the skiing and of their desire to return as soon as possible to sample some more of it. Indeed there is much to approve of, including mile after mile of motorway piste, challenging runs of varied gradient and terrain, steep mogul fields, year-round glacier skiing, and quite outstanding and easily accessible off-piste skiing in every sector. Queues are rarely a problem except during and after a heavy snowfall when much of the mountain is liable to be

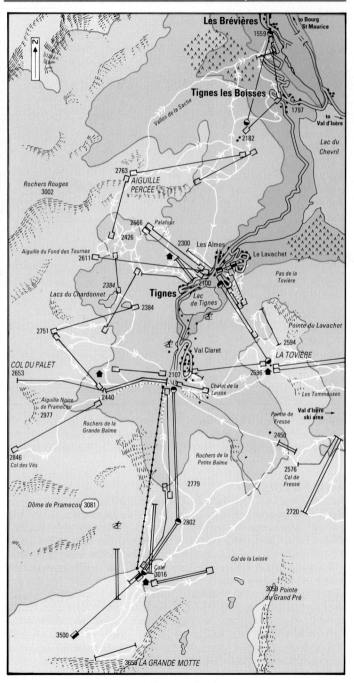

Les Brévières

to Bourg
St Maurice

1559

Tignes les Boisses

1797

to
Val d'Isère

*Lac du
Chevril*

Vallon de la Sache

2182

2763

*AIGUILLE
PERCÉE*

*Rochers Rouges
3002*

2566 *Palafour*

2426

2300   *Les Almes*

Le Lavachet

Aiguille du Fond des Tournes

2611

*Pas de la
Tovière*

2100

2384

Tignes

*Lac
de Tignes*

Lacs du Chardonnet

2384

Pointe du Lavachet

2751

2594

Val Claret

LA TOVIÈRE

COL DU PALET
2653

2107

2696

*Chalet de la
Leisse*

Les Tommeuses

2440

**Val d'Isère
ski area** →

*Aiguille Noire
de Pramecou
2977*

*Pointe de
Fresse*

2450

*Rochers de la
Grande Balme*

*Rochers de la
Petite Balme*

2576
*Col de
Fresse*

2846
Col des Vés

2779

Dôme de Pramecou 3081

2720

2802

Col de la Leisse

*Cote
3016*

3059 *Pointe
du Grand Pré*

3500

3656 *LA GRANDE MOTTE*

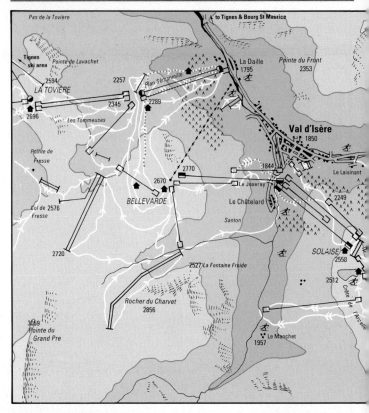

closed off because of the avalanche risk. The Funival funicular in Val d'Isère gives good mountain access in all weather. In the past Tignes has offered little skiing when wind or snow closes in, but the addition of the Grande Motte funicular alleviates this.

The skiing
Top 3439m (11,279ft) bottom 1550m (5,084ft)

Mountain access points abound and a little experience means that you can avoid even the smallest of queues during the morning rush hour. L'Espace Killy divides naturally into six separate sectors. On the Val d'Isère side there are Col de l'Iseran/Pisaillas, Solaise and Bellevarde, which are strung in a row along the curving road to Le Fornet and served by efficient ski-buses mysteriously known as *trains rouges*. The first two sectors are linked by lift at altitude, Solaise and Bellevarde only at valley level just beside the main resort. Bellevarde links with Tignes via the Tovière ridge. The skiing at Tignes divides itself into three areas: Tovière, Grande Motte (going up to the glacier) and Palet/Aiguille Percée. In the depth of winter there is more skiing down to the lower-lying hamlets of Les Boisses at 1850m and Les Brevières at 1550m.

The Solaise cable car was Val d'Isère's first lift, installed in 1943. Two

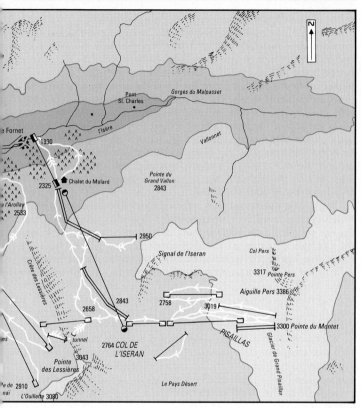

chair-lifts run parallel to it, giving (often quicker) access to the Tête de Solaise. Under these lifts are some steep, challenging, but often stony, runs down through the trees. Above the tree-line, underneath the top half of the cable car and served by its own Le Plan chair, is the wide mogul field which is Val d'Isère's most famous run – the Solaise Bumps. It is neither particularly long nor steep, save for a few pitches of around 30°, but it is a legend. Certainly when there are weeks between snow-falls, the moguls reach daunting dimensions. Descending to the left of the cable car and avoiding most of the moguls, Piste S is one of the most difficult runs in the area. It is longer, steeper, narrower, and almost as bumpy as Solaise.

Beyond the Tête de Solaise a new chair-lift has been built from the beginning of Piste L to the top of Madeleine. This lift, together with the three other existing chairs, provides access to a whole bowl of green and blue cruising runs. The off-piste skiing around the rims of the bowl is often dangerous and, as in the whole of L'Espace Killy, you must pay particular attention to avalanche warnings. The long Cugnai chair gives access to runs down a beautiful off-piste back bowl leading to the chair back up from Le Manchet. The lower part of the Manchet run was widened in time for the 1993 season thus allowing piste-grooming from top to bottom. It is an enormously welcome improvement.

From behind the Tête de Solaise there is some beautiful and usually uncrowded skiing which takes you down to Le Laisinant between Fornet and Val d'Isère, where you catch the bus back to a lift. The runs are marked blue and red, but the blue is tricky in comparison with those higher up, and is another inconsistency in the piste-marking, which can upset early intermediates. The off-piste here is excellent, but beware of cliffs and, in particular, avalanche danger after big dumps of fresh snow.

At the top of the bowl behind Solaise there is a short, steep drag with a run beside it, and a tunnel near the top (rarely open) through to Le Fornet ski area. The run down the other side to the gentle pistes around the Col d'Iseran is always awkward and often closed. Most skiers opt for the dramatic, but frequently chilly, chair ride over the top and down the far side.

The Col de l'Iseran skiing is accessed by a cable car from Le Fornet, which takes you up over steep, wooded slopes to where the ground flattens out for a substantial amount of easy motorway cruising. From the Col, lifts continue up to the Pissaillas Glacier, which offers open easy skiing in winter as well as in summer. Advanced skiers come to this area for the off-piste down from the glacier and through the trees lower down. The Col Pers run from the glacier is long and beautiful, but not very demanding provided you know where you are going. There are two routes down, the more easterly of which ends up at the Refuge de Prariond, a popular ski-touring hut.

After a drink or a simple meal there is a schuss back to Le Fornet with one steeper section through the scenic Gorge du Malpasset. It is important to take note of the ski patrol information at the top of the Cascade chair as to the skiability of the gorge, as it does not always fill up with snow. The off-piste runs behind the Signal drag into the Grand Vallon are wider and steeper, ending in the woods above Le Fornet. From the glacier, blue motorways descend to the top of the Fornet cable car. There is a choice of runs to the valley: the blue involves many traverses and one or two awkward pitches, while the black is narrow, testing, and prone to icy moguls.

On the western side of Val d'Isère, the Rocher de Bellevarde rises steeply and impressively. A long cable car, starting from the same station as the Solaise lift on the edge of town, takes you up 900 vertical metres. The run down underneath is both steep and demanding and it was here on the Face de Bellevarde that veteran Swiss champion Bernhard Russi created the men's downhill course for the Albertville Olympics.

In a brilliantly calculated sop to the environmentalists, he moved the course to preserve the habitat of a rare alpine flower. No one liked the course, not even the winner, and it will probably never be raced again. But the legacy is a piste groomed from top to bottom with a thrilling variety of pitch and terrain, which is regarded by many as the best here.

There are easier ways back to the village. The narrow gunbarrel on the blue Santons run has been widened to allow access by grooming machines, and the piste can now justify its easier colouring. Near the Santons the black Epaule run is usually uncrowded. The long twin drag around the back of the Rocher du Charvet gives access to an off-piste run

called the Tour du Charvet. It is beautiful and not too difficult, but dangerously prone to avalanches after the first section. It offers a series of narrow
couloirs bounded by steep cliffs. Stay to your right as much as you can.

From La Daille the other gentler side of Bellevarde is served by a
variety of lifts, the most important of which is the high-speed underground funicular, which whisks you up to the top in an astonishing
four-and-a-half minutes. It is worth noting that because of the speed,
you can squeeze in more skiing in a morning or an afternoon here than
you can elsewhere in the resort in a whole day. The more leisurely
route is either by gondola or the parallel triple chair. The runs between
the funicular and gondola stations above La Daille are spread around a
wide area and are all very easy with the exception of the OK downhill
course and Orange, a more interesting and less-crowded challenge,
which hugs the Bellevarde rock and is steeper in places.

The area below the gondola station consists mostly of runs both on-
and off-piste through the trees. These are one of the main attractions of
the area, along with a splendid view northwards to Mont Blanc. The main
runs down to La Daille are prone to overcrowding and, despite heavy
banks of snow-cannon, can get very icy and scraped. An interesting off-
piste itinerary is the so-called Piste Perdue, which has been renamed the
Combe Perdue, which roughly follows the tangled course of the river bed.

The main connection with Tignes is a pair of triple chairs. The most
important lift out of Tignes for Tovière is a modern stand-up gondola,
the Aero-Ski from Tignes-Le-Lac. The run straight back down is black
with a steep mogul field at the bottom – and there is an alternative,
even steeper, variant on the top section (the Mur de Paquerettes). The
blue option follows a path for much of the way and can be horribly
overcrowded at the end of the day. Other less severe runs lead down to
Val Claret. Piste H has been widened and is now always well groomed.
These runs join up from the one down from the Col de Fresse and
merge, to the discomfort of beginners, with the Val Claret nursery lifts.
To the south of the Col de Fresse run, a narrow off-piste gully provides
an excellent traffic-free alternative.

The new funicular to Grande Motte should have been completed in
time for the Olympics, but serious engineering problems meant that it
only came into operation in spring 1993. With a capacity of 3,000 people an hour, it takes each load of 670 skiers right through the mountain
from Val Claret at 2100m up to the Panoramic restaurant at 3030m in
just six minutes. A further 70 snow-cannon have been installed on the
Combe de la Grande Motte at a cost of 7mFF to guarantee 1400m of
vertical from as early as the beginning of November. Two new chairs are
designed to cope with the expected increase in skiers here. The notori-
ously unreliable old gondolas and the long two-stage chair running parallel to them are to be dismantled.

On the far side of the glacier, beside the summer ski drag, a marvellous off-piste descent takes you down to the bottom of the double Leisse
chairs. This should only be attempted with a guide because of the huge
ice-falls on the edge of the glacier. The Leisse chairs serve a broad piste
down to the east of the main glacier lift stations, graded blue. It is blue in
character for the most part, but ends in a fierce little mogul field.

From the main glacier lift stations a pleasant wide slope, often mogulled at the bottom, descends down the north face of the mountain beside twin drags and a chair back up. You can continue to Val Claret down a long and not too difficult red, which is often extremely crowded. Next to it is the Wall: one for good skiers to notch up. It is a short, but very steep drop over the end of the glacier. More straightforward ways down are the blue runs down the north-west side of the Motte, which connect with the Col de Fresse lifts taking you back up to Val d'Isère. A particularly fine off-piste run crosses the glacier high up below the Dôme de Pramecou. A 10-minute hike brings you to a col behind the Rocher de Grande Balme from where it is possible to join up with the skiing below Col du Palet.

The Col du Palet/l'Aiguille Percée area above Val Claret and Tignes-Le-Lac is probably the least exciting skiing in Tignes and in the whole Espace Killy, but there is a lot of it and it is a good area for timid intermediates to build their confidence. It is sunny and usually uncrowded, with lots of runs which do not differ greatly. Most are classified as blue with a few easy reds. A quad chair takes you up to the Aiguille du Chardonnet. A superb, very long and beautiful piste takes you down from Aiguille Percée to Tignes-Les-Brevières. Several off-piste alternatives, starting with steep drops off the ridge running west of the Aiguille Percée, follow similar routes to the valley. There is also a blue via Tignes-Les-Boisses which can, however, be very icy and not at all blue at the bottom. The Col du Palet is the starting point for a long run down to Champagny and Plan Peisey. It is not difficult, but is prone to avalanches. A good plan is to stay the night in the Refuge de Palet and set off at first light.

Mountain restaurants

Mountain restaurants and bars are to be found in Val d'Isère rather than Tignes. Indeed new establishments open in increasing numbers each season, but, except for those closest to the slopes, they are poorly frequented during skiing hours. For a ski area the size of Espace Killy, good mountain eating places are sparse. The serious luncher will generally stick to the Val side and more often than not find himself returning to the village itself. We have consistently good reports of the Folie Douce at the top of the first section of the Daille gondola, and La Crech'Ouna at the Funival is a long established family-run affair, which you are only allowed into provided all snow has been removed from your boots. Inside, however, the food, is exceptional and reasonably priced. It is also open in the evening. Beside it, Les Tufs serves similar fare, but with less ambience.

Upstairs at Le Signal, at the top of the Fornet cable car, is pricey but good. Those at the top of Tovière and on the Grande Motte are always crowded, but above average, and the views are spectacular. Les Marmottes in the gentle bowl between Bellevarde and the Col de Fresse, and the one below Col du Palet, are not reliably marked on the piste map, but are worth the journey. One reporter speaks glowingly of l'Arbina in Tignes-Le-Lac as well as the Relais du Lac in Les Brevières and La Cordée at Les Boisses.

Beginners and children

L'Espace Killy has a wide range of ski schools from which to choose. The number is not surprising considering that it was here in the mid-1970s that Patrick and Jean Zimmer, two ex-racers from Alsace, decided to set up their own ski school as an alternative to the traditional ESF. The official school objected, the Zimmers fought their monopoly claim all the way to the French High Court, and won. Today there is a whole gaggle of alternative ski schools in l'Espace Killy, including the Zimmers' Top Ski, Snow Fun, Alpine Experience, Evolution 2 and Mountain Masters.

The competition, though still rife, is now on a sensible scale and has a co-ordinated price structure. This follows a historic meeting on 30 November 1992, when all these rivals managed to sit around a table and agree to work together against the unlicensed cowboy instructors which all major resorts attract. Snow Fun and Top Ski are consistently singled out for praise by reporters. The former is the largest of the alternatives with the emphasis on living up to its title. Top Ski, still run by the charismatic Zimmer brothers, is geared directly to English-speakers and has a cult following among advanced skiers, as well as the reputation for being one of the best off-piste guiding companies in the Alps. Evolution 2 has been described as 'too Gallic in attitude'. Mountain Masters caters mainly for Scandinavian clients. Two reporters said they were not happy about being taken off-piste by their guide on a dangerously warm after-noon. Alpine Experience is a new operation set up by breakaway instructors from Top Ski.

Val d'Isère is not the place to take pre-ski or beginner children. The layout of the village, steep nursery slopes and general lack of facilities simply preclude it. There are many more suitable resort choices, as this guide shows. If you have to take young children, Mark Warner's hotel Cygnaski runs its own crèche for children between six months and six years old; childminders will take children to and from the ski schools. The Isabelle non-skiing garderie, at the foot of the Funival, takes children from two years old. The Petit Poucet kindergarten accepts children aged three to eight years. Snow Fun will take kids out for ski lessons and return them. The ESF runs classes for 4-year-olds upwards. Top Ski takes children from three years old.

Tignes collects a number of unfavourable reports of Les Marmottons kindergarten in Le Lac. The 4- to 6-year-olds who went there were well taught and learnt to ski in a week, but the children were kept out skiing all morning whatever the weather without a rest, refreshments or any form of play-time. The general staff attitude, which we have found in several French resorts, was cool and inflexible. The nursery slopes in Tignes are reliable for snow, but can be crowded, especially at Val Claret. Reporters found the nursery slope at Le Lac to be good.

The resorts

Val d'Isère has grown into a sprawling hotch-potch of a ski town, stretching from the modern apartment buildings of La Daille at one end of the valley to the village of Le Fornet at the other, and the main conurbation of Val d'Isère in the middle. Val d'Isère has in fact developed from an old village, not that the Dukes of Savoie who traditionally owned hunting lodges here would recognise anything but the six-teenth-century stone church. The resort bubbles with excitement by day and by night.

For the past 10 years it has been slowly asphyxiating itself in its own noxious exhaust fumes as more and more car drivers flooded the resort. The snow banked on either side of the road turned grey within minutes of falling and skiers risked their lives every time they crossed the road. The introduction for 1992-3 of the Parc des Lèches covered underground car-park and the gentle phasing out of all cars in the town caused pandemonium among the locals and outrage among visitors, aimed not at the plan itself, but at the cost of parking.

A new roundabout at La Daille and the installation of a parking and information centre were designed to solve the traffic problem. Visitors are granted a two-hour pass in which to unload their vehicles and park them in a designated zone. The initial tariff is 60FF a day, 400FF a week, and 3,200FF a season. Those who choose to ignore the regulations will face a 750FF towing-away fee.

Val d'Isère is set in a remote steep-sided valley, beyond the reservoir which drowned the old village of Tignes 40 years ago. The road emerges from a series of tunnels into the valley at La Daille, a cluster of modern apartment buildings by the Funival lift station. Val d'Isère proper starts half-a-mile up the road, a straggle of petrol stations, ugly concrete apartment blocks and the occasional more pleasing chalet. The road eventually becomes a wide street lined with shops, bars and hotels on either side. Val Village, the new development of shops and hotels opposite the tourist office, has given the whole place a much-needed focal point. The resort is long and strung out, but is by no means huge and nowhere is more than a five-minute walk from the main road bus route. There are a couple of quite large supermarkets in the middle of town and shopping is good for gourmet self-caterers, although queues build up after skiing. The Monday street market here is ever popular.

Tignes is purpose-built and consists of a series of unattractive apart-ment buildings which, despite the recladding of the older ones and the use of more sympathetic materials in the more recent additions, remains unaesthetic. The old village of Tignes disappeared beneath the waters of the Lac de Chevril when the valley was dammed in 1952. In times of drought the church spire occasionally breaks water.

It is a large, mostly self-catering resort split into three parts and though it has a range of year-round sports facilities the village is fairly quiet after dark. Most of the resort is ideal for convenience skiing.

Accommodation

In **Val d'Isère** much of the accommodation is in chalets and self-catering apartments, but there is also a choice of 39 hotels, 30 of them in the two- and three-star categories. At the top of the range, the Latitudes makes a brave attempt but fails to meet, particularly in room size, the standards you might expect of an international four-star hotel. The Sofitel is lacking in soul. The Christiania, noted for its friendly staff, has been redecorated. We received favourable reports of the three-star Blizzard ('new pool, good-size rooms, excellent service, but expensive'). The Tsanteleina has good demi-pension food and has been redecorated. The Bellier, which has been criticised in the past as not worth its three stars, has undergone a facelift.

The Elephant Blanc, run by the Ski Company, and Mountain Lodges, run by Super Solutions, are unquestionably the best chalets in town. These are exquisite holiday homes with first-class cuisine and every whim fully catered for. On a slightly more down-to-earth level of comfort, YSE is the biggest chalet tour operator offering 16 chalets to suit all budgets.

Nearly all the accommodation in **Tignes** is in apartments. Despite attempts to smarten up the old buildings with a bit of recladding, the ghastly aspect of the resort continues to shock visitors. The apartments themselves are generally cramped, although some of the newer more sympathetic buildings are more generously designed. 'Ugly, small apartments giving purpose-built resorts a bad name', remarked one reporter who also commented: 'but you come here to ski, and that's why I keep coming back'.

The hotels Ski d'Or and Curling both manage to inject some luxury into the resort. At the lower end of the scale, the Melèzes at Les Boisses has 18 simple rooms and food at realistic prices.

Eating out

Val d'Isère has 52 restaurants catering for every taste. None of them is cheap. The Perdrix Blanche is renowned for its fresh seafood. The Grande Ourse has a consistently high standard of cuisine. Bar Jacques stays open late, and Crech'Ouna is as welcoming by night as by day. Le Bistro Marseillais is a tiny, but noteworthy newcomer with just a dozen covers tucked away at the back of the Galerie des Cîmes, close to Top Ski. Chez Nano serves excellent fondue and pizza, and La Vieille Maison at La Daille has a warm atmosphere. La Florence and La Luge are noted for their sensibly priced set menus. The choice in **Tignes** is far more limited and largely confined to hotels including the Ski d'Or which is first choice for gourmets. There is also a reasonable choice of less expensive eating places.

Après-ski

Après-ski is more lively in Val d'Isère than in almost any other French resort. Of Tignes, one reporter commented: 'Go to Val, or go to bed.' Dick's Tea-Bar remains the hot-spot in Val. Entry is free after skiing and it is the main Anglo-Saxon meeting place. After dinner it takes on night-club status with a laser disco, and despite a 70FF entrance fee, it is always crowded. Play Bach is its serious rival and is much favoured by resort workers.

Club 21 is expensive and Le Pavillon offers good service and has opened a new champagne bar decorated with English sporting prints. The Taverne d'Alsace is a lively nightspot. Bananas, a small wooden shack with a cellar bar, is busy after skiing.

Skiing facts: Val d'Isère

TOURIST OFFICE
BP 228, F-73155 Val d'Isère, Savoie
Tel 33 79 06 06 60
Fax 33 79 06 04 56

THE RESORT
By road Calais 960km
By rail Bourg-St-Maurice 32km
By air Geneva 3 hrs, Lyon 3 hrs
Visitor beds 25,998 (87% apartments, 10% hotels, 3% chalets)
Transport free bus between La Daille and Le Fornet

THE SKIING
Longest run Verte, 4824m (green)
Number of lifts 51 in Val d'Isère, 102 in l'Espace Killy
Number of trails/pistes 67 in Val d'Isère (33% very easy, 42% easy, 16% intermediate, 9% difficult), 128 in l'Espace Killy
Total of trails/pistes 300km
Nursery slopes 7 lifts
Summer skiing Pissaillas Glacier, 10 lifts
Snowmaking 25 hectares covered

LIFT PASSES
Area pass L'Espace Killy, 870FF for 6 days
Day pass L'Espace Killy, 190FF
Half-day pass L'Espace Killy, 130FF
Beginners 7 free lifts
Children 12 yrs and under, 30% reduction, free for 5 yrs and under
Pensioners 60 yrs and over, as children
Credit cards accepted yes

SKI SCHOOLS
Adults ESF, 950FF for 6 days, Snow Fun, 820FF for 6 days. Top Ski, Evolution 2, Mountain Masters, Alpine Experience, prices on application
Children ESF, 690FF for 6 days, Snow Fun, 650FF for 6 days
Private lessons ESF, 175FF per hr, Snow Fun, 160FF per hr
Special courses snowboarding, ski-touring, telemark, off-piste, slalom, inter-resort safaris, heli-skiing
Guiding companies Top Ski, Evolution 2

CROSS-COUNTRY
Ski schools ESF
Loipe location and size 15km from the centre to La Daille

CHILDCARE
Non-ski kindergarten Isabelle, 2 yrs and over, 8.30am-5.30pm, 210FF per day, including lunch, 1,100FF for 6 days. Snowfun Club Nannours, 3-6 yrs, 80FF for 1½ hrs
Ski kindergarten ESF, 4-6 yrs, 80FF for 2 hrs. Mini Champions, 4 yrs and over, 1,320FF for 6 days including lunch. Petit Poucet, 3-8 yrs, 220FF per day including lunch
Babysitting list from tourist office

OTHER SPORTS
Parapente, snow-shoeing, ice-driving, dog-sledding, snow-mobiling, curling, swimming, fitness centres

WHAT'S NEW
● Car-free centre

FOOD AND DRINK PRICES
Coffee 15FF, bottle of house wine 50FF, beer 15FF, dish of the day 65FF

TOUR OPERATORS
AA Motoring Holidays, Activity Travel, Bladon Lines, Brittany Ferries, Club Med, Crystal, Enterprise, French Impressions, Fresh Tracks, Hoverspeed, Inghams, Ski John Wyatt, Le Ski, Lotus Supertravel, Made to Measure, Mark Warner, Neilson, Sally Holidays, Silver Ski, Ski Airtours, SkiBound, Ski Choice, The Ski Company, Ski Falcon, Ski Olympic, Ski Savoie, Ski Thomson, Ski Val, Ski West, Skiworld, Super Solutions, Touralp, UCPA, Ultimate Holidays, White Roc, YSE

Skiing facts: Tignes

TOURIST OFFICE
BP 51, 73321 Tignes, Savoie
Tel 33 79 06 15 55
Fax 33 79 06 45 44

THE RESORT
By road Calais 960km
By rail Bourg-St-Maurice 25km
By air Geneva, Lyon or Chambéry 3 hrs
Visitor beds 27,158 (96% apartments and chalets, 4% hotels)
Transport free ski-bus between Les Brevières and Val Claret

THE SKIING
Longest run Double M, 1400m (red)
Number of lifts 51 in Tignes, 102 in L'Espace Killy
Number of trails/pistes 61 in Tignes (2% beginner, 57% easy, 33% intermediate, 8% difficult), 128 in L'Espace Killy
Total of trails/pistes 300km
Nursery slopes 2 lifts and a 600m-long slope
Summer skiing Grande Motte Glacier
Snowmaking 17km covered

LIFT PASSES
Area pass L'Espace Killy, 870FF for 6 days
Day pass 190FF
Half-day pass 130FF
Beginners 2 lifts, Le Rosset and Le Claret
Children 5-12 yrs, 615FF for 6 days, free for 5 yrs and under
Pensioners 60 years and over, 160FF per day, 740FF for 6 days
Credit cards accepted yes

SKI SCHOOLS
Adults Ski School International at Val Claret, 900FF for 6 days, ESF at Le Lac, Val Claret and Le Lavachet, Evolution 2 at Le Lac, Val Claret and Le Lavachet
Children ESF at Le Lac, Val Claret and Le Lavachet, 4 yrs and over, 770FF for 5 days, Evolution 2 at Le Lac and Val Claret, Ski School International at Val Claret

Private lessons 155FF per hr, 1,300FF for 6 days
Special courses snowboarding, mono-skiing, telemark, mogul clinics
Guiding companies Evolution 2

CROSS-COUNTRY
Ski schools ESF at Le Lac and Val Claret
Loipe location and size 36km in L'Espace Killy, tracks at Le Lac, Val Claret and Les Brevières

CHILDCARE
Non-ski (and ski) kindergarten Les Marmottons at Le Lac, 2½ yrs and over, Les Petits Lutins at Le Lac, 3 mths-3 yrs, and from 3 yrs at Val Claret, all 1,350FF for 6 days including lunch
Ski kindergarten ESF at Le Lac, Val Claret and Le Lavachet, Evolution 2 at Le Lac and Val Claret, and Ski School International, all from 4 yrs and over, 770FF for 5 days
Babysitting list available from tourist office

OTHER SPORTS
Ice-diving, bowling, skating, squash, tennis, parapente, hang-gliding, climbing walls, husky sleigh rides, heli-skiing, fitness centres

WHAT'S NEW
● Underground funicular at Grande Motte

FOOD AND DRINK PRICES
Coffee 8FF, bottle of house wine 60FF, beer 15FF, dish of the day 55FF

TOUR OPERATORS
Activity Travel, Bladon Lines, Club Med, Crystal, Direct Ski, Enterprise, French Impressions, Hoverspeed, Inghams, Kings Ski Club, Made to Measure, Neilson, Sally Holidays, Ski Choice, Ski Equipe, Ski Olympic, Ski Thomson, Ski Tracer, Ski Val, Ski Weekend, Ski West, Skiworld, STS, Top Deck, Touralp, UCPA , Susie Ward Travel

Sainte-Foy 1550m (5,084ft)

This recent jewel in the Tarentaise crown is neither purpose-built nor part of a large ski area. Set just 15km from l'Espace Killy, the village is made up of a handful of old stone farmhouses clustered around the base of a chair-lift above the village of Sainte-Foy. The skiing, on nine pistes and six marked off-piste runs, served by three quad chairs, is suitable for intermediates to experts. Although there is a nursery drag-lift and a children's village, it is not ideal for beginners.

A road leads up from the village to a car park at the base of the ski area at 1550m. From there the nursery slope drag takes you to the main chair-lift, which rises above the wooded slopes dotted with chalets to a gentle plateau with a small restaurant. Runs back to the car park are mainly red, with the addition of a long green track, Plan Bois. Two further chairs take you up to the Col de l'Aiguille at 2620m. Although there are several black runs from the top chair you can actually ski almost anywhere on the wide mountainside before reaching the woods lower down. From the ridge there is a good off-piste descent on the south-facing side of the Col d'Aiguille. The run then follows the Clou river past a deserted village of the same name, ending at the hamlet of Le Monal, uninhabited during the winter months. From here an easy path brings you back to Sainte-Foy. The unpisted black, Crystal Dark, is particularly recommended by reporters.

The village of Sainte-Foy itself has a couple of simple hotels and rooms for rent, and there are several restaurants including La Becqua, just above the main chair-lift, offering a sunny terrace and panoramic views of mount Pourri on the other side of the valley.

TOURIST OFFICE
Tel 33 79 06 91 70

TOUR OPERATORS

Valloire, Savoie

ALTITUDE 1430m (4,690ft)

● ●

Good points attractive working village, well-groomed slopes,
varied nightlife, family skiing, varied off-piste, child facilities
Bad points relatively low altitude, limited mountain restaurants
Linked or nearby resorts Valmeinier (l), Les Karellis (n)

Set above the Maurienne Valley in an isolated bowl, Valloire is an attractive, reasonably large village that has kept its French spirit. This is still
very much a farming community and the smell of manure is apparent
during the morning walk to the lifts, mingling with the more usual smells
of cooking and baking. It is a reasonably priced and friendly place,
uncrowded except in peak season. The proximity to the Italian border
means that when the resort is crowded it can be very noisy as well.

The skiing
Top 2600m (8,528ft) bottom 1430m (4,690ft)
Valloire's 150km of pisted skiing takes place in two main areas, La Sétaz
and Le Crey du Quart, on two adjacent mountains reached by lifts starting a few minutes from the village centre and going up to 2500m. The
terrain is varied and some of the runs are as long as 1000m vertical. The
skiing is not difficult; even the blacks (difficult runs) would be red
(intermediate) by the standards of many resorts.

Mountain access to La Sétaz is by a six-man gondola from the village up to Thimel, followed by a chair and a drag-lift to the summit. The
main route down to the village is an enjoyable red run. Served by artificial snow-cannon and groomed to a high standard, the area provides a
choice of runs from the wide but sometimes icy red, to the gently
meandering blues (easy runs) towards Les Verneys or Valloire. An alternative is to catch the end of the green (beginner) path of Les Myosotis,
which takes you to the centre of the village. You can also fork right
below the Thimel four-man chair and follow Les Myosotis all the way
down as it gently curves through the trees. Unfortunately, in sunny
weather conditions Les Myosotis quickly becomes badly worn, rutted
and rocky. One reporter commented ruefully that he had taken new
skis down there and ended up wishing he had hired a pair.

Access to Le Crey du Quart ski area is either by the Montissot and
Colerieux chair-lifts via the green Les Myosotis, or directly from Valloire
on two long chair-lifts. The skiing there is mainly of the red motorway
variety with the gentler slopes going down towards Valloire. Le Crey du
Quart pistes give access to Valmeinier and its own small ski area of Gros
Crey which is reached by a lift across the narrow valley. Here there is a
choice of two undemanding black runs, Les Chamois and Les Grandes

Drozes, down to Valmeinier 1500. As might be expected at this altitude, the bottoms of the runs often suffer from poor snow cover. Higher slopes are to be found among the mixed bag of skiing from Gros Crey down to Valmeinier 1800. Lift queues in the area do not seem to be a great problem: the only real bottlenecks occur at the main lift from Valloire to Thimel and at the Thimel four-man chair-lift. Plans to link Valmeinier with Valfréjus, and with Bardonecchia across the Italian border, have yet to materialise but are more than a possibility.

Mountain restaurants

La Sétaz area is adequately covered by its two mountain restaurants, of which the most popular is the Thimel, an unspectacular but reasonably priced restaurant or self-service cafeteria at the top of La Sétaz gondola. Le Crey du Quart area has a restaurant on the ridge at Crey du Quart itself, and one on the run from Pré Rond down to Valloire. Restaurant Pré Rond and Château Ripaille are also recommended.

Beginners and children

There are two ski schools in the resort, Ski Ecole de Valloire and the Ecole de Ski Français. Reports on the ESF included comments on the poor timekeeping of the instructors: 'Our 9am lessons didn't start until 9.35am.' The standard of English is reported as lamentable: 'A lot of English-speakers come here and it's appalling that they don't have more English-speaking instructors. It was like skiing with a Speak Your Weight Machine.' The organisation was heavily criticised: 'Classes seemed to be battling with each other.'

Four nursery slopes cater for beginners and small children. The Garderie Les Aiglons takes non-skiing children, and there are three separate ski kindergartens.

The resort

The resort itself was summed up by one reporter as 'pretty and ideal for families, as children can wander around safely'. Valloire is a traditional French farming village where the highest roof is the church spire.

Accommodation

There are two main hotels in Valloire. The attractive and highly rated Christiania is a three-minute walk from the main Thimel lift and is situated in the heart of the main shopping area. The Grand Hotel Valloire et Galibier is closer to the nursery slopes and Le Crey du Quart lifts. The Club les Carrettes has a swimming-pool, as does the hotel and restaurant La Sétaz. The Plein Sud, run by SkiBound, is a budget hotel with an international staff and a lively bar. There are numerous apartments from which to choose. Several delicatessens offer gourmet fare and supermarkets include Codec, Huit à 8 and Pretty.

Eating out

Le Gastilleur restaurant at the Hotel la Sétaz receives favourable comment for its range of local dishes and good atmosphere. A small hut in front of l'Igloo bar is renowned for its pizzas.

Après-ski

There is no shortage of bars. Le Pub l'Atelier, by the skating rink, serves a fine pint of Guinness, and l'Igloo, the Piano Bar, and Le Centre are all popular meeting places. The Touring Bar and American Dodgers have live music, and Le Mammouth, in the Rapin Hotel, is open until 5am.

Valloire boasts a large outdoor floodlit skating rink, regularly used for ice hockey, with good changing facilities and bar. Ten-pin bowling also takes place in the same building, and parapente and snow-mobiling are available up the mountain. At the end of January, Valloire hosts its International Festival of Ice Sculpture. Each team is given a four-metre block of ice from which to create a sculpture. The impressive results remain on show in the main street for as long as temperatures allow.

Valmeinier 1500 is a small and traditionally built village with a higher satellite at 1800m.

Skiing facts: Valloire

TOURIST OFFICE
73450 Valloire, Savoie
Phone 33 79 59 03 96
Fax 33 79 59 09 66

THE RESORT
By road 937km from Calais
By rail St-Michel-Valloire 4½ hrs by TGV from Paris
By air Lyon 3 hrs
Visitor beds 9,450 (64% apartments, 26% hostels, 10% hotels)

THE SKIING
Longest run Piste des Selles 12km (blue)
Number of lifts 33
Number of trails/pistes 86 (22% beginner, 27% easy, 34% intermediate, 17% difficult)
Total of trails/pistes 150km
Nursery slopes 4
Summer skiing none
Snowmaking 20 hectares covered

LIFTPASSES
Area pass (covers Valloire and Valmeinier, and can be used for 1 day in 8 other Maurienne resorts) 486FF-579FF for 6 days
Day pass 100-118FF
Half-day pass 77-90FF after 12.30pm
Beginners no free lifts
Children under 12 yrs, 486FF for 6 days. Free for under 4 yrs
Pensioners no reduction
Credit cards accepted yes

SKI SCHOOLS
Adults 6 half-days: ESF 490FF, Ski Ecole Valloire 475FF
Children 6 half-days: ESF 350FF, Ski Ecole Valloire 330FF, L'Ourson 370FF
Private lessons 150FF per hr
Special courses snowboarding, off-piste, ski-touring
Guiding companies Compagnie des Guides

CROSS-COUNTRY
Ski schools ESF and Ski Ecole Valloire
Loipe location and size 40km at Bonnenuit Altiport and at Les 3 Croix

CHILDCARE
Non-ski kindergarten Haute Garderie Les Aiglons, 6 mths-7 yrs, 600FF for 6 days, 30FF per day for lunch
Ski kindergarten L'Ourson, Les Marmottons, La Souris Verte all 2½-3 yrs, 370FF for 6 half-days
Babysitting list available through tourist office

OTHER SPORTS
Skating, parapente, sleigh rides, micro-lighting, tobogganing, hang-gliding, snow-mobiling, fitness centre, bowling, snow-shoeing, martial arts, squash

FOOD AND DRINK PRICES
Coffee 10FF, bottle of house wine 60FF, beer 15-20FF, dish of day 60FF

TOUR OPERATORS
Enterprise, SkiBound, Ski Jeannie

Valmorel, Savoie

ALTITUDE 1400m (4,592ft)

••

Good points minimal queues, ideal for family skiing, extensive
nursery slopes, varied off-piste skiing, skiing convenience, freedom
from traffic, resort friendliness, easy road access
Bad points lack of facilities for non-skiers, night-time noise level,
lack of tough runs
Linked or nearby resorts St-François-Longchamp (l)

Valmorel, now well into its second decade, is a prime example of the
second wave of French purpose-built resorts designed to contradict
their ghastly forerunners in Tignes, Flaine and early La Plagne. The idea
was to build a family resort to which the baby-boom generation that
caused the mighty growth of the ski market in the 1960s and 1970s
could return as parents and now indeed as grandparents. At the same
time, as the first grumbles of a collective European 'green' conscience
were making themselves heard, the resort was to blend seamlessly into
the Savoie mountain scenery.

The planners, with a foresight completely unexpected of French
architects in the 1970s, took a couple of old farm buildings in a beautiful valley only 15km from Moutiers. Using local wood, stone and slate
they manufactured a 'traditional' resort. As an experiment it was an
enormous success. It is not, in fact, one resort, but a series of satellites
which the French call *hameaux* and which are not hamlets at all, but
clusters of chalet-style apartments assembled at intervals around the
home piste. These *hameaux* are all self-contained units with their own
reception area perched higgledy-piggledy on different contours of the
mountain, but all focused upon one central and surprisingly picturesque, shopping street. The ski area is, in itself, modest by major
resort standards with 53 pistes served by 31 lifts, but it is connected to
the neighbouring village of St-François-Longchamp in the Maurienne
valley. This easily negotiated link adds a further 31 pistes and 17 lifts to
form a highly respectable ski area of 163km, which is known as Le
Grand Domaine.

St-François-Longchamp's slopes are sunny, wide and gentle, while
the Valmorel side holds the better snow and is both more extensive and
more challenging. It is an ingeniously laid-out resort which, even by the
exalted standards of the Tarentaise and the best piste skiing in the
world, has remarkably few faults. Reporters continue to complain that
the pistes are seriously undergraded. Anyone judging the area by the
local piste map might think it lacking in any challenge for dedicated
skiers. The quality, or rather the user-friendliness, of some of its nursery
facilities, on which much of the resort's reputation is founded, is now

seriously questioned. Parents who are expert skiers will be delighted to discover Valmorel's best-kept secret: outstanding off-piste which, because of the family image of the resort, is unknown to ski-bums and is therefore deserted.

The skiing
Top 2550m (8,364ft) bottom 1250m (4,100ft)

The resort itself sits at the head of a boxed valley surrounded on three sides by sparsely wooded slopes and wide, undulating snowfields above. Although there are tenuous links, the skiing above the village splits naturally into the two main sectors of Baudin and Col du Mottet/Col du Gollet. The Mottet sector faces mainly north, the skiing goes up to 2400m and it therefore has the best snow. Lifts from Hameau du Mottet at the top of Valmorel give access to the 1981m Col du Gollet at the eastern extremity of the lift system. The open and quite steep skiing here – a choice of red (intermediate), black (difficult), or magnificent off-piste in the right conditions – catches the afternoon sun and is also the start of the Nine Valleys tour. You can ski off-piste from here into the Vallée de Belleville and link (with a short taxi ride) into the Trois Vallées ski area at Les Menuires.

The main **mountain access** is via the Pierrafort gondola from the top of the village, which serves a broad slope where the runs are all graded blue (easy), although some are distinctly red in any snow conditions. All reporters comment that the standard of piste-grooming is high overall, but some of these runs are left to become severely mogulled, which would be fine if they were then classified as red. The Mottet chair above the gondola climbs over the most testing pistes to the col of the same name. The wide mogul field under the top part of the chair is quite genuinely black and a good 33° in places, but after an awkward entry it is usually not too intimidating because of the quality of the snow.

A red run skirts around the shoulder and back through its own mogul field to the bottom of the chair; it also gives access via the Riondet drag to an interesting, long, but not too demanding black run down into the Cellier valley. This run is the only east-west on-mountain link between the Mottet and Baudin ski areas. The only alternative is via a lift from the resort centre. As one reporter points out, this results in the lower runs to the resort becoming overcrowded and unnecessarily worn; learners are consequently intimidated by skiers coming off the black and red slopes at Mottet and Gollet.

A long chair-lift goes up to Beaudin from the village. This and the shorter Planchamp chair are subject to 15-minute queues during the morning rush-hour out of season and double that at holiday times. There is a serious need for the Beaudin chair to be upgraded to a gondola. From the top, a series of drag-lifts serve long, easy runs. The blues down into the Celliers valley are again undergraded. These slopes catch the afternoon sun and therefore the moguls here can be intimidatingly hard and icy in the mornings. Another long drag-lift brings you back up to the Combe de Beaudin. From here it is an easy run to the Montagne de Tête. The Valmorel side of the Tête provides plenty of scope for off-piste skiing as well as some tough intermediate skiing below the chair-lift. The other side has a very long green (beginner) trail through the woods to Combelouvière.

From the Celliers valley a two-speed, three-seater chair takes you up to the broad ridge above the road pass of the Col de la Madeleine (closed in winter). One reporter describes this lift as 'infuriating, rather than ingenious. It has two gaps in its line of chairs and when no one is getting on or off, it speeds up. The net result is queues. If half your party catch the lift and the other half do not, this means waiting for them at the top.' The two red runs back down have pitches of nearly 30° and would be graded black elsewhere. There are, however, some easy blue alternatives.

On the sunny side of the ridge the runs down to Longchamp are open and gentle. A combination of schuss and plod take you from the top of the chair to the col, and beyond it to the Lauzière quad chair which goes up to the highest point of the ski area at 2550m on the Longchamp side of the road pass, although it is still covered by the local Valmorel ski pass. This chair is under-used and the off-piste opportunities from here are exceptional. The black run down from this chair is not very steep, but faces south and is often slushy by mid-afternoon; the red back to the col deserves its grading. There are several ways back to Valmorel; one of them, via the Côte 2305m drag-lift to the top of the Madeleine chair, involves a nasty stretch of blue run which should be graded red/black.

A new chair-lift from Longchamp up to the col, designed to improve access to Valmorel, has appeared for some time as a dotted line on the local piste map, but has not left the drawing board. The broad west-facing slopes above the road linking St-François and Longchamp are little used by Valmorel-based skiers. They include some interesting intermediate pistes through light woods above the road and down to the village. It is good confidence-building territory and even the blacks are not intimidating.

Holiday peaks excepted, queuing is not a serious problem in Valmorel. Apart from the village chairs already mentioned, the two drag-lifts, which have to be used to return to Beaudin from Longchamp at the end of the day, suffer from 4pm congestion. The Mucillon lift in particular needs to be upgraded. The snow-cannon covering the blue (easy) run from Beaudin to the village have proved to be an invaluable investment.

Mountain restaurants

It is a pleasure to record that mountain pitstops have improved beyond all recognition in recent years. There are now five in the Valmorel bowl, although perhaps still not enough given the size of the area and volume of visitors; they vary from 'respectable' to 'excellent'. Le Prairion beneath the gondola is lively and 'best for all-day sun and gâteaux'. Refuge 2000, a family-run establishment at the Col de la Madeleine, serves excellent salads and is described as 'very informal'. Les 2 Mazots has the best *croûte du fromage,* but service is said to be slow. Similarly, Le Cheval Noir in Longchamp is criticised for its slow service. L'Alpage was said to be 'unexciting, but efficient'. A considerable percentage of reporters take advantage of the ski-in ski-out convenience of the resort and return to the village for lunch.

Beginners and children

Valmorel has good nursery slopes with three lifts away from the main pistes; however, the blue runs to which novices then progress are not uniformly easy. The ESF has a sound reputation for excellent technical teaching performed with a smile, but it has recently received a few less complimentary reports: 'Organisation chaotic on the first day.' Reporters' biggest gripe is that lessons are given in French in the morning and English in the afternoon, so 'if you can speak French you get the better snow'. However, another visitor in March describes the ESF as 'excellent – the week we went resulted in a remarkable two pupils to one instructor for the English-speaking intermediate group.'

Saperlipopette is the Valmorel kindergarten, which has in the past been hailed as the model for all other such establishments. We have, however, had some contrary reports. In our own experience we have been put off by the rigidity of the hours. If, as a parent, you fail to deliver your children on time before 9am they will not be admitted until the afternoon, thus ruining your skiing. We found the claim that 'all our instructors speak English' is simply not true. The kindergarten is, however, very well-equipped and takes babies from six months old. One reporter speaks of serious understaffing levels: 'Our admittedly demanding and clingy children hated it, the 4-year-old cried incessantly from day one and the 2-year-old from day three. At some times the children were taught skiing with one staff member to 13 children.' It would be unfair to judge Saperlipopette overall on these reports. However, it does seem that the over-serious and not outwardly friendly Gallic attitude toward small children, which we have found more markedly elsewhere in France, highlights cultural differences.

The resort

The heart of Valmorel is Bourg-Morel, a colourful, arcaded pedestrian street full of restaurants, interesting shops, bars and pavement cafés. The free Télébourg gondola connects it to the upper *hameaux* until 11.30pm. It is all modern, but by no means lacking in alpine charm. The supermarkets are said to be overpriced, but well stocked. Anyone with a car is advised to shop in Moutiers, 15km away in the valley. Within the resort a car is not needed at all. Local buses go to Moutiers four times a day during the week and eight times at weekends. There are 20km of cross-country loipes in the area and several kilometres of cleared and signposted walks at the top of Beaudin and Lanchettes.

Accommodation

Most of the accommodation is in apartments, all of which are 'compact' in the French style, with 'apartment for four' really meaning 'just bearable for two.' However, the Planchamp and Fontaine apartments do appear to be of a slightly superior standard. Location is not particularly important. Most of our reporters prefer being close to the main street, despite the fact that we have continuing reports of late-night revelry disturbing those who wish to sleep. Hotel du Bourg is 'very comfortable and clean', although the rooms are 'claustrophobically small'. Hotel Planchamp is slightly smarter, but not so centrally placed. Skiers with cars can stay in the hamlet of Les Avanchers in the simple but pleasant Cheval Noir.

Eating out
For what is by no means a large purpose-built resort the variety of

Skiing facts: Valmorel

TOURIST OFFICE
F-73260 Valmorel, Savoie
Tel 33 79 09 85 55
Fax 33 79 09 89 27

THE RESORT
By road Calais 910km
By rail Moutiers, regular bus service to resort
By air Geneva 3½ hrs
Visitor beds 8,500 (96% apartments, 4% hotels)
Transport traffic-free village centre

THE SKIING
Longest run La Madeleine, 3.5km (blue)
Number of lifts 48 in area
Number of trails/pistes 84 in area (26% beginner, 45% easy, 19% intermediate, 10% difficult)
Total of trails/pistes 162km in area
Nursery slopes 5 lifts
Summer skiing none
Snowmaking 15 hectares covered

LIFT PASSES
Area pass Valmorel, 603-756FF for 6 days. Grand Domaine (covers Valmorel and St-François-Longchamp), 628-793FF for 6 days
Day pass Valmorel 113-141FF, Grand Domaine 116-147FF
Half-day pass Valmorel 84-106FF, Grand Domaine 87-109FF, from 12.30pm
Beginners single and multiple tickets
Children 4-13 yrs: Valmorel 504-637FF for 6 days, Grand Domaine 532-678FF for 6 days. Free for 4 yrs and under
Pensioners 60 yrs and over, as children
Credit cards accepted yes

SKI SCHOOLS
Adults ESF, 9.30am-midday, 494FF for 6 days. Beginners' course, 865FF for 6 days including lift pass
Children ESF, 4-13 yrs, 9.30am-12am, 450FF for 6 days
Private lessons 235FF for 90 mins
Special courses snowboarding, mono-skiing, powder courses, race training
Guiding companies through ESF

CROSS-COUNTRY
Ski schools ESF
Loipe location and size 20km of trails in 3 areas: Aigle Blanc, Le Pré and Les Avanchers

CHILDCARE
Non-ski kindergarten Saperlipopette, 6 mths-3 yrs, 8.30am-5pm, 300-331FF for 6 days including lunch
Ski kindergarten Saperlipopette, 3-8 yrs, 8.30am-5pm, 300-331FF for 6 days including lunch
Babysitting Saperlipopette, or through tourist office

OTHER SPORTS
Parapente, snow-shoeing, dog-sledding, fitness centres, tobogganing

WHAT'S NEW
● Les Sources ski-lift

FOOD AND DRINK PRICES
Coffee 6FF, bottle of house wine 25FF, beer 13FF, dish of the day 40FF

TOUR OPERATORS
Brittany Ferries, Crystal, Direct Ski, Enterprise, Equity Total Ski, French Impressions, Hoverspeed, Made to Measure, Neilson, Sally Holidays, Simply Ski, Ski Airtours, SkiBound, Ski Thomson, Touralp

restaurants comes as a surprise. Reporters recommend Chez Albert ('fantastic – the best pizzas ever'). Pizzeria du Bourg receives equally ecstatic commendations, La Galette is good for pierrade. Le Petit Savoyard has fine fondue and raclette. Le Creuset has 'stupendous' grills. At peak times reservations are necessary in most of the restaurants. One reporter points out that families with small children tend to eat early and it is easier to find a table after 9pm.

Après-ski

Flood-lit skiing on Thursdays is said to be 'good-value fun' as is dog-sledding ('the dog-handler worked harder than the dogs'). There are also toboggan runs and a sauna. Late-night drinking is by all accounts a noisy pastime which particularly upsets those visitors staying in the centre. 'Beware the cheap January weeks when the Spanish come to town and go to town at night,' says one reporter. 'No one can sleep in the early hours; I'd come here again, but not in high season and not without ear-plugs.' Of the bars, the Ski-Roc with live music is highly recommended. La Vadrouille has arm-wrestling contests compèred by the owner. Café de la Gare and Perce-Neige are both lively.

St-François-Longchamp 1650m (5,412ft)

Valmorel's neighbour is a sequence of hamlets below the Col de la Madeleine, linked by a free bus service. These are no-frills resorts, which attract mainly French families. The top hamlet, Longchamp, is an ugly group of A-frame buildings built in the early 1960s surrounded by sunny and gentle slopes. The skiing is ideal for both beginners and intermediates. All the hotels are graded two-star and include La Perelle, managed by British operator SkiBound, and Le Cheval Noir. Longchamp has a kindergarten, skating rink, several restaurants and crêperies, a disco, piano bar, supermarkets and some good specialist food shops. St-François is a group of simple old hotels and hostels at 1450m.

TOURIST OFFICE
73130 Savoie
Tel 33 79 59 10 56
Fax 33 79 59 13 67

TOUR OPERATORS
SkiBound

Bormio, Lombardy

ALTITUDE 1225m (4,018ft)

••

Good points summer skiing, long runs, good artificial snow cover, tree-line skiing, activities for non-skiers, attractive town centre, wide variety of mountain restaurants
Bad points resort-level snow, difficult airport access, heavy traffic, limited child facilities
Linked or nearby resorts Santa Caterina (n)

Bormio is a substantial town rather than a village, with a historic centre and extensive ugly modern suburbs. It stands at the foot of the Stelvio, pass which separates Italian Italy from Germanic Dolomite Italy. Bormio's history as a spa goes back to Roman times in the first century. Its début as an international resort came when it hosted the 1985 World Championships.

The main skiing takes place on one mighty, but gentle mountainside, which is an ideal playground for intermediates. Steady improvements to the lift system and the addition of much-needed extra snow-cannon in recent years have added to the attraction, but failed to open up any new skiing, which might make it of greater interest as a resort for the more advanced. However, the long vertical drop (1787m) does much to compensate. The area lift pass covers neighbouring Santa Caterina, a pretty village with reliable snow, less queuing, and some good intermediate skiing. The pass also includes Livigno, Valdisotto and Valdidentro.

The skiing

Top 3012m (9,879ft) bottom 1225m (4,018ft)

Mountain access to the north-west facing slopes of Monte Vallecetta is by a two-stage cable car from the edge of town. The middle station, Bormio 2000, can also be reached by car, snow conditions permitting. Alternatively you can take the gondola to Ciuk (1620m) and work your way up the mountain by drag and chair. When conditions permit, the longest run from top to bottom is a satisfying 14km. On the open, top half the runs are all fairly long in their own right, but the range of difficulty is limited; the easy runs are a bit tough for skiers just off the nursery slopes, and only when they are icy do the two short blacks (difficult runs) present any serious challenge. A long, flattering off-piste run takes you down to Santa Caterina.

Immediately below the top of the cable car, and to the west of the pistes, a quite steep, wide bowl provides some good off-piste skiing safe from the danger of avalalanches. Return into the lift system is up through the woods via the Ornella drag-lift, which does not always func-

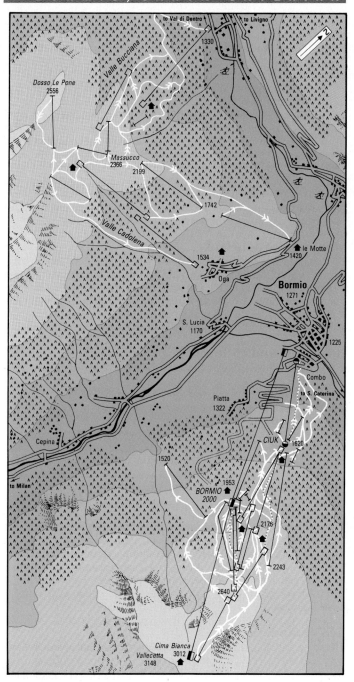

tion. Most skiers spend the day on the top half of the mountain, and the wide, undulating trails through the woods below Ciuk are little used except in bad weather and for skiing home in the afternoon. The FIS downhill course starts steeply just above La Rocca and runs down past Ciuk to near the bottom of the gondola.

On the other side of the valley a worthwhile ski area has been created by the construction of lifts on the west-facing slopes above the villages of Oga and Le Motte, linking up with those above the hamlet of Valdidentro. A chair-lift from the edge of Valdidentro rises over the wooded, north-facing slopes of Masucco (2366m) to a restaurant and a small nursery area. From here two consecutive lifts ascend to the summit, serving pleasant intermediate runs back down the valley, with a couple of blue (easy) alternatives. On the other side of the valley from Masucco is the high point of the ski area, Posse le Pone (2550m), reached by two short drags. From the top, several off-piste routes, and one marked run, take you down the east side of the mountain.

Mountain restaurants

Bormio has 10 mountain restaurants, a considerable number considering the size of the ski area. We have had consistent reports of good mountain fare, including the self-service restaurant at Bormio 2000. La Rocca is recommended for its warm atmosphere in both the self- and waiter-service areas ('wood-burning stoves in both rooms and friendly staff'). Baità de Mario at Ciuk is praised for its *carpaccio* and *polenta*.

Beginners and children

The main ski school is Scuola Italiana Sci 2000 of which we have limited, but positive, reports. Classes do tend to be large at peak times and English is not always spoken well, but '10 out of 10 for an enthusiasm as infectious as chickenpox', said one reporter. Bormio has no less than 5 other small alternative ski schools.

The beginners' lifts are at Ciuk and Bormio 2000. The first is larger and more tranquil, although sometimes short of snow. The latter is said to be marred by a 'dreadful' rope-tow. The area is well suited to children and to family skiing in general, as long as you do not mind having to take a lift up to reach the snow-line for most of the season.

The resort

The medieval heart of the old town is unaffected and very Italian, with a greater variety of shops, cafés and restaurants, tucked away in the back streets, than in most ski resorts, along with interesting open markets. The Via Roma is the main shopping street, cobble-stoned, with historic buildings and a number of antique shops, boutiques and gourmet food shops. The other half of the town is purpose-built with modern hotels – a stark contrast.

Accommodation

The three-star Hotel Nevada is recommended by a regular visitor, along with the Funivia ('clean, with friendly staff'), Larice Bianco and the Aurora. The Ambassador, Derby and the Baità dei Pini all receive good reports. The Cima Bianca is an attractive two-star, and the Piccolo Mondo has a good atmosphere. In the centre, the Posta and Astoria are both comfortable. The most upmarket hotels are the four-star Palace and the Rezia. The Posta, one of the resort's oldest hotels, has been modernised and has a swimming-pool.

Eating out

Taulà is a seventeenth-century barn in the Via Dante specialising in dishes from the Valtellina region. Il Caminetto, the Piccolo Mondo and Osteria de I Magri are all recommended. The Cristall is known for its wonderful pizzas.

Skiing facts: Bormio

TOURIST OFFICE
Via Stelvio 10, 23032 Bormio
Tel 39 342 903300
Fax 39 342 904696

THE RESORT
By road Calais 1146km
By rail Tirano 40km
By air Milan 3½ hrs
Visitor beds 6,100 (52% hotels, 48% apartments)
Transport local bus service

THE SKIING
Longest run Cima Bianca-Bormio, 14km (blue)
Number of lifts 20
Number of trails/pistes 19 (42% easy, 47% intermediate, 11% difficult)
Total of trails/pistes 82km
Nursery slopes 4, up the mountain at Ciuk and Bormio 2000
Summer skiing 20km at Stelvio Pass between May and November
Snowmaking 7km covered

LIFT PASSES
Area pass (covers Bormio, Livigno, Santa Caterina, Valdisotto, Valdidentro) L165,000-185,000 for 6 days
Day pass (Bormio only) L36,000-40,000
Half-day pass L30,000
Beginners no free lifts
Children 12 yrs and under, L30,000-34,000 per day, L120,000-135,000 for 6 days
Pensioners 65 yrs and over as children
Credit cards accepted yes

SKI SCHOOLS
Adults 6 ski schools all with similar times and prices: Anzi, Bormio 2000, Capitani, Nazionale, Sertorelli, Alta Valtellina. Bormio 2000, L100,000-140,000 for 6 lessons (2 hrs each am or pm)
Children Scuola Sci Sertorelli, 5-12 yrs, L120,000 for 6 days
Private lessons L35,000-40,000 per hr for 1 person, L5,000-7,000 per extra person
Special courses snowboarding, off-piste skiing, telemark
Guiding companies Casa delle Guide Alpine Bormio, Ass. Guide Alpine Alta Valtellina

CROSS-COUNTRY
Ski school Scuola Sci Fondo Alta Valtellina
Loipe location and size Pista Alu 12km, Pista Boschetti d'Adda 2km

CHILDCARE
Non-ski kindergarten none
Ski kindergarten none
Babysitting not available

OTHER SPORTS
Swimming, squash, tennis, sports centre, tobogganing, skating, thermal baths

FOOD AND DRINK PRICES
Coffee L1,400, bottle of house wine L10,000, beer L5,000, dish of the day L10,000

TOUR OPERATORS
Enterprise, Neilson, Ski Thomson

Après-ski

You might like to ease your aching muscles in the thermal baths, before trying the generally quiet nightlife, which is limited to a choice of bars and restaurants. The Aurora, Rezia, and Posta all have piano bars. The King's Club and Shangri-là discos start to buzz around midnight. The Mozart bar is recommended.

Santa Caterina 1737m (5,697ft)

Santa Caterina, or San Cat as it is known, is a quiet, attractive village 30 minutes away by bus up a mountain road that is a dead-end in winter when the Gavia pass is closed. It usually has better snow than its larger neighbour and, because of the shared lift pass, a number of reporters prefer to stay here and make the foray on alternate days to Bormio. Local skiing is on the north-east facing slopes of the 3296m Sobretta. The higher slopes are fairly steep and graded black. There are also some winding, intermediate trails down between the trees. Piste maintenance seems to vary from month to month, but the nursery area is covered by snow-cannon. One complaint of the ski area is that the only return on skis to the village is via three red (intermediate) runs; first-year skiers have to take the chair. Out of four mountain restaurants, the Bella Vista and Paradiso are recommended.

Santa Caterina's ski school receives mixed, but generally favourable reviews including 'competent, cautious instruction, although some teachers had a limited command of English'. Another reporter speaks of the school being 'a little disorganised'. An interesting observation that we have often encountered elsewhere is that 'one private lesson was better than the whole week at the ski school'. One reporter claims that the ski school was more interested in group photographs and ski races than in actual teaching. There is good cross-country skiing (10km loipe) beyond the resort, and skating on a natural rink.

The San Matteo Hotel is strongly recommended for comfort and food. Reporters are more muted in the their appreciation of the Park Hotel ('very basic bedrooms, comfortable public rooms and average food'), although the excellent central location was praised. Self-caterers have a choice of two well-stocked supermarkets. Nightlife is limited, with one fairly large disco and a number of cosy bars, which remain open until after midnight.

TOURIST OFFICE
I-23030 Santa Caterina Valfurva
Tel 39 342 93 55 98

TOUR OPERATORS
Enterprise, Neilson, Ski Thomson

Cervinia, Aosta

ALTITUDE 2050m (6,724ft)

••

Good points wide and easy pistes, extensive nursery slopes, resort-level snow, early- and late-season skiing, summer skiing, variety of hotels
Bad points lack of challenging skiing, lack of tree-level skiing, high-season queues, weekend traffic, limited facilities for non-skiers
Linked or nearby resorts Zermatt (I), Valtournenche (I)

Cervinia has in the past been the victim of bad press, and not without justification. But times are changing. Its skiing is connected to Zermatt, but there the similarity ends. While the Swiss resort is rich in alpine charm and varied skiing, the Italian side of the Matterhorn is sunnier, but positively bland in comparison. Once it was the showpiece of Italian ski resorts, a gleaming contemporary development, set high above the tree-line in a sunny south-facing valley. Mussolini changed its name from Breuil to Cervinia, after the Italian name for the Matterhorn. Cable cars swept skiers up to unprecedented heights and Italy's elite flocked to enjoy the novelty. Then they moved on. Other, better resorts developed elsewhere, while poor old Cervinia's lift system lapsed into disrepair, and its grand but utilitarian architecture was eclipsed by more environmentally sympathetic village developments elsewhere.

Today there are positive signs that Cervinia is climbing out of its timewarp and the resort, in recent years, has undergone a major facelift both on- and off-piste. In particular, the addition of one of the biggest cable cars in the world has done much to reduce the queues for access to Plateau Rosa. What one reporter describes as 'hideous examples of neo-brutalist concrete' have given way to wood and stone, and some of the main hotels in the central square have been reclad. But, regardless of cosmetics, nothing can change the basic face of the mountain, which lacks challenge to anyone above the average intermediate level.

Cervinia is extremely popular with beginners or near beginners and has a faithful following of older intermediates who enjoy the open and long pistes which present no hidden horrors. 'Just what the doctor ordered,' said one reporter, 'I cannot stress enough how enjoyable Cervinia skiing is.' Another commented: 'A complete beginner, I have been bragging about the speed of my progress ever since, and my ego had to come back as excess baggage.' Without doubt there are few resorts where beginners might, by the end of the week, find themselves capable of skiing a lengthy 8km through 1500m vertical, from the Plateau Rosa right down to Cervinia with a confidence that will stay with them throughout their years of skiing.

Beginners and intermediates apart, there is really nothing to challenge the experienced skier. Its strongest second attribute is its snow record. Because of its high altitude, resort-level skiing can be relied upon as early as November and well into April. As historical rivals there was no love lost between Cervinia and Zermatt, but both resorts have now finally realised that working together has its advantages and there is a possibility that we will see a joint lift pass in the near future. However, the distances involved mean that day visitors from either resort get no more than a taste of the other's skiing.

The skiing
Top 3490m (11,447ft) bottom 1524m (4,999ft)

The main **mountain access** is via a 6-seater gondola or an ancient 75-person cable car, which takes you up Plan Maison at 2555m. Reporters complain that the climb on foot up to the base station is hard work and tedious, not helped by cars trying to push through the crowds during the morning rush-hour. The alternative is to make your way slowly up the mountain via the more conveniently reached Cretaz drag-lifts, which start from the lower end of the village in what is a huge nursery area lined with rows of deckchairs for sunbathers.

From here, a range of lifts fan out across this wide, open mountain-side including a modern 12-person jumbo gondola, which takes you on up to Laghi Cime Bianche at 2812m. A 140-person state-of-the-art cable car completes the journey to the summer ski area at Plateau Rosa and the link to Zermatt. These new lifts have done wonders in reducing mountain queues and greatly cutting journey time compared to the ancient cable cars which are still operating. The whole lift system is nevertheless erratic in that, for no apparent reason, any one link is liable to close without warning. While the gondola from the village runs all the time, the parallel cable car may not function during low season. Similarly, the Plan Maison-Plateau Rosa cable cars via Cime Bianche may be taken out of service from day to day.

The cable car from Plan Maison to Furggen (3492m) is not always open until later in the season, and is subject to queues when it is. From the top you can see both Zermatt and Cervinia simultaneously. A tedious walk down an internal staircase of nearly 300 steps takes you out on to the broad ledge at the edge of the cliff, and the start of the best black (difficult) run in the resort. After a couple of steep pitches at the top it levels out slightly for the descent to Plan Torrette. A number of off-piste variants here should be attempted only with a guide. From Plateau Rosa the main run down is the famous Ventina, an uninterrupted eight kilometres of easy family skiing for the most part, despite its red (intermediate) grading. It is easily possible to repeat the middle section of the run via the Lago Goillet triple chair. From the top of this (or from Plateau Rosa) a long run with a number of variations takes you all the way down to Valtournenche at 1524m.

To the south-east of Cervinia are the Carosello lifts, little-used chairs and drags starting from the high part of the resort and accessed from the Ventina. Each of the two luxury hotels has a lift outside the front door. The slopes face west and north-west and are fairly steep. They are often unprepared and there is scope for exploring between the pistes.

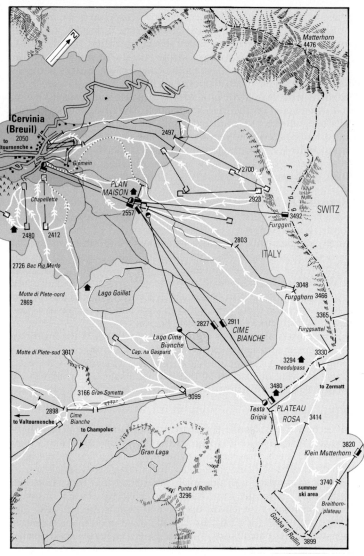

Reporters found sign-posting and piste-grading were accurate in most cases. Queues have been greatly relieved by new lifts, but annoying linkage means that a good deal of poling and side-stepping is required around the mountain. Artificial snow has been installed on the two main home runs back to the village.

Mountain restaurants

Italian mountain fare is better than in most countries and Cervinia is no exception, although prices are high. Reporters were unanimous in their praise of Batia Cretaz da Mario on the blue (easy) run home from Plan Maison, reached from the village by the Cretaz I drag-lift and a two-minute ski. Reports were of a 'wide and imaginative menu' and 'the best plain food in town at not unreasonable prices'. The restaurant at Plan Maison is to be avoided at peak times because of the 'Eastern European multi-queue system much in operation'. Reporters were shocked by the standard of the hole-in-the-ground type of loos in some establishments, and commented on the lack of sanitation. The Chalet Etoile, offering 'charming service, nice soup and pasta', and Plan Torrette just below it, are recommended. One reporter found the best *polenta* he had ever tasted at the Lombard restaurant at the top of Blue 6 on the way down from Plateau Rosa. La Dailhu is also recommended for its 'fresh table linen, good food and friendly service', along with La Baracon du Tenet.

Beginners and children

Cervinia has two ski schools – the Cervino and the Cieloalto. We have received mixed reports of the Cervino, some of them alarming. 'Snowploughers with one week's experience and others with six all herded into the same class, resulting in dissatisfaction', claims one reporter. But another commented that 'the quality of the ski school more than anything else made my week such a success.' Lack of actual instruction and too much 'follow me' is a consistent criticism. In contrast another said there were between eight and ten people to a class, and most instructors spoke adequate English.

The nursery slopes right in the village at the foot of the main runs are extremely good and convenient for parents. Cervinia is very much a family resort and it is not unusual to see three generations of the same family enjoying themselves all over the mountain. The children's ski school takes 5-year-olds and over.

The resort

The centre of the resort is a pedestrian zone. Surrounding roads on the outskirts tend to become clogged with traffic, particularly during high-season weekends. However, most visitors who come here by tour operator coach are not inconvenienced by this. Cervinia is essentially a small and compact village with one main street lined with bars, shops and restaurants. Above the cable car station, buildings (mostly the more expensive hotels) stretch on up the hill towards the Carosello lifts. There is no need for a car here and the more remote hotels tend to operate courtesy mini-buses. The shopping is 'generally good-quality', with a smattering of upmarket boutiques and sports shops interspersed with supermarkets and souvenir shops.

Accommodation

Cervinia boasts a wide range of hotels and some quite new apartments. The Hotel Jumeaux receives glowing recommendations ('clean, roomy, friendly, cheap, civilised and quiet – bliss'). It now has satellite television in its bedrooms. The neighbouring Bucaneve is also praised for its comfort and high standard of cuisine. Lo Stambecco, up the mountain at Plan Maison, is good for convenience and for those who like an early night. The Pelissier and the Joli are described as noisy. Hotel Astoria, next to the cable car station, is 'slightly shabby, but worth it for the location alone'. Hotel Marmore is described as 'basic, but adequate', and the Hotel Cristallo is lavishly recommended with 'everything one could expect of a four-star hotel in a country, which does not have fives'. The four-star Punta Maquignaz receives similar billing. One reporter complains that the Breuil-Centro apartments were 'too cramped, but otherwise there were no real problems'. The Hotel Compagnoni is situated mid-resort, hence 'a little noisy, but simple and comfortable'. The Edelweiss is 'quite small, but smart'.

Eating out

Lino's, beside the skating rink, is recommended for both lunch and dinner, and serves delicious steaks. The Copa-Pan and the Matterhorn are both known for their home-made pizzas. La Bamba is 'more upmarket

Skiing facts: Cervinia

TOURIST OFFICE
Azienda di Soggiorno, Via Carrel 29,
11021 Cervinia
Tel 39 166 949136
Fax 39 166 949731

THE RESORT
By road Calais 1001km
By rail Châtillon 27km, 4 buses daily
By air Turin and Geneva 2½ hrs
Visitor beds 5,700 (53% apartments, 47% hotels)
Transport on foot, car or bus unnecessary

THE SKIING
Longest run the Ventina, 8km (red)
Number of lifts 23 Cervinia, 73 with Zermatt
Number of trails/pistes 58 Cervinia (16% beginner, 25% easy, 40% intermediate, 19% difficult), 118 with Zermatt
Total of trails/pistes 230km, including Zermatt
Nursery slopes extensive, in village centre
Summer skiing on Plateau Rosa, 8 lifts and a cable car
Snowmaking 7 hectares covered

LIFT PASSES
Area pass L205,000 for 6 days
Day pass L41,000
Half-day pass L32,000
Beginners points cards
Children L205,000 for 6 days
Pensioners no reduction

Credit cards accepted yes

SKI SCHOOLS
Adults Cervino and Cieloalto ski schools, both L160,000 for 6 days (3 hrs per day)
Children prices same as adults
Private lessons from L40,000 per hr
Special courses snowboarding, telemark
Guiding companies available through ski schools

CROSS-COUNTRY
Ski schools Cervino
Loipe location and size 2.5km, on edge of village

CHILDCARE
Non-ski kindergarten Cieloalto, prices and times on application
Ski kindergarten Cieloalto, prices and times on application
Babysitting list available from tourist office

OTHER SPORTS
Skating, snow-mobiling, bowling, tobogganing, swimming

FOOD AND DRINK PRICES
Coffee L1,200, bottle of house wine from L10,000, beer L5,000, dish of the day from L10,000

TOUR OPERATORS
Crystal, Enterprise, Inghams, Neilson, Sally Holidays, Ski Thomson

with very friendly staff. One reporter found the cheapest good food was in Petit Monde, 'but the miserable staff drove us away'. The restaurant in the Bucaneve hotel has a fine reputation. The Falcone is described as 'a bit dull and overpriced, especially the wines'. The Petit Palais and the restaurant Valdoran are warmly recommended.

Après-ski

Most reporters are disappointed with the lack of après-ski in Cervinia, which was not at all what they expected. 'The bars lacked atmosphere' according to one reporter. In fact, the nightlife is there, it just starts extremely late, with most bars having their happy-hour between 9 and 10pm. The Dragon Pub in the Hotel Pelissier is the focal point, along with Lino's, Yeti and the Gran Becca. There are two main discos: La Chimera and the Blow-up. The latter is out of the centre, but operates a courtesy bus.

Cortina d'Ampezzo, Dolomites

ALTITUDE 1220m (4,002ft)

Good points large intermediate ski area, extensive nursery slopes, variety of mountain restaurants, long runs, activities for non-skiers, beautiful scenery, skiing for all standards, extensive cross-country skiing, varied off-piste skiing, tree-level skiing, attractive and cosmopolitan resort, variety of restaurants, lively après-ski
Bad points lack of skiing convenience, limited for late holidays, long airport transfer, difficult road access, traffic
Linked or nearby resorts Armentarola (l), San Cassiano (l), San Vito di Cadore (n)

Cortina d'Ampezzo is Italy's only world-class ski resort and at the same time the country's most fashionable and cosmopolitan ski town. Although it is in the Dolomites and indeed links (rather tentatively) into the Sella Ronda circuit and shares its lift pass, it has no hint of the German-speaking, Sud-Tirol atmosphere of its neighbours. Cortina is Italian to its voluptuous core.

It is one of the most remote resorts for visitors from the north and west and the majority of its clientele is Italian. Cortina is a large sunny town, centred on a main shopping street. In style it is the Italian equivalent of Zermatt. It hosted the 1956 Winter Olympics and ranks with St Moritz and Chamonix as one of the world's few all-round winter sports resorts.

Cortina's downhill skiing includes some of the best nursery slopes anywhere, good intermediate skiing and long, challenging runs for accomplished skiers; all of this takes place amid stunningly beautiful scenery. Much of the resort's most 'recent' development was generated by the Olympics almost 40 years ago; some of the buildings are distinctly down-at-heel and it is perhaps time for some drastic cosmetic surgery. The lifts, however, are gradually being upgraded. The skiing areas are far apart on the surrounding mountains, and travelling between them is one of the resort's most irritating points.

Cortina has an upmarket reputation, which can put off those skiers who see Italy as the destination for cheap and cheerful holidays. In high season the ankle-length fur coats can come as a shock, but it is not an exclusive or overtly expensive resort. There are plenty of pleasant, modestly priced hotels, as well as simple bars, which are full of character.

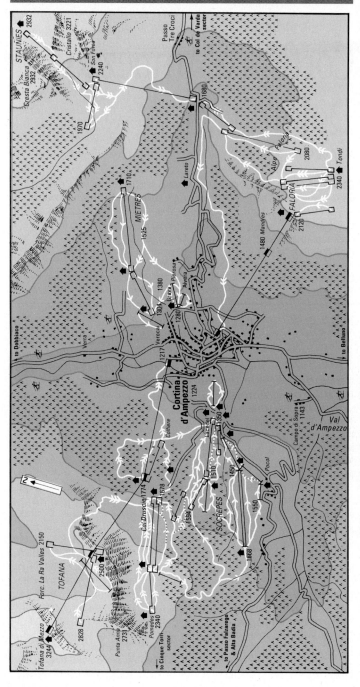

The skiing

Top 2948m (9,669ft) bottom 1224m (4,015ft)

The ski terrain is broken up by typically Dolomite rose pink cliffs. There are open snowfields of easy runs and some gullies so steep and narrow they approach the extreme. Between them is a large variety of intermediate skiing. The main Tofana-Socrepes skiing area is west of the town. On the other side of the large resort, the Staunies and Faloria areas are just about linked, despite the road between them, and provide some interesting runs. A long way out of town, by the Passo Falzarego road, are several unconnected little ski areas, well worth visiting for a change of spectacular scenery. One of them, Passo Falzarego, links into the Sella Ronda circuit.

Mountain access to the Tofana area is via the Tofana cable car, a long trek from the town centre, although buses are frequent. Between the resort and Col Druscie (1774m) the cable car travels over gentle tree-lined terrain and open fields with wide and easy trails, which cross rough roads without much warning for either skiers or drivers. Snow conditions often make these runs testing, which gives them their red (intermediate) and black (difficult) gradings. The second stage of the cable car climbs the sheer, rocky mountainside to Ra Valles, in the middle of a pleasant intermediate bowl. This area is reportedly often closed in poor weather.

The top section of the cable car is designated for sun-bathers and sightseers only. Near the bottom of the bowl there is a gap in the rock giving access to a narrow black trail, which has a reasonably steep south-facing stretch in the middle. The run ends up at the bottom of the Pomedes chair-lifts, about 100m lower than Col Druscie, which is set on a little peak. You can reach here by skiing on down to Colfiere and taking the Col Druscie chair-lift, which itself has an interesting short black run underneath it. The Pomedes chair-lifts, which can also be reached by car, add some excellent runs including a couple of good blacks and the spectacular downhill racecourse, which starts through a narrow funnel between massive pillars of rock. There is also a long serpentine blue from the middle station. The Pomedes runs and lifts link up on long, tree-lined paths with open skiing above Pocol and Lacedel – a huge area of very easy runs and nursery slopes well covered by snow-cannon, called Socrepes.

The Faloria area is reached by cable car from the ring road; the first stage rises over gentle pastureland, the second over a cliff to 2120m. There are no runs under the cable car, but an area of short reds and blues beyond it, all served by a series of chair-lifts. You can ski through the woods to the Tre Croci road at Rio-Gere, either directly from Faloria, or with less effort by means of a little-used red run from Tondi.

On the other side of the Tre Croci road are south-facing slopes, which are served by a long and slow chair-lift going up to the foot of the cliffs of Monte Cristallo. The run back down is wide and easy, continuing down to Rio-Gere and on beside the Tre Croci road back to Cortina. There is no link with the extensive area of easy runs served by a number of lifts beneath Mietres. From the foot of Monte Cristallo a two-stage chair-lift climbs to Forcella Staunies, one of the best couloirs in the area.

The top section of the descent necessitates some good sharp turns, as it is both narrow and very steep. As the run faces south it is, unfortunately, often unskiable.

An isolated two-stage chair-lift (1900-2400m) outside town on the road up to Passo Falzarego serves the little-used north-facing Cinque Torri, with its small area of intermediate runs and beautiful scenery. Further along the road, a dramatic cable car soars up a cliff-face from Passo Falzarego (2105m) to Lagazuoi (2746m). The run back down is mostly blue with a short red section in the middle. Passo Falzarego links into the Sella Ronda via a beautiful 11km red (intermediate) run to Armentarola, near San Cassiano, sprinkled with restaurants. You need to start early in the day in order to achieve any distance on skis. Taxis wait at Armentarola to take skiers up the road to the Lagazuoi gondola, which is one of the ways back to Cortina's distant ski area. There are also buses from Armentarola to Falzarego.

A lot of time is spent travelling around Cortina's ski areas. The ski-bus runs between the two cable car stations and other, less frequent buses travel to and from the furthest ski areas. Morning queues for the Tofana cable car are not a problem due to the late rising-time of the average Cortina skier. There is artificial snow in all the ski areas except Faloria.

Mountain restaurants
Mountain eating is a memorable experience in Cortina and there is a good choice of venues in all the skiing areas, with most restaurants relatively cheap. The ones at Pomedes, Col Druscie and Tondi are particularly recommended. There are several expensive places for serious lunching near the Socrepes lifts, notably El Camineto where, it is vital to make reservations at weekends.

Beginners and children
The nursery slopes and long green runs for quasi-beginners are excellent. Most beginners use the very extensive area above the Falzarego road at Pocol. The Pierosa and Mietres is an equally gentle area, but is rather isolated. There are two non-ski kindergartens in the resort, including Naturalmente, a flexible operation which picks children up from their parents in the morning and returns them after skiing. It also provide a babysitting service.

The main Cortina ski school has an office in the town centre and a meeting place for adult beginners at the Socrepes lift. The Azzurra Cortina is a smaller ski school with an office at the foot of the Faloria cable car.

The resort
Cortina is a stately old town in a stunningly beautiful setting. Its only imperfection is its position on a busy crossroads, which brings with it plenty of traffic. The chic main street, Corso Italia, is pedestrianised and traffic flows around the one-way circuit. People-watching is one of the main early evening pastimes in Cortina, with the Corso Italia alive with promenading, fur-clad Italians looking at the elegant shop windows and

at each other. Outside the centre, the resort extends up and down the valley, with chalets on the main road towards Dobbiaco and some development across the river climbing towards Falzarego.

Accommodation

Hotels range from the large international variety to the very simple, and there is a large number of private apartments and chalets. The most attractive hotel is the comfortable Poste, situated in the heart of Cortina and especially known for its food. Also well-located and stylish, but cheaper, is the Ancora. The elegant Parc Hotel Victoria is centrally situ-

Skiing facts: Cortina d'Ampezzo

TOURIST OFFICE
Piazzetta San Francesco 8, I-32043
Cortina d'Ampezzo, Belluno
Tel 39 436 3231
Fax 39 436 3235

THE RESORT
By road Calais 1200km
By rail Calalzo di Cadore 35km, buses to Cortina every hr
By air Venice 2½ hrs
Visitor beds 22,500 (80% apartments, 20% hotels)
Transport free bus connects the town centre with the main lifts

THE SKIING
Longest run San Marco, 9km (black/red)
Number of lifts 46
Number of trails/pistes 77 (44% easy, 49% intermediate, 7% difficult)
Total of trails/pistes 160km
Nursery slopes 3 lifts
Summer skiing none
Snowmaking 51km covered

LIFT PASSES
Area pass Cortina, L185,000-212,000 for 6 days. Superski Dolomiti, L192,000-221,000 for 6 days
Day pass Cortina, L37,000-43,000, Superski Dolomiti, L39,000-44,000
Half-day pass not available
Beginners coupons
Children 30% reduction for 14 yrs and under
Pensioners 20% reduction for 60 yrs and over
Credit cards accepted yes

SKI SCHOOLS
Adults Scuola di Sci Cortina, 9.30am-

midday, L210,00 for 6 days. Scuola di Sci Azzurra Cortina, 9am-1pm, L380,000 for 6 days, or 1pm-4pm, L250,000 for 6 days
Children Scuola di Sci Cortina, 9.30am-midday, L210,000. Scuola di Sci Azzurra Cortina, 15 yrs and under, 9am-4pm, L600,000 for 6 days
Private lessons L43,000 per hr
Special courses snowboarding
Guiding companies Gruppo Guide Alpine Cortina

CROSS-COUNTRY
Ski schools Scuola Italiana Sci Fondo
Loipe location and size 74km in the valley north of Cortina

CHILDCARE
Non-ski kindergarten Naturalmente, nursery for 1-3 yrs, recreational and sporting activities for 1-14 yrs, from 7.45am. Mini Club, 2-8 yrs, 8am-8pm. No fixed prices available for either
Ski kindergarten Scuola di Sci Cortina and Scuola di Sci Azzurra Cortina, 2 yrs and over, times and prices as children's ski school
Babysitting Naturalmente

OTHER SPORTS
Skating, hockey, curling, indoor tennis, swimming, ski-jumping, tobogganing

FOOD AND DRINK PRICES
Coffee L1,300, bottle of house wine L10,000, beer L2,500, dish of the day L10,000

TOUR OPERATORS
Bladon Lines, Crystal

ated and caters for vegetarians. Two small, attractive chalet hotels within walking distance of the main cable car are the Capannina, with a good restaurant and the inexpensive Barisetti. The Italia is a popular family-run hotel and, although inconveniently positioned, the Menardi is recommended for its good food and reasonable prices. The Montaba and the friendly and informal Olimpia are among the cheapest and most central bed and breakfast hotels. The Fiames is a one-star hotel, conveniently placed for the cross-country loipe.

Eating out

There are more than 40 restaurants ranging from pizzerias to extreme gourmet. The Meloncino al Lago at Laghi Ghedina, north-west of the town, and the expensive Toula, beside the road up towards Falzarego, both offer excellent food. Those in the Capannina and Da Beppe Sello hotels are highly recommended, along with Leone e Anna. The Buca dell'Inferno pizzeria is said to be full of character, the Croda has good pasta and the Passetto serves pizzas.

Après-ski

The nightlife is varied and lively in high season, but quieter in the low season. There are a dozen discos and numerous bars. The Poste hotel is the smartest early evening bar, the Enoteca wine bar is popular and the Orange bar is very central. There is an ice disco on the Olympic rink and the bobsleigh practice and big league ice hockey matches make interesting viewing. The Mietres chair-lift serves a toboggan run.

The cross-country trails are long and varied, although the Fiames base is a long way from central Cortina and the trails do not link with any of the alpine skiing areas. One long trail follows the old railway track to Dobbiaco and another all the way to Villach in Austria. Venice is within reach for a day trip and in Cortina itself the shopping is interesting and varied and includes an art gallery. For non-skiers there are good walks along the valley and to restaurants in and around the ski area.

Courmayeur, Aosta

ALTITUDE 1230m (4,034ft)

••

Good points beautiful scenery, choice of mountain restaurants, alpine charm, easy road access, short transfer, off-piste skiing, big vertical drop, tree-level skiing, extensive artificial snow cover
Bad points lack of skiing convenience, limited nursery slopes, lack of tough runs
Linked or nearby resorts Cervinia (n), Champoluc (n), Chamonix (l), Gressoney-la-Trinité (n), Pila (n), La Thuile (n)

Courmayeur is 35km through the Mont Blanc tunnel from Chamonix, the nearest Italian resort by road from Britain and equally accessible by air from Turin and Geneva. Its attractive ski area offers stunning views of Mont Blanc. Off-piste opportunities include the Vallée Blanche and spectacular powder runs from the 2755m Cresta d'Arp. Its mountain restaurants are some of the most interesting in Europe and the village itself has more than its fair share of alpine charm. The alternative skiing elsewhere in the Val d'Aosta of Cervinia, La Thuile and the remote vastness of Gressonay-la-Trinité and Champoluc are all within easy driving distance. Somewhere there must be a drawback – and there is. Courmayeur's great weakness is its lack of skiing convenience.

The main way up the mountain is by a cable car across the river gorge and the arterial Mont Blanc tunnel road. This takes you up to a sunny plateau, from where you annoyingly have to plod on up to the foot of the lifts. There are equally tiresome alternatives and it is necessary to take the cable car down again at the end of the day. Despite the general efficiency of this modern cable car, queues are inevitable.

But none of this really detracts from the overall appeal of Courmayeur as a ski resort. It is stylish without being exclusive, lively without being rowdy, it has character but not chocolate-box charm. Reporters remark on the friendliness of the locals in startling contrast to the dour Gallic attitude of those on the other side of the tunnel. Extensive investment in snow-cannon in recent years is a welcome bonus. The skiing is not satisfactory for everyone: the pisted runs are short and lack challenge, while at the same time few can reasonably be described as gentle. A car is useful for excursions to other resorts, but parking is difficult and the village is vigorously policed.

The skiing
Top 3470m (11,381ft) bottom 1370m (4,494ft)
The main **mountain access** is by cable car from the edge of the village up to Plan Checrouit at 1706m and skiers have to return the same way in the afternoon. It is possible to store skis and boots at the top. The

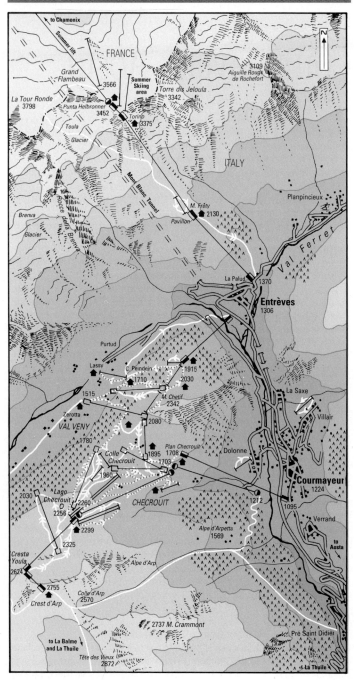

alternatives are a short drive or bus-ride, either across the valley to Dolonne for the old two-seater gondola to Plan Checrouit, or to the Val Veny cable car, near the village of Entreves. The east-facing Checrouit bowl offers a large number of quite short intermediate runs, served by a variety of lifts including a six-seater gondola. The pistes are often crowded, especially near the bottom where they meet. There are surprisingly steep, narrow passages even on some of the blue (easy) runs.

The wooded north-facing Val Veny side of the mountain is linked in a couple of places with the Checrouit bowl. It has longer and more varied pistes with two reds (intermediate) and a black (difficult) following the fall-line through the trees, while a gentle green (beginner) run meanders circuitously down. The pistes served by the Gabba chair, at the top of the ski area and to the west of Lago Checrouit, are reported to keep their snow well and the off-piste run underneath them is testing.

The very inefficient Youla cable car above Lago Checrouit opens up a deep and sheltered bowl, which holds the snow well. It serves a single, uncomplicated red run with plenty of space for short off-piste excursions. It is also possible to ski with a guide off the back of Youla, a long itinerary run down into Val Veny. But the serious off-piste begins at the top of the further short cable car to Cresta d'Arp. The main route of 1500m vertical is down a beautiful and secluded valley, a long and interesting run with some steep and difficult tree-line skiing on the lower stages before finally emerging near the bottom station of the Dolonne gondola or on the river bank near Pré-St-Didier. There is also an interesting run from the top, which takes you southwards through the Vallon de Youlaz to La Balme near La Thuile. There are no pistes from Arp.

The three-stage Mont Blanc cable car begins at La Pallud near the village of Entrèves on the tunnel side of Courmayeur and climbs over 2000m to Punta Helbronner, giving easy access to the Valleé Blanche (see *Chamonix*) without the dreaded ice steps. There is an afternoon bus back from Chamonix. The off-piste run down the Italian side of the massif is steep at the top and involves a clamber along a fixed rope and the hair-raising negotiation of a long, exposed and awkward staircase. But the bottom stage of the cable car from Pavillon has a long, uncomplicated red piste, which is rarely skied.

Queuing both for Plan Checrouit and for Mont Blanc is much worse at weekends when the crowds arrive from Turin. Quad chairs at La Gabba and Zerotta have eased some of the other bottlenecks on the mountain; the Youla cable car can still be a problem. There is a large artificial snow installation covering several pistes down to Plan Checrouit and, over the mountain, down to Val Veny. Both have justified the hefty investment involved for long periods during recent seasons.

Together with the mountain guides, the ski school runs off-piste programmes (including Vallée Blanche outings) and heli-skiing. Courmayeur is a famous mountaineering centre and the scope for ski-touring is vast. The main cross-country trails involve a bus ride, but are excellent.

Mountain restaurants

Eating on the mountain is one of the greatest pleasures of Italy and of Courmayeur in particular. One reporter comments: 'Long before midday delicious smells waft from mountain huts and lure you inside. In bad weather it is easy to persuade oneself to stay all afternoon.' Restaurants are numerous, with a lot of welcoming chalets and converted cowsheds dotted around. Plan Checrouit has simple accommodation and ski shops as well as a number of bars and restaurants. The Château Branlant serves full meals with waiter-service and 'heavenly desserts', the Christiana (downstairs) and La Baita are also recommended. La Grolla at Peindeint on the Val Veny side is outstanding ('expensive, but worth it and difficult to find, thank goodness'). Other recommendations are the Petit Mont Blanc at Zerotta for home-made pasta, 2000 at the altiport for sun-worshippers. The Vieux Grenier is reported to have excellent pasta. On the Mont Blanc side there are bars at each lift stage. The Rifugio Pavillon, at the top of the first stage of the cable car, is reportedly excellent and has a sun-terrace. Rifugio Torino, at the next stage, is also said to be good.

Beginners and children
The nursery slopes are not particularly satisfactory. Those at Plan Checrouit are cramped by buildings; and milling skiers descending from the main pistes are a hazard which novices could well do without. The baby slopes at the top of Val Veny and Dolonne are quieter. We have mixed reports of the Monte Bianco ski school. One reporter was 'amused but mildly disturbed' that his instructor should crash into a tree within minutes of introducing himself. Spoken English among instructors does not appear to be a strong point. Most correspondents agree, however, that private instructors and guides are excellent value. The Kinderheim at Plan Checrouit looks after children from 6 months old.

The resort
Courmayeur is a long, strung-out village and the built-up area has now almost engulfed the neighbouring hamlets of Verrand, Villair and La Saxe, all of them quiet and prosperous second-home areas with some beautiful rough-stone buildings. The heart of the old village is a delightful maze of cobbled alleys partly reserved for pedestrians, full of attractive shops flanked by lively bars, cafés, smart restaurants and fast-food outlets. The main resort bus service, serving cable cars and the cross-country area, runs about every 15 minutes. There are less frequent buses to Dolonne, where the gondola for Plan Checrouit starts; this is a convenient base for skiers, but not for those who want to easily enjoy the considerable nightlife which Courmayeur has to offer.

Accommodation
Much of the great variety of hotel, apartment and chalet accommodation is not well situated for the main cable car. Several reporters stress the undesirability of hotels located on the main road (not to be confused with the main street through the village). The Pavillon is well-situated opposite the cable car; it is comfortable and expensive, with a good swimming-pool and sauna. Hotel Courmayeur is 'friendly, with a roaring log fire in the sitting area'. The two-star Berthod has been partly refurbished and is good value-for-money. The Bouton d'Or is located

just off the main square. The Cristallo is attractive and comfortable, the Edelweiss is friendly, cosy and less expensive.

Other recommendations include the Royal ('smart and expensive') and the Roma ('simple and cheap'). The Télécabine in Dolonne, run by UK operator Mark Warner, has its own crèche and is endorsed by a number of reporters. Bladon Lines operates the Fiocco di Neve chalet-hotel. There is also ample hotel accommodation near the Mont Blanc lifts: the Hotel des Alpes at La Palud and the Aiguille Noire are both

Skiing facts: Courmayeur

TOURIST OFFICE
Piazzale Monte Bianco, I-11013,
Val d'Aosta
Tel 39 165 842042
Fax 39 165 842072

THE RESORT
By road Calais 921km
By rail Pré-St-Didier 5km, regular buses from station
By air Geneva 2 hrs
Visitor beds 20,623 (87% apartments and chalets, 13% hotels)
Transport ski-bus, not included in lift pass

THE SKIING
Longest run Internazionale, 4.5km (red)
Number of lifts 32
Number of trails/pistes 30 (20% beginner, 30% easy, 47% intermediate, 3% difficult)
Total of trails/pistes 100km
Nursery slopes 1 at Dolonne
Summer skiing 2 lifts on the Plateau Colle del Gigante (850m slope) and 1 lift at Colle del Flambeau (800m slope)
Snowmaking 15km covered

LIFT PASSES
Area pass Courmayeur Mont Blanc Funivie (6-day pass covers 1 day in Chamonix and 1 day in Pila), L170,000-200,000
Day pass L40,000
Half-day pass L28,000 after 12.30pm
Beginners Chiecco, Prato and Tzaly lifts are free, points tickets
Children 50% reduction for 1.3m tall and under, free for children under 1m
Pensioners no reduction
Credit cards accepted yes

SKI SCHOOLS
Adults Scuola di Sci Monte Bianco,
L48,000 per day, L160,000 for 6 half-days
Children Scuola di Sci Monte Bianco, 9am-4pm, L340,000 for 6 days including lunch
Private lessons L43,000 per hr
Special courses off-piste, snow-shoeing, ski-touring, ski- mountaineering
Guiding companies Società delle Guide di Courmayeur

CROSS-COUNTRY
Ski schools Monte Bianco
Loipe location and size 35km in Val Ferret

CHILDCARE
Non-ski kindergarten Kinderheim, 6 mths and over, 9am-4pm, L225,000 for 6 days including lunch
Ski kindergarten Kinderheim, 6 mths and over, 9am-4pm, L340,000 for 6 days including lunch and lessons
Babysitting list available from tourist office

OTHER SPORTS
Heli-skiing, parapente, skating, ski jumping, hang-gliding, indoor tennis, fitness centre, dog-sledding, climbing wall, swimming (at Pré-St-Didier)

FOOD AND DRINK PRICES
Coffee L1,200, bottle of house wine from L10,000, beer L5,000, dish of the day L10,000

TOUR OPERATORS
Activity Travel, Bladon Lines, Crystal, Enterprise, Inghams, Interski, Mark Warner, Sally Holidays, Ski Norwest, Ski Thomson, Ski Weekend, Ski West, Ultimate Holidays

praised. Self-caterers are advised to shop at the Desparu supermarket on the Via Regionale directly above the cable car station.

Eating out

Restaurants are plentiful and lively. The Turistica in Via Donzelli is a favourite with reporters ('excellent pasta, huge helpings, very good value'). The Coquelicot is recommended for grills. Le Bistroquet offers 'wonderfully prepared regional dishes'. La Palud is known for its fresh fish and the Pierre Alexis is said by one reporter to be 'the best in town in terms of quality, service and value'. Courmayeur also has plenty of pizzerias. La Maison de Filippo at Entrèves is an institution and dinner here must be experienced once (usually, once is enough) as an exercise in unparalleled gluttony; it offers a fixed-price menu of 36 dishes, served 6 at a time.

Après-ski

This is centred on the lively bars in and around the Via Roma. The Bar Roma with its comfortable sofas and armchairs fills up early. Steve's American Bar and Ziggi's are equally busy and popular. The Abat-Jour Isba Club and Le Clochard are the best discos along with the Tiger Club in Entreves. The swimming-pool at Pré-St-Didier is five kilometres away and is open from 3.30 to 8pm. The ice-rink is open every evening until midnight, with disco music and lights.

For non-skiers there are plenty of interesting excursions. Aosta is recommended for sightseeing and cheap shopping. In fine weather the cable car ride to Punta Helbronner is spectacular and many mountain restaurants are accessible to non-skiers.

Livigno, Valtellina

ALTITUDE 1820m (5,970ft)

∙∙∙

Good points easy runs, extensive nursery slopes, resort-level snow, late-season holidays, sunny slopes, duty-free shopping
Bad points long airport transfer, few tough runs, difficult road access, traffic, limited for non-skiers, lack of special children's facilities
Linked or nearby resorts Bormio (n), St Moritz (n) – *see separate chapters*, Valdisotto (n), Valdidentro (n), Santa Caterina (n)

Livigno is one of the most remote ski resorts in Europe. Easiest access from mother Italy is a one-hour drive over the 2290m pass from Bormio. The five-and-a-half hour transfer from Milan, or similar from Zurich, is enough to put many skiers off, but it is worth the journey, if only for the much-vaunted duty-free shopping.

The high and wide slopes along both sides of the valley above the resort provide a lot of uncomplicated intermediate skiing. The season here is a long one, with almost guaranteed resort-level snow throughout. On a fine day 'Piccolo Tibet', as Livigno is known locally, is extremely welcoming. However, when the weather closes in, few resorts are as bleak. The ski areas are separate, although they are linked by a fast and efficient bus service for those who do not want to walk. The lift system has undergone some improvement in recent years, although it still has considerable shortcomings. What is basically an old and attractive village is, as an estate agent might euphemistically say, in need of care and attention. Its growing popularity as a resort in the British market is because it does give, duty-free shopping apart, astoundingly good value for money.

Thanks to the road tunnel from Switzerland it is possible to reach Livigno from Zurich, thus avoiding the risk of being fog-bound at Milan. A number of our reporters chose to drive 'an easy 11 hours from Ostend', and said that having a car was an advantage for visiting Bormio and Santa Caterina. Both are covered on the area lift pass.

The skiing
Top 2797m (9,174ft) bottom 1816m (5,956ft)
The lower slopes on the south-east-facing slope of the valley are given over to a huge nursery area of 10 drag-lifts and a chair. Above it the slopes of Lago Salin and Carosello provide longer and more challenging runs. The north- and west-facing slopes of Il Mottolino and Monte della Neve above the winding road to Bormio offer a similar amount of skiing. The majority of the skiing is above the tree-line and when the weather closes in, both sides of the valley are inhospitable places in which to find yourself, particularly as the local lift map bears no close

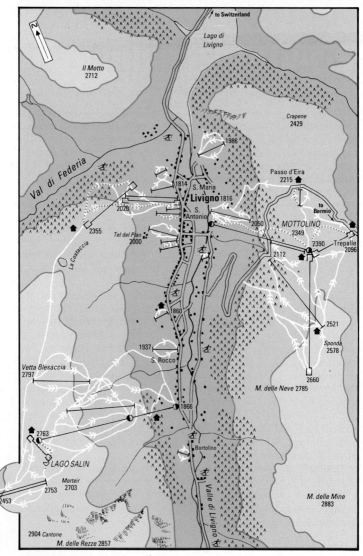

relation to the actual installations on the mountain.

Mountain access is by the two-stage Carosello 3000 gondola from the southern end of town, which takes you up over a wide, open, south-east facing mountainside to 2797m. All the runs back down are graded red (intermediate), but none is severe, at least not until the final descent through the trees to the base. Poor snow cover and somewhat inadequate marking can make these pitches more difficult. Behind the top station is a quiet area of short runs beside the Federia drag-lifts, where the snow is usually at its best. A long, gentle blue (easy) run takes you the whole way along the mountain ridge to link up with the Costaccia chair-lift above the northern end of the resort. This serves a small area of fairly short wooded runs which are covered by snow-cannon.

The Mottolino ski area is accessed by a 12-person gondola which has replaced the old drag-lift and greatly reduced queuing at the only real bottleneck in the entire resort. Other access points along the Bormio road serve a spectrum of intermediate runs complicated only by poor signposting and by the road itself, which cuts awkwardly through the ski area. The wide slope above Trepalle faces east, and the red run beneath the chair-lift can represent a quite serious challenge in certain conditions, particularly at the end of the day when it is icy. A long, satisfying blue takes you from Monte della Neve via Monte Sponda and Mottolino all the way down to the bottom of the gondola. The off-piste opportunities off the Monte della Neve are numerous, but most of the longer itineraries require a bus or a taxi ride back to the resort.

Mountain restaurants

The Costaccia with its outside barbecue area is good, but expensive. Both Mottolino and Carosello are said to offer sound value for money. Ristoro Tea Borch, situated between the bottom and the half-way station of the Carosello 3000 cable car, is an old farmhouse with a lot of character. Tea del Vidal at Mottolino and Tea del Plan (Costaccia) are as popular as ever. The Gatto Nero at Trepalle is highly recommended.

Beginners and children

Livigno has five ski schools. We have mixed reports of the Scuola Italiana Sci Livigno. One reporter described tuition as excellent: 'The instructor spoke perfect English and gave me the best introduction to skiing you could possibly want.' Another complained that his class was 14 in number and the teacher believed in the 'follow-my-leader' technique of learning 'with the occasional monosyllabic word of advice which was only addressed to the women in the class'. Lessons are for a choice of two-hour periods.

The large number of nursery slopes and easy intermediate skiing make Livigno a recommended resort for families, provided the parents ski with the children: the dispersed nature of the skiing makes meeting up quite difficult.

The resort

The three communities of Santa Maria, San Antonio and San Rocco together market themselves as the duty-free ski resort of Livigno. The result is a strung-out series of villages spread out along the floor of this remote valley: an unbroken five-kilometre straggle of hotels, bars, garages, duty-free shops and supermarkets. These commercial enterprises are irregularly interspersed with old barns, working farms and the occasional fine chalet, but there is no real heart to the resort. The lack of alpine charm is disappointing and what is a superb mountain setting has been spoilt by overdevelopment and a general lack of attention to appearance.

Part of the centre is now pedestrianised, but elsewhere traffic remains a hazard. The free ski-buses receive much praise from reporters for their regularity: 'We never waited more than ten minutes for a bus and although some were very full, journeys are tolerable and short.' However, once the ski-buses stop after 6pm, the evening service seems less reliable. There are regular buses to Bormio and to St Moritz. Livigno's *raison d'être* is shopping, with prices for spirits and tobacco reportedly half those on the cross-channel ferry: 'Only £3 for a litre of gin', enthuses one happy shopper. Another points out that it pays to look around carefully as prices vary dramatically. Duty-free status does not appear to have a beneficial effect on bar prices.

Skiing facts: Livigno

TOURIST OFFICE
Via dalla Gesa 65, 23030 Livigno, Sondrio
Tel 39 342 996 379
Fax 39 342 996 881

THE RESORT
By road Calais 1107km
By rail Tirano 3 hrs
By air Bergamo 4 hrs, Milan or Zurich 5½ hrs
Visitor beds 7,896 (55% hotels, 45% apartments)
Transport free ski-bus

THE SKIING
Longest run Federia to Costaccia, 5km (red/blue)
Number of lifts 29
Number of trails/pistes 40 (44% easy, 45% intermediate, 11% difficult)
Total of trails/pistes 85km
Nursery slopes 12
Summer skiing at Stelvio Pass
Snowmaking 4km covered

LIFT PASSES
Area pass (covers Livigno, Bormio, Santa Caterina, Valdidentro, and Valdisotto) L165,000-185,000 for 6 days
Day pass (Livigno only) L34,000-38,000
Half-day pass L25,000
Beginners no free lifts
Children 5-12 yrs, L120,000-135,000 for 6-day area pass
Pensioners 65 yrs and over as children
Credit cards accepted no

SKI SCHOOLS
Adults 5 ski schools: Scuola Italiana

Sci Livigno-Estate, L77,000-87,000 for 6 days (2 hrs per day); Scuola Italiana Estiva Galli Sport, Scuola Italiana Sci Interalpen, Scuola Italiana Sci Livigno Italy, Scuola Italiana Sci Livigno Società Coop, all 9-11am, 11am-1pm or 2-4pm, prices on application
Children Scuola Italiana Sci Livigno-Estate, 5 yrs and over, L72,000-82,000 for 6 days (2 hrs per day)
Private lessons all ski schools, L32,000-51,000 per hr depending on level and season
Special courses monoskiing, snowboarding, telemark, slalom classes, heli-skiing, off-piste skiing
Guiding companies individual guides available through tourist office

CROSS-COUNTRY
Ski schools Scuola Italiana Sci Fondo Livigno
Loipe location and size 40km in valley

CHILDCARE
Non-ski kindergarten none
Ski kindergarten none
Babysitting not available

OTHER SPORTS
Skating, ice-driving, sleigh rides, parapente, snow-mobiling

FOOD AND DRINK PRICES
Coffee L2,000, bottle of house wine L9,000, beer L4,200, dish of the day L10,000

TOUR OPERATORS
Crystal, Enterprise, Inghams, Neilson, Ski Airtours, Ski Falcon, Ski Thomson

Accommodation

Most hotels and apartments are strung along the resort's single axis from Santa Maria to San Rocco. The two-star Hotel Astoria is recommended both for its four-course dinners and its position in San Rocco near the Carosello 3000 gondola. Hotel Sankt Anton, at the other end of town and well positioned for the Costaccia skiing, is described as 'clean and simple'. Camana Veglia is 'small, convenient, family-run, with bags of character'. A regular visitor continues to praise the family-run Silvestri. The Golf Hotel Parc and the Intermonti are the two luxury category hotels and there is a wide choice of three-stars. Much of the tour operator accommodation is in apartments.

Eating out

There is an excellent choice of restaurants ranging from those serving pizzas and pasta to local dishes such as venison and *bresaola*. The Bellavista is strongly recommended for its 'fabulous' pizza. The Vecchia Lanterna and Mario's Pub are both popular. The Pesce d'Oro is a good fish restaurant, unusual in a resort so remote from the sea. Foxi's is praised for its 'great burgers and low prices'. Other recommended eating places are the Ambassador, New Snack and the Ski Grill.

Après-ski

Livigno's after-skiing activity is mainly bar-orientated and lively, but not riotous. There are half-a-dozen discos, but most of these are inconveniently situated on the outskirts of the town. The action begins at the Bar Scuola Sci, headquarters of the main ski school. The British tend to gather at Galli's bar in San Rocco. Other popular nightspots include Foxi's in San Antonio, and Il Ceilo, which attracts a wealthy Italian set. Marco's Video Bar and the Underground Bar are both popular, though too noisy for some reporters' tastes.

The Milky Way

Montgenèvre, Hautes Alpes
ALTITUDE 1850m (6,068ft)

Good points large ski area, resort-level snow, easy runs, skiing convenience, attractive old village centre, extensive tree-level skiing, varied off-piste skiing

Bad points lack of activities for non-skiers, limited après-ski, unreliable late-season snow, limited local skiing, lack of mountain restaurants, lack of tough runs, traffic

Linked or nearby resorts Bardonecchia (n), Borgata (l), Clavière (l), Cesana Torinese (l), Grangesises (l), Jouvenceaux (l), Sansicario (l), Sauze d'Oulx (l), Sestriere (l), Sportinia (l)

Sauze d'Oulx, Piedmont
ALTITUDE 1500m (4,920ft)

Good points large ski area, extensive tree-level skiing, choice of mountain restaurants, sunny slopes, short airport transfer, relatively low prices, varied off-piste skiing, young and lively après-ski

Bad points lack of activities for non-skiers, poor skiing convenience, unreliable resort-level snow, lift queues, unreliable for late-season holidays, limited tough runs, lack of alpine charm, not ideal for families

Sestriere, Piedmont
ALTITUDE 2035m (6,675ft)

Good points reliable snow cover, large ski area, best Milky Way skiing, tough runs, varied off-piste, luxury accommodation

Bad points lack of alpine charm, exposed and windy location

Montgenèvre lies beside a busy main road on a mountain pass a few hundred metres into France from the frontier with Italy. First impression is of a rather untidy and higgledy-piggledy collection of bars, restaurants, shops and hotels, but hidden away from the noisy arterial international thoroughfare is the nucleus of an attractive traditional village which has been developed for tourism in a pleasant enough manner.

The skiing is mainly north-facing and starts at a high altitude; consequently it often has the best snow conditions of the region. It is, however, worth bearing in mind that 1850m this far south in the alpine range does not necessarily mean the same snow cover as you would find in the Mont Blanc massif. Nevertheless, in times of poor snow elsewhere in the region, the resort fills up with skiers from the large Italian resorts of Sauze d'Oulx and Bardonecchia. Montgenèvre is also a popular weekend spot for residents of both Briançon and Turin. Apartments and hotels are reasonably priced by ski resort standards. The skiing and the nursery slopes are conveniently located and were it not for the busy main road which dissects it Montgenèvre could be termed an ideal family resort.

Montgenèvre's own skiing is limited and easy, but it has links with other resorts, providing a large and reasonably varied area known as the Milky Way (Voie Lactée/Via Lattea). This long string of linked resorts is mainly in Italy and is bounded by Montgenèvre at one end and by Sauze d'Oulx at the other. In between lie the villages of Sestriere, Clavière, Cesana Torinese and Sansicario as well as a handful of small hamlets, which are little more than ski lift access points. The area is extremely spread out. It takes a long time to work one's way from one sector of the circuit to another and therefore a car is useful.

Sauze d'Oulx (pronounced Sow-zy Doo) was for years one of the leading alpine resorts for a young British clientele looking for a good time, with some skiing thrown in. It justified its nickname of Benidorm-on-ice by offering budget hotel accommodation coupled with cheap and cheerful après-ski. The inescapable consequences of this were the occasional much-publicised run-ins with the *carabinieri*, which in one celebrated case led to a whole planeload of lager-louts being deported back to Britain. The skiing, for those who made it to the slopes in the morning after the night before, is gentle, but interesting with miles of motorway for cruising intermediates. But it seems that the winds of change are blowing through Piedmont and, as in Benidorm, the yobbo element has moved on to fresh grazing elsewhere.

Recent reporters have been pleasantly surprised to find the resort as a whole far from boisterous, with more of an Italian feel to it than in its recent, troubled past. While British influence is still prevalent, with many of the locals speaking English and some ski shops pricing equipment in sterling, a majority of visitors are Italian. Sauze's fall in international popularity may well be attributed to the sequence of very poor snowfalls it suffered in the mid-1980s which, if that is the reason, acted as a kind of natural cleansing. That meterological hiccup now appears to be over and Sauze d'Oulx, seemingly mindful of its past errors, is trying to win back tourists from abroad.

The resort itself is still not particularly appealing, with a local lift system that appears to have barely altered since the 1960s – tedious, ancient chair-lifts, some of them singles, where in comparable resorts you would expect to find a fast modern gondola. The old village is attractive enough with a fine seventeenth-century church, but the walks around town are steep and icy and the centre is a hotchpotch of mainly ugly modern buildings. The more upmarket apartment blocks are set in the trees on the mountainside.

Sestriere was Europe's original purpose-built ski resort, a joint operation between Mussolini and Agnelli (of Fiat fame). After years of negligence, it has now torn down its rusty cable cars and invested heavily in snow-cannon and new lifts. This, together with its high altitude of around 2000m, makes Sestriere one of the more snow-sure resorts at this end of the Alps. Although it has the reputation of attracting rich Italians from Turin it does not wear its mantle of affluence with any great show of style, a collection of unappealing modern edifices spread

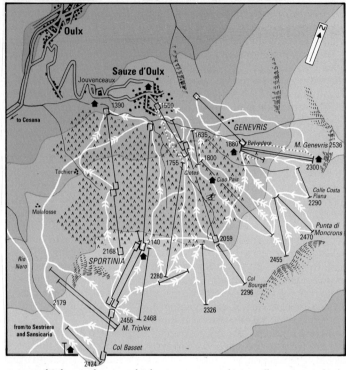

across a high, windy pass which generates a rather soulless atmosphere.

The more shrewd Italians have now swapped Sestriere for nearby Sansicario, a smaller, more sophisticated and modern development with its own ski area, linked to Sestriere and Sauze on the one side and Cesana Torinese on the other.

The skiing
Top 2820m (9,250ft) bottom 1350m (4,428ft)

Montgenèvre's slopes are on both sides of the pass. The south-facing side, Chalvet, is slightly higher with runs up to 2600m, and is usually less crowded than the north-facing slopes, which create the main link with the Italian Milky Way resorts. This area is, however, expanding and in future may well become the more interesting of the two halves. It also provides an easy link with Clavière and a side entrance into the heart of the Milky Way from the top of the Chalvet gondola.

The gondola is a few minutes' walk from the centre and takes you up to an area of treeless, mainly easy runs served by two chairs and three drag-lifts. There are some more difficult runs and also off-piste skiing down to Montgenèvre from the Bélier drag. A choice of red (intermediate) and blue (easy) runs take you back down to the bottom. The blue run beside the drag-lift to the Col de l'Alpet (2430m) is gentle, but the lift gives access to Montgenèvre's interesting additional and developing ski area. The north-east-facing slope behind the col has a chair-lift with

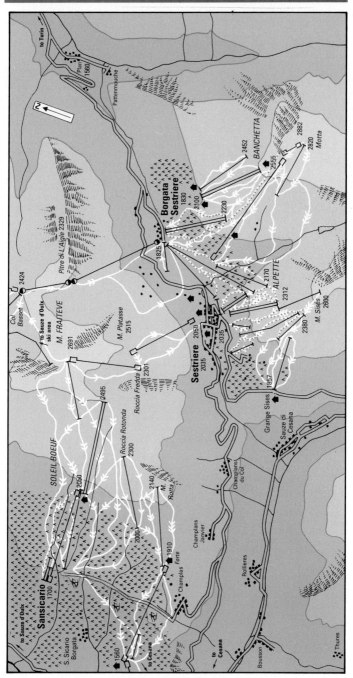

to Turin

Plan 1560

Pattenmouche

N

2452

BANCHETTA

2882
Motta

2820

2555

Borgata
Sestriere

1830

2100

2230

Ptre di L'Aigle 2329

1825

2424

2170

ALPETTE

2312

Col
Basset

to Sauze d'Oulx ski area

M. FRAITEVE

2691

M. Platasse
2515

2050

2035

2035

2380

M. Sises
2600

Sestriere

Roccia Fredda 2301

1857

Grange Sises

2495

Sauze di
Cesana

Roccia Rotonda
2300

SOLEIL BOEUF

2050

2140

M.
Rotta

Champlans
du Col

2000

1910

Champlas
Forte

Champlas
Janvier

Sansicario
1700

to Sauze d'Oulx

S. Sicario
Borgata

1560

to Cesana

Rollieres

Bousson

Thures

to
Cesana

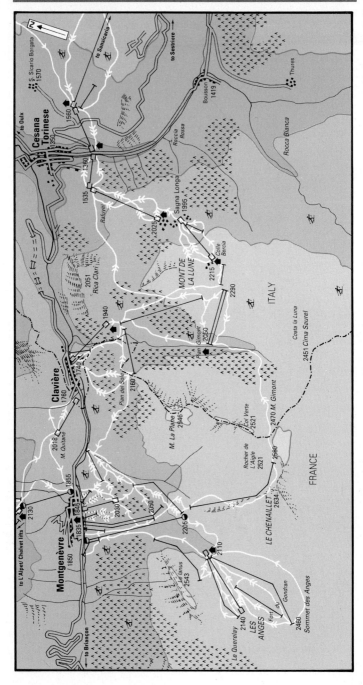

black and red runs beside it and a long, easy run round to Clavière. Future lifts up to 3000m will open up much more challenging skiing.

On the other side of the pass, **mountain access** is on a gondola from the Briançon end of the village as well as by drag-lifts from the centre. These serve easy runs through woods opening into wide nursery slopes above the road. From the top of the gondola there is a choice of three small ski areas. The wide, sheltered bowl of Le Querelay/Les Anges has ruined fortress buildings around the crest and some red and black runs beneath them, but no challenging skiing overall. The Brousset drag-lift serves some difficult skiing in the woods. The long dog-leg drag-lift goes through magnificent rocky scenery to Rocher de l'Aigle, which has a red run beside it and is awkwardly narrow in places, but which is used mainly for access to Clavière.

The Milky Way link from Montgenèvre starts with a poorly signed traverse around the mountain, which is easy to miss in bad light. Otherwise it is not difficult and leads to a long run (beginning red, later blue) past the Gimont drag-lifts and down to Clavière. The more prominent run down from Rocher de l'Aigle is a good off-piste bowl which leads, via some scrub, to the Brousset drag.

The north-facing slopes of Monti della Luna, above Clavière and Cesana Torinese, offer some of the best skiing in the Milky Way: vast and challenging trails through the woods and some good off-piste. The runs to La Comba become steeper as they descend; the section below the bottom chair-lift is never easy and is often too bare to be skied, making a lift ride necessary down to La Comba, beside Cesana. The steep slopes opposite, where a progression of lifts stretches along the Sestriere road on the way up to Sansicario and Monte Fraiteve, are not often skied, for the same reason.

Monte Fraiteve is an exposed crest with impressive views of the French mountains, where the ski areas of Sauze d'Oulx, Sestriere and Sansicario all meet. It is also the start of the famous Rio Nero off-piste run, a long descent, which follows a river gully down to the Oulx-Cesana road, 1600m below. An infrequent bus service takes you back to the lifts at Cesana.

Reporters are unanimous in their opinion that the best skiing in the Milky Way is above Sestriere. The bulk of the skiing around Sestriere is on mainly north- and west-facing slopes on two mountains, Sises and Banchetta, separated by a deep valley. Sises has short, steep runs to below Alpette. The top drag-lift can sometimes offer good off-piste skiing on the shaded side of the peak, but the gorge between the two ski areas looks uninviting. There are intermediate runs down to Grangesises and the Hotel Principi. Banchetta is the intermediate skier's mountain, with longer and more varied runs down to the roadside mini-resort of Borgata. The steep Motta drag-lift and chair serve the highest and toughest of Sestriere's skiing and reach the highest point of the Milky Way at 2823m. Here the slopes beside the drag can be up to 30°, often mogulled. You do not have to tackle these to reach the wide west-facing red itinerary into the dividing valley and on through the woods. Below Banchetta are red and blue runs and some good off-piste above the sunny Anfiteatro area. The north-facing slopes above Borgata are steep and wooded, but the drag-lifts beside the road go up to Sestriere with very easy runs down again, which are ideal for beginners.

The easiest way to Sauze is via the Col Basset gondola from Borgata, but you can also start from Sestriere itself, where chair-lifts go up to Fraiteve with easy south-facing slopes on the Sestriere side, and runs from the top down to Sansicario and Sauze. The open slopes above Sansicario are fairly steep at the top, and the run all the way down to Sansicario, starting off black or red, is a challenging and satisfying descent. Most of the rest of the west-facing skiing is wide, intermediate to easy woodland trails.

The Sauze d'Oulx slopes face west and north, and the majority of them are below the tree-line. The lifts are no longer separately owned – one company now runs all the Sauze and Sestriere lifts, but they are not particularly well placed and the ski area is disjointed by gullies. At the centre of the skiing is Sportinia, a sunny woodland clearing with a few hotels, a small busy nursery area and a variety of restaurants. Above it there is some wide, open intermediate skiing served by several drags, one of which giving access to Col Basset and the run down to Sestriere. The other goes up a shaded mogul slope to the shoulder of Monte Fraiteve. Below Sportinia there are wide runs back through the woods graded red and black, quite steep in places although never really demanding. There are also blue and black runs down to Jouvenceaux.

The Genevris lift system, at one extremity of the Milky Way, starts with a chair-lift from a car-park a long way from most hotels and is alter- natively approached via Clotes. The drag-lifts serve gentle runs below Monte Genevris from the Belvedere mid-station, with Sauze's most dif- ficult pistes below Punta di Moncrons. The run down to Sestriere from Col Basset goes down a valley, which offers some excellent off-piste descents in the right conditions, but a boring road to the mid-station of the return six-seater gondola when they are not.

Queues in Montgenèvre are bad only at weekends and when snow in nearby resorts is poor. The main queue problems at the Italian end of the Milky Way are on the Sauze side of the mountain, which a reporter who was there during an Italian bank holiday describes as 'horrendous'. The lifts in Sestriere are described as much more modern than the ones in Sauze. The local piste map is criticised as being 'very poor with no piste numbers on the map corresponding to the piste-marker boards'.

At Montgenèvre there is artificial snow on several of the lower slopes. Sestriere has a big artificial snow installation, covering many of its north-west-facing runs, from 2500m down to Borgata at 1840m. Sauze has snow-cannon on the runs from the top of Pian Della Rocca (piste no 29) down to Clotes and the village centre. Sansicario has them on two pistes from the mid-station of Soleil Boeuf to the village.

Montgenèvre is better than other resorts in the Milky Way for cross- country skiing, with some easy trails beside the road to Clavière and more difficult runs in the woods on the Briançon side of the resort.

Mountain restaurants

Montgenèvre is seriously short of mountain restaurants with just the Altitude 2000 and Gondrands. The excellent and inexpensive bars and restaurants above Clavière (particularly La Coche) help make up for this shortfall. There are a couple of good restaurants above Borgata for the Sestriere section, but Sauze has more choice, although reporters complain of high prices. Monte Triplex at Sportinia is recommended. The Ciao Pais, tucked away below Moncrons, is said to offer better value and quality. Capanna Kind is also popular.

Beginners and children

Most recent reports speak well of Montgenèvre's ski school ('friendly, helpful, good English') for all grades of skier and for private lessons. The main nursery slope for Sauze is at Sportinia, open and very sunny, but very crowded. There are also nursery slopes at Belvedere on the Genevris side, and in the village when there is snow. We have enthusiastic reports on the standard of instruction in the Sauze Ski School, known as the 'green' ski school, which also uses video analysis: 'Plenty of English-speaking instructors and even a few English instructors; it was excellent value for money, well organised and the teachers seemed to make the most of the lesson time.' The wide Col de Sestriere provides excellent nursery slopes and very easy runs between the resort and Borgata.

In the Italian Milky Way resorts the lift pass is free to children eight years old and younger if skiing with an adult.

The resorts

Montgenèvre is spread along the north side of the busy main road across the high col, now also the main street, with a customs hut at the Italian end of it. On the south side of the pass are open fields, with a row of lifts and a wide area of nursery slopes. Montgenèvre is itself more windswept than its ski areas, which are relatively sheltered. There are three supermarkets but shopping facilities are limited; there is a weekly market which is said to be fun although not cheap.

Sauze stands on the sunny, west-facing flank of a wide valley junction. It is built on a steep slope and is also large and spread out, with everywhere seemingly a long, steep walk from everywhere else including the three lift stations. A crowded and unreliable ski-bus covered by the lift pass circles the village and its lift stations until early evening. Daytime traffic restrictions have done much to ease street congestion.

Sestriere is a bleak and often windswept place, spread around the wide col with a scattering of trees at the bottom of the mountain flanks. The landmarks are the tall, round towers of the old Duchi d'Aosta hotel, now occupied by Club Med, and the Gothic turrets of the recently restored Principi de Piemonte hotel. This is some way from the resort centre, but its has its own lift access to the Sises ski area. Buses run to and from Borgata, Grangsises and the end of the Rio Nero run (on the Oulx-Cesana road). Reporters complain that the resort is bad for changing money ('hotels wouldn't do it and the two banks had very short opening hours') and that the piste map is very hard to obtain.

Accommodation

Montgenèvre's accommodation is mostly in apartments scattered along the road, in the old village and on the lower south-facing slopes;

there are also a few catered tour operator chalets. Access to the skiing is easy from most places, but the Italian end of the village is more convenient. A large new resort development is planned here, along with a new access lift for the south-facing side of the ski area. The pick of Montgenèvre's half-a-dozen less than luxurious hotels are the Napoléon, convenient but basic, and the more attractively Valérie, near the church. Others include the Chalvet and simple La Grange.

Accommodation in **Sauze** is mostly in cheap hotels, which reporters generally find adequate. The best location is around the bottom of Clotes. The hotels in this area are the Hermitage, Stella Alpina and the Sauze. The Sauze is about 100m from the Clotes lift and is described as 'very clean and spacious'. The Gran Baita, next to the church, is recommended as 'excellent – very clean, the staff are pleasant and the hotel is five minutes' walk from everything'. San Giorgio is far from luxurious and badly placed, but friendly and inexpensive. The Chaberton is a simple bed and breakfast place and the Savoia overlooks the Clotes piste and is close to the lifts. The Palace is the biggest and the most expensive hotel, but not particularly stylish. Il Capricorno at Clotes is expensive and attractive. You can be first on the nursery slopes by staying at the Monte Triplex or the Capanna at Sportinia. The Ciao Pais above Clotes also offers cheap and simple accommodation.

Sestriere's accommodation is in hotels, apartments in large new complexes and Club Med. Apart from the Principi, the most luxurious hotel is the modern low-rise Sestriere. The Savoy Edelweiss is simple and central. The Grand Hotel is in the resort centre and five minutes' walk from the lifts. The Miramonti is not very well situated, but friendly, attractive and good value. The recently renovated Biancaneve is just outside town with its own mini-bus service to the slopes.

Eating out

In **Montgenèvre** there are more than a dozen eating places including La Ca Del Sol for pizzas, Les Chalmettes, Le Pichounet, L'Estable, Pizzeria La Tourmente, the smart Le Jamy and Chez Pierrot for pizzas and grills.

In **Sauze**, Kaly's pizzeria is recommended, Osteria da Gigi is an atmospheric wine cellar with live music, Del Borgo serves pizzas, La Griglia pizzeria is good value and Albertino specialises in pasta. Bar Clotes is a snack bar and La Pettegola is a brasserie. On a more expensive level there is the Old Inn and Il Cantun.

Restaurants in **Sestriere** range from pizzerias to smart international restaurants. The Last Tango is for grills and the Fraiteve in the Grand Hotel specialises in local Piedmont cuisine.

Après-ski

Après-ski activity in **Montgenèvre** is extremely limited, but there is a good choice of inexpensive bar-restaurants in which to make merry and three of them have disco-nightclubs attached. The Ca del Sol is a popular bar in the centre and La Graal revolves around satellite television. Stevy Nicks and Play Boy are the two most popular discos. There is little for non-skiers to do, although the skating rink is a good one.

Après-ski in **Sauze** is certainly not what it was. It is still lively with the emphasis on fun, but no longer offensively rowdy. There are plenty of organised activities – torchlight descents, tobogganing and Miss Sauze competitions as well as lively bars and discos. Favourite British haunts are the Derby hotel bar and neighbouring Moncrons cocktail bar; other recommendations include the Cotton Club, the Schuss and the New Life discos. The Andy Capp bar, once the most notorious haunt of British lager-louts, is still the 'in' place after skiing. Walking around Sauze is no great pleasure and there are few non-skiing facilities. The shopping centre in the new part of Sauze contains a range of boutiques and stores including several sports shops.

Sestriere's après-ski is fairly lively and stylish when the Italians are in residence at weekends and in holiday periods, although at other times it is quieter. The Black Sun and Tabata discos are popular at weekends. An ice-driving course can be included in the hotel/lift pass formula, but there is little else for non-skiers here.

Bardonecchia 1312m (4,303ft)

This is a large, traditional and rather dull market town set in a sunny valley and surrounded by beautiful scenery. Although it is not part of the Milky Way it lies close to both Montgenèvre and Sestriere. It is a popular place with Italians who swarm in from Turin at weekends and holidays. The skiing is spread over three areas, linked by free ski-bus, with a total of 140km of piste. Bardonecchia is a good resort for non-skiers as the town has a life independent of skiing, as well as activities including tobogganing, indoor tennis, a sports centre and swimming. The nightlife is lively, with local bars and three discos.

Hotels include La Bettula, close to the shopping centre, the Tabor, close to the ski-bus stop, and the Larici, 250m from the centre. There is a non-ski kindergarten for children up to three years old.

TOURIST OFFICE
Viale della Vittoria 44, Bardonecchia
Tel 39 122 99032

TOUR OPERATORS
Neilson

Borgata 1840m (6,035ft)

This is a small resort five minutes by road from Sestriere with a bus running between the two resorts every half hour. Reporters who stayed in the Nube d'Argenta self-catering apartments praised them as 'clean, modern and convenient for the lifts'. There are complaints about the ski school ('very poor, English language limited, little progress was offered in the lessons, but the teachers were pleasant enough'). The après-ski is almost non-existent with 'a couple of sleepy bars with miserable staff and no (or few) customers'. There is one food shop and a tobacconist.

TOURIST OFFICE
as Sestriere

TOUR OPERATORS

Cesana Torinese 1350m (4,428ft)

Cesana is an attractively shabby old village dating back to the twelfth century, set on a busy road junction at the foot of the Italian approach to the Montgenèvre pass. It is rather confined and sunless, and accommodation is mainly in apartments and a few hotels. The chair-lifts up to the skiing above Clavière and Sansicario are a long walk from the centre and the place can be safely recommended only to those with a car for access to other resorts. Hotels include the three-star Chaberton and half-a-dozen small one-stars. Restaurants include La Selvaggia for regional specialities, La Noblerot for French cuisine, the smart Fraiteve, which specialises in truffles, and the popular Brusachoeur pizzeria. Après-ski spots include the Pussy-Cat pub and the Cremeria Rinaldo e Luciana bar. Local cheese and honey is on sale in the shops.

TOURIST OFFICE
Piazza V.Amadeo 3, 10054 Cesana Torinese, Piedmont
Tel 39 122 89202
Fax 39 122 811315

TOUR OPERATORS
Ski Europe

Clavière 1760m (5,773ft)

Clavière is a small border town in the northern Valle di Susa, with the customs post in the middle. During the eighteenth century it was part of Montgènevre. The village consists of a few hotels and a row of shops (including several good supermarkets) on the Italian side specialising in food and cheap Italian alcohol, with prices in francs and lire. Reporters say the village has a pleasant, relaxed atmosphere and is ideal for families.

The village is tightly enclosed by wooded slopes; and the nursery slope is small and steep, served by two lifts. Lifts give access to the skiing above Montgenèvre and Cesana, with easy runs back from both. Queuing is not usually a problem here, although it does tend to become slightly busier at weekends. Mountain eating places close to the village are the Località Gimont and La Coche.

There are eight hotels along the road. The two-star Hotel Roma, close to the main chair-lift, is recommended ('good value, plenty of food, and comfortable rooms'). Its popular bar is frequented by locals and the hotel attracts school parties. Other hotels include the Passero Pellegrino, Pian del Sole and the Savoia. The restaurants are mainly in hotels, and others include the Bar Ristorante Ski-Lodge, the Sandy and 'I Gran Bouc crêperie. Clavière is 'not a place for those interested in a hectic après-ski'. It has half-a-dozen bars including the Bar Caffé Torino and the Pub Kilt, disco La Scacchiera and there is a floodlit skating rink at the Sports Centre.

TOURIST OFFICE
Via Nazionale 28, Clavière, Piedmont
Tel 39 122 878856
Fax 39 122 878888

TOUR OPERATORS
Equity Total Ski, Masterski

Jouvenceaux 1380m (4,526ft)

This small and charming hamlet is just below Sauze d'Oulx, and is gradually spreading up the road from Oulx to meet it. At the bottom of the lift up to Sportinia is a delightfully unspoilt maze of crumbling alleys with old fountains and medieval paintings on the wall of the church. Most of the accommodation is quite a walk or bus ride from its lift and does not share the charm of the old village. La Chapelle is a three-star hotel, which has a mini-bus to the lift station.

Skiing facts: Montgenèvre

TOURIST OFFICE
F-05100 Montgenèvre, Hautes-Alpes
Tel 33 92 219022
Fax 33 92 219245

THE RESORT
By road Calais 978km
By rail Briançon 10km, Oulx 17km, buses to resort
By air Turin 2 hrs, Grenoble 3 hrs
Visitor beds 6,400 (94% apartments and chalets, 6% hotels)
Transport bus service throughout resort

THE SKIING
Longest run Le Chalvet, 2.5km (red)
Number of lifts 24 Montgenèvre, 101 Milky Way
Number of trails/pistes 42 in Montgenèvre (43% easy, 38% intermediate, 19% difficult), 118 in Milky Way
Total of trails/pistes 60km in Montgenèvre, 400km in Milky Way
Nursery slopes 1 lift
Summer skiing none
Snowmaking 1km covered

LIFT PASSES
Area pass Montgenèvre (covers Montgenèvre-Mont de la Lune), 440-540FF for 6 days, extension pass for Voie Lactée 40FF per day
Day pass 105FF
Half-day pass 80FF after 1pm
Beginners 1 free lift, day passes for limited area
Children Montgenèvre, 4-11 yrs, 320-415FF for 6 days, free for 4 yrs and under
Pensioners 60 yrs and over, as children
Credit cards accepted yes

SKI SCHOOLS
Adults ESF, 9.15-11.45am and

2.15-4.45pm, 766FF for 6 days
Children ESF, 5-12 yrs, 9.15-11.45am and 2.15-4.45pm, 143FF per day, 682FF for 6 days
Private lessons 158FF per hr
Special courses snowboarding, telemark, monoskiing
Guiding companies through tourist office

CROSS-COUNTRY
Ski schools ESF
Loipe location and size 50km on either side of the pass and at Les Alberts 7km away

CHILDCARE
Non-ski kindergarten Halte-Garderie, 1-4 yrs, 9am-5.30am, 440FF for 6 days not including lunch. Village Club du Soleil, free for 3 yrs and under, depending on period, 3-6 yrs from 1,400FF, 6-11 yrs from 1,600FF, both for 6 days
Ski kindergarten Jardin d'enfants, 3-5 yrs, 9am-midday and 2-5pm, 682FF for 6 days not including lunch
Babysitting difficult

OTHER SPORTS
Parapente, snow-mobiling, dog-sledding, ice-driving, skating, swimming

WHAT'S NEW
● Additional drag-lift ● 4 hectares of artificial snow

FOOD AND DRINK PRICES
Coffee 7.50FF, bottle of house wine 30-50FF, beer 10-15FF, dish of the day 60-80FF

TOUR OPERATORS
Enterprise, Made to Measure, Sally Holidays, SkiBound, Ski Thomson

ITALY

TOURIST OFFICE
as Sauze d'Oulx

TOUR OPERATORS
none

Sansicario 1710m (5,609ft)

Sansicario is in a sunny position half-way up a west-facing mountain-side, well placed for exploring the Milky Way. It is a purpose-built resort which consists mainly of apartment buildings linked to a neat commercial precinct by shuttle lift. Facilities are generally good for beginners,

· ·

Skiing facts: Sauze d'Oulx

TOURIST OFFICE
Piazza Assietta 18, I-10050 Sauze
d'Oulx, Piedmont
Tel 39 122 858009
Fax 39 122 850497

THE RESORT
By road Calais 998km
By rail Oulx (5km), frequent buses
By air Turin 2 hrs
Visitor beds 4,350 (64% apartments, 36% hotels)
Transport free bus service

THE SKIING
Longest run Number 12, 6km (blue)
Number of lifts 27 in Sauze
d'Oulx/Jouvenceau, 101 in Milky Way
Number of trails/pistes 33 in Sauze
d'Oulx/Jouvenceau (27% easy, 61%
intermediate, 12% difficult), 118 in
Milky Way
Total of trails/pistes 100km in Sauze
d'Oulx, 400km in Milky Way
Nursery slopes 4 lifts
Summer skiing none
Snowmaking 8km covered

LIFT PASSES
Area pass La Via Lattea (covers Sauze
d'Oulx, Sestriere, Sansicario, Cesana
and Clavière), L185,000-200,000 for 6
days, includes 1 free day in Alpe d'Huez,
Les Deux Alpes, Puy-St- Vincent, Serre
Chevalier. L16,000 per day for a
Montgenèvre extension with a 6-day pass
Day pass L39,000
Half-day pass L26,000 after 1pm
Beginners points tickets
Children L185,00-200,000, free for 8
yrs and under
Pensioners no reduction
Credit cards accepted no

SKI SCHOOLS
Adults Sauze d'Oulx, Sauze Sportinia,
Sauze Project, 10am-1pm, L120,000-
150,000 for 6 days
Children Sauze d'Oulx, Sauze Sportinia,
Sauze Project, 10am-1pm, 5 yrs and
over, L120,000-150,000 for 6 days
Private lessons L35,000 per hr
Special courses snowboarding
Guiding companies through ski school

CROSS-COUNTRY
Ski schools Sauze d'Oulx, Sauze
Sportinia, Sauze Project
Loipe location and size 3km in Sauze
d'Oulx

CHILDCARE
Non-ski kindergarten Pro Loco (tuition
possible), 6 mths-6 yrs, 9am-5pm,
L250,000 for 6 days, not including
lunch
Ski kindergarten Sauze d'Oulx, Sauze
Sportinia, Sauze Project, 5 yrs and
over, L140,000-160,000
Babysitting through Pro Loco

OTHER SPORTS
Heli-skiing, hang-gliding, skating,
tobogganing, bowling, swimming

WHAT'S NEW
● Sports centre as part of hotel/
residence complex

FOOD AND DRINK PRICES
Coffee L1,200-3,000, bottle of house
wine L15,000, beer L2,500-4,000,
dish of the day L12,000

TOUR OPERATORS
Enterprise, Neilson, Ski Falcon,
Ski Airtours, Ski Thomson, Winterski

especially children. There is a good skiing and non-skiing kindergarten (the Junior Club) providing all-day care plus lunch if required for 3- to 11-year-olds. Sansicario has its own ski school. Non-skiing and après-ski facilities are good, but there is little variety – a disco, three restaurants, three bars and few other sporting activities.

Accommodation is of a generally high standard, mostly in apartments, but with a few comfortable, expensive hotels. The most attractive of these is the Rio Envers, a short walk from the centre. Others are the four-star Monti della Luna and the simpler San Sicario.

TOURIST OFFICE
Piazza Garambois 6, 10056 Oulx, Piedmont
Tel 39 122 831596
Fax 39 122 831880

TOUR OPERATORS
Equity Total Ski

Skiing facts: Sestriere

TOURIST OFFICE
I-10058 Sestriere, Piedmont
Tel 39 122 755444
Fax 39 122 755171

THE RESORT
By road Calais 1020km
By rail Oulx 22km
By air Turin 2 hrs
Visitor beds 15,500 (87% apartments, 13% hotels)
Transport no bus service

THE SKIING
Longest run Rio Nero, 7km (black)
Number of lifts 25 Sestriere, 101 in area
Number of trails/pistes 70 in Sestriere (18% beginner, 21% easy, 42% intermediate, 19% difficult), 118 in Milky Way
Total of trails/pistes 120km in Sestriere, 400km in area
Nursery slopes 2
Summer skiing none
Snowmaking 65km covered in area

LIFT PASSES
Area pass Via Lattea (covers Sestriere, Sauze d'Oulx, Sansicario, Cesana and Clavière), L185,000-200,000 for 6 days
Day pass Via Lattea L39,000
Half-day pass L26,000 after midday
Beginners no free lifts
Children L185,000-200,000, free for 8 yrs and under
Pensioners no reduction
Credit cards accepted no

SKI SCHOOLS
Adults Sestriere Ski School, 10am-1pm, L42,000 per day, L160,000 for 6 days
Children Sestriere Ski School, 4 yrs and over, 10am-1pm, L42,000 per day, L160,000 for 6 days
Private lessons L42,000 per hr
Special courses snowboarding
Guiding companies through ski school

CROSS-COUNTRY
Ski schools Sestriere Ski School
Loipe location and size 3km

CHILDCARE
Non-ski kindergarten Neve Sole, 3-11 yrs, 9am-5pm, L10,000 per hr, L35,000 per day including lunch
Ski kindergarten Sestriere Ski School, 4-11 yrs, 10am-1pm, L42,000 per day, L160,000 for 6 days
Babysitting list from tourist office

OTHER SPORTS
Heli-skiing, parapente, ice-driving, skating, go-karting, indoor tennis, squash, fitness centre

FOOD AND DRINK PRICES
Coffee L1,200, bottle of house wine L12,500, beer L2,800, dish of the day L18,000

TOUR OPERATORS
Club Med, Crystal, Neilson

Selva, Dolomites

ALTITUDE 1550m (5,084ft)

••

Good points enormous intermediate ski area, beautiful scenery, wide choice of mountain restaurants, ski-touring, activities for non-skiers, comprehensive beginners' and children's facilities, interesting off-piste skiing
Bad points unreliable snow record, traffic in resort, difficult airport access
Linked or nearby resorts Arabba (I), Armentarola (I), Campitello (I), Canazei (I), Colfosco (I), Cortina d'Ampezzo (n), Corvara (I), La Villa (I), Ortisei (I), Pedraces (I), San Cassiano (I), Santa Cristina (I)

The Dolomites have arguably the most spectacular scenery of any ski area in Europe. The steep cliffs that rise above the snowfields change colour during the day, culminating in their characteristic pinkness at sunset. Although the peaks of these mountains are high, the skiing is virtually all lower down. This is the main cause of the variable snow record of the Dolomites, a handicap that has been offset by heavy investment in modern snowmaking techniques.

Selva, or Wolkenstein as it is also known in this bilingual border area of Italy, is barely more than a fairly small village strung along the main road up the Val Gardena (or Das Grödner Tal). Traffic is therefore heavy and weary skiers are more at risk of injury crossing the street than they ever are while hurtling down the piste. Traffic aside, the resort is quiet, friendly and has an unselfconscious charm to it. It almost seems as if every local practises the regional craft of woodcarving and the results can be found not only in the shops and houses, but also on lamp posts, street corners and at just about every vantage point.

The Sella Ronda, of which Selva is the best-known member, is split into several areas. Selva is in the Val Gardena area along with Ortisei and Santa Cristina. The resorts of Corvara, Colfosco, San Cassiano, Pedraces and La Villa are in Alta Badia. Val di Fassa contains Canazei and Campitello; and Arabba is in Livinallongo.

The skiing

Top 2950m (9,676ft) bottom 1225m (4,018ft)

The skiing in the area is dominated by the Sella Ronda circuit, an enjoyable day out for early intermediates upwards. It can be skied in either direction and takes a reasonable skier about four-and-a-half hours to complete, not counting stops for sustenance or lift queues; the latter can sometimes be a problem. With its mainly blue (easy) and unproblematic red (intermediate) runs, the Sella Ronda is more a way of seeing some wonderful scenery than of trying some really challenging skiing.

The only real problems arise with poor snow conditions, when the south-facing slopes in particular become very worn and unpleasant. One reporter recounted having to remove her skis and walk certain sections of the circuit during a mild spell and indeed short walks between lifts are not uncommon, even when conditions are good. Sign-posting for the Sella Ronda circuit is basically good, but reporters complain that the local piste map is very poor indeed. A decent one can be bought at the tourist office.

Mountain access to the start of the Sella Ronda from Selva is up the Dantercëpies gondola, which is reached via an irritating journey up two drag-lifts that do not quite meet, followed by a perilous walk up a steep and icy road. The alternative, although more crowded, route is up the efficient 12-person Ciampinoi gondola from the centre of the village. From there the Sella Ronda unfolds towards Plan de Gralba, Passo Sella, Arabba and beyond. For a rather more testing run, the hardier skier can take a right turn from the Ciampinoi gondola and ski two of the area's few black (difficult) runs, either back to the bottom of Ciampinoi or, by keeping left, down to Santa Cristina and return by the Sochers lift.

Early intermediates and more advanced cruisers can spend many happy hours in the area between Plan de Gralba and Passo de Sella, an area dominated by gentle blues, but also containing the World Cup downhill course, traditionally second in the racing calendar behind Val d'Isère. There is also the pleasant Gran Paradiso, a good place to rest the tired limbs and bruised egos of would-be downhillers.

A cable car from the southern edge of Ortisei takes you up to Punta Mesdi (2006m). The only way back is down a winding red with some rather terrifying looking drops guarded by safety netting. Otherwise the area is given over to a clutch of gentle blues around the Alpe di Suisi basin, a network of undemanding slopes mixed with several cross-country loops and served by numerous restaurants, among them the Laurinhütte, popular with reporters. Dominated by superb scenery, this area is a deservedly popular place for other activities. There are many good walks and the presence of numerous hotels and eating places, makes it a reasonable resort for non-skiers.

A chair or cable car from the northern edge of Ortisei leads to two long, serpentine red runs back to the village. Unfortunately they are south-facing and rarely have enough snow on them to be anything like skiable. The other side of Seceda has several short and unremarkable reds and a long pretty blue that divides, either past Col Raiser or the Gamsblut restaurant, before joining at Sangon and ending at the top end of St Cristina.

Reached by chair from Santa Cristina, Monte Pana is no more than a series of very short beginners' drag-lifts and almost imperceptible slopes. With no run back down to the village, there is little for all but the very earliest beginner to do but take a drag and a chair to Mont de Seura where a testing red or tricky short black return you to the beginners' slopes once again.

The long blue run from Plan de Gralba to Passo Sella is the Moon Walk, or Rock City, so called because of the enormous boulders by the side of the track. Indeed at times of bad snow the run really does live up to its name: unpleasant to ski or walk and unkind to one's skis. It is here that

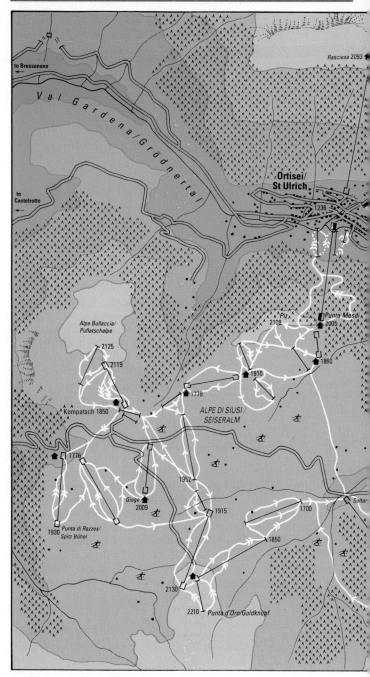

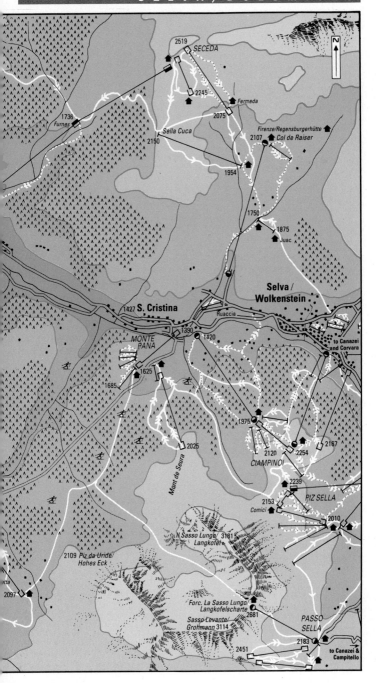

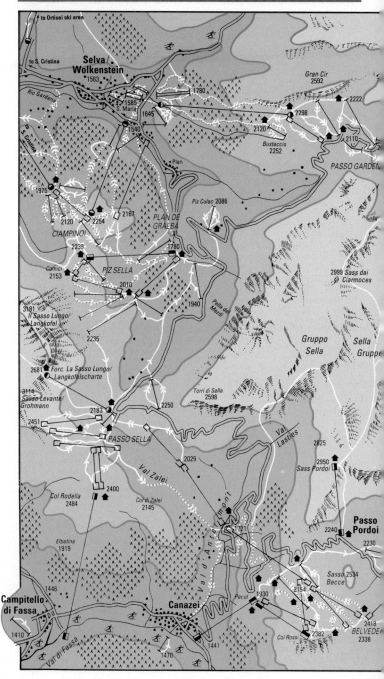

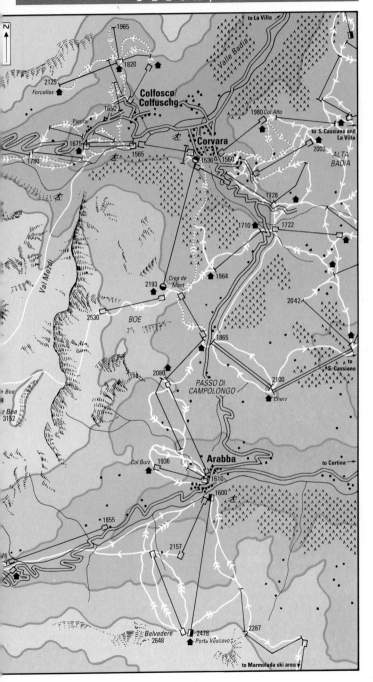

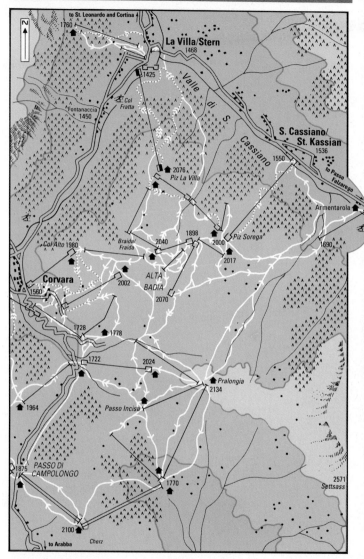

some of the better off-piste skiing in the area is to be found via the Sasso Lungo lift, either by the tricky steep, rocky run, directly under the lift, or the less steep but avalanche-prone run behind the mountain, taking you eventually to Monte Pana and Santa Cristina. Pisted slopes in this area are contained in a Spaghetti Junction of short, easy runs before the long blue runs that link Passo Sella and Plan de Gralba as part of both directions of the Sella Ronda. The Sasso Lungo drag-lift is a regular bottleneck.

From Passo Sella the gentlest possible run goes towards Colfosco, a fine practice place for wobbly schussers, the last third being virtually flat. Colfosco itself, standing slightly removed from the hurly-burly of the Sella Ronda, is an attractive little village with several quiet blue and red runs served by four quite short drags. Colfosco also has one of the classic alpine ski runs, the Val Mezdi, a long couloir which descends between the rocks and should only be attempted by expert skiers accompanied by a guide. The run is accessed by a 45-minute hike. The entry to the couloir is steep and narrow. It widens out then becomes sheer and rocky before ending on the Colfosco meadows.

From the western side of the road over Passo di Campolungo, a series of lifts provide a link with Arabba. South-facing and with a tendency to be icy early in the morning, the runs are enjoyable if unchallenging and rather surprisingly graded red. The long run underneath the new Boè gondola down to Corvara is a wide, fast red with few problems provided it is not too crowded. A longer run can be made by taking the chair from Crep de Munt and skiing the black run from the top back past the Boè Restaurant.

Corvara's ski area is a network of short, gentle blue and red runs on the side of a low, rounded mountain served by three drag-lifts and two efficient chairs. Sharing the ski area with the smaller villages of La Villa and San Cassiano, it has very little to challenge a competent skier, except for the 700km vertical black run above La Villa and its red sister.

One of the main attractions of Arabba's ski area is the fact that the major runs are both challenging and keep their snow much longer than most, because they are both sheltered and north-facing. The best skiing is found by taking the cable car from the village to Belvedere at 2516m, giving a choice of some excellent runs. On the left-hand side the black starts as rather icy, rocky and narrow, but then splits into two testing runs which converge half-way down to the village. To either side of the blacks run winding reds, which provide alternative routes to the same point. The Europe cable car has recently added to the local lift system, rising to Porta Vescovo and connecting with the Marmolada Glacier at 3342m where good late-season and summer skiing can be found.

Having a cable car and very little else, Passo Pordoi is the starting point of an ascent to 2950m and the Sas Pordoi. The terrain here is entirely ungroomed and given over to some excellent off-piste runs. The most skied is the Forcella, which goes virtually straight under the cable car. South-facing, often icy and bare of snow, it is very steep at the top although not too difficult when the conditions are favourable. Longer but more mixed routes include Val Lasties down to the Lupo Bianco restaurant above Canazei. Those with sufficient energy at this altitude can try the 45-minute walk that culminates in the Val de Mesdi and the steep route down towards Colfosco.

The skiing around Canazei is reached from a cable car at the southern end of the village. The area itself is a grid of short red runs served by a variety of drags, chairs and cable cars. The only long run is the red, which dog-legs back down to the village. There are over 30 mountain huts in the Sella Ronda area, over half are open for ski-tourers in winter and spring.

Mountain restaurants

Plentiful, reasonably priced and mostly of excellent quality, the mountain restaurants in the area are crowded, fun and usually have spectacular views of the scenery. The restaurants serve a variety of food to a noisy and discerning Italian clientele and specialise in local dishes rather than the usual frankfurter and chips, chips, chips and chips. Colfosco's ski area contains the pleasant restaurants of Cap Pradat, Cap Edelweiss and Rifuge Forcelles. Waiter-service restaurants include Cherz near Arabba, Crëp de Munt and Pré Ciablun. Scotoni is a recommended self-service, as are Capanna Nera and Santa Croce. In Selva the Gran Paradiso and the Laurinhütte are praised and above Canazei there is the Lupo Bianco.

Beginners and children

The Selva Ski School proudly boasts a spanking new building and is given a favourable report. The standard of tuition appears to be of a high standard. The only drawback in Selva, and in all the Sella Ronda resorts, is the instructors' often limited knowledge of English. One reporter complains of being put in a group of German-speakers, who had to translate the lesson into English for her. The tendency seems to be to push everyone towards the ski school's own expensive hire shop, rather than the cheaper alternatives, but on the whole the ski school is well received.

Selva is an excellent area for children of all ages to learn to ski. The nursery slopes are based below the Dantercëpies gondola at the northern edge of the village. There is a kindergarten at the bottom of the Biancaneve drag-lift where toddlers and small children are taught the rudiments of skiing among cartoon characters and parents. Instructors are plentiful and patient and there seems to be none of the 'here is an entire generation to be put off skiing' attitude that you encounter in some French resorts. The surrounding area is ideal for older children to learn or improve their skiing.

The resort

Selva is a not particularly attractive resort strung out along the road and now virtually joined to Santa Cristina. The sheer volume of traffic on its main street alone would be enough to reduce the charm. But it is a friendly, fun resort based around an attractive church with wood carvings and some pleasing old buildings to make it well worth exploring.

Accommodation

Accommodation consists mainly of small hotels, mostly very comfortable. We have good reports of the Hotel Solaia and in particular its buffet breakfast. The centrally situated Hotel Antares and the Hotel Laurin are also praised. The Aaritz is a comfortable hotel near the Ciampinoi gondola; the Genziana and the simple Stella are recommended. Inexpensive bed and breakfast hotels include the Eden and the Somont and the more comfortable Savoy, which also has a restaurant. Several British tour operators run chalets in the resort, which are mainly of a high standard.

Eating out

Restaurants base their cuisine mainly, and unsurprisingly, on Italian specialities such as pasta and pizzas. Two of the best are the Salfeur Pizzeria and Pizzeria Rino, while a wider selection of food can be found at the recommended Café Mozart and the restaurants of Hotels Laurin and Résidence, both open to non-residents.

Après-ski

At first sight, Selva does not appear to have much of a nightlife. Half-a-dozen cafés serve home-made cakes and pastries, but the resort is quiet in the evening, with few lights, seemingly little activity and without the buzz of a serious party resort. In fact behind the shutters there is a thriving après-ski scene and a good choice of nightspots, but light sleepers are unlikely to have their slumbers disturbed. The liveliest bar is the Luiskeller with its challenge of drinking a line of glasses of the local *grappa*, an activity fondly if vaguely remembered by one of our reporters. Also recommended are Bar Rino, the Hotel Laurin bar, as well as dancing at the Stella and Dali discos. In Santa Cristina Yeti's Ombrella Bar is popular. In Selva the bars include La Stua with folk music evenings, Scoiattolo Stube with live music, the Speckkeller, Sun Valley, Aaritz, l'Médel and Ustaria de Luisl. The best discos are said to be Heustadl in Santa Cristina; and in Selva the Dali, Savoy and the Stella Club rock on into the early hours.

Activities for non-skiers include scenic walks to the ruins of Wolkenstein Castle and Castle Gardena and on the ex-railway track of Val Gardena towards Santa Cristina and Ortisei. However, walkers are warned in the tourist office literature that 'dogs not on leads may be shot by the gamekeepers'. The shops are rather limited, tending to sell food, ski wear or the ubiquitous wooden carvings, all at a reasonable price for a ski resort, but unlikely to excite anyone. There is a weekly market in Selva.

Arabba 1600m (5,249ft)

This small and unspoilt resort is in the Italian-speaking part of the Sella Region and is therefore relatively free of German tourists. Arabba has the Sella Ronda's most demanding pistes overall and therefore attracts serious skiers. Most of the accommodation is in hotels and apartments, with the Sport the most comfortable although not centrally placed. Porta Vescovo is modern and central and houses Arabba's only disco. Bar Peter, Pensione Erica and Albergo Pordoi are the recommended après-ski bars and there is little else to do here but prop them up. A car is useful for visits to livelier Corvara and Cortina, which are not far by road.

TOURIST OFFICE
APT di Belluno, Via R. Psaro 21,
32100 Arabba, Livinallongo
Tel 39 437 940083
Fax 39 437 940073

TOUR OPERATORS
Bladon Lines, Ski Beach Villas

Campitello 1440m (4,723ft)

A small collection of old buildings make up this quiet village set beside a stream, well back from the main road. The Col Rodella cable car (45-minute queues reported) goes up to the ski area and there is no piste back down again. The village is, however, ideal for beginners as some of the area's best nursery slopes are right on its doorstep. Hotels include the Fedora next to the lift station and the Medil, a modern hotel built in traditional alpine style with its own fitness centre and music bar. Hotel Sella Ronda is an alpine-style hotel owned by a priest. It is comfortable, although a reporter recommends avoiding the upper rooms: 'Due to a massive beam, headroom at one end of the rooms is no more than a metre.' Hotel Rubino has a swimming-pool and piano bar among its many facilities.

TOURIST OFFICE
APT di Campitello, CAP 38031
Tel 39 462 61137

TOUR OPERATORS
Crystal, Enterprise

Canazei 1440m (4,724ft)

Campitello's neighbour (2km away) is a large, attractive and lively village on a busy main road in the Italian-speaking Val di Fassa. It is the best place to stay for those in search of non-skiing activities and a good nightlife. The village itself is a tangle of narrow streets with a mixture of old rural buildings, new hotels and some delightful shops. One of the prime places to stay is the Palace Hotel Dolomiti in the centre, built in Grand Hotel style and recommended for its high standard of cuisine and comfort. The Croce Bianca is a popular and central hotel, the Bellevue better placed for the skiing, which is inconvenient from most of the village hotels, involving a cable car a long way from the village centre. The Tyrol and Laurin are both comfortable, the Astoria is an attractive family-run establishment five minutes' walk from the centre and the Azola is a chalet-style hotel in an attractive setting. The Palace Hotel Dolomiti has a pizzeria. The Montanara bar and the Gatto Nero are recommended. Other après-ski activities include bowling, tobogganing, skating and steam baths.

TOURIST OFFICE
APT di Canazei, CAP 38030
Tel 39 462 62466
Fax 39 462 62278

TOUR OPERATORS
Crystal, Enterprise

Colfosco 1650m (5,412ft)

Colfosco has easy access to both Selva and Corvara's skiing, although the village also has a small ski area of its own with good nursery slopes. Recommended hotels are the Kolfuschgerhof and the Centrale. Speckstube Peter, Mesoles, Stria, Matthiaskeller and Tabladel are the most popular eating places. Black Hill Nevada is a pub serving food and the Capella is the smartest eating place.

TOURIST OFFICE
APT, Ciasa de Comun 198,
CAP 39033
Tel 39 471 846176
Fax 39 471 847277

TOUR OPERATORS
none

Corvara 1550m (5,085ft)

Corvara is one of the most centrally placed villages for the Sella Ronda ski area, with access by chair-lift and gondola to both Alta Badia and Arabba. The lifts are easily reached from the village centre. The village itself is a characterless expanse of chalet-style hotels and modern buildings. The biggest and smartest hotel is the Posta, and the Eden and Veneranda are both comfortable. The most popular restaurants are La Tambra, Da Paolo, Adler and Caffé Corvara, the most upmarket La Perla, which also has a piano bar and the Panorama. The Arabesque is an after-skiing bar; the Posta Zirm has tea-dancing and becomes a nightclub later in the evening along with the two other nightspots, Sassongher and Greif. There is cross-country skiing and a skating rink in the village. The ski school has a kinder-garten for 3-year-olds and over, but English is not widely spoken.

TOURIST OFFICE
As Colfosco

TOUR OPERATORS
none

Ortisei 1240m (4,067ft)

This is the major town of the Val Gardena, although not a good base for skiers. The centre is bypassed by the main valley road, but the busy high-way has to be crossed on foot in order to reach the cable car. As in Selva, staying in Ortisei means a lot of walking. The Adler is the prime hotel, with the Posta an old hotel and the Snalterhof an inexpensive hostelry. Nightlife is not as lively as Selva's, but there are some good bars and restaurants.

TOURIST OFFICE
APT, Via Rezia 1, Ortisei, Val Gardena
Tel 39 471 796328
Fax 39 471 796749

TOUR OPERATORS
none

San Cassiano 1537m (5,041ft)

A small, roadside village with mainly new Dolomite-style buildings, San Cassiano has some excellent skiing for beginners and early intermedi-ates who want to avoid challenges. Long, easy runs go into the village from Pralongia and Piz Sorega. Reporters mention the lack of English in a resort which attracts mainly wealthy Italians. The downside of this is being the sole English speaker in a ski school class where lessons become 'laborious, with everything spoken in German and Italian'.

The Rosa Alpina is a large, comfortable hotel in the village centre and is also the focal point for après-ski with a live band. The Ski Bar is recom-mended for good, cheap pizzas and the Capanna Alpina, Saré, Sas Dlacia and Tirol are all busy restaurants. La Siriola, Rosa Alpina, Fanes and the restaurant in Hotel Diamant are the more expensive eating places. There is bowling at the Daimant, but otherwise the village tends to be on the quiet side. Armentarola, with its own hotels and restaurants, is a kilometre away.

TOURIST OFFICE
as Colfosco

TOUR OPERATORS
none

Skiing facts: Selva

TOURIST OFFICE
APT Val Gardena, via Dursan 78,
39047 Santa Cristina
Tel 39 471 79 22 77
Fax 39 471 79 22 35

THE RESORT
By road Calais 1226km
By rail Chiusa 27km, buses from station
By air Innsbruck 1 hr, Verona 3 hrs,
Munich 4 hrs
Visitor beds 11,044 in Selva and
Santa Cristina (51% chalets and farm-
houses, 49% hotels and guesthouses)
Transport free bus between resorts

THE SKIING
Longest run Seceda-Ortisei, 9km (red)
Number of lifts 86 in Val Gardena-Alpe
di Suisi, 464 in Sella Ronda
Number of trails/pistes 29% easy,
57% intermediate, 14% difficult – no
total available
Total of trails/pistes 175km in Val Gardena-
Alpe di Suisi, 1100km in Sella Ronda
Nursery slopes 1 lift beside each ski
school
Summer skiing Marmolada Glacier,
south of Arabba
Snowmaking 78km covered in Val
Gardena, 50km covered in Alta Badia

LIFT PASSES
Area pass Superskipass (covers 464 lifts),
L192,000-221,000 for 6 days. Skipass
(covers Val Gardena/Alpe di Suisi resorts),
L176,000-202,000 for 6 days
Day pass Skipass L35,000-41,000,
Superskipass L39,000-44,000
Half-day pass not available
Beginners points tickets
Children Superskipass, 6-14 yrs,
L134,000-154,000 for 6 days, free for
5 yrs and under
Pensioners 20% reduction for 60 yrs
and over
Credit cards accepted yes

SKI SCHOOLS
Adults Val Gardena Ski School,
9.30am-4pm, L42,000-47,000 per hr
Children Val Gardena Ski School, 4-12
yrs, 9.30am-4pm, L295,000 for 6 days
including lunch, lessons and lifts
Private lessons L42,000 per hr
Special courses mogul clinics,
telemark, snowboarding, monoskiing,
ski-touring, off-piste
Guiding companies Association of
Mountain Guides

CROSS-COUNTRY
Ski schools through Val Gardena Ski
School
Loipe location and size Monte Pana
23km and Vallunga 12km

CHILDCARE
Non-ski kindergarten Verdebello, 15
mths and over, 9am-5pm, L45,000
per day including lunch, L295,000 for
6 days including lunch
Ski kindergarten Selva Ski School,
4-12 yrs, 8.30am-4pm, L295,000 for
6 days including lunch, lessons
and lifts
Babysitting through Verdebello
kindergarten

OTHER SPORTS
Skating, squash, curling, indoor
shooting range, sleigh rides, heli-skiing,
parapente, indoor tennis, swimming,
fitness centre, tobogganing, bowling

WHAT'S NEW
● Free ski-bus between the resorts

FOOD AND DRINK PRICES
Coffee L2,000, bottle of house wine
L12,000, beer L3,000-4,000, dish of
the day L14,000-20,000

TOUR OPERATORS
Bladon Lines, Crystal, Enterprise

La Thuile - La Rosière

La Thuile, Aosta
ALTITUDE 1450m (4,756ft)

Good points compact village, large intermediate ski area, tree-level skiing, extensive nursery slopes, varied off-piste skiing, skiing convenience, low prices
Bad points no childcare facilities, lack of alpine charm, limited for non-skiers, limited après-ski
Linked or nearby resorts Pila (n), La Rosière (l)

La Rosière, Savoie
ALTITUDE 1850m (6,068ft)

Good points large intermediate ski area, ideal for beginners and families, limited for non-skiers, low prices
Bad points lack of tough runs, lack of skiing convenience, limited après-ski
Linked or nearby resorts Les Arcs (n), La Thuile (l)

The road over the Petit-St-Bernard pass, which separates the French Tarentaise from the Italian Aosta valleys, is closed in winter as Hannibal most probably discovered in 218BC when he lost half his army and his elephants here. Of all the alpine routes the Carthaginian general is thought to have taken on his epic journey from Spain to Rome, this is the most likely.

The skiing today takes place mainly on the exposed slopes above the pass at a top altitude of 2642m on the Italian side and 2400m on the French Col de la Traversette. The tenuously linked 135km ski area is equally divided, but certainly the best part of it belongs to Italy, with long intermediate runs, some steeper black runs through the trees and a reputation for severe cold. La Rosière's skiing consists of open, sunny and mainly easy slopes on the south-facing side of Tarentaise above Bourg-St-Maurice and opposite Les Arcs and the Aiguille Rouge. There are also a few steeper runs through the woods below the resort. It is a good place for families, a quiet and friendly village, which is cheap by local standards. Day-trips to the other Tarentaise resorts are possible.

La Thuile is less appealing than its skiing: a purpose-built resort centred on a giant hotel and conference centre, cavernous apartment-blocks and a car park near the site of what used to be an old mining village. The development has attracted considerable investment, which is certainly justified by the skiing. It has the ski-in ski-out convenience and a consequent lack of atmosphere you would expect in a purpose-built resort of this nature. Day trips to Courmayeur and other resorts in the Aosta, as well as Chamonix, are possible with a car.

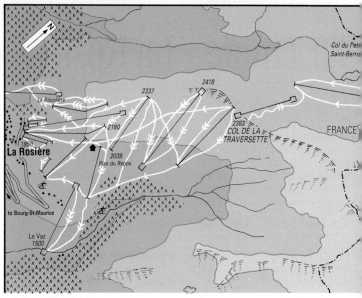

The skiing

Top 2642m (7,938ft) bottom 1150m (3,772ft)

La Thuile's ski area consists of steep, tree-lined slopes above the resort, a wide and gentle east-facing mountain above the trees and steeper north-facing slopes from the top lifts towards the Petit-St-Bernard road. On both sides of the mountain the steeper slopes are surrounded by long intermediate runs giving a good variety of pistes back to the resort. La Rosière's area is a wide, mainly south-facing mountain criss-crossed by easy intermediate runs. The pistes on the pass side of the village, immediately above the tree-line and on down through the woods, are of more interest to good skiers.

The main **mountain access** is by a fast jumbo gondola and chair-lift, which climb steeply from the edge of La Thuile to Les Suches at 2200m, a cluster of buildings above the woods where the mountain flattens out. Three black (difficult) runs drop back down through the woods. Red (intermediate) La Tour provides an easier way back to the resort. Above Les Suches an area of easy wide runs opens into an even wider bowl of intermediate skiing under the rocky peaks of Belvedere and Chaz Dura, the high points of the ski area. Most of the runs under the Belvedere and Cerellaz chairs are wide and gentle, but slightly steeper on the slopes of Chaz Dura. The wide mogul field under the Chaz Dura chair is about the only run which is not constantly groomed. The views from the higher slopes are wonderful, including the Ruitor glacier, which is much used for heli-skiing, and the south side of Mont Blanc. On the easterly side of the ski area is a very long and not much skied run down to the resort through the woods.

Some of La Thuile's best skiing is on the rocky north-facing slopes above the Petit-St-Bernard pass, served by the Fourclaz and the new San

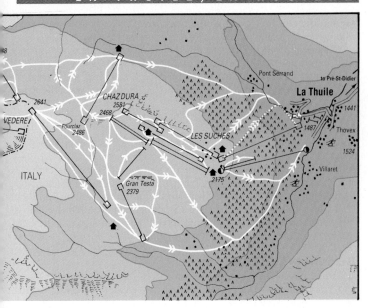

Bernardo chair and accessible from both Chaz Dura and Belvedere. Apart from the marked runs, the off-piste alternatives are interesting and offer a respectable 600m vertical drop. The least direct route is an 11km run, which starts with a choice of black or red runs from Belvedere and ends up following the road into La Thuile.

The link to France is reached either via the San Bernardo chair from the top of the pass, or from the Belvedere chair. A 50m walk from Belvedere takes you to the border and a long schuss into the Bellecombe valley to the Chardonnet quad chair, which climbs steeply over a cliff face to the Col de la Traversette, a gap in the rocky terrain crowning La Rosière's ski fields, complete with Napoleonic fortifications commanding the pass. The start of the red l'Ours run from the top of the San Bernardo also leads down into the Bellecombe valley. Return from La Rosière is only possible via the narrow red Bouquetin piste (less confident skiers can download via the Chardonnet chair), followed by the two Bellecombe drags back up to Belvedere.

Passing below the fort is a blue (easy) run, Choucas, which crosses the mountain and leads directly to La Rosière; several reporters comment on the danger of collision at the frequent crossroads on the piste. Alternatively, you can zig-zag up and down the various lifts beneath the crest, exploring the red runs and the undemanding Chevreuil black. This is a wide, intermediate ski area with short and easy runs and nursery lifts near the village. From the altiport two more testing runs, red and black, skirt the hamlet of Les Eucherts, ending below it at 1500m.

Directly above La Rosière is a wide blue slope, good for beginners and popular with ski school classes, served by a long chair and drag. From the top of the chair two black runs drop down the south-west face of the mountain, across the Petit-St-Bernard road and into the woods. They turn red through the trees down to Les Ecudets at 1150m where a quad chair and drag take you back to the blue run home.

Queues in both resorts are rare except at weekends when linking lifts can become serious bottlenecks. There is artificial snow on a length of north-facing piste down to La Thuile via Les Suches and a total of 10km is covered. La Rosière has one mobile snow-cannon on the main slope above the village.

Mountain restaurants

There are several eating places on the Italian side, the largest being a characterless self-service at Les Suches serving home-made pasta and soups. Le Foyer in the middle of the upper La Thuile bowl has a terrace and good restaurant, and a large bar with an open fire. The Off Shore at the Belvedere chair ('great nautical flavour and sunny position') and the Roxi bar at the Fourclaz chair are recommended. The Altitude Bar is 'the best stopping place on the mountain'. The Plan Repos is the only mountain restaurant on the La Rosière side.

Beginners and children

La Thuile has a small area of nursery slopes near the main lift station and a more extensive area on the easy slopes above Les Suches. Reports of the ski school are all positive; in the spring it organises heli-skiing on the Ruitor Glacier. The resort appears not to have any childcare facilities and the ski school does not accept children under five.

We have mixed reports of the ESF ski school in La Rosière. One reporter complained that the lack of green runs made it difficult for beginners and he did not like the 'couldn't care less' attitude of his instructor. Another said she learned more theory from her husband in half-an-hour than from her instructor in a week. A third was 'very satisfied – I learnt enough to get over into Italy by the end of the week'.

La Rosière has excellent nursery slopes directly above the resort and around the altiport, served by a number of easy lifts. The pistes are kept immaculately groomed and there is an easy slalom course on the blue Renard run. The Village des Enfants has a good reputation and cares for children all day from 9am to 6pm.

The resort

La Thuile stands in a rather austere and enclosed setting 10km from Pré-St-Didier and a further 6 from Courmayeur and the Mont Blanc tunnel. The Petit-St-Bernard climbs no further than here in winter to what was once a prosperous mining village. There are plans to convert the old buildings into a national sports academy. The ski resort is, however, entirely purpose-built with a huge hotel, apartment buildings, a well-equipped sports centre and a range of shops.

La Rosière is little more than a collection of traditional-style buildings lining the hairpin bends of the road up towards the Petit-St-Bernard pass. It has, as one reporter describes it, 'a hint of a real village'. There are several old farming hamlets scattered around the sunny slopes nearby. In winter the road ends with a snow bank at the top of the village beside a pen containing a few sun-bathing St Bernard dogs which pose professionally at the sight of a camera. Access to the skiing is from the roadside at the top of the village, where the first lift was installed in 1962 behind the Relais du Petit-St-Bernard.

Accommodation

La Thuile accommodation is mainly in the Planibel Complex of modern apartments and a large four-star hotel, which houses two swimming-pools and is convenient for the shops. The apartments are built around a courtyard near the main gondola and are 'spacious, chalet-style studios.' Hotel Planibel 'very comfortable'. The Chalet Alpina is set

....

Skiing facts: La Thuile

TOURIST OFFICE
I-11016 La Thuile, Aosta
Tel 39 165 884179
Fax 39 165 885196

THE RESORT
By road Calais 938km
By rail Pré-St-Didier 10km
By air Geneva 2½ hrs, Turin 3 hrs
Visitor beds 3,101 (65% hotels, 35% apartments)
Transport free bus service in the village

THE SKIING
Longest run San Bernardo, 11km (red)
Number of lifts 17 in La Thuile, 35 in area
Number of trails/pistes 27 in La Thuile, 60 in area (13% beginner, 37% easy, 35% intermediate, 15% difficult)
Total of trails/pistes 75km in La Thuile, 135km in area
Nursery slopes 4 lifts
Summer skiing none
Snowmaking 10km covered

LIFT PASSES
Area pass Aosta Valley (covers La Thuile/La Rosière, Pila, and Courmayeur), L218,000 for 6 days. La Thuile/La Rosière, L160,000-177,000 for 6 days
Day pass La Thuile/La Rosière L39,000
Half-day pass La Thuile/La Rosière, L29,000 after 1pm
Beginners free baby-lift in village, points tickets
Children La Thuile/La Rosière, L160,000-177,000 for 6 days. Aosta Valley L218,000 for 6 days. Free for 4 yrs and under
Pensioners no reduction
Credit cards accepted yes

SKI SCHOOLS
Adults Ski School Ruitor, 10am-12.30pm, L123,000-137,000 for 6 days
Children Ski School Ruitor, 5 yrs and over, 10am-12.30pm, L123,000-137,000 for 6 days
Private lessons L43,000 per hr
Special courses heli-skiing on the Ruitor Glacier, snowboarding, telemark
Guiding companies Andrea Perrod, or through ski school

CROSS-COUNTRY
Ski schools Ruitor
Loipe location and size 26.5km total, from Thovex to Promise

CHILDCARE
Non-ski kindergarten none
Ski kindergarten none
Babysitting list available from tourist office

OTHER SPORTS
Heli-skiing, parapente, indoor tennis, squash, bowling, swimming, fitness centre

WHAT'S NEW
● Le Ruitor hotel

FOOD AND DRINK PRICES
Coffee L1,200-1,400, bottle of house wine L12,000, beer L2,500-3,500, dish of the day L10,000

TOUR OPERATORS
Bladon Lines, Crystal, Enterprise, Interski, Neilson, Ski Norwest, Ultimate Holidays

in woodland 500m from the resort with a bus stop outside. Hotel Edelweiss is 'very basic, but OK' and the Ruitor is a new hotel.

La Rosière's accommodation has developed over the years below the Relais du Petit-St-Bernard, but the expansion of the late 1960s and 1970s, which transformed the other Tarentaise resorts, largely passed by this little backwater. A few reasonably sympathetic apartment blocks have sprung up in recent years, but most visitors stay in private chalets hidden in the trees in the Le Gollet area below the main street.

Skiing facts: La Rosière

TOURIST OFFICE
F-73700 La Rosière Montvalezan,
Savoie
Tel 33 79 06 80 51
Fax 33 79 06 83 20

THE RESORT
By road Calais 940km
By rail Bourg-St-Maurice 23km, buses
to the resort
By air Lyon 2½ hrs
Visitor beds 7,000 (91% apartments,
9% hotels)
Transport free bus to lifts

THE SKIING
Longest run Marmottes, 850m (red)
Number of lifts 18 in La Rosière,
35 in area
Number of trails/pistes 33 in
La Rosière, 60 in area (15% beginner,
36% easy, 34% intermediate,
15% difficult)
Total of trails/pistes 60km in La
Rosière, 135km in area
Nursery slopes 2 lifts, 50m
Summer skiing none
Snowmaking 1 mobile snow-cannon

LIFT PASSES
Area pass Domaine International
(covers La Rosière and La Thuile),
666-786FF for 6 days. La Rosière,
501-591FF for 6 days
Day pass La Rosière 112FF, Domaine
International 160FF
Half-day pass La Rosière, 9am-1pm or
12.30-5pm, 80FF
Beginners 2 free lifts (Clarine 1 and
Le Dahu)
Children La Rosière, 4-11 yrs,
333-391FF for 6 days. Domaine
International, 4-11 yrs, 439-519FF for
6 days. Free for 4 yrs and under
Pensioners 60 yrs and over, as

children. Free for 70 yrs and over
Credit cards accepted yes

SKI SCHOOLS
Adults ESF, 9.15-11.45am or
2.30-5pm, 365FF for 6 days
Children ESF, 4-11 yrs, 9.15-11.45am
or 2.30-5pm, 325FF for 6 days
Private lessons 130FF per hr
Special courses heli-skiing,
snowboarding, ski-touring
Guiding companies Nouvelles Traces

CROSS-COUNTRY
Ski schools ESF
Loipe location and size 12km, near
the altiport

CHILDCARE
Non-ski kindergarten Le Village des
Enfants, 1-10 yrs, 9am-6pm, 140FF
per day, extra 30FF per day for lunch
Ski kindergarten Le Village des
Enfants, 1-10 yrs, 9am-6pm, 170FF
per day (includes 1 hr instruction), extra
30FF per day for lunch
Babysitting list available from tourist
office

OTHER SPORTS
Heli-skiing, parapente, dog-sledding,
snow-shoe walks, tobogganing,
fitness centre

WHAT'S NEW
● Fitness centre ● Le Village
des Enfants

FOOD AND DRINK PRICES
Coffee 5FF, bottle of house wine 65FF,
beer 12FF, dish of the day 50FF

TOUR OPERATORS
Equity Total Ski, Enterprise,
Ski Chamois, Ski Olympic

A regular free bus service connects Le Gollet and the outlying hamlet of Les Eucherts to the main ski area. The buses cease running soon after the lifts close and après-ski excursions from Le Gollet involve strenuous hikes up one of the 'short-cuts' to the main road. A number of simple, convenient hotels provide accommodaton nearer the ski area. These include the Plein Soleil and the original Relais. The family-run Hotel Le Solaret is popular with reporters. Le Vanoise is also recommended for families, as the kindergarten is housed in the same building. The Terrasses apartments are 300m from the lifts and are warmly recommended. Self-caterers are pleasantly surprised at the choice and the reasonable prices in the supermarket.

Eating out

La Thuile has an acceptable choice of restaurants. Recommendations include Les Marmottes ('an excellent evening out') and La Bricole, a converted barn between the old and new parts of the resort. Lo Creton and La Grotta pizzerias are both cheap and cheerful. The raclette in the Planibel Complex is said to be 'very reasonable'. The Planibel Hotel is said to be 'smart and expensive'. Others favoured by reporters are La Maison de Laurent and La Tufeja. The Gelateria by the gondola station is justly famous for its ice-cream and cakes.

In **La Rosière**, recommended restaurants include the Terrasse du Yéti ('the greatest pizzas') and La Pitchounette, as well as the Relais du Petit-St-Bernard. Le Christophi is known for its fondue and raclette. La Chaumière is seven kilometres away in the the village of Montvalezan in an old restored Savoyard farmhouse.

Après-ski

After-skiing entertainment is not **La Thuile**'s strong point and there is little to do apart from tour the bars. La Crèmerie, Bar Bricolette and La Brasserie are all crowded when the lifts close. The action later moves to Le Rendez-vous pub and later still to the Bricole disco and LP Disco Music.

Aside from the sports centre in the Planibel Complex, non- skiers are not well catered for. The cross-country trails are not enormously extensive, but are attractively set in the wooded valley that runs down from the Ruitor Glacier to La Thuile.

La Rosière's après-ski usually begins directly after the lifts close at the Relais bar (also known as Toni's). On fine evenings the balcony is packed with people enjoying the view, the *vin chaud*, and the pizzas. Arpin's bar and Le Dahu, are also popular. The Noetiluc disco is for late-night revellers.

There are scenic walks around La Rosière for non-skiers and a regular bus service provides excursions to Bourg-St-Maurice and the other towns and villages dotted along the valley. The 12km cross-country trail winds through the woods and is suitable for all standards.

Andermatt, Uri

ALTITUDE 1447m (4,746ft)

• •

Good points tough runs, alpine charm, extensive off-piste skiing, easy rail access, reliable resort-level snow, ski-touring
Bad points lack of easy runs, limited nursery slopes, poor skiing convenience, lift queues, shortage of mountain restaurants, lack of facilities for non-skiers and children, quiet après-ski, limited tree-level skiing
Linked or nearby resorts Hospental (I), Oberalp-Sedrun (n), Realp (I)

Judging by the lack of tour operator presence in the resort and a consequent lack of readers' letters, we should not be including Andermatt in this book. But its vast off-piste skiing opportunities make it one of Switzerland's little gems which cannot be ignored. Andermatt is a retreat for a dedicated skiing minority, with a relaxed atmosphere and a reputation for heavy snowfalls. Once much favoured by the British, Andermatt is now ignored by all but a devoted few good skiers, many of whom are attracted to the resort by the specialist off-piste ski schools. When conditions are good, weekends, Christmas and Easter can become overcrowded with local Swiss and Italians, but most of the time the resort sleeps peacefully under its blanket of snow.

Andermatt is often depicted as being at the crossroads of the Alps. Indeed it was once one of the busiest of Swiss resorts, on the route to the St Gotthard pass into Italy. Now the high Urseren valley, of which Andermatt, the main settlement, is under-passed by the Gotthard road and rail tunnels, making it a virtual dead-end in winter. The roads from Andermatt over the Furka and Oberalp passes also close when the first snow falls, although tunnel links are maintained for motor-rail.

Andermatt's main business is the military; the village is one of Switzerland's major centres for the training of alpine troops. Indeed, on arrival in the village, visitors' first sight is of bleak barracks and precipitous mountains, although the real Andermatt is an attractive village with cobbled streets, which has retained its traditional character.

The skiing is certainly challenging, with Andermatt a well-known centre for ski-touring and mountaineering; the lift system is limited, and bad weather and weekend queues can make skiing difficult.

The skiing
Top 2965m (9,725ft) bottom 1445m (4,740ft)
There are four ski areas along the sides of the Urseren valley, between the Furka and Oberalp passes. The two main ones lie at either end of Andermatt, the two smaller and less popular areas south-west of Andermatt at the villages of Hospental and Realp.

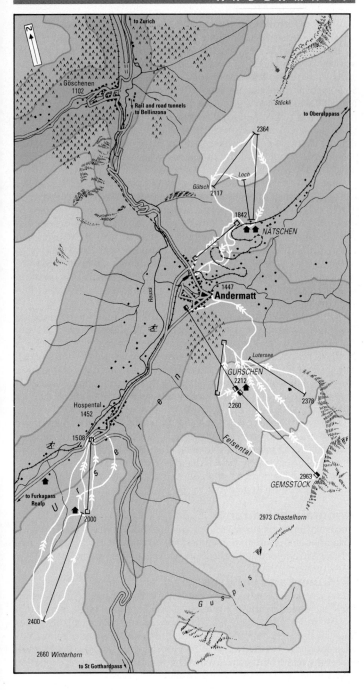

The main **mountain access** is on the two-stage Gemsstock cable car. The Gemsstock itself climbs steeply from the south-western edge of the village to the peak at 2965m. The simple lift system cannot easily manage large numbers of people, despite the recent upgrading of the cable car capacity. There are a couple of lifts around the middle station at Gurschen where the mountainside levels out to provide a small intermediate area. Above and below, the runs are demanding. The steep north-facing slopes keep their snow well, but avalanche danger can close large areas after snowfalls. From the top station, which offers magnificent views, you can traverse to an interesting red (intermediate) run around the shoulder of the mountain, with a fairly steep section followed by a long path back to the Gurschen.

Alternatively you can tackle the options down the shaded face of the Gemsstock which offers 800m of severe vertical. The top half is rugged and tree-less with a mixture of glacier and rocks. Apart from the treacherous off-piste skiing in this bowl, there are some long off-piste alternatives in other directions from the top station, with the Guspis run ending up at the St Gotthardpass, the Felsental near Hospental, or to Andermatt via Unteralp. None of these descents should be tackled without a guide. The bottom half of the main Gemsstock face is no more welcoming than the top, with a single long and challenging black (difficult) run with drops of nearly 30°.

A chair-lift from near the barracks or a short train-ride towards the Oberalp pass brings you to Nätschen, where three drag-lifts serve a small, sunny area of mainly easy south-west-facing pistes. There is plenty of scope for off-piste skiing between the top station and the railway line. The main piste to Andermatt is easy, mostly following the road, which is closed in winter. There is also a direct, unpisted descent under the chairs; this begins moderately, but becomes much steeper towards the village.

Above the village at Hospental, on the south side of the valley, there are just two lifts towards the Winterhorn, with a chair over the steeper lower half of the mountain, followed by a drag serving open blue (easy) runs. The lifts are rarely crowded and give access to some good skiing. Realp, several kilometres further away, at 1538m, has a little-frequented drag-lift suitable for beginners.

Mountain restaurants

Mountain eating places are thin on the ground. There is a waiter-service restaurant at Gurschen, the Gemsstock cable car mid-way station, two at Nätschen and one at the top of the chair above Hospental.

Beginners and children

The main ski school has a few English-speaking instructors. However, there is no kindergarten or nursery. Celebrated local guide Martin Epp is now more often seen teaching powder technique on the slopes beneath the Eiger above Wengen. Another local skier and climber, Alex Clapasson, runs weekly off-piste and touring courses on a weekly basis under the name Mountain Reality. This is subject to tough competition from Canadian guide John Hogg's Alpine Adventures Company.

The resort

Andermatt stretches along a single, curving main street between the two ski areas. The old compact heart of the village receives little sun, hemmed in as it is by mountains, and there is not much traffic and no public transport (both are unnecessary here) on the narrow streets. Accommodation here is a mixture of hotels, some faded relics from the resort's past and others flamboyantly colourful, as well as some appealing old chalets.

Accommodation

This is mainly in hotels, with no location ideal for skiing. For the Gemsstock, the Aurora is most convenient. The central Gasthaus zum Sternen is the most attractive old wooden chalet in Andermatt: cheap, fun and a popular meeting and eating place. The Ochsen is an inexpensive bed and breakfast place. The Bergidyll is a comfortable chalet-style

....

Skiing facts: Andermatt

TOURIST OFFICE
CH-6490 Andermatt, Zentralschweiz
Tel 41 44 67454
Fax 41 44 68185

THE RESORT
By road Calais 805km
By rail station in resort
By air Zurich 3 hrs
Visitor beds 1,200 (58% apartments and guesthouses, 42% hotels)
Transport no bus service, good train service

THE SKIING
Longest run Gemsstock-Andermatt, 4.5km (black)
Number of lifts 12
Number of trails/pistes 23 (30% easy, 26% intermediate, 44% difficult)
Total of trails/pistes 53km
Nursery slopes 1 at Realp
Summer skiing none
Snowmaking none

LIFT PASSES
Area pass (covers the Urseren valley) SF171 for 6 days
Day pass Gemsstock SF46
Half-day pass Gemsstock SF31 after 12.30pm
Beginners coupons or single tickets
Children 6-15 yrs, SF114 for 6 days, whole area, free for 6 yrs and under
Pensioners 62 yrs and over, Nätschen SF25 per day, Winterhorn SF24-31 per day. Gemsstock, no reduction

Credit cards accepted yes

SKI SCHOOLS
Adults Swiss Ski School, 2 hrs in morning and afternoon, SF160 for 5 days
Children Swiss Ski School, 2 hrs in morning and afternoon, SF145 for 5 days
Private lessons SF50 per hr, SF180 per day
Special courses ski-touring
Guiding companies Alpine Adventures, Mountain Reality

CROSS-COUNTRY
Ski schools Swiss Ski School
Loipe location and size 20km between Andermatt and Realp

CHILDCARE
Non-ski kindergarten none
Ski kindergarten none
Babysitting difficult

OTHER SPORTS
Ski-mountaineering, hang-gliding, skating, curling, tobogganing, fitness centre, bowling, sleigh rides

FOOD AND DRINK PRICES
Coffee SF2.80, bottle of house wine SF12.50, beer SF3.80, dish of the day SF18

TOUR OPERATORS
Made to Measure

....

hotel near the station, and popular with the British. The Sonne is comfortably traditional and well placed between the village and the cable-car. Self-caterers can buy provisions at the Co-op supermarket, or at the cheese shop, two bakeries and two butchers.

Eating out

The restaurants, apart from the friendly Tell, are in hotels. The Postillion is recommended, as are the Sternen and the lovely old Hotel St Gotthard at Hospental.

Après-ski

Après-ski revolves mainly around the bars; the Tell and the Adler are packed with locals and soldiers, and others, including the Sternen and cosy Ochsen pub, are popular with skiers. The Postillion Bar, City Bar, Gasthaus Sternen and the Piccadilly Pub are popular with locals and the army. The Café Gotthard has dancing, and Dancing Downhill draws the crowds. Other after-skiing activities include skating, indoor tennis and bowling. Shopping is limited to three sports shops, one boutique, gift and food shops.

Arosa, Graubunden

ALTITUDE 1800m (5,904ft)

••

Good points all-round winter sports resort, easy runs, ideal for family holidays, activities for non-skiers, variety of mountain restaurants
Bad points small ski area, lack of tough runs, spread-out resort, difficult road access
Linked or nearby resorts Davos (n), Klosters (n), Lenzerheide (n) – *see separate chapters*

On a snowy February afternoon in 1883, ski-tourer Dr Otto Herwig-Hold stumbled across the tiny village of Inner Arosa high in the Swiss Graubunden while looking for a place to shelter for the night. The next morning Dr Hold, with seal-skins attached to the soles of his 230cm skis, began his climb of the 2512m Hörnli. Later that day he looked back down at the village and its frozen lake and suddenly saw the enormous business possibilities of the area. This, he realised, would be a prime site for his new tuberculosis sanatorium, where patients could benefit from both the fresh alpine air and the exercise of skiing. The hospital was duly built and, with its wide range of international patients, was to place the name of Arosa firmly on the alpine map.

Today Arosa remains one of the truly all-round ski resorts of the Alps, patronised each season, as it has been for most of the century, by holidaymakers from mainly Switzerland and Germany, although it does have a keen following of British who return year after year.

The skiing

Top 2653m (8,490ft) bottom 1800m (5,904ft)

Arosa's guests are not here to bash the pistes from dawn until dusk; they are more in search of an all-round winter sports experience, part of which is a gentle daily foray on to the piste. The ski area consists of wide, sunny slopes, mostly above the tree-line and covering the three peaks of Hörnli, Weisshorn and Bruggerhorn. It is well linked and, although there are only 16 lifts, there is an encouraging total of 70km of piste. Much of this is made up of blue (easy) and red (intermediate) runs over hilly, rather than mountainous, terrain ideal for beginners and early intermediates.

One of the few hazards of Arosa's skiing is the number of pedestrians and tobogganers on the piste. Non-skiers can buy hiking passes covering gondolas and some chair-lifts. There are paths for walkers and wooden benches all over the pistes. Cross-country skiing is a primary ingredient of the winter formula with the two locations on the Obersee lake and on the scenic golf course at the slightly higher suburb of Maran.

The lift system, by Swiss standards, is modern and efficient with the main **mountain access** by chair-lift or gondola from the centre of Obersee, or by drag-lift from Inner Arosa. A peak-season alternative is to take the free bus to the Hörnli gondola on the far side of Inner Arosa.

This is not a resort for expert skiers, although it is suitable for off-piste enthusiasts. From the top of the Hörnli you can ski the unmarked terrain with a guide all the way to the neighbouring resorts of Lenzerheide, Davos and Klosters. The more difficult piste skiing is reached from the top of the 2653m Weisshorn, a treacherous black (difficult) run which brings you down to the Carmennahütte, the best of half-a-dozen mountain restaurants.

Mountain restaurants

The Carmennahütte is a traditional mountain hut with a weird collection of stuffed animals, old guns and bottles, ancient farm machinery and gigantic cow bells. The excellent Swiss cuisine includes *Rösti* and *Käseschnitte*. Outside the door is a real igloo where, if you stoop through its approach tunnel, you will find yourself inside one of the more unusual bars of the Alps. Work on the igloo starts every October and it takes two months to build. Towards the end of each season it is demolished for safety reasons. The other mountain restaurant of note is the Hörnlihütte with wonderful panoramic views.

Beginners and children

Switzerland's most celebrated extreme skier and mountain guide Sylvain Saudan began his career as a teacher in the Arosa Ski School, which has been in operation for a good 60 years. It claims to have a majority of English-speaking instructors and operates from four different locations around the resort. Reporters praise the classes, which offer 'just the right combination of new challenges yet not pushing one too far'. The children's ski school is less highly commended, with one tale of novice offspring being abandoned half-way down a blue run.

The nursery slope in Inner Arosa, opposite the Kulm Hotel, is the best. Lifts for accompanied children up to 6 years old are free and half-price for those up to 16 years old.

The resort

Arosa is in fact two resorts: a two-kilometre hill separates Inner Arosa, the original village, from the larger, less attractive Obersee area with its grey stone buildings. It is not, however, lacking in ambience. Of the all-round winter resorts which cater for non-skiers, Arosa must merit a place on the podium. This is one of those villages which bustles during the day when other ski resorts are abandoned. Shoppers throng the streets, the coffee houses are crowded and everywhere you look there are families tobogganing, elderly walkers taking their constitutionals and horse-drawn sleighs conveying the well-wrapped, well-heeled couples from one part of this two-centre resort to the other.

The toboggan is an essential form of transport here. Cars are strongly discouraged and indeed banned between midnight and 6am except for arrivals and departures. In the cause of traditional transport, the main road is only partially cleared and the smaller ones not at all. Arosa is therefore well suited to make the world's best (and most expensive) hand-crafted toboggans. You can, however, hire more mundane versions for a few francs per day. Village access is not easy, with no less than 244 bends in 32km up the dramatic road from the busy medieval valley town of Chur. Train travel through stunning scenery is much the easier option.

Skiing facts: Arosa

TOURIST OFFICE
CH-7050 Arosa, Graubunden
Tel 41 81 311621
Fax 41 81 313135

THE RESORT
By road Calais 910km
By rail Obersee station in resort
By air Zurich 3 hrs
Visitor beds 8,245 (59% hotels, 41% apartments and chalets)
Transport bus service between Maran and Hörnli

THE SKIING
Longest run Weisshorngipfel to Tschuggen, 5.5km (red)
Number of lifts 16
Number of trails/pistes 33 (31% easy, 57% intermediate, 12% difficult)
Total of trails/pistes 70km
Nursery slopes 2 lifts
Summer skiing none
Snowmaking none

LIFT PASSES
Area pass SF197 for 6 days
Day pass SF46
Half-day pass SF34 from midday
Beginners free baby lifts at Inner Arosa and Obersee, or points tickets
Children 6-15 yrs, SF99 for 6 days, free for 5 yrs and under
Pensioners 15% reduction for women 62 yrs and over and men 65 yrs and over
Credit cards accepted yes

SKI SCHOOLS
Adults Swiss Ski School, 9.45-11.45am or 2.15-4.15pm, SF115 for 5 half-days
Children Swiss Ski School, 9.45-11.45am or 2.15-4.15pm, SF105 for 5 half-days
Private lessons SF50 per hr
Special courses snowboarding, telemark
Guiding companies through tourist office

CROSS-COUNTRY
Ski schools Geeser
Loipe location and size 25km total at Isel, Pratschalp, Maran and Obersee

CHILDCARE
Non-ski kindergarten day care through various hotels, 9am-6pm (weekdays only), ages and prices on application
Ski kindergarten Swiss Ski School, 4 yrs and over, 9.45-11.45am or 2.15-4.15pm, SF105 for 5 half-days
Babysitting list available from tourist office

OTHER SPORTS
Skating, curling, hot-air ballooning, ice-driving, dog-sledding, luge-ing, sleigh rides, parapente, snow-mobiling, snow-shoeing, hang-gliding, tobogganing, indoor tennis and golf, squash, swimming, fitness centre, bowling

WHAT'S NEW
● Arosa-Weisshorn cable car
● escalator from the Weisshorn cable car station to the Weisshorn peak

FOOD AND DRINK PRICES
Coffee SF3, bottle of house wine SF24, beer SF3, dish of the day SF20

TOUR OPERATORS
Kuoni, Made to Measure, Ski Choice, Ski Gower, Swiss Travel Service

Accommodation

Deciding where to stay in Arosa is particularly difficult because of the diffuse nature of the resort. There is a wide range of hotels, many of which run their own courtesy mini-bus service and some have free crèches. Grand Hotel Tschuggen, above the High Street, receives good reports for its service and food. The modern Arosa Kulm in Inner Arosa replaced the original 1882 building. Its facilities include a nightclub with a live band. The Posthotel is centrally situated for the nightlife and the lifts. The Hotel Hof Maran, a couple of kilometres from the centre next to the cross-country track, is rather dark and depressing at first sight, and after dark it becomes 'like a mortuary', according to reporters, but the staff are friendly and the restaurant is good. The Sporthotel Valsana attracts a loyal following; its facilities include a swimming-pool and a free all-day kindergarten for 3-year-olds and over. The three-star Eden is well positioned in the centre of Arosa and is, according to its management, suitable for 'younger, sportier guests'.

Eating out

Arosa has well over 40 restaurants to suit all tastes and budgets. The Belluga at the Hotel Kulm is a popular restaurant, as are the Restaurant Français in the Hotel Tschuggen and the Säumerstube in the Hotel Eden. The Hof Maran has a pleasant dining-room and Sporthotel Valsana has an à la carte restaurant. Many of the hotels have weekly candlelight dinners, with the one at the Streiff hotel comprising eight courses.

Après-ski

The nightlife is surprisingly lively for a resort where many of the regulars are in their 60s and 70s, varying from noisy bars on the main street to sophisticated nightclubs with live music in a dozen of the major hotels. The average age of holidaymaker appears to be 35 and over. Kaiser's is the main place for tea and cakes, and later on the Brüggli, Taverna and Grischuna bars are popular and the Tschuetta has live music and a good atmosphere. The Barosa Kitchen Club in the Hotel Eden is recommended for dancing, the Garda bar has folklore evenings. Discos include Nuts and Galaxy.

The main shops clustered around the shore of the lake and on the main street include a number of expensive boutiques and jewellers, as well as the usual array of sports shops and a supermarket. For some alternative après-ski there is floodlit cross-country skiing, as well as curling and ice hockey matches to watch.

Crans Montana, Valais

ALTITUDE 1500m (4,920ft)

••

Good points big and well-linked ski area, extensive nursery slopes, easy skiing, tree-line skiing, activities for non-skiers, ski-touring, sunny slopes, cross-country facilities
Bad points heavy traffic, limited tough runs, lack of alpine charm
Linked or nearby resorts Aminona (l), Anzère (n), Bluche (n)

Crans and Montana started life separately, but steadily grew towards each other until, just over 20 years ago, they officially met and became one resort named Crans Montana and at the same time Switzerland's largest ski resort. The town, once a world-famous centre for convalescence after tuberculosis, sprawls across six kilometres of sunny plateau, ideal terrain for the two golf courses the ski area becomes in the summer.

Although the two towns are officially one, Crans and Montana still retain their distinct images. Crans is the more affluent, cosmopolitan resort where the luxury shops sell furs, jewellery, caviar and designer goods. Montana is more of a skiers' resort. But the two have much the same hotel and restaurant quality and prices, as well as sharing the same skiing.

If you decide to come by car, driving is easy in Crans Montana: there is free parking at each lift station and off-street parking in the centre. Having a car is indeed an advantage as day trips to Anzère, and even Verbier, Zermatt and Saas Fee, are all possible.

The skiing
Top 3000m (9,840ft) bottom 1500m (4,920ft)
Crans Montana's skiing is made up of three well-linked ski areas with **mountain access** by gondola from any one of the four base stations: Crans (two gondolas start here), Montana, Les Barzettes and Aminona. The pistes are pleasantly sunny. On a good December day, the south-facing slopes receive eight hours of sunshine, while other Swiss resorts may be lucky to get one. There is however the drawback of poor snow conditions later on in the season. The skiing is split between wide, open slopes and tree-level runs, and although there is some good off-piste to be found, there is only one black (difficult) run and, on the whole, the skiing suits the average intermediate rather than those looking for more advanced thrills. One reporter notes that the skiing is 'ideal for the skier trying to get off the intermediate plateau'.

The main lifts from Crans and Montana meet up at Cry-d'Err, in the middle of the western, and easiest, end of the ski area. From here the run to Chetzeron, where there is a mountain restaurant, is easy enough for second-week skiers to manage. Two drag-lifts take you back up again. The blue (easy) runs from here down to Crans and Montana are on paths which are often congested and in poor condition, with alpine and cross-country skiers as well as walkers all competing for space.

The second sector is Les Violettes in the centre of the ski area, comprising a network of red (intermediate) runs, some of them mogulled, and a red run down to the resort. It is also here that you will find the resort's only black run, served by the Toula chair-lift and drag, which is short and not at all steep. There is a long and attractive run through the trees from here to Plumachit. The focal point of the area, however, is the Plaine-Morte cable car, which climbs from Les Violettes up to the immense, flat glacier of the same name, with its fabulous views of the surrounding peaks. The slopes up here are mainly used for cross-country skiing, summer skiing (on three lifts), and as the jumping-off point for ski touring up to the Weisshorn and Wildstrubel mountains before going over the back towards the resorts of Gstaad, Adelboden and Lenk.

Queuing is not a problem in Crans Montana except at the Plaine-Morte Glacier; the plans to rebuild the cable car for the 1994-5 season should see an end to these in the future.

The Aminona area is the least crowded of the three and also an alternative way up the mountain in the morning via a 10-minute bus ride from Crans Montana. There is easy skiing on the blue runs below Petit Bonvin, served by a couple of drag-lifts, and a blue run home at the end of the day.

For upper intermediates and advanced skiers several challenging runs can be found, including the eastern side of the Cry-d'Err, and beside and below the Nationale lift to Barzettes. There is also scope for a variety of off-piste descents, especially through the trees, with Chetzeron especially good. The area between Les Faverges and Aminona is another interesting off-piste variation, and Col de Poche is praised by one reporter for its 'good steep bumps' and off-piste skiing. Plaine-Morte to Hertentz is another recommended itinerary, as is the Toula area and the back of Bella-Lui. The marked off-piste run from Bella-Lui to Les Violettes is more of a fun, intermediate traverse than anything else.

Crans Montana is an excellent resort for cross-country skiers. There are 6 different loipes to choose from, including 12km on the glacier and 6km on the golf course.

Mountain restaurants

Most of the mountain eating places are convenient rather than atmospheric, and are accessible to walkers and cross-country skiers as well. Merbé, at the mid-station of the Cry-d'Err gondola, is one of the more attractive, and Plumachit is highly recommended by reporters. Chetzeron and Bella-Lui are both waiter-service with sunny terraces, and Petit Bonvin has both self- and waiter-service restaurants. Others include Grand Signal, Violettes and Plaine-Morte.

Beginners and children

The three nursery slope areas are at Grand Signal in the Cry-d'Err area, at Petit Bonvin, high above Aminona, and on the golf course at village

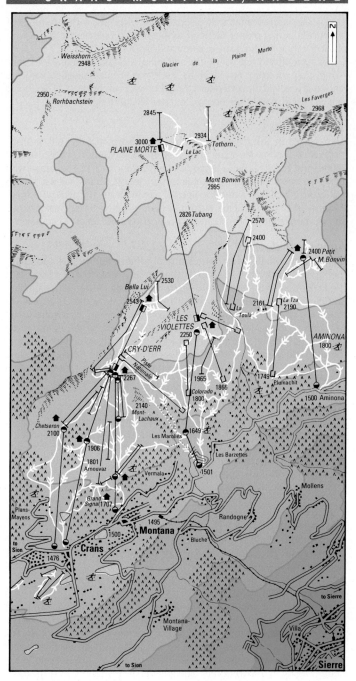

level. Crans and Montana have separate ski schools, with a number of different meeting points. General reports on ski schools are good, with praise for 'helpful, English-speaking instructors'.

We have mixed reports on the suitability of Crans Montana for family skiing, ranging from 'not ideal' to 'everyone seemed satisfied with the kindergarten, with special praise for the crèche run by nuns'. The choice is in fact good, with three non-ski and one ski kindergarten.

The resort

Crans starts in the valley at 1500m and reaches up the hill to Plans Mayens at 1620m. Montana stretches up to the suburb of Vermala at 1600m and across as far as Barzettes. Only Aminona is still separate, with a free ski-bus linking it to the main urban sprawl. Crans has world-class conference facilities, along the lines of the Institute at Davos, and hosts the annual Crans Montana Forum. Indeed wealthy Swiss businessmen and women from Geneva form the major part of the resort's clientèle.

Accommodation

The accommodation here is mainly in comfortable hotels and apartments, with more five-star hotels than in any other Swiss resort, with the exception of St Moritz. The Hauts de Crans, in Montana, is a luxury complex in the woods above the village. The Etoile and the Nationale in Crans are centrally positioned. The Mont Blanc is an atmospheric old hotel above Plans Mayens and conveniently located for the skiing. Hotel de la Forêt is highly recommended with, reportedly, excellent food and the addition of a good annexe across the road. The Olympic is good value, and Le Green has recently been rebuilt and now sports its own fitness centre.

Après-ski

The Amadeus bar is where the ski school groups tend to gather after skiing. Les Granges has a typical alpine atmosphere, and Constellation attracts the resort's large number of snowboarders. The Memphis and the Hotel Forêt both have piano bars, and the New Pub and Le Green are popular drinking spots. Later on, the Pascha disco is for a mainly young clientèle, the Absolut is a new disco, and the 'No 1' is certainly worth a visit.

Eating out

Restaurants include Le Vieux Moulin, Restaurant des Vignettes, and the Continental. The most popular are Restaurant de la Diligence, Le Raccard and Chez Mischa.

Anzère 1430m (4,691ft)

Anzère is a small, modern resort built on a slope to the west of Crans Montana but with its own separate ski area. It is not the most convenient of resorts, but neither is it as unattractive as some purpose-built villages. It has a pleasant village atmosphere with its modern apartments disguised as large traditional chalets, and a car-free zone in the centre, along with two hotels. The lifts depart from both ends of town, so location is not critical, although of the two access routes the gondola is a warmer way to travel up the mountain in winter than by chair.

The sunny little ski area rises to 2420m and has wonderful views across the Rhône valley. The runs are mainly of an easy intermediate standard, set above the tree-line. Apart from the inconveniently positioned small nursery slope at the top of the mountain, there is not a lot to which near-beginners can aspire. Experts are not well catered for,

Skiing facts: Crans Montana

TOURIST OFFICE
CH-3963 Crans, CH-3962 Montana, Valais
Tel 41 27 412132/413041
Fax 41 27 411794/417460

THE RESORT
By road Calais 1012km
By rail Sierre 15km, funicular or bus to resort
By air Geneva 3 hrs, Sion 22km
Visitor beds 40,000 (87% apartments and chalets, 13% hotels)
Transport free bus between Crans and Aminona

THE SKIING
Longest run Plaine Morte, 7.5km (red)
Number of lifts 40
Number of trails/pistes 60 (25% easy, 50% intermediate, 25% difficult)
Total of trails/pistes 160km
Nursery slopes 5 lifts
Summer skiing on Plaine-Morte Glacier, 3 lifts
Snowmaking 800m covered

LIFT PASSES
Area pass (covers Crans Montana-Aminona) SF201 for 6 days
Day pass SF44
Half-day pass SF30, from 11.30am
Beginners 1 free lift in Bluche (2km from Crans Montana)
Children 6-15 yrs, SF120 for 6 days, free for 6 yrs and under
Pensioners women 62 yrs and over, men 65 yrs and over, as children
Credit cards accepted yes

SKI SCHOOLS
Adults Swiss Ski School in Crans, SF219 for 6 days, 4 hrs per day. Swiss Ski School in Montana, SF150 for 5 days, 3½ hrs per day
Children as adults

Private lessons SF48 for 50 mins
Special courses snowboarding, telemark
Guiding companies Swiss Ski School, Swiss Alpine Club

CROSS-COUNTRY
Ski schools Swiss Ski School
Loipe location and size 45km in 6 areas, including Plaine-Morte Glacier

CHILDCARE
Non-ski kindergarten Bibiland, 3-6 yrs, 9am-midday and 2- 6.30pm, SF23 per day, extras SF12 per day for lunch. Fleurs des Champs, 2 mths-12 yrs, 8am-6pm, SF40 per day, extra F7 per day for lunch. Garderie d'Ycoor (Les Coccinelles), 2 yrs and over, SF40 per day, extra SF13 per day for lunch
Ski kindergarten Jardin des Neiges, 3-6 yrs, SF65 per day, SF150 for 5 days, both including lunch
Babysitting list available from tourist offices

OTHER SPORTS
Curling, hot-air ballooning, skating, luge-ing, parapente, hang-gliding, climbing wall, squash, indoor tennis, bowling, tobogganing, fitness centres, swimming

WHAT'S NEW
● 4-seater chair-lift, La Barmaz to Les Violettes ● extension of the children's ski paradise

FOOD AND DRINK PRICES
Coffee SF2.80, bottle of house wine SF30, beer SF3, dish of the day SF16

TOUR OPERATORS
Bladon Lines, Hoverspeed, Inghams, Kuoni, Made to Measure, Neilson, Ski Europe, Swiss Travel Service

although the long runs through the trees to the village offer some variety and challenge. The ski school is well run, but some of its instructors do not speak good English. There are ski and non-ski kindergartens.

Recommended hotels include the Eden, which also has a piano bar, and the self-catering accommodation is of a high standard. The nightlife is on the quiet side with a couple of discos and over a dozen restaurants ranging from pizzerias to more serious dining.

TOURIST OFFICE
CH-1972, Valais
Tel 41 27 382519

TOUR OPERATORS
Made to Measure

Davos-Klosters, Graubunden

Davos

ALTITUDE 1560m (5,117ft)

Good points large intermediate ski area, extensive off-piste skiing, variety of restaurants in town, tree-level skiing, good ski-touring, cross-country skiing possibilities, facilities for non-skiers
Bad points traffic, limited for beginners, large and busy town, lack of alpine charm, quiet après-ski
Linked or nearby resorts Arosa (n), Klosters (l), St Moritz (n) – *see separate chapters*, Gargellen (n), Glaris (l), Wolfgang (l)

Klosters

ALTITUDE 1130m (3,706ft)

Good points large ski area, extensive off-piste skiing, range of mountain restaurants, ski-touring, variety of tough runs, tree-level skiing
Bad points quiet après-ski, difficult mountain access, limited for beginners, traffic
Linked or nearby resorts Arosa (n), Davos (l), Gargellen (n), Küblis (l), Saas (l), Serneus (l), Wolfgang (l)

The mighty Parsenn above Davos and Klosters comprises one of the great ski areas of the world, with natural undulating terrain that is ever changing. Wide-open, steep snowfields and gentle, long cruising slopes lead down to magnificent runs through the trees and on into serenely beautiful sunny pastures. Always at the journey's end is a railway station linked into the region's efficient funicular network, which takes you home, or back to a lift point. The history of skiing is interwoven with the Parsenn and if modern skiing has one birthplace, then this is it. In its 24 November 1883 edition, the local newspaper of the already established spa town of Davos reported: 'It has come to our attention that this winter in Davos people are having a go at the Norwegian sport of skiing. As you probably know, skis are a kind of elongated snowshoe with which you can travel very quickly in deep snow, both up and down mountains. Why should these "skis" not replace the ungainly snowshoes which are commonplace around here?'

Why indeed not? Six years later an Englishwoman, a certain Miss Katherine Symonds, introduced skis to the growing British winter colony in Davos and in 1894 Sir Arthur Conan Doyle wrote passionately

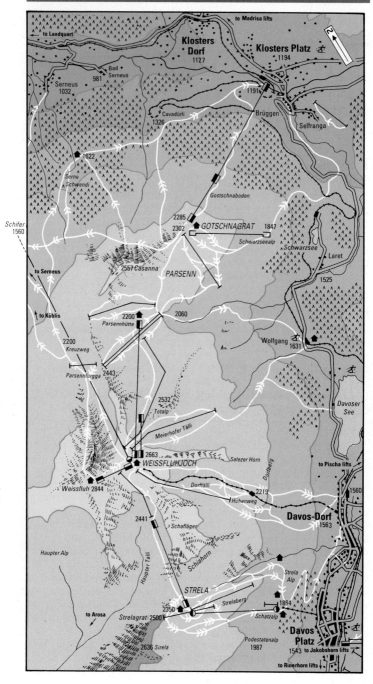

to Madrisa lifts

← to Landquart

Klosters Dorf 1127

Klosters Platz 1194

Bad Serneus • 981

Serneus 1032

1191

Brüggen

Selfranga

Cavadürli 1326

1622

Serne Schwendi

Gostschnaboden

Schifer 1560

2285 2302

GOTSCHNAGRAT 1847

Schwarzseealp

Schwarzsee

to Serneus

2557 Casanna

PARSENN

Laret 1525

↑ to Küblis

2200 *Parsennhütte*

2060

2200 *Kreuzweg*

Wolfgang 1631

Parsennfurgga 2443

2532 *Totalp*

Meierhofer Tälli

Davoser See

Salezer Horn

2663 *WEISSFLUHJOCH*

to Pischa lifts

Dorftälli

Dorberg

2219

1560

Weissfluh 2844

Höhenweg

Davos-Dorf 1563

2441

Schafläger

Schiahorn

Haupter Alp

Haupter Tälli

Strela Alp

STRELA

1864

Strelaberg

Schatzalp

to Arosa

2350

Strelagrati 2500

2636 Strela

Podestatenalp 1987

Davos Platz

1543 to Jakobshorn lifts

to Rinerhorn lifts

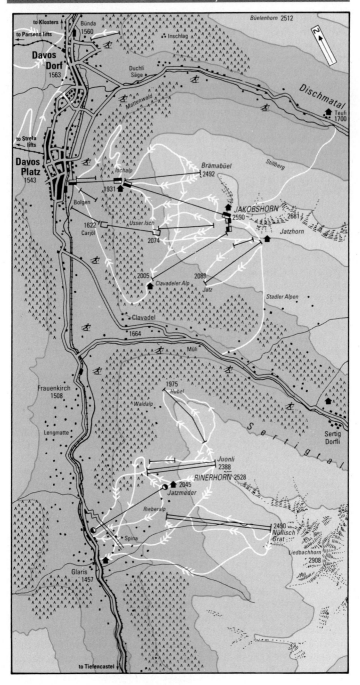

Büelenhorn 2512

to Klosters
to Parsenn lifts
Bünda 1560
Inschlag

Davos Dorf 1563

Duchli Säge

Mattenwald

Dischmatal

Teufi 1700

to Strela lifts

Davos Platz 1543

Ischalp

Brämabüel 2492

Stillberg

1931

Bolgen

JAKOBSHORN 2590

2681

Jatzhorn

1622 Carjöl

Usser Isch

2074

2005

2089

Jatz

Clavadeler Alp

Stadler Alpen

Clavadel

1664

Müli

Frauenkirch 1508

1975

Hubel

Waldalp

Lengmatte

Sertigtal

Sertig Dörfli

Juonli 2388

RINERHORN 2528

2045 Jatzmeder

Rieberalp

2490 Nüllisch Grat

Spina

Liedbachhorn

2908

Glaris 1457

to Tielencastel

of his ski tour from here to Arosa. Apart from their long connection with both skiing and Britain, the large, sprawling, bustling town of Davos, and Klosters, its much more rural neighbour, have little in common. The first winter guest came to Klosters for the 1904-5 season and it has never felt the need to attract package tourism to ensure its existence. Prince Charles' patronage put it firmly on the map of Europe and his narrow escape in an avalanche that killed one and seriously injured another member of the royal party in March 1988 put it on the map of the world.

This publicised the skiing around this charming village in a way that no advertising agency could ever have hoped to achieve. A new cable car was built to alleviate the dreadful queues to reach the top of the enormous north-facing mountainside above it. A couple of hotels were refurbished in response to the increase in visitors, but that apart, the people of Klosters shrugged off the mantle of fame and closed ranks to protect their annual VIP visitor. Its discreetly luxurious hotels and ancient chalets tucked away in the woods exude an air of exclusivity which positively repels any attempts at further commercialisation.

It is important not to confuse the resorts, which have similar-sounding names but are separate and quite different satellites. Klosters Dorf is a hamlet of old farm buildings and the access point to the Madrisa ski area. The next stop on the train is Klosters itself. Down the line, Davos Dorf, which (unlike Klosters Dorf) is a centre for hotels and restaurants, comes before much larger Davos Platz, the heart of the resort. The Parsenn is by no means the only ski area and a car is helpful for making the most of the region, although parking near most of the lifts is usually difficult.

You can make expeditions to St Moritz and Lenzerheide; Arosa and Gargellen (over the Austrian border) are more easily reached on skis with a guide. Apart from the train, frequent but usually overcrowded buses link Davos Dorf and Platz from early morning until late in the evening, with more occasional services running elsewhere. In Klosters, day-time buses every 30 minutes serve the Goschna and Madrisa lifts and points in between. There are buses from Serneus about every hour and regular trains linking all the ski areas except Pischa. With one or two minor exceptions, all these services are covered by the lift pass.

The skiing
Top 2844m (9,328ft) bottom 813m (2,667ft)

Apart from the main Parsenn, the skiing is divided into four distinct areas. The Madrisa, reached by gondola from Klosters Dorf, provides sunny, uncrowded and uncomplicated skiing with a tour over the Austrian border. Jakobshorn, accessed by cable car from near Davos Platz station, has some good challenging runs and great off-piste possibilities in powder conditions. Rinerhorn, reached by gondola from the village of Glaris on the railway line south of Davos Platz, is a mainly mixed intermediate area with a few long runs of over 100m vertical. Pischa, a bus ride from Davos Dorf up the narrow Flüelatal to the cable car station at Dörfji, is always uncrowded with some easy beginner slopes and excellent off-piste.

But the heart of the skiing which has made this area so famous is the huge Parsenn/Weissfluh above Davos Dorf, which links up with the Strela area above Davos Platz and the Gotschna area above Klosters Platz. Most of the lifts are on the Davos side of the mountain, but Klosters has the north-facing slopes and some of the best runs.

Mountain access from Davos Platz is via the Schatzalp funicular railway, which climbs steeply through the woods to the sunny plateau of Schatzalp at 1861m, starting point for the Strelapass ski area, which is in turn a side entrance into the main Weissfluh part of the mountain. A large and comfortable hotel, the four-star Berghotel Schatzalp, is the starting point for a toboggan run down to Platz, a path for walkers and a blue (easy) run for skiers down to Davos Dorf. Above Schatzalp the Strelabahn gondola and two drag-lifts serve the east-facing open bowl with mainly easy skiing down the middle and some steeper runs off to the side in the Guggerbachtäli.

From the Strelapass a cable car and a drag-lift take you along the ridge around the back of the 2709m Schiahorn to Weissfluhjoch, the major lift junction on the mountain and the arrival point of the Parsenn funicular railway, which climbs over 1000m vertical up from Davos Dorf. From here there is an enormous choice of runs in three directions. First, there are those back down to Davos Dorf parallel to the railway line; these runs start gently enough, but below the Höhenweg station the black (difficult) Standard Ersatz and alternative black Unterer Standard can be extremely icy. Secondly, you can explore the extensive, wide, mostly easy motorway pistes behind the Weissfluhjoch, which is also accessed by the much-enlarged cable car from Parsennhütte and the Klosters side of the mountain. Good skiers will enjoy the long run down to the hamlet of Wolfgang from the bottom of the Meierhofer Tälli drag-lift. It is steep in places, but well worth the effort for lunch in the village. Wolfgang can also be reached by a long, easy unless icy, run from Parsennhütte, which starts off blue and quickly becomes red (intermediate).

Thirdly, you can embark on tremendously long runs of over 10km to the villages of Klosters, Serneus, Saas and Küblis. Unless you start from the top of the Weissfluhgipfel, which is reached by another cable car from Weissfluhjoch, none of these is particularly difficult and all are immensely enjoyable. The easiest is a straightforward red run via Cavadürli to Klosters; the trickiest is a slightly more taxing red to Serneus. The mountain is basically north-facing and snow is reliable higher up, but the resorts are low and cover on the lower slopes is often patchy. In between the various marked runs there is some interesting off-piste to be found in the woods. The longer gondola, which rises across these previously unmechanised ski fields from Schifer at 1560m up to Weissfluhjoch, makes it possible to ski repeatedly the top part of the Serneus run.

From Klosters the two-stage Prince of Wales Gotschnagrat cable car is the only way up into the Parsenn and despite being rebuilt is still prone to serious queues. Ridiculously, this second stage has a considerably lower capacity than the first; the result is that skiers race each other across the middle station to avoid missing the cut. There are runs of varying difficulty back down again towards Klosters. The notorious Wang (or to give it is full name, the Gotschnawang) is the direct one down to the Gotschnaboden mid-station. The Wang run is a piste, but is marked on the local piste map by a broken black line. Together with the Swiss Wall above Avoriaz it has the reputation of being awesomely tough, a reputation enhanced by the fatal Royal avalanche, which did not in fact happen here at all, but on an adjacent off-piste slope. The reality is that while it is steep in places, it is by no means intimidating and can be wonderfully enjoyable in the right conditions. Because of the danger of avalanches it is not always open. There is, in fact, a variety of routes down the face and you pick the gradient to suit yourself.

Next along the mountainside is Drostobel, a long, steep and seri- ously challenging black run without all the hype. On the other side of Gotschnagrat an easy traverse takes you across to Parsennhütte and some easy runs beside the Parsennmeder drag-lift. The huge moguls on the black run beneath the Schwarzsee chair provide an interesting chal- lenge for bump-bashers. A red run from the bottom of the chair takes you down through the woods past some discreetly opulent private chalets to the edge of Klosters itself.

The sunny, south-west facing Madrisa area is reached via a gondola from Klosters Dorf and some fine, mainly intermediate skiing, although it is not on a par with the main Parsenn. Most of the skiing is above the tree-line and includes an excellent nursery area near the Saaseralp as well as some long runs from the top of the Madrisa lift, including an unprepared black to Saaseralp and the long and varied 6km Piste Flue black run down through the woods, which links up with the even longer red Schlappin run. The wooded lower slopes beneath Saaseralp are otherwise not skied and lesser beginners must take the lift down at the end of the day.

With a guide you can make a day tour from the Madrisa over to Gargellen in Austria. The return route is via the Gargellen lifts, which are covered by the lift pass, plus a one-hour climb on skins. The best part of the tour is the off-piste run, which follows down to the pretty vil- lage of St Antonien, before taking a bus back to Küblis.

A cable car serves the whole south-west-facing slope of the Pischa area, which goes up to 2485m from 1800m. A simple array of parallel drag-lifts above the tree-line give access to some sunny, intermediate runs beside them, as well as some more challenging runs through the trees. Off-piste opportunities are plentiful behind the Pischahorn and along the shoulder down to the Klosters road at Laret.

The Jakobshorn is the most extensive alternative to the Parsenn/Weissfluhjoch skiing and the most easily accessible from Davos. Above the tree-line is a wide range of long, mostly intermediate runs below the peaks of Jakobshorn and Brämabühel; both are fairly steep at the top. Gentle skiing can be found in the sunny bowl above Clavadeleralp. The wooded paths back to Davos Platz are not appealing, but you can always download by cable car. The north-facing descent of nearly 900m vertical from the Jakobshorn to Teufl in the Dischmatal is a highly recommended off-piste run with an isolated restaurant at the bottom, from where you catch the bus back to Davos.

Rinerhorn is a small area of west- and north-facing slopes now served by a six-person gondola. The pistes above the trees are nothing very special, but there are enough good runs down to the valley to make this a popular tree area when visibility is bad. A stiff 20-minute climb gives access to the steep, north-facing side of the Sertigtal, from where it is possible to ski down to the train station at Frauenkirch. In good powder conditions, the long run down to Glaris, reached from the Nüllischgrat drag-lift, is highly entertaining.

Despite improvements lift queues, particularly at weekends, still remain a serious problem throughout the area. The recent rebuilding of the Klosters cable car has done only a little to relieve the situation and we have continuing reports of long delays at peak times for the Parsenn railway from Davos Dorf, as well as for the Schatzalpbahn from Davos Platz. Reporters recommend escaping to the Pischa at weekends when the main circus in high season becomes 'quite impossible'. Too many long T-bars is also a reporters' complaint, along with poor piste-grooming and inadequate sign-posting ('We found ourselves going down a red run instead of a blue, which was a problem because of the high winds and blizzard conditions').

Mountain restaurants

The area is dotted with mountain restaurants and delightful little *Schwendi* houses off the beaten track in the woods down to Klosters and the other smaller villages of the Parsenn. The Conterser Schwendi in particular is recommended for its 'quite outstanding *Bauernrösti*', as is the Serneus Schwendi, which has recently been revamped. The Rinerhorn and the Pischa self-service are also recommended, as is the Alpina at Klosters.

The restaurant of the Hotel Kulm at Wolfgang (known as Jakob's) makes the long run down all the more worthwhile. The menu consists of simple dishes superbly cooked. The higher restaurants mostly lack character ('the dreadful smell of frying at Parsennhütte and Weissfluhjoch kept us well away').

Beginners and children

Few of our reporters join group lessons in these upmarket resorts, preferring to take private instruction. The Swiss Ski School in both Davos and Klosters has the soundest of reputations and the instructors' standard of English is said to be extremely high. The ski schools will organise off-piste tours from February onwards. Correspondents who have toured to Arosa and across the Austrian border to Gargellen and back are unanimous in their praise of the guiding and instruction.

Neither resort particularly lends itself to beginners. The nursery slopes beside Davos Platz at the bottom of the Jakobshorn are adequate. Klosters has a good, sunny nursery area on the Madrisa at Saaseralp as well as a few small lifts beside Klosters Dorf. The Swiss Ski School in Davos runs a kindergarten, which we are told is 'not particularly impressive'. The Hotel Vereina in Klosters has its own non-ski kindergarten for 2- to 6-year-olds. There is also a ski kindergarten on the Madrisa.

The resorts

Davos is a long, strung-out town with a population of over 13,000, completely devoid of the kind of alpine charm you might associate with one of the great cradles of modern skiing. It is now a major European conference centre and consequently boasts some of the finest four- and five-star hotels in the Alps as well as all the amenities you would expect of a resort which caters for high-spending tourists all year round. Traffic is heavy, but it flows well and away from the main road there are ample pedestrian short-cuts and sedate walks by the river. Indeed the rather blunt, modern Swiss architecture is the root of so much criticism in guidebooks that skiers are pleasantly relieved to discover that the reality is by no means displeasing. Non-skiers will find plenty of marked walks as well as Switzerland's largest natural ice rink and a good swimming-pool. Cross-country skiing is also a popular pastime with 75km of prepared trails in the immediate vicinity.

Klosters Platz remains a charming Swiss village centred on its station, a cluster of established hotels along with more modern interlopers and a number of smart boutiques and expensive sports shops to cater for the needs of its well-heeled guests. A fine wine and Havana cigar shop just across the street from one of the leading hotels is a telling indication of what Klosters' clients consider essentials. Klosters Dorf is a separate sleepy village away from the hub of the resort.

Accommodation

The **Davos** accommodation is mainly in hotels throughout Platz and Dorf, which range from exotic five-stars to the simplest of bed and breakfasts. Central Platz is the most convenient, an easy walk to the lifts for Strela and the Jakobshorn. The Steigenberger Belvedere in Platz has a country-house atmosphere and carved ceilings, but is said to have lost some of its style. The Flüela in Dorf is conveniently situated near the Parsennbahn and according to reporters is 'a lovely hotel, which merits its five-star rating'. The Alte Post is cheerful and reasonably priced. We have good reports of the budget-priced Hotel Bünda in Dorf and the Lohner in Platz. The three-star Montana near Dorf station is popular with reporters. The simple Edelweiss bed and breakfast in Dorf is 'clean and comfortable'.

Many of the visitors to **Klosters** stay in private chalets both in the two villages and in the woods outside, but some of its hotels are as smart (and as expensive) as their Davos counterparts. Hotel Vereina is 'traditionally charming', one of the oldest winter sports hotels in the Alps with huge public rooms, recently modernised bedrooms and a large swimming-pool. The Alpina is built in a modern chalet style and is said to be 'very welcoming'. We have mixed reports of the Kaiser: 'Friendly staff, food adequate to good and an excellent location next to the cable car', but 'The service was impersonal and there was no room at the hotel car-park for our car.'

The Silvretta Parkhotel, which opened in 1990 to cope with the increasing number of visitors to Klosters, is 'discreetly luxurious with comfortable suites and a lovely swimming-pool, but suffers from a soulless dining-room'. The Wynegg, owned by the redoubtable Ruth Guler, is run like a large chalet for its mainly British clients. It has two restaurants: the first is run as a chalet dining-room for residents, the other is open to everyone including Prince Charles, an annual visitor.

Eating out

Davos has an enormous choice of restaurants. The Davoserhof, Waldhaus and the Flüela are all highly recommended. The Bundnerstübli

Skiing facts: Davos

TOURIST OFFICE
Promenade 67, CH-7270 Davos,
Graubunden
Tel 41 81 452121
Fax 41 81 452100

THE RESORT
By road Calais 1000km
By rail station in resort
By air Zurich 2½ hrs
Visitor beds 20,219 (64% apartments and chalets, 31% hotels, 5% guesthouses)
Transport bus serves all lifts in Davos, also to Klosters. Good train service

THE SKIING
Longest run Weissfluhgipfel to Kublis, 12km (black/red)
Number of lifts 29 in Davos, 55 in area
Number of trails/pistes 88 in area (25% easy, 51% intermediate, 24% difficult), no breakdown available
Total of trails/pistes 245km in Davos, 315km in area
Nursery slopes 4 lifts
Summer skiing none
Snowmaking none

LIFT PASSES
Area pass Rega (covers all Davos and Klosters lifts), SF236 for 6 days. Jakobshorn, SF200 for 6 days
Day pass Jakobshorn SF42
Half-day pass Jakobshorn, SF26 after 12.30pm
Beginners coupons, points tickets
Children Jakobshorn, 6-16 yrs, SF120 for 6 days. Rega pass, 6- 16 yrs, SF142 for 6 days
Pensioners 20% reduction for women 62 yrs and over, men 65 yrs and over
Credit cards accepted yes

SKI SCHOOLS
Adults Swiss Ski School, 10am-midday

and 2-4pm, SF180 for 5 days
Children Swiss Ski School, 4-16 yrs, 10am-midday and 2-4pm, SF145 for 5 days
Private lessons SF130 for half-day, SF235 for full day
Special courses snowboarding, ki-touring, telemark
Guiding companies Stephan Welz or Swiss Ski School

CROSS-COUNTRY
Ski schools Swiss Ski School
Loipe location and size 75km of trails along the main valley between Glaris and Wolfgang, and in the Fluela, Dischma and Sertig valleys

CHILDCARE
Non-ski kindergarten Pinocchio (tuition possible with ski school), 2½ yrs and over, 8.30am-4.30pm, SF189 for 5 days, extra SF9 per day for lunch and tea
Ski kindergarten Swiss Ski School, 4-16 yrs, 10am-4pm, SF145 for 5 days
Babysitting list available from tourist office

OTHER SPORTS
Parapente, hang-gliding, skating, curling, ice-hockey, speed-skating, Bavarian curling, indoor tennis, squash, sleigh rides, climbing wall, tobogganing, bowling, swimming, fitness centres

FOOD AND DRINK PRICES
Coffee SF3.20, bottle of house wine SF15-40, beer SF3, dish of the day SF15-25

TOUR OPERATORS
Bladon Lines, Crystal, Inghams, Kuoni, Made to Measure, Ski Choice, Ski Thomson, Ski Weekend, Swiss Travel Service

is reputed to offer regional specialities at affordable prices. A number of reporters found it cheaper and more interesting to eat outside Davos in the evenings. The Gasthof Landhaus in Frauenkirch is recommended, along with the Kulm in Wolfgang.

In **Klosters**, even in low season, it is necessary to book restaurant

Skiing facts: Klosters

TOURIST OFFICE
Postfach 172, CH-7250 Klosters, Graubunden
Tel 41 81 691877
Fax 41 81 694906

THE RESORT
By road Calais 1000km
By rail station in resort
By air Zurich 2= hrs
Visitor beds 8,500 (76% apartments and chalets, 24% hotels and guesthouses)
Transport bus runs to Gotschna and Madrisa lifts. Also to Davos Dorf and Platz. Good train service

THE SKIING
Longest run Weissfluhgipfel to Kublis, 12km (black/red)
Number of lifts 26 Klosters, 55 area
Number of trails/pistes 88 in area (25% easy, 51% intermediate, 24% difficult), no breakdown available
Total of trails/pistes 170km in Klosters, 315km in area
Nursery slopes 1 lift
Summer skiing none
Snowmaking none

LIFT PASSES
Area pass Gotschna/Parsenn, SF190 for 6 days. Madrisa SF177 for 6 days. Rega (covers all Klosters and Davos lifts), SF236 for 6 days
Day pass Gotschna/Parsenn SF48, Madrisa SF39
Half-day pass Gotschna/Parsenn SF35, Madrisa SF29, both after 12.30pm
Beginners coupons, single and return tickets
Children Gotschna/Parsenn, 6-12 yrs, SF114 for 6 days. Madrisa, 6-12 yrs, SF106 for 6 days. Rega, 6-12 yrs, SF142 for 6 days. Free for 6 yrs and under
Pensioners 20% reduction for women 62 yrs and over, men 65 yrs and over
Credit cards accepted yes

SKI SCHOOLS
Adults Swiss Ski School, 10am-midday and 2-4pm, SF120 for 5 days
Children Swiss Ski School, 10am-midday and 2-4pm, SF110 for 5 days, extra SF13 per day for lunch
Private lessons SF140 for half-day, SF230 for full day
Special courses snowboarding, ski-touring
Guiding companies through ski school

CROSS-COUNTRY
Ski schools Swiss Ski School
Loipe location and size 40km, towards Vereina to the Novai Alp and Klosters Dorf to Serneus

CHILDCARE
Non-ski kindergarten Hotel Vereina, 2-6 yrs, 9.30am-4.30pm, SF220 for 5 days including lunch
Ski kindergarten Madrisa, 3-6 yrs, 10am-12.30pm and 1.30-4pm, SF15 per day not including lunch. Hotels Vereina and Steinbock offer lunches for children in ski school for SF13 per day
Babysitting list available from tourist office

OTHER SPORTS
Parapente, hang-gliding, skating, curling, sleigh rides, tobogganing, bowling, swimming, fitness centres

WHAT'S NEW
● Four-star Aldiana Clubhotel Silvretta
● five-star Robinson Club Piz Buin

FOOD AND DRINK PRICES
Coffee SF3.20, bottle of house wine SF15-40, beer SF3, dish of the day SF15-25

TOUR OPERATORS
Bladon Lines, Crystal, Kuoni, Made to Measure, Powder Byrne, Ski Choice, Ski Gower, Ski Unique, Swiss Travel Service

tables at least a day ahead; the exception to this is the Chesa Grischuna where you need to reserve at least three days in advance. The Wynegg, with its unofficial royal seal of appointment, has reasonable prices and a welcoming atmosphere (press photographers apart). It is renowned for its traditional Swiss cuisine.

Après-ski

Neither resort exactly rocks at night. Reporters surprisingly find larger **Davos** to be the quieter of the two later on, although there are more early-evening activities here. There is skating and curling at Dorf, indoor tennis, big-league ice hockey matches in Platz, tea and cakes at Schneider's Café and regular cultural events at the Davos Conference Centre. The piano bar in the Hotel Europe and the Pöstli in the Posthotel Morosani are both popular meeting places. The Chämi-Bar usually draws a big crowd throughout the evening. Late-night revellers move on to the Cabanna Club.

In **Klosters** reporters complain that there are surprisingly few cafés. The nightlife centres on a handful of bars. The cellar piano bar of the Chesa Grischuna is always busy (you can often eat here, even if you cannot obtain a table in the main restaurant). The Silvretta Parkhotel disco attracts a young crowd. Sophisticates move on to the Casa Antica and the Robinson Club. The Madrisa Bar in Klosters Dorf is also recommended by reporters.

Flims, Graubunden

ALTITUDE 1100m (3,608ft)

∙∙∙

Good points large ski area, variety of intermediate skiing, sunny slopes, extensive walking paths, cross-country skiing, tree-level runs
Bad points lack of tough runs, limited for late-season holidays, limited après-ski, lack of resort-level snow
Linked and nearby resorts Falera (l), Laax (l), Lenzerheide (n) – *see separate chapter*

Flims is a resort better-known in Switzerland for its sunny woodland walks than for its skiing, and is hardly known at all in Britain. It does, however, have a big, interconnected ski area which links with Laax and calls itself the White Arena. The resorts are not particularly convenient for skiers, but the overall package is a good one.

The resort sits on a wooded shelf above the Vorderrhein river. The railway follows its course, but the busy main road runs through Flims itself. The mountains here are high, but not steep, and the wide valley makes the setting open and sunny. Flims is divided into two halves: Dorf and Waldhaus.

Laax, five kilometres away, is the smaller village with a purpose-built satellite at Murschetg. The rustic farming hamlet of Falera adds a third alternative village. There are no other major resorts close to Flims, but day-trips to Arosa and Lenzerheide are possible. A car can be useful around the resort, depending on where you are staying.

The skiing
Top 2980m (9,774ft) bottom 1080m (3,542ft)

The ski area stretches across a wide section of the northern valley wall. It faces mainly south-east, but is broken up by a number of deep gullies which face south-west and north-east, making links between the sectors tenuous in bad weather. Most of the ski area is sunny, and the runs down to the resorts become impossible to ski fairly early in the season. The terrain is varied, with long runs through the trees on the lower slopes, an open area above and a small glacier area at the top.

Mountain access from Flims is on the outskirts of Flims Dorf. Of the two main lifts, the more important for the pistes at Flims is the three-seater chair. The runs beneath this lift and the gondola to Startgels are mostly easy, and the red (intermediate) runs from Naraus are not difficult, although they frequently suffer from poor snow cover.

For good skiers, the main attraction of the skiing at Flims is the descent from Cassons, reached by cable car from Naraus up over the cliffs of the Flimserstein. There is an annoying 10-minute walk behind the top station, but it is worthwhile for the view alone, as is the direct black (difficult) descent back to Naraus down the steep but wide face. Only the gentler bottom half is ever groomed. It is of the utmost importance not to leave the marked piste in this area unless accompanied by a qualified guide, as the wrong route could bring you to the edge of the cliff.

The skiing in Flims is connected to the La Siala area, between Flims and Laax, by a cable car from Startgels to Grauberg and a triple chair-lift to Nagens. The runs back down to Startgels are challenging. Most of the skiing on La Siala consists of long, open, featureless pistes, but the top chair-lift serves more interesting runs, with a mixture of motorway and moguls down to Grauberg.

From La Siala there are connections with the Laax skiing either by traversing to or from the Vorab Glacier restaurant, or via Plaun at the bottom of a steep-sided valley with lifts up either side. The awkward paths down to Plaun are graded black, and many skiers prefer to take the chair down. The other side of the valley is much more satisfactory, with longer runs down from Crap Sogn Gion to Plaun.

The unusually named Crap Sogn Gion is where the vast but inadequate cable car from Murschetg arrives. A series of three chairs (the top one a four-seater) make the same slower, but queue-free journey. The run under the cable car from Crap Sogn Gion is a downhill course cut through the woods, with a vertical drop of over 1000m. There are other gentler descents, through Curnius under the chair-lifts, and down to Falera, a useful back way into the lift system.

The cable car to Crap Masegn does not climb very high, but gives access to some long, open runs down to Alp Ruschein, which are usually deserted and good for trying some off-piste at the edge of the marked run. In the other direction, a gondola goes down into a gully then up again to the bottom of the Vorab Glacier, which offers gentle skiing, accessible to all. The great attraction of the Vorab is the run which drops over a saddle near the top down into an attractive, empty valley. It is graded black, although only the beginning could be called steep. The remainder is a wide, fast-cruising piste.

Mountain restaurants

The original part of the ski area, above Flims, is well served with attractive mountain restaurants, many of them accessible to non-skiers. The wait-service Runca, off the piste below Startgels, is among them. Other restaurants include Cassons, Nagens, Segnes and Naraus, all of which are self-service. Foppa has both waiter- and self-service restaurants. On the Laax side there are a few large, functional eating places, with the pleasant exception of the chalet at Larnags. The glacier restaurant has a wonderful view from its sun-terrace.

Beginners and children

There are good, wide nursery slopes beside Flims Dorf, and another nursery lift at the top of the Startgels gondola. There is a small nursery slope at Murschetg, and an easy open slope at Crap Sogn Gion. Skiers with a few days' experience will find plenty of scope. The Parkhotel Waldhaus and the Adula both have crèches. The ski-kindergarten takes children from four years old, lunchtime care is possible, although children must bring their own sandwiches. The ski school is well thought of, with instructors speaking good English and reasonably sized classes.

The resort

Flims-Dorf is a characterless village, spread out along a busy main road. The base station is at the western edge of the village. Half-a-mile or so further south Waldhaus, with no ski-lift of its own, is another traditional resort, which has a large group of hotels among the trees and beside the main road. Waldhaus is a quiet village, Dorf being the livelier ski town. Both stretch down the hill below the road with a few hotels which are mainly of interest to cross-country skiers. The daytime post-bus (covered by the lift pass) serves Flims, Murschetg and Laax, and there are less frequent services to Fidaz and Falera. Many of the hotels have their own courtesy mini-bus.

Accommodation

Accommodation is mainly in comfortable hotels and self-catering apartments. The best location for accommodation is on the edge of Dorf, where the Albanasport, Meiler, Bellevue and the chalet-style Garni Curtgin. are placed. The Crap Ner is the most comfortable hotel in Dorf, but inconveniently situated.

The Parkhotel in Waldhaus is a complete resort of its own, set in the woods above the village ('the overwhelming impression is of spaciousness'). There is a total of five buildings in the grounds, linked by covered paths and underground passages, and you often end up walking long distances from your room to the reception or restaurant. Some of the rooms have curious loos, which also provide a unique washing facility. The Waldeck is a smaller, smart hotel by the main road. The Cresta is recommended. The National hotel runs a mini-bus. The Hotel des Alpes has well-equipped kitchenettes. The Surpunt is ideal for cross-country skiers, and the comfortable Fidazerhof is set above Dorf.

Eating out

Most of the restaurants and bars are in the hotels. The Barga restaurant in Hotel Adula is expensive. Pizzeria Pomodoro and Pizzeria Alpina are also in Waldhaus. The Clavau Vegl and Pizzeria Porta Sut are in Dorf, as is the luxurious Giardino in the Hotel Crap Ner. Other popular places include Little China, the Bellevue, Grischuna, Vorab, Surpunt and Waldeck. An evening at the restaurant Conn includes a horse and carriage ride.

Après-ski

Cafeteria Gloor in Waldhaus is a popular after-skiing spot. Later on in Flims Dorf the main meeting place for young people is the Albana pub and disco. The Waldhaus has a live band. There is tea-dancing in Hotel Meiler, close to the Dorf lifts. The Viva-Club disco is popular.

Laax 1020m (3,346ft)

The most pleasant hotel is the charming and lively Posta Veglia, with a *Stübli* and a piano bar. Murschetg is a large resort complex, most of which is convenient for the slopes. Also well positioned is the expensive

Signina. Like Flims, Laax is a good resort for walkers and cross-country skiers. Of the other communities dotted around the sunny hillsides, Falera is the most important. This is a sleepy, old farming village with a couple of hotels, reached by a narrow road. Falera is linked into the main lift system. The Encarna is a central, simple hotel. You can also stay up the mountain in the modern Crap Sogn Gion Berghotel.

TOURIST OFFICE
CH-7031, Laax, Graubunden
Tel 41 86 34343

TOUR OPERATORS
Kuoni, Made to Measure

Skiing facts: Flims

TOURIST OFFICE
CH-7018 Flims-Waldhaus, Graubunden
Tel 41 81 391022
Fax 41 81 394308

THE RESORT
By road Calais 994km
By rail Chur 17km, hourly buses from station
By air Zurich 2 hrs
Visitor beds 5,350 (64% apartments and chalets, 36% hotels)
Transport regular bus service throughout the Flims-Laax-Falera area

THE SKIING
Longest run White Race (Vorab to Flims-Dorf), 14km (blue/black)
Number of lifts 32
Number of trails/pistes 54 (48% easy, 37% intermediate, 15% difficult)
Total of trails/pistes 220km
Nursery slopes 2km, 3 lifts
Summer skiing none
Snowmaking none

LIFT PASSES
Area pass White Arena (covers Flims-Laax-Falera), SF246 for 6 days
Day pass SF50, SF4 extra on weekends and holidays
Half-day pass SF38 after 12.15pm
Beginners points tickets
Children 6-16 yrs, SF123 for 6 days, free for 5 yrs and under
Pensioners no reduction
Credit cards accepted yes

SKI SCHOOLS
Adults Swiss Ski School Flims, Swiss Ski School Laax-Falera, both 2 hrs

am/pm, SF160 for 5 days
Children as adults
Private lessons Swiss Ski Schools, SF120 per half-day, SF210 per day (1-2 people)
Special courses snowboarding, ski-touring, telemark
Guiding companies Swiss Ski School and Swiss Bergsteigerschule

CROSS-COUNTRY
Ski schools Swiss Ski School
Loipe location and size 60km between Flims and Laax

CHILDCARE
Non-ski kindergarten none, some hotels have crèches
Ski kindergarten Swiss Ski School, 4-12 yrs, SF45 per day, SF160 for 5 days, both not including lunch
Babysitting list available from tourist office

OTHER SPORTS
Hot-air ballooning, hang-gliding, curling, skating, indoor tennis, swimming, fitness centre, bowling, tobogganing

WHAT'S NEW
● Elephant mountain restaurant at Crap Masegn ● hotel museum at the Parkhotel Waldhaus

FOOD AND DRINK PRICES
Coffee SF3, bottle of house wine SF24, beer SF3, dish of the day SF15

TOUR OPERATORS
Kuoni, Made to Measure, Powder Byrne, Ski Unique, Swiss Travel Service

Gstaad, Bernese Oberland

ALTITUDE 1050m (3,444ft)

• •

Good points attractive village, short airport transfer, extensive skiing in region, ideal for non-skiers
Bad points limited for expert skiing, inadequate piste-marking, disjointed ski area, antiquated lift system, traffic in village centre, no snowmaking
Linked or nearby resorts Adelboden (n), Château d'Oex (n), Les Diablerets (n), Gsteig (n), Lauenen (l), Lenk (n), Leysin (n), Rougemont (l), Saanen (n), Saanenmöser (n), Schönried (n), St Stephan (n), Turbach (n), Villars (n), Zweisimmen (n)

In this exclusive playground-on-snow of the rich and famous you do not actually have to own a luxury chalet or stay at the five-star Palace hotel to experience the flatteringly easy skiing and this attractive cosmopolitan resort. The stars come here either to escape the unacceptable price of fame, or to enjoy it. Here they can be seen if they want to, or can hide away if they do not. Gstaad is not a cheap resort. Indeed, economy is not a word in the Gstaad vocabulary. Designer labels are everywhere; here you can buy every top fashion name from Gucci and Cartier to Versace, Yves St Laurent, Dior and Armani.

At a low altitude, Gstaad has a short season; officially it runs from the beginning of December to the end of April, but in reality the prime time to visit is from mid-January to mid-March. Visit any earlier or later and you may find the snow conditions disappointing. The lack of snow cannon is due to the fact that the village areas are too low and generally too warm to make artificial snow.

The skiing
Top 3000m (9,842ft) bottom 1000m (3,280ft)
Gstaad has never been taken seriously by expert skiers, and is never likely to be. However, it is now collectively marketed with nine smaller villages in the area as the Gstaad Super Ski Region, making up a total of 69 lifts and 250km of piste. The other villages of this Gstaad-Saanenland area of the Bernese Oberland are St Stephan, Zweisimmen, Saanenmöser, Schönried, Lauenen, Gsteig, Saanen, Rougemont and Château d'Oex. The weekly lift pass entitles skiers to a day's skiing in Adelboden-Lenk and the Vaudoise Alps (Villars, Les Diablerets. Leysin, Gryon, Les Mosses). The lift system is described by reporters as 'anti-

quated, considering the wealth of the resort', and piste-grooming as 'poor, with no attempt to flatten ruts on drag-lifts'.

The skiing in the immediate Gstaad area is broken up into three segments: Eggli, Wispile and the Wasserngrat. The Eggli interconnects with Rougemont at the top of La Videmanette and you can also ski from Eggli to just outside Saanen on runs which are 'varied, long, and attractive'. The tree-line skiing is also good here, and is particularly important for the poor visibility days. More advanced skiers will not bother to go further than the area around the back of La Videmanette. There is an interesting itinerary run to Gérignoz via La Videman.

The Wasserngrat is the next most advanced skiing area, which hosts the challenging Tiger Run piste. It is here that the famous Eagle Ski Club, with its star-studded membership, is based. Nearby, but not connected, the lower intermediate Hornberg area is a few kilometres out of Gstaad, but within easy reach by bus or train, with tickets included on the lift pass. It is the area's most extensive lift network, with a total of 14 lifts reaching St Stephan at the far end of the valley. Two of the **mountain access** points closest to Gstaad are via the Horneggli lift from Schönried and the Saanerslochgrat gondola from Saanenmöser, both of which are opposite their respective railway stations.

Wispile is the smallest area closest to the town centre. Interesting off-piste routes go from the top of the area down to Feutersoey and to the Chlösterli restaurant for a good lunch. Summer skiing can be found on the glacier at Les Diablerets at 3000m, reached by a three-stage cable car from Reusch. The three summer ski lifts run until the end of August. Both cross-country skiing and heli-skiing are available in the area.

When it comes to mountain eating the choice is extensive with the wait-service Cabane de La Sarouche at Château d'Oex, and the Chemistübli above St Stephan recommended for its 'great home-made sausages'. The Eggli restaurant (also waiter-service) is in the area of the same name, and the two self-service eating places are at the top of Wispile and at the top of Wasserngrat.

The resort

Gstaad is a large cluster of well-preserved ancient wooden buildings with more modern additions, set in a pretty valley. Well placed for both Geneva and Berne airports, it has a compact centre containing alpine branches of designer shops. Attractive private chalets sprawl out from the centre and the elite Palace Hotel sits on its throne at the top of the hill looking down on the village. Traffic is a problem and there are sometimes heavy jams in the centre. A bypass is planned for the near future and should relieve some of the congestion.

The Gstaad Palace dominates the town like Sleeping Beauty's castle. It was here that Peter Sellers as Inspector Clouseau of *Pink Panther* fame asked for a 'rhume'. The five-star Grand Hotel Park, opened in 1991, has a fitness centre, swimming-pool and conference centre. Four-stars include Grand Hotel Alpina, the Arc-en-Ciel and Hotel Bellevue Gstaad, the latter set in its own park and famous for its Chez Fritz restaurant. Sporthotel Rütti is 'clean, basic and friendly with good food'.

Gstaad is a superb resort for an all-round winter-sports experience, with a huge range of activities on offer. The impressive sports centre houses a covered swimming-pool, and there is parapente, tobogganing, skating, curling, hot-air ballooning, sleigh rides, hang-gliding, squash and three indoor tennis courts. A local air service provides fixed-wing flights over the region.

The best restaurants are in the hotels. The Palace has several world-class restaurants, but you will need a very full wallet here. La Cave in the Hotel Olden is good. The sixteenth-century Chlösterli, on the road to Les Diablerets, is recommended for its atmosphere and should not be missed. The Alpenrose at Schönried serves nouvelle cuisine and the Bären at Gsteig has traditional Swiss cuisine. Others include the reason-ably priced Hotel Bernerhof, Cuisine de Saison in Hotel Grand Chalet for its fresh ingredients, and the Chesery for its haute cuisine and good wine cellar. Ristorante Rialto serves Italian food. The restaurant in the Arc-en-Ciel offers good-value pizzas and pasta.

Après-ski

Immediately after skiing skiers gather in the Apple-Pie café, Charlie's Tea Room and Pernet café for a big choice of cakes. The beautiful peo-ple do not usually appear until well after midnight when their chalet dinner parties have ended, but for everyone else the Olden bar is popu-lar at all hours. When the famous finally make an appearance it is at the Greengo disco in the Palace Hotel, or the Chlösterli. The Steigenberger Hotel disco in Saanen is also popular. On the whole, however, the après-ski scene is muted with, according to one reporter, 'lots of private dinner parties in chalets for the residents and pubs for chalet staff, nan-nies, cooks and chauffeurs'. Other nightspots include the Grotte disco in the Hotel Alpenrose, the Hotel Ermitage jazz nights in its Down-Town bar, live music in the Rialto bar, and a piano bar at the Chesery.

TOURIST OFFICE
Gstaad Super Ski Region, Chalet Gstaad,
CH-3780 Gstaad, Bernese Oberland
Tel 41 30 47171
Fax 41 30 45620

TOUR OPERATORS
Kuoni, Made to Measure,
Ski Gower, Swiss Travel Service, The Ski Company

Château d'Oex   1000m (3,280ft)

The resort is better known for its international hot-air balloon festival rather than for its skiing, though it is much used by British tour opera-tors as a cheaper alternative base to Gstaad. It has 14 lifts of its own, 50km of pistes, and mainly blue (easy) and red (intermediate) runs.

TOURIST OFFICE
CH-1837 Château d'Oex, Bernese Oberland
Tel 29 47788
Fax 29 45958

TOUR OPERATORS
Crystal, Kuoni, Made to Measure,
Neilson, Ski Sutherland

The Jungfrau region

Wengen
ALTITUDE 1240m (4,067ft)

Good points alpine charm, variety of easy and intermediate runs, large ski area, tree-level skiing, suitable for non-skiers, easy rail access, excellent nursery slopes, variety of mountain restaurants, freedom from cars, ideal for family holidays
Bad points unreliable snow cover, lack of tough runs
Linked or nearby resorts Grindelwald (l), Grund (l), Lauterbrunnen (n), Mürren (n)

Grindelwald
ALTITUDE 1034m (3,391ft)

Good points spectacular mountain scenery, cosmopolitan resort, large intermediate ski area, wide choice of hotels, easy rail access, ski-touring
Bad points low altitude, unreliable snow cover, lack of tough runs

Mürren
ALTITUDE 1650m (5,412ft)

Good points alpine charm, freedom from cars, lack of crowds, high-altitude skiing, extensive off-piste skiing
Bad points restricted for beginners, limited nursery slopes, limited ski area

No European mountains are more awe-inspiring than the Jungfrau, the Mönch and the Eiger: the Maiden guarded by the Monk from the fearsome Ogre. As generations of skiers and climbers have discovered in this corner of the Bernese Oberland the trio, with their craggy peaks and blue tangle of surrounding glaciers, dominate the sky line. It is impossible to be unimpressed by their majesty and it is their dominant presence and the gentle snowfields beneath and around them which make the villages of Wengen, Grindelwald and Mürren one of the great winter holiday areas of Switzerland.

Centre stage above Wengen and Grindelwald towers the north face of the Eiger, a forbidding 1900m (6,000ft) vertical granite wall, which was considered unclimbable until the first ascent by four Austrians in the summer of 1938. Before and since it has regularly claimed the lives of those prepared to tackle its overhangs and the constant bombardment of snow and stone avalanche. The classic Eigerwand is still considered one of the most difficult winter climbs in the world although it has now been mastered solo in a single day.

It was the mountain railway, still the main means of uphill transport

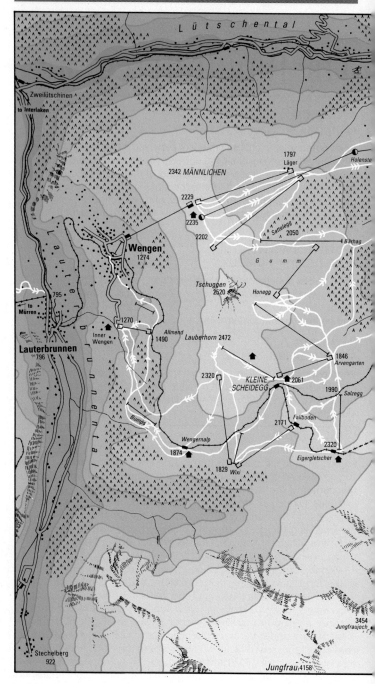

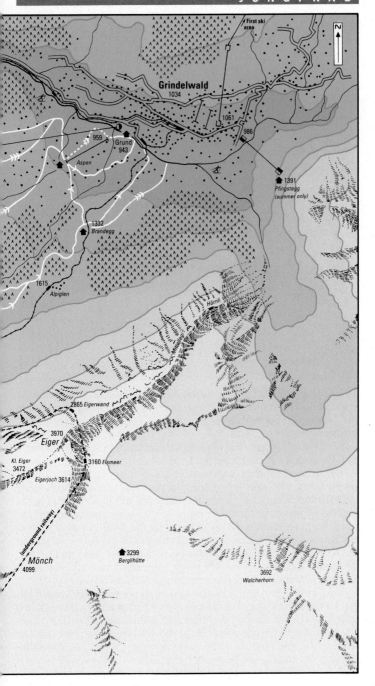

First ski area

Grindelwald
1034

1061

986

959
Grund
943

Aspen

1391
Pfingstegg
(summer only)

1332
Brandegg

1615
Alpiglen

Hörnli

2865 Eigerwand

3970
Eiger

Kl. Eiger
3472

3160 Eismeer

Eigerjoch 3614

Mönch
4099

(underground railway)

3299
Berglihütte

3692
Walcherhorn

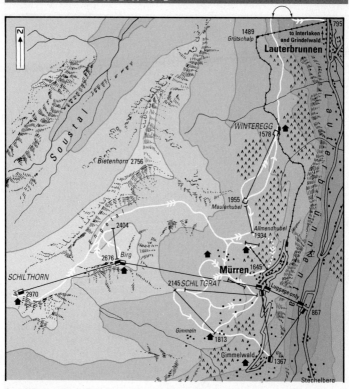

for skiers, which first brought visitors to the area. Grindelwald became a popular holiday resort and the construction of the Wengeralpbahn in the 1880s ensured that the higher resort would also claim part of the summer business. Expansion led to the later building of the Jungfraubahn, Europe's highest funicular railway, which climbs dramatically through the north face of the Eiger to the Jungfraujoch at 3454m.

But in wintertime the visitors went home. It was an Englishman, Sir Henry Lunn, who saw the commercial potential of skiing here, while local farmers regarded it merely as a means of getting about during the months of snow. Sir Henry managed to persuade the owners of the Lauterbrunnen-Mürren railway to run it for the 1910-11 winter season. His Public Schools Alpine Sports Club took over the Palace Hotel and the winter ski holiday package was born. His more distinguished son, Sir Arnold, the father of modern skiing, went on to found the Kandahar Ski Club in Mürren, where slalom racing was first introduced in 1922.

Over in Wengen, British visitors viewed this development with interest. To the amazement of local farmers they had discovered it was much easier to take the train up the mountain, rather than to walk on skins. Their activities were considered to be most definitely unsporting by the standards of the time: to enjoy skiing downhill you should first suffer the pain of climbing up. They called themselves the Downhill Only and both British ski clubs are alive and functioning in the resorts today.

Wengen, Grindelwald and Mürren are all reached on the Swiss railway network from Interlaken. Both Wengen and Mürren are traffic-free and a car is of little or no use in the area. The track divides at Zweilutschinen, with the left-hand fork veering through the Lütschental directly to Grindelwald. The right-hand fork goes to Lauterbrunnen, which is more of a railway halt than a resort, although it does have a number of hotels and some reporters consider it a convenient and much cheaper base for the area. From here trains climb steeply up to Mürren on one side of the valley and up to Wengen on the other. The track carries on up above Wengen to the main ski area at Kleine Scheidegg at the foot of the Eigerwand, before descending to complete the circuit into Grindelwald Grund. The trains stop at wayside halts throughout the area to pick up and set down skiers. They run as accurately as a Swiss watch to a timetable printed on the back of the piste map.

The skiing
Wengen Top 2320m (7,610ft) bottom 943m (3,093ft)
Grindelwald Top 2486m (8,154ft) bottom 943m (3,093ft)
Mürren Top 2970m (9,742ft) bottom 796m (2,611ft)

Grindelwald and Mürren each have their own separate and interesting ski areas, but the main focus of the region is on the joint terrain of Grindelwald and Wengen linked by railway through Kleine Scheidegg and by gondola and cable car through Männlichen.

This main ski circus divides naturally into two, separated by the 2478m Lauberhorn, which lends its name to one of the set-pieces of downhill on the World Cup calendar. Kleine Scheidegg/Männlichen is an undulating, partly wooded area on the Grindelwald side of the mountain, which consists of predominantly easy and intermediate east-facing pistes. **Mountain access** from Grindelwald is either by train to Kleine Scheidegg or gondola from Grund to Männlichen. From Wengen you also take the train up the reverse face of the mountain to Kleine Scheidegg, or a cable car to Männlichen. None of the skiing on this side of the mountain is particularly challenging with the exception of the black (difficult) Aspen racecourse from Männlichen, which has a couple of steep pitches. The runs are otherwise long and confidence-building over a wide area of summer pastureland. Above Kleine Scheidegg the railway climbs to the Eigergletscher station at 2320m before disappearing into the north face on its route up to the Jungfraujoch.

A 20-minute traverse and hike from the top of the Salzegg drag-lift (nicknamed the 'divorce' T-bar because of the difficulty in riding it) takes you to the very foot of the Eigerwand and the start of a spectacular off-piste run, known as the White Hare, which takes you down to the railway and finally to Brandegg. The area is extremely prone to avalanche and should only be attempted in the company of an experienced local guide.

On the other side of the Eigergletscher restaurant, with spectacular views of the ice-falls, is Blackrock. This is probably the best black run in the region, descending towards Wengernalp. Wixi and the Lauberhorn itself provide an endless variety of descents of varying difficulty, although this sector of the mountain is usually the most crowded. The old Lauberhorn drag has been replaced by a quad-chair, but amazingly you still have to plod up to the start from the railway. The run down to Wengen is a mixture of open piste and path, which again becomes very busy. A couple of reporters said they found the path frightening ('too narrow, quite steep and with a number of blind bends'). The Bumps drag serves an easy slope with steeper options at the end and much of the crush can be avoided by skiing on down to the Innerwengen chair.

Grindelwald also has its own sunny, intermediate area of First, which is accessed directly from the village rather than the satellite of Grund. First has been dramatically improved by the replacement of the old, slow chairs with a three-stage gondola, which takes you first up to Bort at 1570m, a south-facing summer pasture with a restaurant. The second stage takes you on up to Grindel at 1955m and access to four drag-lifts serving wide, easy runs. From Oberläger at 1960m, reached by the Hohwald drag, a long and varied red (intermediate) run skirts the boundary of the ski area and takes you all the way down to the Hotel Wetterhorn, from where you can take a bus or ski back into Grindelwald.

A second red follows a more direct route from the Bärgelegg drag to the Bluemlisalp restaurant a few hundred metres further along the road. The third stage of the gondola goes up to First where a drag-lift completes the link with Oberjoch at 2486m. A moderately easy red with a blue (easy) variant brings you back down to the restaurant at First and the start of a black run, steep in places, which roughly follows the path of the gondola back into Grindelwald.

The Mürren skiing is on the slopes beneath the 2970m summit of the Schilthorn. The top offers unquestionably the most challenging piste skiing in the entire Jungfrau and should not be missed by any competent skier visiting the region. There are plans to add at least two more lifts to this sector for 1994-5, which will increase and greatly enhance the skiing. The remainder of the runs, with the exception of the handful of pistes reached by two steep drag-lifts on the Schiltgrat above the village are, however, not worth the effort unless you are staying in Mürren itself. The resort is reached by a steep funicular railway from Lauterbrunnen and, given enough snow, it is possible to ski all the way back down again by means of a long and tortuous path.

Easier and quicker mountain access is via the Schilthornbahn cable car from Stechelberg, a few kilometres by bus along the valley from Lauterbrunnen. The cable car takes you to the southern end of the village, up over a sheer cliff face to Birg at 2676m and finally to the Schilthorn itself, crowned by the Piz Gloria revolving restaurant where some of the 1969 James Bond film *On Her Majesty's Secret Service* was shot.

Just below the restaurant is the starting point for the annual Inferno race, a pro-am downhill open to all who have a helmet and a start number. Some 1,500 racers set off in pairs at 30-second intervals for Lauterbrunnen in the valley below. They must negotiate a handful of gates, climb briefly uphill, but are otherwise free to choose their own hair-raising route down the mountain. The 1928 inaugural contest of what used to be an entirely British race was won by a Mr Harold Mitchell in 72 minutes; today's top skiers complete the course in less than 15.

The one run down from the top of the Schilthorn has rightly been upgraded to black on the piste map, although after the first steep and usually icy mogul field the main piste should present few problems to skiers who normally prefer to stick to red runs. Lift passes are valid for uphill journeys only above Mürren. This in theory means that if a skier decides on arrival that the fairly steep runs from Birg or the Schilthorn black are beyond his or her capability, he or she must pay to come down again. This potentially dangerous policy continues to cause considerable outrage among reporters. However, one correspondent assures us that all is explained on a small notice in German at the cable car station: if you have a lift pass and are carrying skis you will be brought down without charge. Skiers with single journey tickets and pedestrians always have to pay.

After the initial steep pitch the Schilthorn soon opens out into the spectacularly beautiful bowl of the Engetal. A drag-lift from half-way down brings you back up to the cable car station at Birg. From here you can either return to the summit of the Schilthorn or enjoy what is usually the best snow on the mountain on the blue and red runs served by the drag. Lower down the Inferno course the piste provides stunning views of the Jungfrau before entering the Kanonenrohr. At racing speed this narrow rock-walled gulley with unpleasant drop-offs (protected by netting) and harsh moguls is extremely hazardous, but considerably less so when taken at leisure on a sunny day. The run flattens out and leads down to the nursery slope at Allmendhubel, which is otherwise reached by an ancient train from the village centre. Red and blue runs of moderate difficulty descend from here back into Mürren and on to the gentle pastures above the Lauterbrunnen-Mürren railway line at Winteregg.

Lift queues are not a serious problem in the Jungfrau region. Reporters complain that the scramble for the train at Wengen at peak times is annoying: 'Although it looks chaotic the system does actually work well'. The Wengen ski school now has its own reserved trains at peak times. However, one reporter notes that unscrupulous British skiers have been known to take other skis off the train to make room for their own, causing considerable inconvenience and stress. Grindelwald becomes busy at weekends with day visitors. Despite its upgrading, the Lauberhorn chair is also prone to queues.

Mountain restaurants

Many of the restaurants in the area tend to be large and impersonal, but there are some wonderful exceptions. The Hotel Jungfrau at Wengernalp ('incomparably beautiful views') is renowned for its warm atmosphere and Swiss specialities. The Brandegg restaurant is famed throughout the Alps for its 'quite extraordinarily delicious' apple fritters. The Kleine Scheidegg station buffet is much more interesting than it looks, with a variety of Swiss fare and its own *Röstizza*, a cross between *Rösti* and pizza. The Männlichen restaurant has spectacular views, but 'exploits its captive audience with high prices'. A number of reporters prefer to eat in Wengen itself. The Victoria Hotel is 'quiet, and conveniently situated near the nursery slopes and the station'. The *Rösti* in the Stübli of the Eiger Hotel is also recommended.

The restaurant at Bort above Grindelwald is said to be 'very pleasant, reasonably priced, but the food is not exceptional'. The big self-service at First is 'rather large and impersonal'. The Hotel Wetterhorn on the way down to Grindelwald has a convivial atmosphere and good food.

Above Mürren the Birg restaurant is 'nothing to write home about'. The Gimmeln has 'good raclette and *Apfelküchen*'. We have complimentary reports of the revolving Piz Gloria on the summit of the Schilthorn ('not expensive and good value'). One reporter did, however, complain that the 360° panorama made him feel queasy. The Schilthornhütte on the descent from here is a mountain refuge serving simple dishes, with a 'fun atmosphere and wonderful views'.

Beginners and children

We have pleasing reports of high standards of tuition in all three resorts. Mürren Ski School has come in for considerable criticism for the attitude of its often elderly instructors and outdated methods; all that appears to be in the past under the dynamic leadership of Angélique Feuz. All her teachers apparently speak good English and the standard of instruction is said now to be on a par with the ski schools in both Wengen and Grindelwald. Mürren has no easily accessed nursery slope as such and is not a suitable resort for beginners. Wengen, on the other hand, has excellent nursery slopes in the centre of the village.

The non-ski kindergarten at Wengen is strongly recommended. Not all reports on the children's ski school are positive: one reporter found her 4-year-old novice daughter herded into a group of varying experience and ages of up to nine: 'The rather strict discipline imposed by the middle-aged lady instructor did not help.' On complaining was told it was 'uneconomical' to separate groups of children outside the school holidays. We have a positive report of the Wengen Privat independent ski school. Grindelwald children's ski school is also highly thought of by reporters: 'By the end of his first week our 4-year-old could ski all of the beginners' area with us.' The Mini Club at Club Med is strongly recommended by one reporter: 'My 6-year-old daughter loved it and her skiing improved.'

The resorts

Wengen is almost car-free, although a couple of Range Rovers are allowed to operate as taxis. Otherwise, luggage is carried by electric buggy around this charming resort, which despite expansion has lost none of its character and appears to have changed surprisingly little since the foundation of the Downhill Only club nearly 70 years ago. Many of its visitors are still British, the same families who return year after year to create their own entertainment in a decidedly cliquey way. The presence of Club Med at the northern end of town seems incongruous in this otherwise neo-Edwardian setting.

At the heart of it all on a sunny balcony above the Lauterbrunnen valley is the railway. Village life is centred on the comings and goings from the now rebuilt station, which is surrounded by a scattering of largely refurbished hotels built nearly a century ago in the grand manner. The main, indeed only, street stretching southwards from the station is lined with hotels and a modest range of mainly expensive shops and boutiques. The large skating and curling rink beside the nursery slopes forms an integral part of village life.

Grindelwald is the original of the three villages, a large and busy year-round resort spread along the valley floor between the soaring peaks of the Wetterhorn and the Eiger on the one side and the gentler wooded slopes of its First ski area on the other. There are few more cosmopolitan resorts to be found in the world, with every nationality imaginable listed among its guests, not least the Japanese who come here in numbers to visit the Eiger and the Jungfraujoch.

The Kleine Scheidegg ski area is not accessed from Grindelwald at all, but from Grund, a rather soulless suburb five minutes away by train, not aided by the presence of a snow caravan park. The scenery around Grindelwald is spectacular, it has its own small intermediate ski area and many reporters consider it the best place to stay in the Jungfrau: 'Having seen it all and skied for 22 years, I would not consider skiing anywhere else.' Its low altitude does, however, mean that snow cover in the village and on the mountain is uncertain.

Mürren has few rivals as the prettiest and least spoilt ski village in Switzerland. Old chalets and hotels line the paths between the railway station at one end and the cable car at the other. The village is on a sunny shelf perched on top of a 500m rock face above Lauterbrunnen, with extraordinary views across the valley to the Eiger and the Jungfrau. Again, the same British families, nearly all of them members of the Kandahar Club, have been returning here for generations and firm links have been forged with the original village families, although some young Swiss view this British 'ownership' of their resort with undisguised contempt.

Accommodation

In **Wengen** the accommodation is split between hotels and apartments, with some chalets. The resort is quite spread out and distinctly steep. While location is of little importance for the skiing (if staying high up you can ski both down to the train and back to your hotel), a long uphill slog after midnight tends to deter many a holidaymaker from exploring what limited nightlife there is. Hotel Regina is 'spacious, clean and comfortable' and renowned for its English breakfast, although a couple of reporters were otherwise disappointed with the quality of the food. The Park Hotel Beausite by the cable car is the most luxurious, the Victoria Lauberhorn has been completely refurbished and is strongly recommended. The Eiger, now a Best Western, is an institution among long-time visitors.

Hotel Falken, a favourite of Peter Ustinov, is said to be 'delightfully old-fashioned'; however, one correspondent describes it as having 'poor rooms and very poor facilities, although the food was good and the staff pleasant'. Hotel Wengener Hof, five minutes' walk from the station, is said to be 'very comfortable' with good food. Hotel Silberhorn is 'excellent, with multi-national and very friendly staff, superb and substantial food'. Hotel Alpenrose is said to be of an exceptionally high standard ('we particularly liked the large lounge area with log fire').

Hotel Bernerhof and Hotel Bellevue are also both recommended. Club Med here has a fine reputation, although the presence of large noisy French-led classes on crowded pistes can lead to Agincourt-style confrontations with the more conservative British element.

Grindelwald visitors have a wide choice of luxurious hotels as well as simpler accommodation. The Grand Hotel Regina is partly decorated with eighteenth-century antiques and is famous for the ice sculptures in

Skiing facts: Wengen

TOURIST OFFICE
CH-3823 Wengen, Bernese Oberland
Tel 41 36 551414
Fax 41 36 553060

THE RESORT
By road Calais 835km
By rail station in resort
By air Zurich 3½ hrs
Visitor beds 5,000 (50% hotels, 50% apartments and chalets)
Transport traffic-free

THE SKIING
Longest run Mettlen-Grund, 8.5km (blue)
Number of lifts 19 Wengen/Grindelwald
Number of trails/pistes 46 in Grindelwald/Wengen (28% easy, 57% intermediate, 15% difficult)
Total of trails/pistes 98km in Kleine Scheidegg/Männlichen, 165km in Wengen/Grindelwald
Nursery slopes 2 lifts
Summer skiing 1 lift (300m) at Jungfraujoch
Snowmaking 2 snow-cannon on nursery slopes

LIFT PASSES
Area pass Jungfrau pass (covers Wengen, Grindelwald and Mürren), SF210 for 6 days, Kleine Scheidegg/ Männlichen (covers all lifts from Wengen to Grindelwald), SF86 for 2 days
Day pass Kleine Scheidegg/Männlichen, SF48
Half-day pass Kleine Scheidegg/ Männlichen, SF36 after 12.30pm
Beginners points tickets
Children 6-16 yrs, Kleine Scheidegg/Männlichen, SF43 for 2 days. Jungfrau pass, SF105 for 6 days. Free for 5 yrs and under
Pensioners no reduction
Credit cards accepted yes

SKI SCHOOLS
Adults Swiss Ski School, 2 hrs morning and afternoon, SF216 for 6 days
Children Swiss Ski School, 4-12 yrs, 2 hrs morning and afternoon, SF216 for 6 days
Private lessons SF150 for half-day, SF260 per day
Special courses snowboarding, ski-touring, telemark
Guiding companies through ski school

CROSS-COUNTRY
Ski schools Swiss Ski School
Loipe location and size 17.5km in Lauterbrunnen valley

CHILDCARE
Non-ski kindergarten Sport Pavillon, 3-7 yrs, 8.45am-4.30pm, SF125 for 6 days including lunch
Ski kindergarten Gästekindergarten, 3-7 yrs, 8.45-4.30pm, SF110 for 6 days including lunch. Sport Pavillon, 3-7 yrs, 8.45am- 4.30pm, SF125 for 6 days including lunch
Babysitting list available from tourist office

OTHER SPORTS
Heli-skiing, parapente, hang-gliding, dog-sledding, skating, curling, swimming, bowling, fitness centre, climbing wall, tobogganing

FOOD AND DRINK PRICES
Coffee SF3, bottle of house wine SF17, beer SF2.80, dish of the day SF16-22

TOUR OPERATORS
Bladon Lines, Club Med, Crystal, Inghams, Kuoni, Made to Measure, Ski Choice, Ski Europe, Ski Sutherland, Ski Thomson, Ski Unique, Ski West, Swiss Travel Service

its grounds. However, one reporter complains that there is 'nowhere to sit quietly and play bridge away from the very noisy band'. Parkhotel Schoenegg has been in the same family for a hundred years and is said to have excellent four-course dinners. Hotel Hirschen is a family-run three-star in the centre of the village ('very good for children'). The new Hotel Bodmi, situated on the nursery slopes, is very convenient for families.

Skiing facts: Grindelwald

TOURIST OFFICE
CH-3818 Grindelwald, Bernese Oberland
Tel 41 36 531212
Fax 41 36 533088

THE RESORT
By road Calais 835km
By rail station in resort
By air Zurich 3 hrs
Visitor beds 10,800 (59% apartments and chalets, 26% hotels, 15% guesthouses)
Transport bus service between Grund, Grindelwald centre and First lift

THE SKIING
Longest run Mettlen-Grund, 8.5km (blue)
Number of lifts 19 Grindelwald/Wengen
Number of trails/pistes 46 in Grindelwald/Wengen (28% easy, 57% intermediate, 15% difficult)
Total of trails/pistes 98km in Kleine Scheidegg/Männlichen, 165km in Grindelwald/Wengen
Nursery slopes 2 lifts
Summer skiing 1 lift (300m) at Jungfraujoch
Snowmaking 15km covered

LIFT PASSES
Area pass Jungfrau pass (covers Grindelwald, Wengen and Mürren), SF210 for 6 days. Kleine Scheidegg/Männlichen (First area extra), SF86 for 2 days
Day pass Kleine Scheidegg/Männlichen SF48, First SF46
Half-day pass Kleine Scheidegg/Männlichen SF36, First SF34
Beginners points tickets
Children 6-16 yrs, Kleine Scheidegg/Mannlichen, SF43 for 2 days, Jungfrau pass, SF105 for 6 days. Free for 5 yrs and under
Pensioners no reduction
Credit cards accepted yes

SKI SCHOOLS
Adults Swiss Ski School, 2 hrs in morning and afternoon, SF170 for 5 days
Children Swiss Ski School, 3-14 yrs, 2 hrs in morning and afternoon, SF30 for 2 hr lesson, SF180 for 5 days (10 x 2 hr lessons)
Private lessons SF150 for half-day, SF250 per day
Special courses snowboarding, telemark, courses for blind skiers
Guiding companies Bergsteigerzentrum Grindelwald

CROSS-COUNTRY
Ski schools Swiss Ski School
Loipe location and size 30km around the village and at Bussalp

CHILDCARE
Non-ski kindergarten Bodmi, 3 yrs and over, 9.30am-4pm, SF35 per day including lunch
Ski kindergarten Swiss Ski School, 3-14 yrs, 2 hrs in morning and afternoon, SF180 for 5 days
Babysitting list available from tourist office

OTHER SPORTS
Parapente, curling, skating, swimming, fitness centre, climbing wall, tobogganing

WHAT'S NEW
● Three additional hotels: Alpendorf, Bodmi and Steinbock

FOOD AND DRINK PRICES
Coffee SF3, bottle of house wine SF16, beer SF3, dish of the day SF16

TOUR OPERATORS
Bladon Lines, Inghams, Kuoni, Made to Measure, Powder Byrne, Ski Choice, Ski Thomson, Ski Weekend, Swiss Travel Service

In **Mürren** accommodation is split between apartments, hotels and a few tour operator chalets. The Palace Hotel is the smartest and the most expensive. The popular Edelweiss is 'convenient, clean and friendly', although some reporters feel it is in need of modernisation ('very basic for a four-star, but still pleasant'). The Bellevue-Crystal and the Blumental are both recommended, together with the simpler Belmont. The supermarket is said to be adequate and there is also a butcher's shop.

Eating out

Most restaurants in Wengen are in hotels, but Da Mario near Club Med is strongly recommended for pizzas. Mary's Café offers fondue accompanied by alp-horn blowing contests. Restaurant Wengen in the Hotel

Skiing facts: Mürren

TOURIST OFFICE
CH-3825 Grindelwald, Bernese Oberland
Tel 41 36 551616
Fax 41 36 553769

THE RESORT
By road Calais 940km
By rail station in resort
By air Zurich 3½ hrs
Visitor beds 1,960 (33% hotels, 67% apartments, pensions and chalets)
Transport traffic-free

THE SKIING
Longest run Schilthorn to Lauterbrunnen, 15km (black/red)
Number of lifts 12
Number of trails/pistes 18 (33% easy, 45% intermediate, 22% difficult)
Total of trails/pistes 35km
Nursery slopes 1 lift
Summer skiing none
Snowmaking none

LIFT PASSES
Area pass Jungfrau pass (covers Mürren, Wengen and Grindelwald/First), SF210 for 6 days. Mürren/Schilthorn, SF82 for 2 days
Day pass Mürren/Schilthorn, SF46
Half-day pass Mürren/Schilthorn, SF34 after midday
Beginners points tickets
Children 6-16 yrs, Mürren/Schilthorn, SF43 for 2 days. Jungfrau pass, SF105 for 6 days. Free for 5 yrs and under
Pensioners no reduction
Credit cards accepted yes

SKI SCHOOLS
Adults Swiss Ski School, 10am-midday, SF114 for 6 days
Children Swiss Ski School, 4-14 yrs, 10am-midday, SF114 for 6 days
Private lessons SF110 for half-day
Special courses snowboarding, ski-touring
Guiding companies through ski school

CROSS-COUNTRY
Ski schools Swiss Ski School
Loipe location and size 1.5km trail above Mürren on the Blumental plateau

CHILDCARE
Non-ski kindergarten Mürren Day Care Centre, 2 yrs and over, 9.30-12.15am, SF15 (with Guest Card). 3 yrs and over, 9.30am-4pm, SF30 including lunch (with Guest Card). Playroom in Sports Centre
Ski kindergarten Swiss Ski School, 4-14 yrs, 10am-midday, SF114 for 6 days
Babysitting list available from tourist office

OTHER SPORTS
Heli-skiing, skating, curling, squash, indoor tennis, swimming, tobogganing

FOOD AND DRINK PRICES
Coffee SF2.70, bottle of house wine SF17, beer SF2.90, dish of the day SF18

TOUR OPERATORS
Bladon Lines, Kuoni, Made to Measure, Ski Choice, Ski Unique, Swiss Travel Service

Hirschen specialises in fondue *chinoise*. Hotel Victoria-Lauberhorn has a pizzeria and a crêperie as well as a more extensive restaurant. The Felsenkeller in the Hotel Silberhorn is also praised. The Berghaus is known for its fresh fish and the Bernerhof for fondue and raclette. The à la carte restaurant in the Bahnhof, right by the station, is one of the best places to dine in Grindelwald. Reporters also recommend the Schoenegg and the Schweizerhof. In Mürren the Stägerstübi is extremely popular, along with the Eiger and Bellevue-Crystal restaurants.

Après-ski
Wengen is not the place for anyone in search of a riotous nightlife, but there is a lot to do during the early evening. The last ski trains are full of families with toboggans going up to Wengernalp for the four-kilometre descent back to the village. Crowds gather in Café Oberland and in Mary's Café on the home run and the ice-bar outside the Hotel Brunner is busy. In the village itself the skating rink is a centre of activity with curling competitions, hockey matches and often dual slalom racing or ski jumping behind the village. Reporters complain that Wengen has no real tea-and-cakes places apart from Café Gruebi, which is 'very cramped'. The Stuubli, next to the ski school, is cosy and offers snacks. The Eiger Hotel Stübli is packed out, as is the independent Eiger Bar in the main street. You can (for a fee if non-resident) swim at the Mountain Beach Club in the Park Hotel Beausite.

Later night entertainment centres on a few bars. Sina's bar is the most popular (it also has tea-dancing, karaoke and live music). The Carrousel in the Hotel Regina is the best disco in town. At weekends in season Tiffany's in the Hotel Silberhorn and Paradise in the Hotel Belvédère can also be fun. The cinema shows films in English as well as in German and Dutch. There is pool and bowling at the Kegelbahn.

Grindelwald has a large sports centre with swimming, saunas, skating and a climbing wall; it is free to Grindelwald hotel guests. Snow permitting, there are good toboggan runs. The Expresso bar draws the young crowd after skiing, while the Gepsi attracts a slightly older clientele. Later on the Challi bar in the Hotel Kreuz and Post, the Cava in the Derby and Herby's in the Regina are the most popular. The Plaza Club and the Spyder discos rock on into the small hours. The cinema shows films in English.

For such a small village Mürren is surprisingly lively after skiing. It has an excellent sports centre with skating, curling, a swimming-pool, sauna and squash courts. The Ballon bar in the Hotel Palace, together with the Gruebi in the Jungfrau and the Pub in the Belmont, are all popular. The Tächi bar in the Hotel Eiger is one of the main meeting places. The Bliemlichäller disco in the Blumental and the Inferno disco in the Palace are packed at weekends and in season.

Lenzerheide-Valbella, Graubunden

ALTITUDE 1500m (4,920ft)

••

Good points easy runs, extensive cross-country skiing, sunny slopes, tree-level runs, activities for non-skiers
Bad points limited après-ski, lack of tough runs, lack of skiing convenience
Linked or nearby resorts Arosa (n), Churwalden (l), Flims-Laax (n), Davos-Klosters (n), Parpan (l)

These two resorts used to attract a fair number of British families in the 1960s, but for reasons that are not altogether clear they faded in popularity and nowadays the majority of visitors are Swiss and German families. The area has considerable attractions, including magnificent cross-country skiing and a large joint alpine ski area. For piste skiers at least, the extent of the skiing area cannot disguise its lack of variety. The villages are not particularly attractive or convenient.

The distinctive villages lie at either end of a lake in a wide, attractively wooded pass running north-south, with high mountains on either side. The road linking them is an important thoroughfare, which in itself reduces the area's appeal for people with small children and has encouraged the two villages to spread along the valley until they have almost merged. A car is handy for getting to and from skiing, and for evening entertainment; it also gives the chance of some excellent day-trips – St Moritz, Arosa, Flims-Laax, Davos and Klosters are all within range.

The skiing
Top 2865m (9,397ft) bottom 1230m (4,035ft)

The skiing is in two separate areas on either side of the inconveniently wide pass. Both have about half woodland and half open skiing terrain; the Danis/Stätzerhorn area to the west is more extensive and gets the sun in the morning; the Rothorn to the east is higher, more beautiful, more interesting, but more crowded and gets the sun in the afternoon.

There are no particularly difficult pistes, although the Rothorn cable car opens up some off-piste skiing. Runs down to the two villages (or as near to them as they go) are in general gentler than the higher slopes and suitable for inexperienced skiers, except in poor snow conditions, which are said to be not unusual.

Mountain access to the Rothorn skiing is via a two-stage cable car which climbs from a point beside the lake, well away from both villages, to the peak about 1400m above. The panorama from the top is magnificent; the Rothorn drops away in awesome rocky faces, limiting the skiing possibilities to one main piste behind the main crest, through a wooden gallery, then over a ridge giving a choice of descents (red and blue above the Motta chair-lift, red and not very severe black below it) to the lifts above Parpan and back to the cable car mid-station at Scharmoin. From here there is a choice of several gentle, winding descents through the woods taking you back to the bottom station or to the edge of Valbella or Lenzerheide. There are several drags on the northern side of Scharmoin, the longest linking with the sunny Schwarzhorn chair-lift, high above Parpan. If tempted by the open, not very steep unpisted hillsides below the chair-lift, be warned that you risk ending up stranded between Parpan and Churwalden.

The best off-piste run goes from the Rothorn to Lenzerheide via the beautiful Alp Sanaspans; it is long and demanding, with no escape once begun except the variant back to the middle station, which involves a steep and exposed drop over a rocky ridge.

The Danis/Stätzerhorn area is much less impressive, but the rather featureless open hillsides below the peaks have been easy to develop for skiers: a long network of parallel lifts, mostly drags with the exception of the efficient chairs from Lenzerheide to Piz Danis, makes it possible to cover a lot of ground.

Cross-country loipes are extensive with long, mostly linked sectors along the pass, through the woods and around the lake. The Lenzerheide ski school is said to be well organised with small classes.

The resort

The main street of Lenzerheide has some attractive old buildings, but as a whole it has no outstanding charm. Valbella has even less identity, no more than a large community of hotels and concrete-box holiday homes crammed on to a hillside, but it is in some ways a better base, less of a roadside strip, and gives direct access to the western ski area. Accommodation is in apartments and hotels in both villages. The most attractive and best located of the central Lenzerheide hotels is the Danis. The Schweizerhof and Sunstar are recommended. The Guarda Val, out of the centre, is an outstanding hotel with a good restaurant.

Après-ski

The après-ski is fairly quiet, even in Lenzerheide. It is mainly confined to a couple of tea-rooms, live music in some hotels, and a couple of discos. Non-skiers are provided with skating, curling and toboggan runs.

TOURIST OFFICE
CH-7078 Lenzerheide, Grisons
Tel 41 81 343434
Fax 41 81 345383

TOUR OPERATORS
Inghams, Kuoni, Made to Measure,
Ski Choice, Ski Unique, Swiss Travel Service

Saas-Fee, Valais

ALTITUDE 1800m (5,904ft)

• •

Good points alpine charm, long ski season, variety of nursery slopes, spectacular setting, freedom from cars, resort-level snow, ski-touring, summer skiing, children's facilities
Bad points long airport transfer, lack of skiing convenience, difficult road access, lack of tree-level skiing
Linked or nearby resorts Saas-Almagell (n), Saas-Balen (n), Saas-Grund (n), Zermatt (n) – *see separate chapter*

Saas-Fee is an old farming village which has grown over the years to become one of Switzerland's most popular resorts. Like Zermatt, it is one of the few completely car-free resorts and has been so since 1951, but unlike its exalted neighbour it has remained a quiet family resort. The attractive chalet-style buildings have been carefully maintained, and all the new buildings blend in well. Add to the characterful village of small, winding streets a stunning glacial backdrop and you have the perfect chocolate-box resort. Beautiful the setting may be, but it can be harsh in mid-winter when only minimal sunshine reaches the village.

Many visitors to Saas-Fee find the skiing is limited, despite the substantial skiing provided by the Metro Alpin underground railway. Avalanche safety measures mean that no further construction is possible on the mountain. There are good nursery slopes next to the village, and wide, easy glacier slopes up to the mountain, but much of the skiing is on the steep side and there are no blue (easy) runs to the village from the main areas. The off-piste skiing is limited by severe glacier danger, although Saas-Fee is a major departure point for organised ski-tours with mountain guides and forms part of the Haute Route.

The skiing

Top 3600m (11,800ft) bottom 1800m (5,904ft)

Saas-Fee is one of the most snow-sure resorts in Europe, with all-year-round glacier skiing. But at lower altitudes the glacier is a hindrance, dividing the north-facing skiing into two segments. The new Alpin Express jumbo gondola taking skiers from near the car park up to the mid-station of the main Felskinn ski area has greatly improved **mountain access** from the village and relieved what was, until recently, a serious queuing problem. The only remaining bottlenecks are at the Felskinn cable car in high season, where queues are reported to be up to 45 minutes long, and when the snow lower down is poor there can be queues for the high glacier drags and for the Längfluh chair.

Access to the Längfluh area is by gondola from the outskirts of town. This takes you up to Spielboden, where a cable car goes up to Längfluh with its steep mogul fields. There are tenuous links at the top of the area to the main Felskinn sector. The Plattjen area is a north-east-facing slope, close to the village and much favoured by ski school classes.

Good, challenging red (intermediate) and black (difficult) mogul runs go under the gondola at Längfluh, but most people go up the cable car to ski the easier reds served by the top chair-lift. The only way back down to the top gondola station from the bottom of this chair is on a black run, so many skiers prefer to ride up it and come down by cable car. From the top of the cable car, you can pay six francs to take the Fee-Chatz snow-cat (a cramped trailer), or to be towed on skis behind it, gently uphill across the glacier to Felskinn.

Felskinn's skiing, reached either by a cable car which starts a drag-lift ride away from the edge of the resort, or on the new Alpin Express, is more extensive. The easy skiing is served by drags on the top half; lower down it becomes more bumpy, and inexperienced skiers can join the cable car at Maste 4. Reporters recommend the itinerary runs under Felskinn. The Metro to Mittelallalin opens up more skiing and makes it possible to ski across to Längfluh. The steep black starts immediately from the top of the Metro, the red begins with a short walk up the mountain, and the blue even higher with a 15-minute uphill walk. The two drag-lifts on the glacier serve these pistes, enabling you to ski them repeatedly without using the Metro.

You can reach the Metro on the drags to Egginerjoch and Kamel. These served the pre-Metro summer skiing and are often closed during the early season. The lower drag-lift serves a wide red, and the upper one serves two short and steep blacks. Access to the Metro is via a path from the top of the lower drag, or on the Kamel black from the top of the upper one. The black run is not steep, but it does involve a walk.

The Metro's mid-station has a tunnel leading out to the far side of the mountain for the start of some off-piste descents. The lift does not normally stop here, but will do so when off-piste conditions are good.

The Plattjen gondola runs from the same building as the Längfluh. It gives access to some easy intermediate skiing. The main slope, above the trees, is served by a chair which often has a short queue. From here the runs to the village are through the trees, with the choice of a black run or a narrow (and sometimes icy) blue. The former Hannig ski area has been transformed into a hiking and tobogganing area.

Mountain restaurants

According to reporters, eating and drinking is excellent and cheaper on the mountain than in the village. The Gletschergrotte, among the trees off-piste from Spielboden, has good food, but slow service. The Alpenblick is a waiter-service restaurant. The Metro takes you to the highest revolving restaurant in the world, although it has limited views.

Beginners and children

The nursery slopes are wide, gentle and well-placed for lunches and meeting up with other skiers, but the bottom parts are not very sunny in mid-winter and can be glacially cold. There is a capacity for artificial snow on these slopes, although it is unnecessary for much of the season. The

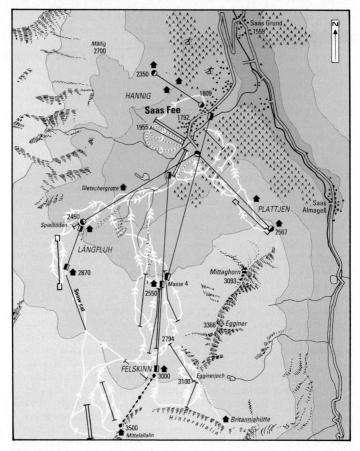

ski school does not generally receive good reports; class sizes are too big at busy times, organisation is bad, English is not widely spoken.

The Glückskäfer in the Waldrain House takes non-skiing babies and children up to six years old. Skiing children from five years old can join the special children's classes at the ski school.

The resort

The traditional village of Saas-Fee spreads for over half a mile along a couple of narrow, car-free roads which converge to form a village centre. Shopping facilities are adequate, with food shops at various points in the village. Transport is on foot or via expensive electric taxis.

Accommodation

This is mainly in the form of traditional-looking hotels which are comfortable but not luxurious, and self-catering chalets. The bulk of the resort is near the entrance to the car parks. The hotels over the river at the far end of the village are the most convenient for skiers. Two chalet-style hotels which are well placed for the lifts are the Waldesruh and the Derby, both comfortable yet lacking in atmosphere. The neighbouring Belmont is smarter. Further away from the lifts, the Dom is a friendly hotel. The Beau-Site is recommended for its food, as is the Aparthotel Zurbriggen. The Tenne is a cosy place. The Walliserhof has a good restaurant serving nouvelle cuisine, as well as a swimming-pool and a nightclub. The Alphübel is a 10- to 15-minute walk from the lifts, but very popular with families as it contains an all-day crèche which is free to guests.

In a class of its own is the Waldhotel Fletschhorn, a 20-minute walk through woods to the north of the resort. It is comfortable and its restaurant serves excellent nouvelle cuisine. The newest hotels in town are the Schweizerhof, Hotel Garni Artemis and Hotel Atlantic. The Allegra House is a new apartment building, and the Amici apartments are spacious and in an excellent location. Self-caterers can buy their provisions at the Supermarket Saas-Fee or Konsum Saas-Fee.

Eating out

The most popular eating places include La Ferme, Arvu Stube, La Gorge, Del Ponte, Käse-Keller, Feeloch, and Schäferstube. The restaurant at the Tenne is famous for its grills. The Alp-Hitta is recommended for traditional Swiss food, Zur Mühle for fondue *chinoise*. The Gourmet-Stübli Hohnegg is recommended for those who want a memorable evening out, as is the Waldhotel Fletschhorn.

Après-ski

The limited after-skiing activities include tea at the Skihütte and Hotel Belmont. Nesti's Ski Bar ('very crowded') and the Pic-Pic Bar are both popular. Later on there are live bands in a couple of the hotels; the tiny bar of the Christiania is usually crowded and the Sissy bar of the Tenne is cosy. The Go-Inn, the Fee Pub, the Sandokan and the Happy Bar are all recommended. There are three discos – Crazy Night, Disco Club Yeti and Dancing Le Club – none of which charge entrance fees.

Saas-Grund 1559m (5,117ft)

Saas-Grund is the valley village strung out along the road up to Saas-Almagell, a five-minute bus ride from and a cheaper alternative to Saas-Fee. It is not as attractive as Saas-Fee, and nor is it car-free. The skiing is high and sunny, suited mainly to intermediates and off-piste skiers.

The skiing takes place on the high, sunny shelf of Kreuzboden at 2400m, and is reached by gondola. The only runs back to the valley are an off-piste itinerary and a long, narrow path with an exposed drop off the side. A popular red run from the top of the gondola is served by a chair-lift, while above Kreuzboden a pair of long drags serve broad, gentle red and blue pistes. The top section of the gondola goes up to Hohsaas at 3098m, serving a long and varied red piste. Off-piste opportunities abound. Saas-Grund has adequate nursery slopes as well as gentle runs at Kreuzboden. There is a big restaurant at Kreuzboden, and a little hut at Hohsaas with a wonderful view of Saas-Fee, and good food to go with it. The accommodation is in chalets, apartments and modest hotels, including the Ruby, recommended for 'excellent quality and quantity of food, and catering for vegetarians'.

Saas-Almagell, at a slightly higher 1672m, also has its own small ski area serviced by five short drag-lifts and one chair.

TOURIST OFFICE
3910 Saas-Grund, Valais
Tel 41 28 57 24 03
Fax 41 28 57 11 43

TOUR OPERATORS
Ski Europe, Ski Thomson

Skiing facts: Saas-Fee

TOURIST OFFICE
CH-3906 Saas-Fee, Valais
Tel 41 28 591111
Fax 41 28 571860

THE RESORT
By road Calais 1072km
By rail Brig, frequent buses from station
By air Geneva or Zurich, both 3½ hrs
Visitor beds 8,500 (71% apartments and chalets, 29% hotels)
Transport traffic-free village

THE SKIING
Longest run Mittelallalin-Felskinn-Saas-Fee, 14km (red)
Number of lifts 26
Number of trails/pistes 35 (23% easy, 46% intermediate, 31% difficult)
Total of trails/pistes 80km
Nursery slopes 4 lifts
Summer skiing 15km of runs on the Feegletscher
Snowmaking 1.6km covered

LIFT PASSES
Area pass (covers all lifts except the Fee-Chatz snow-cat, extra SF6) SF230 for 6 days
Day pass SF48
Half-day pass SF40, from midday
Beginners single tickets available for nursery lifts
Children 6-16 yrs, SF140 for 6 days (extra SF2 for Fee-Chatz), free for 5 yrs and under
Pensioners no reduction
Credit cards accepted yes

SKI SCHOOLS
Adults Swiss Ski School, SF165 for 5 days
Children Swiss Ski School, SF160 for 5 days
Private lessons SF50 per hr
Special courses snowboarding
Guiding companies through Swiss Ski School

CROSS-COUNTRY
Ski schools Swiss Ski School
Loipe location and size 8km loop through woods starts at Wildi. Further trails in the Saas valley (25km)

CHILDCARE
Non-ski kindergarten Glückskäfer, 0-6 yrs, 8.30am-5pm, SF65 per day
Ski kindergarten Swiss Ski School, 5-12 yrs, 9.45am-3.30pm, SF45 per day, SF19 extra for lunch
Babysitting Glückskäfer, or through tourist office

OTHER SPORTS
Skating, curling, ice-hockey, indoor tennis, swimming, fitness centre, tobogganing

WHAT'S NEW
● Hannig only open for tobogganing and walkers

FOOD AND DRINK PRICES
Coffee SF2.80, bottle of house wine SF24, beer SF3, dish of the day SF25

TOUR OPERATORS
Bladon Lines, Crystal, Enterprise, Inghams, Kuoni, Made to Measure, Ski Choice, Ski Gower, Ski Thomson, Swiss Travel Service

St Moritz, Engadine

ALTITUDE 1800m (5,904ft)

∙∙

Good points beautiful scenery, big ski area, reliable resort-level snow, extensive facilities for non-skiers, excellent cross-country skiing, lively après-ski, variety of mountain restaurants, sunny slopes, late-season skiing
Bad points lack of skiing convenience, limited nursery slopes, difficult road access, long airport transfer, lift queues, heavy traffic
Linked or nearby resorts Celerina (l), Champfèr (n), Pontresina (n), Samadan (n), Sils Maria (l), Silvaplana (l), Surlej (l), Zuos (n)

In 1864, four Englishmen were enjoying a summer evening in the Kulm Hotel after a day of walking in the mountains and taking the spa water for which the village was renowned. With winter fast approaching they sadly discussed their return to England. Their friend, hotelier Johannes Badrutt, proposed they might return at the end of the year rather than wait until the following summer. He even suggested that their winter holiday of tobogganing and various sports on the frozen lake would be financed by him, should there turn out to be less sunshine than in the summer. With the good winter climate in St Moritz, Badrutt knew his money would be safe. His gamble paid off and the resort has never looked back.

One hundred and thirty years later, the international rich are still coming here in the winter. The resort still revolves as much around tobogganing and horse-riding on the frozen lake as it does around skiing. St Moritz now fills only five per cent of its beds with British occupants, and regulars say that the place has lost its style, as the original core of well-to-do British has been gradually replaced by other Europeans and Americans. Certainly the Palace, most expensive of the luxury hotels, seems flashy, but the Carlton and Kulm still have the quiet formality, the card tables, and the worn leather of London clubs. Under the continuing directorship of Colonel Digby Willoughby, the St Moritz Tobogganing Club remains defiantly British.

St Moritz has always been the place to see and be seen. It is to skiing what Bond Street is to London, but the official line is that you do not have to be rich to enjoy the resort – although it certainly helps. It is, however, possible to stay here on a similar budget to that needed for other fashionable Swiss resorts: Zermatt, Verbier or Davos, and the many skiers who never give St Moritz a try are making a mistake. The scenery is superb, with beautiful lakes set against a backdrop of the soaring Piz Nair and Piz Corvatsch peaks; the skiing, in one of the highest of alpine resorts, is surprisingly extensive and varied, and the non-skier and cross-country skier are extremely well catered for.

All approaches to the resort, except that from Austria, involve high passes. The Julier pass from Chur is kept open, but is often snowy. A car is valuable for getting around the ski areas, and for après-ski if you are not staying centrally. Socialites, however, need never stray from Dorf and the Corviglia ski area above it. The past is still alive in the form of a special train service from London, and rail is still the best means of access to the resort. St Moritz is also one of the stops on the Glacier Express, which runs to and from Zermatt via Andermatt, a spectacular journey not to be missed.

The skiing

Top 3303m (10,834ft) bottom 1720m (5,642ft)

The setting in this south-western corner of Switzerland on the Italian border is a stunning one. There are wide, open sunny slopes to flatter intermediates, steep and gentle descents through the woods, long, steep pitches with moguls, excellent glacier skiing with beautiful views, and plenty of scope for long off-piste excursions, which few skiers make use of. This variety of skiing is found on the mountains spread around the two valleys, which meet at Celerina, just below St Moritz.

Corviglia is the sunny, south-facing mountain immediately above St Moritz. **Mountain access** to these wide slopes is by the funicular railway from the top of Dorf, or the cable car from the edge of Bad. On the slopes a series of drag-lifts serve unchallenging intermediate runs. The cable car up to Piz Nair gives access to off-piste runs down the Suvretta valley towards Bad, and to long and beautiful pistes down to Marguns. This bowl, reached more directly from Corviglia, offers long and varied runs down from Trais Fluors and Glüna. The fast chair-lift on Piz Grisch provides an alternative route to the off-piste Val Silvretta run. The only skiing exclusively served by the cable car is the short, steep front face, often unskiable. From Marguns there is an occasionally narrow and awkward run ending at Celerina, where a gondola takes you back up to Marguns.

The Corvatsch area is accessible from both ends at valley level and consists of connected drag-lifts above the tree-line, serving intermediate skiing, with a single cable car climbing much higher. But the skiing is more varied and challenging across to the glaciers of Piz Bernina. The direct piste is an exhilarating slope, either bumpy or hard and very fast. The less direct route is manageable by most intermediates. Another great joy is the beautiful long Hahnensee run through the woods to St Moritz Bad via a secluded mountain hut. There is good off-piste skiing to Champfèr, Surlej and into the Roseg valley. A piste down from the Corvatsch mid-station connects with the Furtschellas skiing above Sils Maria via a long chain of lifts stretching across rocky mountainsides. At the other end there are some excellent long runs from Furtschellas itself to the isolated base station. Although not particularly steep, none of the lower runs is easy.

A single, long cable car goes up from the Bernina pass road to the magnificently situated hotel, restaurant and sun-terrace of Diavolezza, amid marvellous glacier scenery. There is an easy open slope beside the drag-lifts at the top, and a long intermediate run back down under the lift. However, the great attraction is the much skied off-piste run over

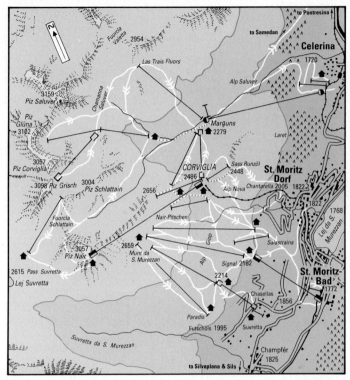

the back, across the glacier and through woods to Morteratsch. It involves some walking, and there are narrow passages between crevasses and an awkward icy drop to negotiate at the end of the glacier; these should not deter reasonably competent skiers.

Lagalp is a consistently steep, conical mountain opposite Diavolezza, which presents long runs from top to bottom, ranging from the very steep and challenging to the fairly easy. A run from the top station links up with a couple of drag-lifts at the Bernina pass. There are a few short, sunny, easy runs near the top of a funicular and one run down through the woods, intermediate except for one steep section. Alp Languard is directly accessible from Pontresina; it has a nursery area and a long drag-lift serving a red (intermediate) run.

Large areas of skiing depend on few lifts, especially the cable cars, where there are often long queues not only at weekends, despite the high proportion of non-skiers in the resort. A system of stamping numbers on skis has been in operation for many years at the Corvatsch cable car so that you do not have to stand in line while waiting for your number to come up, but you still have to wait nearby to ensure you do not miss your turn. The Sils Maria cable car is reported to be queue-free, unlike the more direct and easily accessible Surlej one. There may be half-hour queues for Piz Nair above Corviglia even in January. There can be irritating queues for many of the chair- and drag-lifts caused by single

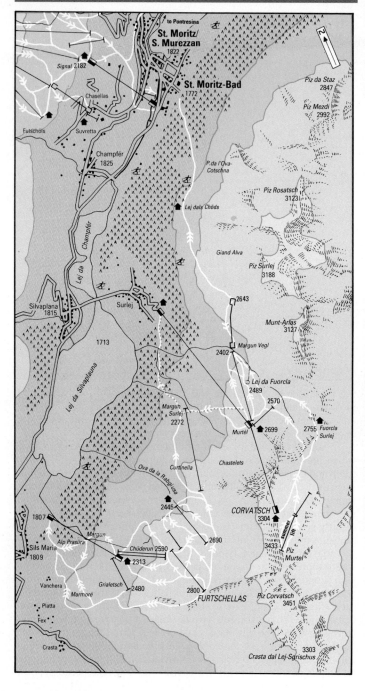

to Pontresina

St. Moritz/
S. Murezzan
1822

St. Moritz-Bad
1772

Signal 2182

Chasellas

Futschöls

Suvretta

Champfèr
1825

Piz da Staz
2847

Piz Mezdi
2992

P.da l'Ova-
Cotschna

Piz Rosatsch
3123

Lej dals Chöds

Giand Alva

Piz Surlej
3188

Lej da Champfèr

Silvaplana
1815

Surlej

2643

Munt Arlas
3127

Margun Vegl
2402

1713

Lej da Fuorcla
2489

2570

Margun
Surlej
2272

Lej da Silvaplauna

Murtèl   2699

2755 Fuorcla
Surlej

Ova da la Rabgiusa

Margun
Surlej
2272

Curtinella

Chastelets

CORVATSCH
3304

1807

2445

Margun

Alp Prasüra

Sils Maria
1809

Chüderun 2590

2313

2690

3433 Piz
Murtèl

Vanchera

Grialetsch
2480

Marmoré

2800

FURTSCHELLAS

Piz Corvatsch
3451

Platta

Fex

Crasta

3303
Crasta dal Lej Sgrischus

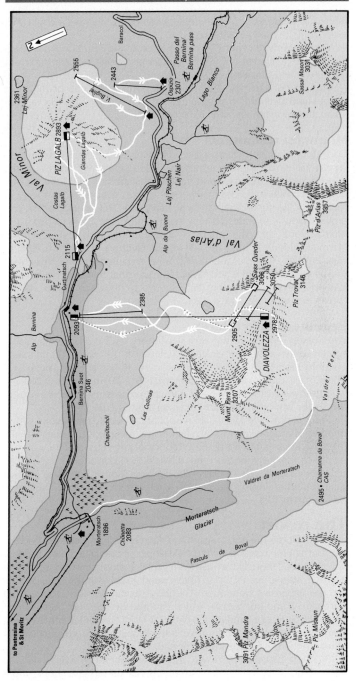

riders not being forced to alternate – something the Swiss could well learn from the American resorts.

The snowmaking here is very extensive, with cannon on a long, lower piste on Corvatsch, several shorter pistes on Corviglia, and from the bottom of Diavolezza.

The frozen lakes and side-valleys here make up one of the most famous and beautiful cross-country areas in Europe, and the annual 42km marathon attracts over 10,000 entrants.

Mountain restaurants

Corviglia's mountain eating places are plentiful and varied, from self-service cafeterias to very attractive chalets. On the Corvatsch side, Fuorcla Surlej, Hahnensee and the cosy restaurant behind the top-station self-service have charm. There is a good restaurant on the Crap Nair run below the Murtèl cable-car station. In the Corviglia sector, recommendations include the new restaurant in the Piz Nair bowl, the Alpina Hütte and the Marmite, where booking is essential. The Marmite, hidden behind the self-service cafeteria, which you have to walk through, is one of the most famous restaurants in the Alps and is said to sell more truffles and caviar than any other restaurant in Europe. The price is commensurably high, and prices elsewhere on the mountain are not for those on a budget.

Beginners and children

The nursery slopes are not very satisfactory, as there is little available space on the valley floor except at Celerina at the foot of the Marguns gondola. Most St Moritz beginners start on slopes at Corviglia around Chantarella and Salastrains where there is a beginners' roundabout; when snow conditions are good they can progress to long easy runs in this sector, but often the transition is an awkward one.

Reports of the St Moritz ski school are generally favourable, with a number of American and Australian instructors, and the others speaking good English, but we do have reports of large classes. One reporter mentions that beginners are not allowed to ski on the nursery slopes unless with a ski school class. The Suvretta House hotel has its own drag-lift and children's ski school. Many other hotels have their own private instructors.

The resort

St Moritz Dorf is the hub of the resort, layered on to the steep hillside to the north of the lake, beneath the ski slopes of Corviglia. This is fashionable St Moritz, more like a busy town centre (complete with traffic) than a village. Monstrous Victorian hotels stand guard over the lake; outside are the expensive boutiques (Giorgio Armani, Versace, Hermès and Cartier to name but a few), which can also be seen on Bond Street, Faubourg St Honoré and Rodeo Drive. St Moritz is neither attractive nor convenient; distances on foot are considerable and parking is difficult, although there is a multi-storey car-park.

St Moritz Bad, the spa village, sprawls without much style beside the lake on the valley floor. There are hotels, restaurants and shops, and it is ideally situated for cross-country skiers. There is also direct access from here to Corviglia by cable car. The bus service between Bad and Dorf is often crowded, and more often than not it is easier, if not quicker, to walk between the two.

From the top of Dorf a road winds down an attractive wooded slope, following the course of the Cresta and bob runs to the edge of the quiet village of Celerina. Trains and buses between ski stations are reliable but not frequent. There are no evening buses, and trains stop running at about 11pm.

Accommodation

The accommodation is spread out around Dorf and Bad, with most beds in four- and five-star hotels. For ski-lift convenience the best locations are on the edge of Bad near the Signal lift, site of the luxurious Chesa Sur L'En, or high up in the centre of Dorf. In Bad, the Parkhotel Kurhaus on the far side of the village is well positioned for cross-country skiing. Club Med has two hotels in Bad, with the usual extensive facilities. They have excellent food, and their own instructors.

In Dorf, the Steffani is one of the more attractive of the smaller hotels. The Kulm is the most appealing of the five-stars. The Eden and the Languard are simpler, but still comfortable bed and breakfast hotels in the centre. Centrally positioned in Dorf is the Schweizerhof, which is recommended for its good food and service, and the Crystal is also praised for its service. Celerina is a cheaper base, yet is still convenient for the skiing on Corviglia, with the English-owned Chesa Rosatsch hotel recommended. Self-caterers can buy their provisions at the Co-Op supermarkets in Bad and in Dorf.

Eating out

There are a few simple restaurants and pizzerias on the main square in Dorf, and in Bad. Recommendations include the Cascade, a large bar with a good restaurant attached, the smart Chesa Veglia and the Engadina. The Kulm and Palace hotels are renowned for their restaurants. It is worth noting that these and a number of other restaurants in St Moritz require men to wear a jacket and tie.

Après-ski

For tea and cakes immediately after skiing Hanselmann's, arguably as famous as St Moritz itself, should not be missed. Glattfelders is recommended for caviar, tea and coffee. There is tea-dancing at the Zuber Hütte and at the Chantarella on the way down from Corviglia. Most of the après-ski is hotel-based, with formal dress requirements in several establishments including the Palace Hotel's King's Club disco, where photographers and bouncers crowd the door, and Dracula's (members only). Other nightclubs include Vivai and Absolut. The Steffani bar is popular, a more casual and less expensive venue for drinking and dancing. The Schweizerhof has two bars, of which the Stübli is particularly recommended. Other bars include the Cava, Charly's and Cascade.

St Moritz is also an ideal resort for non-skiers, both active and inactive. There are long and beautiful walks to restaurants in the Corviglia ski area, and up the Roseg, Morteratsch and Fex valleys. In season, (until the end of February) there are lots of spectator sports including the Cresta and bob runs, together with golf and polo on the frozen lake using red balls.

Skiing facts: St Moritz

TOURIST OFFICE
CH-7500 St Moritz, Graubunden
Tel 41 82 33147
Fax 41 82 32952

THE RESORT
By road Calais 1047km
By rail station in resort
By air Zurich 4 hrs
Visitor beds 12,771 (55% apartments, chalets and guesthouses, 45% hotels)
Transport bus service between Bad and Dorf

THE SKIING
Longest run Hahnensee, 8km (black)
Number of lifts 60 in area
Number of trails/pistes 55 (10% easy, 70% intermediate, 20% difficult) local
Total of trails/pistes 350km in area
Nursery slopes 1 lift (50m)
Summer skiing 2 lifts each on Corvatsch and Diavolezza
Snowmaking 11km covered

LIFT PASSES
Area pass Upper Engadine (covers St Moritz, Celerina, Silvaplana, Pontresina, Sils), SF236 for 6 days
Day pass St Moritz/Celerina SF44, Upper Engadine SF47
Half-day pass St Moritz/Celerina SF37, Upper Engadine SF39, after 11.45am
Beginners points tickets
Children 15-20% reduction for 6-15 yrs, free for 6 yrs and under
Pensioners no reduction
Credit cards accepted yes

SKI SCHOOLS
Adults St Moritz Ski School, 10am-midday or 1.30-3.30pm, SF175 for 6 half-days. Ski School Family Card (parents with children), SF173 each
Children St Moritz Ski School, 12 yrs and under, SF55, 10am-midday or 1.30-3.30pm, SF175 for 6 half-days. Suvretta, 12 yrs and under, 10am-midday or 2-4pm, SF158 for 6 half-days, extra SF12 per day for lunch

Private lessons St Moritz Ski School, SF130 for half-day, SF240 per day. Suvretta, SF260 per day (5 hrs) for up to 3 people
Special courses snowboarding, telemark
Guiding companies The St Moritz Experience

CROSS-COUNTRY
Ski schools St Moritz Ski School
Loipe location and size 80km in St Moritz, 150km in Upper Engadine

CHILDCARE
Non-ski kindergarten Hotel Schweizerhof, Carlton Hotel and Parkhotel Kurhaus, 3 yrs and over, 9am-5pm, SF35 per day including lunch
Ski kindergarten St Moritz Ski School, 4 yrs and over, 10am- 3.30pm, SF200 for 6 days, extra SF20 per day for lunch
Babysitting list available from tourist office

OTHER SPORTS
Olympic bob run, Cresta run (skeleton), hot-air ballooning, skating, curling, parapente, hang-gliding, winter golf, winter cricket, winter polo tournaments, horse-racing and riding on the frozen lake, climbing wall, indoor tennis, squash, fitness centres, swimming, bowling, tobogganing

WHAT'S NEW
● chair-lift on Corvatsch from Alp Surlej to Murtèl middle station
● renovated Muottas Muragl cable car

FOOD AND DRINK PRICES
Coffee SF3.50, bottle of house wine SF27, beer 5SFR, dish of the day SF20-25

TOUR OPERATORS
Club Med, Inghams, Kuoni, Made to Measure, Powder Byrne, Ski Gower, Ski Thomson, Ski Weekend, Swiss Travel Service

Pontresina 1800m (5,904ft)

Pontresina is a self-sufficient resort with a completely different atmosphere from glittering St Moritz. It is a rather staid village with a single main street, patronised by visitors who return year after year to the same comfortable hotels. Although it is closer than St Moritz to some of the best skiing at Diavolezza and Lagalb, there is no significant skiing from the village itself.

The Steinbock and Engadinerhof are comfortable and traditional hotels. Pontresina is one of the best locations in the region for cross-country skiers, and also has a good skating/curling rink and swimming-pool (covered by the lift pass). One reporter complains of little English being spoken in the ski school.

TOURIST OFFICE
CH-7504 Pontresina
Tel 41 82 66488
Fax 41 82 67996

TOUR OPERATORS
Club Med, Made to Measure,
Ski Gower, Swiss Travel Service

Verbier, Valais

ALTITUDE 1500m (4,920ft)

••

Good points resort atmosphere, big ski area, tough skiing, off-piste skiing, late-season skiing, children's facilities, après-ski, attractive scenery, non-skiing activities, easy airport transfer
Bad points lift queues and bottlenecks, antiquated lift system, high prices, traffic
Linked or nearby resorts Nendaz (l), Veysonnaz (l), La Tzoumaz (l), Thyon, (l), Bruson (n), Champex-Lac (n)

Verbier is a cult resort which, on international reputation alone, grabs itself a top-10 place in world rankings. There is a strong argument that this is unjustified, and that the bad points cancel out the good points. However, whatever we say here will not sway a single one of its hard-core of devoted fans (one described it as 'possibly the best resort in the world') who would not be seen, either on or off the slopes, in any other resort. Verbier has some of the most challenging piste skiing and the most radical off-piste (and après-ski) to be found anywhere in the Alps. It also has a shamefully antiquated lift system for a resort which sees itself in an international context. This leads to unacceptable queuing even in low season, both for mountain access and at several points on the mountain. At Christmas, New Year, and over Easter, only masochists, or those who simply don't know any better, will bother to battle with the crowds. At these times the locals don't ski at all, or they ski elsewhere.

The tourist board argument is that if you know your way around the mountain, it is possible to avoid the queues (which it now accepts do exist). Our argument is twofold. Firstly, the majority of visitors do not know their way, and indeed, if they did, the queues would reform else-where. Secondly, if you are paying one of the highest lift pass prices in Europe you are entitled to value for money, which, during a large part of the season, you do not get.

One Saturday in January we queued for 30 minutes at Tortin. The following day it took 75 minutes to reach the Olympique restaurant at Attelas 1, which is only 1220m above the village – and it took a further 40 minutes to go down to Verbier again by gondola. Reports of two-hour queues on the busiest days of the year are unsubstantiated and probably exaggerated, but any resort which has a sign outside the main mountain access lift saying '60 minutes from this point' has a problem, and signposting is otherwise abysmal. Much of the queuing takes place in dank, concrete corridors without even a ski video to alleviate the boredom.

The tourist board protests that we must all make the best of what there is. Such is the strength of the environmental lobby in Switzerland that no new lifts can be built, and there are severe strictures on what can be replaced. And while the people are prepared to queue, there may be little incentive on Téléverbier, the sole lift operator at the resort, to further invest in the lift system to rid the resort of this inconvenience. Jumbo gondolas cost about the same to install as a wide-bodied airliner costs to build and, unlike France, Switzerland provides no state aid to the development of ski resorts on either a cantonal or a federal level. Jumbo gondolas and detachable quad chairs are what are needed here to replace much of the network of antique gondolas and cable cars. Unless that investment is forthcoming, discerning skiers will wisely take their trade elsewhere, even if it means missing out on these wonderful mountains.

A jewellery advertisement in the 30-person Attelas 1 cable car warns 'Don't crack under pressure'. Anyone getting to read this on a high-season weekend is surely close. The British are second behind the Swiss in the table of nationalities who ski here, but the figure has dropped from 18 to 12 per cent since 1987 and the recession cannot take the full blame.

The resort itself is more of a wooden city than a village, a not altogether unpleasing collection of post-war buildings perched on a sunny balcony above the town of Martigny, within easy reach of Lac Léman and Geneva Airport. Chamonix and the French Alps are an hour away on the other side of the Col du Forclaz.

The skiing
Top 3330m (10,925ft) bottom 820m (2,690ft)
With the integration in 1991 of Les Collons/Thyon into the system, the Four Valleys ski area now comprises 400km of piste served by 97 lifts. Thyon, Veysonnaz, Nendaz, La Tzoumaz and Verbier itself, together with Bruson and Champex-Lac, offer an extraordinary diversification of skiing which is hard to match. It is just a shame about the lift system.

Verbier's local skiing takes place in two separate areas, Savoleyres and the larger Les Ruinettes, with **mountain access** at opposite ends of the resort. The two are linked by gentle off-piste runs which are often skied into a pisted state, and by regular ski-buses. The larger area links into Nendaz, Thyon and Veysonnaz. It is important to note that while these resorts are not far away as the crow flies, they are a considerable distance by road via Martigny. Taking a taxi after the lifts have closed is an exorbitant option. In planning a day's itinerary you should remember to build the lift queue factor into the timing.

Savoleyres is the smaller and less popular of the two areas, reached by lifts starting high above the centre. The runs down on the sunny Verbier side of the mountain are mostly open and intermediate, but steep enough to accommodate the resort's slalom racecourse. Off-piste there is some good spring snow skiing and powder in the best mid-winter conditions. The lower pistes into the resort are unreliable, often with poor snow cover. On the north-facing side there is a Super-G course and long trails down to La Tzoumaz, a little-skied area but a useful snow pocket even when the front of the mountain has poor snow.

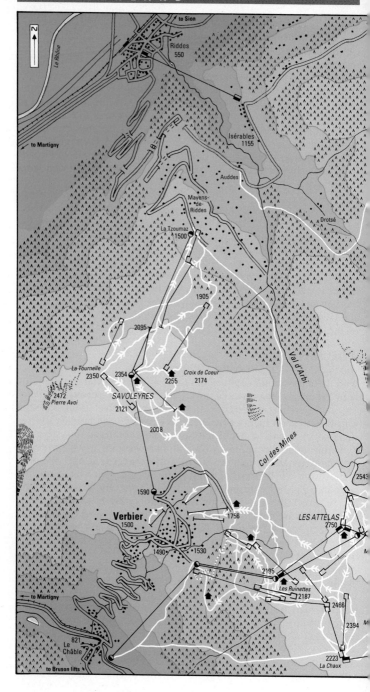

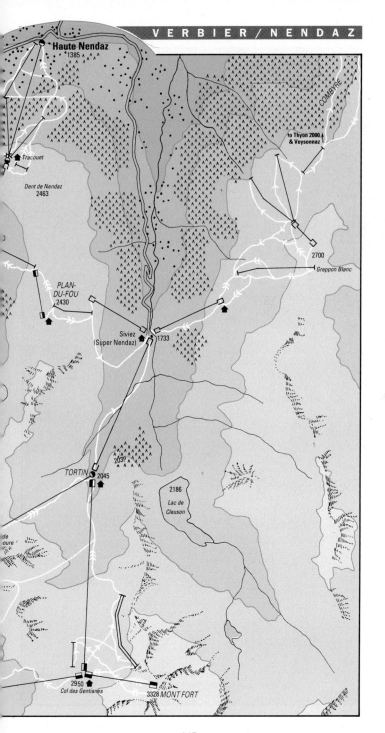

Haute Nendaz
1385

Tracouet

Dent de Nendaz
2463

COMBYRE

to Thyon 2000
& Veysonnaz

2700

Greppon Blanc

PLAN-
DU-FOU
2430

Siviez
(Super Nendaz) 1733

2039

TORTIN 2045

2186
Lac de
Cleuson

de
oure

2950
Col des Gentianes   3328 MONT FORT

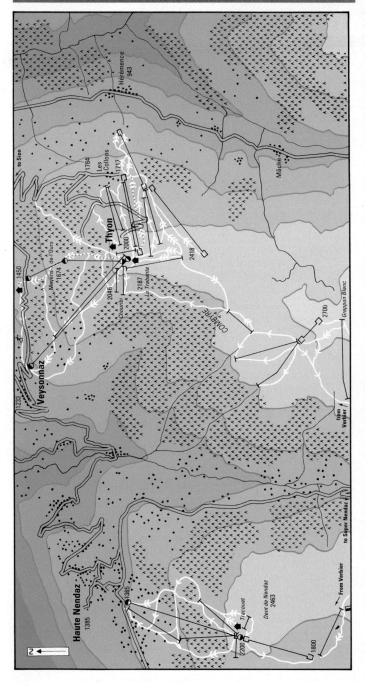

Hérémence 943

to Sion

Les Collons 1784

717

Mâche

Thyon 2000

1450

Mayens-de-l'Ours 1674

2046

2187

La Trabanta

2418

Chouribi

Greppon Blanc

COMBYRE

2700

Veysonnaz 1233

from Verbier

to Super Nendaz

Haute Nendaz 1385

1365

Tracouet

Dent de Nendaz 2463

From Verbier

2200

1800

2

The dog-leg drag to the top station is steep and there is some tough skiing here in the form of big moguls when conditions are right. The speed-skiing course beside the Taillay chair is open to all, with possible speeds in excess of 80km for the brave on ordinary 205cm skis. Savoleyres is also the area where you will find the main beginner slopes.

At the far end of the village, various alternative lifts go up from Medran to the main ski area around Les Ruinettes beneath the ridge of Les Attelas. The chair-lift route is under-used and the ancient four-man gondola, which stops here on its way up from Le Châble, is painfully slow. At weekends the day-tripper crowds flock in from Geneva and Berne, and to say that access is difficult is a masterly piece of understatement. The six-seater alternative is still spoken of as a 'recent' addition by the tourist office. It did in fact come into service in 1986 and is a prime example of superannuated technology. What is needed here is a major jumbo gondola. The six-seater takes you only to Les Ruinettes, from where you can take a 30-person cable car or a chair-lift. The cable car, Attelas 1, mercifully comes to the end of its long life in 1995 and will, we hope, be replaced by a jumbo gondola.

To the east of the Attelas ridge, the skiing in the sheltered bowl of Lac des Vaux is limited in extent but ideal for intermediates. The area is popular with ski school classes which have graduated from the nursery slopes of Savoleyres and is therefore prone to overcrowding. To the west of the ridge the skiing down past Ruinettes is tougher and more extensive. For many competent but not expert skiers this area, served by a series of three chairs, is the centre of Verbier's skiing. It is testing terrain with no easy way down, although there is nothing intimidatingly steep, even on the black (difficult) run. However, it is all prone to overcrowding.

A wide variety of runs stretch down from Les Ruinettes to Verbier itself. A blue (easy) path provides the easy option and tough mogul runs take you down through the trees towards the hamlet of Clambin. These wooded slopes provide some of the best skiing in the area when visibility is bad elsewhere.

An attractive way home from Lac des Vaux is on the Col des Mines route which runs around from the bottom of the lifts before crossing over the ridge to the south-facing slopes above the nursery lifts. The run is most definitely off-piste and great care should be taken, but it is not difficult to ski and the route is understandably popular. It is, however, often closed after a new snowfall until the snow is cleared off the path. An alternative off-piste run is the Vallon d'Arbi which winds down through the woods to La Tzoumaz.

By keeping to the left on the way down from Attelas to Ruinettes you can make your way over to the sunny open bowl of La Chaux, where various intermediate pistes go down to the bottom station of the cable car up to the Col des Gentianes and the glacier skiing of Mont-Fort. These pistes and the cable car can also be reached by chair from Ruinettes and from Verbier. The small cable car from Attelas to Mont Gelé was replaced for 1992-3, much to the surprise of those critics of the lift system who felt that the money might have been better spent elsewhere on queue dispersement. Mont Gelé, open only in the safest of conditions, provides Verbier with its most famous skiing – all of it off-piste. This is serious ski territory and only expert skiers should attempt it. In icy conditions a fall here can prove fatal. The couloirs down to Attelas provide extreme skiing, while the main runs down the back, which are both longer and less severe, take you down to Tortin or La Chaux.

The main link with the eastern half of the skiing is the chair from Lac des Vaux to Col de Chassoure at the top of a dauntingly long, wide and steep mogul field, too often congested with intermediates in trouble. The run down ends on the plateau of Tortin and is usually known by that name. Again, in icy conditions, great care has to be taken here. By any standards this is a difficult, but eminently rewarding piece of skiing.

A cable car climbs from here to the Col des Gentianes and the Mont-Fort cable car takes you on up to 3330m. The views here from the top of Mont-Fort are spectacular (you can see the Matterhorn and Mont Blanc). The off-piste option for the adventurous, and fit, is to traverse 30 to 40m, without falling, to one of the two spectacular couloirs which lead down the back of Mont-Fort. These finish with a long walk-out alongside Lac de Cleuson and the dam, finally ending in Siviez. Back on the piste, the black run down underneath the cable car is steep (35°) and usually heavily mogulled. A roundabout alternative is marked red (intermediate) on the piste map but, although a couple of degrees less severe, it should also be graded black.

Below the Col des Gentianes there are some wonderful open runs served by drag-lifts. This is where you will find the summer skiing area served by the two parallel drags, Glacier I and II, which also make up a good area for near-beginners. Off-piste opportunities also abound, but the dangers of crevasses and avalanches should never be underestimated.

It should be remembered that the cable car to Col des Gentianes is not open to skiers with a Four Valleys lift pass, and if you want to ski this area you must buy the Mont-Fort supplement. The lift pass is the most expensive in Europe; in order to soften the impact on families a number of reductions are available.

The long, north-facing run down from Col des Gentianes to Tortin is a good black, testing because of popularity and occasional narrowness rather than because of its steepness, with some excellent off-piste variants. The run down from Col des Gentianes to La Chaux, under the cable car, is much less difficult but also much less interesting; the top part is a zig-zag path, except when good snow permits corner-cutting. It provides breath-taking views of the Grand Combin and neighbouring glaciers. A couple of times a year, in the best of snow conditions, it is possible to ski off-piste to Le Châble from the top of Mont-Fort. The run is 18km with a vertical drop of 2500m.

From Tortin, easy runs take you down to Siviez (formerly known as Super-Nendaz), where lifts branch east for Thyon and Veysonnaz, and west for Nendaz. A long chain of short lifts and easy runs along the upper slopes of the mountainside lead to Thyon, which has broad nursery slopes. In the right snow conditions a number of excellent long runs lead down through the woods to Veysonnaz and Mayens-de-l'Ours. On the other side of Siviez a steep drag-lift and a chair to Plan-du-Fou give access to an easy off-piste run to Prarion and on down through the woods to Auddes, where a special bus links up with lifts from La Tzoumaz up to Savoleyres. The Nendaz skiing is a simple arrangement of long, intermediate, north-facing runs above the resort, served by the long Tracouet gondola or alternative drags, and shorter south-facing slopes behind Tracouet down to Prarion. The Plan-du-Fou cable car, above Prarion, makes it possible to get to Siviez on skis for access to Tortin and Mont-Fort.

Snowmaking operates on the final path through the woods down to Verbier. Thyon and Veysonnaz both have snow-cannon along the full length of a major piste, and Nendaz has a short stretch.

Mountain restaurants

These tend to be, on the whole, functional filling stations that provide food and a place to sit in the sun rather than a place to linger and savour your lunch. The Cabane de Mont-Fort is a popular spot with a good terrace. It is wise to get here early to ensure a place in the sun. Chez Dany, on a run down from Les Ruinettes, serves good pizzas and local food. It is small without being claustrophobic, and is also open in the evening. La Marmotte, at the bottom of the Savoleyres Sud drag-lift, and the reasonably priced Chez Simon also in the Savoleyres area, are both recommended by reporters. L'Olympique, at the top of Attelas I, has a big sun terrace with self-service food, and an upstairs waitress service restaurant. The Carrefour at the top of the nursery slopes and at the bottom of the pistes down to the resort is friendly and popular. The octagonal restaurant at Plan-du-Fou between Siviez and Nendaz has a particularly solid following.

Beginners and children

The Swiss Ski School here has a sound reputation for teaching both on and off the piste. Nearly all the instructors speak good English and their attitude is friendly and helpful. The resort also has l'Ecole du Ski Fantastique, which specialises in off-piste and heli-skiing. Neither of the nursery slopes is in the centre of the village. Les Moulins is half-a-mile away, and La Camargue one mile by bus.

We have had good experiences and favourable reports of the children's classes at the Swiss Ski School. Although our visit was in low season and there were few English children, the instructors were kind, friendly and spoke good English. The skiing day can be as flexible as you like, with the possibility of half the day spent in the Schtroumpfs non-ski kindergarten (next to the ski school meeting place) and the other half at the ski school. The Schtroumpfs staff will accompany children between the kindergarten and ski school, and are very flexible about timing.

The Schtroumpfs kindergarten is a cosy place with a friendly atmosphere. Two staff look after babies, however young, up to seven-year-olds, mainly indoors, with a good choice of toys. They serve a hot lunch, have a rest room with cots for afternoon naps and a small outdoor play area.

The resort

This post-war chalet-style village, set on a sunny ledge at 1500m and commanding spectacular views of the surrounding mountains, has managed to retain its charm despite its steady increase in size. Based around a busy central square, the resort is governed by a rather quirky one-way system which often makes short journeys quicker on foot. The modernistic steeple of the English church is an eyesore rather than a landmark.

Accommodation

The accommodation offered by British tour operators is mainly of the chalet variety. Chalet Mont-Clair, run by Ski Thomson, is recommended by reporters. Be warned, though: a wrongly positioned chalet or apartment can mean very long walks. The Hotel Farinet in the main square is warmly recommended by several reporters for its comfort. It is described as 'good for families as long as they are not on a budget'. The Hotel de Verbier, the Mazot and the Parc all receive favourable reports. The Rosalp and the less central Montpelier head the four-star category. Self-caterers have a choice of four supermarkets of which the Co-op seems to have the most reasonable prices.

Eating out

Roland Pierroz's Rosalp is one of the finest restaurants in Switzerland. Al Capone, Borsalino and Fer à Cheval are good for pizzas. La Luge is the place for steaks. Braconnier, Le Caveau and Channe Valaisanne are all praised. At the cheapest end of the scale, La Crêperie continues to be 'cheap, cheerful, and worth every franc'. The Hotel Phénix has an interesting Chinese restaurant.

Après-ski

The shops are good, but generally expensive, consisting mainly of ski shops selling designer ski wear. Mountain Air and Ski Xtreme are just two of them; the latter we found very helpful for ski hire. Ski Adventure sells ski wear and other designer fashion. L'Igloo is for children's clothing, and Davis is the place to go for unusual gadgets, leather and watches. Evening action centres equally on the noisy and overcrowded Pub Mont-Fort, the Nelson, the Aristo, La Chaumière, Big Ben Pub, King's and the Scotch Club. Later still the scene moves on to Marshal's, the Venue and the Farm Club. Marshal's is the noisiest and attracts a younger age group. The Farm Club is for older sophisticates.

Nendaz 1365m (4,478ft)

This is a long, hilly hairpin resort without much village atmosphere, and with most of its self-catering apartments a 15-minute walk from the lifts. The lift system is inadequate and for many skiers the day starts with a queue for the bus up to Siviez, no more than a cluster of service buildings at the foot of the lifts up to Tortin. This gives quick access to Mont-Fort, allowing the keen skier to reach the best powder before the Verbier crowd is able to. Accommodation is in three hotels and two pensions as well as a wide choice of apartments and chalets. The

Spaghettaria des Flambeaux and Spaghettaria du Mazot are the cheaper eating places. The Mont Rouge, the Grenier and Robinson's are noted for their good value. Après-ski centres on the London Pub, Le Parapluie, Tahin-Tahin and Pub La Phénix. Discos Les Flambeaux and Le Privé both charge a SF15 entry fee, which includes one free drink.

Skiing facts: Verbier

TOURIST OFFICE
Case Postale 300, CH-1936
Tel 41 26 31 62 22
Fax 41 26 31 32 72

THE RESORT
By road Calais 998km
By rail Le Châble 15 mins
By air Geneva 90 mins
Visitors beds 23,200 (95% apartments and chalets, 5% hotels)
Transport free ski-bus

THE SKIING
Longest run Mont-Fort to Le Châble
Number of lifts 97
Number of trails/pistes 100 (40% easy, 40% intermediate, 20% difficult)
Total of trails/pistes 400km
Nursery slopes baby-lift des Moulins, 300m, and La Camargue, 200m long
Summer skiing limited runs at Mont-Fort
Snowmaking 20km in Four Valleys area

LIFT PASSES
Area pass SF284 for 6 days, SF247 for Four Valleys only without Mont-Fort
Day pass SF53
Half-day pass SF46 after 11am, SF40 after 12.30pm
Beginners no free lifts
Children 40% reduction for 3-16 yrs. Family reductions: full price for father, 40% discount for mother, 40% reduction for 16- 20 yrs, 70% reduction for under 16 yrs
Pensioners 40% reduction for 60 yrs and over
Credit cards accepted yes

SKI SCHOOLS
Adults Verbier Swiss Ski School, SF101 for 6 mornings, SF101 for beginners and low intermediates (afternoons only)
Children SF196 for 10 lessons
Private lessons SF52 per hr, SF290 per day. Ecole de Ski Fantastique, SF270 per day
Special courses off-piste, snowboarding, telemark
Guiding companies Ecole de Ski Fantastique

CROSS-COUNTRY
Ski schools Swiss Ski School
Loipe location and size 4km in Verbier, 4km Ruinettes-La Chaux, 43km of other trails in Four Valleys

CHILDCARE
Non-ski kindergarten Chez les Schtroumpfs, up to 7 yrs, SF40 per day including lunch
Ski kindergarten Club Mini-Champions, 3-10 yrs, SF50 per day, SF250 for 6 days
Babysitting list available from tourist office

OTHER SPORTS
Sports centre with skating, swimming, squash, and outdoor tennis, 2 parapente schools, hang-gliding, climbing wall, bowling

WHAT'S NEW
● Refurbishment of Mont Gelé cable car ● baby-lift at Les Moulins ● ice-climbing pyramid

FOOD AND DRINK PRICES
Cup of coffee SF2.70-2.90, bottle of house wine SF25-28, beer SF3-4, dish of the day SF17-19

TOUR OPERATORS
Activity Travel, Bladon Lines, Crystal, Enterprise, Flexiski, Kuoni, Made to Measure, Mark Warner, Silver Ski, Ski Beach Villas, Ski Choice, Ski Equipe, Ski Esprit, Ski Jeannie, Ski Thomson, Lotus Supertravel, Susie Ward Travel, Swiss Travel Service, Ski West, Ultimate Holidays

TOURIST OFFICE
1997 Nendaz, Valais
Tel 39 27 881444
Fax 39 27 883900

TOUR OPERATORS
Bladon Lines, Hoverspeed, Ski Choice

Bruson 1100m (3,608ft)

Although there are medium-term plans to build a lift up from Le Châble to Bruson, thus linking it to Verbier, this quiet mountainside community is at present reached by infrequent, but free, ski-buses from Le Châble station. From the hamlet of Bruson a chair goes up over gentle slopes to Mayens-de-Bruson, no more than a scattering of chalets at present. A short drag and a path across the mountainside, via a welcoming and reasonably priced restaurant, take you to the Pasay chair. This goes up over a broad piste through the forest, graded black on the piste map but in reality red (intermediate), except for a short pitch at the top. From the western side of the ridge reached by this chair a short run southwards across the mountainside takes you to the Grand-Tsai drag. This gives access to a small bowl on the western side of the ridge, as well as to both on- and off-piste runs back towards Mayens on the eastern side. When the snow is good you can ski down from Layens to Le Châble; direction-finding is not always easy, and some of the paths involved are unpleasantly narrow, although the powder can be good.

TOURIST OFFICE
as Verbier

TOUR OPERATORS

Villars-sur-Ollon, Vaud

ALTITUDE 1300m (4,264ft)

••

Good points attractive scenery, short airport transfer, facilities
for family skiing, open and sunny slopes, easy resort access,
cross-country facilities
Bad points lack of tough runs, no artificial snowmaking, limited
après-ski
Linked or nearby resorts Arveyes (n), Barboleusaz (l), Chesières (n),
Gryon (n), Les Diablerets (l), Gstaad (n)

Villars is a traditional resort set on a sunny balcony above the Rhône
Valley. Originally bestknown as a base for British boarding and finishing
schools, it has over the last few years regained its popularity as a family
resort. The village is set on a through-road with chalets and hotels scattered along it. The modern additions blend well with the older buildings, and there are a number of chalets of ornate and original design.

The quite small ski area has little to offer the expert, apart from a
good introduction to off-piste skiing, but it is perfect for the intermediate who prefers the individuality of a small resort with manageable skiing rather than an endless, impersonal ski circus. The Diablerets link
adds to the size of the ski area, although this is not always easily negotiated and can sometimes be closed in poor snow conditions. A car is a
mixed blessing: Les Diablerets can be reached by road when the skiable
connection is closed, as can Gstaad and Verbier, but local parking
restrictions make movements around town difficult.

The skiing
Top 2970m (9,742ft) bottom 800m (2,624ft)
Mountain access to the hub of ski area at Bretaye is by railway from
the west side of the resort and there are two other access points: the
Roc d'Orsay gondola at the northern edge of the village and the gondola from the nearby village of Barboleusaz. Bretaye is the main cross-
road for the lifts and runs, which makes for some congestion. It does,
however, have the advantage of being the main meeting point for skiers
of all standards and the ski schools, further adding to the benefits of
Villars as a family resort.

The east-facing runs from Grand and Petit Chamossaire are open red
(intermediate) slopes, which are very exposed at the summit, averagely
steep, but short. Grand Chamossaire, as well as being approached from
the Roc d'Orsay gondola, can also be reached by a drag from Bretaye. It
has a couple of good runs served by a short drag on the back of the hill.
The long blue (easy) run from Grand Chamossaire down to Col de
Soud is recommended. The west-facing runs from Chaux Ronde to

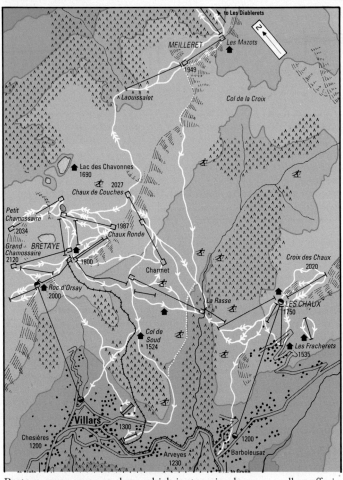

Bretaye cover an open slope which is steep in places, as well as offering a blue route. This is surprisingly praised by one reporter for its mogul field ('enables beginners to feel challenged').

The ungroomed black (difficult) run from Chaux Ronde, served by a chair-lift, is soon skied into a pisted state after a snowfall; it is not too steep and can be tackled by confident intermediates with relative ease. The pistes from Roc d'Orsay and Bretaye go down to the village, the latter linking with the wide and sunny slopes to La Rasse at 1350m. The chair from here to Chaux de Conches opens up some good blue and red runs from its mid-station and a black mogul field on the upper part. Some gentle off-piste can be found on the slopes around La Rasse and Charmet. The drags from La Rasse link with the separate, intermediate-level skiing on Les Chaux. The sunny run from Les Chaux to the tiny village of Les Fracherets loses its snow early, as does the run down to the bottom of the gondola at Barboleusaz.

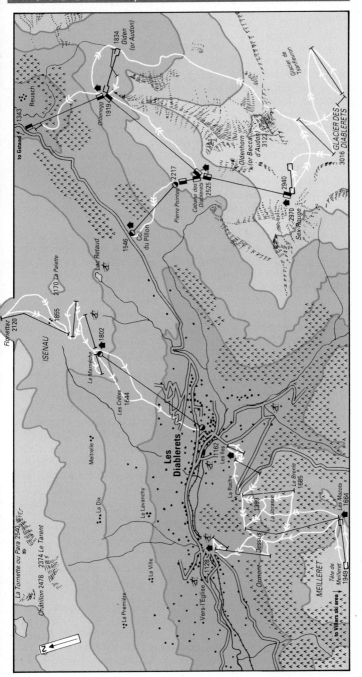

The Chaux des Conches chair provides the sometimes elusive link to Les Diablerets. The run is graded black because of the steep and ungroomed mogul field near the top. However, most of the run is an easy blue motorway. Most of the Villars-Les Diablerets pistes vary between blue and red and are all on north-facing slopes through the trees. The return to Villars is across open mountainside. The Les Diablerets Glacier is actually part of Gstaad's ski area, although it can be approached either on the Col du Pillon gondola in the Isenau area or by cable car from Reusch. The glacier can be crowded when snow is poor in Villars and Gstaad. The runs are wide and easy, with the highlight being the long run down the Combe d'Audon. A drag-lift from here goes to Oldenegg, opening up an interesting run to Reusch. A post-bus returns you to the various lift stations along the valley.

Isenau is the separate ski area of Les Diablerets and is approached by gondola from the far side of the village. The skiing here is on limited, gentle slopes.

General reports on the Villars ski area suggest the chair-lifts are 'a little long in the tooth', and too many drag-lifts have 'a tendency to have a dog-legged course requiring you to perform ski-ballet to avoid being unceremoniously dumped half-way up the mountain'. Special mention goes to the drag at the back of the Roc d'Orsay where 'the top part goes up through a neat chicane and then pulls the skier on tip-toes up a steep bank'. Lift queues are not generally a problem, with the only bottleneck on weekend afternoons at Lift 10 from Lac Noir to Chaux Ronde. The lift map is confusing, as it gives inaccurate information on runs and type of lifts. There is no snowmaking in Villars.

Mountain restaurants

The main restaurant at Bretaye is conveniently placed but lacks charm and is expensive, although a reporter recommends its 'great hot-dogs'. The Lac des Chavonnes has a good reputation, but reservations are essential in high season. The Buffet Col de Soud is an attractive chalet with a large sun-terrace giving superb views of the Diablerets Glacier. It is particularly recommended for its home cooking. The Refuge de la Rasse, also known as Chez Mic's, is a rustic mountain eating place where you grill your own sausages.

Beginners and children

The two ski schools have their offices in the village centre and at Bretaye. The Swiss Ski School is well spoken of with English-speaking, friendly instructors. The Ecole de Ski Moderne uses the *ski évolutif* method of teaching beginners, and specialises in snowboarding and parapente, as well as giving lessons for the disabled. Club Med has its own ski school in Villars.

We have favourable reports of 'sensitively manned lifts', with operators slowing down the chairs for children to get on. The Swiss Ski School children's classes are praised by reporters ('children have fun'). Pré-Fleurie ski kindergarten is said to be 'quite excellent'. Children can be picked up from their hotel in the morning, provided with identical one-piece ski suits, and parties are thrown for birthdays which fall during the holiday.

The resort

This pleasant village is spread along a road which at the moment still allows cars, but in the near future should be traffic-free. As the mountain railway has to be reached by bus, it doesn't really matter where you stay between Col de la Croix at one end of town and up the hill by the station at the other. The same road runs through the villages of Chesières and Arveyes, both of which are bus-linked satellites of Villars. Villars is one of the few Swiss resorts which over the years has allowed the British to buy property, and a number of the chalets are British-owned.

Skiing facts: Villars

TOURIST OFFICE
PO Box 148, CH-1884 Villars, Vaud
Tel 41 25 353232
Fax 41 25 352794

THE RESORT
By road Calais 952km
By rail station in village, connects with main line at Aigle or Bex. Regular buses from either station
By air Geneva 1½ hrs
Visitor beds 9,750 (82% apartments and chalets, 18% hotels)
Transport free bus from railway station to Roc d'Orsay télécabine

THE SKIING
Longest run Les Bouquetins, 2.5km (blue)
Number of lifts 45
Number of trails/pistes 82 (37% easy, 46% intermediate, 17% difficult)
Total of trails/pistes 120km
Nursery slopes 400m, 3 lifts
Summer skiing on Glacier des Diablerets
Snowmaking none

LIFT PASSES
Area pass (covers Villars and Les Diablerets, except the glacier) SF190 for 6 days
Day pass SF38
Half-day pass SF29, 8.30am-1pm or 1.30pm-5pm
Beginners limited lift pass included in ski school price
Children 6-16 yrs, SF23 per day, SF114 for 6 days, free for 6 yrs and under
Pensioners 65 yrs and over, as children
Credit cards accepted yes

SKI SCHOOLS
Adults Swiss Ski School, 10.15am-midday, SF110 for 6 days. Ecole de Ski Moderne, 10.30am-midday, SF95 for 6 days
Children Swiss Ski School, 12 yrs and under, 10.15am-midday, SF110 for 6 days. Ecole de Ski Moderne, 3-12 yrs, 10.30am-midday, SF85 for 6 days
Private lessons at both ski schools, SF50 per hr
Special courses snowboarding, monoskiing, telemark
Guiding companies through ski schools

CROSS-COUNTRY
Ski schools Swiss Ski School
Loipe location and size 44km, at Bretaye and from the village up to Col de la Croix

CHILDCARE
Non-ski kindergarten Koala, 2½-6 yrs, 8.15am-11.45 and 2- 5pm, SF33 per day, not including lunch
Ski kindergarten Swiss Ski School, 3-12 yrs, 9am-4.30pm, SF275 for 6 days including lunch. Pré-Fleuri, 9am-5.30pm, SF65 including lunch
Babysitting list available from tourist office

OTHER SPORTS
Heli-skiing, parapente, luge-ing, hang-gliding, skating, curling, indoor tennis, squash, bowling, swimming, fitness centres, climbing wall, sleigh rides

FOOD AND DRINK PRICES
Coffee SF2.50, bottle of house wine SF15, beer SF2.80, dish of the day SF20

TOUR OPERATORS
Bladon Lines, Club Med, Hoverspeed, Kuoni, Made to Measure, Neilson, Ski Esprit, Ski Weekend, Swiss Travel Service

Accommodation

The Hotel Bristol has a comfortable and modern interior, although some reporters found it too formal. Hotel du Cerf is family-run with 'lots of home-style cooking'. The large, modern Eurotel is something of an eye-sore, but its apartments are 'spacious, clean, and the staff excellent'. Club Med is housed in the old Villars Palace, a leviathan of a hotel. The Hotel Panorama has well-equipped self-catering apartments, but suffers from being up a steep slope from the main street. The Elite, next to the Roc d'Orsay gondola, has a children's playroom. La Crémaillère in Barboleusaz is a good-value option. Self-caterers will find the Supermarket Viret has a good range of food and wine, and there are many small delicatessen, cheese shops, butchers and bakers.

Eating out

Dining varies between informal *Stüblis* and fine restaurants. Café de la Gare, also known as Chez Jo's, serves fondue, La Francis crêpes and pizza, and the Alpe Fleurie is praised by reporters for its efficiency. Hotel Bristol is recommended for 'wonderful food in a rather formal atmosphere'. Similarly, the Grand Hotel du Parc, set in its own spacious grounds, offers excellent cuisine.

Après-ski

Reporters say the nightlife is disappointing and very quiet: 'Walking around town after 6pm is a lonely experience as it is deserted as soon as the last train of the day has brought skiers down from Bretaye.' What nightlife there is centres mainly on the bars, with the Mini Pub ('cosy and atmospheric'), Le Sporting ('for those who like to be looked at'), the Bridge Pub and Charly's Bar, which attracts a young and lively clientèle, all recommended. The discos are the El Gringo and New Sam, the latter with a space-age interior. Immediately after skiing the tea-rooms near the station serve home-made cakes. The shops offer a good variety of sports equipment, clothing (mainly sporty designer wear) and souvenirs, and the nearby town of Bex offers greater scope at lower prices.

Les Diablerets 1162m (3,811ft)

Les Diablerets is a sprawling village, with mainly chalet accommodation. The few hotels are modern and seem out of place, but the overall atmosphere is relaxed and ideal for families. The ski school runs Club Pinocchio at the Hotel des Sources, for 3-year-olds and over. Hotels include the modern Eurotel, Le Chamois and Hotel Mon Abri ('family-run and cosy'). The resort's après-ski is quiet, with the 200-year-old Auberge de la Poste a good place for an after-skiing drink or evening meal. The Buvette du Pillon is popular for its cheese specialities.

TOURIST OFFICE
CH-1865, Les Diablerets, Vaud
Tel 41 25 531358

TOUR OPERATORS
Bladon Lines, Kuoni, Made to Measure,
Ski Gower, Ski la Vie

Zermatt, Valais

ALTITUDE 1620m (5,314ft)

••

Good points beautiful scenery, exceptional village charm, large ski area, activities for non-skiers, tree-line skiing, early and late ski holidays, summer skiing, great variety of mountain restaurants, lively après-ski, wide range of shops
Bad points lack of skiing convenience, limited nursery slopes, ski school, high prices
Linked or nearby resorts Cervinia (l), Grächen (n)

Zermatt is one of those rare places in the world where the combination of terrain, village and facilities gel to produce a colossus. On sheer charm alone it has to be guaranteed a top 10 placing in anyone's list of world resorts. Arriving off the evening mountain train, which winds up from Täsch to this car-free resort, you cannot help being overwhelmed by the winter magic of it all. Outside the Edwardian station well-heeled passengers surrounded by piles of luggage queue for taxis or await the horse-drawn sleighs and liveried coachmen from the smarter hotels. All the while the high street, a pleasing blend of older chalets and well-designed modern buildings, bustles with the throng of après-skiers and window shoppers.

Zermatt has grown in recent years and changed considerably for the better. Avalanche-safe building plots have been exhausted and it can expand no more, leading to sky-high property prices on a par with Manhattan and Mayfair. Recent additions have, however, been largely in keeping with the traditional chalet style, which makes the place so enchanting. Somehow, from every street corner, the majesty of the Matterhorn is inescapable; the most distinctive peak in the world is also the most beautiful.

In conquering it for the first time on 14 July 1865, Victorian mountaineer Edward Whymper put the village of Zermatt on the world map. 'One crowded hour of glorious life' was how he described the time he spent on the summit. For several of his companions it was also their last. During the descent the rope parted and his friend Lord Francis Douglas plunged to his death on the glacier below. Relics of the climb, including the frayed rope, are on display in Zermatt's small museum.

Like Chamonix, Zermatt does more business in summer than in winter. It is a resort which, save for a few weeks in May and November, has no really low or closed season. Skiing on the glacier at the top of the Klein Matterhorn is open all year. The lift system, by Swiss standards, is good. Unlike some other major Swiss resorts where lip-service to the environmentalists has been an excuse for not reinvesting in mountain access, Zermatt has done much to smooth the bottlenecks created by

600,000 winter hotel visitors and the skiing occupants of 12,000 apartments. Nevertheless it has its faults. The ski area, which is good for experts, excellent for intermediates, and ghastly for beginners, is naturally disjointed and does not lend itself to family skiing or to couples or groups of varying standards. Despite those improvements it is prone to bad queueing at New Year and on certain other high-season weeks (particularly for the Trockener Steg/Klein Matterhorn area). According to reporters the Swiss Ski School, a target of criticism over several years, shows no signs of improvement. With a supplement to your lift pass you can ski over the top and down into Cervinia in Italy. The skiing is, however, much more interesting on the Swiss side.

The skiing
Top 3899m (12,788ft) bottom 1620m (5,314ft)

Once on the slopes, even if there is a queue for access from the village, you can lose the crowds. The three contrasting ski areas are Gornergrat/Stockhorn, Sunnegga/Blauherd, and Schwarzsee/Klein Matterhorn. The best way to enjoy Zermatt's skiing is to settle for one sector and spend the day there. Crossing town from one to another involves at least a 15-minute walk or an expensive taxi ride, as well as the time involved in regaining altitude.

In both Sunnegga and Trockener Steg a couple of major motorway pistes have now lost their graded colour status and are known as 'downhill routes'. This means that while they are marked runs which are swept by the ski patrol at the end of the day, they are not prepared by piste machine.

Mountain access to the Gornergrat/Stockhorn area is via the Gornergrat railway, part of the Swiss rail system and eligible for all kinds of discounts applicable to rail travellers. Like all Swiss trains, the Gornergrat runs on time and the timetable published on the back of the ski map is rigidly adhered to. The trip is spectacularly beautiful and, at 40 minutes, spectacularly slow. The journey starts right in the town centre and winds slowly up the mountain passing an area of good, easy runs above Riffelberg with, on a fine day, extraordinary views of the Matterhorn. The wise traveller sits back with his morning paper occasionally glancing at the scenery. You could be a commuter heading for work instead of play.

The run down to Zermatt has some steep sections, which are prone to ice. But in good conditions it is not difficult. There is a tough and scenic intermediate run towards Gant and Findeln, as well as some extremely challenging off-piste, which should only be attempted in the company of a guide. Beyond Gornergrat three cable cars span a narrow rocky crest which climbs barely 180 vertical metres, but serves the wide north-facing slopes above the Findeln Glacier. This area is rarely open before February and comprises one of the genuinely tough ski areas of the Alps which, if not actually pisted, is marked as such on a piste map. Because of its height (slightly below 3300m), good snow is guaranteed into the spring. However, great care should be taken owing to the risk of avalanche and rockfalls. From the top of the Hohtälli at 3286m, long challenging runs take you all the way down to Gant and Riffelalp. A second cable car takes you along the ridge to Stockhorn at the extremity of the piste map from where there are a number of on- and off-piste alternatives. A third cable car takes you from Hohtälli to Rote Nase, which is the starting point for Triftji, one of the great textbook black (difficult) runs of Europe, with gradients of around 34° in the steepest parts.

Access to the Blauherd/Sunnegga sector is reached by the Sunnegga Express underground railway, a forerunner and slower version of those in Val d'Isère and Les Deux Alpes, but nevertheless an efficient and trouble-free form of transport. There are easy and sunny slopes between Blauherd and Sunnegga, served by a gondola which can attract unpleasant queues at peak times. A slightly steeper run takes you down to the hamlet of Findeln and return is by double chair, while a variation of blue (easy) runs wind around the mountainside through the woods back down to the resort itself.

Steeper descents include the National, a downhill course which is prone to crowds and subsequent icy patches. A high-speed detachable quad at Patrullarve has replaced the troublesome drag-lift and has greatly relieved the bottleneck of skiers trying to get back up to Blauherd. The Unterrothorn cable car gives access to an interesting open face, which needs a heavy covering to be properly skiable. Around the back of the peak some pleasant intermediate runs go down to Blauherd and to Gant to form a tenuous link (by no means always open) to the Triftji drag in the neighbouring Gornergrat/Stockhorn ski area. On the north face, the Kumme chair serves some long, entertaining pistes of mainly intermediate standard, as well as some harsh off-piste itineraries.

Access to the Trockener Steg/Schwarzsee lift starts with a brisk 15-minute walk or a ski bus ride from the centre. A cable car and a gondola climb gently over the lower pastures to Furi from where three cable cars fan out. One of them climbs on to Trockener Steg from where the Klein Matterhorn cable car spans ice-falls and an almost vertical cliff face to the highest lift station in Europe. A long tunnel leads to the easiest of glacial slopes where snow, even in the greenest of winters, is guaranteed. At the turn of the year the temperature can be so low as to make skiing unbearable. The Cervinia area joins at Testa Grigia, now reached on the Italian side by a 140-person cable car, which greatly eases the return journey for day-trippers to Italy.

Several long drag-lifts here, on top of the world, are open all the year round when weather permits (which is by no means always). A particularly beautiful run in this sector heads gently west across a heavily crevassed glacier from just below the Furgsattel towards the Matterhorn, and from there either sharply round and back to Furgg or up to the top of the Hörnli lift.

Intermediates can ski down to Furgg on-piste to the top of the second cable car from Furi. More difficult pistes and good off-piste slopes are served by the Garten drag, and the run down from Furgg to Furi is an awkward red (intermediate). In general, good skiers find the runs down from Schwarzsee more satisfying. A cluster gondola now connects Furgg and Schwarzsee. A new unpisted itinerary route, the Aroleid, gives direct access to Furi. Two blacks plunge through the

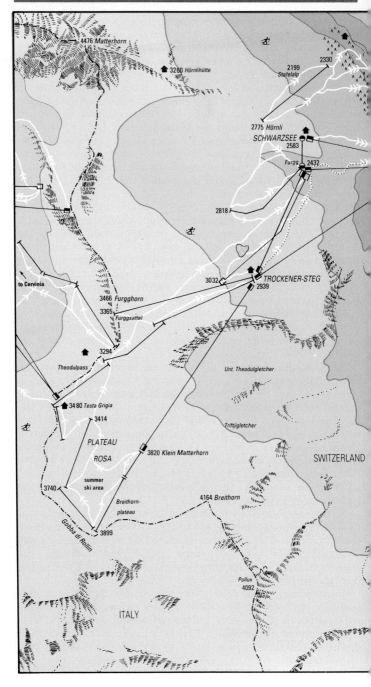

4476 Matterhorn

3260 Hörnlihütte

2199 Stafelalp

2330

2775 Hörnli

SCHWARZSEE
2583

Furgg 2432

2818

3032

TROCKENER-STEG
2939

to Cervinia

3466 Furgghorn
3365 Furggsattel

3294

Theodulpass

Unt. Theodulgletcher

3480 Testa Grigia

3414

PLATEAU

ROSA

Triftjigletcher

3820 Klein Matterhorn

SWITZERLAND

summer
ski area

3740

Breithorn-
plateau

4164 Breithorn

Gobba di Rollin

3899

Pollux
4092

ITALY

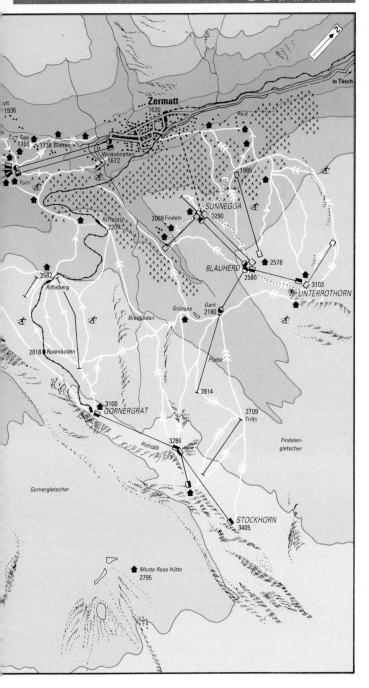

woods, including the tough and narrow Tiefbach, arriving at the same destination. Both runs are often mogulled. A couple of easier and longer ways down take you past the Hörnli drag-lift, which itself serves interesting north-facing gullies, but once you drop below this drag, the only way up is via the cable cars from Furi.

Although there are few wide, open slopes (apart from Stockhorn), Zermatt offers enormous off-piste opportunities, which rank among the best in Switzerland for good skiers who are prepared to pay for local guides. The rocky nature of the mountains and the presence of crevassed areas makes the terrain extremely hazardous and the need for caution cannot be emphasised enough. The local heli-ski operation is worth the money, but drops need to be booked well in advance.

Mountain restaurants

If there is one resort which excels above all others at providing sympathetic mountain eating at not necessarily outrageous prices, then that resort is Zermatt. Not only the visitors, but locals as well, treat lunch with as much importance as the skiing itself. The indicator board at the Sunnegga lift station shows which restaurants, as well as which lifts and pistes, are open. Each area has its modern self- and waiter-service lift station restaurants, which provide more than adequate fare, but the real joy of Zermatt's eating lies in the mountain huts with their sunny terraces, which abound on the lower slopes and in neighbouring hamlets where plates piled with *Rösti* or *Käseschnitte* beckon. Chez Vroni's at Findeln reigns supreme following the demise of Enzo's in its original form (Enzo went home to Italy). In its place is Chez Heidi und Franz, of which we have received no reports. Othmars above Ried is consistently good, Zum See on the way down from Furi, run by Max and Grettl, is a top runner. 'Just thinking of lunch at Aroleid makes my mouth water,' says an enthusiastic reporter. Simi's is part of the Zermatt tradition. Other recommendations include Tony's Grotta at Riffelalp, which serves 'great Italian food', Blatten, Gandegg Hütte, Rote Nase Hütte and Farmer Haus at Furi ('especially good for an early supper').

Beginners and children

The Swiss Ski School here has been the butt of criticism for many years for its lackadaisical attitude. The tourist board protests that this is without foundation, but sadly we are still receiving negative reports. Zermatt is definitely not a place for beginners. It has nothing that can properly be called a nursery slope and, from our own experience with an adult beginner we enrolled in classes, there is a very real danger of a novice being put off the sport altogether. At the 'meeting place', at the top of the Sunnegga Express, absolute chaos ruled with no class markers and no one visibly in charge. Lessons eventually began 25 minutes late and the instructor spoke no English. Over the ensuing three days the teacher changed three times and the majority of pupils dropped out of the class. On the plus side, the actual standard of teaching itself was high. What the Swiss Ski School in Zermatt needs is competition.

The ski school takes children from six years old, but the nursery slopes are, as we have already said, very limited. Because of the layout of the resort and the disparate ski areas, parents will find the inconvenience factor high. Zermatt is not recommended for holidays with young ski-aged children.

The resort

The busy main street which winds gently uphill from the station is lined with largely new hotels, luxury shops and numerous banks to cater for some of the wealthiest skiers in Europe and the US who holiday here each season. The more exotic hotels are clustered around the church.

The town straddles both banks of the river, with most of the up-market hotels on the same side as the high street. As the village has expanded over the years, so the hotels, chalets and apartment buildings have spread as far as the Sunnegga railway and far beyond at one end of town, and to the Klein Matterhorn cable car at the other. Wherever you are staying you will always need to walk a long way somewhere and, if there is an ideal point of the village at which to lodge, it would be right next to the main bridge on either side of the river. Zermatt is traffic-free; visitors must leave their car in Täsch and continue their journey by train or taxi. Travel around the village is on foot, by ski bus, electric taxi, or horse-drawn sleigh. Pedestrians should take particular care to avoid being run down by the taxis, which travel in near silence at dangerous speeds.

Accommodation

Some of Switzerland's most exotic and upmarket hotels can be found in Zermatt. The five-star Mont Cervin and Zermatterhof are the most luxurious, the Alex Schlosshotel Tenne and the Monte Rosa the most unusual. The Schlosshotel Tenne has an *art nouveau* interior complete with caryatids, frescoes and unusual furniture. The ancient, but comfortable, Monte Rosa is where Edward Whymper stayed before climbing the Matterhorn. There is a huge range of accommodation to choose from, including the Bristol, which is warmly recommended by reporters for its good food and friendly atmosphere. The Albana Real has a growing reputation as 'the unstuffiest four-star in town'. Much of tour operator accommodation is in chalets and apartments. Five supermarkets look after the needs of self-caterers.

Eating out

Zermatt is a gourmet's dream with dozens of fine restaurants. Recommendations include, as always, Le Mazot. The Spaghetti Factory and Tony's Pizzeria are popular and cheap by Zermatt prices. Le Gitane and Chez Gaby are good for grills. Zamoura, in the Hotel Post, is renowned for its seafood. The Walliserstübli and the Whymperstube are both mentioned by our reporters for their good food and value for money.

Après-ski

You might be forgiven for thinking that all of Zermatt's après-ski is aimed at teenagers. Certainly much of it is. The North Wall bar is recommended as 'the place in town where it all happens'. The Papagallo is the 'in' pub where British chalet staff throng after skiing, and The Village is

Skiing facts: Zermatt

TOURIST OFFICE
Bahnhofplatz, CH-3920 Zermatt, Valais
Tel 41 28 66 11 81
Fax 41 28 66 11 85

THE RESORT
By road Calais 1076km (parking
3 miles away in Täsch)
By rail station in resort
By air Geneva 3½ hrs by road,
4 hrs by train
Visitor beds 12,500 (50% hotels,
50% chalets and apartments)
Transport ski-bus costs SF2 (weekly
tickets available), electric taxi and
horse-drawn sleigh

THE SKIING
Longest run Klein Matterhorn to
Zermatt, 15km (red/black)
Number of lifts 37 in Zermatt,
73 with Cervinia
Number of trails/pistes 60 in Zermatt
(5% beginner, 25% easy, 40% interme-
diate, 30% difficult), 118 with Cervinia
Total of trails/pistes 230km including
Cervinia (no breakdown available)
Nursery slopes limited, on Sunnegga
and Riffelalp
Summer skiing extensive, with 8 lifts
on Klein Matterhorn Glacier
Snowmaking 85 hectares covered

LIFT PASSES
Area pass SF264 for 6 days, Cervinia
extension SF29 per day
Day pass SF58
Half-day pass not available
Beginners no free lifts
Children 50% reduction for 6-15 yrs
Pensioners 25% reduction for men over
65 yrs and women over 62 yrs
Credit cards accepted no

SCHOOLS
Adults Swiss Ski School, SF195 for 6
days
Children 6-12 yrs, SF225 for 6 days
including lunch, 12-17 yrs, SF175 not
including lunch
Private lessons SF260 per day for
1-2 people
Special courses powder lessons,
racing, moguls, snowboarding
Guiding companies Mountain Guides
Office

CROSS-COUNTRY
Ski Schools Swiss Ski School
Loipe location and size Furi-
Schweigmatten 7km, Täsch-Randa
14km

CHILDCARE
Non-ski kindergarten Seiler's Children-
Paradise at Hotel Nicoletta, 2-8 yrs,
SF45 per day including lunch, Mini-Club,
2½ yrs and over, SF22 per day (closed
Sundays), Kinderclub Pumuckel (see
below)
Ski kindergarten Kinderclub Pumuckel
at Hotel Ginabelle, 2-6 yrs, SF85 per
day including ski lessons for older chil-
dren. Swiss Ski School, 6-12 yrs,
SF225 per week including lunch
Babysitting list available from tourist
office

OTHER SPORTS
Skating, curling, luge-ing, tobogganing,
sleigh rides, parapente

WHAT'S NEW
● 4-star Hotel Berghof and 3-star
Hotel Kronig ● open-air artificial ice-rink
● Mini-Club kindergarten ● parapente
lessons

FOOD AND DRINK PRICES
Coffee SF2.20-2.50, bottle of house
wine SF17-22, beer SF3, dish of the
day SF14-16

TOUR OPERATORS
Activity Travel, Bladon Lines, Crystal,
Enterprise, Inghams, Kuoni, Lotus
Supertravel, Made to Measure, Mark
Warner, Neilson, Powder Byrne, Ski
Gower, Ski Choice, Ski La Vie, Ski Scott
Dunn, Ski Thomson, Ski Weekend,
Super Solutions, Swiss Travel Service,
Ultimate Holidays

a disco complex, again strictly aimed at the under-20s.

The over-20s will find Elsie's Bar to be one of the most sympathetic après-ski places in town, accommodated in a small crooked house on the high street. It serves Champagne and oysters as well as a variety of drinks and snacks in a warm, crowded atmosphere. The Hotel Alex, sister hotel of the Alex Schlosshotel Tenne, has a well laid-out, but rather staid nightclub where guests sit in comfort in armchairs and sofas. Beck's is popular for non-alcoholic après-teas. UG2, below the Hotel Pollux, is one of the more middle-of-the-road discos.

Grächen 2114m (6,934ft)

This is a small farming village with an old centre and modern chalet-style additions, extremely popular with the Swiss, Germans and Dutch, but still largely unknown to the British. Its biggest disadvantage, in the eyes of tour operators, is the narrow access road to the resort, which makes coach transfers difficult. The 40km of skiing is on interesting terrain going up to 2813m, which is extremely rocky and therefore plenty of snow is needed. In good conditions the off-piste skiing at this resort is sensational.

Grächen, with its many unusual facilities, is an ideal resort for families. As well as having its own ski school and a kindergarten for skiing and non-skiing children from two to six years old, there is also a big enclosed children's area. The Schnöö Ski Paradise, at the top of the main gondola, is supervised by trained staff and has its own lifts and pistes, toboggan runs, igloos to play inside, a ski roundabout, heated indoor accommodation and mini hang-gliding. Hotels include the unsophisticated Abendruh, the Zum See at the edge of a lake and the two-star Alpina.

TOURIST OFFICE
CH-3925 Grächen, Valais
Tel 41 28 56 13 00

TOUR OPERATORS
Ski Sutherland, Ski Unique,
Swiss Travel Service

Aspen, Colorado

ALTITUDE 7,945ft (2422m)

••

Good points caters for all grades of skier, excellent children's facilities, extensive nursery slopes, extensive cross-country skiing, ideal for non-skiers, variety of skiing, range of restaurants and après-ski, shopping
Bad points high prices, traffic in resort, limited access to beginner slopes from Aspen
Linked or nearby resorts Aspen Highlands (n), Snowmass (n)

Aspen's history as a silver-mining town goes back to 1879 when prospectors made their way down the steep slopes of Hunter's Pass, later to be known as Independent Pass, looking for pastures new in the Roaring Fork Valley. They came from Leadville, then Colorado's second largest city with a population of 15,000, where vast silver deposits had been found that year. The dozen or so prospectors who stayed that winter put up tents at the foot of Aspen Mountain where the future town would later stand.

Aspen's renaissance as a ski town began across the ocean in Germany's Garmisch-Partenkirchen during the 1936 Winter Olympics. It was there that Theodore Ryan, a wealthy American from the East Coast, met bob-sleigh champion William Fiske III and complained about the lack of good ski resorts in America. They agreed to keep in touch should any opportunities for development arise in the near future.

The following summer, Thomas J. Flynn, a mine owner and one of the original Aspenites, met Fiske at a party in California and described to him the geography of Aspen Mountain and its snowfields. When the two men arranged to meet again in Aspen, Fiske was enchanted by the mountain, took out an option on land there, returned with Ryan and other investors, and started to build a 16-bedroom lodge, which was to house the area's first ski holidaymakers. In 1947 Aspen finally opened as a ski resort with a three-and-a-half mile ski lift – the world's longest.

Today Aspen is one of the world's best-known ski resorts, with the skiing on four separate mountains each with its own base: Aspen Mountain (also known as Ajax after Ajax Mine), Tiehack/Buttermilk, Aspen Highlands and Snowmass. Confusingly, Aspen Highlands is a totally separate resort, which is privately owned. Only Aspen and Snowmass could be called villages, with Aspen, at the base of Aspen Mountain, being the biggest and smartest of the four bases, as well as part-time home to celebrities such as Michael Douglas, Jack Nicholson and Chris Evert. The average age of the well-heeled visitors here is closer to 40 than 30 and the skiing is for good intermediates upwards.

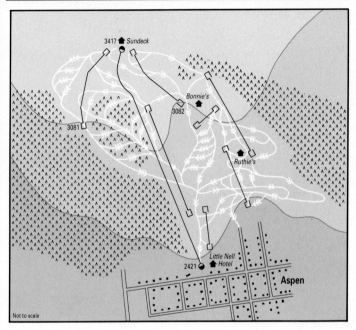

Tiehack/Buttermilk, next to Aspen Highlands along the valley and 10 minutes from Aspen by road, is the beginners' mountain with one hotel and a ski shop. Many of the skiers here are children. Finally there is Snowmass, 20 minutes from Aspen and a resort in its own right, with a pedestrian shopping mall, hotels, condominiums, restaurants and the biggest ski area of the four mountains. It attracts skiers of all standards who have chosen to shun the glamour of Aspen.

The skiing
Aspen Top 11,212ft (3418m) bottom 7,945ft (2422m)
Snowmass Top 12,310ft (3750m) bottom 8,223ft (2507m)
At present the skiing is divided into four entirely separate ski areas, though there are plans to join Snowmass and Buttermilk by creating East Village resort, which will connect with the top of the High Alpine\Big Burn ski area in Snowmass, thereby creating America's biggest ski area. All the ski areas are reached by free bus from the Rubey Park terminal in the centre of town.

Snowmass is a mainly intermediate area of immaculately groomed slopes and big wide runs. Naked Lady is a good cruising slope. Several reporters recommend the blue Turkey Trot as 'a wonderful intermediate run'. The more difficult runs on the mountain include Zugspitze and others in the Sam's Knob area and the Hanging Valley Wall section on the top of Baldy Mountain, the latter being experts' terrain often closed in windy weather conditions. When the area is open it offers some very testing skiing: 35° to 45° chutes, cliffs of up to 100ft (30m), and some great tree-line skiing. The beginner runs are long and wide and include

469

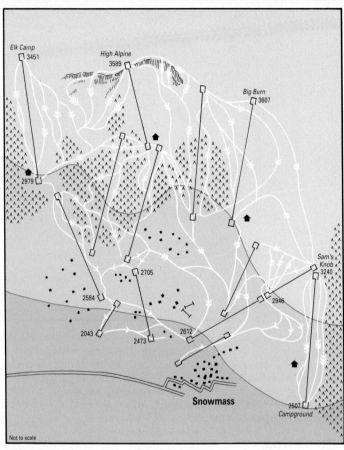

Elk Camp 3451

High Alpine 3589

Big Burn 3607

2979

Sam's Knob 3240

2705

2584

2946

2043

2612

2473

2507 Campground

Snowmass

Not to scale

those under the Funnel and Wood Run lifts.

Fanny Hill is a popular beginners' trail next to the Mall, however it does tend to become crowded. Assay Hill is the easiest skiing at Snowmass. More confident beginners will enjoy a long run, which starts at the Max Park bowl, continues into Lunchline and then Scooper. Again, it can be crowded at peak periods. Mountain access is mainly on the Fanny Hill chair, which is close to the Snowmass Village Mall and which has a maximum waiting time of up to 10 minutes during the end-of-the-day rush hour. Other access points are the Wood Run and Assay Hill chairs, both a little further away from the Mall.

Tiehack/Buttermilk is the best learning and children's ski area we have come across. A whole mountain designated to easy skiing, with wide slopes cut through the trees. Ten entire trails are devoted to beginners. The terrain is divided into three sections with West Buttermilk generally the easiest skiing, Main Buttermilk the most central and Tiehack the most advanced. All three have beginner runs and each of the areas has its own base.

The mountain access to Tiehack is by the Lower Tiehack chair, to West Buttermilk by the Buttermilk West chair, and to Main Buttermilk by the Main Buttermilk, chair. There are two beginners' lifts at Main Buttermilk base, the Ski School lift and the Panda Peak chair. The trails for each section are marked with different coloured arrows: red for Tiehack, white for Main Buttermilk and blue for West Buttermilk. One reporter took two 5-year-olds from the top of Main Buttermilk down to the base of the mountain, and mentioned the huge sense of achievement the children felt at being able to ski a whole mountain. Their only criticism is that a couple of the chair-lifts did not have safety bars, even though they are supposedly for inexperienced and often timid skiers. At the top of Main Buttermilk above the No Problem run is the new Fort Frog children's village.

Aspen Mountain is the one for experts, a challenging collection of over 40 black diamond (difficult) and double black diamond (expert) runs. The main **mountain access** is by the Silver Queen gondola, centrally placed in town next to the Little Nell hotel. It whisks skiers to the summit in 15 minutes. Alternative routes up the mountain are by Lifts 1A, 8 and 3. Lift 3 is a high-speed quad, which is used more than any other chair on the mountain. Aspen Mountain is not for children, beginners, or timid intermediates. It is entirely made up of mogul slopes, steep gullies and ungroomed tree-line skiing, which will certainly frighten the faint-hearted.

Walsh's is considered to be one of Aspen's finest runs. It is steep enough for skiers to have to put in some very exact turns, and after a new snowfall the trail keeps its powder intact. The run-out into Lud's Lane, however, is rather flat and necessitates a hearty push with ski poles. Another run well-loved by the locals is Jackpot, which has a mixture of mogulled terrain and off-piste tree-line skiing, sometimes rocky at the top and bottom. Other expert runs include Glade 2 and 3, Shoulder of Bell and Ridge of Bell, the double black diamond runs coming off International and the runs which are parallel to Walsh's starting at Sundeck.

Silver Queen, at the very end of International, is where you can find unspoilt powder due to its northern exposure and out-of-the-way position. It is a good idea to avoid the sometimes crowded Spar Gulch and Copper Bowl when skiing back down the mountain. Wide cruising runs include Seibert's, which leads into Copper Trail.

Mountain restaurants

On Aspen Mountain, Sundeck and Shlomo's are both popular restaurants. Sundeck, at the top, provides wonderful panoramic views. Shlomo's is in the Little Nell hotel at the base. Bonnie's is our favourite eating place here, a self- and waiter-service restaurant with a sun terrace, which is favoured by Aspen's jet-set. The food, as we have found everywhere in Aspen, is of a high standard, and the friendliness and service first class. Ruthie's is set lower down the mountain with a good view of the town below.

At Snowmass, Gwyn's High Alpine restaurant offers the best food on this mountain, with a choice of self- or waiter-service. Reporters found the quality and choice of food in the self-service to be just as good as in the more expensive restaurant. Other mountain eating places in Snowmass are Dudley's, Ullrhof, Krabloonick's and Café Suzanne. At Up 4 Pizza you can order your meal to be ready on arrival. The Ullrhof is cosy, with a wood-burning stove, and is the obvious stop-off point for skiers in the popular Big Burn area. Buttermilk has Café West, the Inn at Aspen, Cliffhouse and the Tiehack Café.

Beginners and children

All the mountains have their own ski school, although the one at Aspen Highlands is separately run. There is also a huge variety of ski workshops on offer on all the Aspen Skiing Company mountains (Aspen, Snowmass and Buttermilk).

The main children's ski area is at Buttermilk/Tiehack, where the Indian village and Fort Frog are the newest attractions. Fort Frog is a specially designed cowboy fort with look-out posts, a jail and a saloon bar. It is also the new on-mountain children's centre where skiers of all ages can be video-taped while they are skiing and watch the playback. The fort and village were created by the same designer as Vail's Fort Whippersnapper. Specially illustrated children's lift maps for Buttermilk and Snowmass make the whole idea of skiing here even more fun.

Snowmass has excellent nursery slopes and kindergartens. Two young British reporters at the Big Burn Bears ski kindergarten comment: 'We love the Bears so much we want to stay here for ever'. Schedules are flexible enough to alter according to the weather or even the child's stamina – an example that could well be followed by the equivalent ski schools in France.

The resort

The nineteenth-century silver-mining town of Aspen is laid out on a grid, so shops, hotels and other landmarks are all easy to locate. The streets are wide, with a number of shopping malls sets back from them. The buildings in downtown Aspen are mainly well-preserved Victorian brick. The main historical landmarks from Aspen's boomtown heritage are the Elk's Club building, the Pitkin County Courthouse, Wheeler Opera House and the Hotel Jerome. On the outskirts of town the buildings become smaller, clad in pastel-coloured weatherboarding. In the centre, horse-drawn carriages take tourists around the town and contrast starkly with the busy Rubey Park bus station. In stark counterpoint to Aspen, Snowmass is a modern, attractive pedestrian mall surrounded by a sprawl of condominium blocks.

Accommodation

Aspen is the liveliest place to stay, with a range of accommodation for all price levels. The luxury hotels here are the stylish Jerome, the Little Nell, and the new Ritz Carlton at the base of Aspen Mountain. At a slightly more reasonable price are the Hotel Aspen, the Independence Square and the Aspen Club Lodge. We have received reports on unhelpful staff at the Grand Aspen Hotel . The bed and breakfast inns and condominiums slightly further from the centre are cheaper, but still well connected by bus. Recommendations include the Innsbruck Inn, the Limelight Lodge, the Christmas Inn and the Ullrhof. Almost all accommodation in the area has either a swimming-pool or an outdoor hot-tub. Self-caterers staying in condos can shop for food at Clark's Market, and at City Market for fresh organic products.

At Snowmass the Silvertree Hotel, the Wildwood and the award-winning Snowmass Lodge and Club are all recommended. The Club has a fitness centre. Buttermilk has one main hotel, the Inn at Aspen.

Eating out

Of the four bases Aspen has the biggest variety of restaurants, including two sushi bars, Takah Sushi and Kenichi. The 'in' place is Trattoria Farfalla, across the road from the Jerome, a new addition to Aspen's wealth of eating places. Smuggler serves Cajun and Creole food and has a warm atmosphere. The restaurants in the Jerome and the Little Nell are both popular, but pricey, places to eat. Synergy serves mainly fish. Su Casa is a busy Mexican restaurant, Anguilla is a new Caribbean restaurant, and Little Annie's specialises in fish and has a particularly wide following.

Good-value eating places include the Hard Rock Café, which displays Madonna's sexy sequinned basque among other prized rock memorabilia. Hickory House fills the gap, as does the sparsely decorated McDonald's.

Unusual eating places include Woody Creek Tavern and the rustic Pine Creek Cook House at Elk Mountain in Snowmass. Krabloonick, on the piste at Snowmass, is reached by dog-sled; its specialities are smoked meats, wild game and home-made preserves. Also at Snowmass is the Cowboys Restaurant featuring South-Western cuisine, and the Brothers' Grille, both at the Silvertree Hotel, and Mountain Dragon for Mandarin and Szechuan cuisine.

Après-ski

Après-ski drinking takes place at Shlomo's and Tippler, both at the base of Aspen Mountain, and at Timbermill in Snowmass, which has popular karaoke evenings. Other much frequented après-ski places are the Hotel Jerome bar, Legends of Aspen, the Red Onion and Bentley's. Shooters Country and Western bar is recommended by one reporter. Tatou is a popular disco, Tippler also has a disco and the Caribou Club plays host to the visiting stars. Aspen's main activity outside skiing is shopping. Here you can buy everything, from designer fashions at Polo Ralph Lauren, to less expensive clothing at Banana Republic and at Esprit for younger fashions. Indian jewellery can be found at Columbine, and the Miners Building sells everything from fishing tackle to cut-price computer games. Curious George sells an unusual collection of Western artifacts, including exotic leather belts.

Aspen Highlands 8,000ft (2439m)

Aspen Highlands, just six minutes by bus from Aspen, is a privately owned mountain. Proprietor Whipple Van Ness Jones, a one-time stockbroker, opened the ski area in 1957. Its no-frills atmosphere is in com-

Skiing facts: Aspen

TOURIST OFFICE
PO Box 1248, Aspen, CO 81612
Tel 1 303 925 1220
Fax 1 303 925 9024

THE RESORT
By road Denver 4 hrs
By rail Glenwood Springs 40 miles
By air Aspen airport 5 mins from
Aspen, 25 mins from Snowmass
Visitor beds 16,000 in area(hotels,
condominiums, guesthouses, and
lodges - no breakdown available)
Transport free bus between 4 moun-
tains from 8am to 4.45pm (or earlier
depending on route), pay bus between
Aspen and Snowmass runs until 1am

THE SKIING
Longest run Green Cabin from the top
of High Alpine in Snowmass, 4.6 miles
(blue)
Number of lifts Aspen 8, Snowmass
16, Tiehack/Buttermilk 7
Number of trails/pistes Aspen 76 (35%
intermediate, 35% difficult, 30%
expert), Snowmass 72 (10% easy, 51%
intermediate, 18% difficult, 21%
expert), Tiehack/Buttermilk 45 (35%
easy, 39% intermediate, 26% difficult)
Total of trails/pistes Aspen 631 acres
(1388 hectares), Snowmass 2,500
acres (5500 hectares).
Tiehack/Buttermilk 410 acres (902
hectares)
Nursery slopes 2 lifts at
Tiehack/Buttermilk, 2 lifts at
Snowmass
Summer skiing none
Snowmaking Aspen 210 acres (462
hectares), Snowmass 62 acres (136
hectares), Tiehack/Buttermilk 108
acres (238 hectares)

LIFT PASSES
Area pass (covers Aspen Mountain,
Snowmass and Tiehack/Buttermilk)
$222 for 6 days
Day pass (Aspen Mountain, Snowmass
and Tiehack/Buttermilk) $35-45
Half-day pass $30-40 after midday
Beginners no free lifts
Children $26 per day for 7-12 yrs, free
for under 6 yrs
Pensioners 65-69 yrs, as children, free
for over 70 yrs
Credit cards accepted yes

SKI SCHOOLS
Adults Aspen Mountain Ski School,
Tiehack/Buttermilk Ski School, and
Snowmass Ski School, $45 per day. Vic
Braden Ski College at Buttermilk, prices
on application
Children Kids Ski Weeks for 7-12 yrs,
Teens Ski Weeks, both $280 for 5 days
Private lessons $105 for 1½ hrs
Special courses snowboarding,
women's seminars, off-piste, Mountain
Masters, teen classes, mogul clinics,
style clinics, telemark
Guiding companies Ramer Adventure
Skiing

CROSS-COUNTRY
Ski schools Snowmass Lodge and Club
Touring Center
Loipe location and size 80km track
between Aspen and Snowmass

CHILDCARE
Non-ski kindergarten Snowcubs at
Snowmass, 18 mths-3 yrs, 8.30am-
4pm, $60 per day, $280 for 5 days,
including lunch. Little Feet Day Care, 6
wks-18 mths, 7.30am to 5.30pm. Little
Red School House at Snowmass, 3-5
yrs; both prices on application
Ski kindergarten Big Burn Bears at
Snowmass, 4-6 yrs, and Powder
Pandas at Tiehack/Buttermilk, 3-6 yrs,
both $60 per day or $280 for 5 days
including lunch, lifts and lessons
Babysitting Nighthawks at Snowmass,
Super Sitters at Aspen and Snowmass

OTHER SPORTS
Hot-air ballooning, snow-mobiling,
skating, dog-sledding, indoor tennis,
swimming, fitness centres, bowling

WHAT'S NEW
● Aspen/Vail Premier Passport joint
lift pass ● Fort Frog
children's learning area at Tiehack/
Buttermilk ● Ritz-Carlton hotel at Aspen

FOOD AND DRINK PRICES
Coffee $1, bottle of house wine $10-
14, beer $2, dish of the day $9-15

TOUR OPERATORS
Activity Travel, American Independence,
Bladon Lines,Crystal, Lotus Supertravel,
Made to Measure, Ski world

plete contrast to sparkling Aspen's. A visit here is well worth while for those in search of some unpretentious skiing. New lifts are unheard of, and indeed it is like stepping back into the 1960s.

Highlands has one hotel, the Maroon Creek Lodge, and Schwannie's cafeteria at the ski area base. The skiing is for all standards although it particularly attracts hardened skiers and snowboarders. The average age here is 25, considerably lower than at Aspen Mountain. The old-fashioned blue-painted chairs travel sedately up the mountain, and the view below is reminiscent of parts of the Salzburgerland in Austria. Designer ski-suits are completely out of place: regulars wear strictly practical clothing.

Mountain access is on the Exhibition 1 chair-lift, followed by Exhibition II to the Merry Go Round Restaurant. Intermediates and experts can take the Grand Prix or Golden Horn drags to get up the mountain more quickly. From the top, Kessler's Bowl is wild and unpisted, strictly for experts who are prepared to go for it in any snow condition. The upper part is treeless with some moguls, and when you do reach the trees the trail becomes open and steep. The bottom of the run flattens out as you go left through the trees and on into more moguls at the bottom of Sodd Buster. Kessler's Bowl, Sodd Buster and Snyder's Ridge are named after three patrolmen who died in an avalanche in Highland Bowl in 1984. These runs, together with Steeplechase, Garmisch, St Moritz and The Wall, are some of the more challenging runs.

The Olympic lift gives access to more expert and intermediate terrain. Another recommended cruise is the wide Golden Horn/ Thunderbird area on the lower part of the mountain. Exhibition is a popular beginner's run under Lift 2, which is very wide and open.

Unfortunately, the standard Aspen Skiing Company lift pass does not cover Aspen Highlands. You can, however, buy a book of tickets which covers all four. The Merry Go Round restaurant has good value food. Apart from the normal group ski classes, Aspen Highlands ski school holds racing and mogul technique clinics and snowboarding lessons. Snowpuppies kindergarten has a ratio of four children to one instructor and serves hot, nutritious lunches.

TOURIST OFFICE
1600 Maroon Creek Road, Aspen, CO
Tel 1 303 81611 3352

TOUR OPERATORS
None

Banff, Alberta

ALTITUDE 5,350ft (1631m)

••

Good points reliable snow record, wide range of skiing for all
standards, extensive child facilities
Bad points lack of skiing convenience, very low temperatures
Linked or nearby resorts Lake Louise (n), Mystic Ridge/Mount
Norquay (n), Sunshine Village (n)

As far as Europeans are concerned, Canada's most popular skiing area
lies in the Banff National Park two hours' drive to the west of Calgary.
The climate is continental, rather than maritime as it is at Whistler,
which results in the dry, fluffy powder that tempts enthusiasts to spend
approximately £3,000 a week on heli-skiing in the Bugaboos and the
Monoshees on the other side of the Rogers Pass. Those who prefer a
more traditional holiday have the choice of staying in Lake Louise, a
top-class ski area in its own right, or in the small town of Banff, with its
regular bus services to Lake Louise, Sunshine Village and Mystic
Ridge/Mount Norquay.

Although Lake Louise has plans to build a residential lodge at the
base of its lift system within the next three years, all existing accommodation is 5 to 10 minutes' drive away. As there is no village as such,
there is no feeling of being in a ski resort and little opportunity for leaving the hotel in the evenings. Banff has the advantage of being a real
town, albeit rather a tourist-orientated one as it is even more popular
with summer visitors than winter ones. On the plus side, it has a central
grid of wide, attractive streets lined with restaurants, bars and shops
and roamed by elk herds who make short work of the contents of dust-
bins with unattached lids.

The skiing
Lake Louise Top 8,650ft (2637m) bottom 5,393ft (1644m)
Sunshine Village Top 8,954ft (2730m) bottom 5,440ft (1659m)
Mount Norquay Top 7,000ft (2941m) bottom 5,350 ft (1631m)
Of the three ski resorts in the Banff catchment area, Lake Louise is
indisputably the best. From the base area at Whiskyjack Lodge, moun-
tain access is via a choice of three chair-lifts – Olympic, Glacier and the
Friendly Giant Express – which take skiers up to the mid-station at
Whitehorn Lodge. Anyone who has to wait for more than 10 minutes to
get onto one of these lifts can reclaim the cost of their lift pass, but Lake
Louise has not yet had to pay out.

From Whitehorn, all lifts lead to the Back Bowls and on to the Larch
and Ptarmigan chairs. This layout effectively gives Lake Louise four
linked ski areas. It is the resort's proud boast that all its lifts have at least

one green (easy) run down. This is often the kiss of death as far as advanced skiers are concerned, although Lake Louise offers interesting off-piste challenges on such runs as Brown Shirt, Paradise and East Bowl as well as testing mogul fields on Raven, Exhibition and Ptarmigan. Nor will intermediates be disappointed by long blue (intermediate) cruisers such as Meadowlark and Juniper. All in all, Lake Louise's 4,000 acres (1619 hectares) have been intelligently developed to provide plenty for everyone.

Attempts have been made to do the same at Sunshine Village and Mystic Ridge/Mount Norquay, but neither has the acreage nor the vertical drop to achieve comparable results. Sunshine Village, set high on the Continental Divide, lives up to its name, but has the disincentive of a ferocious wind-chill factor that often drives temperatures down to -30°C for days on end. This makes for excellent snow on predominantly gentle terrain. Such short, sharp tests as there are may be found off the Standish and Tee Pee Town chairs. In 1990, Mount Norquay, the town hill for Banff, consisted of a selection of black bump runs off the North American chair, plus a tiny network of beginner slopes. The area has now been upgraded by the addition of the Mystic Ridge intermediate area and a bright new base station. This provides terrain for skiers of all levels off a total of five lifts, with 90 per cent snowmaking coverage, but experienced skiers will soon exhaust its 25 runs.

All three resorts offer adult ski schools backed up by extensive family services. Lake Louise has a nursery for babies from 18 days to 18 months old, plus programmes for toddlers (19 to 35 months old), Daycare (3 to 6 years old) and Kids Ski (7 to 12 years old). Sunshine Village offers Daycare (19 months to 6 years old) and Kids Kampus (Wee Angels, 3 to 6 years old, and Young Devils, 6 to 12 years old). Mystic Ridge/Norquay caters for Tiny Tigers (3 to 6 years old) and Scamps (6 to 8 years old).

The resorts

Canadian Pacific Hotels and Resorts, the company that transported the concept of the British Railways Victorian Gothic hotel into the Canadian wilderness at the end of the last century, has two flagships in the area. The Banff Springs Hotel rises like a fortress on the outskirts of Banff, while the newly renovated Chateau Lake Louise enjoys a fairy-tale setting on a lake about 10 minutes' drive from the slopes. Both offer 5-star luxury and full resort facilities in the shape of outdoor heated swimming-pools, fitness centres, shopping malls and assorted bars and restaurants. Those in search of something a bit more like home, and a bit closer to the action, should consider the Banff Park Lodge or the Mount Royal Hotel.

Après-ski

Banff's Beaujolais restaurant offers an unusual degree of sophistication for Alberta, and Wild Bill's Saloon is the top shot for pool and live music. Non-skiers can try ice-fishing for lake or rainbow trout or winter casting for brown trout on the open waters of the Bow River. Alternatives include sleigh rides, dog-sled tours, bathing in sulphur hot springs and skating, both indoors and outdoors. Banff has its own cinema and 18-hole indoor mini-golf course.

TOURIST OFFICE
Ski Banff/Lake Louise,
Box 1085, Banff, Alberta
Tel 1 403 762 4561
Fax 1 403 762 8185

TOUR OPERATORS
Crystal, Frontier Ski, Lotus Supertravel,
Neilson, Ski Tal, Ski the American Dream,
Ski Thomson, Activity Travel,
All Canada Travel, Canada Air Holidays

Beaver Creek, Colorado

ALTITUDE 8,100ft (2470m)

•••

Good points compact resort, facilities for children, unusual mountain restaurants, skiing convenience
Bad points small ski area, high-priced accommodation
Linked or nearby resorts Vail (n) – *see separate chapter*

Beaver Creek, once thought of as Vail's elegant little sister, has come of age. Although only in its second decade, this little village with a permanent population of only 150, situated a 20-minute bus ride from Vail along the shore of the Eagle River, is in danger of eclipsing the exclusive image of its sibling. It is reached via a private road from the outskirts of Avon, a functional valley town, which has all the ambience of Moutiers and which serves as a dormitory for the majority of the workforce in Vail Valley.

Like most other Colorado ski resorts, Beaver Creek first staked its claim to fame through its gold, although it is proving to be far more successful as a resort than as a mining village. James Lyons and his partner, Frederick Westlotom, first struck pay-dirt here on 16 March 1881 while prospecting in the boulder-strewn cascade of water, which empties off the mountain into the Eagle River. They called the stream Beaver Creek. Eking a living out of the earth here, 10,000ft up in mountains often covered by snow for six months of the year, was far from easy. Their Aurora Mine never produced a decent strike and the settlers who followed the miners fared little better with their attempts to grow cauliflower and rhubarb.

Ex-US President Gerald Ford made his home here and helped put the resort on the map. Today Beaver Creek exudes an air of sophistication and wealth, which makes it probably the smartest family resort in the America.

The skiing
Top 11,440ft (3488m) bottom 8,100ft (2470m)
The skiing has been greatly by the addition in 1991-2 of Grouse Mountain, with a 550m (1,804ft) drop and half-a-dozen runs mainly geared towards experts. It is served by the Grouse Mountain Express high-speed quad. Previously critics suggested that serious skiers had to commute to Vail. In fact, Beaver Creek, while offering no real surprises, has delightfully varied skiing, albeit best suited in the main to accomplished intermediates.

The main **mountain access** is by the Centennial Express lift from outside the Hyatt Regency hotel, which takes you up to Spruce Saddle, the mid-station restaurant area, which at 10,200ft (3110m) is nearer the top than the bottom. The Stump Park lift takes you up to the summit Elevation at 11,440ft (3488m). Some of the best gentle runs are situated in this top section. A long cruise takes you down into Rose Bowl on the eastern edge of the ski area.

More accomplished skiers will head off westwards towards Red-Tail Camp at the base of Grouse via a choice of interesting double black diamonds (expert runs): Golden Eagle, Peregrine and Goshawk. Alternatively, you can return to the village down the 1989 World Championship men's downhill course beneath the Centennial Express. The Larkspur lift takes you up from Red-Tail Camp to Larkspur Bowl, which has four short but exciting blacks as well as a choice of gentler blue (intermediate) runs.

Spruce Saddle has an outdoor barbecue and a cafeteria. Rafter's offers a full waited lunch, but Beano's is the biggest name here. The latter, situated near the foot of Larkspur, is named after Frank Bienkowski, a settler who left Chicago to live here as a farmer in 1919. At lunchtime it is open only to members of the exclusive Beaver Creek Club. By night it opens its doors to tourists for gourmet dinners with live music and can be reached by motorised sleigh. One reporter mentioned that the evening was 'spoiled by the fumes from the snowcat, which pulled the sleigh, and the food was a disappointment'.

Vail and Beaver Creek Ski Schools are part of the same school, and the same teaching techniques are used. One reporter mentions that 'the enthusiastic instructor actually made me enjoy skiing crud'. All types of course are on offer, including women-only ski classes, freestyle lessons, snowboarding classes and off-piste skiing.

Like Vail, Beaver Creek has some excellent children's ski facilities. A ski-through area with Western attractions (children trace the footsteps of a fictional character called Sourdough Pete in his search for gold and ski through the Indian village), a specially illustrated children's map, and a children's ski centre with play area, lunch room and all-day supervision, show that Beaver Creek is well-organised for families with small children. For older children, snowboard classes are offered for 8-year-olds and over.

The resort

Beaver Creek calls itself 'the most luxurious and comfortable ski resort in America'. Well-designed shopping precincts and condominiums are clustered around the exclusive Hyatt Regency to form the heart of the village at the foot of the slopes. The pampering never stops. The village has a free limousine service and complimentary hot chocolate, coffee and biscuits are served at the bottom of the Centennial Express lift each morning. As the village is purpose-built, there is almost no walking and the skiing is on your doorstep wherever you are staying. Even so, many of the hotels offer a form of valet parking for your skis, which are taken from you when you arrive, placed out on the snow in front of you before skiing each morning, and whipped away from you at the end of the day. All this and more, but at a price.

Beaver Creek is not known for its cut-price accommodation – indeed most of it falls into the luxury bracket. The Hyatt Regency is the hotel chain's US flagship, with a central post-modern baronial hall dominated by a roaring log fire and a huge elk-antler chandelier. The ski valet service here means you do not handle your skis at all. Other accommodation, all of it luxury, includes the Camberley Club Hotel, the Charter hotel and the Chateau, which is Beaver Creek's recently built centrepiece, comprising condominiums, detached chalets and a central spa with Olympic-sized swimming-pool.

The Inn at Beaver Creek, the Creekside Lodge, and the Highlands condos are on a marginally more reasonable price level, but if you want to ski Beaver Creek the cheapest way possible, stay down at Avon in the valley. For those who are holidaying in self-catering condos, the City Market supermarket in Avon is recommended.

For an experience that is a little different (and even more expensive) Trapper's Cabin, reached off-piste from the top of the Strawberry Park lift, is one of the world's great romantic hideaways. Superficially it resembles a local trapper's cabin *circa* 1880. It was, in fact, built in 1986 and has en-suite bathrooms and the kind of mod cons not to be found a century ago.

Après-ski

Crooked Hearth in the Hyatt has some of the best pizzas in town, and the Patina Bar and Grill specialises in Californian food. Other restaurants include the Terrace, Legends, Mirabelle and Golden Eagle Inn. Leroy's is a friendly eating place ideal for the family.

The Coyote Café is one of the livelier bars, and the Crooked Hearth attracts a slightly older clientele. Cyrano's and Nick's in Vail are worth the journey for those who want to dance. A moonlight snow-shoe tour with dinner at Leroy's is one of the more unusual evening activities. Other ways to spend the evening include a visit to one of the cinemas or art galleries.

Breckenridge, Colorado

ALTITUDE 9,594ft (2925m)

• •

Good points wide choice of easy runs, tough runs, efficient lift
system, reliable resort-level snow, family skiing, tree-level skiing,
attractive town centre, variety of shops
Bad points inconveniently strung-out village, traffic in centre
Linked or nearby resorts Arapahoe Basin (n), Copper Mountain (n),
Keystone (n)

Breckenridge is rich in contrasts. The lovingly preserved, turn-of-the-
century miners' shacks stand beside modern hotels and apartment
buildings, and even the street names are a dichotomy. The town takes
its name from a Civil War general who fought on the Confederate side
and was ultimately defeated by Grant, Sherman and Lincoln. These
Unionist generals receive the lesser accolade of having streets named
after them. Breckenridge officially joined the United States only in in
1936, making it one of America's 'newest' old towns.

Gold was first discovered here in 1859. Second and third rushes followed around the turn of the century, but by 1910 most of the mines
were empty. The boom years seemed to be over until in 1961 a consor-
tium from Wichita, Kansas, which already owned much of the mountain, launched the Breckenridge ski area, preserving the town's unique
character. Today Breckenridge is owned by a Japanese company. It is
marketed under the Ski the Summit banner along with Copper
Mountain, Arapahoe Basin and Keystone, all accessible within an hour
by free shuttle-bus and all sharing a lift pass.

Breckenridge is not intimidatingly smart or cosmopolitan like Vail or
Aspen. Instead it offers a wide variety of accommodation and a good,
but not enormous, ski area famed for its moguls. It is an ideal resort for
families who want to try American skiing for the first time in a place
where the locals are both helpful and friendly.

The skiing
Top 12,204ft (3720m) bottom 9,594ft (2925m)
The skiing is on three interconnecting, mainly north-east facing mountains, unoriginally named Peak 8, Peak 9 and Peak 10 by the miners. A
fourth mountain, Peak 7, which is approached via Peak 8, is currently
being assessed by the United States Forestry Commission for the possibility of turning it into a ski area. No lifts would be constructed and it

would be purely off-piste country. In common with other Rocky Mountain resorts Breckenridge's tree-line is high, meaning that most runs are protected from occasional high winds and, even in low cloud, visibility is good. There is also some good off-piste skiing among the trees. Most of Breckenridge's skiing is on fairly short, easy slopes, many of which are indistinguishable from the next. There are, however, some excitingly steep chutes and awesome mogul fields.

Peak 8, with 65 per cent of its terrain classed as difficult, is the steepest and the least busy of the three mountains. Lehman's Run on Peak 8 is recommended for its length, variety and lack of crowds. It has greens (easy) and blues (intermediate) on its front face, easy black (difficult) runs through the woods, some real blacks, namely the Back Bowls high up on the south side of the peak, and the double black diamond (advanced) trails, Contest and Horseshoe, offering mogul slopes. Mach 1 is steep but wide, and is ideal terrain for the regular freestyle competitions which are held here. Much of the remaining steeper skiing is found on both sides of the gulch separating Peak 8 and Peak 9.

Peak 9 is the easiest and most central of the three mountains, rising to 11,480ft (3500m), with **mountain access** to all the areas from here via the Quicksilver high-speed quad chair, which starts from just outside the resort complex and arrives at mid-point on Peak 9. At midpoint there is the option of switching to Peak 10. The lower area around the Quicksilver and the Mercury chair consists of mainly wide, green runs. The skiing on Peak 9 includes some smooth, intermediate cruising runs, although it is also suitable for more timid skiers who want to avoid a challenge. Devil's Crotch and Mineshaft double black diamond trails should only be attempted by experts, as the moguls here are always big and the runs claustrophobically narrow.

Peak 10 has only one lift, but this serves some tougher skiing for good intermediates and upwards, including The Burn, a mainly off-piste area. The mountain's easiest trail is Flapjack. Contest Bowl and Horseshoe Bowl at the top of Peak 8 offer some of the resort's best powder skiing when conditions are right. Horseshoe is served by a T-Bar, an anachronism within the otherwise state-of-the-art lift system, but installed for practical reasons – the high winds above the tree-line would often make a chair impossible to run. The best descents begin after a short walk from the top. Breckenridge's other bowl skiing includes Imperial, North and the Back Bowls.

The pistes, or trails, are well groomed here as they are all over North America, although many of the upper slopes are left unbashed for mogul lovers. Reporters complain that signposting is not always clear, and it is 'sometimes too easy to miss a green run and end up on a black'. Queues develop at peak ski school hours and the resort is more crowded at weekends. Reporters suggest avoiding the Quicksilver and Mercury lifts early in the morning and Peak 9 in the afternoon.

Mountain restaurants

The mountain eating places are all adequate, but no single one is particularly memorable. Reporters remark that they are 'generally self-service, of good standard, but lack the ambience of Austria or Switzerland', and

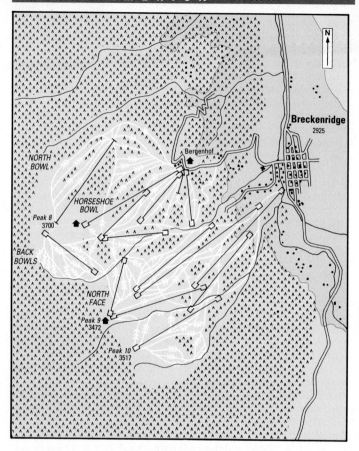

also that they are 'large cafeteria-style places which sell reasonably priced, if unvaried, food with extremely quick (maximum of five minutes) service'. Peak 8 has three restaurants to choose from, Peak 9 five and Peak 10 just one.

Beginners and children

The Breckenridge Ski School is highly regarded: 'Our instructor treated us as individuals. There were never more than eight to a group, we never felt rushed and lessons were always on time, unlike some Austrian ski schools.' Others remarked upon the pleasing lack of 'technical bullshit'. As in most other Colorado resorts, you choose the class you think will suit your ability; no terrifying tests where you are bound to ski at your very worst. Special courses include ski clinics with video analysis. The mogul tuition is particularly recommended by our reporters.

As Breckenridge is a particularly high resort, very young children (and indeed, the elderly) may tend to suffer from the altitude. They may become dehydrated and will need to drink a lot of extra fluid. Parents should use plenty of sun-tan cream and after-sun moisturisers on their children's skin. However, these small details are made up for by the excellent child facilities, with Kids' Castle, the children's complex at the base of Peak 8, having recently being expanded by 30 per cent. The building incorporates warming areas and a lunch room. The Children's Center here cares for children from two months to five years old. Peak 9's Children's Center takes children between three and five years old for skiing or just for play.

The resort
In the mining years, Main Street was a rutted dirt-road lined with wooden boardwalks and false-fronted buildings. The town enjoyed several gold and silver booms and at one time some of the house exteriors were even decorated in silver-based paint. Since those days Breckenridge has been carefully preserved. More than 250 authentic buildings still remain and have become restaurants, bars and shops. We have reports of 'quite heavy traffic in peak hours on Main Street'.

Accommodation
The Village at Breckenridge Resort, right next to the Quicksilver chair, is said to be 'modern and clean, with very large rooms'. It has a wealth of facilities including its own athletic club, skating rink, the ubiquitous 'hot tub' (whirlpool), a swimming-pool, and 40 shops and restaurants. The Breckenridge Hilton and the Beaver Run Resort both have pools and hot-tubs; the former also houses the Cuddly Bear Toddlers' Center where children from one to three years old are looked after all day. The Beaver Run Resort is well positioned for the skiing. Ridge Street Inn is recommended as 'friendly and well run'. The Brown Hotel dates from 1890, when it boasted Summit County's only bath tub. Today, it is also known for its restaurant. Breckenridge Mountain Lodge offers good, cheap accommodation a short walk from the centre; the Powderhorn apartments and Pine Ridge condos are both recommended. The Liftside Inn is praised for its 'spacious apartments and excellent location', and it also has a pool and hot tubs.

Eating out
Mexican food is popular in Colorado and Mi Casa, a couple of minutes' walk from the lifts base, has an informal atmosphere. Across the road, Fa-Heatas Bar and Grill is a Mexican café with a relaxed atmosphere. Santeramo's has live music at weekends as a backdrop to its Italian cuisine, while there is piano music at Stein Erikson's, where fresh seafood and prime rib are the specialities. The Breckenridge Brewery is praised for its good-value food and 'brilliant beer', and Pasta Jays is an affordable place which is aimed at families. The Whale's Tail is praised for its excellent food and service. At Bernard's Inn you eat well, but the service has been strongly criticised. The Hearthstone is highly recommended for its 'unbelievably good Jalepeno prawns'. The cosy Ski Tip Lodge at nearby Keystone is well worth a visit even if you are staying at Breckenridge. The evening begins with a sleigh ride from the village and a bottle of cham-

Skiing facts: Breckenridge

TOURIST OFFICE
PO Box 1058, Breckenridge, CO 80424
Tel 1 303 453 5000
Fax 1 303 453 7302

THE RESORT
By road Denver 85 miles (137km)
By rail Denver station
By air Denver Airport 1½ hrs
Visitor beds 23,000 (in hotels, condominiums, guesthouses and lodges – no breakdown available)
Transport free shuttle service to all three base areas, town and most lodging, runs from 8am-10pm, and free bus service to Copper Mountain, Keystone and Arapahoe Basin

THE SKIING
Longest run Four O'Clock Run, 3½ miles (5.6km) – blue/green
Number of lifts 16
Number of trails/pistes 112 (19% easy, 35% intermediate, 46% difficult)
Total of trails/pistes 1,600 acres (648 hectares) in Breckenridge
Nursery slopes at the bottom of Peak 8 and 9
Summer skiing none
Snowmaking 335 acres (136 hectares) covered

LIFT PASSES
Area pass (covers Peak 8,9 and 10) $180 for 6 out of 8 days. Ski The Summit ticket coupons (covers Breckenridge, Keystone, Copper Mountain and Arapahoe Basin), $198 for 6 days
Day pass (Breckenridge only) $38
Half-day pass $29 after 12.30pm
Beginners ski school lessons include lift pass in price
Children 6-12 yrs, $90 for a 6 out of 8 day pass, free for 5 yrs and under
Pensioners 60-69 yrs as child, free for 70 yrs and over
Credit cards accepted yes

SKI SCHOOLS
Adults Breckenridge Ski School, $180 for 6 days
Children Breckenridge Ski School

(6-12 yrs), Teens (13-17 yrs), both S180 for 6 days
Private lessons $70 per hr
Special courses snowboarding, telemark, monoskiing, advanced clinics (powder, moguls), racing clinics, women's seminars, disabled skiing
Guiding companies Colorado Heli-Ski

CROSS-COUNTRY
Ski schools The Nordic Centre
Loipe location and size 23 miles (38km) of track, ½ mile (1km) from Peak 8 base

CHILDCARE
Non-ski kindergarten Children's Center at Peak 8, 2 mths-1 yr, $45 per day, Snow Play at Peak 8, 2-5 yrs, Peak 9, 3-5 yrs, $38 per day including lunch, all 8.30am-4.30pm
Ski kindergarten special ski school for 3 yrs and over at Peak 8 and 9, 8.30am-4.30pm, $42 per day including lunch. Junior Ski School, Peaks 8 and 9, 4-5 yrs, 8.30am-4.30pm, $45 per day including lunch, $200 for 5 days
Babysitting available through childcare operations on Peaks 8 and 9, also through some hotels

OTHER SPORTS
Heli-skiing, snow-mobiling, sleigh rides, skating, indoor tennis, swimming, fitness centre, climbing wall

WHAT'S NEW
● snowboard terrain garden
● children's facilities expanded at Kids' Castle at Peak 8 base

FOOD AND DRINK PRICES
Coffee $1, bottle of house wine $16, beer $2, dish of the day $5.95

TOUR OPERATORS
Activity Travel, American Independence, Bladon Lines, Crystal, Enterprise, Inghams, Lotus Supertravel, Made to Measure, Neilson, Ski Equipe, Ski The American Dream, Ski Thomson, Ski Val, Skiworld

pagne before the wholesome four-course dinner. The pastel-painted clapboard buildings on Breckenridge Main Street house a range of boutiques, art galleries and a tacky surfeit of T-shirt shops.

Après-ski

Breckenridge has a choice of authentic nightspots including the original Gold Pan Saloon, which has been here since 1859 and is said to be, the oldest continually operated bar west of the Mississippi. It has a smoky, old-time atmosphere and dancing. Meach's Mogul also has dancing every night and, less energetically, time can be spent sampling the local brew at the Breckenridge Brewery and Pub or the *pastis* at French Pierre's. Jake T Pounders has cowboy music to entertain its yuppie crowd, and the Whale's Tail attracts an older, more affluent clientèle. Shamus O'Toole's Roadhouse Saloon is reported to be 'extremely dull on the two occasions on whichx we visited it'. Downstairs At Eric's has 'a brilliant band', and Joshua's at the bottom of Peak 9 is 'a good place for noisy music and cheap, gassy beer'.

Nightly guided snow-mobile tours into the backwoods are a popular après-ski activity. The culmination is an unappetising alcohol-free group dinner in an abandoned mining camp, but it does not detract from the overall experience. The organisers, Tiger Run Tours, provide huge padded suits and biker-style boots for the journey.

Copper Mountain, Colorado

ALTITUDE 9,593ft (2926m)

● ●

Good points range of easy and intermediate skiing, ideal for families, easy road access, Extreme Experience area for off-piste skiing, excellent child facilities
Bad points lack of resort charm, limited après-ski
Linked or nearby resorts Keystone (n)

Like so many Rocky Mountain resorts, Copper Mountain might never have existed were it not for the gold beneath the snow, which drew miners here from all over the world in the latter half of the nineteenth century. John S. Wheeler, who founded the original settlement of Wheeler Junction off what is now Interstate-70, described his boom town, which supplied lumber to the surrounding mines, as 'a summer resort, which may attract thousands'. One hundred years later his prophecy was fulfilled, even if he got the season wrong. On 5 December 1972 Copper Mountain resort opened for visitors with 5 lifts and an initial 26 miles (42km) of trails.

Copper Mountain, on the Denver side of the Vail Pass, was purpose-built as a ski resort. None of the original buildings remains and it therefore lacks the charm of Breckenridge and Keystone, its more traditional neighbours in Summit County, collectively marketed worldwide under the Ski The Summit banner. Indeed, the village itself ominously reminds one of the first-wave French purpose-built resorts of the 1960s, which may explain why Club Med chose it as their introduction to the US winter market. However, what it loses in its plain architectural style it wins in the friendliness of the locals and its facilities as a family resort.

The skiing
Top 12,360ft (3768m) bottom 9,600ft (2926m)
Mountain access is from five points in and around the village. Most of Copper Mountain's skiing is on tree-lined trails, with a total of 76 runs and extensive snowmaking. The majority of the difficult runs are below Copper Peak and there are some interesting bowls for experts. Union Peak presents some challenges while there is also plenty of fast cruising terrain for intermediates. Copper has a lot of easy skiing, with certain sections designated as slow ski areas. Snowboarders are catered for with a half-pipe (a purpose-built snow wall for freestyle turns).

The newest ski area is Extreme Experience, a 350-acre (140-hectare) sector with a vertical drop of nearly 2,000ft (610m) on the south side of Copper Peak. This provides a choice between open powder bowls and unpisted clearings through the trees. Access is via the Storm King lift followed by a short hike to the summit at 12,360ft (3768m) from where qualified guides take you all the way down to Highway 91. A shuttle-bus service takes you back to the resort. Users of the area are provided with avalanche bleepers.

Copper Mountain, like too many American and French resorts, has suffered from the incompatibility of snowboarders (or 'shredders' as they are called in the US) sharing the same slopes as skiers. It has also experienced the much more sinister problem of 'packboarding', a lethal game of 'chicken' invented by young members of the board whereby they intentionally ride too close to other snowboarders or skiers. To overcome this menace, Copper has introduced a safety programme and 'shrediquette' brochure listing snowboarding rules.

The ski school offers group and private lessons, along with bumps and powder workshops, beginner packages, and Junior and Senior Ranch (ski programmes for children). The Belly Button Bakery takes skiers from three years old.

The resort

The resort is ideally suited to families. Being purpose-built, it involves no walking and the childcare facilities are said to be excellent. The Belly Button Babies nursery is right by the slopes, catering for those of two months old and upwards, while the Belly Button Bakery takes non-skiing children. Activities at the Bakery include cooking and baking, arts and crafts and outdoor snow play. Lunch is provided for all ages and evening babysitting is available.

Most of Copper's accommodation is in apartments and condominiums. Copper Junction was the first condo, The Lodge is right by the slopes, Village Square and Telemark Lodge are also recommended. O'Shea's Copper Bar offers a good selection of fast food and salads, Pesce Fresco specialises in fish and pasta, and Farley's is known for its ribs and steaks. Rackets, in the Racquet and Athletic Club, offers some of the resort's better food, based on American and French cuisine.

Après-ski

Après-ski here is not dissimilar to that of the French purpose-built resorts, with a limited choice of bars and not a lot more. Those who choose to can carry on exerting themselves after skiing at the Copper Mountain Racquet and Athletic Club, well equipped with facilities including a swimming-pool, weight-training, tennis and racquetball courts. Skating on West Lake is free from midday until 10pm.

TOURIST OFFICE
Copper Mountain Resort, PO Box 3001, CO 80443
Tel 1 303 968 2882
Fax 1 303 968 2711

TOUR OPERATORS
American Independence, Club Med, Inghams, Lotus Supertravel

Crested Butte, Colorado

ALTITUDE 9,100ft (2774m)

• •

Good points extensive tough runs, varied off-piste skiing, interesting cross-country skiing, old town atmosphere, variety of restaurants, children's facilities
Bad points resort accessibility, separate ski area and village
Linked or nearby resorts none

It was a geologist travelling through the area in 1873 who gave the coal-mining town its unusual name, sounding more like an exotic bird than what was to become an important Colorado ski resort. A 'butte' (pronounced as 'beauty') is, in fact, a mountain which is isolated from the rest of a range. Today there is a historic village and a completely separate modern ski station three miles (5km) away.

Crested Butte is 28 miles (45km) from Gunnison airport, which is served by small passenger aircraft from Denver, 230 miles (268km) away by road on one of the most beautiful drives in the Rockies.

The skiing
Top 11,945ft (3918m) bottom 9,100ft (2774m)
Crested Butte has some of the easiest skiing in Colorado as well as some of the most difficult. Its 12 lifts serve 82 trails spread over 1,150 acres (460 hectares) of ski terrain. A high 58 per cent of the runs are classed as difficult, 29 per cent intermediate and 13 per cent easy.

Mountain access is via the Keystone triple chair-lift, which takes you from the middle of the base area to a central point, where blue (intermediate) and green (easy) trails stretch out ahead. From the mid-station Peanut and Roller Coaster are two easy runs for finding your ski legs. From the top, Houston connects with the Painter Boy triple chair, serving a secluded area of green and blue runs.

The new Silver Queen high-speed quad takes skiers to the most difficult part of the main ski terrain as well as to Paradise Bowl and the smooth blue Upper Treasury under the Paradise lift. From here the Twister lift runs parallel to the top half of Silver Queen and offers some black diamond (difficult) trails such as Jokerville, Twister and Crystal.

The Extreme Limits area comprises some 260 acres (104 hectares) of ungroomed extreme skiing, which locals claim is some of the best in Colorado. It comprises Spellbound Bowl, Phoenix Bowl, Teocalli Bowl, the new Third Bowl and, best known of all, the North Face. This challenging skiing was, until recently, enjoyed only by the ski patrol and the most dedicated skiers prepared to walk for 30 minutes to reach it. However, the new Silver Queen quad takes a slightly different route to the former chair, making the old tedious trek unnecessary.

Irwin Lodge, 12 miles (19km) away and set at 10,700ft (3262m), offers snowcat skiing on 2,400 acres (960 hectares) of terrain. This is a cheaper and more leisurely way than heli-skiing of exploring virgin powder slopes far off the beaten track. The Lodge is reached only by snowcat or snow-mobile and offers accommodation, meals and transport for its skiers.

Although a relatively small percentage of the runs at Crested Butte are graded easy, these are long and gentle, perfect for the large section of the clientèle, which is made up of families and beginners. The resort caters for them with special 'Learn to Ski Free' weeks, where first-time skiers are given complimentary tuition, rentals and lift tickets while they learn the basics. Crested Butte Ski School offers group and private lessons, as well as ski programmes for the disabled, telemarking, race programmes, women's ski adventures with US ski team veteran Kim Reichhelm, bump and powder workshops, ski extreme and intermediate workshops.

There is a kindergarten for children aged between six months and six years old at the Buttetopia Nursery in the Whetstone Building close to the Grande Butte Hotel. Butte Busters offers lessons for children aged seven to twelve years old.

In all, 235 acres (94 hectares) are covered by snow-cannon. Several reporters praise the resort for its clear signposting and lack of queues ('very orderly, well organised and no pushing'). However, the chair-lifts are reported to be rather slow, but adequate. Paradise Lodge is the only recommended mountain eating place in an area short on altitude restaurants. Crested Butte links in to an extensive cross-country network of 100 miles (160km) of trails.

The resort

The difficult choice, as in many American ski resorts, is whether to stay in the historic and attractive old town away from the ski area where there is atmosphere and après-ski, or in the convenient purpose-built ski village at the base of the lifts where there is little ambience and few evening activities. Most skiers choose to stay in the new village and eat out in the old one. One reporter describes the purpose-built ski satellite as 'quiet, with little traffic apart from snow-ploughs' and 'not for party-goers'. Whichever one you decide upon, the free bus service connects the two villages at frequent intervals. The main ski area hotel is the large and quite expensive Grande Butte next to the lifts; reporters praise it as 'excellent, with huge rooms and doorstep skiing'. The other hotels are the Crested Butte Lodge where you can experience fireside dining at Jeremiah's, the Norwegian-style Nordic Inn and the Manor Lodge. The Plaza condominiums are fully equipped for self-caterers.

In the old town's Main Street, 40 of the original nineteenth-century buildings with their colourful wooden façades have survived to be converted into shops ('upmarket and not cheap') and give the place a fine Victorian feel to it. Hotels and guesthouses are scattered around the town, including the Nordic, a family-run ski lodge which is recommended by reporters, Rozman's Motor Lodge and the more expensive Crested Butte Club, an attractive Victorian hotel and spa. The old town also has some attractive bed and breakfast accommodation with prices to match. The Claim Jumper is a log cabin furnished with antiques, the Gothic Inn is decorated with hand-painted furniture and the Crested Beauty offers a wholesome breakfast and a relaxed atmosphere. Moderate prices can be found at the Elk Mountain Lodge, which was a miners' hotel built in 1919 and the British-owned Cristiana Guesthaus. Irwin Lodge, 12 miles (19km) from Crested Butte, has 23 bedrooms set on a gallery around the large central hall with an open fireplace.

Après-ski

Diners are offered a good choice of locations, with some three dozen restaurants mainly in the old town. The Soupçon, which concentrates on French cuisine, is in a small Victorian building hidden in an alley. The Idle Spur has good prime ribs, but is said to be noisy. The Bacchanale has a quiet ambience and serves pasta and other Italian food. Gulf Coast Grill has fresh seafood. Penelope's and Le Bosquet are recommended and the Rib Parlor Pit restaurant specialises in ribs and sea food. Both the Bakery Café and the Forest Queen serve good breakfasts.

The Wooden Nickel is the oldest saloon in town. Rafters, near the lifts, is a crowded bar with a live band and the Roaring Elk Saloon in the Grand Butte hotel is a popular after-skiing meeting place. Dancing takes place at the Eldorado. Other nightspots include the Talk of the Town and Kochevars. More unusual après-ski possibilities include snow-mobile 'dinner tours' to Irwin Lodge and snowcat tours to the Paradise Lodge restaurant on the mountain.

There is also dog-sledding, ice-fishing, snow-mobiling, racquetball, fitness centres, swimming, sleigh rides, parapente, winter mountain-biking and horse-riding in the snow.

TOURIST OFFICE
Crested Butte Mountain Resort, PO Box A,
12 Snowmass Road, CO 81225
Tel (Freephone) 0800 894085
Fax 1 303 349 2250

TOUR OPERATORS
Activity Travel, American Independence,
Crystal, Ski the American Dream, Skiworld

Jackson Hole, Wyoming

ALTITUDE 6,311ft (1924m)

••

Good points real cowboy-town atmosphere, tough skiing, lively après-ski, ideal for non-skiers, beautiful scenery, attractive town, well-run kindergarten
Bad points distance from Jackson to main ski area, bottleneck at cable car, short ski season, lack of easy runs
Linked or nearby resorts Snow King (n), Grand Targhee (n)

Jackson Hole is, in our opinion, one of the top half-dozen resorts in the world. What it lacks in size, it makes up for in the raw excitement generated by some of the steepest skiing in North America. Jackson Hole is Teton Village, the base of the ski area, which is a full 20-minute ride from the cowboy town of Jackson, Wyoming. Jackson has its own small ski resort of Snow King above the town and is in turn 15 minutes from Jackson Airport. It is all slightly confusing, not helped by the fact that there is another separate resort called Snow King actually in Jackson itself. A nineteenth-century trapper named Davey Jackson is responsible for the first half of the name; the Hole is a 50-mile section of the Snake River, which twists its way between the Teton and Gros Ventre mountain ranges.

The skiing

Top 10,450ft (3186m) bottom 6,311ft (1924m)

The skiing here is renowned for its difficulty and excitement, and so it should be. Rendezvous, the steepest mountain, is about as serious skiing territory as you can get, but Jackson Hole also has some good nursery slopes: long, beautifully groomed fairways, which converge on the village at the foot of Après-Vous Mountain, the resort's second and much tamer peak. **Mountain access** is on the Teewinot or Crystal Springs chairs. Plenty of intermediate skiing is on offer, although those unable to cope with sudden and harsh changes in the gradient, as well as the odd vicious couloir, should carefully follow the blue (intermediate) trail signs. Occasionally you may find a run or section of the mountain closed because of a moose on the loose. This is really no joke; anyone who comes between a mother and her young can expect a ferocious attack. Skiing in the Wild West is an altogether different experience from anywhere else.

The 10,450ft (3186m) peak of Rendezvous Mountain is directly reached by the 63-man aerial tram (cable car), which is now 30 years old, although it has undergone a refit. Rather unfairly, like the Grands Montets in Argentière, you are charged a small supplement to ride it. The new owners of Jackson Hole Ski Corporation have already drawn up plans to replace the tram, but at the moment queuing at peak times can almost rival that of its French sister. Wise skiers will take the Crystal Springs double chair and the triple above it. You can then work your way across to the Thunder double chair and on to the steep face of the mountain. Many of the chairs are old and slow, but most will be upgraded over the next three seasons. At present Thunder appears to be a particular bottleneck.

The choice of steep bowls includes Cody, Cheyenne, Rendezvous and Tensleep, and rocky mogul chutes like the Alta series under the aerial tram. Nearly all the skiing is steep, and in powder conditions, quite extraordinary.

Jackson Hole is one of the few US resorts where there is at least an approximation of in European off-piste skiing. The Hobacks is a steep, tree-studded snowfield on the edge of the ski area, which is never pisted. It is best skied in the early morning when the snow is at its lightest and indeed the run is closed at 2pm. Like much of Jackson, it is south-facing and in mild weather conditions the going can get heavy by late morning. A short climb with a guide opens up vast tracts of powder on Headwall and Green River, especially in spring.

Good out-of-bounds or off-piste skiing it may have, but Corbet's Couloir is Jackson Hole's main claim to fame. Corbet's is a notorious chute at the top of Rendezvous Mountain, accessed by a 20ft (6m) jump off a cornice. All but the bravest of skiers are satisfied with walking to the edge of the couloir and looking down into it.

Mountain restaurants

A small warming hut at the top of the aerial tram does what it says. The only other refreshment centre on the mountain is Casper Restaurant, an adequate self-service near the bottom of the Casper Bowl triple chair. Most skiers lunch at the Alpenhof, a Tyrolean-style restaurant at the base of the mountain, or elsewhere in Teton Village.

Beginners and children

Jackson Hole ski school's philosophy is to make learning a pleasure. A sense of fun is brought to all ski lessons, both child and adult, so that everyone feels happy. After tackling the long, gentle nursery slope, you progress up the mountain to steeper, but still pleasingly wide, trails. It must be said, however, that the jump from nursery to intermediate trails in Jackson Hole is a large one.

Unless you are staying in Teton Village, getting to the slopes is not particularly convenient for a family. The kindergarten is right at the base area in Teton Village, and has its own ski shop, an enclosed outdoor play area, and a kiosk selling hot chocolate. The Kinderschule is one of the better ski kindergartens we have come across. Children are taught with the excellent 'Edgie Wedgie' technique in which ski tips are clipped together with a brightly coloured, bendy strip of plastic. This

stops the skis from crossing and encourages children to make a 'wedge'
or snowplough. Children are taken to and from the nursery slopes in a
snow-mobile trailer.

The resort

Others have tried, but only Jackson Hole has succeeded, in seamlessly
welding the dusty gun-slinging charisma of a Western frontier town to
the high-tech facilities of a modern ski resort. Jackson is the summer
host to two million visitors, who arrive in their campers on their way to
or from Yellowstone National Park. In the winter it returns to its natural
state, a small market-town with an interesting range of shops, restaurants and vast country bars. Here, cowboys who may not be cowboys at
all, but renegade dentists from Omaha, gulp shots of Wild Turkey,
shoot pool and dance a wild rock rhythm called the Western Swing.

The central square is crowned by a triumphal arch of elk antlers, naturally harvested from what is the largest elk refuge in North America, a
couple of miles out of town. Night revellers returning with a skinful of
bourbon shouldn't be surprised to encounter stray elks roaming the
streets. Wooden boardwalks and shops selling western clothing all add
to the atmosphere.

Teton Village, the alternative accommodation base, is a cluster of
hotels and condos centred on a picturesque clock tower and the cable
car, or 'aerial tram' as they call it here, at the foot of Rendezvous
Mountain. Fervent skiers will opt for Teton Village and avoid the daily
commute, but to stay here is to miss out on the overall experience that
helps to make Jackson Hole such an important all-round resort.

For some years, development in Jackson Hole has been in limbo
while founder Paul McCollister was locked in lengthy litigation over the
future ownership of the resort. Jackson Hole changed hands in summer
1992 and the new owners have already started on a multi-million-dollar
expansion programme. This will include upgrading the lift system.

Accommodation

You can either stay in Jackson where all the action is, or in Teton Village
right next to the slopes. We prefer the former because its great atmosphere makes it worth putting up with the 20-minute drive to and from
the slopes. If you are looking for a traditional half-board hotel, then the
Wort Hotel in Jackson is the one which comes closest to it. The big
advantage is its position right in the centre of town, near all the shops
and nightlife. Other hotels include the Rusty Parrot Lodge and the Days
Inn. Motels include the comfortable Parkway Inn, with a swimming-pool
and two hot tubs, but no restaurant. The Inn at Jackson Hole is, in fact, at
Teton Village, well positioned at the base of the slopes. Self-caterers
need to go to Jackson for the supermarkets, which include Albertsons
and Foodtown. Further afield on a hill overlooking the valley is Spring
Creek Resort, the most unusual place to stay in the area.

Eating out

Breakfast is a serious business in cowboy country. The real McCoy of
eggs over easy, stacks of pancakes, hash browns and grits found at

Skiing facts: Jackson Hole

TOURIST OFFICE
PO Box 290, Teton Village, WY 83025
Tel 1 307 733 2292
Fax 1 307 733 2660

THE RESORT
By road Salt Lake City 250 miles
(400km)
By air Jackson Airport 15 minutes from
Jackson and 20 minutes from Teton
Village. Airport shuttle bus for a
nominal fee
Visitor beds 7,148 (70% hotels,
25% apartments, 2% guesthouses,
3% other)
Transport free bus service operates
day and evening between Jackson and
Teton Village

THE SKIING
Longest run Gros Ventre, 4.5 miles
(7km) – blue
Number of lifts 9
Number of trails/pistes 65 (10%
beginner, 40% intermediate, 50%
advanced)
Total of trails/pistes 2,500 acres
(1011 hectares)
Nursery slopes 1 lift and a 2,260ft-long
slope. The Kinderschule building is
located at the base of Eagle's Rest
slope
Summer skiing none
Snowmaking 80 acres (176 hectares)
covered

LIFTPASSES
Area pass $192 for 6 days
Day pass $39
Half-day pass $30 after 12.30pm
Beginners Eagle's Rest, free for
beginners' first lesson
Children free for under 5 yrs on Eagle's
Rest, $19 per day for 14 yrs and under
Pensioners $19 per day for 65 yrs
and over
Credit cards accepted yes

SKI SCHOOL
Adults Jackson Hole Ski School at
Teton Village, $40 per day
Children Skiwee, 6-14 yrs, $53 per day
including lessons, lunch and snacks

Private lessons $45 per hr
Special courses snowboarding,
women's ski clinics, race camps,
mogul clinics, Meisters lessons (high
level), senior ski programme (over 50
yrs), mountain experience (off-piste),
disabled skiing
Guiding companies Alpine Ski Guides

CROSS-COUNTRY
Ski schools Jackson Hole Nordic
Center
Loipe location and size 25km of track
and skating lanes at the base of
Jackson Hole resort

CHILDCARE
Non-ski kindergarten infant care for
non-ski children 2-18 mths, childcare
for 1½ yrs and over, both at
Kinderschule, 8.30am-4.30pm, $45
per day including lunch and snacks
Ski kindergarten One-on-One and
childcare at Kinderschule, 3-5 yrs, $53
including lunch, snacks, and 1 hr
lesson. Minimeisters group lessons,
3-5 yrs, $53 for lesson with childcare
Babysitting Kinderschule

OTHER SPORTS
Skating, dog-sledding, sleigh rides,
snow-mobiling (with tour to
Yellowstone National Park), snowcat
skiing at Grand Targhee, night skiing at
Snow King resort, indoor tennis,
swimming, fitness centres, bowling,
heli-skiing, elk sleigh rides

WHAT'S NEW
● Ownership of Jackson Hole ● 2
hotels in Jackson ● luxury condos at
Teton Village

FOOD AND DRINK PRICES
Coffee 50c, bottle of house wine $10,
beer $2.50, dish of the day $5-10

TOUR OPERATORS
Activity Travel, American Independence,
Collineige, Crystal, Lotus Supertravel,
Made to Measure, Neilson, SkiBound,
Ski Scott Dunn, Ski the American
Dream, Ski Thomson, Ski Val, Skiworld

Bubba's Bar-B-Que in Jackson or the Mangy Moose in Teton Village. In the evening the art deco-style Cadillac Grille in Jackson is a good place for hamburgers, seafood and fresh pasta; it is also fun for children. JJ's Silverdollar Bar and Grill in the Wort Hotel has the ubiquitous ribs, in various forms. The Blue Lion is a more expensive option and Stiegler's serves Austrian cuisine.

Après-ski

Unless you are over 21 and can prove it, you are not going to enjoy yourself here outside skiing hours. So strict are Wyoming's licensing laws that anyone who could be taken for under 40 should carry their identification at all times. The Million Dollar Cowboy Bar, the Silver Dollar Bar, and The Rancher in Jackson are where the action is. You can dance in all three to live music for most of the season. The Cowboy Bar has the most atmosphere with real leather saddles as bar stools and a full-size, stuffed grizzly bear.

Teton Village has the Mangy Moose, one of the finest post-slope bars in the Rockies. It has live music in the evenings and a video room for those under age. The Wingback Lounge at the Inn is a quieter option, and the Stockman's Lounge at the Sojourner usually has ski videos and free appetisers. If you have hired a car you should drive to Wilson on the road towards the Teton Pass for an authentic Western evening at the Stagecoach Inn, with live music, cowgirls in flounced dresses and good-value food. It is the kind of place where you eat with your hat on and go easy on the eye contact with strangers.

Other après-ski activities include night skiing at the Snow King resort in Jackson, and visits to Yellowstone National Park. There are also cinemas and art galleries to visit. Shopping is another important après-ski activity here, and prices tend to be good. The Polo Ralph Lauren Factory Store sells end-of-line designer clothes at a fraction of normal prices.

Grand Targhee   8,000ft (2439m)

Forty-two miles northwest of Jackson, and just inside the Wyoming border, is the small resort of Grand Targhee. Targhee is blessed with a good snow record, which is why the main attraction here is snowcat skiing in the virgin powder. This is by previous arrangement only, as the cat (a passenger-carrying rat-track) takes a maximum of 10 passengers, plus the guide and a patrolman. The resort has 1,500 skiable acres (607 hectares), and a further 1,500 acres available for snowcat skiing.

TOURIST OFFICE
PO Box Ski Alta, Wyoming 83422
Tel 1 307 353 2304

TOUR OPERATORS
American Independence

Keystone, Colorado

ALTITUDE 9,300ft (2835m)

••

Good points extensive snowmaking, variety of restaurants, skiing
for all standards, night-skiing, variety of tough runs
Bad points strung-out resort, lack of resort charm, lack of skiing
convenience
Linked or nearby resorts Arapahoe Basin (n), Copper Mountain (n)

Keystone came into existence not because of a gold strike but because
it was the end of the line. Old Keystone was the name given to the railhead here in the 1880s and the mountain above it was called Keystone
Mountain. In the late 1960s a group of developers won permission from
the US Forest Service to create a new mountain resort to meet the
growing demand by skiers. Today Keystone has become one of
Colorado's top intermediate ski areas.

Keystone, along with Copper Mountain and Breckenridge, is part of
the Ski The Summit group of resorts. It is located 75 miles (120km)
from Denver off Interstate 70. The resort is set around a lake, which in
winter claims to be North America's largest natural skating rink.
Keystone has no real centre; the few kilometres between the far end of
the village and the skiing are an untidy arrangement of condos and
shopping malls. Accommodation is in hotels and apartments and the
slopes are served by a frequent and free shuttle bus-service.

The skiing
Top 11,657ft (3554m) bottom 9,300ft (2835m)
The 1,105 acres (442 hectares) of skiing are covered by a huge 849 acres
(340 hectares) of snowmaking, giving Keystone a long season. Indeed
the whole of Keystone Mountain is covered by snow-cannon. There are
two bases for **mountain access** – Mountain House, the original village
centre, and River Run at the eastern end of the resort. This is the starting point for the longest of the lifts. Keystone has three mountains, with
the main area (Keystone Mountain) designated for intermediates, with
tree-lined trails as well as some more demanding blue runs.

More experienced skiers can ski North Peak, behind the main mountain, which offers a good choice of mogul runs and off-piste descents.
The Outback, even further back, is the newest area, opened during the
1991-2 season, offering some of the resort's most testing skiing with 70
per cent intermediate terrain and the remainder advanced. The area
also has tree-less bowl-skiing.

The skiing is not, however, a nine-to-five occupation here. With 205
acres (82 hectares) of groomed trails lit by high-pressure sodium lamps,
Keystone has North America's biggest night-skiing operation. The night

skiing takes place on Keystone Mountain and is entirely covered by snow-cannon. The Noon 'til Moon lift pass allows you to ski until 10pm.

Serious skiers will head for the East Wall, five miles (8km) up the canyon in Arapahoe Basin, owned by Keystone, which has another 490 acres of skiing. This is a separate ski area with a base lodge, but without a resort as such. It opened in 1969 and has a top lift station of 12,448ft (3795m), 27 trails and provides skiing well into June. The skiing is mainly for good intermediates to experts, with some narrow descents. In mid-winter it can be extremely cold at this high altitude. Face masks and neck warmers can be essential items of clothing here. On high wind-chill factor days we have reports of skiers being checked at the start of each lift to make sure no skin is left exposed.

In Keystone's ski area restaurants include the Summit House, offering self- and waiter- service dining during the day and in the evening for night skiers. The Outpost, near the summit of North Peak, contains two restaurants – the smart Alpenglow Stube and the lively Timber Ridge. A-Basin has a hut at the top of its Exhibition chair-lift, offering outdoor barbecues on warm spring days.

Keystone Nursery is a non-ski kindergarten for infants and upwards. Mini-Minors is the ski kindergarten for 3- to 4-year-olds and Minor's Camp is for children from five to twelve years old; both offer packages which include lifts, lunch, equipment rental and lessons. There are also teen programmes and race-training courses.

The resort

The original village centre is Mountain House, at the base of the lifts, which incorporates a ski school, kindergarten and rental shops. Keystone today is a resort without a real centre and indeed without much character. Although it is purpose-built, lift access can be inconvenient from many of the hotels and condos. Keystone's accommodation includes the luxurious lakeside Keystone Lodge, which has a swimming-pool, restaurant and fitness centre.

Mid-priced accommodation includes the Ski Tip Lodge, just outside the village, which retains some of the atmosphere of the 1860s stagecoach inn that it was. Its bedrooms have large antique beds with traditional patchwork quilts and the sitting room is wood-panelled and cosy. The Inn at Keystone, at the Nordic Centre but away from the alpine skiing, is a pleasant country inn. The disadvantage of both the Inn and the Ski Tip Lodge is their seclusion from the village and ski area, despite courtesy transport. Cheaper accommodation can be found at nearby Silverthorne, where the Alpen Hütte is recommended. A bus service operates around the village, but a hire car is useful for visiting Breckenridge and other resorts in the area.

Après-ski

Keystone Ranch is a restored ranch-house serving six-course dinners. The Bighorn Steak House in the Keystone Lodge is known for its fresh seafood. The Ski Tip Lodge offers a wholesome four-course dinner in a wood-beamed dining-room. Apart from horse- and dog-sleigh rides, most of the après-ski activities are confined to bars. The Last Chance

Saloon has live entertainment and pool tables. Snow-mobiling and skating are also offered in the village, along with 86km of cross-country trails and indoor tennis.

TOURIST OFFICE
Keystone Resort,
Box 38, CO 80435
Tel 1 303 468 4242
Fax 1 303 468 4343

TOUR OPERATORS
American Independence, Inghams,
Lotus Supertravel, Made to Measure,
Ski the American Dream, Skiworld

Killington, Vermont

ALTITUDE 1,045ft (319m)

∙∙

Good points extensive artificial snowmaking, variety of runs for all
standards, late-season skiing, tree-level skiing, facilities for
beginners and families
Bad points extremely low temperatures, weekend crowds, lack of
skiing convenience, lack of village atmosphere, limited for
non-skiers, no off-piste skiing
Linked or nearby resorts Pico (n)

Where the name Killington came from is not officially recorded. The
mountain was formerly known as Mount Pisgah, which is not, as the
locals suggest, an ancient Indian word meaning 'muddy mountain', but
the name of the mountain ridge from which Moses first spied the
Promised Land. With the colonial market town of Woodstock 20 minutes down the road, Killington is more likely to be a corruption of
Kidlington, Woodstock's Oxfordshire neighbour in England. Oscar
Wilde stayed here in 1882 and wrote in the hotel visitors' book: 'Kind
reader, if you ever come in sight of old Mount Killington, leave business, pleasure, home and friends.'

Killington Ski Area was invented by skier Preston Smith, who saw the
mountain's potential in 1954. With no fortune of his own, Smith succeeded in raising the money to open the resort in December 1958, after
three years of sleeping rough on the mountain to plan its first trails. The
original ticket booth was a converted chicken coop.

Today Killington is the biggest ski resort in Vermont. Combined with
neighbouring Pico, 10 minutes' drive away, the area offers eight mountains served by 27 lifts and 147 trails. The major disadvantage is that
there is no resort of Killington as such. Hotels, condominiums and
shopping centres straggle along the 5-mile (8km) road from the highway. Although there are hotel courtesy cars and a regular shuttle service, visitors soon learn that a car is a major asset. The main visitors to
Killington are from Boston and New York, but the resort is becoming
more and more popular with the British who come because of the relatively short flight to Boston and the reliable snow conditions.

The skiing
Top 4,220ft (1287m) bottom 1,045ft (319m)
Killington has a total of 107 trails, with an extra 40 in neighbouring Pico.
Although the resort advertises six mountains, they are, in fact, com-
pressed into a small area. Killington does, however, do some things on
a large scale: it is the proud owner of the world's biggest snowmaking
operation. Here the snow-cannon cover an incredible 40 miles (64km)

of trails and are dependent on ultra-low temperatures. Indeed temperatures of –30°F (–36°C) are not uncommon. This means snow can be easily made but skiing is an extremely unpleasant exercise. Face masks, neck warmers, boot and glove heaters are essential in order to avoid frostbite. The season is commensurably long, running from mid-October to early June.

This harsh environment is reflected in the quality of the snow. Skiing in New England is not easy. The diamond-hard pistes mean you generally need a higher standard of technique than almost anywhere else and, as in Stowe, you will usually find a better than average skiing ability on the mountain. The trails, as is common in all North American resorts, are beautifully groomed.

Snowshed, at the end of the access road, is the main **mountain access** point served by a series of chairs taking you up towards Killington Peak, Snowdon and Rams Head Mountains. The Killington Gondola, the second access point at the base of Bear Mountain, claims at three-and-a-half miles (six kilometres) to be the longest ski lift in North America. Certainly it is the most antiquated and the slowest. At times the lift queues which form at the base station are quite unacceptable. A third, more reasonable means of access to this vast area, is by triple chair from the bottom of Sunrise Mountain. The ski area is well connected and the signposting is excellent with large maps at all major points and stocks of piste maps all over the mountains.

The wide, gentle green and blue runs of Rams Head will suit beginners and intermediates, while the tougher skiing is found on Snowdon, Killington and Skye. Bear Mountain has the awesome mogul run Outer Limits, with Devil's Fiddle, Wildfire and Bear Claw all testing. But the runs are generally wide enough to make nothing seem impossible. Most of the area's skiing is on fast, cruising terrain. Dream Maker is recommended as a good, steep black and very well groomed.

Mountain restaurants

In past editions of this book the mountain restaurants have been heavily criticised. There is, in fact, a good variety of food at reasonable prices and restaurants vary between cafeteria-style and waiter-service. One reporter paid an average of $12 per day for lunch for two (a filling clam chowder soup or enormous sandwich, yoghurts, cookies and soft drink). Bear Mountain Deli is recommended for its selection of over 90 beers, the waiter-service Pegonips has a relaxed atmosphere and Peak Restaurant, on Killington Peak, is a cafeteria-style eating place. On the down side, long queues are reported at lunchtime and it can be difficult to find a seat.

Beginners and children

Video analysis is used in ski teaching here and there is a high proportion of instructors to pupils. All in all, Killington tries very hard to win over the new skiers. Reporters remark that European ski schools could learn a lot from the American attitude towards customer service, since they 'mix a sense of humour with an apparent genuine concern, so that all pupils get the most out of lessons'. Groups rarely have above eight skiers and more usually seem to take four or five pupils at a time.

The Children's Centre cares for a wide age range, from babies of 6 weeks old up to children of 12 years old; ski lessons start at 3 years old. Fresh Tracks takes children from 3 to 8 years old and reporters praise the kind and helpful staff, adding that their children received excellent tuition. The Superstars Ski School takes slightly older children from 6 to 12 years old and is highly recommended by our reporters. Children will receive individual lessons at no extra cost if there is no one else of their level.

The resort

Killington Ski Area is two-and-a-half hours' drive from Boston and five hours from New York, so weekend crowding is very much in evidence. Killington is a car-orientated resort; the accommodation is spread out over several miles, but location is not critical even if you do not have a car since there is a free shuttle bus running from the main ski areas all the way along the main road. There is no resort as such, and hotels, condominiums, shops and restaurants are scattered along the main road, with Mercedes and Jaguars parked alongside pick-up trucks and older cars. Snowshed, the main lift base area, is probably the most convenient place to stay.

Accommodation

The accommodation seems to be of a unilaterally high standard, with most of the hotels and condominiums having a hot tub, sauna, a living room with an open fire, and even a swimming-pool, as standard facilities. The Pinnacle Condominiums are close to both the Snowshed and Ramshead lift stations and are well equipped. The Mountain Green condominiums are conveniently placed for the slopes ('accommodation near enough the slopes to be able to nip back for lunch') and have a health club, a restaurant and shops. The Summit Lodge is 'extremely comfortable and very welcoming, the sort of place people go back to time and time again'. The Inn of the Six Mountains is of a high standard with a well-equipped health club. Roaring Brook Inn is well situated, with a free après-ski buffet and live entertainment at weekends. Chalet Killington, a mile from the ski lifts, is reported to be 'reasonably comfortable, with pub-style evening meals'. Chalet Salzburg is run by an Austrian couple.

Eating out

The New World Grill in the Inn of the Six Mountains offers one of Killington's best fine-dining experiences. Food is traditional American (steaks, seafood and chicken) with a French influence. Grist Mill can be crowded at weekends, but the wait is worth it. Hemingway's, a couple of miles out of town, is considered by reporters to be one of the best but most expensive, haute cuisine restaurants in northern Vermont. Reservations are essential. Goucho's Mexican Restaurant serves Tex-Mex cuisine. Charity's 1887 Saloon has a lively atmosphere and a good selection of American fare. Other recommended eating places include Casey's Caboose, Red Clover Inn and the Vermont Inn. Ppeppers is a diner-style eating place.

Après-ski

The Wobbly Barn has extremely good live acts. The Mallard's Lounge in the Grist Mill has live Country and Western music and a frozen lake outside where you can hire skates on any evening for night-time skating. Madhatters Lounge is recommended, as is McGrath's Irish Pub at the Inn at Long Trail.

The shops are fairly basic with one large supermarket and a smattering of sports shops and art and craft outlets. It is, however, worth driving to the nearby town of Rutland to look for excellent seconds at bargain prices in the Timberland Factory Outlet Store. Other non-alpine

Skiing facts: Killington

TOURIST OFFICE
Killington, Vermont 05751
Tel 1 802 422 3333
Fax 1 802 422 4391

THE RESORT
By road Boston 2½ hrs, Burlington 1½ hrs
By rail White River Junction
By air Burlington airport 1½ hrs
Visitor beds 13,638 (60% condominiums, 23% hotels, 17% guesthouses/ chalets)
Transport bus between lodging and base areas

THE SKIING
Longest run Juggernaut, 10 miles (16km) – green
Number of lifts 19
Number of trails/pistes 107 (45% easy, 20% intermediate, 35% difficult)
Total of trails/pistes 77 miles (123km)
Nursery slopes extensive area at Snowshed
Summer skiing none
Snowmaking 535 acres (214 hectares) covered

LIFT PASSES
Area pass (covers 6 mountains) $203-227 for 6 days
Day pass $41
Half-day pass $32 after 12.30pm
Beginners no free lifts
Children 50% reduction for 12 yrs and under, free for 6 yrs and under if skiing with a parent on Snowshed area
Pensioners 50% reduction for 65 yrs and over
Credit cards accepted yes

SKI SCHOOLS
Adults Killington Ski School, $22 for 2 hrs

Children Superstars Ski School, 6-12 yrs, 9.30am-3pm, $69 per day, $269 for 5 days
Private lessons $55 per hr
Special courses snowboarding, telemark
Guiding companies through ski school

CROSS-COUNTRY
Ski schools none
Loipe location and size none in Killington

CHILDCARE
Non-ski kindergarten the Children's Center (Snowshed), 6 wks-12 yrs old, 8am-4.30pm, $41 per day, $164 for 5 days, $4.75 per day extra for lunch
Ski kindergarten First Tracks at the Children's Center (Snowshed), 3-8 yrs, 8am-4.30pm, $55 per day, $218 for 5 days, $4.75 per day extra for lunch
Babysitting available through most hotels

OTHER SPORTS
Snow-mobiling, wagon rides, skating, swimming, fitness centres

WHAT'S NEW
● 2 additional quad chair-lifts
● 30% increase in snowmaking
● 8 new grooming vehicles

FOOD AND DRINK PRICES
Coffee $1, bottle of house wine $8, beer $2.75, dish of the day $8-12

TOUR OPERATORS
American Independence, Ski the American Dream, Ski Thomson, Virgin Holidays

skiing activities include skating on the Summit Lodge pond, tobogganing at the Mountain Top Inn at Chittenden, sleigh rides at the Hawk Inn
and Mountain Resort, snow-mobile rides and telemarking.

Pico 2,000ft (610m)

Pico, a 10-minute drive from Killington, is a quiet family resort best-
suited to intermediates and a world away from the big-time commercial
success of its famous neighbour. The first T-bar in America was installed
here in 1937 on Pico Mountain, which offers 2,000ft (610m) vertical of
interesting and sunny glade skiing. The main mountain access is via two
quad chairs, which take you up to the summit at 4,000ft (1220m) and
give access to a series of fairly steep black diamond pistes down the
front face as well as a meandering blue alternative. The lower flanks of
the face are served by an updated version of the original T-bar and a
variety of modern triple and quad chairs. It is a pleasant little ski area
claiming 40 trails of which 20 per cent are easy, 60 per cent intermediate and 20 per cent difficult.

The village itself is a pleasant collection of modern buildings in the
New England weather-boarded style, clustered around a pedestrian
main street. Accommodation is mainly in condominiums. A considerable number of guests stay in the lodges and inns around Killington.

TOURIST OFFICE
Sherburne Pass, Rutland, VT 05701
Tel 1 802 775 4346

TOUR OPERATORS

Lake Tahoe, California/Nevada

HEAVENLY 6,500ft (1982m)
SQUAW VALLEY 6,200FT (1890m)

••

Good points beautiful scenery, variety of skiing for all standards, large choice of nearby resorts, children's facilities, tree-level skiing, après-ski at South Lake Tahoe
Bad points no resort centre at Heavenly, lack of non-skiing activities, lack of resort atmosphere
Linked or nearby resorts Alpine Meadows (n), Boreal Ski Area (n), Diamond Peak at Ski Incline (n), Granlibakken Ski Area (n), Homewood (n), Kirkwood (n), Mount Rose/Slide Mountain (n), Northstar-at-Tahoe (n), Sierra Ski Ranch (n), Sierra Summit (n), Sugar Bowl (n), Tahoe Donner Ski Bowl (n)

Squaw Valley and Heavenly are the largest and best known of the 14 alpine skiing resorts and 7 cross-country resorts set in the mountains above the shores of Lake Tahoe. This stretch of cobalt blue water on the borders of California and Nevada justly lives up to its reputation as the second largest and most beautiful alpine lake in the world behind Lake Titicaca in Peru. Granlibakken Ski area with its two lifts is the oldest, Squaw has the toughest skiing, but it is Heavenly (it recently dropped the 'Valley' from its name) which stands out from the pack because of its stunning scenery and unusual nightlife. On one side of Monument Peak the view is of the arid vastness of the Nevada desert, on the other the lush beauty of Lake Tahoe.

Off the slopes, serenity switches to frenzy amid the green baize of the tables, the clunk of one-arm bandits in the 24-hour casinos of South Lake Tahoe on the Nevada side of the state line. At breakfast-time it is possible to glimpse the occasional bleary-eyed gambler heading for the slopes metaphorically minus his shirt, but still with a pair of skis to his name.

Squaw Valley, which hosted the 1960 Winter Olympics, has more challenging slopes above the north shore of the lake in a corner of the Sierra with a long skiing tradition. Surprisingly skis were in use here, more as a means of transport than for recreation, at least 35 years before they made their debut in the Austrian and Swiss Alps. As far back as 1856 John 'Snowshoe' Thompson, a Norwegian immigrant, was carrying the mail on skis between the mining camps in these mountains. Until the railroad was built in 1872 he was the miners' only winter link with the outside world.

The skiing

Heavenly Top 10,100ft (3079m) bottom 7,200ft (2195m)
Squaw Valley Top 9,050ft (2759m) bottom 6,200ft (1890m)

Heavenly is one of America's largest ski areas, with almost all of the skiing in the tree-line. It also has one of America's most extensive snow-making programmes, with 37 miles (59km) of terrain covered by snow-cannon. The skiing is divided between the Nevada and the Californian sides of the mountain. The Nevada face consists mainly of blue (intermediate) runs, although there is expert skiing in the Mott Canyon area, a north-facing wall with a selection of chutes through the trees. The green (easy) trails are mostly on the lower and middle slopes. The upper Californian side is mainly blue, fast cruising terrain. The most difficult skiing on the Californian side is just above the Base Lodge and on the bowl runs. Higher up the mountain there are some blacks (difficult) off Skyline Trail.

The skiing at Squaw Valley takes place on six peaks: Granite Chief, Red Dog, KT-22, Squaw, Emigrant and Broken Arrow. The area is divided into three sectors, with the lifts rather than the runs colour-graded. All the main lifts on Red Dog, KT-22 and Granite Chief are black, Squaw and Emigrant's are blue; the uphill transport to Broken Arrow is either by gondola or cable car. Intermediates will find a huge amount of skiing, with the highlight a three-mile (5km) trail from the High Camp area down to the mountain base.

Squaw's nursery slopes are in the centre of the ski area up on the mountain. The recent addition of the Papoose chair-lift behind the Children's World at Papoose is a great convenience; parents can deposit their offspring before buying their tickets and proceeding up the mountain on the Papoose chair. At Heavenly there is a mini-clinic and junior ski school.

The resorts

The ski area of Heavenly and the town of South Lake Tahoe are separate, although Tahoe Seasons Resort hotel complex is close to the lifts at the California base. Harrah's and High Sierra Casino Hotel in South Lake Tahoe are two of the bigger casino hotels, along with Caesars Tahoe, the Horizon Casino Resort and Harvey's Resort. Much of the accommodation is in condominiums. On the quieter Californian side motels are stacked side by side with little to choose between them. Station House Inn and the Timber Cover Lodge are singled out by reporters. At the Nevada base there are also condominiums.

The Squaw Creek Resort is a large ski-in ski-out complex at the base of Squaw Valley with its own restaurants, bars, fitness centre and ice rink. Squaw Valley Lodge is also close to the base lifts and the Olympic Village Inn is nearby. The Squaw Valley Inn is opposite the cable car. There are also lodges in and around Tahoe City.

Après-ski

Restaurants at South Lake Tahoe include the Sage Room at Harvey's, the Summit at Harrah's and the Edgewood Terrace restaurant. Carlos Murphy's is an Irish/Mexican restaurant, while Zachery's and Dixie's specialise in Cajun cooking. The gaming tables attract money and money attracts the top names in show business. The Tahoe region is renowned for its Vegas-like celebrity shows, although some of the big bills from television may mean little to Europeans. Turtle's has dancing and the Christiania Inn, close to the ski area, has a good atmosphere.

Glissandi at the Squaw Creek Resort is recommended for its food and the Olympic Village Inn has two restaurants. Further afield in Tahoe Vista, Captain Jon's specialises in seafood and Le Petit Pier in French cuisine. La Cheminée in Kings Beach serves nouvelle cuisine. At Homewood there is Christy Hill and the Swiss Lakewood Restaurant. The Cal-Neva Lodge in Crystal Bay has two restaurants and an oyster bar. There is dancing at Bar 1 in the Squaw Valley Mall, as well as at the Olympic Village Inn at weekends.

Squaw and Heavenly have a distinct lack of non-alpine skiing activities, with cross-country skiing, ice-fishing, skating and snow-mobiling the only other sports at Squaw and nothing at Heavenly, although snow-mobiling, ice-fishing and cross-country can all be enjoyed nearby.

TOURIST OFFICE
Heavenly Central Reservations,
PO Box 2180, Stateline, NV 89449
Tel 1 702 588 4584
Fax 1 702 588 5517

TOUR OPERATORS
Ski the American Dream

TOURIST OFFICE
Squaw Valley Ski Corporation,
Olympic Valley, CA 96146
Tel 1 916 583 6989
Fax 1 916 583 8184

TOUR OPERATORS
American Independence,
Ski the American Dream, Virgin Holidays

Mammoth Mountain, California

ALTITUDE 7,953ft (2425m)

• •

Good points runs for all standards, long ski season, large ski area, extensive snowmaking, late-season skiing, activities for non-skiers
Bad points long airport transfer, quiet après-ski, scarcity of mountain restaurants, weekend lift queues
Linked or nearby resorts June Mountain (n)

Mammoth Lakes, four miles (7km) down the road from Mammoth Mountain's main lodge, is a neat little town which supports a year-round tourist business. Although the lodge now boasts a huge sculpture of a prehistoric tusked beast, the mountain owes its name to the Spanish, who dubbed this extinct volcano the 'big mountain'. Long after the Spaniards, Jackie Collins (a non-skier) wrote one of her early blockbusters here while the rest of her family were out skiing.

Mammoth Mountain is one of the few major American ski areas still run by its founder rather than by an anonymous corporation. Dave McCoy, who set up the first lift here towards the end of the 1940s, still controls it all with his family. Most days he is out on the slopes riding lifts or punching tickets. Mammoth has multiplied somewhat since those early days and now boasts 30 lifts, all of them chairs except for two gondolas, one drag-lift and one T-bar.

The icing on the cake is the nearby June mountain ski area, 30 minutes or 22 miles (35km) away by road, rather nearer as the crow flies. The McCoys opened this up in the 1980s and today it has one state-of-the-art large cabin gondola, two detachable quads and five double chairs. The same lift ticket covers both regions.

Mammoth and June are popular with southern Californians, who head for the slopes on sunny weekends. The ski resorts lie 300 miles (480km) to the north of Los Angeles, a spectacular six-hour drive past the Mojave desert and up into the Sierra Nevada mountains. Richard Branson rates Mammoth as one of his favourite family ski destinations, which may in part explain why Virgin flies into Los Angeles. While a car is useful, an efficient shuttle bus plies to and from the ski area.

The skiing
Top 11,053ft (3370m) bottom 7,953ft (2425m)
In the 1992-3 season Mammoth had a better snow record than anywhere else in the world. Its average annual snowfall is over 27ft (8m) and it has a

large skiable area with trees growing up to about 9,000ft (2743m). Above the tree-line the skiing is of the open bowl variety. The green (easy) runs are all among the trees, as are most of the blue (intermediate) runs.

Above the trees there are five small peaks, all of which are reached by one or other of the chair-lifts. These can be tackled by intermediate skiers. Running right across the skyline from any of these peaks is the rim of the old volcano. The six-seater Gondola 2 takes you up to the highest point while, a little further to the right as you look up the mountain, the three-person Grizzly chair takes you up to the next highest point on the redoubtable Mammoth cornice. Between the two lifts there are three double diamond (very difficult) trails – Climax, Hangman's Hollow and Drop Out – while for those of a more cautious frame of mind a single diamond (difficult) trail takes you down a less forbidding gradient into Cornice Bowl.

Just over the right flank of the ridge a long twin chair takes you to another, rather lower, point from where there is a choice of three more doubles and one single diamond, or you can join the long blue trail, Number 87 (also called Road Runner), which runs all the way down from the highest point on the ridge. This starts from the top of Gondola 2. You can also turn left at the summit and again pick your place to drop off the cornice. Intermediates should not hesitate too long as the further you go the steeper the drop-off points become. All the cornice runs start on wide slopes, so a skier's choice will largely depend on snow conditions at the time. Long traverses can get you out of most of the tight spots.

Even though Mammoth is known for its sunny days and mild temperatures, the mountain does not receive its fantastic snowfalls without its share of white-outs and storms. And it is then that the many trails among the trees, quite a few of them blacks, come into their own.

There are four easy **mountain access** points into the lift system, each served by one or other of the shuttles. Mountain hosts help you find your way around. No one should miss the more gentle skiing at June Mountain. Both summits here, Rainbow and June itself, are just over 10,000ft (3049m) with trees right to the top. There are magnificent views to the more jagged peaks in the Sierras. The gondola whisks everybody up to the Meadows plateau and there are greens, blues and blacks down from the very top. This 500-acre (200-hectare) ski area is a great place to ski at weekends when Los Angelinos are crowding out Mammoth, large as it is. Both areas allow snowboards and in June there is even a special snowboarders' park.

After some very unusual late and lean snow years, both mountains installed artificial snowmaking just in time for the capricious weather to return to its old self and start throwing down overnight three-foot dumps of the white stuff. In a good year the skiing can stretch into July.

Mountain restaurants

There are few actually on the slopes. Mammoth has two and June has one on-hill snack bar. The four base areas all have cafeterias. Prices generally are reasonable, with soup and a hefty sandwich setting you back about $5, hot chocolate a dollar, beer slightly more, coffee rather less.

There is waiter-service in the pleasant Yodler, a Swiss chalet which was brought over and reconstructed plank by plank in the base area. The Mammoth Mountain Inn is also recommended. The Mountainside Grill serves breakfast, lunch and dinner and offers everything from steak and seafood to pasta and salad.

Beginners and children

There are special learn-to-ski packages for one, two or three days. Prices include lifts, lessons and equipment rental. The three-day package at Mammoth costs $182.

Children under seven years old ski free, which is a higher than average age for a ski resort, making Mammoth a more economical place than some to bring small children who ski. For children between four and six years old there is a special half- or all-day Funland programme.

Older children up to 12 years old can enroll in the Mammoth Explorers programme, which divides entrants into groups of differing abilities. For teenagers up to 17 there are ski clinics with hand-picked instructors who can cope with first-timers, snowploughers or even fast cruisers. The very young, between 6 weeks and 4 years, can be enrolled in the Mountain Inn's Small World daycare centre. Safe hands free anxious parents for a full day's skiing.

The resort

In European terms there is no resort as such. Mammoth Lakes is the nearest small town. The road from it passes a few hotels and condominiums before terminating at the main base lodge. Facing the lodge is the Mammoth Mountain Inn complex. Its three separate blocks look rather like an alpine military barracks. Inside, most of the rooms are vast and this is certainly the most convenient place to stay for keen skiers without a car. There is a choice of six main lifts just across the road.

Accommodation

There is a large number of hotels, guesthouses, apartments and rooms to be found in Mammoth Lakes, many of them with whirlpools, exercise spas and other American goodies. The Alpenhof, on the right as you leave town by the road to the mountain, is a cheerful place that looks as Tyrolean as its name suggests. Jägerhof Lodge is another, just out of town on the ski-shuttle route. The Austrian influence on the early days of American skiing is reflected in some other more economical establishments such as Holiday Haus and the Kitzbühel Lodge. The newest establishments are Sierra Lodge (a non-smoking hotel), Shilo Inn and the Quality Inn bed and breakfast. The luxury Silver Bear condos are within walking distance of the lifts. Self-caterers can shop at Von's supermarket, which sells a large variety of food, Pioneer Market (a smaller alternative) or the Gourmet Grocer.

Eating out

Mammoth Lakes comes into its own here with well over 40 restaurants, delicatessens, ice-cream parlours and pizzerias. There are six steak and seafood establishments, three Mexican restaurants, four Italian, one

Chinese and one Japanese. The Lakefront (nouvelle cuisine in a historic lodge), Natalie's and The Mogul (high-quality steaks) are among the more expensive while Goats Bar, Las Sierras and the Swiss Café are three of the least costly.

Slocums Italian and American Grill is a good place for dinner out. The Shogun is the resort's sushi bar, Roberto's offers some of the best Mexican cuisine in town, and The Good Stuff has healthy and wholesome food. Angel's has creative cooking in a cosy atmosphere.

• •

Skiing facts: Mammoth Mountain

TOURIST OFFICE
PO Box 24, Mammoth Lakes, California 93546
Tel 1 619 934 2571
Fax 1 619 934 0602

THE RESORT
By road Los Angeles 300 miles (480km)
By air Mammoth/June Lake airport 10 miles (16km)
Visitor beds 8,200 (72% apartments, 25% hotels, 3% chalets)
Transport shuttle service throughout Mammoth Lakes to the ski area

THE SKIING
Longest run Road Runner, 2½ miles (4km) – blue
Number of lifts 30
Number of trails/pistes 150 (30% easy, 40% intermediate, 30% difficult)
Total of trails/pistes over 3,500 acres (1,400 hectares)
Nursery slopes 1,000 acres (400 hectares)
Summer skiing none
Snowmaking 200 acres (80 hectares) covered

LIFT PASSES
Area pass (covers Mammoth and June Mountains) $148 for 5 days
Day pass $37
Half-day pass $27 from 12.30pm
Beginners free lifts for beginner ski school classes
Children 7-12 yrs, $74 for 5 days, free for 7 yrs and under
Pensioners free for 65 yrs and over
Credit cards accepted yes

SKI SCHOOLS
Adults Mammoth Mountain, 10am-midday and 1.30-3.30pm,

$150 for 5 days
Children Mammoth Explorers, 4-12 yrs, 10am-3.30pm, $48 per day including lunch
Private lessons $55 per hr
Special courses snowboarding, senior ski camps, advanced and mogul clinics, women's ski seminars
Guiding companies through ski school

CROSS-COUNTRY
Ski schools Tamarack Ski Center
Loipe location and size 35km of trails around the lakes

CHILDCARE
Non-ski kindergarten Small World Day Care, infants/toddlers 2½ yrs and under, $39 per day including lunch. Preschool, 2½-12 yrs, $36 per day including lunch, 8am-5pm
Ski kindergarten Small World Day Care, 4-12 yrs, $50 for half-day including lunch, 8am-12.30pm or 12.30-5pm
Babysitting list available from tourist office

OTHER SPORTS
Hot-air ballooning, snow-mobiling, dog-sledding, sleigh rides, tobogganing, tube-ing, swimming, indoor tennis, fitness centre

WHAT'S NEW
● Expanded day-care on mountain
● additional snow-cannon ● more quad lifts

FOOD AND DRINK PRICES
Coffee $.75, bottle of house wine $8, beer $2, dish of the day $6

TOUR OPERATORS
American Independence, Ski the American Dream, Virgin Holidays

• •

Après-ski

Directly after skiing the Yodler offers a good selection of cocktails, and Hof's at the base of Hut II has spiced wine and a variety of cocktails. When it comes to late-night drinking, dancing and pool-playing the scene is not so varied. It might be worth looking in on Grumpy's, the Ranch House or Gringo's, but mid-week they can be quite subdued. Whiskey Creek offers live entertainment; Rafters, Ocean Harvest and Stogie's are the other main nightspots. The pace hots up at weekends when Los Angelinos hit town.

If shopping is your kick there is plenty to choose from including a Ralph Lauren Polo factory outlet and a dozen other clothing shops. No fewer than seven hairdressers and four florists give one an idea of the requirements of skiers from Los Angeles.

Park City, Utah

ALTITUDE 6,900ft (2104m)

••

Good points extensive intermediate skiing, safe and accessible beginners' slopes, wide choice of restaurants and shops, vibrant nightlife, international clientèle, plenty of activities for non-skiers, cross-country facilities
Bad points inconvenient resort layout, limited expert terrain, uninspiring scenery
Linked or nearby resorts Deer Valley (n), Park West (n), Sundance (n)

As the crow flies, it is barely six miles from Snowbird to Park City, yet Utah's two leading resorts could hardly be more different. Where Snowbird is confined in its canyon and trapped in its purpose-built glitz, Park City sprawls along a much wider valley with little regard for convenience and none at all for land conservation. Like many of its Colorado rivals, it has artfully converted a colourful mining past into a colourful touristic present. Its focus is Main Street, home to the Wasatch Brewery, the Egyptian Theater and a host of art galleries and boutiques. Between them there are bars and more bars, too many for a single pub crawl, no matter how determined the crawler. Or so it is often claimed.

The skiing
Top 10,000ft (3049m) bottom 6,900ft (2104m)

Park City's ski area lies on rolling wooded terrain on the slopes of Jupiter Peak. Although the United States Ski Team has used the resort as its headquarters since 1973, the skiing is much less challenging than Snowbird's. This is partly because the lower altitude makes for a greater percentage of glade skiing on trails cut from the forest and partly because the slopes are less steep. Although a triple chair-lift takes skiers directly from the downtown area to the Angle Station half-way up the mountain, the best **mountain access** is from the Resort Center on the outskirts of the town. Park City is a moderately well-designed complex on three levels, with shops and cafés set around an open-air skating rink.

This area also serves as the loading point for the Silver Queen gondola, which rises directly to the Summit House restaurant in 23 minutes. From here, skiers of all grades will find suitable runs to the bottom of the resort's newest lift, the Prospector high-speed quad. The easiest is Claimjumper, a broad green (easy) boulevard curving round the mountain towards the Snow Hut restaurant. Confident intermediates will not find themselves unduly tested by Hidden Splendour, Mel's Alley, Powder Keg and Assessment, but Prospector, Single Jack, Sunnyside and Parley's Park take rather more direct routes down the mountain.

Advanced skiers have a choice of easy black runs, including The Host, Thaynes, Double Jack, Ford Country and Glory Hole, all leading into the Thaynes Canyon, a blue (intermediate) cruiser that marks the eastern boundary of the ski area. Half-way down, they can take the Motherlode chair-lift back to the Summit House or continue down to the King Consolidated chair-lift, the access point for 10 short blue runs leading into Broadway and Hot Spot. This is American skiing at its most uniform; confidence-building factory territory where it is often hard to tell one run from the next.

Those in search of adventure should take the Jupiter Access trail from the Summit House to the Jupiter chair-lift. This goes up to the top of the resort, a wind-blown ridge with a variety of ungroomed options. Shadow Ridge and Fortune Teller go straight down under the chair through sparsely wooded snowfields, but a 10-minute walk along the ridge to the east brings skiers to the top of Scott's Bowl. Alternatively they can head for Portuguese Gap, a narrow, often heavily mogulled field between trees.

A 20-minute walk along the ridge to the west leads to Jupiter Peak and the choice between the steep descent into Puma Bowl via the East Face, or back to the chair-lift via the West Face. All these runs are well worth the walk, but expert skiing in Park City is too dependent on the Jupiter chair-lift being open. When the wind gets up, as it frequently does, or the cloud closes in, the options are drastically reduced. The black (advanced) alternatives to the west of the resort are six parallel descents through aspen trees and are also prone to closure because of poor snow conditions.

Beginners can profit from a three-and-a-half-mile (five-and-a-half-kilometre) high-quality green descent from the Summit House to the Resort Center, via the top of Claimjumper, Bonanza and Sidewinder. This is broad, flat, open territory, perfect for discovering the pleasures of keeping going on beautifully groomed snow. The less experienced should avoid it late in the afternoon, when it becomes a race-track back to base as the lifts close. There is a less frenzied beginners' area at the bottom of the resort, served by the First Time and Three Kings lifts.

Mountain restaurants

The Mid Mountain restaurant, a low wooden cabin built to serve the miners in 1898 and moved to its present site in 1987, offers high-quality fast food in pleasant, light surroundings. It is open only at lunchtime whereas its rivals, the Summit House at the top of the gondola and the Snow Hut at the bottom of the Prospector high-speed quad, serve breakfast as well. Steeps, a cavernous, modern ski-in ski-out bar at the bottom of the main run back to the Resort Center, has table service at lunchtime. It is also an essential après-ski stop, with live music, happy hour prices and a party atmosphere, especially when the weather allows revellers to sit out in the sun.

Beginners and children

The Park City Ski School uses the American Teaching System as pre-scribed by the PSIA (Professional Ski Instructors of America). There are full-day and half-day adult group lessons for visitors aged 14 and over. The Mountain Experience programme takes good intermediate to advanced skiers into the high bowls on Jupiter Peak. Private lessons are also available. Beginner and early intermediates meet at the bottom of the mountain, intermediate to advanced at the Summit Ski School area at the top of the Prospector high-speed quad.

The Park City Ski School divides its programme into Youth (seven to twelve years) and Kinderschule (three to six years). The Youth programme offers group lessons on the same terms as the adult programme but the Kinderschule package includes lunch and indoor supervision. The Kinderschule Mountain Adventure is for children aged three to six who are capable of stem christies or better.

The resort

Since mining began in the mid-nineteenth century, silver to the value of $400 million has been extracted from the hills surrounding Park City. George Hearst, father of William Randolph Hearst, was one who made his fortune in the 1880s, the era of maximum prosperity. Today Park City has a permanent population of 5,800 and a reputation for being rather more than a ski resort. In recent years, its aspirations on the cultural front have been enhanced by the emergence of the Sundance Film Festival. This event, which takes place over the last 10 days in January under the patronage of Robert Redford's Sundance Institute, is now recognised as the premier showcase for American independent films that compete for prizes on the international festival circuit throughout the rest of the year. Park City also has a Foundation for the Arts and Humanities, which arranges a full programme of concerts and lectures and a City Library in the renovated Miner's Hospital.

Accommodation

The most convenient place to stay is undoubtedly the Silver King Aparthotel, a complex offering 85 units ranging from studio to penthouse. Each has a fully equipped kitchen, a wood-burning fireplace, a double-sized whirlpool bath and a washer/dryer. It also has indoor and outdoor swimming-pools, a sauna and a therapy pool. However, its greatest plus is that it is only 100 yards from the gondola station. The Prospector Square Hotel, about 15 minutes away by free shuttle bus, resembles a collection of Nissen huts and is priced accordingly, but the management is extremely welcoming and it does have a superb athletics club, with an Olympic-size indoor swimming-pool, four racquetball courts and an impressive mechanised gym. The recently refurbished Yarrow Hotel has luxurious rooms and a more central location, plus a heated outdoor swimming-pool and two hot-tubs.

Eating out

An evening on Main Street could have no more traditional a start than dinner at The Claimjumper, an all-American establishment serving portions of surf and turf and buffalo so huge that a 'wolfie bag' is the only way to clear your plate. Alex's is another popular Main Street haunt. The menu includes decidedly non-American ingredients such as frogs' legs and sweetbreads. They tend to be over-sauced but both the raw material and the cooking are good. The Ichiban Sushi and Japanese Cuisine, newly located opposite the Claimjumper, has Japanese dishes and a wide selection of fresh fish.

Après-ski

By Utah's strict Mormon standards, Park City is Sin City. This means that a degree of polite rowdiness that would be frowned upon in Snowbird is tolerated on Main Street. This is especially true at the Alamo, a low-life dive that serves as the headquarters for the Park City Rugby Club, a well-established institution that sends touring teams all over the United States and Canada. Its memorabilia share the walls with stuffed moose and elk heads, those omnipresent symbols of the Great American West. The Alamo has pool, table football, darts and occasional live music. Although it is a private club, it has relaxed approach towards sponsorship. This means that strangers ask the barman if he can find them a sponsor and he turns to the nearest drinker and asks him to oblige. He nods, you buy him a drink and you and your party are members for the evening, as Utah's idiosyncratic licensing laws require.

Cisero's Club, further up Main Street on the opposite side, is owned by a pair of musicians who use their expertise to maintain high standards for their nightly live music sessions. It, too, is a private club, so again sponsors must be found. Exceptions to this rule include Park City Billiards, a new pool hall near the Resort Center, The Shaft and the Wasatch Brew Pub at the top of Main Street. By 1.30am Main Street is as quiet as Bond Street on Christmas Day.

Main Street is also the shopping area where specialities are pottery and Indian artifacts. The Factory Stores at Park West, four miles away, is a large shopping centre selling end-of-line designer clothing.

Deer Valley 7,200ft (2195m)

This is one of the most self-consciously grand resorts in the Rockies, lying three miles to the north-east of Park City up a winding mountain road. It is a place where grooming counts, both on slopes that are meticulously smoothed and on clients who are immaculately clothed. Many are of an age at which they welcome Deer Valley's boast that uniformed employees are in place to carry skis from car to chair-lift. And many are on the kind of incomes that can buy the best that the exclusive Stein Eriksen Lodge has to offer.

TOURIST OFFICE
Deer Valley Ski Area, Park City,
Utah 84060
Tel 1 801 649 1000

TOUR OPERATORS
none

Park West 6,800ft (2073m)

At the other end of the spectrum, and indeed at the other end of Park City, there is Park West, an ugly downmarket development on the road

Skiing facts: Park City

TOURIST OFFICE
Park City Ski Area, PO Box 1630,
Park City, Utah, 84060
Tel 1 801 649 6100
Fax 1 801 649 4132

THE RESORT
By road Salt Lake City 30 miles (48km)
By air Salt Lake City International
Airport 45 mins
Visitor beds 3,410 (44%
condominiums, 37% other
accommodation, 19% hotels)
Transport free shuttle bus around town,
every 20 mins, 7.40am-1am. Main
Street trolley bus to and from The Town
lift, every 15 mins, 10am-11pm

THE SKIING
Longest run from the Summit House to
Resort Center, 3½ miles (5.6km) – green
Number of lifts 13
Number of trails/pistes 83 (17% easy,
48% intermediate, 35% difficult)
Total of trails/pistes 2,200 acres (890
hectares)
Nursery slopes 2 lifts
Summer skiing none
Snowmaking 375 acres (152 hectares)
covered

LIFT PASSES
Area pass $190 multi area voucher
book, any 5 out of 6 days (covers Park
City, Deer Valley, Alta, Brighton,
Snowbird, Solitude, Sundance, night
skiing). $180 pass (for any 5 out of 6
days) covers Park City and night skiing
Day pass $40
Half-day pass $27
Beginners no free lifts
Children 12 yrs and under, $15-18
Pensioners 65-69 yrs, $20 per day,
free for 70 yrs and over
Credit cards accepted yes

SKI SCHOOLS
Adults Park City Ski School, $38 for 4
hr day, $170 for 5 days
Children Park City Ski School Youth
School group lessons or Mountain
Experience, 7-13 yrs, $38 for 4 hr day,
$61 including lunch

Private lessons $113 for 2 hrs, $10
per additional person
Special courses ski-touring
(Interconnect off-piste 1-day adventure
from Park City to Snowbird, via
Solitude, Brighton and Alta), heli-skiing,
snow-shoeing, snowboarding
Guiding companies Utah Powderbird
Guides

CROSS-COUNTRY
Ski schools White Pine Touring, group
and private lessons available, children
and senior citizens free. Norwegian
School of Nature Life, tours in the
Wasatch and Uinta Mountains, plus
lessons and treks
Loipe location and size 19km in Park
City

CHILDCARE
Non-ski kindergarten Night Owls,
24-hour babysitting services with
trained minders
Ski kindergarten Kinderschule, 3-6 yrs,
$59 per day, 8.30am-4.30pm,
including snack, lunch, lesson, and
organised play. Kinderschule Mountain
Adventure, 3-6 yrs, $68 per day,
10am-noon and 2-4pm, including
lesson and lift pass
Babysitting Night Owls, Creative
Beginnings, Miss Billie's Kids Campus,
Professional Sitters Service, Country
Care

OTHER SPORTS
Snow-shoeing, hot-air ballooning,
skating, snow-mobiling, sleigh rides,
spectator ski jumping, indoor tennis
and racquetball, fitness centres,
swimming, night skiing (4pm-10pm)

FOOD AND DRINK PRICES
Coffee from 50c, bottle of house wine
from $10, beer $1.50, dish of the day
$9.95

TOUR OPERATORS
Activity Travel, American Independence,
Crystal, Lotus Supertravel,
Made to Measure,
Ski the American Dream

back to Salt Lake City. Because it is known as Utah's snowboarding headquarters it is particularly popular with families and itinerant workers with winter jobs in Park City. The slopes are never too busy. One reporter remarks that 'the very small number of skiers meant that even as the day progressed the condition of the slopes did not deteriorate noticeably'. Another sums it up as 'good intermediate skiing on uncrowded, well-groomed slopes'.

TOURIST OFFICE
Park West Ski Area, Park City, Utah 84060
Tel 1 801 6495400

TOUR OPERATORS
none

Sundance 6,100ft (1860m)

This small and remote resort is most famous for its owner, film star Robert Redford. But that is where the glitter ends. It is a small village of wooden buildings nestling in the trees, offering skiing mainly for intermediates, with just 4 lifts and 39 runs. Reporters recommend it for a short trip while visiting the area, rather than a longer stay.

The one mountain restaurant, the Bearclaw Cabin at the top of the Arrowhead triple chair, is an alpine-style hut with a log fire and panoramic views over the Wasatch Peaks and the Uinta Mountains. The Grill Room is recommended for evening meals in a rustic setting. It serves local specialities, which include Utah trout. The Tree Room offers more formal dining.

TOURIST OFFICE
Sundance Ski Area, Provo, Utah 84604
Tel 1 801 225 4100

TOUR OPERATORS

Snowbird, Utah

ALTITUDE 8,100ft (2468m)

••

Good points skiing convenience, efficient lift system, steep skiing, varied runs, reliable snow record, late-season skiing, off-piste skiing
Bad points unwelcoming architecture, lack of atmosphere, limited après-ski, crowded nursery slopes, limited choice of accommodation, lack of activities for non-skiers, children's facilities
Linked or nearby resorts Alta (n), Brighton (n), Solitude (n)

Snowbird and Alta, the extravagantly modern and the resolutely traditional, are separated by a mile of winding highway and a philosophical divide of continental proportions. Snowbird opened in December 1971, the brainchild of voluble Texan oil millionaire Dick Bass, who commissioned a design in his own irrepressible image. Its focus is the Cliff Lodge, a monumental 11-storey building set firmly in the centre of Little Cottonwood Canyon, 25 miles (40km) from Salt Lake City. Alta, which opened for business back in 1938, is ferocious in defence of its understated alpine village style against the intrusions of the brash interloper down the valley. Bass dreams of turning the two resorts, along with neighbouring Brighton and Solitude, into a Utah version of the Trois Vallées, served by an integrated lift system and a single lift pass. In Alta, the word is that it could happen if Salt Lake City succeeds in its bid for the 2002 Winter Olympic Games.

Between them, Snowbird and Alta provide what is arguably the best advanced skiing area in the United States. Snowbird lies at the bottom of Hidden Peak, a steep north-facing mountain, with richly varied terrain. Alta, on the slopes of Mount Baldy and Sugarloaf, is justly famous for its opportunities for dedicated powderhounds. This sector of the Wasatch Mountains receives an average of 500in (12.7m) of snow a year, compared with 300 to 325in (8 to 8.5m) in the Colorado Rockies, which allows Snowbird and Alta, along with Robert Redford's resort Sundance, to use Utah's favourite slogan, 'The Greatest Snow on Earth', at every opportunity.

The skiing
Top 11,000ft (3352m) bottom 8,100ft (2468m)
The uniformity imposed by tree-line skiing, the dominant factor in so many of America's resorts, is minimal in Snowbird. The terrain on Hidden Peak is partly wooded, partly bowls and partly chutes, a mixture that provides runs for all levels, but with a definite bias towards the expert. One less experienced reporter noted that 'the grooming was poor, causing many mogul fields to develop'. As most skiers are intermediate, the resort tries to play down the expert bias by claiming that

50 per cent of its trails are for beginners and intermediates, but there is no denying that it is the advanced skier who will profit most from this impressive mountain.

The aerial tram (cable car) is the main **mountain access** for the network of black (difficult) runs, a single blue run (intermediate), and Chips, a confidence-building three-and-a-half-mile (five-kilometre) descent back to the tram station. Turning left off Chips, after the initial few hundred yards down the ridge, provides confident skiers with a choice between Primrose Path and Silver Fox, both of which stretch all the way to the bottom. Alternatively, the Cirque Traverse gives access to Great Scott, Upper Cirque and Peruvian Cirque, single or double black diamond (expert) runs on steep but open terrain. Turning right off the ridge brings skiers to High Baldy and Peruvian Gulch, an expert loop that joins Chips a third of the way down the mountain.

It is also possible to reach the top of Hidden Peak via the Little Cloud chair-lift, the ski-off point for a second steep, sparsely wooded hillside. The easiest runs are Little Cloud and Shireen, the toughest the Gad chutes, with Regulator Johnson somewhere in between. However, all the options are black. So, too, are Barry Barry Steep, Wilbere Bowl and Wilbere Chute, three parallel expert runs on open terrain in the mid-mountain area. Dalton's Draw and Mach Schnell are formidable glade runs leading directly back to the resort.

Intermediate skiers are best served by the Gad 1 and 2 chair-lifts. The blue runs, Bassackwards and Election, wind away from the top of Gad 2 to join the Lunch Run above Snowbird's only mountain restaurant, while Bananas takes a similarly circuitous route in the opposite direction before joining Lower Bassackwards for the long return to base. Beginners take their first lessons on Chickadee, an uncomfortably busy slope between the Cliff Lodge and the Snowbird Center. They then progress to the Mid Gad and Wilbere chair-lifts, the starting points for a very limited network of gentle runs on the lower slopes. Once they have exhausted the possibilities of Big Emma, Snowbird's only decent green (intermediate) run, the choice is limited to the Bass Highway, Miner's Road and West Second South, not so much runs as convenient links to different parts of the resorts.

Mountain restaurants

Lunchtime eating on the mountain at Snowbird is extremely limited. The attractively wood-clad Mid Gad restaurant at the bottom of the Lunch Run is the only mountain eating place, although the whole resort is ski-in ski-out, which means that all restaurants are easily accessible at lunchtime.

Beginners and children

The Snowbird Ski School has 139 instructors registered with the PSIA (Professional Ski Instructors of America) out of a total of nearly 200. Programmes are provided for every ability and discipline, including specials for seniors, racers and mogul skiers. The daily Adult Super Class matches skiers of similar abilities in group lessons. The Bumps and Diamonds Workshop takes ambitious skiers onto challenging terrain while the Style Workshop concentrates on improving elegance on groomed runs.

Ninety-minute Chickadee lessons for pairs of children aged 3 and 4 provide a safe introduction to the sport. Camp Snowbird Children's Center offers a mixed programme including skiing, arts and crafts, sledding, movies and playing for children aged 3 to 12.

The resort

Officially, the heart of the resort is the Snowbird Center, the departure point for the aerial tram that carries 125 skiers to the top of Hidden Peak in eight minutes, but it is the mirrored walls of the aptly named Cliff Lodge that dominate the long, narrow sprawl of contemporary buildings and car-parking facilities. The Center consists of the Plaza Deck, an open space surrounded by limited shops on three levels. When the weather is fine, people sit on the ground drinking beer from cans, a rather uncomfortable form of conviviality that is forced on them by the absence of neighbourhood bars. Outlying buildings house condominiums and the overall impression is of a single-function resort with no alternatives for non-skiers.

Accommodation

The best accommodation in Snowbird is in the Cliff Lodge, which offers large, luxurious, if somewhat impersonal, rooms and suites with views of the mountain or the canyon. One reporter describes it as 'externally abysmal, internally comfortable and well appointed'. The top floor has a fully equipped gym, an aerobics area, outdoor lap-pool and an overheated 30-person whirlpool that is standing room only at peak times. The Lodge has extensive spa facilities. The alternatives, the Lodge at Snowbird, the Inn and Iron Blosam Lodge, have a choice of bedrooms or condominiums. Groceries can be bought at General Gritts on Level 1 at the Snowbird Center.

Eating out

When it comes to restaurants, Snowbird is limited and, for the most part, expensive. In the Aerie, on the tenth floor of the Cliff Lodge, influences range from French to Japanese, but the resulting dishes are well cooked and the wine list is rewarding. The Atrium, which rises through the Cliff's 11 floors, is more American in tone, with buffet breakfasts and lunches, while the Mexican Keyhole caters for the upmarket taco trade. Down at the Snowbird Center, the very hungry appreciate the huge portions at the Steak Pit (dinner only). More modest alternatives include Pier 49 San Francisco Sourdough Pizza in the Snowbird Center and an outpost of the Taco Bell empire, at the bottom of the Gad 1 lift (breakfast and lunch only).

Après-ski

Due to Utah's licensing laws, all Snowbird's bars are designated as private clubs and those who wish to drink in them must buy a resort membership card. The price is modest at $5 for two weeks, and each member may be accompanied by three friends. Clearly this is more a

Skiing facts: Snowbird

TOURIST OFFICE
Snowbird Ski and Summer Resort, Snowbird, Utah 84092-9000
Tel 1 801 742 2222
Fax 1 801 742 3300

THE RESORT
By road Salt Lake City 25 miles (40km)
By air Salt Lake City International Airport 40 mins
Visitor beds 1,800 (59% hotels and lodges, 41% condominiums)
Transport free shuttle bus from Gad Valley to the Snowbird Center, 8am-5pm. Free evening shuttle between the Snowbird Center and the Iron Blosam Lodge, every 30 mins, 5.30pm to 11pm

THE SKIING
Longest run Chips, 3.5 miles (5km) – blue
Number of lifts 8
Number of trails/pistes 48 (20% beginner, 30% intermediate, 50% advanced)
Total of trails/pistes 2,000 acres (809 hectares)
Nursery slopes 1 lift
Summer skiing none
Snowmaking none

LIFT PASSES
Area pass $190 Utah multi area voucher book, (covers Snowbird, Alta, Park City, Deer Valley, Solitude, Sundance, Brighton), any 5 out of 6 days. $150 pass, (covers Park City only), any 5 out of 6 days
Day pass $37 with tram, $30 without tram
Half-day pass am or pm, $30 with tram, $24 without tram
Beginners free Chickadee lift
Children 12 yrs and under, $22 with tram, $17 without tram. Half-day, am or pm, $17 with tram, $15 without tram
Pensioners 62-69 yrs as children, free for 70 yrs and over
Credit cards accepted yes

SKI SCHOOLS
Adults Snowbird Ski School, 2-5 people, $90 for 1 hr, $215 for 3 hrs, $350 for 6 hrs
Children 5-15 yrs, $60 per day including lunch, $155 for 3 days, $275 for 5 days
Private lessons $65 for 1 hr, $165 for 3 hrs, $275 for 6 hrs
Special courses snowboarding, telemark, disabled skiers, Powder Plus (on Atomic wide-bodied skis), Silver Wings (50 yrs and over), race clinics, heli-skiing, women's workshops, ski touring with the Interconnect off-piste adventure between Park City and Snowbird, via Solitude, Brighton and Alta
Guiding companies Wasatch Powderbird Guides

CROSS-COUNTRY
Ski schools nearest is Solitude Nordic Ski School
Loipe location and size nearest is Solitude Nordic Center with 16km of track

CHILDCARE
Non-ski kindergarten state-licensed Infant Center, 6 mths – 3 yrs, $39 per half-day, $45 per day
Ski kindergarten Camp Snowbird mixed programme, $27 per half-day, $35 per day, $155 for 5 days, $6 per hr (must be reserved 14 days in advance during the ski season). Chickadee ski lessons (2 children 3-4 yrs), $40 per session
Babysitting list available from all lodges

OTHER SPORTS
Climbing wall, squash, indoor tennis, racquetball

FOOD AND DRINK PRICES
Coffee $1.50, bottle of house wine $10, beer $2.50, dish of the day $5-10

TOUR OPERATORS
Activity Travel, American Independence, Crystal, Made to Measure, Ski the American Dream

bureaucratic nonsense than a deterrent, but Snowbird's bars are few and formal enough to deter all but the most enthusiastic nightlifers. Sitting in the Aerie bar until closing time at 1am is about as exciting as an insurance convention on a wet Saturday in Chicago. The Comedy Circuit, a showcase for American stand-up comics and television comedians, has replaced Snowbird's only disco.

Alta 8,500ft (2591m)

Alta's skiing is deliberately of the rugged, undergroomed variety, with many places where skiers can get the best 'shot' down the mountain. The Wildcat and Collins chair-lifts take roughly parallel routes up Mount Baldy. From Wildcat, experts ski out along Peruvian Ridge, the starting point for Punch Bowl, which one-third of the way down divides into Rock Gully and Wildcat Face, black trails in wide glades often made all the more challenging by large bumps. Intermediates can cruise back to base from the top of Collins down user-friendly Meadow and Corkscrew. Reporters recommend the cheap lift pass and lack of queues in Alta, but the transfer tow-rope separating the two main areas was 'unpleasant and tiring on the arms'.

Chic's Place is recommended as one of the best mountain restaurants in the Rockies. The Alpenglow is described by one reporter as being 'on the lines of an Austrian mountain restaurant – wooden, steamy, with long bench tables'. The Albion, however, had 'a chaotic self-service system converging on three overworked cashiers'.

Those in search of adventure head for the long, slow Germania chair-lift. This is the access point for the Greely area, with its five demanding bowls Cecret Saddle, Glory Hole, Yellow Trail, East Greely and Greely, and for the West Rustler area, with its supreme challenge, Alf's High Rustler, the awesome descent overlooking the resort. Reporters mention the confusing lift map which made Germania look like a gentle traverse when it was, in fact, 'an exposed face with howling winds', and 'many novices lost their footing, sliding downhill, with little risk of injury, but the prospect of a very tiring climb'. The Supreme chair-lift offers a choice of narrow runs in gulleys among rocks on one side and two welcoming blues, Big Dipper and Rock 'n' Roll, on the other.

Beginners may find Snowbird more attractive than Alta because its three green runs, Crooked Mile, Sunnyside and Sweet 'n' Easy, are served by three chair-lifts and well separated from the rest of the resort.

As far as architecture is concerned, Alta mixes the old with the new. The buildings are spread along the valley between twin focal points the Wildcat Ticket Building, at the bottom of Collins and Wildcat, and the Albion Ticket Building, the meeting point for the Alf Engen Ski School and the Children's Center. Alta has five privately owned lodges and four condominium complexes totalling 1,136 beds.

TOURIST OFFICE
PO Box 8007, Alta
Tel 1 801 742 3333

TOUR OPERATORS

Steamboat, Colorado

ALTITUDE 6,900ft (2104m)

••

Good points family skiing, efficient lift system, extensive
snowmaking, tree-line skiing
Bad points lack of tough runs, lack of resort charm
Linked or nearby resorts none

If you are expecting a genuine cowboy ski resort then the reality of
Steamboat comes as a shock – a purpose-built condo village dating
from the 1960s rather than the 1860s. The old town of Steamboat
Springs is 3 miles (5km) away, a 10-minute drive or half-an-hour by
shuttle bus. The resort began operating on 12 January 1963, with one
double chair on Storm Mountain. The following year Billy Kidd won
America's first ever silver medal at the Innsbruck Olympics and
returned to oversee Steamboat's development as a major US ski resort.

During the intervening three decades Steamboat has kept on
expanding. It now has 21 lifts, 100 trails and a total of 2,500 acres (1000
hectares) of ski terrain and a top lift at 10,500ft (3201m). A vast 365
acres (146 hectares) of trails are covered by artificial snowmaking.
Steamboat is less smart and less cosmopolitan than its two Colorado
counterparts, Aspen and Vail. The downtown area has a raw, western
cowboy-town atmosphere.

Stolport Airport, 3 miles (5km) away, and Yampa Valley Airport, 22
miles (35km) away, both connect with Denver International Airport.

The skiing
Top 10,500ft (3201m) bottom 6,900ft (2104m)

The skiing takes place on four intermediate mountains: Sunshine,
Storm, Christie and Thunderhead. There is some good tree-level skiing,
but little to liven up the experts; most of the trails are fairly steep, but
wide enough to suit intermediates. The main **mountain access** is by
the Silver Bullet gondola to Thunderhead, from where you can reach
Sunshine and Storm peaks. There are few green (easy) runs on the
upper slopes, although most of the resort's runs are long, wide blues
(intermediate), which are not particularly taxing. The runs from the top
of Storm Peak, High Noon on Sunshine Peak and from Heavenly Daze
to the ridge of Thunderhead are ideal for fast cruising.

Steamboat has two on-mountain eating centres, at Rendezvous
Saddle and at the top of the Thunderhead gondola, each containing a
number of restaurants. Ragnar's at Rendezvous Saddle serves a wholesome lunch in atmospheric surroundings and Western BBQ at
Thunderhead features an all-you-can-eat buffet.

The Kiddie Corral Nursery, at the bottom of the gondola, is a non-ski kindergarten for children between six months and six years. Buckaroos takes children from two-and-a-half to three-and-a-half years old; a one-hour private lesson (even for the youngest) is included in the daily package. Sundance Kids is for skiing children of three-and-a-half years and over. There is an enormous variety of other programmes offered, including special classes for teenagers, learn-to-ski weekends, race-training and powder lessons. You can also learn to telemark and snowboard, and the resort runs women's ski seminars and a programme for handicapped skiers. The Steamboat Ski Touring Center has 30km of cross-country trails along Fish Creek and on Rabbit Ears Pass.

The resort

Steamboat itself is a functional, modern village of multi-storey condominiums and hotels surrounding the main lifts. The old town of Steamboat Springs has cowboy origins, but is not as attractive as some ('rather moth-eaten and dowdy'); the main road bisects the whole town and loses it any form of pedestrian appeal. Steamboat's major upmarket hotel is the Sheraton Steamboat Resort in the ski village centre and close to the gondola. The Ptarmigan Inn is also comfortable and well positioned. The Holiday Inn offers medium-priced accommodation one mile from the ski area. The Harbor Hotel is in the old town of Steamboat Springs and is furnished with 'antique-style furniture and Victorian wallpaper coverings'. The Alpiner in Steamboat Springs is a good-value Bavarian-style inn. There are over a dozen good condominium buildings from which to choose.

Après-ski

L'Apogée is a smart downtown restaurant serving French cuisine. In the ski resort, Cipriani's in the basement of the Thunderhead Lodge provides northern Italian fare, and Mattie Silks is recommended for its puddings. Hazie's at Thunderhead Lodge is a good spot for dinner. It specialises in American cuisine and involves a gondola ride. The Sheraton has Remington's. For après-ski the Inferno, Dos Amigos, the Tugboat Saloon, Buddy's Run and Steamin' Jacks bars are all popular. Downtown, the Old Town Pub is one of the busiest nightspots, as is the Red Dog Saloon. BW3 has live music and Gorky Park has live gypsy music and a Russian theme with 27 different vodkas served. Snowcat and snow-mobile excursions are also available. Other sports include ice-driving, hot-air ballooning, bungee-jumping, sleigh rides, bob-sleigh, dog-sledding, ice-fishing, skating, tennis, handball, racquetball and a hot-springs pool in town.

TOURIST OFFICE
Steamboat Ski Corporation, 2305 Mt Werner Circle,
Steamboat Springs, CO 80487
Tel 1 303 879 6111
Fax 1 303 879 7844

TOUR OPERATORS
Activity Travel, American Independence,
Crystal, Enterprise, Lotus Supertravel,
Ski the American Dream, Ski Thomson

Stowe, Vermont

ALTITUDE 1,300ft (396m)

....

Good points variety of restaurants, tough runs, New England
ambience, extensive snowmaking,cross-country facilities, children's
facilities, tree-level skiing
Bad points weekend lift queues, distance from village to ski slopes
Linked or nearby resorts Smuggler's Notch (l)

Picture red barns, weatherboarded houses, an attractive main street, a
white steepled church, old coaching inns peopled by wealthy
Bostonians and you will have a very clear image of Stowe. The usual
giant shopping malls, hamburger joints and neon signs are all pleasingly
absent from the 200-year-old village.

Skiers began to come here from Manhattan and Boston in the late
1930s, and the first lift opened in 1937. Today Stowe has 10 lifts and 45
trails cut through the woods, covering more than 378 acres (152
hectares). The ski area is seven miles (11km) away from the village centre, and although there are regular shuttle buses, a car is a distinct
advantage. Boston is three-and-a-half hours away by road and makes an
interesting day-trip.

The skiing

Top 3,650ft (1113m) bottom 1,300ft (396m)

If you can ski the Front Four at Stowe, you can ski anywhere. Goat,
National, Starr and Liftline are double black diamond (expert) runs
equal to the steepest runs in Europe's top resorts. Skiers have to
learn to cope with the additional problems of what here they call
'frozen granular patches' and we call ice, for most of the winter, in
numbingly low temperatures. Consequently, the standard of skier
found in Stowe is higher than almost anywhere in the United States.
Apart from the big four trails, the ski terrain is best suited to intermediate cruising, with Gondolier being a fine example of the best of this
type of run.

Stowe is home to Vermont's highest mountain, Mount Mansfield,
with **mountain access** by high-speed gondola. A total of 10 lifts serve
the ski area, although at peak season the lift queues can make even
Verbier look inviting. Because of this an early-morning start is a necessity. At weekends the locals will be up on the first lift and finish skiing
before 10am, when the queues can become unacceptable.

Cross-country skiers are well catered for in Stowe, with four interconnected ski centres and the largest groomed trail network in the
USA. The kindergarten takes children from two months to three years
old and the Children's Learning Centre takes 3- to 12-year-olds.

The resort

Accommodation in Stowe is an easy choice between modern American hotels and over-the-top New England inns, torn from a Laura Ashley catalogue carelessly left on a Cotswolds hillside near Moreton-in-the-Marsh. Ye Olde England Inne is a lot more comfortable than the average English pub. Topnotch is a hotel with condos and indoor tennis courts, and Ten Acres Lodge is a lovingly restored 1840s farmhouse. The Green Mountain Inn, with four-poster beds and stripped wooden floors, is the old coaching inn in the village centre, which affords the best location. Stoweflake Resort is a resort within a resort, with a choice of straightforward bedrooms or your own separate house in the grounds. Trapp Family Lodge, four miles (six kilometres) out of town, is where the real Trapp Family Singers, immortalised in *The Sound of Music*, came to live after fleeing Salzburg in 1938. The lodge, rebuilt after a fire in the 1980s, is a cross-country resort with easy access to the alpine ski area of Mount Mansfield.

Après-ski

Stowe has a good selection of restaurants. Winfield's in the Snowflake is recommended for fish, Copperfields at Ye Olde England Inne serves game and seafood, the Salzburg Inn offers typical alpine dishes and HH Bingham's is reachable on skis at the end of a gentle run. Later on, the main attractions are the live bands at the Rusty Nail and BK Clark's.

TOURIST OFFICE
PO Box 1320, Stowe, Vermont
Tel 1 802 253 7321
Fax 1 253 2159

TOUR OPERATORS
Ski the American Dream, American Independence,
Ski Thomson, Virgin Holidays

Smuggler's Notch, Vermont 1,001ft (305m)

The resort gained its name when the pass was used for the illicit passage of goods to and from Canada before the War of Independence. It was not until the 1930s that it became a ski resort. Today it is one of the best family skiing resorts in North America, and indeed won the Family Ski Resort of the Year Award given by the US *Family Circle* magazine. Our reporters give the resort glowing reports. The village has a compact centre, comprising condominium buildings and some hotels. The skiing is mainly for intermediates, with 56 trails on three interconnected mountains: Madonna, Morse and Sterling. You can ski over the back of Sterling to Stowe.

TOURIST OFFICE
Smugglers Notch, Vermont 05464
Tel 1 802 644 8851

TOUR OPERATORS

Taos, New Mexico

ALTITUDE 9,207ft (2807m)

••

Good points choice of restaurants, extensive difficult skiing, off-piste skiing, cultural activities in Taos town, tree-level skiing, excellent ski school
Bad points skiing convenience from Taos town, poorly linked runs, remote ski area
Linked or nearby resorts none

Taos Ski Valley is a curious mixture of chalet and cactus, set in the arid New Mexican desert. The ski resort with its alpine architecture is situated up in the Carson National Forest 20 miles (32km) from the town of Taos, a straggle of authentic adobe and utilitarian concrete, which provides the only break in the desert scenery. The fact that it was two Europeans who discovered the area near the old mining town of Twinings may explain this dichotomy. Ernie Blake, a German-born Swiss, planted the seeds of a ski resort here in 1955. A year later, Jean Mayer, a French racer, set up the ski school and the St Bernard hotel. What they created was an alpine-style village on a mountain top in the middle of the United States.

The skiing
Top 11,819ft (3603m) bottom 9,207ft (2807m)
Much of the skiing is difficult and timid intermediates are not immediately inspired with confidence. Al's Run, the steep mogul field beneath the main chair (also the main **mountain access**), is not encouraging on first sight. A sign at the bottom of the lifts reads: 'Don't panic! You are looking at ⅛₀th of Taos Ski Valley. We have many easy runs too.' Indeed, Taos does have slopes for lower levels, although the terrain is rated overall 51 per cent expert. The tree-line stretches to the top of the mountain, with most of the runs carved out of the woods. From the main ridge there are green (easy) routes back to base and the groomed blue (intermediate) runs give access to some tougher options. Several black (difficult) trails are left ungroomed, enabling experts to tackle everything from moguls to powder. Toughest of all are the chutes off the High Traverse.

Taos' out-of-bounds (off-piste) skiing starts at the top of Chairlift 2, with a 20-minute hike carrying skis along the Highline Ridge. This gives access to some short and fairly easy chutes. More energetic skiers can make an hour-long trek up Kachina Peak. Safety is paramount and groups (singles not allowed) have to sign themselves out before 2pm.

For those who are not yet at this stage, the Ernie Blake Ski School offers Learn-to-Ski-Better packages, which include full-board accommodation, a lift pass and instruction. The ski school has an outstanding reputation. Bébékare is for babies from six weeks to one year old, Kinderkare for one- and two-year-olds, Kinderkäfig is the ski kindergarten, and Junior Elite is for children between seven and twelve years old.

The resort
The accommodation choice is between staying in the Taos Ski Valley or in Taos town, a 30-minute drive away. The town is the more culturally attractive proposition, as well as offering a wider choice of restaurants and hotels, but is less convenient for the skiing. Beds are quick to fill up in the Ski Valley, especially at the original St Bernard hotel. Other Ski Valley accommodation includes Hotel Edelweiss, Thunderbird Lodge and Chalets and the Kandahar Condominiums. The luxurious Taos Inn has cosy bedrooms, each with its own fireplace. The Quail Ridge Inn, on the road to the Ski Valley, has indoor tennis and racquetball courts. Katchina Lodge is a beautifully decorated adobe-style building. The Sagebrush Inn, on the road to Santa Fe, is moderately priced. Even cheaper is Chile Azul, a former artists' residence and studio, and there is a large range of motel accommodation.

Après-ski
The varied eating places include Doc Martin's, in the Taos Inn, for south-western dishes and seafood. The Sagebrush Inn offers American specialities, the Brett House in Ski Valley Road has lamb and seafood. Others include Tim's Stray Dog, a cantina-style bar with Tex-Mex cooking, and the popular Rhoda's Restaurant.

Après-ski starts at the Martini Tree Bar and goes on to the St Bernard, the Edelweiss and the Thunderbird bars. The Sagebrush has dancing to live Country and Western music and the Adobe Bar in the Taos Inn is popular. Live entertainment is available on certain nights at the Kachina Lodge and at Ogelvie's Bar and Grill on the main plaza. The craft shops and art galleries offer plenty of scope for browsers.

TOURIST OFFICE
PO Box 85, Taos Ski Valley, NM 87525
Tel 1 505 776 2291
Fax 1 505 776 8591

TOUR OPERATORS
American Independence , Ski Scott Dunn

Telluride, Colorado

ALTITUDE 8,725ft (2660m)

••

Good points tough runs, wide variety of intermediate terrain, tree-line skiing, beautiful scenery, lack of lift queues, resort-level snow, authentic old town
Bad points difficult resort access, lack of activities for non-skiers, purpose-built village at base area out of keeping with town
Linked or nearby resorts Purgatory-Durango (n)

Telluride is an atmospheric old mining town at the end of a remote and beautiful box-canyon with a colourful and epic history, and a spectacular back-drop of the mighty and desolate Don Juans. Reborn as a cult ski resort, it became the haunt of hippies from California who retreated here in the early 1970s just as the first proper ski-lifts were being installed, and stayed on. It is they who have recently protested against the radical changes being made in an attempt to transform this picturesque old town into America's number one ski resort.

Telluride is deeply divided over the route it is taking into the twenty-first century, in particular the issue of its new ski villages. Should it remain funky and old-fashioned, or pander to progress? To a large extent that decision has already been taken, and the new Mountain Village is rapidly taking shape. Wealthy businessmen and celebrities have been buying up property and land, and the locals and visitors now fear Telluride could take on the commercial glitz of Aspen, though its remoteness may prevent this happening.

The skiing
Top 11,890ft (3625m) bottom 8,725ft (2660m)
Mountain access is via either the Coonskin or the Oak Street lifts. Telluride has the reputation for being 'steep and deep', which should not put off beginners and intermediates. Skiers using Chair 10 on Sunshine Peak, for example, can only access easy terrain. If they turn right at the top above San Joaquin Village, their options are Double Cabin, Bridges and Galloping Goose, all wide, smooth and gentle green (easy) runs. In the other direction Sundance, a mild blue (intermediate), is almost as benign. But the principal skiing is divided between Gorrono Basin and Telluride Face. The Face is dominated by double-black (very difficult), black (difficult) or testing blue bump runs, some of which are steep enough to be intimidating. However, Telluride has a welcome policy of grooming one side or the other of half-a-dozen of these runs. Thus, those who want to hit the bumps on Plunge, for example, can do so, while skiers who like their steep runs to be smooth can ski the same run, but stick to the groomed section.

Intermediates will enthuse about See for Ever, a long, quite steep but not difficult, blue trail with outstanding scenery, including a wonderful view of the Lasal mountain range almost 100 miles (169km) away in Utah. Many of the runs on the Face have dramatic glimpses of Telluride's old town spread-eagled below, where there are two base facilities: Coonskin, where Lift 7 returns you to mid-mountain, or Oak Street, where Lift 8 links with Lift 9 to bring you back to Gold Hill and the Gorrono Basin area. Here one large network of mainly blue trails is centred on Lifts 2, 3 and 4, and another based on lift 5. There is an extensive 'extreme' area on the lower section of Gold Hill reached from Lift 6, which will provide Telluride with what will arguably be some of the most dramatic tree-line skiing in the Rockies.

The new San Joaquin Bowl lift will access Little Rose chute, Dynamo, Electra, Buzz's Glade and Happy Thought, which until now could only be reached properly by hiking up the mountain. Another new lift at Prospect Bowl will provide substantial intermediate terrain on Bald Mountain and in Palmyra Basin, eventually almost doubling the size of the ski terrain.

Mountain restaurants
The Gorrono Ranch Restaurant, reached via Lifts 3 and 4, specialises in ranch-style Western cooking, barbecues, and salads. With its large sun terrace, this is the main meeting point at lunchtime. Next door, the Gorrono Ranch Saloon is a good-value eating place for soups and chilli. Giuseppe's at the top of Lift 9 is a small, European-style lunch spot with spectacular scenery. South-Western regional cooking is available at the Cactus Café in the Mountain Village. At the bottom of Lifts 1 and 10, the Day Lodge restaurant specialises in 'deli' sandwiches, soups, salads and burgers. Evangeline's in the Mountain Village serves Cajun/Creole cuisine. The Alpenglow Restaurant combines South-Western and alpine cuisine. You can get salads, soups, sandwiches and light meals at the Sundance, and The Plunge serves grills.

Beginners and children
The ski school has over 80 instructors and a solid reputaton for being friendly and relaxed, but at the same time effective in its teaching methods. You can sign up for lessons at the Coonskin, Gorrono and Mountain Village offices. Private lessons are available by the hour or for a whole day, including guided tours. There is also a free guided tour each morning lasting about 90 minutes. Skiers can join speciality clinics such as 'steep and deep', moguls, snowboarding, telemarking, racing and video analysis. Group instruction is available for children between 3 and 12 years old.

The resort
The old town has the air of a Wild-West film set. Indeed the main street, lined with colourful old timber bars, restaurants and shops, looks structurally much the same as it must have done when Butch Cassidy robbed the San Miguel Valley Bank in 1889 to launch his criminal career. The 'New' Sheridan Hotel, celebrating its centenary in 1995, still dominates

Colorado Avenue, along with the Court House, the Sheridan Opera House and an extraordinary contraption parked nearby called the Galloping Goose. This is a bizarre hybrid van/railway engine, used in the 1950s in a final and fruitless attempt to keep the unprofitable Rio Grande railway running. Ajax Mountain and Telluride Peak, part of the massive San Juan range, tower above the town like a theatrical back-cloth, giving it an almost surreal beauty. As well as the new mountain village at the base of the main ski area there are plans for further devel-opment at the top of Lifts 3 and 7, to be known as St Sophia.

Although a gondola for skiers and pedestrians linking the new vil-lage with the old town is due to open this winter, the anti-expansionist lobby is grateful that the new mountain village cannot be seen from downtown Telluride.

Accommodation

The big choice is between staying in the old town and the new village. Most reporters suggest that unless easy ski access is an absolute prior-ity, the new village should be avoided. In town, the New Sheridan is a haven of genuine faded Victoriana revamped to a suitable standard of en-suite finery. On a smaller scale, there is Dahl Haus, once a miners' boarding house. The Doral is a luxury hotel in the new village that had staffing problems in its first year; its big plus is a vast and superbly equipped spa and sports complex. Bed-and-breakfast options include the Alpine Inn, in town. Pennington's at the Mountain Village is one of the more comfortable but more expensive. Other accommodation includes the Ice House Lodge in the old town and Lulu City condomini-ums in the new. The Skyline Guest Ranch in the old town has good food and excellent views of the Wilsons. The Viking Suites are reported to offer simple accommodation, and are well-situated near the Coonskin lift. Self-caterers can buy supplies from a choice of two well-stocked supermarkets and two good bakeries.

Eating out

There is a wide selection of smart restaurants as well as a choice of more reasonably priced diners. La Marmotte has French cuisine, the PowderHouse, specialising in crab legs and prime rib, is rated by many as the best in town, as well as one of the most expensive. Good-value eating places include Floradoras for all-American food, the Roma for Italian cuisine, and the more basic Downstairs Deli-Diner.

Après-ski

One World Bar has live music, a lively atmosphere and serves snacks. If you want a smokey Wild-West bar room experience, try a game of pool in the Last Dollar saloon. The Roma Bar was once one of the wildest saloons in town and still retains its 1860 bar. The boisterous San Juan Brewing Company, located in the old Rio Grande Southern Railroad Depot on the banks of the San Miguel River, offers fresh food and home-brewed beers. The Bear Creek Saloon has live music, and O'Bannons is cheap and cheerful.

Purgatory-Durango 8,793ft (2663m)

This is the closest resort to Telluride, but is many miles apart in style and atmosphere. Instead of the technical and designer ski suits of their neighbours, skiers at Purgatory tend to dress a lot less glamorously. The resort handbook suggests: 'Ski wear should keep you warm and comfortable regardless of style or flair.'

The town of Durango, with its skiing at Purgatory 25 miles away, was formerly a railroad hub in the late nineteenth century. Purgatory

Skiing facts: Telluride

TOURIST OFFICE
PO Box 453, Telluride, CO 81435
Tel 1 303 728 3041
Fax 1 303 728 4475

THE RESORT
By road Montrose 65 miles (104km),
Denver 330 miles (528km)
By rail Grand Junction 127 miles
(203km)
By air Telluride airport 15 mins
Visitor beds 4,055 (hotels and
apartments – no breakdown available)
Transport free shuttle bus in town and
to the Telluride Mountain Village Resort

THE SKIING
Longest run See Forever, 2.85 miles
(5km) – blue
Number of lifts 10
Number of trails/pistes 62 (21% easy,
47% intermediate, 32% difficult)
Total of trails/pistes 1,050 acres (420
hectares)
Nursery slopes 2 lifts
Summer skiing none
Snowmaking 155 acres (62 hectares)
covered

LIFT PASSES
Area pass (covers Telluride Face,
Gorrono Basin and Sunshine Peak)
$204 for 6 out of 7 days
Day pass $39
Half-day pass $30 after 9am
Beginners no free lifts
Children 6-12 yrs, $132 for 6 days, free
for 6 yrs and under
Pensioners women 65 yrs and over,
men 69 yrs and over, $23 per day. Free
for 70 yrs and over
Credit cards accepted yes

SKI SCHOOLS
Adults The Telluride Ski School,
10.20am-1pm or 1.20-4pm,
$35 for a half-day
Children Snowstar (3-5 yrs), Telstar (6-
12 yrs), 9am-4pm, $225 for 5 days
including lunch. Teen Club (13-18 yrs),
special dates only
Private lessons $65 per hr
Special courses snowboarding, telemark
Guiding companies Telluride Outside

CROSS-COUNTRY
Ski schools Telluride Nordic
Association
Loipe location and size 50km at the
Telluride Nordic Centre

CHILDCARE
Non-ski kindergarten Village Nursery:
infant care, 2-12 mths, 8.30am-4pm,
$40 per day; toddler care, 1-3 yrs,
8.30am-4pm, $35 per day
Ski kindergarten Snowstar, 3-5 yrs,
9am-4pm, $50 per day including lunch
and instruction, $225 for 5 days
Babysitting through the Village Nursery

OTHER SPORTS
Heli-skiing, hot-air ballooning,
snow-mobiling, snow-shoeing, skating,
sleigh rides, climbing wall, swimming,
fitness centres, ice-climbing

WHAT'S NEW
● Eight-passenger gondola will
link the town of Telluride to the
Mountain Village

FOOD AND DRINK PRICES
Coffee $1, bottle of house wine $10-
14, beer $2.50, dish of the day $9-15

TOUR OPERATORS
Activity Travel, American Independence,
Lotus Supertravel, Ski Discovery, Ski
the American Dream, Skiworld

opened to skiers in 1965 and has now grown to include 9 chair-lifts, 70 trails, and a ski area of 675 acres (270 hectares). Purgatory Village Center is the slope-side village. The accommodation here comprises the Purgatory Village Hotel, the Best Western Lodge and a handful of self-catering condominiums.

Purgatory's skiing is for all standards but the resort is particularly renowned for The Legends, 150 acres of expert terrain reportedly as steep as 35° in places, but still groomed by an automated piste-basher. There is also some worthwhile tree-level skiing as well as a series of challenging chutes. Family ski facilities are particularly good with a special 36-acre (15- hectare) Family Ski Zone and a separate adventure park for young children. Teddy Bear Ski Camp is for skiers aged three-and-a-half years and over, and there is a choice of four non-ski kindergartens. Harris Park is the main intermediate area, and a popular expert trail is Pandemonium, which takes you steeply back down to the base area. Recommended off-piste descents include the back of the Snag run.

TOURIST OFFICE
1 Skier Place, Durango, CO 81301
Tel 1 303 247 9000
Fax 1 303 385 7989

TOUR OPERATORS
Lotus Supertravel

Vail, Colorado

ALTITUDE 8,200ft (2500m)

••

Good points resort ambience, easy introduction to powder skiing, mixed ability groups, children's ski area, efficient lift system, well-marked runs, ski school, large ski area, resort charm, beginners facilities
Bad points lack of steep terrain, homogenised skiing, high-priced accommodation
Linked or nearby resorts Beaver Creek (n) – *see separate chapter*

If you have never skied in North America then you must go to Vail and to its smart, and no longer so little sister resort, Beaver Creek. Regardless of your standard of skiing, no matter whether you hail from Manchester, Madrid or Miami, this is where you should begin skiing in the United States. That is not necessarily to say that the Vail Valley offers the best skiing in the United States, or even in Colorado, but it is some of the best developed; a slick commercial operation as far as lifts, the ski area and accommodation go, in a beautiful setting which serves Europeans as a staging post between the Alps and the Rockies.

For all that, the first-time visitor to the States who has learned his skiing in the Tyrol before progressing to the Trois Vallées will be astonished by the fact that, in the land where big is beautiful, the skiing in the USA is, in comparison, small-scale.

Consider that the Trois Vallées has 200 lifts, Val d'Isère and Tignes a total of 102, and even a more modest area like Kitzbühel has 61. It comes as a shock to discover therefore that Vail, which together with Beaver Creek is unquestionably the biggest resort in terms of ski area in the USA, has only 24.

The ski terrain of Vail was shaped, according to legend, back in the mid-1880s when settlers and miners forced the peaceful Ute Indians from their tribal lands. In retaliation they adopted a scorched earth policy. They started spite fires which cleared the mountainside of trees and thereby created its celebrated powder snow Back Bowls.

Whatever the truth of it, ski fanatic Peter Siebert saw the potential in 1962 to create not a wholly American but a European-style resort here. Within a year there were three lifts, eight ski instructors, and a $5 lift pass. Today the resort employs 800 teachers at peak times and runs an efficient lift system which is geared on paper to cope with 35,000 skiers an hour. The old two-lane track to the highland sheep pastures is now an interstate freeway.

In the early days Vail could cater for 300 visitors in basic conditions. Now it can put up more than 32,000 in hotels and condos. Yet, despite the number of skiers in a relatively small area, the lift system is efficient, with Vail having more detachable quad chair-lifts than anywhere else in the world. Lift lines are organised with a firm but polite precision unheard of in the Alps. The lines of waiting skiers group in fours and alternate into position under the guidance of a lift marshal, with lone skiers being channelled in through a feeder lane to make up incomplete fours. Never is a chair permitted to go up empty.

Euro-style pushing is greeted with vociferous disbelief and the politeness of your fellow skiers is completely overwhelming. Consequently, even on the busiest of weekends, lift queues are generally bearable in length and fast-moving. However, the main Vista Bahn Express gets very busy at high season and is best avoided during the main morning rush-hour. The other bottleneck is the Orient Express chair-lift, although problems here have been alleviated by the introduction of a new triple chair in Sun Up Bowl.

The skiing
Top 11,450ft (3491m) bottom 8,200ft (2500m)

Vail's skiing is typical of most in America, with gentle and well-marked trails cut through the trees and perfectly groomed slopes, making the terrain ideal for beginners to intermediates. Most of the advanced skiing in Vail is on the higher slopes at the eastern end of the resort. The Back Bowls, on the blind side of the mountain from the resort, have an awesome reputation for fine powder. They are unpisted, and when conditions are right they certainly offer some extraordinary deep-snow skiing. But the Back Bowls are, in general, not steep, save for certain optional pitches, and provide a good introduction to powder.

The skiing is basically divided into two areas: the wooded front face with its series of trails which criss-cross the mountain from above East Vail through to Cascade Village, and on the far side the Back Bowls.

Mountain access from Vail to the front face is firstly by the Vista Bahn Express lift from Vail Village, which whisks you up to Mid Vail, a sunny plateau tucked between Summit Elevation and Wildwood. The alternative routes are via the Lionshead gondola and Born Free Express lifts. At peak holiday times wise skiers can work their way up and eastward from Cascade Village lift, or in the opposite direction from the eastern end of the resort via the Golden Peak lift. The valley lifts can be very busy from 9.30am to 11am, so start early or late. One reporter suggested skiing the upper half of the mountain early and the lower half later in the day.

The runs down the front face start along a ridge made up of three peaks: The Far East, Summit Elevation and Wildwood. All provide you with over 3,000ft (900m) of vertical – not bad by American standards.

The beauty of the skiing in Vail is that a group of different standards can all ski together. The trails are so cut through the strands of spruce and aspen that for every advanced run there is an alternative intermediate or easy trail to the same lift station. Expert skiers will head immediately for North-east Bowl between Far East and Summit where Blue Ox, Highline and Roger's Run are all testing double black diamond (expert) runs. The Northwoods Express lift takes you up to Summit from Roger's. Here you can head down to Mid Vail and work your way westwards via the Hunky Dory lift for Kangaroo Cornice, Look Ma and Challenge. Less confident skiers will be able to ski almost everywhere by the gentlest of green (easy) trails. Game Creek Bowl has a series of easy but satisfying intermediate trails. Lost Boy run is particularly recommended as a confidence-building cruise.

For longer runs the most satisfying options are those that drop from Eagle's Nest Ridge all the way down to the resort. The most direct of these, from the top of the Avanti lift, is used as a Women's World Cup downhill course. There are various easier alternatives to the two steepish runs down to the Vail Village lift stations, and it is not difficult to ski back to any part of the resort. On the eastern side of Mid Vail most of the runs home converge into Riva Ridge. Flapjack, followed by Riva Ridge from the top of the Highline Chair to the resort itself, is, at four-and-a-half miles, Vail's longest run.

On the far side of the mountain lie the Back Bowls, only open when snow cover is sufficient, and which offer as near an equivalent to off-piste skiing as is allowed in most of US resorts. Around 64 per cent of the skiing here, on what is the south-facing side of the ridge and reached from almost any point along it, is rather unjustly classified as advanced. Despite the size of the bowls, fresh powder does not last long here and it is the early bird after a big snowfall who will get the best of it.

In the beginning there was just one lift, the High Noon chair, which returns skiers around 2,000ft (600m) back up to the ridge between Sun Down and Sun Up bowls which each offer about 10 named runs including Wow and Headwall. In the nature of bowl-shaped ski areas there is a wide range of orientation and snow conditions, though the bowls are generally sunny. The last places to be tracked involve a lot of traversing for only short sections of steeper skiing before you end up on the Sun Down and Sun Up catwalks which feed all skiers in the bowl into the High Noon lift. The steepest and most interesting runs are close to the lift on the eastern side of Sun Down Bowl.

To the east the high-speed Orient Express lift, taking you up near the Far East, has opened up the vast area usually referred to as China Bowl, although the uneven undulations of the mountain naturally subdivide the zone into five identifiable areas: the main bowl, China, with the chair up its eastern flank; Siberia; Inner Mongolia and Outer Mongolia to the east –the most distant corners of Vail's ski area, served by a short linking Mongolia drag-lift which takes you up to the top of the ski area at 11,450ft (3490m)– and dainty little Tea Cup Bowl, tucked away between China and Sun Up, with just three named runs – Morning Thunder, Red Zineger and Emperor's Choice. This extension now provides some of the best and most varied skiing in the Back Bowls.

A new triple chair from Yonder in Sun Up now takes skiers across to Jade Glade in China Bowl. This adds 120 acres (48 hectares) of skiing and you can hop on the West Wall lift, a two-way surface lift which allows skiers to reach either the expanded Two Elk Restaurant at the Far East or Tea Cup Bowl. This reduces queuing time for the Orient Express, which can be a bottleneck when conditions are good. Another new drag-lift, the Wapiti (the Indian word for elk), takes you back up to

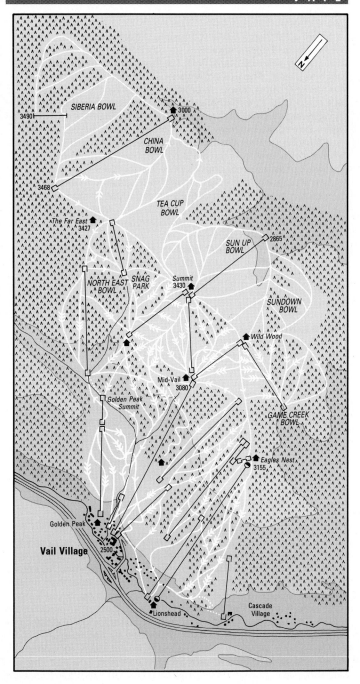

SIBERIA BOWL

3490

CHINA
BOWL

3000

3468

TEA CUP
BOWL

3427
The Far East

SUN UP
BOWL

2865

NORTH EAST
BOWL

SNAG
PARK

Summit
3430

SUNDOWN
BOWL

Wild Wood

Mid-Vail
3080

Golden Peak
Summit

GAME CREEK
BOWL

Eagles Nest
3155

Golden Peak

Vail Village

2500

Lionshead

Cascade
Village

Two Elk Restaurant from Upper West Poppy Fields in China Bowl.

Silk Road is a very gentle run making a huge tour to the east of the bowls sector. Poppy Fields is a groomed blue (intermediate) piste through the heart of China Bowl for those who find the powder too tough to handle. The western slopes of China are not quite such go-as-you-please territory. Rocks and cliffs around Dragon's Teeth have to be negotiated with care. The biggest and steepest slopes are Jade Glade and the mighty Genghis Khan, which is easier than it looks from the Orient Express lift, but tough enough to raise most adrenalin levels.

It must be said that the international hype generated about the Back Bowls is considerable. In the finest powder conditions the skiing here is glorious, but at any other time you may find the slopes just don't live up to their reputation. There is really very little variation in the terrain and the newcomer will spend a considerable amount of time poring over his lift map trying to work out whether he is on Après Vous, Cow Face or Chicken Yard. Indeed, cynics would argue that the names are the best bit of the Back Bowls.

Vail is no Jackson Hole or Chamonix, but then nor does it pretend to be. Vail is a resort for all standards, especially beginners and intermediates. It has great, though not too steep powder skiing but one can't help getting a niggling feeling that it is all, like the whole area, slightly homogenised.

Mountain restaurants

Two Elk Restaurant at the Far East has undergone a major expansion and now has 700 seats as well as an outdoor barbecue in good weather conditions. It has a baked potato bar, salad bar and a pasta bar. There are seven up-mountain restaurants in all and four ski-by food stands, including the Wine Stube and the Cook Shack at Mid Vail, which both have waiter-service. The former serves ethnic dishes and the latter American cuisine. Booking is advisable at the Cook Shack. Wildwood Shelter, at the top of Chair 3, offers health-food specialities, and Wok'n'Roll Express is a ski-by pagoda serving Chinese chicken and fried rice. Two Elk has done much to improve mountain eating as, until recently, on-slope restaurants were not Vail's strongest point, offering little variety. An alternative is to go down to resort level, which is easy to reach and is where good eating abounds at reasonable prices.

Beginners and children

The Vail Ski School has a formidable reputation as one of the best in the world. Certainly, with 800 instructors at peak times, it is the biggest. The whole American philosophy of ski teaching is refreshing and never more so than in Vail. The emphasis is on having fun, rather than, at least in the early stages of tuition, seeking stylistic perfection. If you learned your basic skiing in Austria or Switzerland, do not be surprised to be told on Day One that you ski with your legs far too close together and 'If you're having fun, tell the world about it and start hollerin''.

The school meets at seven locations in the valley including Vail Village and Lionshead, and uses SyberVision video as a teaching aid. Skiers look at a split-screen television and can compare their technique to that of a role model. Reporters who have taken lessons here appear boundless in their praise both for the teaching methods and the cheerful enthusiasm and friendliness of the teachers.

Vail's children's ski school is the best in the USA, according to the American *Family* magazine. Families are well catered for on the mountain with designated Slow Skiing areas. Persistent and reckless speedsters are liable to forfeit their lift ticket. There are two children's ski centres, at Golden Peak and at Lionshead, and an enclosed 15-acre (6-hectare) area around Fort Whippersnapper on Golden Peak. Here children can experience 'ski-through adventures', a touch of Disneyland on skis with a dragon's lair, silver mine, look-out tower, post office, jail, saloon serving hot chocolate on cold days, and an Indian village.

The resort

Vail Village was Bavarian in architectural design. Post-Tyrolean would be a more realistic description of the attractive collection of wood-clad buildings which lend themselves to the environment, albeit they are positioned on the edge of Interstate 70. With a tree-line that rises over 10,000ft (3048m), the mountains are tame and generally reminiscent of Austria with a touch of the Cairngorm range.

Lesson One for the Euroskier is that there are no hazardous drives up a series of icy hairpin bends to reach most US resorts. With Denver's Stapleton Airport at 1800m, you don't have to climb dramatically to reach the ski areas. Vail is situated west of the Continental Divide, which is good for snowfall, sometimes too good, and even though a freeway cuts through the pass, it can be blocked for short periods. If you have bothered to come all this way, take a stretched limo from the airport and settle back in your seat to enjoy the 90-minute ride. It is time to discover that the American ski experience is not just about skiing, but an all-encompassing winter holiday.

The village itself is Austrian in appearance with a distinct lack of Wild West atmosphere. If you want the raw gold-mining experience you must look towards Breckenridge or Telluride. Instead, the emphasis on gasthofs, *Weinstubel*, *Wedel* courses, and *glühwein* is symptomatic of a region which believes that sophistication comes from Europe. In fact, modern skiing has as many nineteenth-century roots buried in the USA as in Europe and, for the country which invented the chair-lift, apeing the Alps must always be a mistake. Nevertheless, the result is a resort with few rivals in popularity.

The resort stretches for more than a mile from East Vail, westwards through Vail Village, and on to Lionshead and Cascade Village in the direction of Avon and Beaver Creek. The whole, generally pleasing, conurbation is sandwiched between the freeway and the foot of the Gore mountains. Vail Village is the heart of it all, a collection of wood-clad buildings beside the Gore Creek. It has all the trappings of an upmarket alpine village, with lavish window displays in exclusive shops. The Lodge at Vail and other luxury hotels and condominiums are to be found here. The focal point is a photogenic central clock tower. The centre is pedestrianised. Free buses run every few minutes between the different parts of Vail from approximately 6am to 2am. Parking is not

Skiing facts: Vail

TOURIST OFFICE
PO Box 7, Vail, CO 81658
Tel 1 1000 303 476
Fax 1 6008 303

THE RESORT
By road 100 miles west of Denver, Interstate West to Vail Village
By rail Glenwood Springs 45 minutes
By air Eagle County Airport 45 minutes. Denver airport 90 minutes
Visitor beds 32,100 (50% hotels, 40% condominiums, 5% guesthouses, 5% chalets)
Transport complimentary bus between Vail and Beaver Creek runs from 6am to 2am

THE SKIING
Longest run Flapjack to Riva Ridge, 4.5 miles (blue/green – intermediate at the top, beginner at the bottom)
Number of lifts 24
Number of trails/pistes 121 (front side 32% beginner, 36% intermediate, 32% advanced. Back Bowls 36% intermediate, 64% advanced)
Total of trails/pistes 3,992 acres (1596 hectares)
Nursery slopes at Golden Peak with 2 lifts and a 15 acre ski-through adventure area, and at Lionshead
Summer skiing none
Snowmaking 297 acres (120 hectares) covered

LIFT PASSES
Area pass (covers Beaver Creek) $234 for 6 days
Day pass $42
Half-day pass $37 after midday
Beginners no free lifts
Children 30% reduction up to 12 yrs
Pensioners $32 per day for 65-69 yrs, free for 70 yrs and over
Credit cards accepted yes

SKI SCHOOLS
Adults Vail Ski School (at Lionshead and at Golden Peak), $50 for 1 day, $70-92 for 1 day including lifts, $211-251 for 3 days including lifts
Children Vail Ski School (at Lionshead and at Golden Peak), 3-12 yrs, $64 per day including lesson, lifts and lunch
Private lessons $85 per hr for 1-5 persons. $355 per day for 1-5 persons
Special courses snowboarding, telemark, ski courses for women
Guiding companies Colorado Heli-ski

CROSS-COUNTRY
Ski school at Golden Peak, base of Chair 12
Loipe location and size Strawberry Park Nordic Skiing Center and a 32km track in McCoy Park

CHILDCARE
Non-ski kindergarten Small World Play School Nursery at Golden Peak, 2 mths-6 yrs, 8am-4.30pm, $50 per day including lunch
Ski kindergarten 3-6 yrs: $40 for half-day, $64 per day including lesson, lifts and lunch. 6-12 yrs: $50 per day, $64 per day including lifts
Babysitting list available from most lodges

OTHER SPORTS
Heli-skiing, hot-air ballooning, snow-mobiling, skating, bob-sleigh, dog-sledding, indoor tennis, swimming, fitness centres and exercise rooms

WHAT'S NEW
● Triple chair-lift in the Back Bowls, 2 surface lifts in China Bowl, children's surface lift at Golden Peak ● Two Elk Restaurant expanded by 200 seats
● 2 new hotels under construction
● plans afoot for Peach Bowl and Super Bowl extensions to the Back Bowls

FOOD AND DRINK PRICES
Coffee $1, bottle of house wine $10-14, beer $1.50-2.00, dish of the day $9-14

TOUR OPERATORS
Ski the American Dream, Activity Travel, American Independence, Bladon Lines,Crystal,Enterprise,Inghams, Lotus Supertravel,Neilson,Ski Equipe, Ski Thomson, Ski Val, Skiworld, Ski Discovery

always easy and a car is not really necessary. Lionshead, half-a-mile to the west, has now become a second centre to Vail, with equally good mountain access. Much of the accommodation is here.

Accommodation

The elegant Lodge at Vail, owned by Orient Express Hotels Inc, is close to the Vista Bahn Express lift and centrally located in Vail Village. It is recommended for those looking for luxury. The Westin has spacious rooms and free access to all the fitness facilities at the adjoining Cascade Club. The Chateau Vail Holiday Inn is built in traditional Colorado inn style and is centrally situated in town. The more basic Vail Village Inn is also well placed, close to the Vista Bahn Express lift. Most of the cheaper accommodation is found outside Vail centre and includes Roost Lodge, a family-run lodge, and the Days Inn, both in West Vail.

If you are self-catering in one of the many condominiums (Vail Village Condominiums are the most centrally located), Safeway is one mile out of Vail's centre in West Vail and is the biggest and most reasonably priced supermarket. The smaller supermarkets in town are generally more expensive.

Eating out

The choice of restaurants in Vail is comprehensive. The bistro-style Sweet Basil has New American cuisine and Ostello serves Italian food. Wild Flower in the Lodge at Vail and Chanticler at Lionshead are considered the most luxurious. Try the Uptown Grill at Lionshead for excellent South-Western cuisine. Blue's serves good-value Italian fare. The Hub Cap Brewery is all-American. The Saloon at Minturn, a five-mile taxi ride, has a great evening atmosphere. At the Minturn Country Club you can cook your own steaks and seafood. Boca's, also in Minturn, specialises in beef. The 4 Eagle Ranch, 12 miles to the west, serves cowboy dinners and there is a good range of ethnic eating places including Mexican, Cajun, Thai, Japanese, Moroccan and Chinese. Vegetarians are well catered for in Vail, with a choice of salads and pasta at almost all restaurants. Casual eating places include Cassidy's Hole in the Wall in Avon, an authentic Western saloon serving South-Western specialities and hickory-smoked barbecues. Café Arlberg in the Lodge at Vail is more expensive, but has a good atmosphere and good food. The dozen or so fast-food joints include the ubiquitous McDonald's.

Après-ski

Vendetta's and the Red Lion are among the main après-ski meeting places. Sheika's attracts a slightly more mature set than the other bars. Cyrano's and Nick's are the best discos and the Altitude Club is also recommended by reporters. Minimum age rules in clubs (usually 21) tend to be strictly enforced. There are cinemas and art galleries, as well as Vail's fascinating museum on the history of skiing. Other sports facilities include heli-skiing, hot-air ballooning, snow-mobiling, skating at the Dobson Ice Arena, dog-sledding, bob-sledding, snow-shoeing, sleigh rides, ice hockey, eight indoor tennis courts, and three fitness centres. There are no public swimming-pools but some hotels have their own.

Whistler and Blackcomb, BC

ALTITUDE 2,214ft (675m)

••

Good points skiing for all standards, long ski season, extensive off-piste skiing, ideal for family skiing, tough runs
Bad points low temperatures, lack of sunshine, heavy weekend and high-season queues
Linked or nearby resorts Whistler Creek (I)

Combine the best of North American skiing – an efficient lift system, beautifully groomed slopes, friendly and helpful resort staff – with the best of European skiing – a big vertical drop, plenty of varied runs and challenging off-piste skiing – and the result is Whistler/Blackcomb. Apart from a low number of sunny days and bone-achingly cold weather, with temperatures at times low enough to make frost-bite a common occurrence, it is hard to find fault with Whistler and the adjacent Blackcomb resort and mountain. America's *Snow Country* magazine voted it North America's number one resort for 1992-3, edging Vail out of its traditional number one slot.

Whistler was originally known as Alta Lake, a wild and beautiful area north of Vancouver, accessible only by train or on horseback. Minerals were first mined here in 1901 and the timber industry moved in four years later. By 1915 the first lodge had been built to house holiday-makers who came here for the fishing. The first road to Whistler was completed in the 1950s, but it was not until 10 years later that people started to come to the area for skiing weekends using the handful of gas-driven drag-lifts. At the beginning of the 1979-80 season, Whistler finally took off as a major ski resort when the new purpose-built village was linked to the growing ski area on Whistler Mountain. Neighbouring Blackcomb Mountain opened up as a ski area the same year. Over the next two years around 200 million Canadian dollars were invested in the resorts and mountains, turning them into a world-class ski area.

For years the image of this premier Pacific Rim resort has been plagued by rivalry between the two opposing camps of Whistler and Blackcomb. Neither would see fit to mention the other in its publicity, thus halving the size in the eyes of the world of what essentially is one resort. Today they have almost buried the hatchet to manage a joint international marketing operation. Here you will find two of North America's biggest vertical drops, an ultra modern lift system and endless trails and bowls serving skiers of every standard. The pedestrianised villages (separated by the main road) are just two hours from Vancouver and attract a truly international clientèle. Thirty per cent of the skiers are Japanese, and the rest an eclectic selection of Americans, Australians and Europeans.

The skiing
Top 7,495ft (2284m) bottom 2,214ft (675m)

Mountain access to Whistler is on the Whistler Village gondola and to Blackcomb on the Wizard Express quad. Queuing can be a problem at weekends (particularly after a fresh snowfall) because of the resort's proximity to Vancouver. The two mountains are linked via a low traverse from Blackcomb Mountain to the bottom of the Whistler Village gondola (accessed via the short Magic chair if setting out from the base). Skiers wanting to go in the opposite direction take the Fitzsimmons triple chair up to a point a couple of hundred metres above the Blackcomb base area. The alternative is to walk between the two, which takes 10 minutes. Whistler and Blackcomb share some of the most varied skiing to be found in one area. Together they offer glaciers, steep chutes, wide open bowls and miles of tree-line skiing.

Skiers will always argue about which is the best mountain – Whistler or Blackcomb. The truth is that they both have excellent marked runs for all standards and it is only the off-piste which differs. At Blackcomb you will find as good fast cruising runs as you will at Whistler, but you will also experience some steep off-piste couloirs and stunningly beautiful glacier skiing.

At Blackcomb there is smooth and easy skiing on runs such as the green (easy) Jersey Cream and Crystal Road. Ridge Runner and Blue Line are good, fast blue (intermediate) runs. Rendezvous Restaurant is the mid-point of the mountain to which many of the lifts come back and where fast blue runs like Wishbone and Springboard begin. Cruiser and School Marm are good, fast runs back down to the village. Overbite, a single diamond black (difficult) run, often has monster-sized moguls. A whole series of tricky couloirs are easily accessed from the Blue Line run which starts at the top of Horstman Glacier. Sylvain Saudan, the Swiss extreme skier, has given his first and second names to two double black diamond (very difficult) runs here. Both are steep and narrow descents through the rocks, which are only possible when there is plenty of snow. They in turn give access to Jersey Cream Bowl, a wonderfully steep open slope. Pakalolo is another extremely difficult gully off the same ridge, which brings you out in the blue Glacier Drive beneath the Glacier Express lift.

This quad chair, new for the 1992-3 season, takes skiers up to the Blackcomb and Horstman Glacier areas and gives access to two T-bars and the summer skiing. Blackcomb Glacier has a very long blue run which starts from the top of Showcase T-bar and goes all the way around the outside perimeters of the ski area. The scenery at the top section of the run is stunning, wide open, and there is often fresh, ungroomed powder to ski through down the long, gentle slope. The next section continues through the trees, and the run finishes in the main part of the ski area where it joins Honeycomb and Zig Zag.

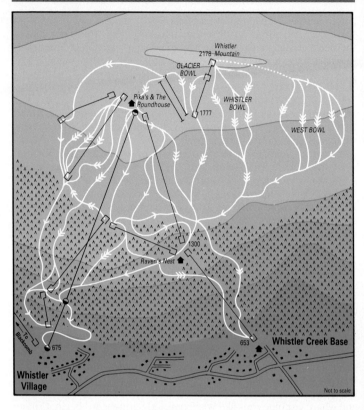

The Seventh Heaven area, a wide open face above the tree-line, is transformed into a mighty powder field after a snowfall. Southern Comfort, Panorama and Cloud 9 are easy blues served by the Seventh Heaven detachable quad, which takes you up to Horstman Hut at 7,494ft (2285m). Xhiggy's Meadow is a more demanding black alternative. This part of the mountain is particularly exposed and bleak when the weather closes in. Even on a warm, sunny day, you may need to put on a hat and neck-warmer at this point.

The mid-section of the mountain is made up of a series of tree runs of varying difficulty (but mainly advanced), which bisect the front face. These are served by two quads and two triples. Gearjammer, Undercut, Freefall, Black Magic and Sorcerer are all challenging blacks together with the top half of the longer Stoker. Cruiser is the blue alternative, which takes you all the way down to Blackcomb Base.

Whistler also has good, fast cruising runs and gentle greens, but it is best known for its endlessly challenging bowl skiing. There are two base areas to Whistler: Whistler Village itself, and Whistler Creek, two miles down the valley. The two-stage Whistler Village gondola is the main artery of Whistler Mountain. It takes you first to Olympic Station where the children's and beginners' ski area is based. The second stage brings

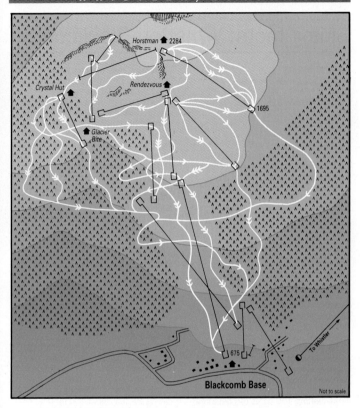

you to Pika's and the Roundhouse at the top of the tree-line. The short T-bar run drops down to the base of Peak Chair, which gives access to the bowls off the front and back faces for which Whistler Mountain is so justly famous. Because of the high risk of avalanche danger, some or all of the bowls are frequently closed by the ski patrol.

From the summit, a long blue run, Burnt Stew Trail, winds gently all the way round the mountain to the north into Symphony Bowl: a long easy powder field. The trail hugs the perimeter of the ski area, bringing you down to the bottom of Blue or Green chair for the return ride to Pika's. Beyond Symphony, and reached by an off-piste hike from the top of Burnt Stew, are the open slopes of Piccolo, Flute and Singing Pass. From the summit, in the opposite direction, Highway 86, another long blue run, again skirts the perimeter fence before joining Franz's, a long exciting blue, which takes you down to Whistler Creek base. Alternatively you can carry on across Franz's and take the Redline Express quad back up to Pika's. A strong bonus point for Whistler Mountain is that, by taking either of the perimeter trails, any intermediate skier has a chance to experience the whole mountain without having to tackle slopes beyond his or her capabilities.

The front face bowls are all black, and some of them very black

Skiing facts: Whistler/Blackcomb

TOURIST OFFICE
4010 Whistler Way, Whistler,
BC V0N 1B4
Tel 1 604 932 3928
Fax 1 604 932 7231

THE RESORT
By road Vancouver 2 hrs
By rail North Vancouver station 2½hrs
By air frequent coach service between
Vancouver airport and the resorts.
Visitor beds 2,945 (52% hotels, 41%
apartments, 6% hostels)
Transport free bus service operates
around Whistler/Blackcomb. Whistler
Creek to Whistler Village, $1.25 for
adults, $1 for children, free for under 5 yrs

THE SKIING
Longest run Burnt Stew
Trail-Sidewinder-Olympic, 7 miles
(11km) – blue/green
Number of lifts 28
Number of trails/pistes 200 (20%
beginner, 55% intermediate, 25%
expert)
Total of trails/pistes 3,657 acres
(1480 hectares)
Nursery slopes 2 baby-lifts
Summer skiing mid-June–August, on
Blackcomb and Horstman Glaciers
Snowmaking 100 acres (40 hectares)
covered on Whistler Mountain

LIFT PASSES
Area pass $234 for 6-day dual
mountain pass
Day pass $42 one mountain only, $44
dual mountain pass
Half-day pass Whistler $35, Blackcomb
$34, afternoon only
Beginners no free lifts
Children 7-12 yrs, Whistler $18 per
day, Blackcomb $19 per day, $99 for
6-day dual mountain pass. 13-18 yrs,
Whistler $33 per day, Blackcomb $34
per day, $204 for 6-day dual mountain
pass. Free for 6 yrs and under
Pensioners over 65 yrs, Whistler and
Blackcomb both $30 per day,
Credit cards accepted yes

SKI SCHOOLS
Adults Whistler Mountain Ski School,
$32 per day, Blackcomb Ski School,
$33 per day, Ski Esprit dual mountain
guiding/instruction, $155 for 3 days

Children 12 yrs and over as adults.
Kids Kamp Devo programme (14-16
yrs) for advanced skiers
Private lessons Whistler Mountain $63
per hr, Blackcomb Mountain $65 per hr
Special courses women's programme,
heli-skiing, snowboarding, Ski Esprit,
Dave Murray race clinics and summer
ski camp, freestyle, bumps clinics
Guiding companies Whistler Alpine
Guides Bureau

CROSS-COUNTRY
Ski schools through ski schools
Loipe location and size 22km at Lost
Lake, beginner trails around golf course

CHILDCARE
Non-ski kindergarten Chateau Whistler
and Delta Mountain Inn, both all ages,
24 hrs per day, 7 days a week, $7-9 per
hr. Whistler Fairway $6 per hr, Kids
Kamp at Blackcomb, 18 mths to 3 yrs,
$50 per day
Ski kindergarten Ski Scamps on
Whistler Mountain, 2-12 yrs, $51 per
day, $230 for 5 days, including
lessons, equipment and lunch. Wee
Wizard at the Kids Kamp on Blackcomb
Mountain, 3-4 yrs, $45 for 5 hr day,
$185 for 3 days, including 3 hrs of
skiing per day, lunch and rentals. Kids
Kamp, 4-12 yrs, $36.50 for 5 hr day,
including 4 hrs of skiing and rentals
Babysitting Chateau Whistler and Delta
Mountain Inn. List from other hotels

OTHER SPORTS
Snow-shoeing, swimming, sleigh rides,
indoor tennis, skating, parapente,
snow-mobiling, fitness centres

WHAT'S NEW
● Glacier Express high-speed quad
chair on Blackcomb Mountain

FOOD AND DRINK PRICES
Coffee 80c-$1.40, bottle of house wine
$10-18, beer $4.25, dish of the day $6

TOUR OPERATORS
Activity Travel, All Canada Travel and
Holidays, Canada Air Holidays, Crystal,
Frontier Ski, Jean Stanford Ski Holidays,
Made to Measure, Neilson,
Ski the American Dream, Ski Tal,
Lotus Supertravel

indeed. Everything depends on the weather conditions and it is vitally important to heed avalanche warnings and not to attempt any closed run. Cockalorum and Stephan's, an icy chute with rocks on either side, give dramatic entry to West Bowl and on down to Highway 86. Whistler Bowl, straight off the top, provides extraordinary powder skiing either back to the base of Peak chair via Shale Slope or Left Hook, or down through Doom and Gloom and Grand Finale to Highway 86. To the left of the local piste map, Glacier Bowl provides the ultimate double black diamond challenges in The Saddle and The Cirque.

From the base of Peak chairs, parallel T-bars surmount the ridge leading down into Harmony Bowl, a long blue run to the bottom of Blue Chair. Harmony Horseshoes, Boomer Bowl and Gun Barrel are all interesting black variations. The mid-section of the mountain below Pika's is given over to a huge network of trails through the trees. A number of good runs start from the top of Black Chair, including Jimmy's Joker, which is a mogully black diamond run, the black Wild Card and Raven, the blues Orange Peel and Ptarmigan, and wide beginner run Papoose. Bear Cub is another gentle and wide green slope ideal for near-beginners. Bear Paw is a good black run down to Olympic Station and the Dave Murray Downhill is a very long black run named after a local ski teacher. Goat's Gully is an ungroomed run going straight down under Orange Chair and often having variable snow conditions.

Mountain restaurants

At Whistler we have found a mountain eating place that is unique outside Japan. Pika's is one of the two large restaurants in the hub of the ski area on Whistler Mountain comprises two restaurants and a sushi bar. On Blackcomb Mountain, Rendezvous Restaurant is the most popular place with a choice of self- or waiter-service, and there is also a choice of the Horstman Hut, Crystal Hut and Glacier Bite. Reporters find the general standard of catering here to be high.

Beginners and children

A huge range of ski classes are available on Whistler and Blackcomb mountains. Whistler's ski school offers ski lessons for beginners and upwards, with the addition of bumps and powder clinics, all-day cruiser classes and race clinics. Blackcomb's school has class lessons for all standards: the intermediates' Cruiser Club, Superclass for fast-paced skiing on double black diamond runs, and a range of workshops for bumps, powder, snowboarding and parallel perfection. The two ski schools combine to provide their unique Ski Esprit programme, which gives skiers the best of both mountains, together with video analysis, fun races and après-ski activities. As well as this, Dave Murray Ski Camps include recreational ski courses, race techniques and snowboarding.

Both Whistler and Blackcomb mountains have their own ski and non-ski kindergartens. Blackcomb's Kids Kamp is at the bottom of the mountain at the base of the Magic chair-lift, adjacent to the main Wizard Express lift. It provides childminding for children from 18 months and tuition for skiers from 3 to 13 years. Whistler has Ski Scamps beside the Olympic Station and next to the nursery slopes. Children are taken up here and brought back down again for hand-over to and from parents at Whistler Village and Whistler Creek village bases.

The resorts

Whistler and Blackcomb are separated by a main road and a 10-minute walk. Whistler is the bigger, livelier, and more developed village with most of the accommodation. Blackcomb, based around the Chateau Whistler Resort luxury hotel, is the quieter, more sophisticated option. Both villages are built in a modern, yet attractive style with painted wood-clad buildings and pedestrian-only centres. The resorts call their architecture 'European style', although we have never seen this style in the Alps. The centre of Whistler is a square filled with shops, bars and restaurants. A regular bus service operates between the villages and also to Whistler Creek, a small base area with accommodation at the bottom of the Quicksilver Express chair.

Accommodation

The landmark hotel of the area is the ski-in ski-out Chateau Whistler Resort, a 100-year-old crenellated building with sumptuous interior and exclusive shops on its ground floor. It contains a health club, two ball-rooms and two restaurants. The many bed-and-breakfast lodges are a cost-conscious option, including Carney's Cottage, Chalet Beau Séjour, Brio House and Chalet Luise. Whistler Chalets offer a variety of enormous condominiums right on the slopes. The Mountainside Lodge is also comfortable. Other hotels include the Glacier Lodge and Nancy Greene Lodge in Whistler centre. Self-caterers can shop for provisions at Nester's Shop Easy and the Grocery Store.

Eating out

The Trattoria di Umberto at Whistler serves excellent Italian food in an upmarket, but cosy, atmosphere. Monk's Grill in Blackcomb is a large brasserie-style place offering ribs, steaks, hamburgers, and salads. The Keg is a lively place serving American food. Other popular places include Chez Joel's and Fiorentyna's. To satisfy its large Japanese clientèle, the sushi restaurants include Sushi Village at the Westbrook Whistler Hotel and Teppan Village at the Delta Mountain Inn. The Wildflower, at the Chateau Whistler Resort, is open for Sunday brunch. Other recommended eating places are Subway Stop, Settebello's and Misty Mountain Pizza for good-value food. For a more upmarket eating experience, try the Val d'Isère, La Rua, Il Caminetto, and Les Deux Gros.

Après-ski

The Longhorn Saloon is undoubtedly the most popular after-skiing place in town. Garfinkel's, Peter's Underground, the Mad Café, Citta, Merlin's at Blackcomb and Mogul's are also popular meeting places. Later in the evening the crowd moves over to Black's pub, and Nancy's Lounge. The Savage Beagle Club has dancing, as do Buffalo Bill's and Tommy's Africa, the latter outside the village centres but on the bus route. Each of these offers the all-Canadian après-ski experience bars with dancing in an atmosphere which is sedate by European standards.

Andorra

Resorts include Arcalis, Arinsal, El Tarter, Grau Roig, Pal,
Pas de la Casa, Soldeu

The Principality of Andorra has a reputation for 'supermarket skiing', a duty-free, basic way for the rowdier end of the British market to don their anoraks, reverse their baseball caps, give the art of snowploughing a try and ' 'ere we go, 'ere we go' long into the night. While the price of a ski trip to Andorra is comparable with those to Romania or Bulgaria, the quality of equipment and facilities is years ahead. But Andorra is stuck with a 'budget skiing' tag which is a liability for an area trying to attract new winter visitors.

Bordered by Spain to the south and west, and by France to the north and east, this small chunk of the Pyrenees only covers 464km². Architecturally disappointing, with most of the buildings being concrete eyesores, Andorra still derives most of its income from the summer season when visitors come from all over Europe to take advantage of its tax-free status. Even this is misleading because, while alcohol, perfumes and tobacco are still astonishingly cheap, other prices seem similar to those in Britain. However, bargains can be found, especially in ski wear and equipment, but they are the exception rather than the rule.

Andorra is a good starting point for those new to skiing. It is cheap, friendly, and has a uniformly excellent standard of ski instruction and hire equipment. It is neither quaint, nor does it provide testing skiing for the expert, especially off-piste, but with a careful choice of resort and an expectation level to match your purse, anyone from a good intermediate downwards can have an enjoyable and rewarding trip.

Pas de la Casa
ALTITUDE 2095m (6,872ft)
The first impression of Pas de la Casa is of a Gibraltar-on-ice, a view endorsed by the architecture, which is both modern and ugly. Supermarket shelves are piled high with incredibly cheap alcohol, much of it produced locally. This includes the local 'port' available in two-litre plastic bottles for a handful of pesetas. Like the gallons of sangria consumed daily in the many bars, Pas de la Casa is an unassuming kind of a place, with a warm glow to it. The village does not feel like a resort which owes its total existence to skiing. As most of the money is made in summer, winter here has a more relaxed air than many of the more traditional alpine ski resorts.

The skiing
Top 2818m (9,243ft) bottom 2091m (6,860ft)
The skiing in the Pas de la Casa and Grau Roig area, except for three

small runs, is based within two main bowls dominated by the peak of Cabanettes at 2818m. Served by a modern and very efficient lift system and well-groomed slopes, the area is covered by a network of snow-cannon, used whenever temperatures permit, to supplement the sometimes insufficient supplies from Mother Nature.

Most of the lifts start in the same area at the top end of the resort, leading to a variety of slopes for differing abilities. On the right-hand side is the La Solana drag-lift taking hardier beginners to the gentle blue (easy) and green (beginner) runs, which go back to the resort at the end of the Tubs and Directa 2 runs. However, it is to the main Pas de la Casa quad chair that most people head, for the option of skiing either the Pas de la Casa or Groi Roig valleys. The queues for this lift can look quite long, especially at peak times, but the wait is rarely more than 10 minutes. From there, the most popular route is to return to Pas de la Casa via Directa 1. This is supposedly black (difficult) at the top, descending almost immediately into a red (intermediate) run. The only real problem is the steepish gully at the beginning, and the mixed abilities of other skiers.

A better option for those who have progressed beyond the snow-plough is to turn right at the top of the chair. From here you can either choose the black FIS run, with its optional mogul field, or meander down the enjoyable Gavatxa red run, taking you past the towers of the Radio des Vallées Andorra broadcasting station and back down to the resort. Return to the top is via the four-seater Costa Rodona chair-lift.

Next to the Pas de la Casa quad is the surprisingly under-used Coll Blanc double chair. Even at peak times, this lift is virtually empty, even though it takes you almost to the same point. From here the gentle Llac red takes you back to the resort or you can traverse towards the Coll dels Isards series of lifts. These, set apart and rather higher than the main lifts, give access to the nursery slopes and to Isard, a long, flat, rather unrewarding blue, much loved by fledgling bombers.

Instead of returning immediately to the resort from the top of the Pas de la Casa, Costa Rodona or Coll Blanc lifts, another option is to head over the ridge to the runs into Grau Roig. On the whole less congested than the Pas de la Casa side, with fewer beginner classes, these form an enjoyable, but somewhat monotonous network of runs. The exceptions are the Antenes and Pastora blacks.

Down in Grau Roig, with its one hotel, one apartment block and one restaurant, there are two more areas to be skied. The Del Cubil chair-lift gives access to five red and two blue runs; all are fairly short and the snow tends to disappear quickly here. The better alternative is to catch the drag up to Mont Malus, from where two short but very enjoyable reds or (snow permitting) the black Granota take you back to Grau Roig.

Mountain restaurants in the Pas de la Casa/Grau Roig area are cheap and functional. With the possible exception of the Refugi de Pessons below Mont Malus, they are little more than snack bars.

Andorra attracts a much higher than average percentage of beginners to its slopes and this is reflected in the high quality of tuition at the ski school. Classes are kept to a maximum of 12 people and the standard of English spoken is praised by several reporters, possibly due to the large amount of BASI-qualified English and Antipodean instructors. The fact that all of the runs end in one area is a big advantage for meeting children after lessons. Both ski and non-ski kindergartens are available between 9.30am and 5pm for 3- to 6-year-olds. It is advisable to book well in advance.

The resort

Pas de la Casa is not the prettiest of resorts and its popularity is due more to the success of its supermarkets than its village charm. It has a large variety of accommodation ranging from the very comfortable to the very basic. Two of the more expensive hotels, which receive favourable comment from reporters, are the Sporting and the Central, both at the lower end of the resort. The budget hotel Llac Negre has a varied local menu and friendly staff. Reporters speak of its excellent value and it is said to be 'warm, clean and friendly'.

Of the many self-catering apartments, Paradis Blanc is clean and modern although, as seems typical of this kind of accommodation, not over-generous with space. The Lake Placid apartments are among the cheapest on offer, but seem to have few admirers; reporters complain about their small size, lack of soundproofing, inadequate hot water and temperamental lifts. As one commented, 'It is no joke carrying your ski gear down six flights of steps'.

Après-ski

Most of the bars in Pas de la Casa are cheap, and even the ones with dancing seem to have resisted the urge to charge for entry. Most are of the strip-lit, deafening music variety, although the classy Le Pub and lively Marseilles bar are places where you can both drink and talk at the same time. The Discoteca Bilboard is a small, lively disco for those with pre-1980s musical tastes. A much commented-on nightspot is Bar 11 and its 'Drink Frenzy', which takes place from 9pm until 2am each night, when, for a set 120FF, you can drink as much beer, wine or spirits as you like.

Restaurants are cheap (three-course set menus from 35FF) and usually good. The food is mainly Spanish, with fresh seafood and the ubiquitous paella, although some concessions have been made to the French. By choosing carefully, you can eat well at a reasonable price.

TOURIST OFFICE
Pas de la Casa-Grau Roig Estació d'Esqui, Andorra
Tel 33 628 20399
Fax 33 628 23036

TOUR OPERATORS
Enterprise, Neilson, Panorama's
Ski Experience, Ski Falcon,
Ski Thomson, Skiworld, Top Deck Ski

Soldeu
ALTITUDE 1800m (5,904ft)
For many years there has been talk of linking Pas de la Casa with its

nearest neighbours, Soldeu and El Tarter, but as yet this has not advanced any further than a dotted line on the piste map. Thirty minutes by road from Pas de la Casa, the linked resorts of Soldeu and El Tarter (1710m) provide a marked contrast to their nearest neighbour. They consist of little more than a ribbon of stone and wood buildings alongside the main road, although new, more environmentally sympathetic regulations mean that more recent constructions, notably the Hotel Sporting, are much more attractive.

The skiing
Top 2560m (8,397ft) bottom 1710m (5,609ft)

From Soldeu, the ski area is reached by a single-span bridge that would make Indiana Jones think twice. The Edelweiss restaurant is situated between the resort and the bridge for those in need of duty-free Dutch courage along the way. Once the crossing has been negotiated, **mountain access** is via the Espiolets lift, which whisks you up to Pla dels Espiolets and the main skiing area. Reporters complain of heavy queues at the El Tarter access lift on weekend mornings.

The ski area of Soldeu and El Tarter is made up of mainly long cruises and 'nice, wide-open terrain at the top, and forest from mid-mountain down'. The skiing is typified by Gall de Bosc, an 8200m green (very easy) run, which winds between Pla dels Espiolets and Soldeu. Tree-lined and gentle, it is a pleasant run when the snow is good and can provide a flattering end to the day. By branching right underneath the Espiolets lift it is also possible to ski back to Soldeu.

A quicker return route is via a choice of reds and blues, which link with the Llebre and Abet blacks ('exhilarating runs through the woods'). Both runs are well groomed with artificial snow, and provide a challenging descent. Narrow in places, they tend to become congested after ski school hours.

Above Pla dels Espiolets is the Solana del Forn ski area, a series of long, straight green runs leading soporifically back to the more challenging runs towards Soldeu. Above the tree-line, and to the right of Solana del Forn, is the Riba Escorxada ski area, a network of long, mainly red runs towards the slopes above El Tarter. The pick of these gliding runs is the fast, black El Voltor leading on to the end of the Esparver red. Usually uncrowded, they are steep enough to be interesting, and hold their snow well. From the bottom of the run the enjoyable blue Esquirol or the testing black end of Aliga take you down to Soldeu itself, and the Riba Escorxada chair returns you to Pla dels Espiolets.

We have good reports of the nursery slopes, which are 'well prepared and fenced off from the rest of the pistes'. The ski school is also well spoken of, with good children's instruction from English staff. The Esqui Calbo restaurant, across the bridge from the bottom ski-lift, is highly recommended for its good service and value for money food.

The resort
The atmosphere of this aesthetically unappealing roadside resort is alleviated by the presence of a few well-run hotels. The El Duc is a comfortable chalet-style hotel in the village centre, opposite the ski slopes.

Beside it is the traditional-style Sporthotel with sauna and gym. Apart-hotel Edelweiss and the Cabo apartments share the Sporthotel's facilities. The Naudi is a small family-run hotel with a good sun terrace.

Après-ski

The busy nightlife centres around the Pussycat, Aspen and El Duc discos. The Xalet Sol i Neu, right beside the slopes, is well positioned for the après-ski. The Esquirol and the Hard Rock Café are reporters' favourite restaurants and the Hotel Bruxelles has good food. The El Pi is said to be good value at 1400 pesetas for a four-course meal.

TOURIST OFFICE
Soldeu-El Tarter, Andorra
Tel 33 628 21197
Fax 33 628 61982

TOUR OPERATORS
Enterprise, Freedom Holidays,
Panorama's Ski Experience, Ski Falcon,
Ski Thomson, Skiworld, Top Deck Ski

Arinsal

ALTITUDE 1550m (5,084ft)

Arinsal does not look like a ski resort at all, with its small row of shops and bars, and apartment buildings scattered along the road. With rarely any snow in the resort itself to provide a clue, the only sign that this is a winter sports centre is the two-person chair-lift.

The skiing

Top 2572m (8,436ft) bottom 1550m (5,084ft)

Mountain access is via the double chair-lift, which takes you to the start of the main ski area at 1950m, a bleak, treeless series of slopes on one face of Pic Negre, rising to 2572m. The two main pistes, the black La Devesa and the blue Les Marrades 1, running from the top of the main Arinsal lift down to the resort, are sometimes closed due to lack of snow. This limits the remainder of the area to beginner and lower inter-mediate terrain. As all the runs are channelled into a V-shape, which ends on the nursery slopes, even beginners will feel the pressure of the limited runs. One reporter comments that he has never seen such a mixture of abilities, with skiers from L'Estadi and Les Fonts Roges skiing at speed and colliding with beginners' classes on El Cortal and Escola.

From the main chair-lift, the best option is to take the Les Fonts lift towards the right-hand side of the ski area. From there the option for all but beginners is either to take the gentle, but usually crowded, Les Fonts Roges blue run back to where you started, or, by skiing the end of Port Vell, to catch the drag-lift up to the ridge between Pic Negre and Pic Alt de la Capa. This is the highest point of the skiing, and very bleak it is too. The choice from here is to return via the blues of Port Vell and El Tubo, or on La Solana and Les Fonts Roges. Alternatively, the more testing option is to turn left off the drag and take the short blacks, Coll or l'Alt de la Capa via another short lift. These tend to be icy and mogulled, but too short to be really frightening, before giving access to the bulk of the slopes. From here, the way to avoid the crowds is to stick to the long red La Tossa, returning by the lift of the same name.

Mountain restaurants are, on the whole, 'shabby and over-priced', say reporters, although there are one or two exceptions. At the bottom of the Arinsal chair-lift the self-service Asterisc serves good food and a full English breakfast, as does its sister establishment Obelisc at the Bambi chair-lift. For such a small place, Arinsal is well supplied with good off-slope restaurants and bars. Pick of the resort is the Red Rock, serving beer, burgers and chilli with a good atmosphere and a welcome warmth after the bleakness of the skiing.

The resort

Again the motto seems to be 'cheap and basic'. The Poblado apartments come in for particular praise ('clean, well-kept and newly built'), while Hotel Rossell receives quite serious criticism: 'evening meal was just adequate, breakfast was totally inadequate – one croissant and Melba toast (small), and one cup of coffee,' and 'at best could be described as basic'. Attitude and service at the hotel Font is 'on a par with the Rossell'. We also have mixed views of the Hotel Erts: 'basic and friendly', yet 'dreadful food, raw pork being served up one evening, and the rooms left much to be desired'. The Hotel Diana, 15 minutes from the centre, is new. Hotel Janet is a small, family-run place on the outskirts. The large, modern Hotel St Gothard is one of the village's main nightspots. The Hotel Solana has a new indoor swimming-pool and sauna, and the Coma Pedrosa has good food and is run on a more personal basis.

Après-ski

Skydance at the St Gothard hotel is a popular disco, the Red Rock bar has live music and is recommended for its food, and the Solana disco pub has a good atmosphere. Cisco's is recommended for Mexican food.

TOURIST OFFICE
Arinsal Information Office, La Massana,
Andorra
Tel 33 628 35822
Fax 33 628 36242

TOUR OPERATORS
Crystal, Neilson, Panorama's
Ski Experience, Ski Falcon,
Ski Thomson, Snowcoach

Arcalis

ALTITUDE 1940m (6,363ft)

At 1940m, with runs going up to 2600m, this is one of the higher resorts with skiing on wide runs above the tree-line. The village is 25 minutes from Pal ('very pretty scenery, brilliant for beginners') and neighbouring La Massana. The nine drags and three chairs serve runs which suit all standards of skier. Reporters are lavish in their praise: 'The sheer variety of the skiing makes it a great place. No lift queues, one of the best, smaller resorts we have been to.'

TOURIST OFFICE
Camp de Neu Ordino, Arcalis, Andorra
Tel 33 628 64154
Fax 33 628 62540

TOUR OPERATORS
Panorama's Ski Experience

Pal
ALTITUDE 1780m (5,838ft)

This smartly equipped resort a few kilometres south of Arinsal has a greater variety of skiing in prettier scenery than most other Andorran villages. A total of 15 lifts including two quad chairs serves 30km of mainly beginner and intermediate runs. 8km of piste are covered by an impressive battery of 136 snow-cannon.

The ski area starts at Els Amorriadors, a bus ride up the road from the village of Pal. From here a chair and a series of drags serve an easy area of glade skiing going up to the Pic del Cubil at 2358m. More challenging runs take you down through the woods to the Coll de la Botella at 2087m.

TOURIST OFFICE
Pal Estació d'Esqui, Andorra
Tel 33 628 36236
Fax 33 628 35904

Eastern Europe

Countries included Slovenia, Bulgaria, Romania, Slovakia, Poland

The political changes of the late 1980s and early 1990s throughout Eastern Europe did much to change the perspective of skiing in a part of the world which has, until now, struggled without any independent finance for development. Skiing has continued to survive against all the odds here. The mountains of Georgia, the Czech Republic and Slovakia, Poland, Bulgaria and Romania all lend themselves to skiing, as of course does, or rather did, Yugoslavia. It seems incredible that poor beleaguered Sarajevo actually hosted the Winter Olympics as recently as 1984. Quite when the slopes there will re-open for business is a question lost in the chaos of civil war. But in general, as we head towards the twenty-first century, the mountains of Eastern Europe represent one of the great future holiday areas for skiers.

Already these countries have their own, sometimes over-full, domestic markets, but at the moment the biggest plus point of skiing in Eastern Europe is the price. Skiers on a budget tend to look to Bulgaria, Romania and to plucky Slovenia. Not yet well-known by tourists are Slovakia and Poland, which to date only attract the more adventurous skiers from abroad, including a large number of former East Germans. The facilities in these two countries still lag far behind those of Western Europe.

Despite their emergent state of capitalism and movement towards the establishment of market economies, Eastern European countries have much in common with each other as ski destinations, but still remain in most ways quite different from the major Western alpine countries. The skiing of some resorts can compete happily with that of minor counterparts in Austria and the accommodation is built to suit foreign visitors. However, in other respects Eastern Europe can be disappointing. These countries do not offer the opportunities for self-indulgence that many skiers have become used to in resorts elsewhere. Of course these shortcomings are of less importance to some: leaders of school parties, for example, may consider a shortage of tempting bars to be a blessing.

Not only do these countries offer a cheap holiday and a fascinating cultural experience, but there is also the potential for combining a sightseeing trip with a few days' skiing. The local people are trying hard to adjust to the rapid changes and particularly to a market economy. Things do not always run as smoothly as tourists have come to expect. There are still shortages, delays, slow service and sometimes only basic facilities. The majority of reporters have, however, been exceptionally impressed by the friendliness and generosity of the Eastern Europeans.

We have not given the address or telephone numbers of the local tourist offices as we have done for other countries. We recommend that you travel through a bonded tour operator or via a country's own state travel agency.

Slovenia

This independent state continues to promote itself as a ski destination despite the cruel civil war in other parts of what was once Yugoslavia. Slovenia in the extreme north-west has some good skiing and those tour operators who stuck with it protest correctly that their resorts are untouched by and are a long way from the fighting.

Like other Eastern European countries Slovenia is reasonably priced. Food, drink and internal travel are about one-third of British prices. Reports of the ski schools are generally favourable, with English widely spoken and the video analysis helpful.

Kranjska Gora 810m (2,667ft)

Positioned close to the Italian and Austrian borders, Kranjska Gora is the best-known resort in the region, offered by mainstream tour operators as well as Eastern European specialists. It is Austrian in ambience, even down to an onion-domed church, although its modest hotels are not comparable to cosy Austrian gasthofs and its chalets are more severe than their Tyrolean equivalents. The setting, in a flat-bottomed valley between craggy wooded mountains, is a pretty one.

The nursery slope runs are fairly short, wide and gentle, set right on the edge of the village, but the transition to real pistes is rather abrupt, with the mountains rising quite steeply from the valley floor. One run, from the 1630m Vitranc summit, is particularly testing. There are lots of drag-lifts serving intermediate pistes on the Vitranic, but they go no more than half-way up what is in any case a small mountain, which means not only limited skiing, but also a danger of poor snow. A two-stage chair-lift goes further to 1570m, presenting a fairly challenging descent of over 750m vertical to the valley.

There are swimming-pools and saunas in several of the slightly institutional hotels, as well as some discos and bars. The bar of the Slavec hotel is said to have a good local atmosphere. The Hotel Larix is recommended for its location, rooms and facilities. The Garni is conveniently situated, clean and spacious. The Prisank has good food, but not much variety.

TOUR OPERATORS
Balkan Holidays, Ski Slovenia Choice,
Ski Thomson

Bled 880m (2,887ft)

While Kranjska Gora is the largest Slovenian ski resort, the attractive old spa town of Bled looks on to a seventeenth-century church on an island in the middle of a lake. Its simple skiing is eight kilometres away at Zatrnik, where there is a total of five lifts serving easy wooded slopes, ideal for beginners in good snow conditions, but providing little challenge to intermediates. The Golf, a quiet hotel set slightly away from the main centre, is recommended.

TOUR OPERATORS
Balkan Holidays, Ski Slovenia Choice,
Ski Thomson

Bovec 520m (1,706ft)

Of the other Slovenian resorts accessible to the British package-holiday skier, Bovec, just south of Kranjska Gora, is the most interesting for skiers. It does not have many lifts, but they do include a three-stage gondola rising to 1750m and serving some moderately challenging slopes. When there is snow down to the village, the run from top to bottom is memorable. Bovec was rebuilt after World War II and is a town, rather than a resort. Après-ski revolves around hotels and lively local bars. Hotels include the Alp and the Kanin, a short distance from the centre.

TOUR OPERATORS
Ski Slovenia Choice

Bohinj 1725m (5,658ft)

The only tour operator which offers holidays at Mount Vogel and Mount Kobla sells them under the collective title of Bohinj. Bohinj is a lakeside town with skiing above it at Mount Vogel. A cable car takes you to a plateau where seven lifts conveniently connect a handful of easy intermediate runs among the trees and a small nursery area. If the conditions are good you can ski all the way down to the lake.

There is accommodation available to package-holidaymakers right at the base of Mount Vogel, in the Zlatorog hotel near the Vogel cable car station. It is recommended for convenience for the slopes, although it is rather isolated in the evenings as it is not really part of a village. The Ski Hotel Vogel at the top of the cable car is a good place to stay, as are the hotels Jezero in Bohinj and Kompass, both above Lake Bohinj.

The other skiing area close to Bohinj lake is Mount Kobla and the adjacent mountain Savnik; it consists of a mixture of easy and intermediate runs, entirely below the tree-line between 550m and 1500m. Kobla quickly becomes crowded at weekends.

TOUR OPERATORS
Ski Slovenia Choice

Rogla 1500m (4,921ft)

Rogla, a purpose-built resort 45km from the Austrian border, has a modern lift system, two FIS downhill courses and reliable snow conditions. The Hotel Planja, overlooking the ski area, is recommended and has its own sports hall with tennis courts, squash and basketball.

TOUR OPERATORS
Ski Slovenia Choice

Bulgaria

Anyone planning a holiday in Bulgaria should first find out what they are letting themselves in for. Although many changes have taken place over the past few years, all our reporters are agreed that the experience of skiing here bears no comparison to skiing in the mainstream alpine countries, and indeed no comparison should be attempted. It is worth listing a number of primary concerns.

First, currency: hard currency is still much sought after although a harsh crack-down on the currency black market has led to more uniform exchange rates and the disappearance of 'touts' pestering you for pounds. Some hotel bars and restaurants are said only to accept hard currency. One reporter notes that the cost of the kindergarten proved on arrival to be not only double the price listed in the brochure, but had to be paid for locally in hard currency, leaving her desperately short of holiday money. It seems that the Bulgarians, at least those in ski resorts, have emerged from their enforced crash course in capitalism with first-class degrees. While everything is still cheap by Western standards, prices (in Borovets in particular) appear to double each year. It would appear that the Bulgarians are shooting themselves in the foot, because the one advantage that these resorts unquestionably had in the past was unmatchable low prices.

Secondly, food: reporters speak of 'the same monotonous fodder every day'. The main problem with the food is not the lack of it, but the washed-out tastelessness: 'A choice of omelette or a type of stew', 'a piece of meat about the size of an egg in its shell', 'sludgy coffee and orange juice diluted beyond dilution'. Food at the caravans which serve as mountain restaurants is usually of a higher standard with an emphasis on chips ('sausage and chips, chicken and chips, and plain chips'). One more adventurous reporter spoke of discovering 'good, cheap food' by finding a restaurant away from the main tourist centre. Self-catering in a studio rather than a hotel room, as one reporter found, has its problems: 'The supposed benefits are a larger balcony, a hob, a fridge, some cooking utensils and some cutlery, but there were no food shops.'

Thirdly, medical facilities: the hospitals are reported to be very basic, unclean and lacking facilities that we in the West take for granted. On the other hand, mountain rescue seems to be efficient, with minor injuries treated speedily and effectively. Simple medications such as aspirin are not readily available. Loo paper is scarce and you are still advised to bring your own bath plug.

Fourthly, hire equipment: skis are locally made and not of the high quality you would find elsewhere in Europe. They tend to come in shorter-than-average lengths. It is possible to purchase skis and bindings for £100 or less; some of these sets have Atomic cosmetics, but you cannot be certain of the quality of what you are buying.

If you are concerned by the considerations above, you should perhaps consider a holiday elsewhere. To most people they mattered very little and were easily made up for by the beauty of the country, the enormous friendliness of the locals, the excellence of the ski schools, and the all-round good value of the holiday: 'Did we make a mistake? No, we wanted a cheap skiing holiday and we got one.'

Borovets 1323m (4,339ft)

This is one of the most popular destinations for the British in Eastern Europe. Spectacularly situated among pine forests high in the Rila mountains, the resort is more a spread-out collection of hotels than a village. But with the highest point of the ski area at 2430m, reached by the 5km Yastrebets six-seater gondola, Borovets' skiing compares favourably with that of many of the smaller alpine resorts. It is divided into three areas: a variety of wooded runs on the mountain directly above the resort; more wooded intermediate runs reached by gondola to the right of the resort; and open skiing between 2150m and 2540m, above the top gondola station, served by a series of parallel drag-lifts. There is a limited nursery area at the foot of the main mountain and some long, meandering trails, including one of 6km from the top of the ancient single chair, but the skiing is generally more suited to intermediates who have the choice of some fairly testing red and black runs.

There is little in the way of really challenging skiing or off-piste scope for the expert. Mountain restaurants are basic and not high in number, but are incredibly cheap. There is a lovely old café on the six-kilometre blue run, which is well worth a visit. The gondola is closed for maintenance on Friday mornings and reportedly all day on the last Friday of each month. It is the only means of mountain access to the higher slopes and is prone to serious queuing problems ('an hour-long wait in the mornings is commonplace'). The quality of piste-grooming is said to be very poor: 'The uphill runs beneath the drag-lifts would give a self-respecting French *pisteur* an apoplectic fit.' Pistes are unmarked and there are few direction signs. Piste maps are hard to come by and as one correspondent noted 'a black market in these is surely only a matter of time'. It would appear that the cartographer was supplied only with a red pen and it is therefore impossible to judge the degree of difficulty of runs from the map.

The ski school is highly commended by most reporters: 'The ski school was outstanding. I cannot praise the instructors enough, especially the one teaching our children.' However, another described teaching as 'abysmal – one instructor went on strike on day three and was never seen again'. The kindergarten receives good reports.

Most of the hotels are within five minutes' walking distance of the slopes and lifts. Horse- or donkey-drawn carts do a circuit of the main hotels and are remarkably cheap. The Rila is huge and rather impersonal ('looks like a French apartment block inside and out'). The more recently built Samakov (with swimming-pool) has better food by Bulgarian standards and is comfortable, but again large and impersonal. It is well placed for the gondola, but less so for the chair-lifts. The smaller twin hotels of Ela and Mura offer comfortable accommodation.

Après-ski relies upon the local bars, discos and floor-shows, with the Rila and Samakov acting as principal entertainment centres. Karaoke and 'Russian' strip-shows are much in evidence. The Ela has an English bar with English prices to match. The Breza bar is recommended, as is Peter's opposite the gondola. Various excursions are available. One reporter took a trip to the opera in Sofia which 'cost £12 including transport with a good meal thrown in. Entrance to the opera itself was 17½p.'

As one reporter summed it up: 'Potential visitors to Borovets should be aware of the differences between this Eastern European resort in terms of food and drink, and the culture and lifestyle of the Bulgarians and weigh up whether the savings are worth it in comparison to other low-cost Western European ski resorts.'

TOUR OPERATORS
Balkan Holidays, Balkan Tours, Crystal,
Enterprise, Inghams, Neilson, Ski Falcon

Pamporovo 1620m (5,314ft)

To the south-west of Borovets is Pamporovo, a large resort suited to first-time skiers. The nearest airport, Plovdiv (about one and three-quarter hours away), is very basic. The lift system consists entirely of chairs and drags serving mainly easy pistes on the Snezhanka mountain (1925m). There are several good nursery areas and a number of confidence-building pistes through the trees, including one from the top height of 1925m to the lowest point at 1450m. There are two more difficult runs, including the Wall, which is not as steep as it sounds, but is used as a slalom racecourse; advanced skiers would probably find little to maintain their interest after the first two or three days.

Snack bars on the mountain are apparently numerous, but of poor quality and one reporter commented: 'The burger was probably horse.' The pizza caravan near Stoudnets gets a strong recommendation. Rental equipment is first-class and we have very favourable reports of the ski school: the instructors take an obvious pride in their English and instruction is reportedly clear and technically sound ('tuition was outstanding in terms of enjoyment and friendliness'). Pamporovo is the southernmost mountain resort in Eastern Europe, and snow conditions can be unreliable in the latter part of the season.

The resort consists of a handful of unattractive modern hotels, lacking atmosphere, but of a high standard, a five-minute (free) bus-ride from the slopes. The Perelik is adequate, though slightly faded. Reporters note that the food is 'not great, but buffets are excellent and the Cabernet Sauvignon is fantastic value'. Its swimming-pool is 'huge, like Hackney municipal baths rather than a leisure pool'.

Après-ski, in alpine terms, is limited to a few folksy restaurants and hotel discos, although there are nightclubs at the hotel Perelik and at the Somolyan (a 45-minute bus-ride away). One reporter recommends the bar at Molina and the White Hart is reputed to have good food. Also Thoroughly recommended are the traditional local evenings laid on for tourists; folk barbecues at the Cheverme restaurant and 'game' evenings sampling local fare. One reporter notes: 'The instructors even invited us to their homes.'

TOUR OPERATORS
Balkan Holidays, Balkan Tours, Crystal,
Enterprise, Ski Falcon, SkiBound

Vitosha 1800m (5,904ft)

Bulgaria's highest resort is on Mount Vitosha, overlooking Sofia. The resort consists of a couple of comfortable hotels, old hunting lodges, a hire shop and lift station on a wooded ledge. Sofia is 20km away by an extremely cheap bus service. The skiing consists of a total of 22km of runs on north-facing slopes above the tree-line, served by a small network of lifts, which are apparently closed one day a week for maintenance. It is an ideal resort for beginners and early intermediates. Experts would, however, easily become bored by the very limited skiing. There are some cross-country trails in the forest. Vitosha's proximity to the capital means that it is inundated with people at weekends and lift queues can be a problem. The ski school is said to be excellent.

Hotels include the Hunting Lodge, unique accommodation set in its own grounds in a forest clearing 700m from the nearest ski lift. The Proster is the largest hotel with good facilities including a swimming-pool. One reporter commented that 'the view was fabulous, maintenance was appalling, it was very noisy, and the food was poor.' Hotel Moreni is 'basic, with no frills'. Nightlife is said to be minimal, apart from the Proster disco.

TOUR OPERATORS
Balkan Holidays, Enterprise,
Inghams, Ski Falcon

Romania

Prices in Romania are even lower than Bulgaria. All our reporters found it difficult to spend more than £30 in a week's holiday, and that is with a fairly active nightlife. As in other Eastern European countries, hire equipment is in short supply and you are strongly advised to bring your own. English is widely spoken in the tourist centres. The lifts are old-fashioned, in serious need of upgrading and prone to long technical delays. The standard of ski tuition is generally high.

Poiana Brasov 1020m (3,346ft)

Romania's top ski resort is Poiana Brasov, about two hours north of Bucharest in the centre of the country. It is an unusual purpose-built resort, with its hotels and other facilities dotted around a wooded plateau at the foot of the skiing. It resembles more of an enormous holiday camp than a village. This means that much of the skiing day is spent on buses, which are said to be intermittent, but free.

The main ski area is reached by gondola or cable car (do not expect them both to be running at the same time) up to 1775m, and consists of three main elements: satisfying intermediate runs roughly following the line of the lifts from top to bottom; a good open nursery area at altitude; and a long roundabout run away from the lifts. This is graded black only because it is not prepared and is used as a downhill race-course. There is also a separate, gentle nursery area in the resort.

Mountain restaurants are few and far between, with cheap food, but 'shocking toilet facilities'. The Outlaws Hut in the resort is the best restaurant, which our reporters found 'lively, cheap and full of atmosphere'. There is no shortage of ski school instructors, who speak excellent English and are keen to show you a good time, 'even if it means buying them all their drinks in the bar at night and then coping with their hangover the next day at class'.

Of the hotels, the Alpin is particularly recommended, the Teleferic is adequate but basic, and the Soimul is comfortable, although one reporter found the management 'very rude, as I was accused of not paying a 'phone bill which had been duly paid'. Hotel Cuicas is 'of surprisingly good standard for the cost of the holiday with en-suite facilities and a balcony, but the food is appalling and it cannot cater for vegetarians'. Non-skiing and early evening après-ski are fairly limited, apart from a big public swimming-pool; other sports facilities include skating and bowling. The nightlife varies from discos to cabarets and karaoke nights.

Excursions are organised to 'Dracula's castle', and there are cheap buses and taxis which can take you into the town of Brasov, where there is limited shopping. One reporter was surprised to find a cheap Chinese restaurant in the main square of Brasov, which was 'a nice change from the standard Romanian fare that did not cater for vegetarians, unless they were on an egg diet'. The Dacia restaurant is said to specialise in 'excellent wild boar and bear'. The Neagre nightclub is said to be fun 'if you like Russian strippers'.

The ski school is unanimously recommended, 'exceptionally good value and the teachers are of an excellent standard'. Reporters speak of a dated feeling about the resort. One warned he found it 'full of British yobbos on cheap drunken sprees', but at the same time described his holiday as 'a culturally fascinating experience'.

TOUR OPERATORS
Balkan Holidays, Balkan Tours,
Crystal, Enterprise, Inghams,
Neilson, Ski Romanian Holidays,
Seasun School Tours,Ski Falcon

Sinaia 800m (2,624ft)

Sinaia is a small town stretching along the main road through the mountains from Bucharest to Brasov. Its role as a ski resort is relatively minor. A two-stage cable car from the town, its top section duplicated by a chair-lift, serves long intermediate runs down the front of the mountain. These are poorly marked and are consequently quite challenging in poor visibility. The main area is on exposed, tree-less slopes behind the mountain and on subsidiary peaks beyond – short intermediate runs with some variety, and plenty of scope for skiing off-piste. The town is quiet and although there are a few bars and restaurants après-ski revolves mainly around tour operators' hotels.

TOUR OPERATORS
Crystal, Ski Romanian Holidays

Slovakia

Slovakian skiing is the least developed we have come across in Eastern Europe. The lifts are limited and ancient, causing horrendous queues. The advantages over other Eastern European countries is that the food is plentiful and wholesome, while still cheap. The resorts are also attractive and unspoilt. Slovakian skiing is a very long way from Prague. The daily, two-and-a-half hour flight via Bratislava takes you to Tatry Poprad airport in the High Tatras, with its primitive runway and small terminal building. The latter was closed when we arrived during an evening blizzard and our luggage was unceremoniously dumped on to the snow before the battle to hire one of the three taxis followed.

Vysoke Tatry are the highest mountains in the Carpathians, which stretch from Bratislava almost to the Black Sea. The High Tatras is the only alpine-type massif in the range and runs for just 26km of it. Six of the peaks, including Lomnicky Stit, the best ski mountain, rise above 2600m. The small ski resorts are reached from Poprad by a mountain railway, which is as efficient as the Swiss trains of the Bernese Oberland, but costs just 10p a ride.

The picturesque villages, set in the trees at the foot of the mountains, have an olde worlde charm. The Edwardian stations and *fin-de-siècle* splendour of the hotels brings alive the memories of another era. The High Tatras are an increasingly popular destination not only for Slovaks, but also for the new tourist trade of former East Germany. At present the skiing is too primitive to satisfy the Western visitor, but everything is changing at such a rate that it is easy to imagine the High Tatras developing within a few years.

Stary Smokovec 1018m (3,339ft)

Stary Smokovec, reached by train or road from Poprad, is the most attractive village to stay in. The Grandhotel, which looks like it could have been transported from Biarritz, is adequate. Its best point is the restaurant, which serves delicious food of a surprisingly higher standard and lower price than its Austrian alpine counterparts. The more luxurious Grandhotel Praha at Tatranská Lomnica has room prices more in keeping with its Western European equivalents.

Stary Smokovec's access lift is a slow funicular which takes you up into the ski area where there is a modern hotel. A couple of drag-lifts allow you to explore what there is of the mountain, before going down a green (beginner) trail through the trees for a £2-per-head lunch.

Further down the valley is Strbské Pleso, a small resort with four lifts and a cross-country circuit.

TOUR OPERATORS
Cedok, 49 Southwark Street,
London SE1 1RU
Tel 071-378 6009

Tatranská Lomnica 850m (2,788ft)

Fifteen minutes away by ski train lies Tatranská Lomnica, which offers the best skiing in the area, accessed by a 1950s cable car. The lift queues for this are so horrific that rarely more than one ride a day is possible. Tickets are sold with a pre-set travel time. From the top of the cable car a two-seater chair-lift takes you up to 2600m and offers an acceptable run down with limited off-piste variations back to the lift station. From here the descent to the valley can be spectacular, given the right snow conditions.

TOUR OPERATORS
Cedok

The Low Tatras 1400-2024m (4,592-6,639)

The Low Tatras, in particular the Ziarska Valley, is Slovakia's second ski region, which offers less spectacular mountains, but more lifts. There is no village to speak of, just hotels dotted along the valleys to the north and south of Mount Chopok at 2045m. On the north side there is a fairly extensive and varied ski area, vulnerable to wind. The only way down is by black run or chair-lift.

It is essential to bring your own skis and boots to the Tatras, as the hire equipment is of a frighteningly low standard. The variety of equipment seen on the slopes includes lace-up or metal clip leather boots, and wooden skis with fixed bindings. At the moment no British tour operators offer holidays here.

Poland

Again, no tour operator has ventured to Poland. The lift system is similar to Slovakia's and Zakopane, the major resort, offers a ski area comparible in size to an Austrian glacier's summer skiing. One local told us it was quicker to put on skins and climb to the pistes than to wait in the lift queues.

Zakopane 1986m (6,514ft)

On the other side of the Slovakian High Tatras is Zakopane, Poland's leading ski resort. Zakopane is about two hours' drive south of Krakow, right on the Slovakian border. It is surrounded by breathtaking scenery and delightful outlying villages, with traditionally carved and decorated wooden churches.

The best of the skiing starts just outside town at Kuznice, best reached by taxi from the hotels at the centre of the village. A cable car with appalling queues takes you up to just below the 1990m summit of Kasprowy Wierch, the major of the four small ski areas. Here there is some good, open bowl skiing, which is served by a couple of ancient chair-lifts. At the end of the day, provided there is enough snow, it is possible to ski all the way down to the cable car base station.

In Zakopane itself, the second area, Gubalowka, is reached by funicular from the bottom of the high street, which gives access to some practice slopes and a choice of wide runs around the trees. The steep Nosal runs are Zakopane's main racing slopes and are reserved in the morning for slalom practice. There are also some gentle nursery slopes on the outskirts of town. Day lift passes are reported to be uneconomical; it is better to pay by the ride.

TOUR OPERATORS
Polorbis Travel, 82 Mortimer Street,
London W1N 7DE
Tel 071-580 8028

Norway

Resorts included Geilo, Hemsedal, Lillehammer, Oppdal, Trysil, Voss

Still largely ignored by British skiers, Norway has been brought firmly into the spotlight by its staging of the 1994 Winter Olympics around Lillehammer. The country that invented the ski, and whose downhill racers are, with impeccable timing, back up among the best in the world, will no doubt orchestrate an efficient, if not spectacular Games. They take place not four years but only two years after Albertville, so that in future the Summer and Winter Olympics will not be held in the same year, thus relieving pressure on the International Olympic Committee. The choice of Lillehammer as the sandwich venue before Japan is nevertheless surprising.

It is frequently said that Norwegians can ski before they can walk, but this refers to cross-country skiing, a necessity in rural areas and more of a way of life than a sport. Downhill skiing is treated with a degree of bemusement by most Norwegians and this is reflected in the resorts; these tend to be small towns which happen to have a ski area nearby. An exception to this is Kvitfjell, the Bernardt Russi-designed Olympic men's downhill course, which has no town nearby.

Norway is expensive. Eating out is roughly twice the price of London, petrol about double the UK price and alcohol about three times the price. A litre of beer costs an amount that most alpine night-club owners can only dream of charging. Hotel accommodation, clothes and virtually everything else are well above UK prices; ski passes and ski hire are also dearer than in comparable resorts elsewhere.

Despite its high cost and limited downhill skiing, there is plenty to recommend Norway for a winter holiday. Although most of its resorts are at low altitude, Norway has a good snow record due to its northerly latitude, backed up by modern and efficient snowmaking equipment. The people are friendly and speak excellent English, the environment is a safe one and children are positively welcomed. The standards of food, accommodation and equipment are superb.

It is, however, the sheer difference of Norway that attracts those more used to the popular European resorts. The landscape has none of the drama of the Mont Blanc massif, nor the gentle beauty of the Dolomites. Instead, its harsh but haunting hills are an ideal setting for those who want to try the Norwegian national sport of cross-country skiing. Equipment is relatively cheap to hire, and basic technique can be quickly grasped with the minimum of tuition. There are hundreds of kilometres of prepared tracks to explore in every corner of the country, and the speed of travel is up to the individual (not always the case in downhilling). At any age, it is an excellent way to escape from the crowds and explore the countryside at a leisurely pace.

Lillehammer
ALTITUDE 200m (656ft)

Host to the 1994 Winter Olympics and birthplace of the cheese slicer, little Lillehammer looks more like an American Wild-West frontier town with its clapboard-fronted houses and one main street. Quiet and friendly, it gives the impression of a community going about its business unaware that it is supposed to be a ski resort. In fact the nearest downhill skiing is based 15km away at Hafjell, and the men's downhill course at Kvitfjell is 50km away; hardly a ski-in ski-out resort.

The skiing
Top 1050m (3,333ft) bottom 200m (656ft)

Hafjell is the larger of the two centres, but its skiing is hardly extensive, with only 23km of prepared pistes, 7 lifts and 9 runs (with some variations), and although enjoyable, it is unlikely to keep anyone but the most undemanding of intermediates occupied for more than a couple of days. The best runs are from Hafjelltoppen, at 1050m down either the Kringelas or Hafjell runs. Both are graded black (difficult) and form part of the Olympic men's and women's slalom courses. Like all the runs here they are extremely well groomed, with artificial snowmaking if needed, but provide a limited challenge to the expert. Night skiing is also available once a week.

Kvitfjell is an unusual ski area, to say the least. It was created specifically for the 1994 Winter Olympics by veteran Swiss racer Bernhardt Russi and the men's downhill course, which effectively is the whole ski area, is said to be the most technically demanding ever built. The area is so small that on race days its 4km of pistes are closed to everyone but competitors and officials.

The resort
Accommodation in the area is almost entirely in hotels, with the Hotel Lillehammer highly praised, especially for its roast reindeer. The Quality Hafjell is also well reviewed (its disco is the only one in the area). Described by one reporter as 'a very comfortable hotel, with some of the most bizarre décor I have ever seen', the Oyer Gjestegard is a suitable hotel for children, who will love the stuffed animals in the reception as well as the nearby Lilliputhammer model village. The Rica Victoria is also recommended.

TOURIST OFFICE
Utvikling, PO Box 85, 2601 Lillehammer
Tel 47 61 266443
Fax 47 61 256585

TOUR OPERATORS
Made to Measure, Norwegian Travel Service,
Norwegian State Railways, Waymark

Geilo
ALTITUDE 800m (2,624ft)

Situated in the Halling Valley, at the foot of the Hardanger Plateau,

250km from Oslo and the same from Bergen, Geilo is a sprawling resort without an obvious focal point or any striking charm.

Its 18 lifts and 24km of piste are grouped in 2 areas, one adjacent to the village and the other, Vestlia, reached by bus. Runs are short due to the limited 265m vertical drop (the longest is 1.5km) but, 130km of carefully prepared loipe provide excellent cross-country skiing.

The resort

Accommodation is in hotels or apartments. We have positive reports of the Dr Holms Hotel as well as the traditional Geilo Hotel next to the main lifts. On the subject of après-ski, one reporter comments: 'What après-ski? There is only one bar and that is very expensive.'

TOURIST OFFICE
PO Box 85, N-3581 Geilo
Tel 47 320 86300
Fax 47 320 86850

TOUR OPERATORS
Dawson and Sanderson, Inntravel,
Made to Measure, Norwegian Travel Service,
Norwegian State Railways

Voss

ALTITUDE 91m (300ft)

Like Lillehammer, Voss is a ski town where the skiing does not dominate. Approximately one-and-a-half hours by train from Bergen, six from Oslo and based on the edge of Lake Vangsvatnet, the old farming village is dominated by Mount Hangur with its 40km of piste and eight cross-country trails.

The resort

The varied range of accommodation includes a number of camp-sites which stay open all-year-round. Fleischers Hotel, Park Hotel Voss and Vinje Turisthotel are all recommended by reporters.

TOURIST OFFICE
PO Box 57, 5701 Voss
Tel 47 56 511716
Fax 47 56 511715

TOUR OPERATORS
Dawson and Sanderson, Made to Measure,
Norwegian Travel Service, Norwegian
State Railways

Hemsedal

ALTITUDE 650m (2,132ft)

Situated 30km north of Geilo, Hemsedal is a scattered resort with some of the most testing runs in Norway. Its 30km of piste, divided into 19 runs and served by 14 lifts, are described by one experienced reporter as 'the most immaculately groomed pistes I have encountered'. An efficient lift system composed mainly of modern high-speed triple and quad chairs reduces queuing to a minimum.

The resort

The disparate nature of the resort and scarcity of ski-buses make a car more of a necessity than a bonus. Accommodation appears to be of a high standard. The Hemsedal Hotel is praised as 'very comfortable, the food is excellent'. The more central Skogstad Hotel and the smaller and more far-flung Liostova Hotel receive favourable comment.

TOURIST OFFICE
Hemsedal Turist Kontor, 3560 Hemsedal
Tel 47 320 78156
Fax 47 320 78537

TOUR OPERATORS
Made to Measure, Norwegian Travel Service,
Norwegian State Railways, Waymark

Trysil
ALTITUDE 600m (1,428ft)

This is a fast-growing resort three hours by road from Oslo. Its 75km of piste served by 23 lifts are spread across the wooded slopes of Trysilfjellet at 1132m. In common with many Norwegian resorts, the lifts are several kilometres from the resort centre. The skiing varies from easy beginner trails to some more challenging red (intermediate) runs, with a maximum vertical drop of 650m.

The resort

Accommodation is mainly hotel- and apartment-based, although mountain cabins, notably the Trysilfjellet, make a pleasant change for hardy self-caterers. The Hotel Soria Moria, 2km from the lifts, is a clean and modern hotel which is favoured by reporters.

TOURIST OFFICE
N-2420 Trysil
Tel 47 624 50511
Fax 47 624 51165

TOUR OPERATORS
Norwegian State Railways

Oppdal
ALTITUDE 545m (1,788ft)

This is Norway's most northerly downhill resort, 120km south of Trondheim. It is also the country's largest resort with 78km of pistes and 15 lifts spread over four interlinking mountains and a longest run of 1.6km. The top height of the downhill skiing is 1300m. The modern, and rather scattered, resort enjoys a long ski season and has in the past staged World Cup events. There is a ski school, ski kindergarten and a childcare service.

The resort

Hotel Nor Alpin is set in the village centre, and contains a disco and pub. Its restaurant has a good reputation. The Hodvin hotel is right next to the piste and has superb views of the mountain. It has an après-ski centre containing a disco, and apartments as well as hotel accommodation. Stolen Terrasse is a recently built apartment block close to the lifts; the larger apartments have private saunas. The resort's facilities include swimming-pools, curling, a sports hall, snow-mobiling, sleigh rides and a 400m skating rink. Oppdal has 186km of cross-country trails covering a variety of terrain. Five floodlit tracks cover 11km.

TOURIST OFFICE
PO Box 50, N-7341
Tel 47 24 21760
Fax 47 24 20888

TOUR OPERATORS
Norwegian Travel Service,
Norwegian State Railways

Scotland

There are now three main skiing centres in Scotland – Aviemore, Glenshee and Nevis Range – as well as a further two more areas on a much smaller scale – Glencoe and The Lecht. Each of the main centres is different in character. The skiing area of Aviemore is about 10 miles (16km) due east of the village itself, but the village is quite substantial and is a better centre than most for après-ski.

Glenshee is based around a lodge perched near the top of a 2,199ft (670m) pass, nine miles (14km) from Braemar. Nevis Range, which has sensibly changed its name from impossible-to-pronounce Aonach Mor, is the newest and is somewhat reminiscent of a small local skiing area in North America. Again it is a place only to ski, with all off-slope activities and evening entertainment centred six miles (10km) away at Fort William. Glencoe is a small and remote area to the south of the town and is only open for part of the week. The Lecht, between Ballater and Grantown-on-Spey, is little more than a giant 'wet' dry ski slope, which is mainly suitable for beginners.

The resorts are not particularly close to one another. Travelling by road in a clockwise direction it takes 40 minutes from Glencoe to Nevis Range and a further 90 minutes to Cairngorm, one hour on to The Lecht and a further hour to Glenshee. Overnight trains from London to Aviemore and Fort William, as well as regular flights, make access fairly painless in terms of time, if not of cost.

Skiing in Scotland should neither be dismissed nor its standard over-estimated. It is infinitely preferable to dry slope skiing, but no one should seriously suggest that a one-week skiing holiday in the Highlands could rival the same in most recognised alpine villages or in North America, or even in Andorra. The ski areas are comparable in size to those, for example, of Alpbach and Niederau, and none of them has a proper base with accommodation and all the other trappings of a ski resort at the foot of its slopes. The vagaries of the weather are such that it is impossible to plan and book ahead in the certain knowledge of adequate snow cover. The Cairngorm is on the same latitude as Labrador and above 2,000ft (610m), where the skiing takes place, the weather is similar. The British maritime climate has a high proportion of wind and cloud and a low proportion of the stable, dry, bright weather that contributes so much to the beauty of the alpine winter.

Skiing often takes place in extremely unfriendly conditions, with no shelter provided by trees, higher mountains or enclosed lifts (the Nevis Range gondola gives access to the skiing, but is not a part of it). Weather conditions can deteriorate in minutes and it is important to wear technical rather than fashion clothing to maintain body warmth. Cairngorm continues to operate with a compassionate unwritten policy of offering partial refunds when the weather completely closes in during the course of a day.

At its very best, as in any resort in the world, Scottish skiing can be magnificent; unfortunately, these days are the exception rather than the norm. The ski schools, all with BASI-qualified instructors, are excellent and the advantage of learning from a native English-speaker is enormous. But at its worst, sampling the slopes of Scotland can be a miserable, cold experience which, unless you happen to live within a short drive, many would consider to be simply not worth the effort or the expense.

For the English skier who lives within easy reach of an international airport it is usually quicker and overall cheaper to take a package to the Alps, where he will find an infinitely greater variety of skiing coupled with an ambience that is arrogantly lacking in Scotland. It is almost as if the lift companies and indeed the hoteliers take a perverse pride in avoiding any of the atmosphere of an alpine resort, which to many holidaymakers is as important as the skiing itself (and that is nothing to write home about).

Reporters again complain of the shortcomings of Scottish piste-marking, lift maps and general maintenance, with the notable exception of Nevis Range. They groan about the weather and the queues on the piste and in the limited restaurants, but stoically accept both. Few actually regret their visits: 'We thought we knew what to expect. We were right, it was tough.'

The 1992-3 season was a good one, with the first runs opening as early as October and the last of the resorts closing well after Easter. But when the snow falls at any time during the season it still melts faster than in the Alps. More importantly, the whole of the Highlands are subject to stronger winds. The real problem of skiing in Scotland is not only limited and irregular snowfall, but snow retention, a problem that even snowmaking will not overcome. Artificial snow blows away just as fast as natural. Chestnut paling fencing is used to some beneficial effect down the side of the runs. When conditions are good the resorts are prone to spectacular overcrowding, particularly at weekends. Daylight hours are longer in spring and conditions on the mountain are less likely to be unbearable than in the depth of winter. From Easter onwards the range of other tourist attractions in the Highlands widens significantly.

Aviemore, Inverness-shire

ALTITUDE 1,804ft (550m)

....

Good points easy access from Scotland and north of England, extensive cross-country skiing, BASI skiing tuition, variety of activities for non-skiers
Bad points unpredictable weather, small ski area, lack of atmosphere in the resorts, weekend lift queues, lack of skiing convenience, unappealing mountain restaurants

---

Aviemore is still, by the skin of its teeth, the main Scottish ski centre, with a major attack on its hands presented by the stylish newcomer in the shape of Nevis Range, alias Aonach Mor. Aviemore lies in the wide Spey valley on the A9 about 120 miles (192km) north of Edinburgh and Glasgow and 30 miles (48km) south of Inverness on the main road and rail line heading to the north of Scotland. There are direct day-time trains from the Lowlands, Inverness and London, as well as overnight trains from London. An adequate bus service operates from the village to the slopes 10 miles (16km) away on the Cairngorm mountain. When conditions are good the resort is inundated with weekend visitors from the Scottish cities and queues become unbearable. Weekday skiing is infinitely preferable.

The skiing

Top 3,608ft (1100m) bottom 1,804ft (550m)
By alpine standards this is a small ski area, but it is impressive when compared with the dry slopes with which most British skiers have to be content for 51 weeks of the year, with top-to-bottom runs approaching 2 miles (3km) in length when snow conditions permit. The area divides into two parts with a car park each, the Day Lodge and the Coire Caf. **Mountain access** is from both of these, with the lifts going up to Shieling and to Coire Na Ciste respectively, from where they rise again to meet below the 4,084ft (1245m) Cairngorm peak. Coire Na Ciste gives access to the most difficult skiing, the Westwall, which can be a lot of fun. Many of the 17 lifts are chairs, which are excellent for carrying skiers over the patchy snow, but are prone to closure when the wind picks up.

Congestion can be serious when the ski area is only partly open. Strong winds often close the chair-lifts or confine skiers to the lower slopes. Alternatively, poor snow cover closes the lower runs and limits the lift capacity from the car park. Queuing is conducted in methodical ranks, but can be a seriously frustrating business. The number allowed on the mountain is restricted, so when the car parks are full the ticket offices close. When conditions are good it is wise to arrive early as the car parks can be filled to capacity by 9.30am.

When there is a lot of snow, the forest land around Glenmore provides plenty of scope for cross-country skiing, as the mountains do for Nordic ski-touring and winter climbing. Danger resulting from the unpredictability of the weather should not be underestimated. Access to the cross-country trails is at Inverdruie, just outside Aviemore.

Mountain restaurants

If the mountain restaurants were inviting they would add greatly to the appeal of the ski area in bad weather. They are not, although there have been recent improvements. All of them are self-service. The Day Lodge restaurant is in the Coire Cas car park; it has a bar beneath it with a log fire. There is the Coire Na Ciste snack bar, the licensed Shieling snack-bar is higher up and higher still is the unlicensed Ptarmigan snack-bar.

Beginners and children

The nursery slopes are good, although often crowded, and dismal weather does not provide the ideal conditions in which to learn. There are several ski schools in Aviemore and elsewhere in the Spey Valley. Reports are generally favourable.

The resort

Aviemore established itself as a modest summer holiday centre in the second half of the nineteenth century. The old village is not particularly impressive rows of shops with a few hotels and guesthouses lining the road near the station. The resort largely consists of a modern development, the Aviemore Centre, which has extensive facilities including an artificial ski slope, a go-kart circuit and a skating rink. These really come into their own when skiing is not possible, especially for families with children. The bus service to and from the slopes is said to be erratic. There are also daily buses from more distant villages in the Spey valley.

Accommodation

Accommodation is mainly in hotels and self-catering apartments, with some simple bed and breakfast houses in the village. The Coylumbridge is a large hotel with a holiday-camp atmosphere outside Aviemore on the way to the ski area. It has a log-cabin bar and dancing in the evening, swimming-pool and tennis courts. Outside Aviemore, the Osprey in Kingussie and the Ard-Na-Coille in Newtonmore are good, small family hotels. There are other small towns and Highland villages in the Spey Valley, including Boat of Garten, Carrbridge, Dulnain Bridge and Grantown-on-Spey, all of which have accommodation.

Eating out

Aviemore alone has 15 restaurants ranging from fish and chips fast-food outlets to much smarter à la carte establishments and the same number again in the nearby villages. Many of the restaurants are in hotels, including the Cairngorm Hotel, which is recommended for its bar food. There is an Indian restaurant and two bistros – La Taverna and the Gallery – as well as the Ecclefechan Bistro in Carrbridge. Booking is essential at the restaurant in the Dunvegan Hotel in Grantown-on-Spey. Generally, restaurants tend to close early, with last orders between 8 and 9pm.

Après-ski

This is not the place to find either the small atmospheric bars of Switzerland and Austria or the huge pounding discos of Italy or France. The choice lies between noisy, often rowdy, hotel bars, and coffee shops and tea-rooms for non-alcoholic relaxation. The Aviemore Centre has a disco, a skating disco and a cinema.

Glenshee 2,162ft (659m)

Glenshee is situated on the main A93 spanning the border of Aberdeenshire and Perthshire on a mountain pass, which can often be temporarily closed by snow. The ski area lies 9 miles (14km) south of Braemar. The nearest railway station is Perth and the nearest airport is Aberdeen.

The trouble with Glenshee is that it lacks both snow-holding gullies and exceptional altitude, but its 26 lifts and 40km of runs offer plenty of scope for an entertaining day's skiing in fine weather. The pistes are short, but the variety of terrain is interesting. The season is a brief one, rarely extending into April. The top station is 3,502ft (1068m) and the vertical drop 1,342ft (409m). The skiing is on both sides of the main road and covers three valleys. There is a large car park, but as in Aviemore when it is full you are turned away or told to drive straight through and you will not be skiing that day. When conditions are good it is important to arrive early.

To the west of the road is the older area of Cairnwell, including the short and sometimes icy Tiger run and the bowl below Carn Aosda. To the east of the road are the lifts to Meall Odhar, which have been extended into the next valley and up to the top station on Glas Maol. The uphill transport is almost entirely by drag-lift. The best and longest-lying snow and the most satisfying runs are on Glas Maol, but early and late in the season there may not be enough snow in the two intervening valleys for access to it by drag.

What is needed is a chair-lift to run parallel to the present drag-lifts. Of the 38 runs, 60 per cent are classified as easy, 34 per cent intermediate and 6 per cent difficult. The longest piste is one mile (2km) and it is graded black/red. A total of 1,312ft (400m) of piste is covered by five snow-cannon. There are two ski schools and a children's ski school. A crèche was introduced for the first time last year.

TOURIST OFFICE
Glenshee Tourist Association,
Perthshire
Tel (0339) 741320
Fax (0337) 41665

TOUR OPERATORS
Scottish Tourist Board

Nevis Range   2,148ft (655m)

Nevis Range was hailed as the future of Scottish skiing when it opened in December 1989, and reporters unanimously agree that, uncertain weather apart, it is living up to its early promise. The skiing is on Aonach Mor, which is Britain's eighth-highest mountain and the close neighbour of Ben Nevis. It lies seven miles (11km) north of Fort William and a little over a mile (2km) along its own access road off the main A82 to Inverness 120 miles (192km) north of Glasgow. This new concept in British skiing is reached by six-person gondola from a car-park and base station at just 90m above sea-level. It takes you speedily up to 2,150ft (655m) to a restaurant ('surprisingly good and reasonably priced'), ski shop and ski school complex.

Two drag-lifts serve the nursery area and a chair gives access to a series of further drags across the wide Snowgoose bowl, which has a vertical drop of 1,856ft (566m). Occasionally it is possible to ski all the way down to the car-park. Eight lifts (not including the gondola) in total serve 24 pistes, which divide equally between easy, intermediate and difficult. Reporters overall are greatly impressed with this small ski area and in particular with the quality of the piste-grooming, and on a clear day the views are magnificent. Nevis Range ski school has 20 full-time and 15 part-time instructors.

There is a bus service from Fort William to the cable car station every three hours. Regular train services operate to Fort William from Glasgow and an overnight train brings skiers from London. The crèche at the base station takes children from three to seven years old; booking is essential.

Fort William is an old lochside town at the foot of Ben Nevis which is well used to tourism although it is taking time for the locals to adjust to having a winter as well as a summer season. It combines a degree of holiday resort liveliness with the unaffected atmosphere of an ordinary small country town with a few hotels and a range of everyday shops and pubs. Reporters recommend the Crannof Seafood restaurant on the pier and the Indian Garden. The Snowgoose restaurant at the top of the gondola is often open in the evening, with weekend discos and ceilidhs; and no charge for the gondola. The Lochaber Leisure Centre has a good pool, squash courts, sauna and climbing wall. The bus to the ski area leaves from outside Presto, near the Nevisport centre, a complex including a bar, café, bookshop and sports shop at the heart of the town.

TOURIST OFFICE
Fort William and Lochaber Tourist Board,
Cameron Square Fort William, Inverness-shire PH3 6AJ
Tel (0397) 703781
Fax (0397) 705184

TOUR OPERATORS
Scottish Tourist Board, Ski Norwest

Glencoe   2,001ft (610m)

The White Corries ski area at Glencoe, 26 miles (42km) from Fort William and 85 miles (136km) north of Glasgow is open only five days a week (not Tuesday or Wednesday) and is limited in appeal. An access chair-lift takes you from an isolated car park at 1,099ft (335m) up to 2,201ft (671m) and a drag-lift takes you up on to the Plateau and the main ski area, which goes on up to the 3,637ft (1109m) summit of Meall A'Bhuirid. It is served by a further chair-lift and three drags. Occasionally it is possible to ski down to the low car park, which provides a total vertical drop of 2,486ft (758m). Although the ski area is small it can boast genuinely easy runs on the Plateau, a short sharp challenge in the Flypaper piste from the summit, as well as intermediate runs above the café. There are 6 miles (10km) of marked pistes, 6 lifts

Skiing facts: Aviemore

TOURIST OFFICE
Aviemore and Spey Valley Tourist Board
Grampian Road
Aviemore PH22 1PP
Tel (0479) 810363
Fax (0479) 811063

THE RESORT
By road London 550 miles (880km)
By rail station in Aviemore
By air Inverness 1 hr
Visitor beds 6,627 in Spey valley (48% hotels, 38% apartments and chalets, 9% guesthouses, 5% hostels)
Transport bus from Aviemore to Cairngorm lifts, £3 return

THE SKIING
Longest run Westwall, 1.6km (black/red)
Number of lifts 17
Number of trails/pistes 25 (32% easy, 32% intermediate, 36% difficult)
Total of trails/pistes 40km
Nursery slopes 4 lifts
Summer skiing none
Snowmaking none

LIFT PASSES
Area pass full area, £60-75 for 6 days
Day pass limited area £8-10, full area £12-15
Half-day pass limited area £6-7.50, full area £9-11, after 1pm
Beginners single and return tickets, vouchers
Children full area, 5-17 yrs, £40-50 for 6 days. Free for 5 yrs and under
Pensioners women 60 yrs and over and men 65 yrs and over, as children
Credit cards accepted yes

SKI SCHOOLS
Adults Aviemore Ski School (one of

many ski schools), 10.30am-12.30pm and 1.30-3.30pm, £64 for 6 days
Children Aviemore Ski School, 8-17 yrs, 10.30am-12.30pm and 1.30pm-3.30pm, £64 for 6 days
Private lessons £50 for a half-day
Special courses snowboarding, telemarking
Guiding companies through ski schools

CROSS-COUNTRY
Ski schools Highland Adventure
Loipe location and size 60km of forest trails

CHILDCARE
Non-ski kindergarten Mercury Freedom Inn Hotel for residents and non-residents, 2-8 yrs, 9am-4pm, £1.25 per hr
Ski kindergarten Aviemore Ski School; Penguin Ski School, 5-7 yrs during Feb half-term and Easter, 10.30am-12.30pm and 1.30-3.30pm, £18 per day, £88 for 6 days not including lunch
Babysitting list available from tourist board

OTHER SPORTS
Skating, curling, indoor tennis, squash, mountain biking, climbing, clay pigeon shooting, golf, fishing, riding, go-karting, swimming

FOOD AND DRINK PRICES
Coffee 60-80p, bottle of house wine £5.75-7.95, beer £1.30-1.50, dish of the day £3.95

TOUR OPERATORS
Hi-Line, Highland Guides, Scottish Tourist Board, Ski Norwest, Ski Treks, Skisafe Travel

and 15 pistes of which 27 per cent are difficult, 33 per cent intermediate and 40 per cent easy. There is also a ski school.

Base facilities have, we are told, been considerably upgraded. The Isles of Glencoe Hotel at nearby Ballachulish is a new and comfortable hotel with swimming-pool. There is simple bed and breakfast accommodation at Glencoe village. The King's House Hotel, which claims to be Scotland's oldest inn, is about a mile (2km) from the car-park. The other nearest hotels are a 30-minute drive away at Fort William.

TOURIST OFFICE
White Corries Ltd, The Ridges,
Glencoe, Argyll PA39 4HT
Tel (08552) 303
Fax (08552) 765

TOUR OPERATORS
Scottish Tourist Board

The Lecht 2,109ft (643m)

The Lecht is a small area best suited to complete beginners and locals who want to practise their technique. It is situated at 2,114ft (645m) on the A939 between Tomintoul and Ballater. It has a top station of 2,600ft (793m) and a vertical drop of 491ft (150m). There are 11 small lifts and pistes, which are all easy to intermediate in standard. There is a café, ski school, hire shop and crèche.

TOURIST OFFICE
Moray District Tourist Board,
17 High Street, Elgin, Morayshire IV30 1EG
Tel (0343) 552075
Fax (0343) 552982

TOUR OPERATORS
Scottish Tourist Board

Spain

• •

Resorts included Baqueira-Beret, Formigal, La Molina, Sierra Nevada

Spain does not have any historical connection with skiing and indeed it seems surprising that a country associated with beaches and summer sunshine should have any skiing at all. It does in fact have two quite separate mountain ranges, which both receive adequate winter snowfalls, regardless of whatever is happening in the countries in the main alpine chain.

Spain is arguably the only country in Europe in which skiing is a growth industry. The number of Spanish skiers continues to increase and it is no longer possible to spend a week in any major ski resort in France or Switzerland without hearing Spanish. The happy result is that ski facilities within their own country are being greatly improved.

Baqueira-Beret remains the most important of the Pyrenean resorts, a small but smart development much loved by King Juan Carlos which attracts wealthy skiers from Madrid and Barcelona. Sierra Nevada in the deep south of the country has an entirely different character and clientele. In preparation for the 1995 Ski World Championships the resort, which used to be called Sol y Nieve, has undergone a complete transformation. It has a solid snow record and nowadays you are far more likely to encounter the Spanish king on the piste here (he has an apartment in the best hotel) than anywhere in the Pyrenees.

The mountain atmosphere in Spain is not markedly dissimilar to that of the mainstream skiing countries, notably Italy. The Spanish are avid holiday-makers, determined to squeeze every available drop of enjoyment out of the day (and the evening). Lunch is a serious business and the sight of three generations of the same family tucking into a huge cauldron of paella and flagons of local wine at a mountain restaurant is wonderfully incongruous and refreshing. The chatter in the cable cars is deafening, noise on the piste is considerable, but it is all thoroughly good-natured.

The low standard of equipment hire has caused considerable disquiet in the past. In the bigger resorts there have been definite improvements and you no longer have to accept skis 10cm too short for your level of technique, nor rental boots of obscure manufacture that feel as old as they look.

The Spanish eat late and party even later, which British skiers sometimes find difficult to keep up with. After a hard day on the slopes it can be disconcerting to discover that restaurants do not begin to fill up before 9pm and the discos are 'dead' until well after midnight. One reporter to Sierra Nevada said he found the evening entertainment 'limited and not particularly interesting', while another raved about the 'action' to be found after 3am.'

Baqueira-Beret, Lérida

ALTITUDE 1500m (4,920ft)

••

Good points efficient lift system, typically Spanish après-ski
Bad points limited tree-level skiing, lack of resort charm
Linked or nearby resorts Llessui (n), Port-Ainé (n), Super Espot (n)

Baqueira is a genuinely exclusive resort in the Spanish Pyrenees, a small, modern development with upmarket hotels and an abundance of furs and Ferraris. It lies at the head of the beautiful Val d'Aran, near Viella on the northern side of the Pyrenees, which means easy access from France and more reliable snow than in other Spanish resorts. Its skiing is in a reasonably large area with a mixture of tree-lined and open terrain and varied grades of runs. The original ski station is at the foot of the lifts, comprising modern apartment blocks and hotels. Many regular visitors prefer to stay in the more traditional hotels further down the valley. There are good inns in both Viella and Arties. Because it is not cheap, Baqueira attracts few tour operators, although it does have a small and loyal British following.

The skiing

Top 2510m (8,233ft) bottom 1510m (4,953ft)
There are 43 pistes at Baqueira-Beret, a total of 73km of ski terrain and 22 lifts. The ski area is cut into two by a narrow valley. The main mountain, Cap de Baqueira (2500m), is directly above the resort and consists of a compact network of chair- and drag-lifts serving mainly intermediate runs on the west face of the mountain. Three triple chair-lifts below the Cap de Argulls make up a notable area of mainly blue (easy) runs, with a couple of steeper descents graded red (intermediate) and black (difficult) on the right-hand side. There are some longer, challenging slopes on the north side of the Cap de Baqueira and a couple of itineraries down the tree-lined valley that separates it from the wider and gentler slopes above Beret. From Orri in the valley a series of chair-lifts and easy pistes of 1800-2500m take you across Tuc det Dossau, which has two steep descents and an indirect blue one. The longest run is 5.5km from Cara Norte to Cascada.

There is a quad chair from Baqueira to the nursery area at Torre de Control, where there are two baby-lifts and a total of 100m of slopes. A lift pass is necessary for children from the age of 6, although there is a 45 per cent reduction up to the age of 11. We have enthusiastic reports of the Baqueira-Beret ski school (although little English is spoken); snowboarding is taught and heli-skiing is also possible. The ski kindergarten, Guarderia 1500, is for babies from 6 months and Guarderia 1800 is for 3-year-olds and over. Babysitting is available through the hotels.

Mountain restaurants include the waiter-service Restaurant 1800, Bosque, Restaurant 2200 and Audeth. Queues are not a problem here except on public holidays. The efficient lift system is said to be modelled on Vail's and has a high number of chair-lifts including some fast quads. There is artificial snow-making.

The resort

The resort itself lies beside the road up to the very high Bonaigua pass, often but not always closed in winter. Recent sympathetic development has increased its appeal as a base with some good shops, hotels, restaurants and a leisure centre. The atmosphere is relaxed and friendly. There are just under 3,000 tourist beds in the resort, of which 45 per cent are in apartments, 31 per cent in chalets and 24 per cent in hotels. The Tryp Royal Tanau is a new 5-star hotel complete with swimming-pool, fitness centre and an indoor golf simulator. There are two supermarkets for self-caterers.

Après-ski

The après-ski is genuinely Spanish; the numerous *tapas* bars fill up as soon as the lifts close. The Escornacrepki is said to be one of the more popular restaurants and the best-value places include the Borda Lobato, Perdiu Blanca and Ticolet. The restaurant in the new Tryp Royal Tanau hotel and the Casa Irene are two of the smartest eating places. The most popular evening bars are the Nolotil at Baqueira, the Luna and the Carpa at Arties. Elurra and Tiffany's are the discos which are based at Viella. Despite its exclusive reputation, reporters were pleasantly surprised to find resort prices lower than they had expected.

Other activities include dog-sledding, parapente, bowling, a total of three fitness centres and seven kilometres of cross-country loipe at Pla de Beret. The small nearby ski resorts of Super Espot, Llessui and Port-Ainé are all within easy driving distance.

TOURIST OFFICE
PO Box 60, 25530 Viella, Spain
Tel 34 73 644455
Fax 34 73 644488

TOUR OPERATORS
Ski Miquel

Sierra Nevada, Granada

ALTITUDE 2100m (6,888ft)

••

Good points skiing for beginners and intermediates, mountain scenery, lively après-ski, varied choice of restaurants
Bad points weekend crowds, frequent bad weather conditions, lack of tree-level skiing, lack of resort charm
Linked or nearby resorts none

Sierra Nevada lies in the Andalusian mountain range of the same name, 32km from the ancient Moorish city of Granada, and constitutes Europe's most southerly skiing. Unlike the other Spanish ski resorts, which are nearly all in the Pyrenees, in the north-east of Spain, Sierra Nevada is out on a limb, a stark contrast to the surrounding area and nearby resorts of Marbella and Malaga with their yacht clubs and golf courses. The resort used to be marketed under the name of Sol y Nieve (Sun and Snow) and the purpose-built village in which most skiers stay (at 2100m) is known as Pradollano.

The ski area is extremely vulnerable to bad weather and the mountain range as a whole is exposed to Atlantic gales. When the weather here is bad everything stops, but when conditions are good the skiing can be excellent and the views stunning. On a clear day you can even see Morocco. However, because of the proximity to Granada and the Costa del Sol, the resort suffers from crowding at weekends and on public holidays.

Mountain access to the main skiing area is by a choice of three lifts (including a gondola) from the edge of the village. To the right of the top gondola station is a small nursery area, consisting of four short green (beginner) runs served by drag-lifts. Most of the skiing is on the wide, easy and intermediate slopes of Veleta, above Borreguiles at 2645m. Of more interest to experts is the skiing around Loma de Dilar, a ridge served by chairs and drags with short, steep black runs down the face. These provide some challenge, but the resort is more suitable for beginners and intermediates ('not suited for advanced skiers looking for a challenge – I'd be bored if I spent a week here').

The mountain restaurants tend to become crowded as soon as the morning ski school finishes, although queues to be served appear to be no longer than five minutes. The restaurants are praised by reporters as 'unglamorous and excellent value' and 'the quality of food was better than expected'. Eating places include the cheap and cheerful Borreguiles close to the top gondola station.

There are competing ski schools and English is widely spoken. The Escuela Espanola de Esqui comes in for a mixed reception: 'The instructor's initial reluctance to teach beginners wore off as our level of skiing improved throughout the week.' There is one nursery drag-lift, a kindergarten in the resort and a ski kindergarten up at Borreguiles.

The resort

Most of Pradollano's buildings date from the 1960s and 1970s, but some are more recent. It is not an attractive place ('just like Torremolinos with snow and litter'), but the atmosphere is 'quiet, with quite a Spanish feel to the resort'. The accommodation is mainly in hotels. The Melia Sol y Nieve and the four-star Melia Sierra Nevada, both near the main square, are convenient and pleasant. The Melia Sol y Nieve has a mini-club for children from 5 to 11 years old. Melia Sierra Nevada has a swimming-pool, disco and its own shops. The Kenia Nevada is recommended by a reporter as 'a quiet hotel, most guests were Spanish but the service was generally friendly and attentive and the bedrooms comfortable and clean'. The chalet-style Parador, set on its own above Pradollano (accessible by chair-lift and piste), is fairly functional but has exceptional views. The Albergue Universitani is said to be excellent value and clean. One reporter recommends staying in a cheap hostel in Granada ('very easy to drive up to the resort in the morning and significantly cheaper than staying in the resort'). Self-caterers can buy provisions at the single supermarket.

Après-ski

Alternative sports include tobogganing near the Parador, ski-jumping and two cross-country loipes. The bars tend to fill up as soon as the lifts close, with the British-run Crescendo Lodge bar reportedly a friendly place. There is a small range of restaurants serving local, French, Turkish and Italian cuisine. The Borreguiles is one of the most popular eating places and the Sierra Nevada 53 disco is recommended.

Excursions can be made to Granada, famous for the spectacular Alhambra Palace as well as for its beautiful renaissance and baroque buildings. The shops in the resort are limited and sell mainly expensive ski wear. There is little else for non-skiers.

TOURIST OFFICE
Sierra Nevada Information, Pradollano, Granada
Tel 34 58 48 05 00

TOUR OPERATORS
Ski Thomson

Formigal 1500m (4,920ft)

The resort of El Formigal lies in the Tena Valley in the centre of the Pyrenees and 8km from the French border. Formigal has 18 lifts (including one gondola) and 27 pistes in an open and sunny area rising to Pico Tres Hombres at 2350m. The gentle runs are mainly suited to beginners and intermediates, although there are also a couple of more difficult runs. There is a ski school, ski and non-ski kindergarten (English is spoken by about 25 per cent of the instructors), two nursery slopes and five mountain restaurants.

The village itself is modern, with stark concrete and wood architecture. Most of the hotels, cafés and bars line a central main street. The Nieve Sol is a large hotel close to the village centre with its own disco. The Meson Arrigal is a typically Spanish restaurant serving good-value *tapas*. The resort of Panticosa, with its small ski area of 7 lifts and 14 pistes, is a short drive away in the same valley as Formigal.

TOURIST OFFICE
Formigal Information, Sallent de Gállego, Huesca
Tel 34 74 48 81 25

TOUR OPERATORS
Ski Thomson

La Molina 1400m (4,592ft)

The resort is in the eastern part of La Cerdeña and 14km from the French border. It connects with neighbouring Masella (1600m) via a chair over the peak of Tossa d'Alp.

La Molina has 21 lifts, most of which are on the open, intermediate slopes of Puig Llancada. La Molina itself has 21 lifts including one nursery drag-lift; Masella has 10 lifts and a mixture of runs including five blacks from the Tossa summit. The straggling old village of La Molina lacks any real centre and there is a newer purpose-built satellite, Supermolina, higher up the mountain at 1700m.

TOURIST OFFICE
La Molina Information, Alp Gerona
Tel 34 72 89 21 76

TOUR OPERATORS

Skiing safety

The mountains are like the sea: they give enormous pleasure, but they can also be dangerous and should be treated with the utmost respect at all times. Only when you find yourself in an awkward and potentially dangerous situation or witness an accident at first hand do you properly realise what the risks can be. Below are a few useful tips:

Weather and exposure

The weather can change at a moment's notice and vary dramatically at different altitudes. Always dress with this in mind and be prepared for all conditions. Several layers of clothing are best. Never set off without sunglasses or goggles, and a hat or headband. It is always preferable to be too hot than too cold.

All children under the age of 14 years should wear helmets. Unfortunately they are not yet compulsory and you will still see more helmets in certain ski countries than others. They can be worn on their own or over a thin balaclava or hat on extremely cold days.

Never ski with a baby or small child in a backpack, however warm and sunny the weather. Even the best skiers can catch an edge, or someone could ski into you.

Exposure in bad weather can result in frostbite or hypothermia. Frostbite is the excessive cooling of small areas of the body, usually of the fingers, toes, nose, cheeks or ears. The affected tissue first turns white and numb. This is called first-degree frostbite and can be dealt with by immediate, gentle re-warming. In cold conditions watch out for signs of frostbite in each other. Hypothermia is a condition resulting from a drop in the whole body's temperature. It is difficult to diagnose, with some of the more obvious symptoms being physical or mental lethargy, sluggishness, slurring of speech, spurts of energy and abnormal vision.

Accident procedure

Speed is essential when an accident has occurred:

- Mark the accident site by placing crossed skis about 10m uphill of the casualty
- If the casualty is not breathing, administer artificial respiration (mouth-to-mouth resuscitation). Make sure there is nothing obstructing the mouth or throat
- If the casualty is breathing but unconscious, turn him/her on to their side to minimise the risk of choking. Protect any fractured limb from movement
- If the casualty is bleeding, apply direct pressure to the site of the wound using a cloth pad if possible

- Do not remove the ski boot if there is injury to the lower leg as it acts as a splint
- Keep the casualty warm, comfortable and as cheerful as possible. Alert the ski patrol immediately
- If the casualty appears to be in shock, by going pale, cold and faint, he/she should be encouraged to lie with their head lower than their feet. Do not administer food or drink.

Safety on the piste

A set of rules for skiers is drawn up by the International Ski Federation. These rules aim to keep skiing accidents to a minimum, and are increasingly forming the basis of legal judgments in both civil and criminal actions in European courts. If you do cause an accident while in breach of these rules, you could be in serious trouble. A list of the rules is printed below:

FIS rules for the conduct of skiers

1 Respect for others: a skier must behave in such a way that he does not endanger or prejudice others.
2 Control of speed and skiing: a skier must ski in control. He must adapt his speed and manner of skiing to his personal ability and to the prevailing conditions of terrain, snow and weather as well as to the density of traffic.
3 Choice of route: a skier coming from behind must choose his route in such a way that he does not endanger skiers ahead.
4 Overtaking: a skier may overtake another skier above or below and to the right or the left, provided that he leaves enough space for the overtaken skier to make any voluntary or involuntary movement.
5 Entering and starting: a skier entering a marked run or starting again after stopping must look up and down the run to make sure that he can do so without endangering himself or others.
6 Stopping on the piste: unless absolutely necessary, a skier must avoid stopping on the piste in narrow places or where visibility is restricted. After a fall in such a place, a skier must move clear of the piste as soon as possible.
7 Climbing and descending on foot: both climbing or descending skiers on foot must keep to the side of the piste.
8 Respect for signs and markings: a skier must respect all signs and markings.
9 Assistance: at accidents, every skier is duty-bound to assist.
10 Identification: every skier and witness, whether a responsible party or not, must exchange names and addresses following an accident.

General comments on the rules

Skiing, like all sport, entails risks. The FIS rules must be considered an ideal pattern of conduct for a responsible and careful skier; their purpose is to avoid accidents on the piste. The rules apply to all skiers, who are obliged to be familiar with them and to respect them. If he fails to do so, his behaviour could expose him to civil and criminal liability in the event of an accident.

Rule 1   Skiers are responsible not only for their own behaviour, but also for their defective equipment. This also applies to those using newly developed equipment.

Rule 2   Collisions usually happen because skiers are travelling too fast, are out of control or have failed to see others. A skier must be able to stop, turn and move within the ability of his own vision. In crowded areas, or in places where visibility is reduced, skiers must ski slowly, especially at the edge of a steep slope, at the bottom of a piste and within areas surrounding ski lifts.

Rule 3   Skiing is a free activity sport where everyone may ski where and as they please, provided that they abide by these rules and adapt their skiing to their own personal ability and to the prevailing conditions on the mountain. The skier in front has priority. The skier behind another in the same direction must keep sufficient distance between himself and the other skier so as to leave the preceding skier enough space to make all his movements freely.

Rule 4   A skier who overtakes another is wholly responsible for completing that manoeuvre in such a way as not to cause a difficulty to the skier being overtaken. This responsibility rests with him until the overtaking manoeuvre has been completed. This rule applies even when overtaking a stationary skier.

Rule 5   Experience proves that entering a piste and starting to ski again after stopping are the cause of accidents. It is absolutely essential that a skier finding himself in this situation enters the piste safely and without causing an obstruction or danger to himself or others. When he has started skiing properly again, even slowly, he has the benefit of Rule 3 against faster skiers coming from above or behind.

Rule 6   Except on wide pistes, stops must be made at the side of the piste. One must not stop in narrow places or where it is difficult to be seen from above.

Rule 7   Moving against the general direction poses unexpected obstacles for the skiers.

Rule 8   The degree of difficulty of a piste is indicated in black, red, blue or green. A skier is free to choose whichever piste he wants. The pistes are also marked with other signs, showing direction or giving warnings of danger or closure. A sign closing a piste, like one denoting danger, must be strictly observed. Skiers should be aware that warning signs are posted in their own interests.

Rule 9   It is a cardinal principal for all sportsmen that they should render assistance following an accident, independent of any legal obligation to do so. Immediate first aid should be given, the appropriate authorities alerted and the place of the accident marked to warn other skiers. The FIS hopes that a hit-and-run offence in skiing will incur a criminal conviction similar to a hit-and-run offence on the road, and that equivalent penalties will be imposed by all countries where such legislation is not already in force.

Rule 10 Witnesses are of great importance in establishing a full and proper report of an accident; therefore, everybody must consider that it is his duty as a responsible person to provide information as a witness. Reports of the rescue service and of the police as well as photographs, are of considerable assistance in determining civil and criminal liability.

Safety off-piste

No one should ski off-piste without a properly qualified local guide, particularly in glacial terrain where the risk of crevasse is added to that of avalanche. Always wear a recognised avalanche bleeper and take the time to learn how to use it and carry out a grid search *before* you set off. The chances of survival after an avalanche deteriorate rapidly after the first five minutes. Listen to your guide, learn basic snowcraft and how to read a slope. Remember you may be many kilometres from a resort or a pisted run with no trail markers to guide you.

In the event of an avalanche, try to ski to the side. If you fall, get rid of your skis, poles, and backpack if possible. Swim and fight to stay on the surface.

Tips to remember when skiing off-piste

- Always ski in a group, never alone
- Always ski in control
- Always stop behind the guide (there may be cliffs or other hazards ahead)
- In deep snow use powder cords – three-metre ribbons attached to your skis – to enable you to find a lost ski after a fall
- Carry a map of the area and a compass. Know how to use both
- Be wary of slopes where the run-out is not clearly obvious from the start. Following other skiers' tracks does not necessarily mean the route is safe.

Equipment report

These days skiers face an unprecedented and bewildering choice of boots. Until recently, boot manufacturers satisfied themselves with making one, or at most two, types of shell. Now the two market leaders, Nordica and Salomon, manufacture no fewer than four different categories of boot with many choices of model within each one.

The recent move away from rear-entry boots, more dictated by fickle fashion merchants than any sense of logic or skier practicality, has led to a host of 'mid-entry', traditional but revived 'overlap', and redesigned overlap designs. If you have bought rear-entry in the past few years (and up to 80 per cent of skiers were doing so until recently) it is best to think carefully before making any rash moves. Many new designs are being rushed out and relatively few of them have a good design pedigree.

Indeed, it is perhaps as well to get back to the basics of what a boot is designed to do. There are four criteria, all with a capital 'C', which should be uppermost on your shopping list when boot buying:

● **Comfort** Always the primary factor unless you want to torture your feet to obtain the tightest control through a set of slalom gates. For most people, rear-entry boots are more comfortable than overlap or mid-boots because the foot is held firmly across the instep (the lower part of the shell is fixed in volume). The more traditional boots with clips controlling an overlapping shell bring the shell closer to the foot. Additional uncomfortable pressure-points often result

● **Control** A ski boot is designed to transmit your side-to-side and ankle bending movements to the ski. The best boots achieve this with the minimum loss of energy and movement into the padding or shell of the boot. It is therefore vital that your inner boots are not too thick or mushy once your technique improves. The most critical part of a boot's transmission function is the top of the shell and cuff, so make sure that the boot grips the lower leg firmly here

● **Convenience** In this area there is really no competition between rear-entry and front-entry boots. All rear-entry boots are entered and tightened quickly with a maximum of two clips. In some cases (notably Salomon) the tightness you skied with the afternoon before is memorised for the morning after – a handy benefit. Nordica, Raichle and Rossignol are the only manufacturers to have put fresh design work into rear-entry so far and their models are also worth trying

● **Custom-fit** Custom foam-injected boots have been around ever since the change from leather to plastic in the early-1970s. When expertly foamed (make sure you visit a highly experienced retailer with a technician who has performed many successful fittings) this provides a comfort and quality of ski control that cannot be equalled with an off-the-shelf boot. Customised 'orthotic' insoles, notably Sidas Conformable, are also worth investigating.

The ultimate control

Notwithstanding the above, there is no disputing that the vast majority of racers, instructors and other professional skiers have spurned rear-entry in favour of boots that in many cases are only marginally different to those which predominated 15 years ago; classic two-part shell, four-clip boots. The research and design resources of boot companies have now swung back into these boots, with some interesting results for 1993-4.

The classic Lange shell continues from year to year with minor changes and is a firm favourite. Tecnica has emulated this style of design with even better results in the form of the TNT, with an unusually well-made inner. Nordica revived the Grand Prix for the 1992-3 season, but its new Vertech looks more interesting.

The Salomon Integral was a controversial new boot in 1992-3 because of its unconventional design, but the Evolution models look most promising and have a good forward-lean release for easy walking. The new Raichle Flexon Comp has much improved clips and overall design, as do the Dynafit 3F series.

For those strong enough to want a very serious (stiff) flex pattern in their boots, the Rossignol and Nordica racing models are probably about the best.

Skis: new widths/new shapes

Compared to other forms of transport, skis do not traditionally vary much in terms of dimensions: 190cm long (give or take 20cm) and 66mm wide (give or take 4mm) are the sizes which tend to prevail. For optimum all-round performance in terms of speed, stability and turning in all snow conditions, there can be little variation. This is not to say that dramatic and interesting options in performance cannot be served up by altering lengths and shapes. While the world's fastest skiers, of the Flying Kilometre, use skis tall enough to touch a ceiling (240cm), a lot of people are having fun skidding and spinning around on 'Figl' skis which are only 60cm long. One amusing version of these is the Big Foot, made by Kneissl, which is shaped like a big pink foot. It has been successfully marketed into a craze in Austria. Rent a pair for a day for a novel experience.

The compact skis that swept the market in the mid-1970s, 20 to 30cm shorter than normal ski lengths, revolutionised the ease with which people could learn to ski, tackle moguls and other trickier conditions. For slower, more timid skiers they were, and still are, a most valid concept. Atomic and Head (in the form of an old favourite, the Hot Head) have sensibly revived the idea for 1993-4. If you ski slowly, there is no reason to feel ashamed of skiing with 160cm, 170cm or 180cm skis – the experience is a lot easier and the only gain from longer skis is stability at speed, which you will not need anyway.

A ski of bizarre dimensions which caused much comment in 1993 was the Atomic Powder Plus (Fat Boy). Again on the short side, it is generally skied at a 180cm length, but comes in 4 sizes from 150cm to

200cm, and has the difference of being 80 per cent wider than a regular ski. This ski therefore has exceptional floating qualities in powder, slushy and cruddy snow, qualities that monoskiers have enjoyed for years with a similar overall surface area.

The buoyancy of super-wide skis (Volkl is also making one called the Explosiv) makes turning in tricky snow far easier and lighter, with hardly any need to 'unweight'. Like the monoski, the design of the Powder Plus or Explosiv compromises piste performance somewhat because the edge-to-edge speed is slow and turning is therefore sluggish. The bindings are uniquely mounted off-centre toward the inside edges and both ski brakes have to be sawn off so leashes, as the top surface of the ski states bluntly, are mandatory. Mike Wiegele Helicopter Skiing in British Columbia uses Fat Boys with custom-built ski brakes fitted to the bindings. It seems likely that these will now be marketed throughout Europe.

Equally wide at the tip and tail, but with extreme curvature toward the waist (which is narrower than slalom skis at 60mm), the Kneissl Ergo is designed more for piste use and is made to turn very quickly with minimum effort. Super-curved edges like this may be a trend for future ski design (Elan are also making a ski of this type).

Which tour operator?

For many of us a ski holiday is one of the highlights of the year, a time when we can relax and leave the worries of everyday life behind as we set off down the slopes in the clear mountain air. But if the tour operator you have booked with goes into liquidation, either after you have booked the holiday and paid in full or, worse still, while you are actually at your resort enjoying your holiday, it can be a nightmare. The only way to protect your interests is to make sure the operator with which you book with is fully bonded.

A bonded company will have been financially assessed by a Government-approved bond organiser and will have provided a legal guarantee to the bond administrators, via its bank or an insurance company, to provide a cash sum on liquidation. The bond administrators have back-up insurance as a fail-safe and will organise the refund of money owed to you by the tour organiser. If you are already abroad, the bond administrators will arrange for you to complete your holiday and return to the United Kingdom.

Since January 1993 it has been illegal to trade as a tour operator without offering financial protection to customers in the case of insolvency. Any tour operator doing so lays itself open to criminal liability, which is not of much comfort to customers if they lose their holiday or their money and have no prospect of recovering either.

Skiers should therefore ascertain that their chosen operator is fully bonded before parting with any money. A number of trade organisations are acceptable to the DTI but the main ones for companies involved with the ski travel industry are:

● **ABTA**, the Association of British Travel Agents, represents about 90 per cent of the travel industry in Britain
● **AITO**, the Association of Independent Tour Operators, which has over 130 members. A number (eight at the time of going to press) of its 31 ski members are protected by AITO's own bonding arm. Other members may be and often are bonded through ABTA and ATOL (see below) but membership of AITO does not confirm that the company is bonded
● **The Civil Aviation Authority** is responsible for the issue of Air Travel Organisers' Licences. Any company offering air-inclusive holidays is required to have one. Any company that is an ATOL holder can be considered fully bonded, provided you are travelling by air. If you intend to self-drive with a company bonded only by ATOL your holiday is technically not financially safe in the event of any liquidation
● **The Passenger Shipping Association**, representing ferry and cruise lines.

Below is a list of ABTA-, AITO- and ATOL-bonded ski operators offering holidays from Britain:

AA MOTORING HOLIDAYS
Fanum House
Basingstoke
Hants
HHRG21 2EA
Reservations (0256) 493878
Bonding ABTA
Travel self-drive
Accommodation apartments
Small operator specialising in ski-drive holidays to France. AA Five Star vehicle cover inclusive in package.
Children under four years travel free

ACTIVITY TRAVEL
23 Blair Street
Edinburgh
EH1 1QR
Reservations 081-541 5115.
Fax (031) 220 4185
Bonding ABTA, ATOL
Travel air, departing Gatwick, Heathrow, Edinburgh, Glasgow, Manchester, Newcastle, Plymouth, Stansted
Accommodation hotels, apartments, chalets, lodges
Large range of resorts in the Alps and the Rockies. USA ski and sun combinations, family discounts, ski guiding, fly-drive, flights only package. Separate group skiing brochure

ALL CANADA TRAVEL AND HOLIDAYS
90 High Street
Lowestoft
Suffolk
NR32 1XN
Reservations (0502) 565176.
Fax (0502) 500681
Bonding ABTA
Travel air, departing Gatwick. Also self-drive
Accommodation hotels
Operator offering ski holidays to Canada. Resorts include Banff, Lake Louise and Whistler. Offers learn-to-ski packages and fly-drive

ALPINE EXPRESSIONS
4 Belsize Crescent
London
NW3 5QU
Reservations 071-794 1480.
Fax 071-431 4221
Bonding AITO Trust
Travel air, any UK airport. Also self-drive
Accommodation hotels
French specialist with tailor-made holidays in hotels of character to resorts including Megève, Châtel, and Samoëns

ALPINE TOURS
54 Northgate
Canterbury
Kent
CT1 1BE
Reservations (0227) 454777.
Fax (0227) 451177
Bonding ABTA, ATOL, AITO member
Travel air, departing Gatwick, Heathrow, Birmingham, Bournemouth, Bristol, Glasgow, Leeds-Bradford, Luton, Manchester, Stansted.
Also coach and self-drive
Accommodation hotels
Specialising in holidays to the Austrian Tyrol. Excellent race clinics for intermediates with Olympic medallist Heini Messner, powder clinics, mogul clinics, summer skiing, schools

AMERICAN INDEPENDENCE
The Gables
42b High Street
Great Dunmow
Essex
CM6 1AH
Reservations (0371) 874848.
Fax (0371) 874543
Bonding ABTA
Travel air, departing Gatwick, Heathrow, Glasgow
Accommodation hotels and apartments
Specialist US operator offering ski holidays to 20 USA resorts. Child discounts and fly-drive packages available

AUSTRIAN HOLIDAYS
50-51 Conduit Street
London
W1R 0NP
Reservations 071-439 7108.
Fax 071-437 0343
Bonding ABTA, ATOL
Travel air, departing Gatwick, Heathrow, Birmingham, Manchester
Accommodation hotels
Specialises in Austrian holidays

BALKAN HOLIDAYS
Sofia House
19 Conduit Street
London

W1R 9TD
Reservations 071-493 8612.
Fax 071-491 7068
Bonding ABTA, ATOL
Travel air, departing Gatwick,
Heathrow, Birmingham, Manchester
Accommodation hotels
*Holidays in Bulgaria, Romania and
Slovenia with the emphasis on
beginners to early intermediates, and
cheap après-ski. Discounts of up
to 50% for children sharing a room with
adults*

BALKAN TOURS
37 Ann Street
Belfast
BT1 4EB
Reservations (0232) 246795.
Fax (0232) 234581
Bonding ABTA, ATOL, AITO member
Travel air, departing Belfast, Dublin
Accommodation hotels
*One of Ireland's biggest ski operators
offering holidays to Bulgaria and
Romania. Offers school and group
holidays*

BEACH VILLAS
8 Market Passage
Cambridge
CB2 3QR
Reservations (0223) 311113.
Fax (0223) 313557
Bonding ABTA, ATOL, AITO member
Travel air, departing Gatwick, Glasgow,
Luton, Manchester. Snow train to
French and Austrian resorts
Accommodation chalets
*Small operator with wide-ranging
programme which includes St Anton,
Arabba and Verbier. Child and group
discounts*

BLADON LINES
56/58 Putney High Street
London
SW15 1SF
Reservations 081-785 3131.
Fax 081-788 3543
Bonding ABTA, ATOL, AITO member
Travel air, departing Bristol, Gatwick,
Glasgow, Luton, Manchester. Also
snow train
Accommodation mainly chalets, also
hotels and apartments
*One of the major chalet operators
offering ski holidays to more than
20 resorts. Child, granny and nanny
discounts make it a good choice for
families. Offers ski guiding and a
crèche in Tignes*

BRITTANY FERRIES
The Brittany Centre
Wharf Road
Portsmouth
PO2 8RU
Reservations (0705) 751833
Bonding PSA (Passenger Shipping
Association)
Travel ferry from Portsmouth to Caen
Accommodation apartments
*Ferry company offering ski-drive
holidays to France. Free ferry crossing
and accommodation for children
under 14 years on holiday with two or
more adults*

CANADA AIR HOLIDAYS
50 Sauchiehall Street
Glasgow
G2 3AG
Reservations 041-332 1511/(0345)
090905. Fax 041-353 0135
Bonding ABTA
Travel air, departing Heathrow, Gatwick
Accommodation hotels
Specialises in Canadian holidays

THE CLUB
1st Floor
Devonshire House
29-31 Elmfield Road
Bromley
Kent
BR1 1LT
Reservations 081-313 9900
Bonding ABTA, ATOL
Travel air, departing Gatwick,
Birmingham, Manchester. Also coach
and self-drive
Accommodation hotels, apartments,
and chalets
*Emphasis on fun and après-ski for
young skiers, singles holidays, group
reductions, beginners' holidays with
video instruction*

CLUB MED
106/110 Brompton Road
London
SW3 1JJ
Reservations 071-581 1161.
Fax 071-581 4769
Bonding ABTA, ATOL
Travel air, departing Heathrow,
Gatwick, Manchester
Accommodation club-hotels
*Specialist in upmarket holiday villages
in France, Switzerland, Italy, Colorado
and Japan. Baby clubs in three resorts,
mini clubs (4 years and over) in 20
resorts. Extensive in-house après-ski,
own ski school*

CONTIKI
Wells House
15 Elmfield Rd
Bromley
Kent
BR1 1LS
Reservations 081-290 6422.
Fax 081-290 6569
Bonding ABTA, ATOL
Travel coach, departing London
Accommodation hotels and
club-chalets
*Coach holidays for ages 18-35
years in Hopfgarten, Austria.
Emphasis on the social scene as
well as skiing*

CRYSTAL
Crystal House
The Courtyard
Arlington Road
Surbiton
Surrey
KT6 6BW
Reservations 081-399 5144.
Fax 081-390 6378
Bonding ABTA, ATOL
Travel air, departing Gatwick,
Birmingham, Bristol, Exeter, Glasgow,
Leeds/Bradford, Luton, Manchester,
Newcastle, Southampton,
Southend. Also coach, snow train and
self-drive
Accommodation hotels, apartments
and chalets
*Major operator offering ski holidays to
over 43 resorts including Europe,
Eastern Europe, USA and Canada.
Offers crèches, learn-to-ski packages.
Separate Ski Value brochure*

DAWSON AND SANDERSON
60 Middle Street
Consett
County Durham
DH8 5QE
Reservations (0207) 591261.
Fax (0207) 591262
Bonding ABTA, ATOL
Travel air, departing Heathrow,
Newcastle. Also by ferry
Accommodation hotels
*Small operator which did not produce
a brochure for 1992-3 season, but
sends clients to Voss and Geilo
in Norway*

DIRECT SKI
Halliburton House
5 Putney Bridge Approach
London
SW6 3JD

Reservations 071-371 0060.
Fax 071-371 8616
Bonding ABTA, ATOL
Travel air, departing Gatwick,
Heathrow, Glasgow, Manchester
Accommodation hotels and
apartments
*Small French specialist operator with
nine resorts. Ski clinics and learn-to-ski
packages available. Budget and luxury
apartments*

ENTERPRISE
Groundstar House
London Road
Crawley
RH10 2TB
Reservations London (0293) 560777
Manchester 061-745 7000.
Fax (0293) 588680
Bonding ABTA, ATOL
Travel air, departing Gatwick,
Heathrow, Birmingham, Bristol,
Glasgow, Manchester, Newcastle,
Stansted. Also snow train
and self-drive
Accommodation hotels, apartments
and chalets
*Major operator, offering ski holidays
in over 85 resorts in 9 countries. Group
discounts, good family and child
facilities*

EQUITY TOTAL SKI
Norwood House
9 Dyke Road
Brighton
East Sussex
BN1 3FE
Reservations (0273) 203202.
Fax (0273) 203212
Bonding ABTA, ATOL
Travel air, departing Glasgow,
Manchester. Also coach and self-drive
Accommodation hotels and
apartments
*Comprehensive packages offered to
resorts in Austria, France, and Italy*

FLEXISKI
55 Old Church Street
London
SW3 5BS
Reservations 071-352 0044.
Fax 071-376 3730
Bonding ATOL
Travel air, departing Gatwick,
Heathrow, Birmingham
Accommodation chalets and hotels
*A small specialist operator for Verbier
and Courchevel 1850. Offers weekend
skiing*

FREEDOM HOLIDAYS
30 Brackenbury Road
Hammersmith
London
W6 0BA
Reservations 081-741 2345/4471.
Fax 081-741 9332
Bonding ABTA, ATOL, AITO member
Travel air, departing Gatwick,
Heathrow, Manchester. Also self-drive
Accommodation hotels and
apartments
*Small operator offering ski holidays in
Andorra and Châtel*

FRENCH IMPRESSIONS
31 Topsfield Parade
London
N8 8PT
Reservations 081-342 8870.
Fax 081-342 8860
Bonding ABTA
Travel self-drive, departing Dover,
Newhaven, Southampton, Harwich
Accommodation apartments and
chalets
*Ski-drive holidays to 10 different
resorts in France. Offers family
discounts and accommodation for
all budgets*

FRESH TRACKS
McMillan House
Cheam Common Road
Worcester Park
Surrey
KT4 8RH
Reservations 081-335 3003.
Fax 081-330 6819
Bonding ABTA, ATOL
Travel air, departing Gatwick,
Heathrow, Manchester
Accommodation hotels and
apartments
*Small operator offering learn-to-ski
powder programmes, mountain
guiding using local guides, and special
family weeks. Holidays in Flaine and
Chamonix. Agent for Mike Wiegele
Helicopter Skiing in British Columbia*

FRONTIER SKI
Winge Travel Ltd
3 Whitcomb Street
London
WC2H 7HA
Reservations 071-839 5341.
Fax 071-839 5761
Bonding ABTA, ATOL, AITO
Travel air, departing Heathrow,
Glasgow, Manchester
Accommodation hotels, self-catering

chalets and apartments
*Specialises in holidays to Whistler,
Banff and Lake Louise in Canada.
Offers tailor-made holidays and
heli-skiing*

GTF TOURS
182-186 Kensington Church Street
London
W8 4DP
Reservations 071-792 1260.
Fax 071-221 0390
Bonding ABTA, ATOL
Travel air, departing Gatwick
Accommodation hotels and
snowhouses
*Goes to five Austrian resorts. Offers
weekend skiing and short breaks,
child and group reductions, flight-only
packages*

GO WORLDS APART HOLIDAYS
Global House
31 Brixton Road
Watford
Herts
WD2 5AB
Reservations (0923) 817698
Bonding ABTA
Travel coach, remains with you
throughout the duration of the holiday
Accommodation apartments
*Small operator specialising in holidays
based in Kirchdorf, Austria. Beginners
ski Kirchdorf whilst intermediates and
above go to Steinplatte or St Johann.
Also offers holidays in Isola 2000*

HEADWATER HOLIDAYS
146 London Road
Northwich
Cheshire
CW9 5HH
Reservations (0606) 48699.
Fax (0606) 48761
Bonding ABTA, ATOL, AITO member
Travel air, departing Gatwick,
Heathrow, Belfast, Birmingham, Bristol,
Edinburgh, Glasgow, Manchester,
Newcastle. Also rail and self-drive
Accommodation hotels
*Specialises in cross-country and alpine
ski holidays in France, Norway and
Canada for all ages and stages. Also
offers gourmet ski weeks*

HOVERSPEED HOLIDAYS
Travelscene House
11-15 St Ann's Road
Harrow
Midds
HA1 1AS

Reservations 081-424 2929.
Fax 081-863 0545
Bonding ABTA,ATOL
Travel self-drive
Accommodation apartments
Small operator offering ski-drive holidays to France and Switzerland

INGHAMS
10-18 Putney Hill
London
SW15 6AX
Reservations 081-785 7777.
Fax 081-785 2045
Bonding ABTA, ATOL
Travel air, departing Gatwick, Heathrow, Bristol, Birmingham, Dublin, Glasgow, Luton, Manchester, Newcastle, Stansted. Also snow train and self-drive
Accommodation hotels and apartments
One of the original major operators, which visits 77 resorts in 8 different countries. Group and child discounts available. Also offers a separate luxury brochure

INN TRAVEL
The Old Station
Helmsley
Yorks
YO6 5BZ
Reservations (0439) 71111.
Fax (0439) 71070
Bonding ATOL, AITO Trust
Travel air, departing Gatwick, Heathrow, Birmingham, Manchester
Accommodation hotels
Specialises in cross-country ski holidays for the independent traveller in Switzerland, Italy, Norway and France

INTERSKI
95 Outram Street
Sutton-in-Ashfield
Notts
NG17 4BG
Reservations (0623) 551024.
Fax (0623) 440742
Bonding ABTA, ATOL
Travel coach, departing throughout Britain. Flight-only seats available
Accommodation hotels and apartments
Specialises in Courmayeur and La Thuile in Italy. Offers skiing packages for schools

JEAN STANFORD SKI HOLIDAYS
Ridge House
Chilmark
Salisbury
Wilts
SP3 5BS
Reservations (0747) 870708.
Fax (0747) 871426
Bonding AITO Trust
Travel self-drive for all French destinations, with option to go by air. Clients for Whistler fly on a scheduled flight from Gatwick
Accommodation chalets, hotels and apartments
Small, flexible company which goes to Megève, Chamonix, the Portes du Soleil and Whistler

KEY TO AMERICA
15 Feltham Rd
Ashford
Middx
TW15 1DQ
Reservations (0784) 248777.
Fax (0784) 256658
Bonding ABTA
Travel air, departing Heathrow, Gatwick
Accommodation hotels and apartments
Specialises in ski holidays to America

KINGS SKI CLUB
24 Culloden Road
Enfield
Middx
EN2 8QD
Reservations 081-342 0303.
Fax 081-363 4605
Bonding ABTA, ATOL
Travel coach, departing London, regional departures for large groups on request. Also air and self-drive
Accommodation mainly chalets, also apartments
A ski club offering holidays to France and Austria. Group discounts available. Most of the chalets belong to the club

KUONI
Kuoni House
Dorking
Surrey
RH5 4AZ
Reservations (0306) 742500.
Fax (0306) 740719
Bonding ABTA, ATOL
Travel air, departing Heathrow, Gatwick, Birmingham, Manchester. Also self-drive
Accommodation hotels and apartments
Upmarket operator which specialises in ski holidays to a large number of Swiss resorts

LE SKI
25 Holly Terrace
Huddersfield
Yorks
HD2 1DX
Reservations (0484) 548996.
Fax (0484) 548996
Bonding ATOL, AITO Trust
Travel air, departing Gatwick, Bristol,
Edinburgh, Glasgow, Manchester,
Newcastle. Also self-drive, rail and
coach
Accommodation chalets, hotels and
apartments
*Specialises in good-value holidays to
Courchevel 1650 and Val d'Isère*

LOTUS SUPERTRAVEL
Hobbs Court
Jacob Street
London
SE1 2BT
Reservations 071-962 9933.
Fax 071-962 9932
Bonding ABTA, AITO member
Travel air, departing Heathrow.
Also self-drive
Accommodation chalets and hotels
*Not the same company as the old
Supertravel. Lotus offers ski holidays to
high-altitude resorts including
Courchevel, Méribel and Zermatt, the
USA and Canada*

MADE TO MEASURE
43 East Street
Chichester
West Sussex
PO19 1HX
Reservations (0243) 533333.
Fax (0243) 778431
Bonding ABTA, ATOL
Travel air, scheduled flights departing
Gatwick, Heathrow, Birmingham,
Manchester. Also rail and self-drive
Accommodation hotels and
apartments
*Wide variety of tailormade holidays that
incorporate 98 different resorts in
Europe and USA. Fun ski courses are a
big feature of the programme, as are
off-piste instruction and ski-touring*

MARK WARNER
20 Kensington Church Street
London
W8 4EP
Reservations 071-938 1851.
Fax 071-938 3861
Bonding ABTA, ATOL
Travel air, departing Gatwick,
Heathrow, Glasgow, Manchester. Also

self-drive
Accommodation chalets and club-
hotels
*Holidays to seven top European
resorts. Ski guiding available and
crèches in three of the club-hotels*

MASTERSKI
Thames House
63-67 Kingston Road
New Malden
Surrey
KT3 3PB
Reservations 081-942 9442.
Fax 081-949 4396
Bonding ATOL
Travel air, departing Gatwick, Belfast,
Glasgow, Manchester, Newcastle
Accommodation hotels, apartments,
and chalets
*Christian specialist for singles and
groups. Austrian and French hotel
programme is operated by
Kaleidoscope, Italian hotel programme
by Equity Total Ski. Chalets and
apartments operated by Masterski
Christian leadership and chalet staff*

NEILSON
Arndale House
Otley Road
Headingley
Leeds
Yorks
LS6 2UU
Reservations (0532) 394555.
Fax (0532) 752609
Bonding ABTA, ATOL
Travel air, departing Gatwick,
Heathrow, Belfast, Birmingham,
Bradford, Bristol, East Midlands,
Glasgow, Leeds, Luton, Manchester,
Newcastle, Stansted. Also snow train,
and self-drive
Accommodation hotels, apartments,
chalets
*Major operator to 80 resorts in 9
different countries. Family and group
discounts and learn-to-ski weeks
available*

NORWEGIAN STATE RAILWAYS TRAVEL BUREAU
Trafalgar Square
21/24 Cockspur Street
London
SW1Y 5DA
Reservations 071-930 6666.
Fax 071-321 0624
Bonding ABTA, ATOL, AITO member
Travel air/rail, departing Heathrow,
Gatwick

Accommodation hotels and apartments
Specialises in holidays in Norway combining travel with Scandinavian Airlines and Norwegian State Railways. Cross-country and telemarking offered, as well as child facilities

NORWEGIAN TRAVEL SERVICE
Southern House
Guildford Road
Woking
Surrey
GYU22 7UY
Reservations (0483) 756871.
Fax (0483) 755120
Bonding ABTA
Travel air, departing Heathrow, Aberdeen, Glasgow, Newcastle,
Accommodation hotels, apartments, chalets
Norwegian specialist. Cross-country, dog-sledding and good child facilities offered

PANORAMA'S SKI EXPERIENCE
29 Queens Road
Brighton
East Sussex
BN1 3YN
Reservations (0273) 206531.
Fax (0273) 205338
Bonding ABTA, ATOL, AITO member
Travel air, departing Gatwick, Birmingham, Manchester. Also self-drive and rail
Accommodation hotels and apartments
Small operator specialising in budget holidays to Andorra, Bulgaria and Livigno in Italy

PASSAGE TO SOUTH AMERICA
41 North End Road
London
W14 8SZ
Reservations 071-602 9889.
Fax 071-371 1463
Bonding AITO Trust
Travel air, departing Gatwick, Heathrow
Accommodation mainly hotels, also chalets and apartments
Specialises in holidays in South America, ranging from Chile to Bolivia. Offers cross-country holidays and babysitting

PGL YOUNG ADVENTURE LTD
Alton Court
Penyard Lane
Ross-on-Wye
Herefordshire

HR9 5NR
Reservations (0989) 768768.
Fax (0989) 765451
Bonding ABTA
Travel air, departing Gatwick, Heathrow. Also self-drive and coach
Accommodation hotels
Specialist in family holidays to Austria, mainly beginners' resorts. Teenage ski adventure and school holidays also available

POWDER BYRNE
50 Lombard Road
London
SW11 3SU
Reservations 071-223 0601.
Fax 071-228 1491
Bonding ATOL
Travel air, departing Heathrow, Birmingham, Manchester
Accommodation mainly hotels
Swiss specialist upmarket operator. There is a Junior Club in Flims, a crèche, and nearly all other resorts offer weekend skiing and mountain guides

RAMBLERS
PO Box 43
Welwyn Garden City
Herts
AL8 6PQ
Reservations (0707) 331133.
Fax (0707) 333276
Bonding ABTA, ATOL
Travel air, departing Heathrow, Birmingham, Glasgow, Manchester
Accommodation hotels
Operator specialising in walking holidays, with a small cross-country skiing programme in the Vercors in France and the Salzkammergut in Austria

SALLY HOLIDAYS
Basted Lane
Basted
Borough Green
Kent
TN15 8BA
Reservations (0732) 780499
Bonding ABTA, ATOL
Travel self-drive
Accommodation hotels, chalets and apartments
Ferry company offering self-drive holidays to France, Italy and Austria. Child and group reductions available

SEASUN SCHOOL TOURS
Seasun House
4 East Street

Colchester
Essex
CO1 2XW
Reservations (0206) 871181.
Fax (0206) 871361
Bonding ABTA, ATOL
Travel coach, departing anywhere in
UK. Flights also available from Gatwick,
Heathrow, Luton, Stansted
Accommodation hotels and pensions
Specialises in holidays for schools.
Resorts in France, Austria, Switzerland,
Andorra and Romania

SILVER SKI

Conifers House
Grove Green Lane
Maidstone
Kent
ME14 5JW
Reservations (0622) 35544.
Fax (0622) 38550
Bonding ABTA, ATOL, AITO member
Travel air, departing Gatwick,
Manchester
Accommodation chalets
Holidays in France and Verbier. Children
half-price when sharing parents' room.
Ski guiding available

SIMPLY SKI

8 Chiswick Terrace
Acton Lane
London
W4 5LY
Reservations 081-742 2541.
Fax 081-995 5346
Bonding ABTA, ATOL, AITO member
Travel air, departing Gatwick,
Heathrow, Manchester. Also self-drive,
snow train and coach
Accommodation mainly chalets,
also hotels
Small operator with holidays in
Courchevel, La Plagne and Valmorel.
Crèche in Montchavin (La Plagne)

SKI AIRTOURS

Wavell House
Holcombe Road
Helmshore
Rossendale
Lancs
EB4 4NB
Reservations (0706) 260000
Bonding ABTA
Travel air, departing Gatwick,
Manchester. Also snow coach and
self-drive
Accommodation hotels, apartments
and chalets
New mainstream ski operator going to

33 resorts in Austria, France and Italy

SKI THE AMERICAN DREAM

1/7 Station Chambers
High Street North
London
E6 1JE
Reservations 081-552 1201/ 081-470
1181. Fax 081-552 7726
Bonding ABTA, AITO
Travel air, departing Gatwick,
Heathrow, Glasgow, Manchester
Accommodation hotels and
apartments
American ski specialist offering
holidays in more than 20 different
resorts in America and Canada. Child
reductions available

SKI AUSTRIA

Austro Travel
11-15 St Ann's Road
Harrow
Middx
HA1 1AS
Reservations 081-427 4445.
Fax 081-861 4151
Bonding ABTA, ATOL, AITO member
Travel air, departing Gatwick,
Birmingham, Glasgow, Luton,
Manchester
Accommodation hotels
Austrian specialist offering holidays in
nine resorts. Learn-to-ski weeks, child
and group discounts and weekend
skiing

SKIBOUND

Olivier House
18 Marine Parade
Brighton
East Sussex
BN2 1TL
Reservations (0273) 696960.
Fax (0273) 676410/600999
Bonding ABTA, ATOL, AITO member
Travel air, departing Gatwick, Belfast,
Bristol, Glasgow, Luton, Manchester,
Tees-side. Also self-drive
Accommodation chalets, hotels, and
apartments
Large operator which visits more
than 40 resorts in four countries. Group
discounts available

SKI CAMPUS

Llangarron
Ross-on-Wye
Herefordshire
HR9 6PG
Reservations (0989) 770701/
770757. Fax (0989) 770752

Bonding ABTA, AITO member
Travel air, departing Heathrow
Accommodation own hotel in Megève
*Owns and operates the Hotel
Belle Etoile on the piste in Mègeve.
Offers group holidays and scheduled
flights*

SKI CHOICE
27 High Street
Benson
Wallingford
Oxon
OX10 6RP
Reservations (0491) 37607
Bonding ABTA
Travel air, departing Gatwick.
Also coach, rail and self-drive
Accommodation catered and
uncatered chalets, hotels, snow-homes
*Offers individual ski holidays to France,
Austria and Switzerland. Budget
holidays, families and groups*

SKI ESPRIT
Oaklands
Reading Road North
Fleet
Hants
GU13 8AA
Reservations (0252) 616789.
Fax (0252) 811243
Bonding ABTA, ATOL, AITO member
Travel air, departing Gatwick. Also
self-drive
Accommodation chalets
*Operator specialising in catered
chalet holidays for families in eight
resorts in France and Switzerland.
Extensive childcare facilities in all
resorts, with qualified nannies.
Group and child discounts are
available*

SKI EQUIPE
27 Bramhall Lane South
Bramhall
Stockport
Cheshire
SK7 2DN
Reservations 061-440 0010.
Fax 061-440 0080
Bonding ATOL
Travel air, departing Gatwick,
Birmingham, Edinburgh, Glasgow,
Manchester. Also self-drive
Accommodation apartments, chalets
and hotels
*Ski Adventure and Première Neige
weeks in Verbier and Courchevel, also
offers Alpe d'Huez. Group discounts
available*

SKI EUROPE
Northumberland House
2 King Street
Twickenham
Middx
TW1 3RZ
Reservations 081-891 4400.
Fax 081-892 3454
Bonding ABTA
Travel coach, departing throughout UK.
Also air and self-drive
Accommodation hotels and youth
hostels
Specialises in school group holidays

SKI FALCON
Groundstar House
London Road
Crawley
West Sussex
RH10 2TB
Reservations London 071-221 0088,
Birmingham 021-666 7000, Glasgow
041-248 7911, Manchester 061-831
7000
Bonding ABTA, ATOL
Travel air, departing Gatwick,
Heathrow, Birmingham, Bristol,
Glasgow, Luton, Manchester,
Newcastle. Also snow train and
self-drive
Accommodation apartments and
hotels
*Mainstream operator for over 25
resorts in six countries. Beginner weeks
and group and child discounts available*

SKI GOWER
2 High Street
Studley
Warwicks
B80 7HJ
Reservations (0527) 854822.
Fax (0527) 857236
Bonding ABTA
Travel coach, departing from the
school. Also by air
Accommodation hotels, youth centres
and holiday villages
*Specialist school holidays operator. All
resorts offer good recreational activities*

SKI HILLWOOD
2 Field End Road
Pinner
Middx
HA5 2QL
Reservations 081-866 9993.
Fax 081-868 0258
Bonding ATOL
Travel air, departing Gatwick,
Birmingham, Luton. Also self-drive

Accommodation hotels, apartments and snow homes
Specialist in family holidays to the Tyrol with crèches in Hopfgarten and Neustift

SKI JEANNIE
21 London Road
Great Shelford
Cambs
CB2 5DB
Reservations (0223) 840680.
Fax (0223) 844435
Bonding ATOL
Travel air, departing Gatwick, Glasgow, Manchester. Also self-drive
Accommodation mostly chalets, also self-catering and hotels
Ski holidays to Morzine, Méribel and Verbier. Ski guiding available

SKI JOHN WYATT
PO Box 168
Shrewsbury
Salop
SY1 1ZZ
Reservations (0743) 236832
Bonding ABTA, ATOL
Travel air, departing Gatwick, Manchester. Also snow train and self-drive
Accommodation chalets
Small family-run operator specialising in holidays to La Plagne, Méribel, Val d'Isère and St Anton. Ski guiding available, and gourmet packages offered at some chalets

SKI LA VIE
28 Linver Road
London
SW6 3RB
Reservations 071-736 5611.
Fax 071-371 8059
Bonding ATOL
Travel air, departing Gatwick, Heathrow, and some regional airports. Also self-drive
Accommodation mainly catered chalets
Small operator to Champéry, Zermatt and Les Diablerets in Switzerland. Ski guiding available, and crèches in three resorts

SKI MIQUEL
Derwent House
Alexandra Business Centre
Uppermill
Nr Oldham
Lancs
OL3 6HT
Reservations (0457) 820200.
Fax (0457) 872715
Bonding ATOL
Travel air, departing Gatwick, Manchester. Also self-drive
Accommodation hotels and chalets
Long-established operator for France, Austria, Switzerland and Spain

SKI NORWAY
Church Gate
Church Street West
Woking
Surrey
GU21 1DJ
Reservations (0483) 756871/6.
Fax (0483) 755120
Bonding ABTA
Travel air, departing Heathrow, Gatwick, Aberdeen, Birmingham, Glasgow, Manchester, Newcastle. Also ferry between England and Norway
Accommodation hotels and apartments
Specialises in ski holidays to Norway including cross-country weeks and dog-sledding. Child reductions of up to 80 per cent

SKI NORWEST
8 Foxholes Cottages
Foxholes Road
Horwich
Bolton
Lancs
BL6 6AL
Reservations (0204) 668468
Bonding ABTA
Travel luxury coach, departing Manchester, Leeds and Newcastle areas
Accommodation hotels and apartments
Holidays to Scotland and Italy. Group and child reductions, ski guiding, ski weekends and school holidays offered

SKI OLYMPIC
Pine Lodge
Barnsley Road
Doncaster
Yorks
DN5 8RB
Reservations (0302) 390120.
Fax (0302) 390787
Bonding ABTA, ATOL, AITO member
Travel air, departing Gatwick, Manchester. Also rail, coach and self-drive
Accommodation mainly chalets
Specialists in ski holidays to France. In-chalet nanny service available on request, and ski guiding

SKI PARTNERS
Friary House
Colston Street
Bristol
BS1 5AP
Reservations (0272) 253545.
Fax (0272) 293697
Bonding ABTA, ATOL, AITO member
Travel air, departing Gatwick, Belfast,
Bristol, Luton, Manchester. Also by
coach
Accommodation hotels
*Austrian specialist visiting a wide
variety of resorts from St Anton to Maria
Alm. Group and child reductions
available. Snowboarding and
cross-country weeks offered*

SKI PEAK
Hangerfield
Witley
Surrey
GU8 5PR
Reservations (0428) 682272.
Fax (0428) 685369
Bonding ATOL, AITO Trust
Travel air, departing Gatwick,
Manchester. Also self-drive
Accommodation hotels (including own
British-managed hotel), and chalets
*Small, specialist operator going to
Vaujany in the Alpe d'Huez region.
Ski guides, off-piste and crèche
facilities. Also has chalet in Méribel*

SKI ROMANIAN HOLIDAYS
34 Burrowfields
Welwyn Garden City
Herts
Reservations (0800) 515828/(0707)
330209. Fax (0707) 331576
Bonding ABTA, ATOL
Travel air, departing Gatwick,
Heathrow, Manchester, Stansted
Accommodation hotels and villas
*Romanian and Bulgarian specialist.
Group and child reductions, learn-to-ski
weeks, fly-drive and flight-only packages*

SKI SAVOIE
362-364 Sutton Common Road
Sutton
Surrey
SM3 9PL
Reservations 081-715 1122.
Fax 081-644 3068
Bonding ABTA, ATOL
Travel air, departing Heathrow.
Also self-drive
Accommodation hotels, apartments
and chalets
*Specialises in ski holidays to the
Savoie region of France.
Made-to-measure holidays and family
discounts available*

SKI SCOTT DUNN
Fovant Mews
12a Noyna Rd
London
SW17 7PH
Reservations 081-767 0202.
Fax 081-767 2026
Bonding ABTA
Travel air, departing Gatwick, Glasgow.
Also self-drive
Accommodation hotels, apartments
and chalets
*Flexible, upmarket operator with
holidays in Courchevel, Zermatt,
Champéry and Jackson Hole. Agent for
Mike Wiegele Helicopter Skiing in
British Columbia. Crèches provided in
all its European resorts, heli-skiing in
Zermatt and Jackson Hole*

SKI SLOVENIA CHOICE
Chesham House
150 Regent Street
London
W1R 6BB
Reservations 071-439 7233
Bonding ABTA, ATOL
Travel air, departing Gatwick,
Heathrow, Manchester
Accommodation hotels and
apartments
*Holidays to five resorts in Slovenia.
Group and child reductions, free ski
instruction offers, emphasis on après-ski*

SKI SUTHERLAND
Church Gate
Church West Street
Woking
Surrey
GU21 1DJ
Reservations (0483) 755766.
Fax (0483) 755120
Bonding ABTA
Travel air, departing Gatwick,
Heathrow, Birmingham, Bristol
Glasgow, Manchester, Newcastle. Also
coach and rail, and ferry to Norway
Accommodation mainly hotels
*Specialises in school skiing, with group
and low-season discounts. Resorts in
Europe, USA and Norway*

SKI TAL
2 Criterion Buildings
Wintersbridge
Portsmouth Road
Thames Ditton

Surrey
KT7 0SS
Reservations 081-398 9861.
Fax 081-398 7153
Bonding ATOL
Travel air, departing Gatwick. Also
self-drive
Accommodation mainly chalets,
also hotels and apartments
*Operator to Austria, France and
Canada. Ski improvement programmes
in Leogang and in Canada*

SKI THOMSON
Greater London House
Hampstead Road
London
NW1 7SD
Reservations 021-632 6282.
Fax 071-387 8451
Bonding ABTA, ATOL
Travel air, departing Gatwick,
Heathrow, Bristol, Birmingham,
East Midlands, Glasgow, Leeds-
Bradford, Luton, Manchester,
Newcastle, Stansted. Also snow
train and self-drive
Accommodation hotels, apartments
and chalets
*The biggest tour operator of all,
Thomson offers ski holidays to over
70 resorts in 10 different countries.
Family and group discounts, crèches,
ski guides, learn-to-ski weeks available
as well as separate Skistyle budget
brochure. Accommodation to suit all
budgets*

SKI TOTAL
10 Hill Street
Richmond
Surrey
TW19 1TN
Reservations 081-948 6922/3535.
Fax 081-332 1268
Bonding ATOL
Travel air, departing Gatwick. Also rail
and self-drive
Accommodation chalets
*Operator specialises in holidays to
Austria and France. Ski guiding
available, and families catered for in all
resorts*

SKI TRACER
41 North End Road
London
W14 8SZ
Reservations 071-602 7444.
Fax 071-371 1463
Bonding ABTA, AITO member
Travel air, departing Gatwick,

Manchester. Also rail, coach and
self-drive
Accommodation chalets and
apartments
*Small operator to Tignes, La Plagne and
Les Deux Alpes. Snowboarding weeks
in Tignes offered*

SKI TRAX
Henry Bell House
Gilesgate
Hexham
Northumberland
NE46 3NJ
Reservations (0434) 606488.
Fax (0434) 608197
Bonding ABTA
Travel sleeper coach, departing
Newcastle upon Tyne. Flights
available on request
Accommodation hotels, apartments
and chalets
*Small operator specialising in ski
holidays to France, Austria and
Scotland. Offers weekends and
summer skiing in Austria*

SKI UNIQUE
Church Gate
Church Street West
Woking
Surrey
GU21 1DJ
Reservations (0483) 755766.
Fax (0483) 755120
Bonding ABTA
Travel air, departing Gatwick,
Heathrow, Birmingham, Manchester
Accommodation hotels and
apartments
*Offers mainly made-to-measure group
holidays to Austria, France, Switzerland
and Norway*

SKI VAL
39a North End Road
London
W14 8SZ
Reservations 071-371 4900.
Fax 071-371 4904
Bonding ATOL
Travel air, departing Gatwick,
Manchester, Plymouth. Also snow
train, ski-drive and coach
Accommodation hotels, apartments
and chalets
*Varied programme including Val d'Isère,
Jackson Hole in Wyoming, and Whistler.
Ski guiding available*

SKI WEEKEND
Winster

25 Hambidge Lane
Lechlade
GL7 3BJ
Reservations (0367) 241636.
Fax (0367) 253488
Bonding ATOL
Travel air, departing Heathrow.
Also self-drive
Accommodation hotels
*Offers long or short weekend breaks in
France and Switzerland, off-piste
courses, ski safaris and local mountain
guiding*

SKI WEST
1 Belmont
Lansdown Road
Bath
Avon
BA1 5DZ
Reservations (0225) 44516.
Fax (0225) 481876
Bonding ABTA, ATOL, AITO member
Travel air, departing Gatwick, Bristol,
Glasgow, Luton, Manchester,
Newcastle. Also coach and self-drive
Accommodation hotels, apartments
and chalets
*Offers a comprehensive range of ski
holidays in Europe and America.
Ski clinics, off-piste weeks, group
discounts available*

SKIWORLD
41 North End Road
London
W14 8SZ
Reservations 071-602 4826.
Fax 071-371 1463
Bonding ABTA, ATOL, AITO member
Travel air, departing Gatwick,
Heathrow, Glasgow, Manchester.
Also rail, coach and self-drive
Accommodation hotels, apartments
and chalets
*Ski holidays to France, Andorra and the
USA. Ski guiding, tailor-made holidays
and discounts available*

SNOWBIZZ VACANCES
69 High Street
Maxey
Cambs
PE6 8EE
Reservations (0778) 341455.
Fax (0778) 347422
Bonding ABTA, ATOL, AITO member
Travel air, departing Gatwick,
Manchester
Accommodation hotels and
apartments
A small, specialist operator to Puy

*St Vincent and Serre Chevalier. Offers
learn-to-ski weeks*

SNOWCOACH CLUB CANTABRICA
Holiday House
146-148 London Road
St Albans
Herts
AL1 1PQ
Reservations (0727) 866177.
Fax (0727) 43766
Bonding ABTA, ATOL, AITO member
Travel coach, departing throughout
England and Wales. Also air
and self-drive
Accommodation hotels and
apartments
*Coach holidays to Austria, France, Italy
and Andorra. Offers family and group
discounts*

SNOWLINE HOLIDAYS
PO Box 141
Deal
Kent
CT14 6UR
Reservations (0304) 381551.
Fax (0304) 381546
Bonding ATOL, Bond Plus Protection
Travel air, departing Gatwick,
Manchester. Also rail and self-drive
Accommodation hotels, apartments
and chalets
*Offers flexible breaks, ski guiding,
crèche and children's club*

SNOWPIPER
Sandpiper House
19 Fairmile Avenue
Cobham
Surrey
KT11 2JA
Reservations (0932) 868658
Bonding AITO Trust
Travel self-drive
Accommodation apartments and
hotels
*Small operator with no-frills self-drive
holidays to France. No resort reps or
ski guides*

SNOWTIME
96 Belsize Lane
London
NW3 5BE
Reservations 071-433 3336.
Fax 071-433 1883
Bonding ATOL
Travel air, departing Gatwick, Glasgow,
Manchester. Also self-drive and snow
train
Accommodation chalets, hotels and

apartments
*The original Méribel specialist.
Snowtime has its own crèche with
nursery nurses, making this is a good
choice for families*

THE SKI COMPANY LTD
41 Hyde Vale
Greenwich
London
SE10 8QQ
Reservations 081-305 2299.
Fax 081-858 0971
Bonding ATOL
Travel air, departing Heathrow
Accommodation chalets
*Exclusively marketed by Abercrombie
and Kent. Specialists in luxury holidays
in France and Switzerland. Good child
facilities, weekend skiing, off-piste and
powder weeks, ski guiding from local
ski schools*

STS
24 Culloden Road
Enfield
Middx
EN2 8QD
Reservations 081-367 9090
Bonding ABTA, ATOL
Travel luxury coach, departing all over
Britain. Also by air from Gatwick,
Heathrow, Luton, Stansted
Accommodation hotels and
apartments
*Old-established operator to a wide range
of resorts in Austria, Italy and France,
including some lesser-known ones.
Specialist in school skiing holidays*

SUPER SOLUTIONS
206 Heythorp Street
London
SW18 5PA
Reservations 081-944 1155.
Fax 081-879 1762
Bonding ABTA
Travel air, departing Gatwick,
Heathrow, Glasgow, Manchester
Accommodation chalets
*Operator offering luxury accommodation
in Val d'Isère, Méribel and Zermatt.
Personal, flexible service, gourmet food
and à la carte holidays*

SWISS TRAVEL SERVICE
Bridge House
Ware
Herts
SG12 9DE
Reservations (0920) 463971
Bonding ABTA, ATOL

Travel air, departing Gatwick,
Heathrow, Birmingham, Manchester.
Also self-drive
Accommodation hotels and
apartments
*Swiss specialist offering upmarket
holidays in over 20 resorts, including
some lesser-known ones. Offers
tailor-made holidays, child reductions
and fly-drive*

TOP DECK SKI
133 Earls Court Road
London
SW5 9RH
Reservations 071-370 4555.
Fax 071-373 6201
Bonding ABTA, ATOL, AITO member
Travel air, departing Gatwick,
Manchester. Also coach, rail and
self-drive
Accommodation hotels, apartments
and chalets
*Aimed at the 18-35 age bracket, with
holidays to Andorra, France,
Switzerland and Austria. Ski guiding
available*

TOURALP
1 Berghem Mews
Blythe Road
London
W14 0HN
Reservations 071-602 1952.
Fax 071-602 1957
Bonding ABTA, ATOL
Travel air, departing Gatwick,
Heathrow, Manchester. Also coach,
snow train and self-drive
Accommodation hotels and
apartments
*Large operator which specialises in
ski holidays to major French resorts.
Group reduction for those staying
in apartments*

ULTIMATE HOLIDAYS
Ultimate House
Twyford Business Centre
London Road
Bishops Stortford
Herts
CM23 3YT
Reservations (0279) 755527.
Fax (0279) 655603
Bonding ABTA, ATOL
Travel air, departing Gatwick,
Manchester
Accommodation hotels, chalets and
apartments
*Small ski operation serving four
resorts in Mont Blanc area, plus*

Val d'Isère

VIRGIN SNOW
Galleria
Ground Floor
Station Road
Crawley
West Sussex
RH10 1HY
Reservations (0293) 617181.
Fax (0293) 536957
Bonding ABTA
Travel air, departing Gatwick, Heathrow
Accommodation hotels
*Ski holidays to USA, flying with
Virgin Airlines. Combined sun and ski
holidays offered*

WAYMARK
44 Windsor Road
Slough
SL1 2EJ
Reservations (0753) 516477.
Fax (0753) 517016
Bonding ATOL
Travel air, departing Gatwick,
Heathrow, Birmingham, Glasgow,
Manchester
Accommodation hotels, lodges and
farmhouses
*Cross-country specialist offering
holidays in the Alps, Norway, Germany,
Canada, Bohemia and Russia.
Also ski touring and telemarking*

WHITE ROC SKI
69 Westbourne Grove
London
W2 4UJ
Reservations 071-792 1188.
Fax 071-792 1956
Bonding AITO Trust
Travel air, departing Heathrow,
Birmingham, Manchester. Also
self-drive
Accommodation hotels and chalets
*Specialises in ski holidays to France.
Weekend skiing and local ski guiding
available*

WINTERSKI
38 Ship Street
Brighton
East Sussex
BN1 1AB
Reservations (0273) 204541.
Fax (0273) 620222
Bonding ABTA, ATOL
Travel coach, departing from schools
or clubs throughout UK. Also by air
from Gatwick
Accommodation hotels and a

chalet-hotel
*Specialises in schools and club skiing
to Italy. Package prices include
equipment hire and tuition*

YSE
The Business Village
Broomhill Road
London
SW18 4JQ
Reservations 081-871 5117.
Fax 081-871 5229
Bonding ATOL
Travel air, departing Gatwick
Accommodation apartments and
chalets
*Specialist upmarket operator to
Val d'Isère. Ski-guiding available.*

··

Tour operators which have applied for bonding

COLLINEIGE SKI
32 High Street
Frimley
Surrey
GU16 5JD
Reservations (0276) 24262.
Fax (0276) 27282
Travel air, departing Heathrow,
Manchester
Accommodation chalets
*A small, flexible operator offering ski
holidays in Chamonix. Weekend skiing,
childcare, a variety of ski courses and
instruction available, as well as First
Tracks off-piste skiing programme
for groups. Chalets have a homely
atmosphere*

MERISKI
Fovant Mews
12a Noyna Road
London
SW17 7PH
Reservations 081-682 3883.
Fax 081-682 2346
Travel air, departing Gatwick
Accommodation chalets
*Small operator which specialises in
Méribel, with a wide range of chalets.
Offers Pat Graham's Ski Venture for
intermediates*

NICKSKI
6 Sedley Place
London

W1R 1HG
Reservations 071-493 5869,
Fax 071-493 4317
Travel air, departing Gatwick,
Heathrow, Birmingham, Bristol,
Glasgow, Manchester, Newcastle.
Also rail and self-drive
Accommodation mainly chalets
Operator which specialises in
Avoriaz. Ski guiding, monoskiing,
snowboarding and off-piste skiing
available

SKI BEL AIR

35 Adam and Eve Mews
Kensington High Street
London
W8 6UG
Reservations 071-251 2077.
Fax 071-937 1991
Bonding applied for
Travel air, departing Gatwick, regional
departures available on request.
Also self-drive
Accommodation mainly chalets
Small operator specialising in Méribel.
Ski guiding and nannies available

UCPA

30 Brackley Road
Stockport
Cheshire
SK4 2RE
Reservations 061-442 6130
Travel coach, departing London,
Birmingham, Manchester
Accommodation hotels with 2-8-
bedded rooms
French company which organises
activity holidays for young people.
No hidden extras. Lift pass, instruction,
après-ski, equipment, coach travel and
full board all included in holiday
package

SUSIE WARD TRAVEL

Little End
St Agnes
Cornwall
TR5 OXD
Reservations (0872) 553055.
Fax (0872) 553050
Travel by air, departing Gatwick,
Heathrow. Also snow train, self-drive
Accommodation hotels and chalets
Small operator to Verbier and four
resorts in France. Instructor foundation
courses, ski weekends and ski guiding
offered

All information was correct at the time
of going to press.

Skiing by numbers

Travel to Ski

NATIONAL TOURIST OFFICES
The tourist offices listed below are for countries with recognised ski resorts.

Andorran Delegation
63 Westover Road
London
SW18 2RS
Tel 081-874 4806

Australian Tourist Commission
10-18 Putney Hill
London
SW15 6AA
Tel 081-780 2227 **Fax** 081-780 1496

Austrian National Tourist Office
30 St George Street
London
W1R 0AL
Tel 071-629 0461 **Fax** 071-499 6038

Bulgarian National Tourist Office
18 Princes Street
London
W1R 7RE
Tel 071-499 6988 **Fax** 071-321 0025

Canadian High Commission
Canada House
Trafalgar Square
London
SW1Y 5BJ
Tel 071-930 8540 **Fax** 071-258 6322

Cedok
(represents Czech Republic and Slovakia Republic)
49 Southwark Street
London
SE1 1RU
Tel 071-378 6009 **Fax** 071-403 2321

Chilean Embassy
12 Devonshire Street
London
W1N 2DS
Tel 071-580 6392 **Fax** 071-436 5204

Finnish Tourist Board
Greener House
66 Haymarket
London
SW1Y 4RF
Tel 071-839 4048 **Fax** 071-321 0696

French Government Tourist Office
178 Piccadilly
London
W1V 0AL
Tel 071-491 7622 **Fax** 071-493 6594

German National Tourist Office
65 Curzon Street
London
W1Y 7PE
Tel 071-495 3990 **Fax** 071-495 6129

Italian State Tourist Office
1 Princes Street
London
W1R 8AY
Tel 071-408 1254 **Fax** 071-493 6695

Japan National Tourist Organisation
167 Regent Street
London
W1R 7FD
Tel 071-734 9638 **Fax** 071-734 4290

New Zealand High Commission
New Zealand House
Haymarket
London
SW1Y 4TQ
Tel 071-973 0360 **Fax** 071-839 8929

Norwegian Tourist Board
Charles House
5-11 Lower Regent Street
London
SW1Y 4LR
Tel 071-839 2650 **Fax** 071-839 6014

Romanian National Tourist Office
17 Nottingham Street
London
W1M 3RD
Tel 071-224 3692 **Fax** 071-487 2913

Scottish Tourist Board
23 Ravelston Terrace
Edinburgh
EH4 3EU
Scotland
Tel 031-332 2433 **Fax** 031-343 1513

or:
19 Cockspur Street
London
SW1Y 5BL
Tel 071-930 8661 **Fax** 071-930 1817

Slovenian Embassy
Heather Lodge
Kingston Hill
Kingston-upon-Thames
Surrey
KT2 7LX
Tel 081-974 8300 **Fax** 081-974 6552

Spanish Tourist Office
57 St James's Street
London
SW1A 1LD
Tel 071-499 0901 **Fax** 071-629 4257

Swedish Tourist Board
73 Welbeck Street
London
W1M 8AN
Tel 071-487 5007 **Fax** 071-935 5853

Swiss National Tourist Office
Swiss Centre
New Coventry Street
London
W1V 8EE
Tel 071-734 1921 **Fax** 071-437 4577

United States Travel and Tourism
PO Box 1EN
London
W1A 1EN
Tel 071-495 4466 **Fax** 071-495 4377

SKI TRAVEL AGENTS AND CONSULTANTS

Chalets and Hotels Unlimited
50a Friern Barnet Lane
London
N11 3NA
Tel 081-343 7339 **Fax** 081-445 2528
Ski travel agent specialising in chalet holidays

Erna Low Consultants
9 Reece Mews
London
SW7 3HE
Tel 071-584 2841 **Fax** 071-589 9531
British-based agent for Flaine and La Plagne in France

Ski Travel Centre
311 Byres Road
Glasgow

G12 8UQ
Scotland
Tel 041-357 3945 **Fax** 041-357 4283
Specialist ski travel agency

Ski Solutions
206 Heythorp Street
London
SW18 5PA
Tel 081-944 1155 **Fax** 081-879 1762
Specialist ski travel agency

Skiers Travel Bureau
Marco Polo Travel
79 Street Lane
Roundhay
Leeds
LS8 1AP
Tel (0532) 666876
Fax (0532) 693305
Specialist ski travel agency and Aspen reservations

Snowline
PO Box 9
Market Harborough
Leics
LE16 7QS
Tel (0858) 84786 **Fax** (0858) 84570
Specialist ski travel agency

HELI-SKI COMPANIES

Austria

Lech Ski School
A–6764
Tel 43 5583 2355
Fax 43 5583 3781
Flies three skiers at a time, with a guide, from the resort up to 2400m on a choice of two peaks

Italy

Helitecnica
Quart, Aosta
Tel 39 165 765 418
Wide range of flights around Courmayeur and Valgrisenche

Lacadur Heliski
11010 Valgrisenche
Aosta
Tel 39 165 97 138
Some of the most wide-ranging heli-skiing in Europe

Switzerland

Air Glaciers Trans Heli
Box 236 1868 Colombey

Tel 41 2571 2626 **Fax** 41 2571 9453
Part of the REGA rescue helicopter association. Organises flights from Swiss resorts

Bohag
3814 Gsteigwiler
Tel 41 3622 9230 **Fax** 41 3622 0972
Variety of packages and day-trips in Bernese Oberland

Canada

CMH Heliskiing (UK agent)
61 Doneraile Street
London
SW6 6EW
Tel 071-736 8191 **Fax** 071-384 2592
The original heli-ski company, with nine locations in British Columbia. Packages include accommodation, all meals, transfers and a guaranteed drop of 100,000 vertical feet (3049 vertical metres) per week

Kootenay Helicopter Skiing
PO Box 717
Nakusp
BC VOG 1RO
Tel 1 604 265 3121
Fax 1 604 265 4447
Various packages available from two to seven days in the Selkirk and Monashee ranges of British Columbia

Mike Wiegele Helicopter Skiing
Box 249
Banff
Alberta
Canada
Tel 1 403 762 5548
Fax 1 403 762 5846
Operation based at Blue River in British Columbia between the end of November and May. Various length packages include luxury chalet accommodation, all meals, 100,000 vertical feet (3049 vertical metres) for 7 days, and 2 guides per group

Fresh Tracks (UK agents)
McMillan House
Cheam Common Road
Worcester Park
Surrey
KT4 8RH
Tel 081-335 3003 **Fax** 081-330 6819

Ski Scott Dunn (UK agents)
Fovant Mews
12a Noyna Road
London
SW17 7PH
Tel 081-767 0202 **Fax** 081-767 2026

Selkirk Tangiers Helicopter Skiing
Box 1409
Golden
BC VOA 1H0
Tel 1 604 344 5016
Fax 1 604 344 7102
Tough skiing image. Accommodation in a roadside motel in Revelstoke

TYAX Heli-Skiing
PO Box 849
Whistler
BC VON 1B0
Tel 1 604 932 7007
Fax 1 604 932 2500
Based at Whistler, this is suitable for first-time heli-skiers, with the addition of the resort's own pistes.

USA

High Mountain Heli-Skiing
Box 2217
Jackson
WY 83001
Tel 1 307 733 3274
Fax 1 307 733 0645
Based at Jackson Hole, Wyoming. Day-trips only in groups of four

Watsatch Powderbird Guides
PO Box 57
Snowbird
UT 84092
Tel 1 801 742 2800
Fax 1 801 742 2802
Based in Snowbird, Utah. Day-trips only with an average of six lifts per day

Telluride Heli-Trax
PO Box 1560
Telluride
CO 81435
Tel 1 303 728 4904
Fax 1 303 728 3807
Based in Telluride, Colorado. Day trips

Colorado Heli-Ski
PO Box 64
Frisco
CO 80443
Tel 1 303 668 5600
Fax 1 303 468 1144
Based in Colorado, with flights out of Breckenridge, Copper Mountain and Vail

Ruby Mountain Heli-Ski
PO Box 1192
Lamoille
NV 89828
Tel 1 702 753 6867
Fax 1 702 753 7805
Largest US operation, three-day packages with a guaranteed 39,000 vertical feet (11,890 vertical metres)

SKI GUIDED COURSES

The companies listed below specialise in ski clinic holidays and do not appear in the tour operators list. Note, several of the tour operators in the main list do offer ski clinic-type courses. The best idea is to read the brochure first and discover what they offer and for what level of skier.

Fred Foxon

81 Divinity Road
Oxford
OX4 1LN
Tel (0865) 723743
Personal performance snow weeks based in Val d'Isère, catering for intermediates, advanced and off-piste skiers. Programme includes video analysis, equipment maintenance and snowcraft

Fun Ski

43 East Street
Chichester
West Sussex
PO19 1HX
Tel (0243) 533333
Fax (0243) 778431
Jo Dent runs personalised ski development courses at Altenmarkt, Austria, for basic intermediate to advanced skiers. Six- and twelve-day courses include video analysis and off-piste skiing

Pat Graham Ski Clinics

8 Calverley Court
Oulton
Leeds
LS26 8JE
Tel/Fax (0532) 824 793
Pat Graham of the International Ski School in Méribel runs several ski clinics in the resort. Transform Your Skiing Clinics helps recreational skiers get the maximum enjoyment out of their skiing, and there are also break-through clinics, powder clinics, and seniors clinics. Accommodation can also be arranged

McGarry The Ski System

Cumballa
Hyde Road
Dalkey
Co Dublin
Ireland
Tel 081-399 5823
Fax 353 1 2859139
Ski clinics for intermediates upwards, although groups of six beginners or more will be allocated a coach. Programme includes video analysis

Masterclass

Birchview
Railway Terrace
Aviemore
PH22 1SA
Scotland
Tel (0479) 810814/33 79 08 22 00
Fax (0479) 811659
Sue and Ken Dickson and Alan Hole formed Masterclass in 1992, which has now merged with Ski Cocktail to provide English-speaking classes for British clients in Courchevel

Heini Messner Clinics

54 Northgate
Canterbury
Kent
CT1 1BE
Tel (0227) 454777   **Fax** (0227) 451177
Marketed through Alpine Tours. Offer race training, not for racers but to help intermediates on 'the plateau'. Winter courses in Steinach, summer and winter on the Stubai glacier

Mountain Experience

The Cottage
Whitehough Head
Chinley
Stockport
Cheshire
SK12 6BX
Tel (0663) 750160
Brian and Louise Hall run a guiding service based in Chamonix, France and an assortment of ski-touring courses including an introduction to the sport in Chamonix, the Haute Route and traversing the Bernese Oberland

Optimum Ski Courses

PO Box 708
London
E3 5HX
Tel 081-980 3911
Offers ski clinics in the Tarantaise, France, marketed through Skiworld, and in Keystone, Colorado, through Ski the American Dream

Ali Ross

Ski Solutions
206 Heythorpe Street
London
SW18 5PA
Tel 081-944 1155   **Fax** 081-879 1762
Specialist intermediate and advanced courses based in Tignes, with video analysis and specialist seminars

Ski Club of Great Britain

118 Eaton Square
London

SW1W 9AF
Tel 071-245 1033 **Fax** 071-245 1258
*Ski courses for various standards of
skier. Off-piste weeks and ski safaris*

The Ski Company
13 Squires Close
Bishop's Stortford
Herts
CM23 4DB
Tel (0279) 653746
Fax (0279) 654705
*Special ski weeks based in La Clusaz,
France. Includes courses for beginners/
improvers and the 'Not So Young', as
well as mogul clinics and family weeks*

Roland Stieger
Route de Taconnaz
74310 Les Houches
France
Tel 33 50 54 43 53
Fax 33 50 54 46 26
*Chamonix-based courses and mountain
guiding, also bookable through White
Roc (see* Which Tour Operator?*)*

Top Ski
Galerie des Cîmes
BP 41
73150 Val d'Isère
France
Tel 33 79 06 14 80 **Fax** 33 79 06 28 42
*One of the leading alternative ski
schools in the Alps, set up in the mid-
1970s with English-speaking clients in
mind. Off-piste courses, summer skiing
and piste clinics*

SKI INSURANCE COMPANIES

American Express
Sussex House
Burgess Hill
West Sussex
Tel (0444) 239900
Fax (0444) 235257

Douglas Cox Tyrie Ltd
Central House
High Street
London E15 2PF
Tel 081-534 9595 **Fax** 081-519 8780

Endsleigh Insurance Services Ltd
97-107 Southampton Row
London
WC1B 4AG
Tel 071-436 4451

Fogg Travel Insurance Ltd
Fullerton Lodge
Crow Hill Drive

Mansfield
Notts
NG19 7AE
Tel (0623) 631 331/5
Fax (0623) 420 450

Hamilton Barr
Bridge Mews
Bridge Street
Godalming
Surrey
GU7 1HZ
Tel (0483) 426600 **Fax** (0483) 426382

•••••••••••••••••••••••••••••••
Skiing organisations

Artificial Ski Slope Instructors (ASSI)
The English Ski Council
The Area Library Building
The Precinct
Halesowen
West Midlands
B63 4AJ
Tel 021-501 2314 **Fax** 021-585 6448

**British Association of Ski Instructors
(BASI)**
Grampian Road
Aviemore
Inverness-shire
PH22 1RL
Tel (0479) 810407
Fax (0479) 811222

British Ski Federation
258 Main Street
East Calder
West Lothian
Scotland
EH53 0EE
Tel (0506) 882952 **Fax** (0506) 884343

SKI COUNCILS
These bodies govern the sport as a
whole, taking responsibility for
promoting and developing skiing and
skiers' interests with the aid of grants
from the Sports Council.

English Ski Council
Area Library Building
The Precinct
Halesowen
West Midlands
B63 4AJ
Tel 021-501 2314 **Fax** 021-585 6448

Scottish National Ski Council
Caledonia House
South Gyle

Edinburgh
EH12 9DQ
Scotland
Tel 031-317 7280 **Fax** 031-339 8602

Ski Council of Wales
240 Whitchurch Road
Cardiff
CF4 3ND
Wales
Tel (0222) 619637 **Fax** (0222) 619637

Ulster Ski Council
8 Abercorn Park
Hillsborough
County Down
Northern Ireland
Tel (0846) 683243 (evenings only)

SKI CLUBS

There are a variety of special interest ski clubs, covering areas such as junior race training, disabled skiers, snowboarding and ski-touring. Several ski resorts also have their own clubs. We have also added the larger regional ski clubs, although a full list is available from the Ski Club of Great Britain.

Alpbach Visitors Club
Barhaus
6236 Alpbach
Austria
Tel 43 5336 5282

Alpine Club
55 Charlotte Street
London
EC2A 3QT
Tel 071-613 0755

Austrian Alpine Club
PO Box 43
Welwyn Garden City
Herts
AL8 6PQ
Tel (0707) 324835 **Fax** (0707) 333276

British Alpine Racing Ski Clubs (BARSC)
St James' House,
Frederick Road
Edgbaston
Birmingham
B15 1JJ
Tel 021-456 3445 **Fax** 021-456 3165

British Deaf Ski Club
19 Starling Close
Woosehill
Wokingham
Berks
(no telephone number available)

British Ski Club for the Disabled
Springmount
Berwick St John
Shaftesbury
Wilts
SP7 0HQ
Tel (0747) 828515

British Snowboarding Association
c/o Edge
6 Sedley Place
London
W1R 1HG
Tel 071-408 1187 **Fax** 071-493 4317

Downhill Only
Scale Hill
Congleton Road
Alderley Edge
Cheshire
SK9 7AB
Tel (0280) 702571
Ski club based in Wengen, Switzerland. Junior race training also offered

Eagle Ski Club
22 Flask Walk
London
NW3 1HE
Tel 071-794 9341
Ski-touring club, which arranges a variety of tours in Austria, France, Switzerland and Morocco

Kandahar Ski Club
Woodside
Benenden
Cranbrook
Kent
TN17 4EZ
Tel (0580) 240606
Fax (0580) 241684
Ski club based in Mürren, Switzerland

K Racing
11 Brookfields
Stebbing
Dunmow
Essex
CM6 3SA
Tel (0371) 856734
Fax (0279) 680543
Junior race training branch of the Kandahar Ski Club

Ladies Ski Club
40 Aynhoe Road
London
W14 0QD
Tel 071-603 7464

Mardens
Southridge House
Streatly

Berks
RG8 9SG
Tel (0491) 872710
Ski club based in Klosters, Switzerland

Midland Ski Club
23 The Grove
Little Ashton
Sutton Coldfield
B74 3UB
(no telephone number available)

Scottish Ski Club
The Cottage
New Gilston
Leven
Fife
KY8 5TF
Tel (0334) 84401

Ski Club of Ireland
Hotel Kilternan
Kilternan
Co Dublin
Ireland
Tel 353 1 955658

Ski Club of Manchester
210 Bramhall Moor Lane
Hazel Grove
Stockport
SK7 5JJ
Tel 061-483 3139

The Uphill Ski Club
12 Park Crescent
London
W1N 4EQ
Tel 071-636 1989 **Fax** 071-436 2601
Organisation for disabled skiers

Ski Club of Great Britain
118 Eaton Square
London
SW1W 9AF
Tel 071-245 1033 **Fax** 071-245 1258

Now the dominant club for British skiers, the SCGB was formed in 1903 by a group of 11 pioneers of downhill skiing 'to encourage the sport of skiing, assist novices, give information to members and bring together persons interested in the sport'. In the Club's early days, the organisation of ski racing formed a significant part of its activities (first World Championships in alpine downhill and slalom racing were organised by the Club at Mürren in 1931). Although the original aims remain, it concentrates now on recreational skiing, and offers its members a wide range of services and benefits to help them get the most out

of their skiing holidays.

The aspect of the Club best known to non-members is its gathering of information about skiing conditions: its snow reports are widely published during the skiing season. These reports come from the Club's representatives, who are present in over 30 major resorts throughout the season to help visiting members. The reps organise weekly programmes, as part of which they lead groups of different standards around the slopes, on- and off-piste. Members who like the idea of skiing for the whole of their holiday in a compatible group led by a qualified person, perhaps with the intention of improving a particular aspect of their skiing, are catered for by the Club's programme of organised skiing parties.

The Club also administers the British Ski Tests, designed to provide skiers with a measure of their skiing competence, and runs an Information Department at its London headquarters, staffed by experienced skiers with access to extensive files of detailed information on resorts and on other aspects of skiing including, for example, equipment stockists.

The clubhouse is also a social centre, with a popular bar serving snacks. There is a year-round programme of events (social and ski-related) here and around Britain. The Club has a network of regional and local representatives, and links with many dry ski slopes. As well as an annual Members' Handbook, members receive five issues of *Ski Survey*, Britain's oldest skiing magazine. Among other benefits for members are discounts (commonly 5 or 10 per cent) on the cost of ski holidays and equipment from a wide range of suppliers, in the Alps as well as Britain. Resorts expected to have SCGB representatives in the 1993-4 season include:

Andorra
Soldeu

Austria
Igls
Kitzbühel
Mayrhofen
Obergurgl
St Anton
Schladming

France
Alpe d'Huez

Avoriaz
Chamonix/Argentière
Flaine
Isola 2000
La Plagne
Megève
Serre Chevalier
Tignes
Val d'Isère
Val Thorens

Italy
Cervinia

Switzerland
Arosa
Crans Montana
Grindelwald
Gstaad
Klosters
Mürren
St Moritz
Verbier
Villars
Wengen
Zermatt

USA
South Lake Tahoe, California

Edinburgh
Tel 031-333 1000

Glasgow
Tel 041-887 1111

Leeds/Bradford
Tel (0532) 509696

London Gatwick
Tel (0293) 531299

London Heathrow
Tel 081-759 4321

Luton
Tel (0582) 405100

Manchester
Tel 061-489 3000

Newcastle
Tel 091-286 0966

Stansted
Tel (0279) 662520

Main airlines in the UK
Those listed below offer international
scheduled flights to airports close to
the ski areas.

American Airlines
Tel 081-572 5555

Austrian Airlines
Tel 071-439 1851

Air Canada
Tel 081-759 2636

Air France
Tel 081-742 6600

British Airways
Tel 081-897 4000

Continental Airlines (USA)
Tel (0293) 776464

Delta Airlines (USA)
Tel (0800) 414767

Lufthansa
Tel 071-408 0442

Northwest Airlines (USA)
Tel (0345) 747800

Swissair
Tel 071-439 4144

United Airlines (USA)
Tel (0800) 888 555

Virgin Atlantic Airlines (USA)
Tel (0293) 747747

• •

Getting there

GOING BY AIR
Air travel is probably the most popular
and fastest way of getting from Britain
to the Alps, and nearly all tour
operators offer holidays based on it.
There are scheduled and charter flights,

Major UK airports

Aberdeen
Tel (0224) 722331

Belfast Aldergrove
Tel (0849) 422888

Birmingham
Tel 021-767 7145/6

Bristol Lulsgate
Tel (0275) 474444

Cardiff
Tel (0446) 711111

Dublin
Tel 353 1 370191

East Midlands (Derby)
Tel (0332) 810621

GOING BY RAIL

Going by rail to the Alps is becoming popular. It is often easier for families, financially and luggage-wise, and the added bonus is an extra day's skiing. A group of tour operators offer the Snow Train option to France and Austria, leaving Calais on Friday evenings and arriving in time for skiing the following morning. Below are a few useful telephone numbers for those travelling by rail.

British Rail International
Tel 071-834 2345

European Rail Travel Centre
Tel 071-834 2345

French Railways
Tel 071-409 3518

German Railways
Tel 071-290 1135

Swiss Rail
Tel 071-734 1921

The Snow Train

Tour operators using the service (contact them direct):
Austria - Bladon Lines, Crystal, Enterprise, Inghams, Neilson, Ski Falcon, Thomson Skistyle
France - Bladon Lines, Crystal, Enterprise, Inghams, Neilson, Simply Ski, Ski Falcon, Ski Thomson, Skiworld, Snowtime, Touralp, John Wyatt Travel

GOING BY COACH

This is the best-value way of travelling to the Alps, although standards of comfort vary. The main coach station in Britain is:

Victoria Coach Station
Tel 071-730 0202

GOING BY CAR

Travelling to the Alps by car has become an increasingly popular option and, no doubt, will become more so with the advent of the Channel Tunnel. Once there, you have the freedom to move from resort to resort to find the best snow. It is also an economical way of travelling for a family or group. Remember to work the cost of petrol and motorway tolls into your budget, and do not forget to obtain a Green Card from your insurance company. Breakdown insurance is advisable (see below).

Brittany Ferries (Portsmouth-Caen)
Tel (0705) 827701

Hoverspeed (Dover-Calais, Dover-Boulogne)
Tel (0304) 240241

North Sea Ferries (Hull-Zeebrugge, Hull-Rotterdam)
Tel (0482) 795141

Olau Line (Sheerness-Vlissingen)
Tel (0795) 666666

P & O European Ferries (Portsmouth-Le Havre, Dover-Calais, Dover-Ostend, Felixstowe-Zeebrugge, Portsmouth-Cherbourg)
Tel (0304) 203388

Sally Lines (Ramsgate-Dunkerque)
Tel (0843) 595522

Sealink Stena Line (Dover-Calais, Harwich-Hook, Newhaven-Dieppe, Southampton-Cherbourg)
Tel (0233) 647047

BREAKDOWN INSURANCE

The two main motoring organisations, the AA and RAC, offer various services to their members.

Automobile Association (AA)
Tel (0256) 24872

Royal Automobile Club (RAC)
Tel 081-686 2525

Autohome Ltd
Tel (0604) 232334

Europ Assistance
Tel 081-680 1234

Mondial Assistance
Tel 081-681 2525

National Breakdown Recovery
Tel (0532) 393666

CAR RENTAL COMPANIES

Avis
Tel 081-848 8733

Budget Rent-a-Car
Tel (0800) 181181

Europcar
Tel (0532) 422233

Hertz
Tel 081-679 1799

Reporting on the resorts

Reporters to the Guide stand a good chance of winning a free copy of the next edition. Resort reports should use the structure set out below and be sent to: Dept CD, Consumers' Association, FREEPOST, 2 Marylebone Road, London NW1 4DF. No stamp is needed. Please write as clearly as you can or, if at all possible, type your reports. Use separate sheets for different resorts, however short each report may be.

Resort report checklist

Basics
Your name and address

Your skiing background (experience, competence)

Resort name/country

Date of visit

Tour operator used

Hotel/chalet/apartment block stayed in

Verdicts
Your reaction to our 'good points' and 'bad points' verdicts on the resort.

Operation of lifts
New lifts, upgraded lifts, lift queues, lift passes and other payment systems.

Operation of runs
Remarks on piste-marking, piste-grooming, piste closure, artificial snow, accuracy of resort piste map. Name any favourite runs and interesting off-piste descents.

Mountain restaurants
General comments, specific named recommendations.

Ski schools
Remarks on organisation, tuition, language, use of time, allocation of pupils to classes, group size etc. Cover private lessons, guiding, and special courses if you tried them. It is vital to specify which school.

Children's facilities
Remarks on skiing and/or non-skiing kindergartens: facilities, staff competence and attitude, language, approach to ski tuition, meals, hours, cost etc. Specify which kindergarten or ski school.

Local transport
Transport within the resort, where you can get to and where you cannot, frequency, reliability, convenience, cost, crowding, value of a car.

Accident/medical facilities
Your experience of any mountain rescue and subsequent hospital treatment.

Shopping
Range of everyday (food/supermarket) shops, including quality, service and prices. Range of other (clothing/jewellery/gift) shops.

Non-skiing facilities
Range, quality, convenience, price of sporting and other non-skiing facilities in the resort; excursion possibilities.

Eating out
Range and type of restaurant, general comments. Specific recommendations essential.

Après-ski
Range and style of bars, restaurants, discos, clubs; what happens in the resort after skiing, from tea-time until the small hours. Specific recommendations essential.

Access
Remarks on airport arrival/departure, coach transfer, car access/ parking, rail connections.

Accommodation
Remarks on particular hotels, chalets or apartments – must be named. Advice on choice of location within the resort.

Prices
General observations on the cost of meals and drinks (village and mountain), entry fee to and drink prices in discos and clubs. Please give examples whenever possible, for example price of a beer, soft drink, bottle of house wine, cup of coffee, dish of the day.

Summary
What did you particularly like and dislike about the resort? What aspect of the resort came as a surprise (pleasant or otherwise)? Who does the resort suit, and who does it not suit? On the whole, do you regret choosing this resort? If so, why?

Resort index